MOTORIST
BRITAIN

C000274294

Contents

Map pages	inside front cover
Route planner	*II–VII*
Motorways	*VIII–XIV*
Restricted junctions	*VIII–XI*
M25 London Orbital motorway	*XII*
M6 Toll motorway	*XIII*
Smart motorways	*XIV*
Road map symbols	**1**
Road maps	**2–115**
Britain 1:250,000 scale Some islands are shown at slightly smaller scales	2–111
Ireland 1:1,000,000 scale	112–115
District maps	**116–127**
Birmingham	116–117
Glasgow	118–119
London	120–123
Manchester	124–125
Tyne & Wear	126–127
Street map symbols	**128**
Town plans	**129–141**
Central London	**142–157**
Central London street map	142–151
Central London index	152–157
Index to place names	**158–194**
County, administrative area map	158

42nd edition June 2019

© AA Media Limited 2019

Revised version of the atlas formerly known as *Complete Atlas of Britain*. Original edition printed 1979.

Cartography: All cartography in this atlas edited, designed and produced by the Mapping Services Department of AA Publishing (A05688).

This atlas contains Ordnance Survey data © Crown copyright and database right 2019 and Royal Mail data © Royal Mail copyright and database right 2019.

Contains public sector information licensed under the Open Government Licence v3.0

Ireland mapping contains data available from openstreetmap.org © under the Open Database License found at opendatacommons.org

Publisher's Notes: Published by AA Publishing (a trading name of AA Media Limited, whose registered office is Fanum House, Basing View, Basingstoke, Hampshire RG21 4EA, UK. Registered number 06112600).

ISBN: 978 0 7495 8134 3

A CIP catalogue record for this book is available from The British Library.

Disclaimer: The contents of this atlas are believed to be correct at the time of the latest revision, it will not contain any subsequent amended, new or temporary information including diversions and traffic control or enforcement systems. The publishers cannot be held responsible or liable for any loss or damage occasioned to any person acting or refraining from action as a result of any use or reliance on material in this atlas, nor for any errors, omissions or changes in such material. This does not affect your statutory rights.

The publishers would welcome information to correct any errors or omissions and to keep this atlas up to date. Please write to the Atlas Editor, AA Publishing, The Automobile Association, Fanum House, Basing View, Basingstoke, Hampshire RG21 4EA, UK.
E-mail: *roadatlasfeedback@theaa.com*

Acknowledgements: AA Publishing would like to thank the following for information used in the creation of this atlas: Cadw, English Heritage, Forestry Commission, Historic Scotland, National Trust and National Trust for Scotland, RSPB, The Wildlife Trust, Scottish Natural Heritage, Natural England, The Countryside Council for Wales. Award winning beaches from 'Blue Flag' and 'Keep Scotland Beautiful' (summer 2018 data): for latest information visit *www.blueflag.org* and *www.keepscotlandbeautiful.org*. Transport for London (Central London Map), Nexus (Newcastle district map).

Ireland mapping: Republic of Ireland census 2016 © Central Statistics Office and Northern Ireland census 2016 © NISRA (population data); Irish Public Sector Data (CC BY 4.0) (Gaeltacht); Logainm.ie (placenames); Roads Service and Transport Infrastructure Ireland

Printer: Walstead Peterborough, UK

Scale 1:250,000
or 3.95 miles to 1 inch

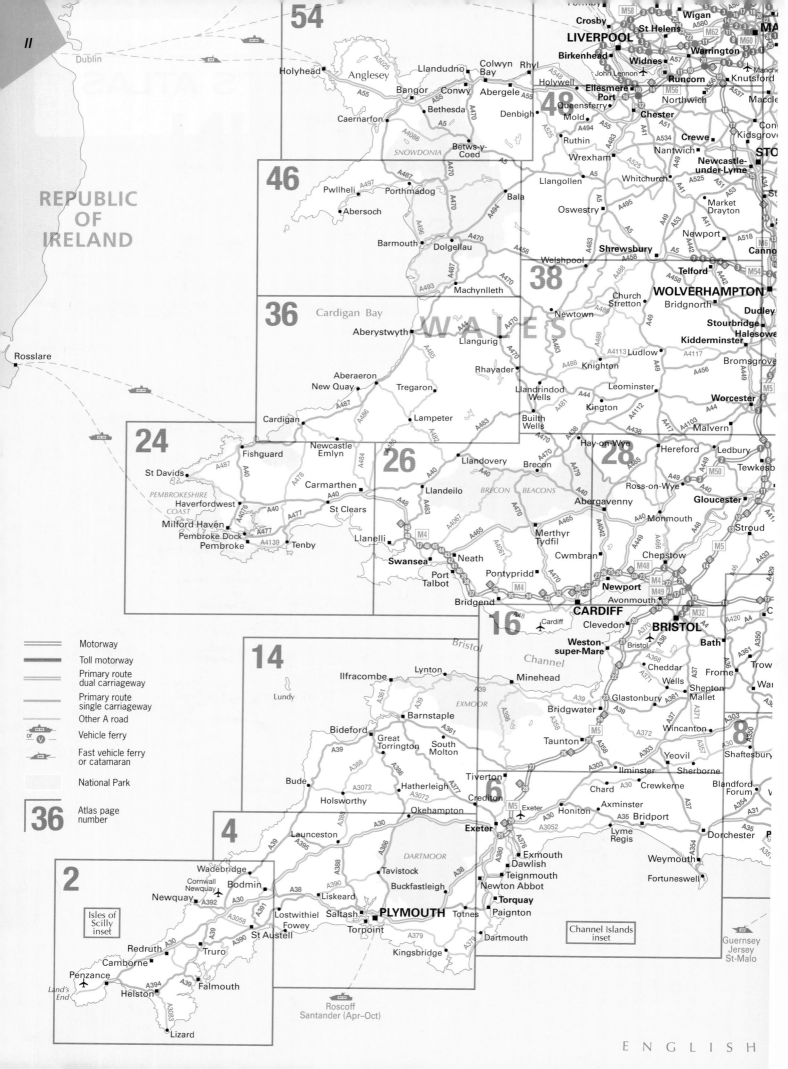

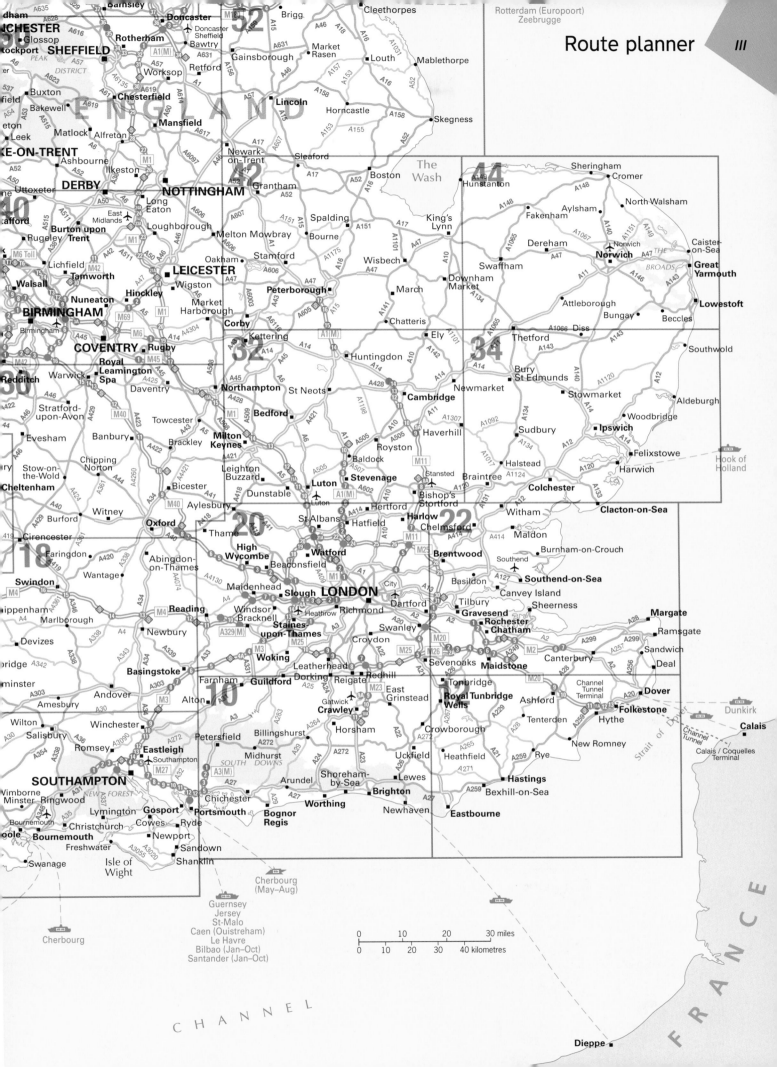

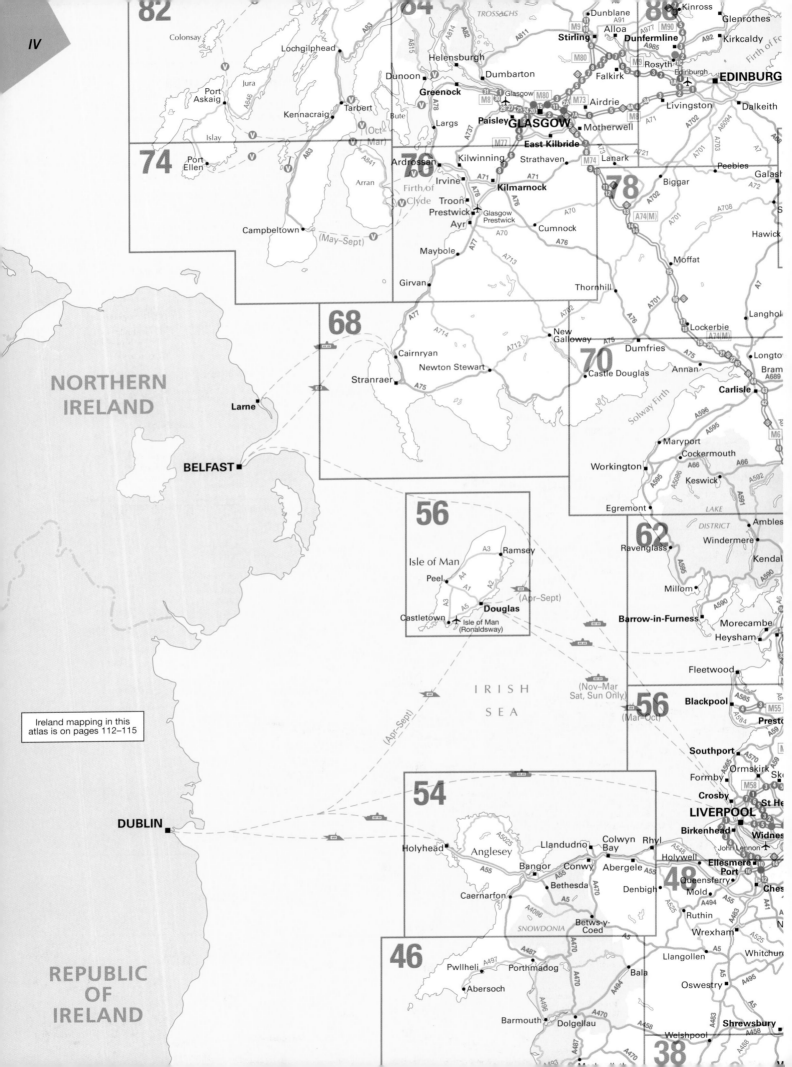

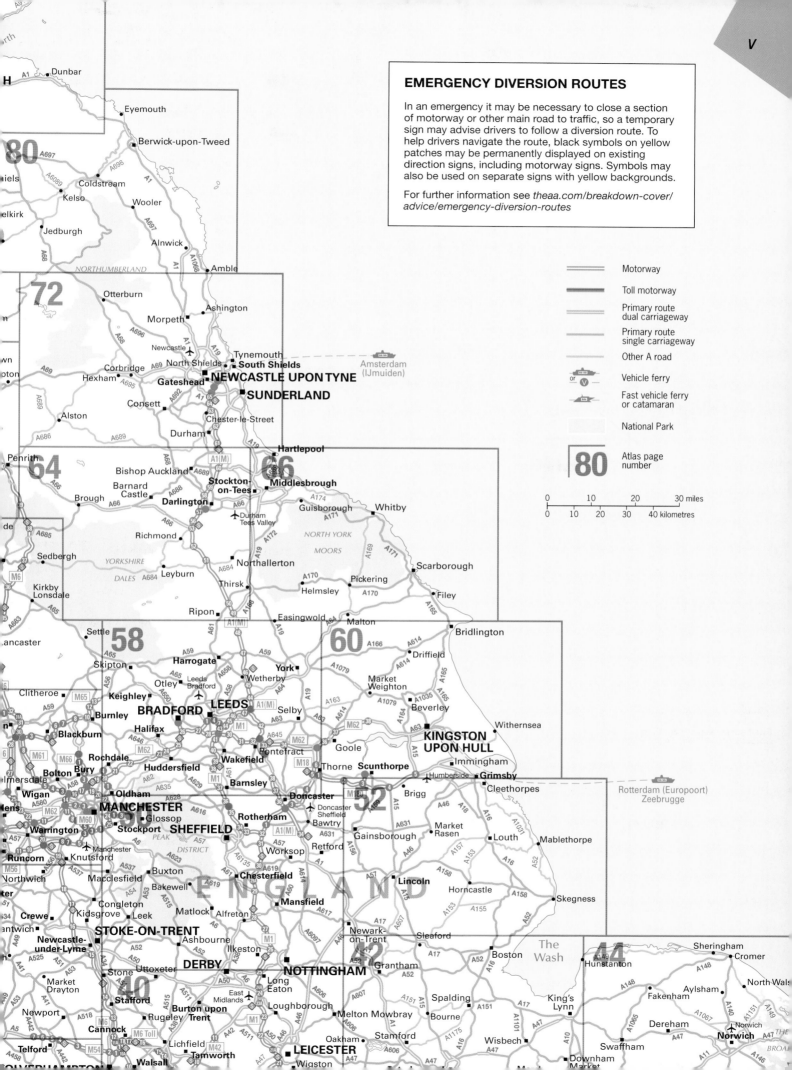

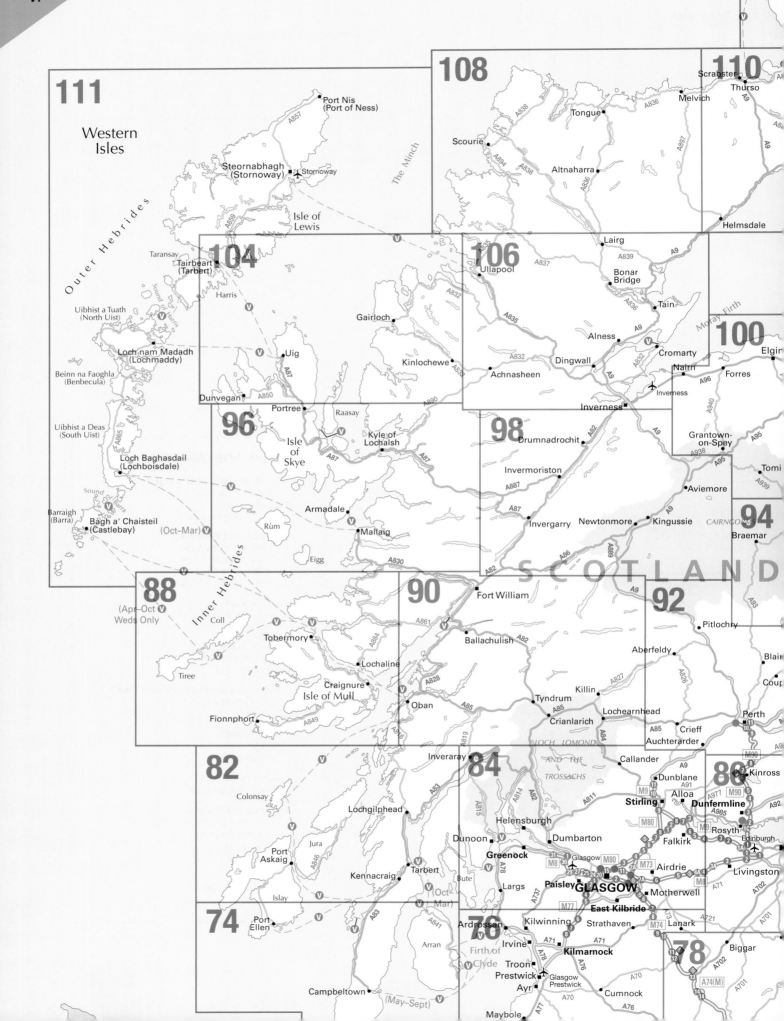

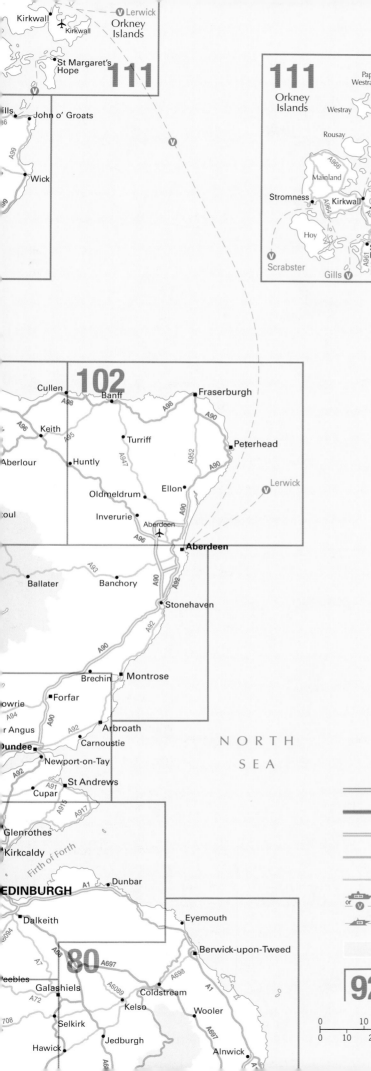

FERRY OPERATORS

Hebrides and west coast Scotland
calmac.co.uk
skyeferry.co.uk
western-ferries.co.uk

Orkney and Shetland
northlinkferries.co.uk
pentlandferries.co.uk
orkneyferries.co.uk
shetland.gov.uk/ferries

Isle of Man
steam-packet.com

Ireland
irishferries.com
poferries.com
stenaline.co.uk

North Sea (Scandinavia and Benelux)
dfdsseaways.co.uk
poferries.com

Isle of Wight
wightlink.co.uk
redfunnel.co.uk

Channel Islands
condorferries.co.uk

France and Belgium
brittany-ferries.co.uk
condorferries.co.uk
eurotunnel.com
dfdsseaways.co.uk
poferries.com

Northern Spain
brittany-ferries.co.uk

Legend:

Motorway

Toll motorway

Primary route dual carriageway

Primary route single carriageway

Other A road

Vehicle ferry

Fast vehicle ferry or catamaran

National Park

92 Atlas page number

0   10   20   30 miles
0 10 20 30 40 kilometres

Restricted junctions

Motorway and primary route junctions which have access or exit restrictions are shown on the map pages thus:

M1 London - Leeds

Northbound
Access only from A1
(northbound)

Southbound
Exit only to A1
(southbound)

Northbound
Access only from A41
(northbound)

Southbound
Exit only to A41
(southbound)

Northbound
Access only from M25
(no link from A405)

Southbound
Exit only to M25
(no link from A405)

Northbound
Access only from A414

Southbound
Exit only to A414

Northbound
Exit only to M45

Southbound
Access only from M45

Northbound
Exit only to M6
(northbound)

Southbound
Exit only to A14
(southbound)

Northbound
Exit only, no access

Southbound
Access only, no exit

Northbound
No exit, access only

Southbound
Access only from
A50 (eastbound)

Northbound
Exit only, no access

Southbound
Access only, no exit

Northbound
Exit only to M621

Southbound
Access only from M621

Northbound
Exit only to A1(M)
(northbound)

Southbound
Access only from A1(M)
(southbound)

M2 Rochester - Faversham

Westbound
No exit to A2
(eastbound)

Eastbound
No access from A2
(westbound)

M3 Sunbury - Southampton

Northeastbound
Access only from A303,
no exit

Southwestbound
Exit only to A303,
no access

Northbound
Exit only, no access

Southbound
Access only, no exit

Northeastbound
Access from M27 only,
no exit

Southwestbound
No access to M27
(westbound)

M4 London - South Wales

For junctions 1 & 2 see London district map
on pages 120–123

Westbound
Exit only to M48

Eastbound
Access only from M48

Westbound
Access only from M48

Eastbound
Exit only to M48

Westbound
Exit only, no access

Eastbound
Access only, no exit

Westbound
Exit only, no access

Eastbound
Access only, no exit

Westbound
Exit only to A48(M)

Eastbound
Access only from A48(M)

Westbound
Exit only, no access

Eastbound
No restriction

Westbound
Access only, no exit

Eastbound
No access or exit

Westbound
Exit only to A483

Eastbound
Access only from A483

M5 Birmingham - Exeter

Northeastbound
Access only, no exit

Southwestbound
Exit only, no access

Northeastbound
Access only from A417
(westbound)

Southwestbound
Exit only to A417
(eastbound)

Northeastbound
Exit only to M49

Southwestbound
Access only from M49

Northeastbound
No access, exit only

Southwestbound
No exit, access only

M6 Toll Motorway

See M6 Toll motorway map on page *XIII*

M6 Rugby - Carlisle

Northbound
Exit only to M6 Toll

Southbound
Access only from M6 Toll

Northbound
Exit only to M42
(southbound) and A446

Southbound
Exit only to A446

Northbound
Access only from M42
(southbound)

Southbound
Exit only to M42

Northbound
Exit only, no access

Southbound
Access only, no exit

Northbound
Exit only to M54

Southbound
Access only from M54

Northbound
Access only from M6 Toll

Southbound
Exit only to M6 Toll

Northbound
No restriction

Southbound
Access only from M56
(eastbound)

Northbound
Exit only to M56
(westbound)

Southbound
Access only from M56
(eastbound)

Northbound
Access only, no exit

Southbound
Exit only, no access

Northbound
Exit only, no access

Southbound
Access only, no exit

Northbound
Access only from M61

Southbound
Exit only to M61

Northbound
Exit only, no access

Southbound
Access only, no exit

Northbound
Exit only, no access

Southbound
Access only, no exit

M8 Edinburgh - Bishopton

For junctions 7A to 29A see Glasgow district
map on pages 118–119

Westbound
Exit only, no access

Eastbound
Access only, no exit

Westbound
Access only, no exit

Eastbound
Exit only, no access

Westbound
Access only, no exit

Eastbound
Exit only, no access

M9 Edinburgh - Dunblane

Northwestbound
Access only, no exit

Southeastbound
Exit only, no access

Northwestbound
Exit only, no access

Southeastbound
Access only, no exit

Northwestbound
Access only, no exit

Southeastbound
Exit only to A905

Northwestbound
Exit only to M876
(southwestbound)

Southeastbound
Access only from M876
(northeastbound)

M11 London - Cambridge

Northbound
Access only from A406
(eastbound)

Southbound
Exit only to A406

Northbound
Exit only, no access

Southbound
Access only, no exit

Northbound
Exit only, no access

Southbound
No direct access,
use jct 8

Northbound
Exit only to A11

Southbound
Access only from A11

Northbound
Exit only, no access

Southbound
Access only, no exit

Northbound
Exit only, no access

Southbound
Access only, no exit

M20 Swanley - Folkestone

Northwestbound
Staggered junction; follow
signs - access only

Southeastbound
Staggered junction; follow
signs - exit only

Northwestbound
Exit only to M26
(westbound)

Southeastbound
Access only from M26
(eastbound)

Northwestbound
Access only from A20

Southeastbound
For access follow signs -
exit only to A20

Northwestbound
No restriction

Southeastbound
For exit follow signs

Northwestbound
Access only, no exit

Southeastbound
Exit only, no access

M23 Hooley - Crawley

Northbound
Exit only to A23
(northbound)

Southbound
Access only from A23
(southbound)

Northbound
Access only, no exit

Southbound
Exit only, no access

M25 London Orbital Motorway

See M25 London Orbital motorway map on
page *XII*

M26 Sevenoaks - Wrotham

Westbound
Exit only to clockwise
M25 (westbound)

Eastbound
Access only from
anticlockwise M25
(eastbound)

Westbound
Access only from M20
(northwestbound)

Eastbound
Exit only to M20
(southeastbound)

M27 Cadnam - Portsmouth

Westbound
Staggered junction; follow
signs - access only from
M3 (southbound). Exit
only to M3 (northbound)

Eastbound
Staggered junction; follow
signs - access only from
M3 (southbound). Exit
only to M3 (northbound)

Westbound
Exit only, no access

Eastbound
Access only, no exit

Westbound
Staggered junction; follow
signs - exit only to M275
(southbound)

Eastbound
Staggered junction; follow
signs - access only from
M275 (northbound)

M40 London - Birmingham

Northwestbound
Exit only, no access

Southeastbound
Access only, no exit

Northwestbound
Exit only, no access

Southeastbound
Access only, no exit

Northwestbound
Exit only to M40/A40

Southeastbound
Access only from
M40/A40

Northwestbound
Exit only, no access

Southeastbound
Access only, no exit

Northwestbound
Access only, no exit

Southeastbound
Exit only, no access

Northwestbound
Access only, no exit

Southeastbound
Exit only, no access

M42 Bromsgrove - Measham

See Birmingham district map on pages
116–117

M45 Coventry - M1

Westbound
Access only from A45
(northbound)

Eastbound
Exit only, no access

Westbound
Access only from M1
(northbound)

Eastbound
Exit only to M1
(southbound)

M48 Chepstow

Westbound
Access only from M4
(westbound)

Eastbound
Exit only to M4
(eastbound)

Westbound
No exit to M4 (eastbound)

Eastbound
No access from M4
(westbound)

M53 Mersey Tunnel - Chester

Northbound
Access only from M56
(westbound). Exit only to
M56 (eastbound)

Southbound
Access only from M56
(westbound). Exit only to
M56 (eastbound)

M54 Telford - Birmingham

Westbound
Access only from M6
(northbound)

Eastbound
Exit only to M6
(southbound)

M56 Chester - Manchester

For junctions 1,2,3,4 & 7 see Manchester
district map on pages 124–125

Westbound
Access only, no exit

Eastbound
No access or exit

Westbound
No exit to M6
(southbound)

Eastbound
No access from M6
(northbound)

Westbound
Exit only to M53

Eastbound
Access only from M53

Westbound
No access or exit

Eastbound
No restriction

M57 Liverpool Outer Ring Road

Northwestbound
Access only, no exit

Southeastbound
Exit only, no access

Northwestbound
Access only from A580
(westbound)

Southeastbound
Exit only, no access

M58 Liverpool - Wigan

Westbound
Exit only, no access

Eastbound
Access only, no exit

M60 Manchester Orbital

See Manchester district map on pages
124–125

M61 Manchester - Preston

Northwestbound
No access or exit

Southeastbound
Exit only, no access

Northwestbound
Exit only to M6
(northbound)

Southeastbound
Access only from M6
(southbound)

M62 Liverpool - Kingston upon Hull

Westbound
Access only, no exit

Eastbound
Exit only, no access

Westbound
No access to A1(M) (southbound)

Eastbound
No restriction

M65 Preston - Colne

Northeastbound
Exit only, no access

Southwestbound
Access only, no exit

Northeastbound
Access only, no exit

Southwestbound
Exit only, no access

M66 Bury

Northbound
Exit only to A56 (northbound)

Southbound
Access only from A56 (southbound)

Northbound
Exit only, no access

Southbound
Access only, no exit

M67 Hyde Bypass

Westbound
Access only, no exit

Eastbound
Exit only, no access

Westbound
Exit only, no access

Eastbound
Access only, no exit

Westbound
Exit only, no access

Eastbound
No restriction

M69 Coventry - Leicester

Northbound
Access only, no exit

Southbound
Exit only, no access

M73 East of Glasgow

Northbound
No exit to A74 and A721

Southbound
No exit to A74 and A721

Northbound
No access from or exit to A89. No access from M8 (eastbound)

Southbound
No access from or exit to A89. No exit to M8 (westbound)

M74 and A74(M) Glasgow - Gretna

Northbound
Exit only, no access

Southbound
Access only, no exit

Northbound
Access only, no exit

Southbound
Exit only, no access

Northbound
No access from A74 and A721

Southbound
Access only, no exit to A74 and A721

Northbound
Access only, no exit

Southbound
Exit only, no access

Northbound
No access or exit

Southbound
Exit only, no access

Northbound
No restriction

Southbound
Access only, no exit

Northbound
Access only, no exit

Southbound
Exit only, no access

Northbound
Exit only, no access

Southbound
Access only, no exit

Northbound
Exit only, no access

Southbound
Access only, no exit

M77 Glasgow - Kilmarnock

Northbound
No exit to M8 (westbound)

Southbound
No access from M8 (eastbound)

Northbound
Access only, no exit

Southbound
Exit only, no access

Northbound
Access only, no exit

Southbound
Exit only, no access

Northbound
Access only, no exit

Southbound
No restriction

Northbound
Exit only, no access

Southbound
Exit only, no access

M80 Glasgow - Stirling

For junctions 1 & 4 see Glasgow district map on pages 118–119

Northbound
Exit only, no access

Southbound
Access only, no exit

Northbound
Access only, no exit

Southbound
Exit only, no access

Northbound
Exit only to M876 (northeastbound)

Southbound
Access only from M876 (southwestbound)

M90 Edinburgh - Perth

Northbound
No exit, access only

Southbound
Exit only to A90 (eastbound)

Northbound
Exit only to A92 (eastbound)

Southbound
Access only from A92 (westbound)

Northbound
Access only, no exit

Southbound
Exit only, no access

Northbound
Exit only, no access

Southbound
Access only, no exit

Northbound
No access from A912
No exit to A912 (southbound)

Southbound
No access from A912 (northbound).
No exit to A912

M180 Doncaster - Grimsby

Westbound
Access only, no exit

Eastbound
Exit only, no access

M606 Bradford Spur

Northbound
Exit only, no access

Southbound
No restriction

M621 Leeds - M1

Clockwise
Access only, no exit

Anticlockwise
Exit only, no access

Clockwise
No exit or access

Anticlockwise
No restriction

Clockwise
Access only, no exit

Anticlockwise
Exit only, no access

Clockwise
Exit only, no access

Anticlockwise
Access only, no exit

Clockwise
Exit only to M1 (southbound)

Anticlockwise
Access only from M1 (northbound)

M876 Bonnybridge - Kincardine Bridge

Northeastbound
Access only from M80 (northbound)

Southwestbound
Exit only to M80 (southbound)

Northeastbound
Exit only to M9 (eastbound)

Southwestbound
Access only from M9 (westbound)

A1(M) South Mimms - Baldock

Northbound
Exit only, no access

Southbound
Access only, no exit

Northbound
No restriction

Southbound
Exit only, no access

Northbound
Access only, no exit

Southbound
No access or exit

A1(M) Pontefract - Bedale

Northbound
No access to M62 (eastbound)

Southbound
No restriction

Northbound
Access only from M1 (northbound)

Southbound
Exit only to M1 (southbound)

A1(M) Scotch Corner - Newcastle upon Tyne

Northbound
Exit only to A66(M) (eastbound)

Southbound
Access only from A66(M) (westbound)

Northbound
No access. Exit only to A194(M) & A1 (northbound)

Southbound
No exit. Access only from A194(M) & A1 (southbound)

A3(M) Horndean - Havant

Northbound
Access only from A3

Southbound
Exit only to A3

Northbound
Exit only, no access

Southbound
Access only, no exit

A38(M) Birmingham Victoria Road (Park Circus)

Northbound
No exit

Southbound
No access

A48(M) Cardiff Spur

Westbound
Access only from M4 (westbound)

Eastbound
Exit only to M4 (eastbound)

Westbound
Exit only to A48 (westbound)

Eastbound
Access only from A48 (eastbound)

A57(M) Manchester Brook Street (A34)

Westbound
No exit

Eastbound
No access

A58(M) Leeds Park Lane and Westgate

Northbound
No restriction

Southbound
No access

A64(M) Leeds Clay Pit Lane (A58)

Westbound
No exit (to Clay Pit Lane)

Eastbound
No access (from Clay Pit Lane)

A66(M) Darlington Spur

Westbound
Exit only to A1(M) (southbound)

Eastbound
Access only from A1(M) (northbound)

A74(M) Gretna - Abington

Northbound
Exit only, no access

Southbound
No exit

A194(M) Newcastle upon Tyne

Northbound
Access only from A1(M) (northbound)

Southbound
Exit only to A1(M) (southbound)

A12 M25 - Ipswich

Northeastbound
Access only, no exit

Southwestbound
No restriction

Northeastbound
Exit only, no access

Southwestbound
Access only, no exit

Northeastbound
Exit only, no access

Southwestbound
Access only, no exit

Northeastbound
Access only, no exit

Southwestbound
Exit only, no access

Northeastbound
No restriction

Southwestbound
Access only, no exit

Northeastbound
Exit only, no access

Southwestbound
Access only, no exit

Northeastbound
Access only, no exit

Southwestbound
Exit only, no access

Northeastbound
Exit only, no access

Southwestbound
Access only, no exit

Northeastbound
Exit only (for Stratford St Mary and Dedham)

Southwestbound
Access only

A14 M1 - Felixstowe

Westbound
Exit only to M6 & M1 (northbound)

Eastbound
Access only from M6 & M1 (southbound)

Westbound
Exit only, no access

Eastbound
Access only, no exit

Westbound
Exit only to M11 (for London)

Eastbound
Access only, no exit

Westbound
Exit only to A14 (northbound)

Eastbound
Access only, no exit

Westbound
Access only, no exit

Eastbound
Exit only, no access

Westbound
Exit only to A11
Access only from A1303

Eastbound
Access only from A11

Westbound
Access only from A11

Eastbound
Exit only to A11

Westbound
Exit only, no access

Eastbound
Access only, no exit

Westbound
Access only, no exit

Eastbound
Exit only, no access

A55 Holyhead - Chester

Westbound
Exit only, no access

Eastbound
Access only, no exit

Westbound
Access only, no exit

Eastbound
Exit only, no access

Westbound
Exit only, no access

Eastbound
No access or exit.

Westbound
No restriction

Eastbound
No access or exit

Westbound
Exit only, no access

Eastbound
No access or exit

Westbound
Exit only, no access

Eastbound
Access only, no exit

Westbound
Exit only to A5104

Eastbound
Access only from A5104

Refer also to atlas pages 20–21

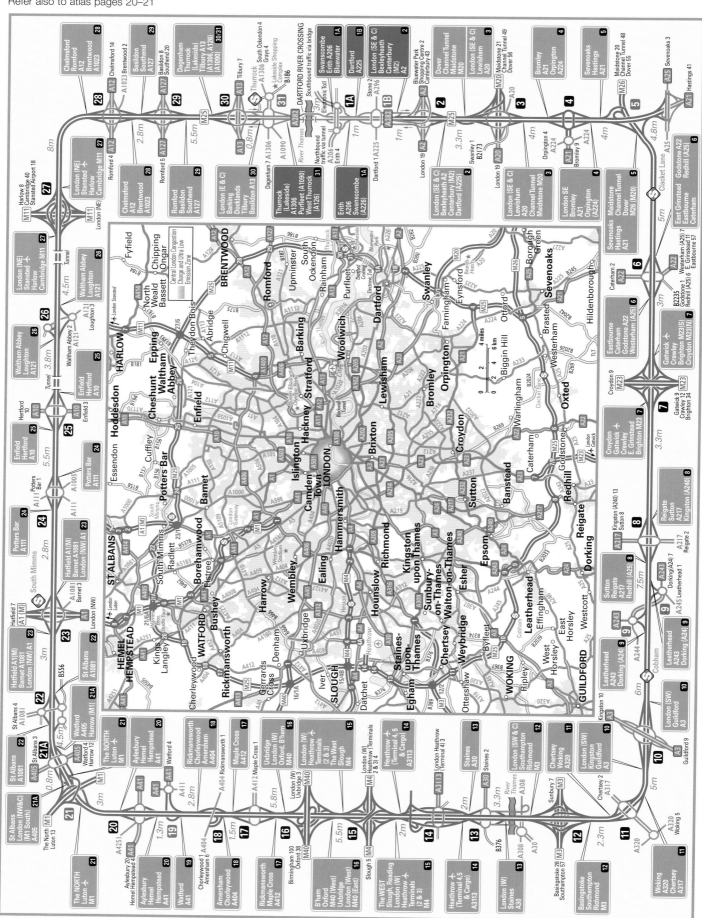

Refer also to atlas page 40

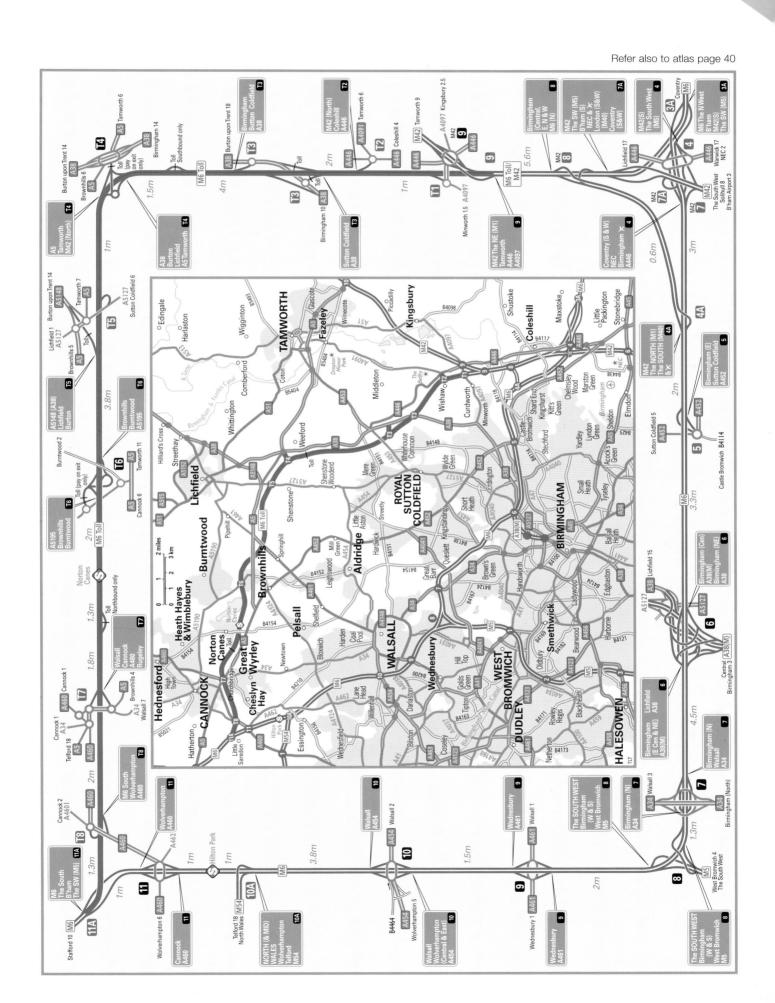

Smart motorways

Since Britain's first motorway (the Preston Bypass) opened in 1958, motorways have changed significantly. A vast increase in car journeys over the last 61 years has meant that motorways quickly filled to capacity. To combat this, the recent development of **smart motorways** uses technology to monitor and actively manage traffic flow and congestion.

How they work

Smart motorways utilise various active traffic management methods, monitored through a regional traffic control centre:

- Traffic flow is monitored using CCTV
- Speed limits are changed to smooth traffic flow and reduce stop-start driving
- Capacity of the motorway can be increased by either temporarily or permanently opening the hard shoulder to traffic
- Warning signs and messages alert drivers to hazards and traffic jams ahead
- Lanes can be closed in the case of an accident or emergency by displaying a red X sign

- Emergency refuge areas are located regularly along the motorway where there is no hard shoulder available

The map shows the main motorway network with the three different types of smart motorway in operation or planned to open over the next five years:

Controlled motorway
Variable speed limits without hard shoulder (the hard shoulder is used in emergencies only)

Hard shoulder running
Variable speed limits with part-time hard shoulder (the hard shoulder is open to traffic at busy times when signs permit)

All lane running
Variable speed limits with hard shoulder as permanent running lane (there is no hard shoulder); this is standard for all new smart motorway schemes since 2013

Standard motorway

Quick tips

- Never drive in a lane closed by a red X

- Keep to the speed limit shown on the gantries
- A solid white line indicates the hard shoulder – do not drive in it unless directed or in the case of an emergency
- A broken white line indicates a normal running lane
- Exit the smart motorway where possible if your vehicle is in difficulty. In an emergency, move onto the hard shoulder where there is one, or the nearest emergency refuge area
- Put on your hazard lights if you break down

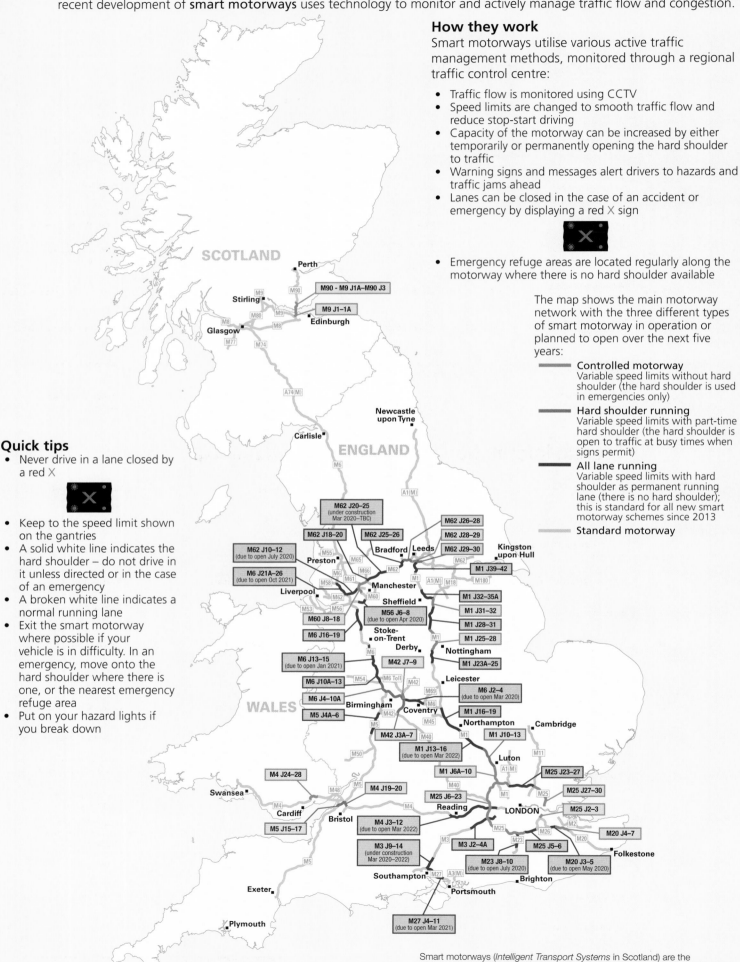

Smart motorways (*Intelligent Transport Systems* in Scotland) are the responsibility of Highways England, Transport Scotland and Transport for Wales

Motoring information

M4	Motorway with number	S	Primary route service area	Road tunnel	F	International freight terminal
Toll T4	Toll motorway with toll station	BATH	Primary route destination	Toll →	Road toll, steep gradient (arrows point downhill)	H	24-hour Accident & Emergency hospital
6	Motorway junction with and without number	A1123	Other A road single/dual carriageway	5	Distance in miles between symbols	C	Crematorium
5	Restricted motorway junctions	B2070	B road single/dual carriageway	or V	Vehicle ferry	P·R	Park and Ride (at least 6 days per week)
Fleet S R	Motorway service area, rest area		Minor road more than 4 metres wide, less than 4 metres wide		Fast vehicle ferry or catamaran		City, town, village or other built-up area
	Motorway and junction under construction		Roundabout		Railway line, in tunnel	628 637 Lecht Summit	Height in metres, mountain pass
A3	Primary route single/dual carriageway		Interchange/junction	—o—X—	Railway/tram station, level crossing		Snow gates (on main routes)
1	Primary route junction with and without number		Narrow primary/other A/B road with passing places (Scotland)	+++++++	Tourist railway		National boundary
3	Restricted primary route junctions		Road under construction	⊕ ✈ Ⓗ	Airport (major/minor), heliport		County, administrative boundary

Touring information To avoid disappointment, check opening times before visiting

	Scenic route	✿	Garden	Waterfall		Motor-racing circuit
i	Tourist Information Centre	♣	Arboretum	Hill-fort		Air show venue
i	Tourist Information Centre (seasonal)		Country park	Roman antiquity		Ski slope (natural, artificial)
V	Visitor or heritage centre		Agricultural showground	Prehistoric monument		National Trust site
♣	Picnic site		Theme park	Battle site with year 1066		National Trust for Scotland site
⊕	Caravan site (AA inspected)		Farm or animal centre	Steam railway centre		English Heritage site
▲	Camping site (AA inspected)		Zoological or wildlife collection	Cave or cavern		Historic Scotland site
▲⊕	Caravan & camping site (AA inspected)		Bird collection	Windmill, monument		Cadw (Welsh heritage) site
♠	Abbey, cathedral or priory		Aquarium	Beach (award winning)	★	Other place of interest
♠	Ruined abbey, cathedral or priory		RSPB site	Lighthouse		Boxed symbols indicate attractions within urban areas
♜	Castle		National Nature Reserve (England, Scotland, Wales)	Golf course	◉	World Heritage Site (UNESCO)
	Historic house or building		Local nature reserve	Football stadium		National Park and National Scenic Area (Scotland)
	Museum or art gallery		Wildlife Trust reserve	County cricket ground		Forest Park
	Industrial interest		Forest drive	Rugby Union national stadium		Sandy beach
	Aqueduct or viaduct		National trail	International athletics stadium		Heritage coast
	Vineyard, brewery or distillery	☼	Viewpoint	Horse racing, show jumping		Major shopping centre

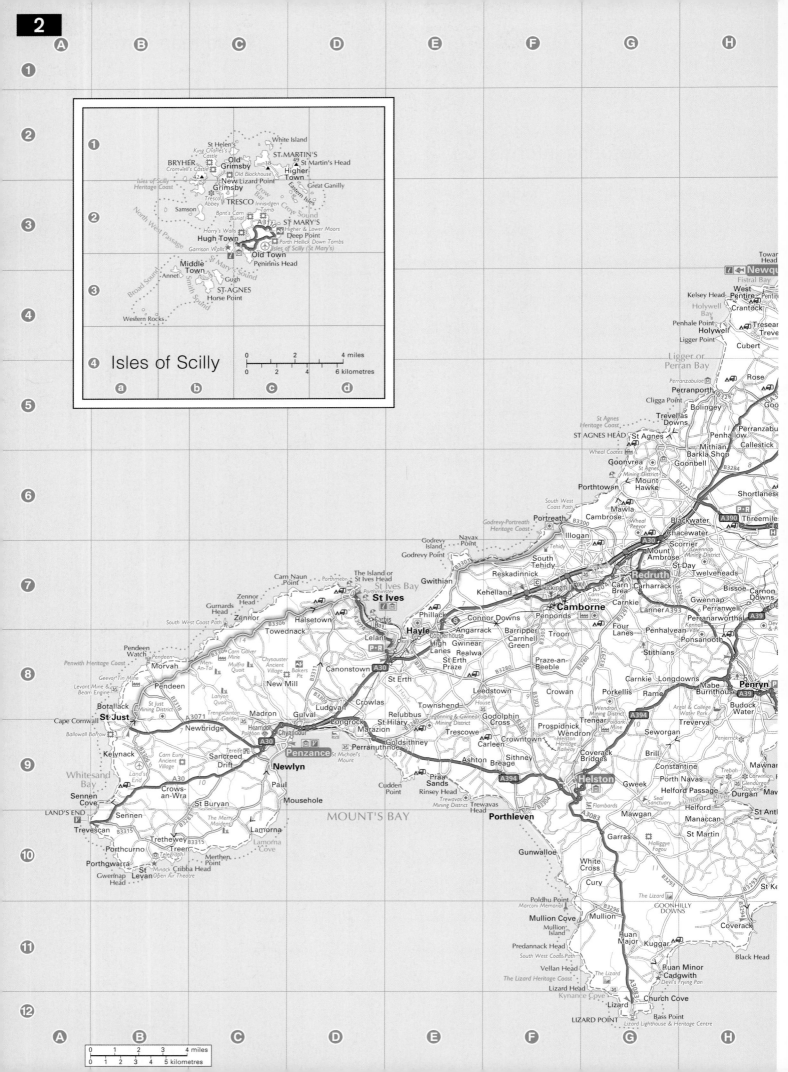

2

Isles of Scilly

St Helen's
White Island
King Charles's Castle
ST MARTIN'S
St Martin's Head
BRYHER
Cromwell's Castle
Old Grimsby
Old Blockhouse
Higher Town
New Grimsby
Lizard Point
Isles of Scilly Heritage Coast
Great Ganilly
Eastern Isles
North West Passage
Tresco Abbey
TRESCO
Innisidgen Tomb
Crow Sound
Samson
Bant's Carn Burial
ST MARY'S
Higher & Lower Moors
Harry's Walls
Deep Point
Hugh Town
Porth Hellick Down Tombs
Garrison Walls
Isles of Scilly (St Mary's)
Old Town
Peninnis Head
Middle Town
St Mary's Sound
Broad Sound
Annet
Gugh
ST AGNES
Smith Sound
Horse Point
Western Rocks

0   2   4 miles
0   2   4   6 kilometres

Isles of Scilly

Towan Head
Newquay
Fistral Bay
Kelsey Head
West Pentire
Pentire
Holywell Bay
Penhale Point
Crantock
Tresean
Treve
Holywell
Ligger Point
Cubert
Ligger or Perran Bay
Perranzabuloe
Rose
Perranporth
Cligga Point
Bolingey
Perranzabu
Trevellas Downs
St Agnes Heritage Coast
Penhallow
Perranzabu
Callestick
ST AGNES HEAD
St Agnes
Mithian
Barkla Shop
Wheal Coates
Goonvrea
Goonbell
Mount Hawke
Porthtowan
Mining District
Shortlanes
South West Coast Path
Mawla
Cambrose
Wheal Peevor
Blackwater
Threemile
Godrevy-Portreath Heritage Coast
Portreath
Illogan
Chacewater
Navax Point
Tehidy
Mine
Scorrier
Mount Ambrose
Godrevy Point
South Tehidy
Reskadinnick
Redruth
St Day
Twelveheads
The Island or St Ives Head
Gwithian
Nickingmill
Carn Brea
Carharrack
Bissoe
Carnon Downs
Carn Naun Point
Porthmeor
St Ives Bay
Kehelland
Camborne
Carn Brea
Gwennap
Perranwell
Porthminster
St Ives
Phillack
Penponds
Carnkie
Lanner
Perranarwortha
Zennor Head
Carbis Bay
Hayle
Angarrack
Barripper
Troon
Penhalvean
Ponsanooth
Gurnards Head
Zennor
Lelant
High Lanes
Carnhell Green
Four Lanes
Stithians
Kennall
Halsetown
Gwinear
Realwa
Praze-an-Beeble
South West Coast Path
Towednack
St Erth Praze
Carnkie
Longdowns
Mabe Burnthouse
Penryn
Pendeen Watch
Carn Galver Mine
New Mill
Canonstown
Crowan
Wendron Mining District
Porkellis
Rame
Penwith Heritage Coast
Morvah
Men-An-Tol
Mulfra Quoit
St Erth
Townshend
Leedstown
Godolphin House
Crowan
Prospidnick
Trenear
Poldark Mine
Argal & College Water Park
Budock Water
Geevor Tin Mine
Pendeen
Chysauster Ancient Village
Bakers Pit
Godolphin Cross
Wendron
Treverva
Levant Mine & Beam Engine
Lanyon Quoit
Madron
Gulval
Ludgvan
Crowlas
Relubbus
St Hilary
Tregonning & Gwinear Mining District
Crowntown
Helston Heritage Railway
Coverack Bridges
Sewogan
Botallack
Trengwainton Garden
Heamoor
Poltair
Longrock
Marazion
Trescowe
Carleen
Sithney
Penjerrick
St Just Mining District
Newbridge
Chyandour
St Michael's Mount
Carnmenellis
Ashton
Breage
Carras
Constantine
Trebah Garden
Mawnan
St Just
Teneriffe
Penzance
Perranuthnoe
Helston
Gweek
Porth Navas
Glendurgan Garden
Cape Cornwall
Ballowall Barrow
Sancreed
Drift
Newlyn
Cudden Point
Praa Sands
Rinsey Head
Flambards
Seal Sanctuary
Helford Passage
Durgan
Mav
Kelynack
Carn Euny Ancient Village
Paul
Rinsey Head
Trewavas Head
Mawgan
Helford
St Anth
Whitesand Bay
Land's End
Mousehole
Mount's Bay
Porthleven
Manaccan
St Martin
Sennen Cove
Crows-an-Wra
St Buryan
Lamorna
Cudden Point
Praa Sands Mining District
Gunwalloe
Halliggye Fogou
LAND'S END
Sennen
The Merry Maidens
Lamorna Cove
White Cross
Garras
St Keve
Trevescan
Trethewey
Treen
Merthen Point
Cury
The Lizard
Coverack
Porthcurno
Minack Open Air Theatre
Cribba Head
Poldhu Point
Marconi Memorial
GOONHILLY DOWNS
Porthgwarra
St Levan
Mullion Cove
Mullion
Gwennap Head
Mullion Island
Ruan Major
Kuggar
Predannack Head
South West Coast Path
Ruan Minor
Cadgwith
Vellan Head
Devil's Frying Pan
Black Head
The Lizard Heritage Coast
The Lizard
Lizard Head
Lizard
Church Cove
Kynance Cove
LIZARD POINT
Bass Point
Lizard Lighthouse & Heritage Centre

0   1   2   3   4 miles
0   1   2   3   4   5 kilometres

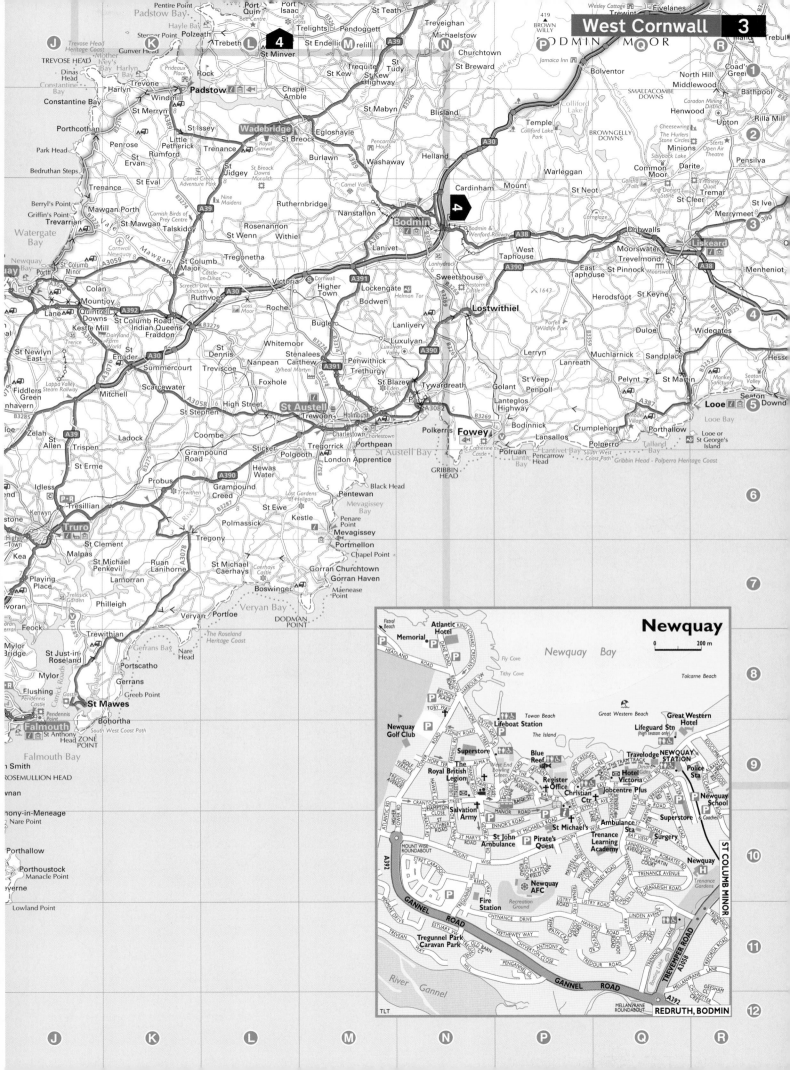

BODMIN MOOR

Newquay

Newquay Bay

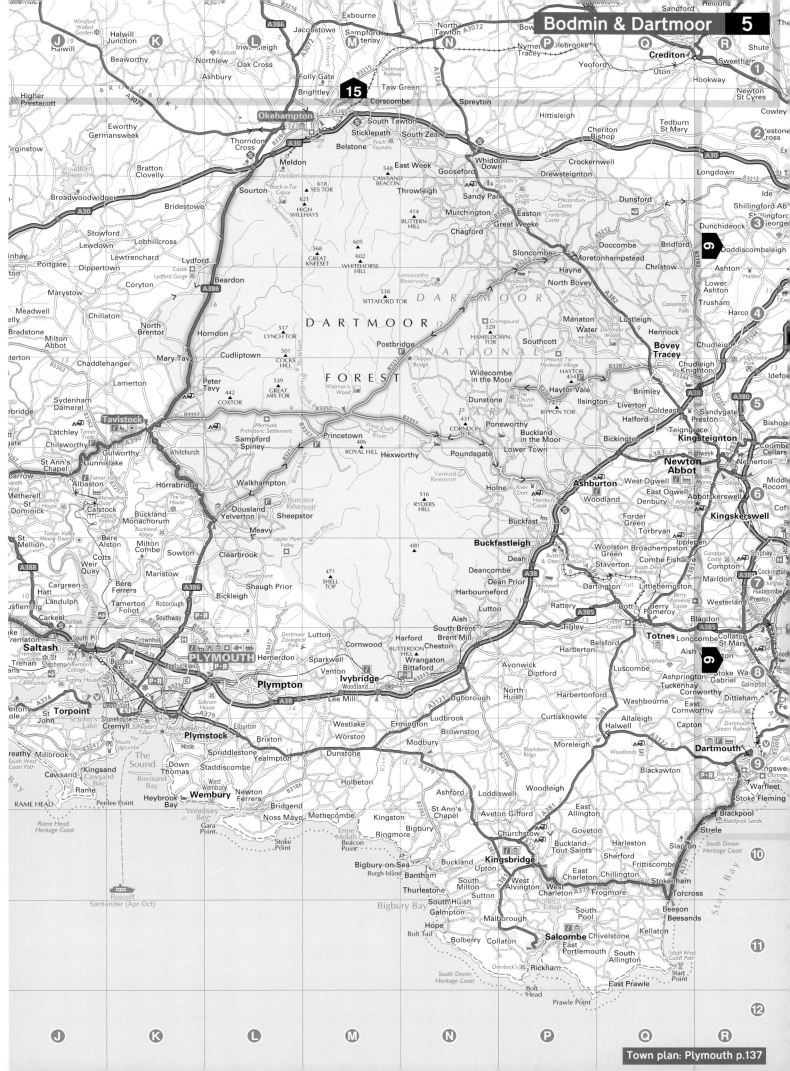

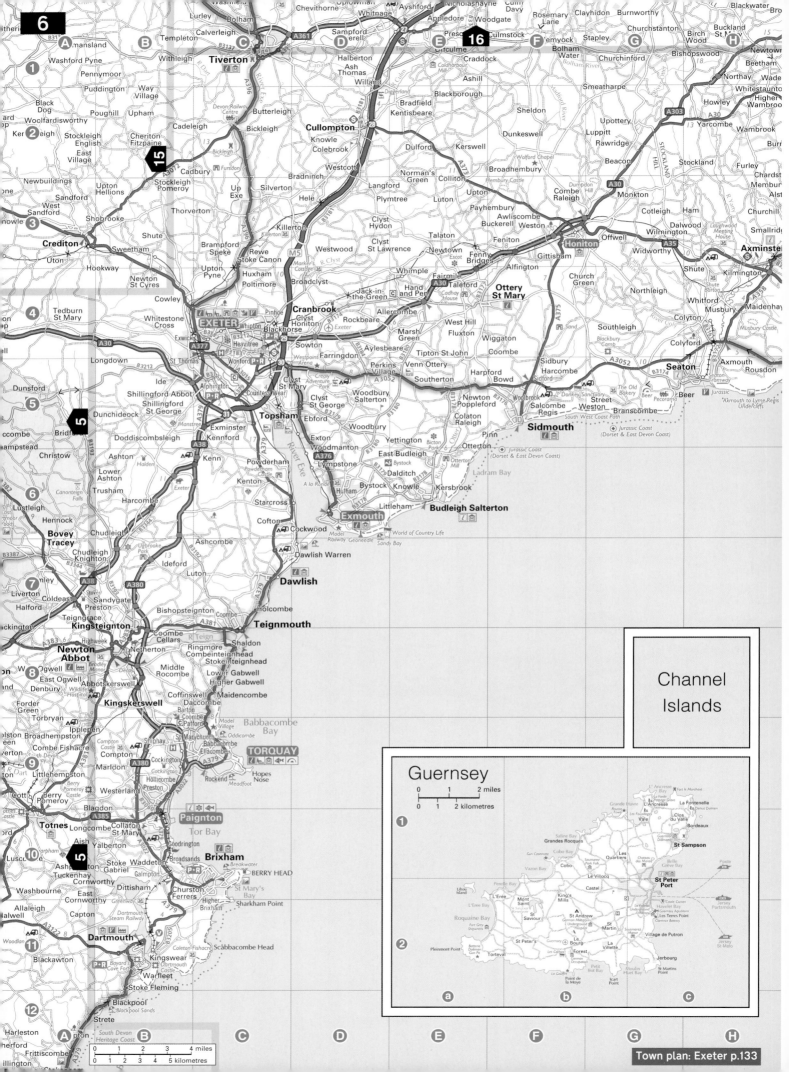

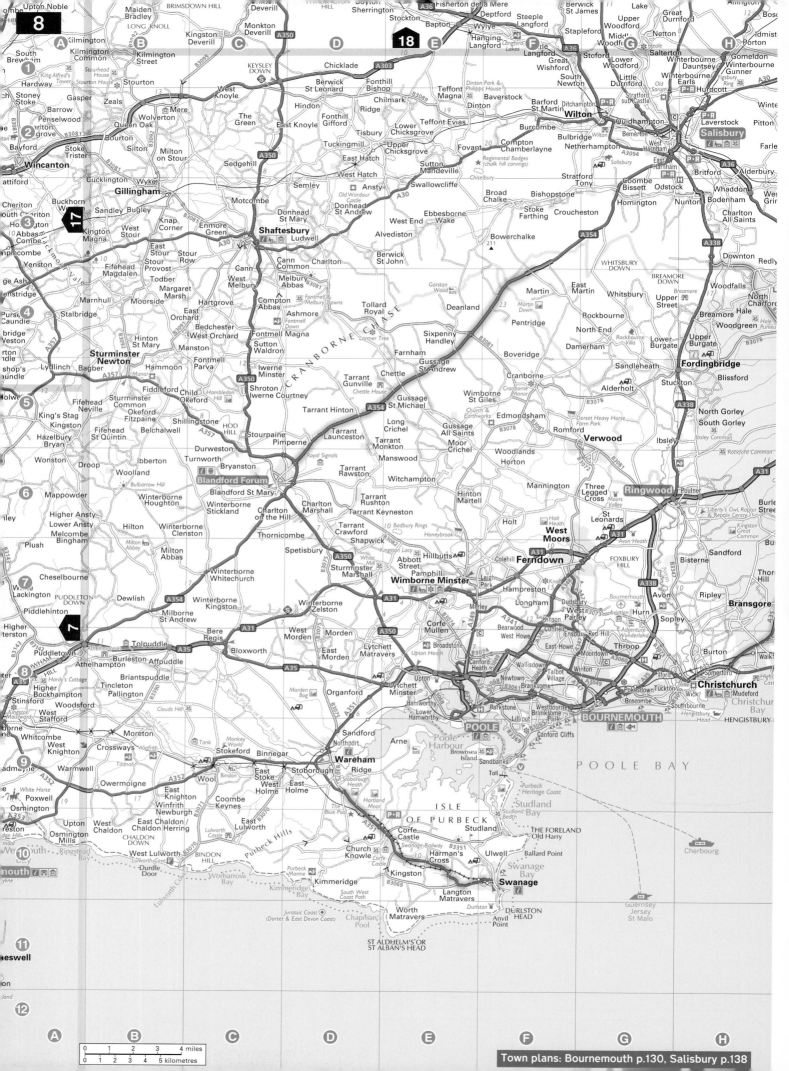

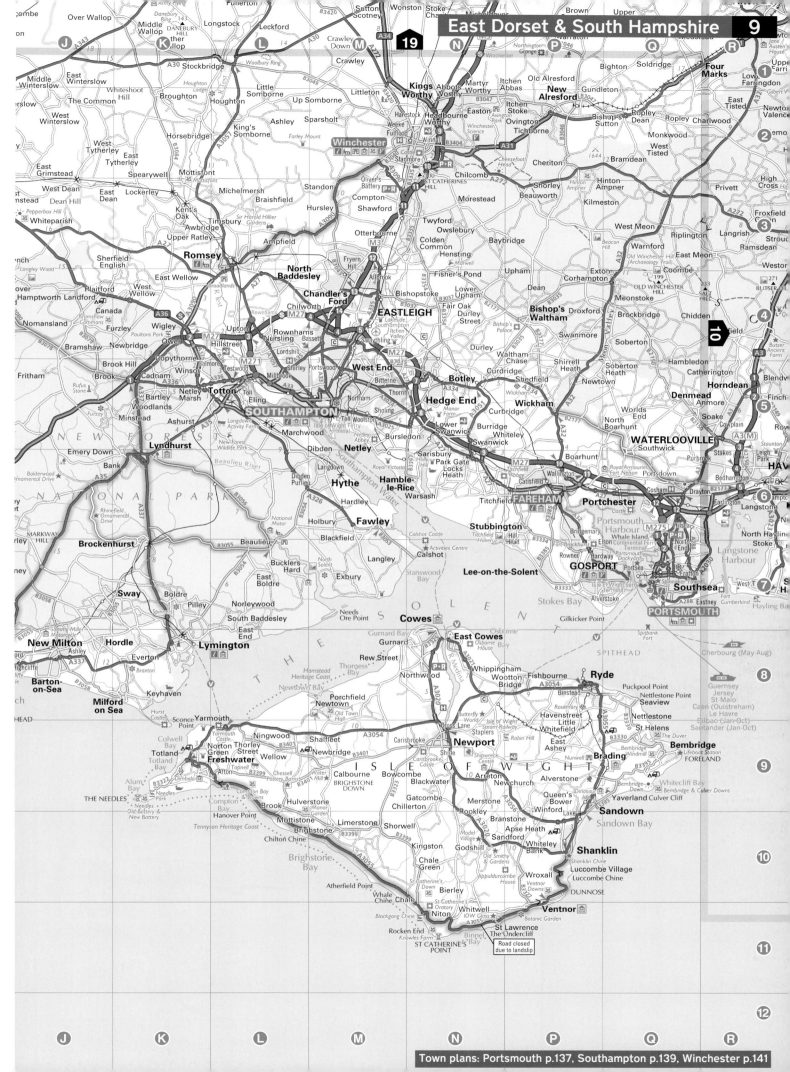

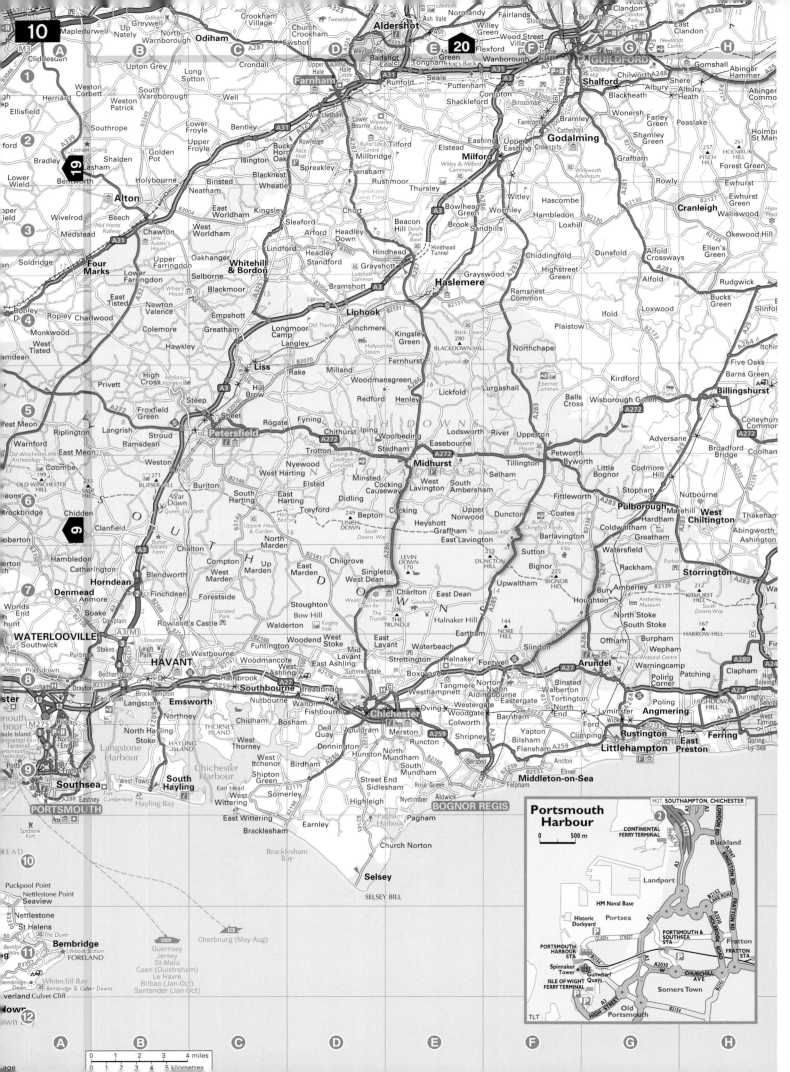

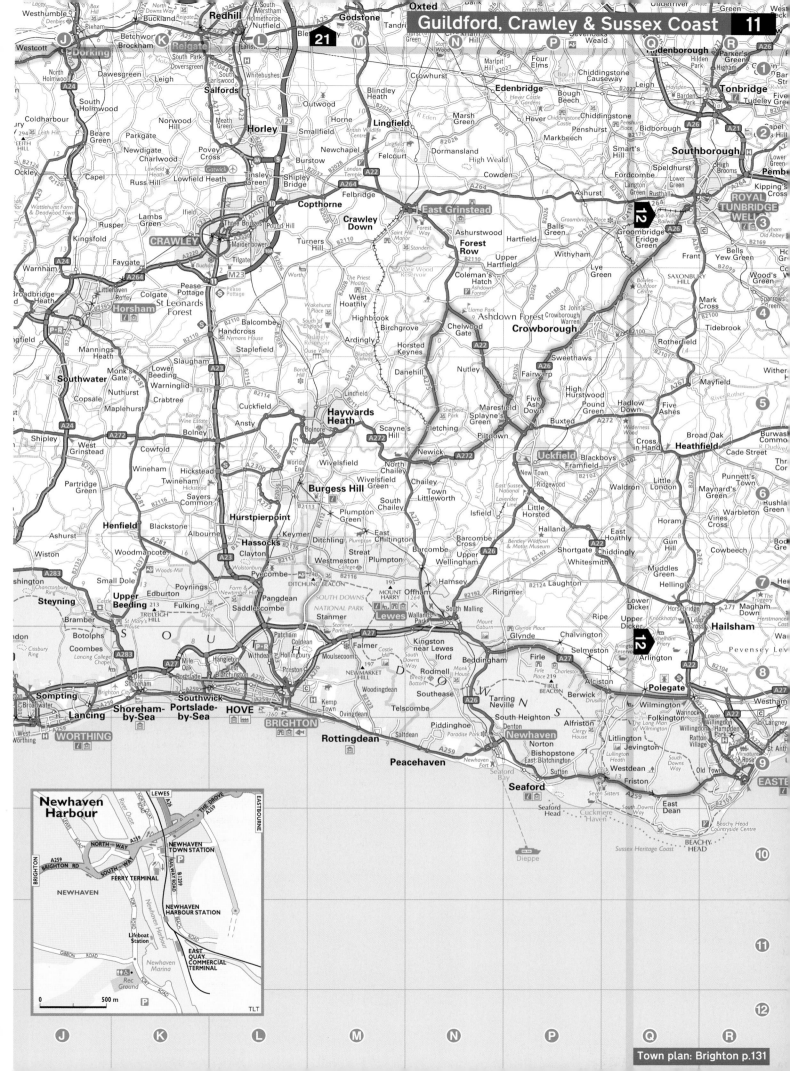

Town plan: Royal Tunbridge Wells p.138

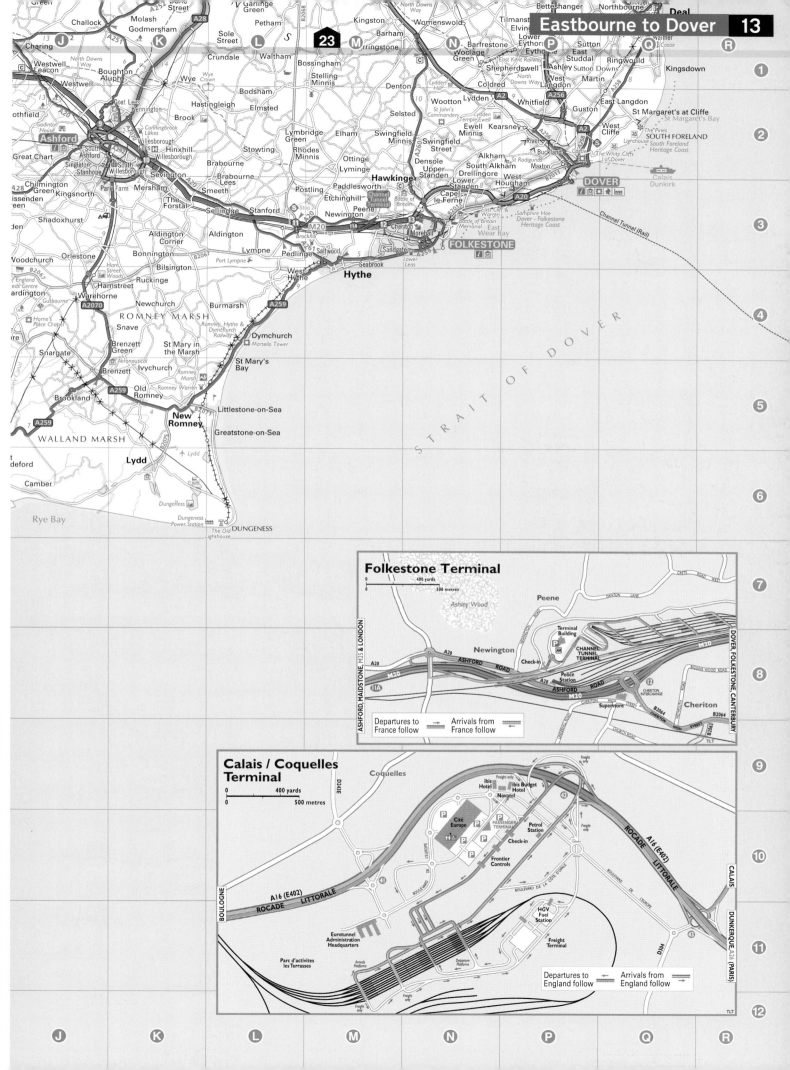

Folkestone Terminal

Departures to France follow →
Arrivals from France follow

Calais / Coquelles Terminal

Departures to England follow ←
Arrivals from England follow

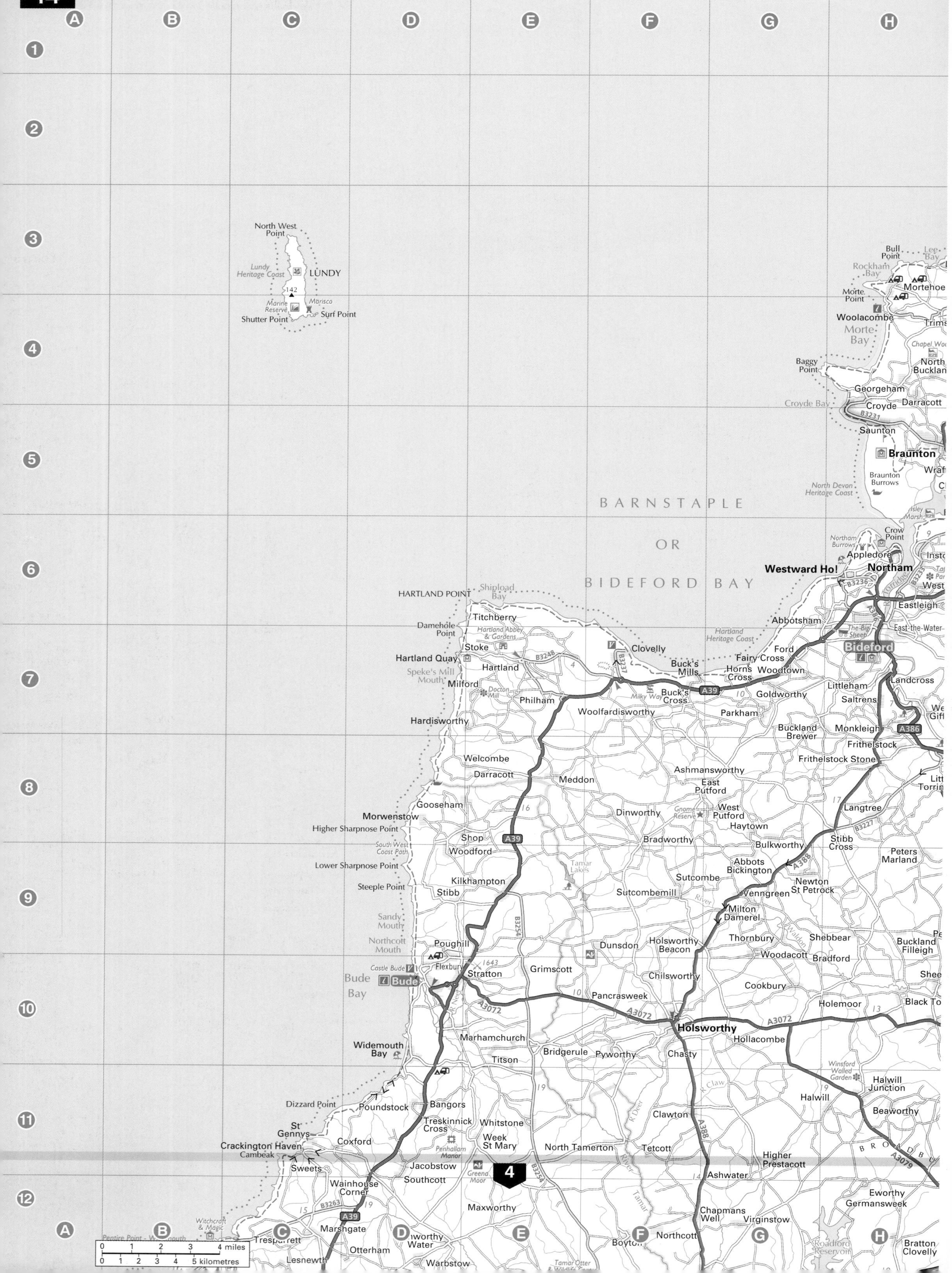

A B C D E F G H

1
2
3
4
5
6
7
8
9
10
11
12

A B C D E F G H

North West
Point
Lundy
Heritage Coast   LUNDY
•142
Marine   Marisco
Reserve
Shutter Point   Surf Point

BARNSTAPLE

OR

BIDEFORD BAY

Bull
Point   Lee
Rockham   Bay
Bay
Morte
Point   Mortehoe
Woolacombe
Morte
Bay   Chapel Wood

Baggy
Point   North
Bucklan
Georgeham   Darracott
Croyde Bay
Croyde
B3231
Saunton

North Devon
Heritage Coast
Braunton
Braunton   Wra
Burrows
Isley
Marsh

Northam
Burrows   Crow
Point
Westward Ho!   Appledore Northam   Insto
Eastleigh   East-the-Water
Abbotsham   Bideford
The Big
Sheep
Ford
HARTLAND POINT   Shipload
Bay   Fairy Cross   Woodtown
Titchberry   Buck's   Horns
Mills   Cross
Damehole   Hartland Abbey   Clovelly   Goldworthy   Littleham
Point   & Gardens   Saltrens
Stoke   Buck's
Hartland Quay   B3248   Milky Way   Cross   10
Hartland   Parkham
Milford   Docton
Speke's Mill   Mill   Philham   Woolfardisworthy   Buckland   Monkleigh
Mouth   Brewer
Hardisworthy   Frithelstock
Frithelstock Stone
Welcombe   Ashmansworthy
Darracott   Meddon   East   West
Putford   Putford
Gooseham   Dinworthy   Gnome   Haytown   Langtree
Morwenstow   Reserve
Higher Sharpnose Point   Shop   Bradworthy   Bulkworthy   Stibb
South West   Woodford   Cross   Peters
Coast Path   Sutcombe   Marland
Lower Sharpnose Point   Tamar
Lakes   Sutcombemill   Abbots
Bickington   Newton
Steeple Point   Kilkhampton   Venngreen   St Petrock
Stibb   Dunsdon   Milton
Sandy   Damerel
Mouth   Holsworthy   Thornbury   Shebbear   Buckland
Northcott   Beacon   Woodacott   Filleigh
Mouth   Poughill   Chilsworthy   Bradford   Shee
Castle Bude   Grimscott
Flexbury   Cookbury
Bude   Stratton   Holemoor   Black To
Bude   Pancrasweek
Bay   A3072   Holsworthy
A3072   Hollacombe
Widemouth   Marhamchurch   Halwill
Bay   Titson   Bridgerule Pyworthy   Chasty   Junction
Clawton   Halwill
Dizzard Point   Poundstock   Bangors   Beaworthy
St   Treskinnick   Whitstone   Tetcott   Higher
Gennys   Coxford   Cross   Week   North Tamerton   Prestacott
Crackington Haven   St Mary   Penhallam   Ashwater
Cambeak   Manor   Green
Sweets   Wainhouse   Jacobstow   Moor   Chapmans   Eworthy
Corner   Southcott   4   Well   Germansweek
Virginstow
Maxworthy
Marshgate   Bratton
Witchcraft   Clovelly
& Magic   Otterham   Iworthy
Trespurrett   Water   Boyton   Northcott
Lesnewth   Warbstow   Tamar Otter
0 1 2 3 4 miles   & Wildlife Cen
0 1 2 3 4 5 kilometres

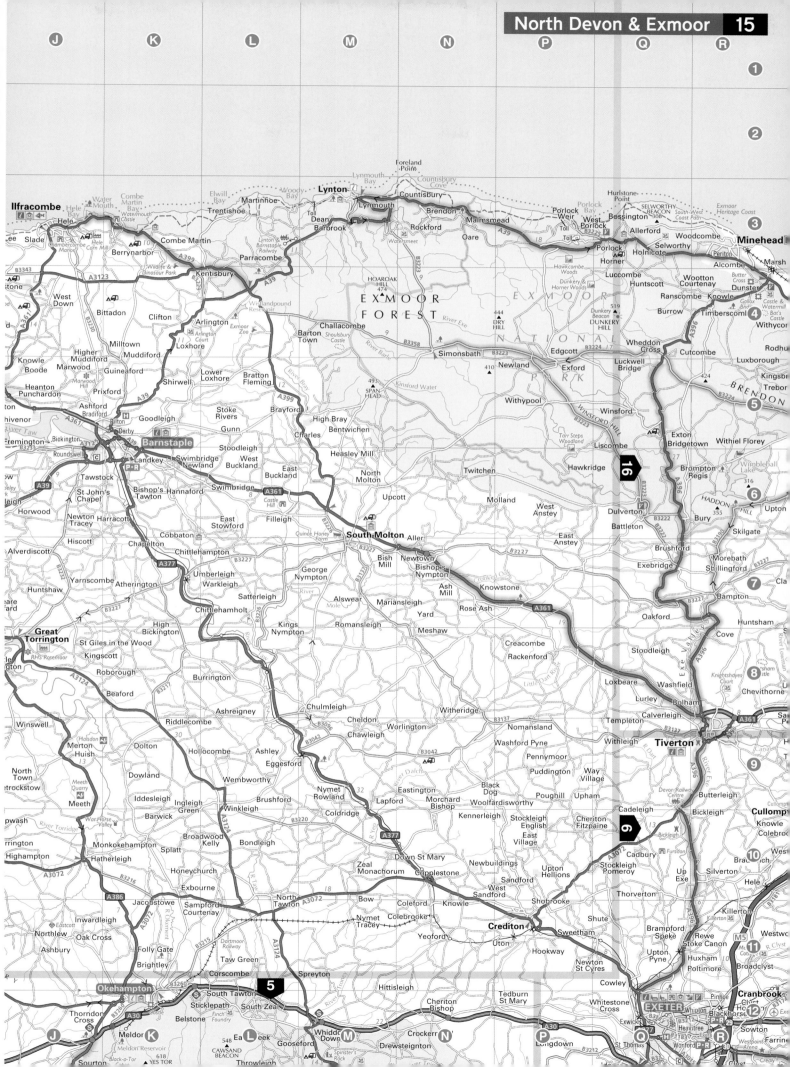

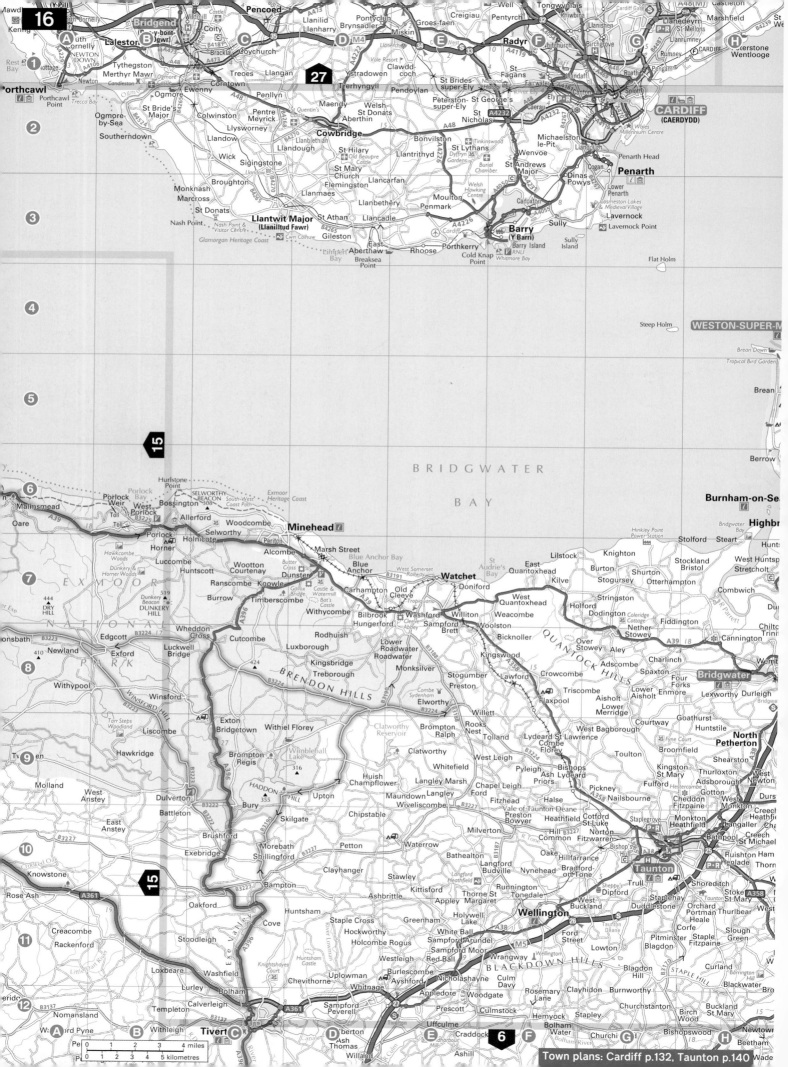

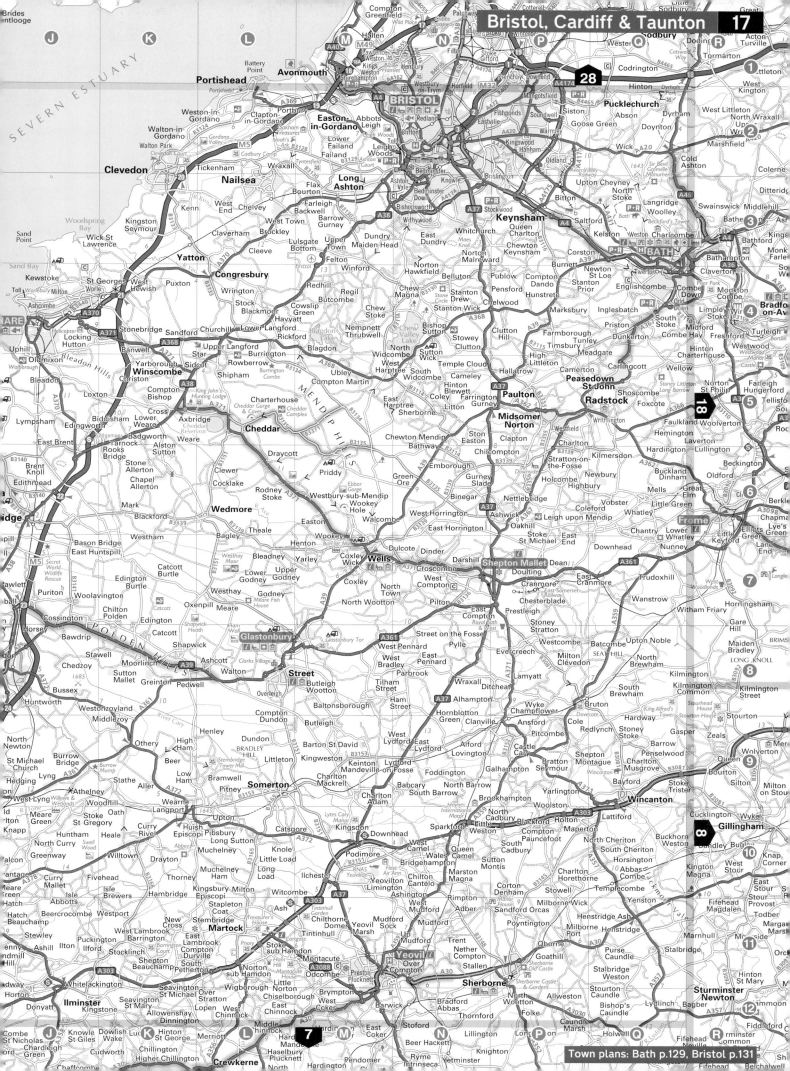

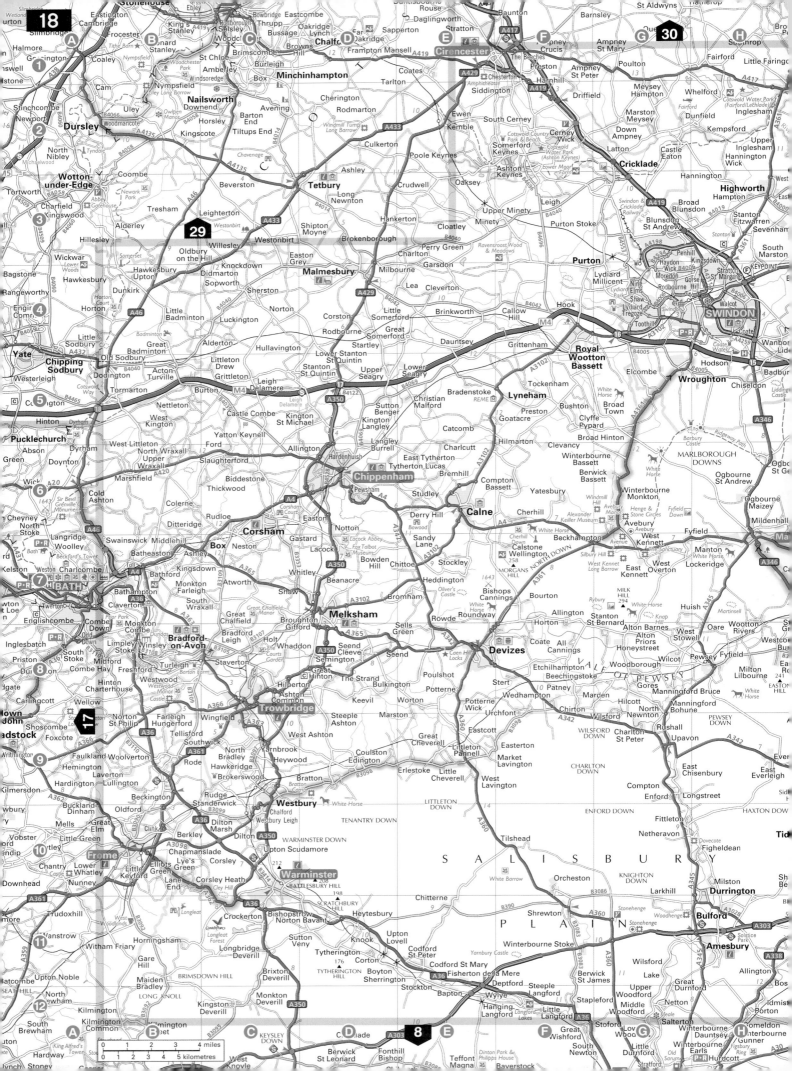

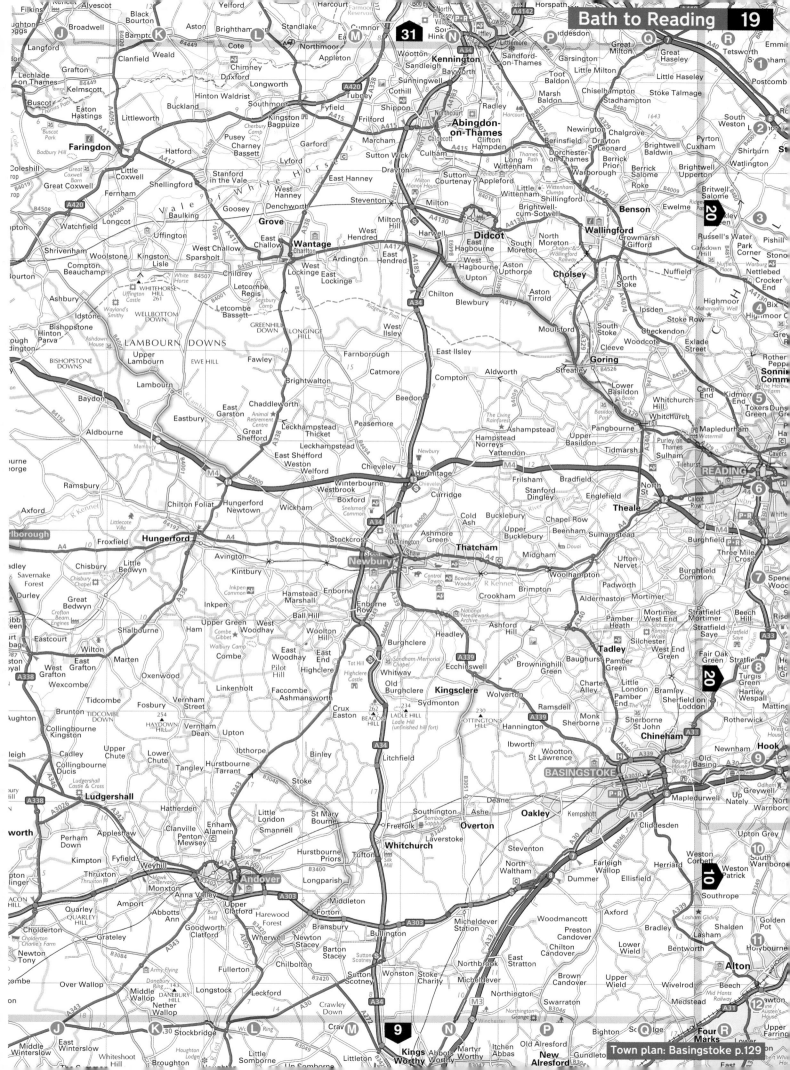

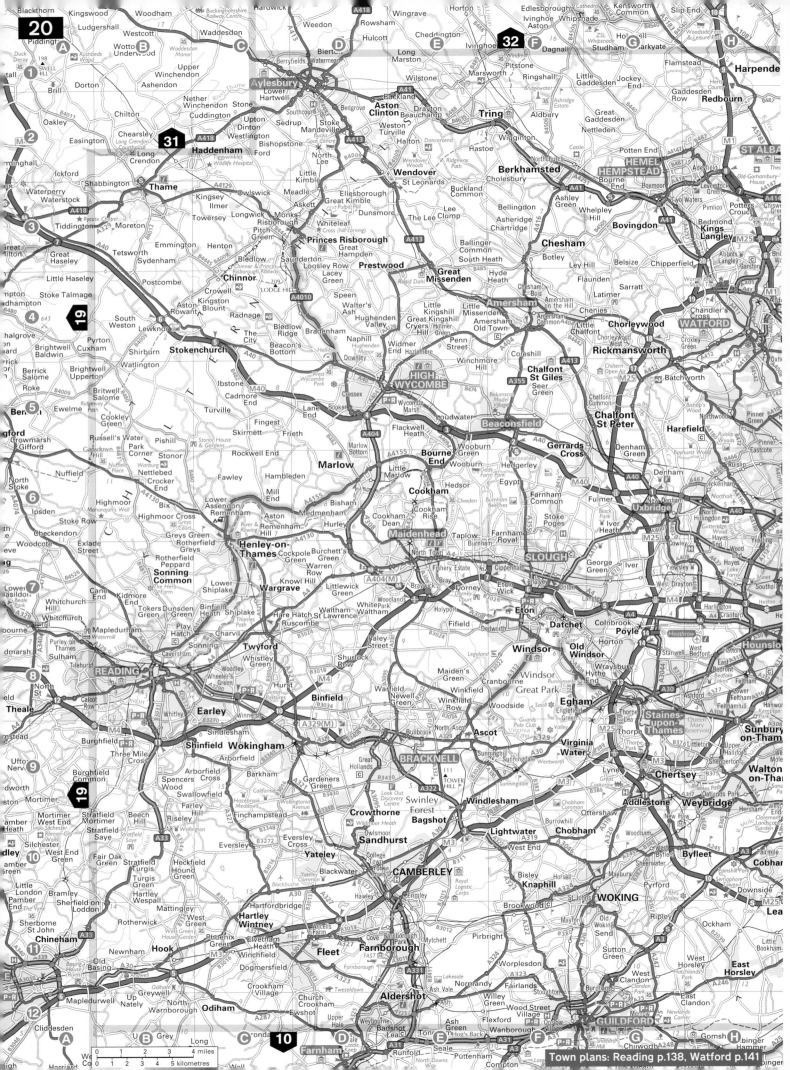

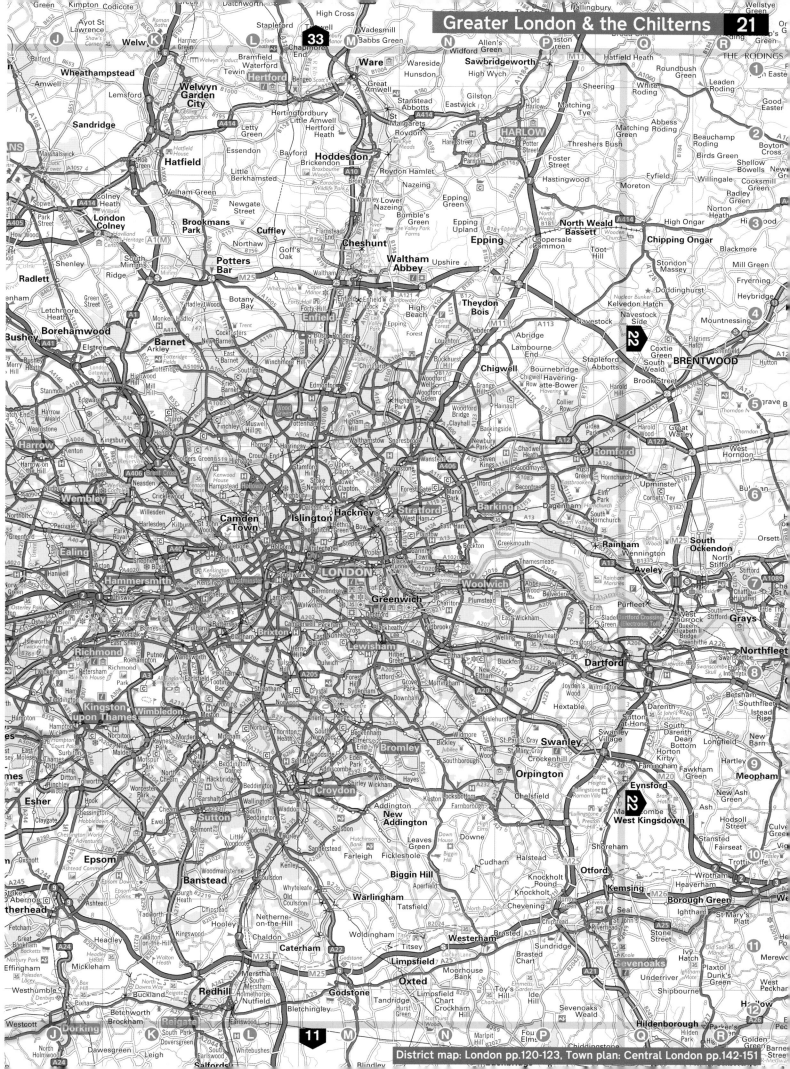

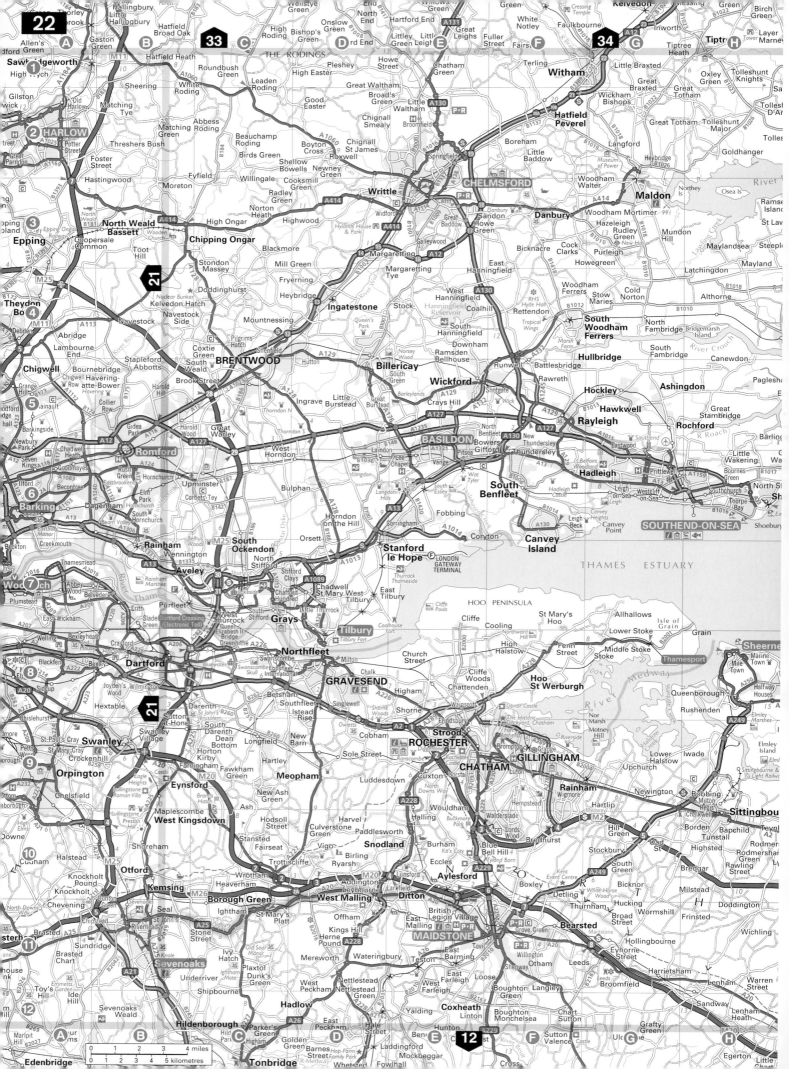

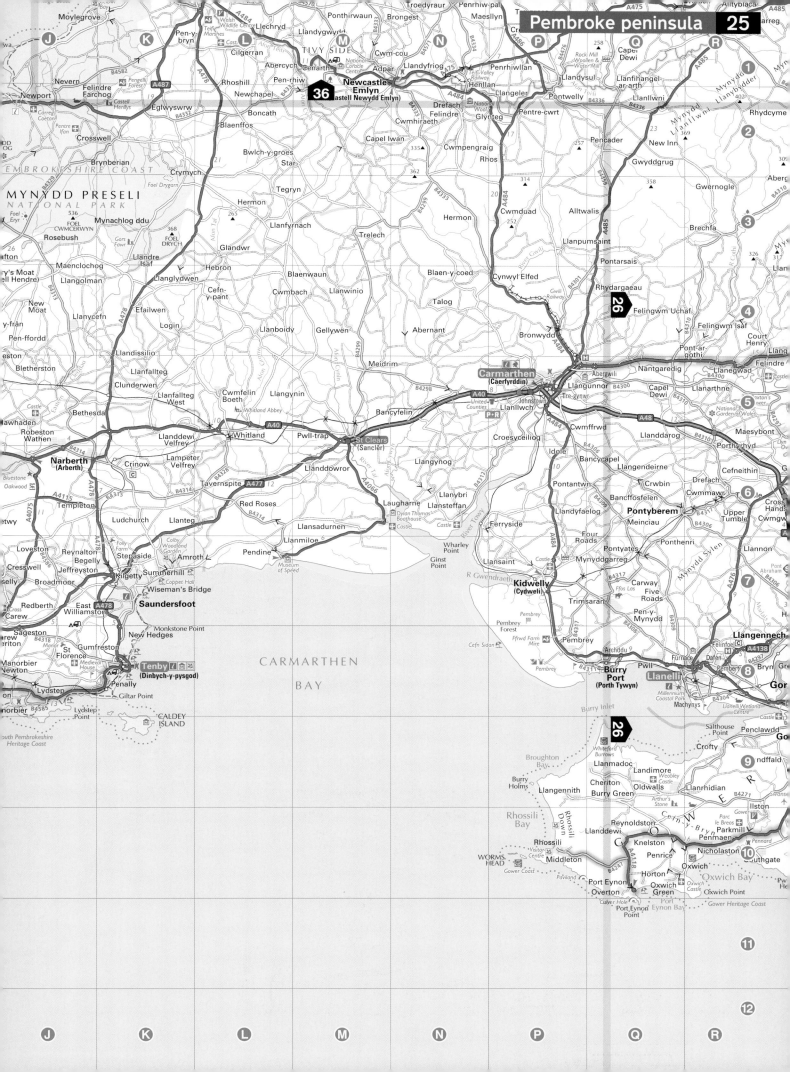

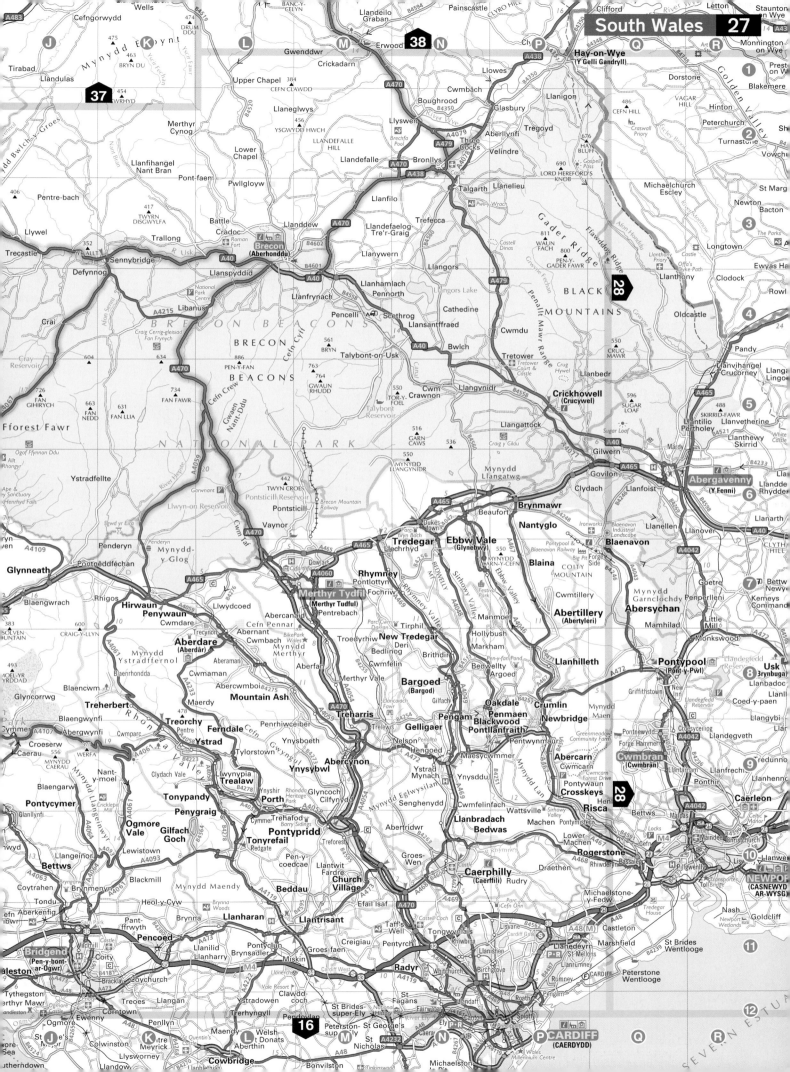

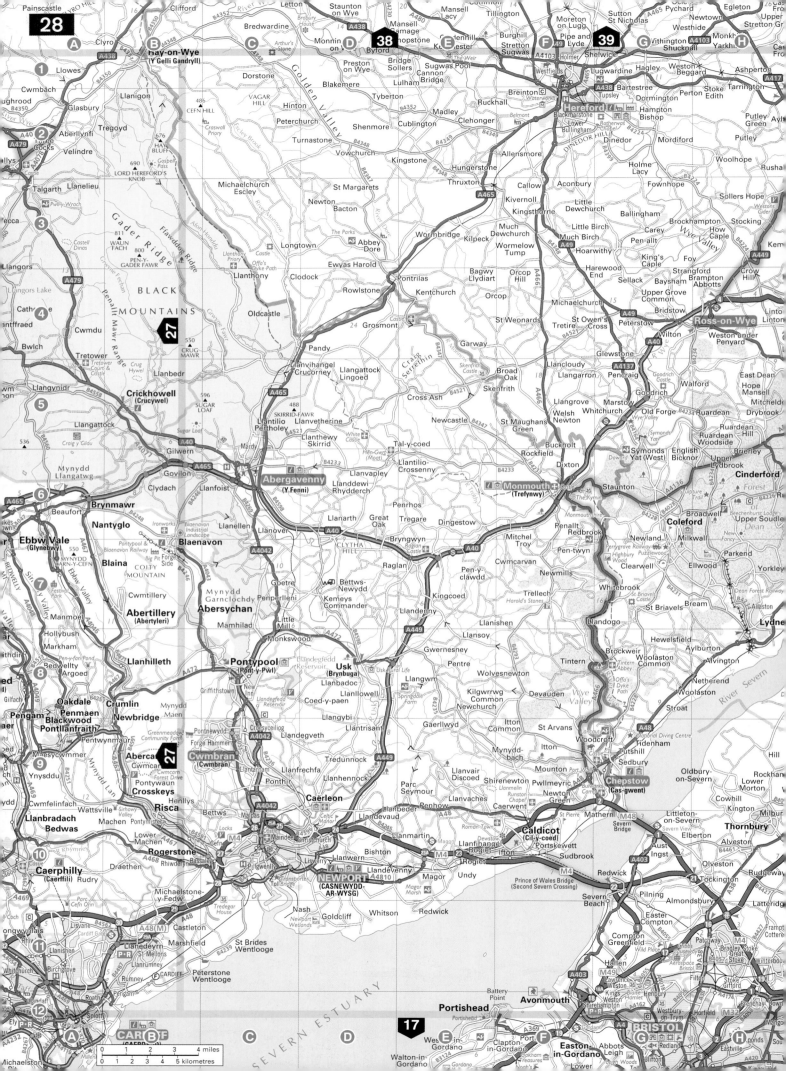

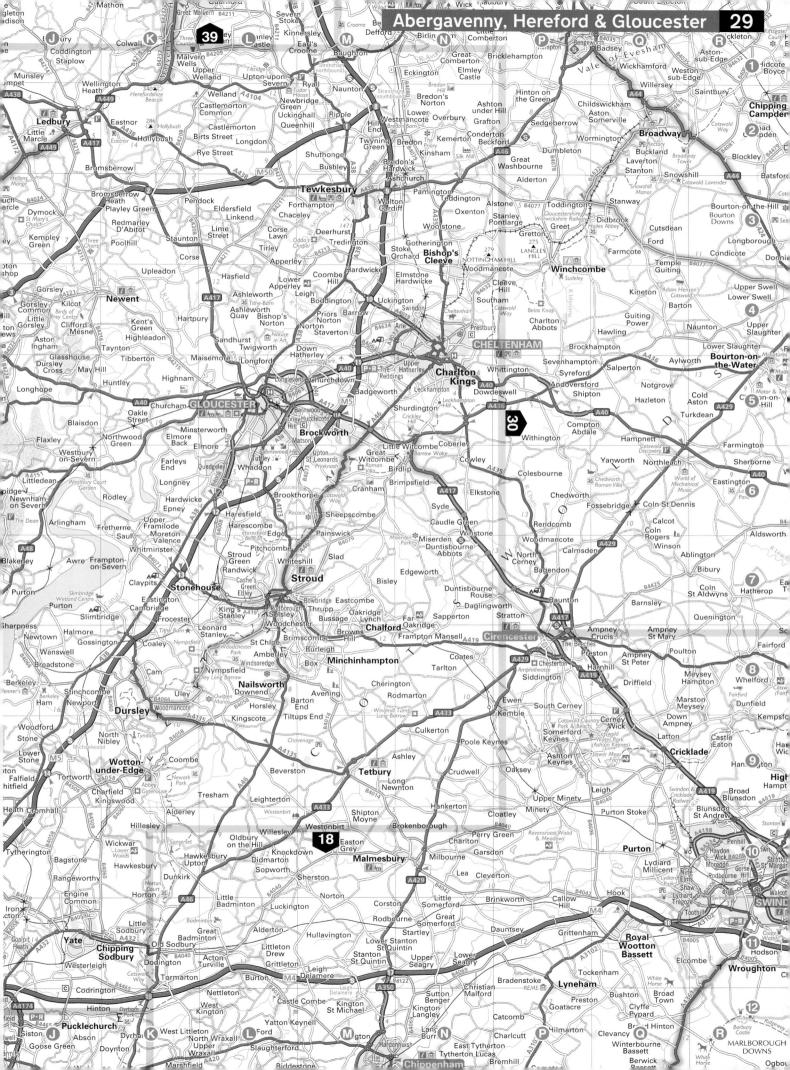

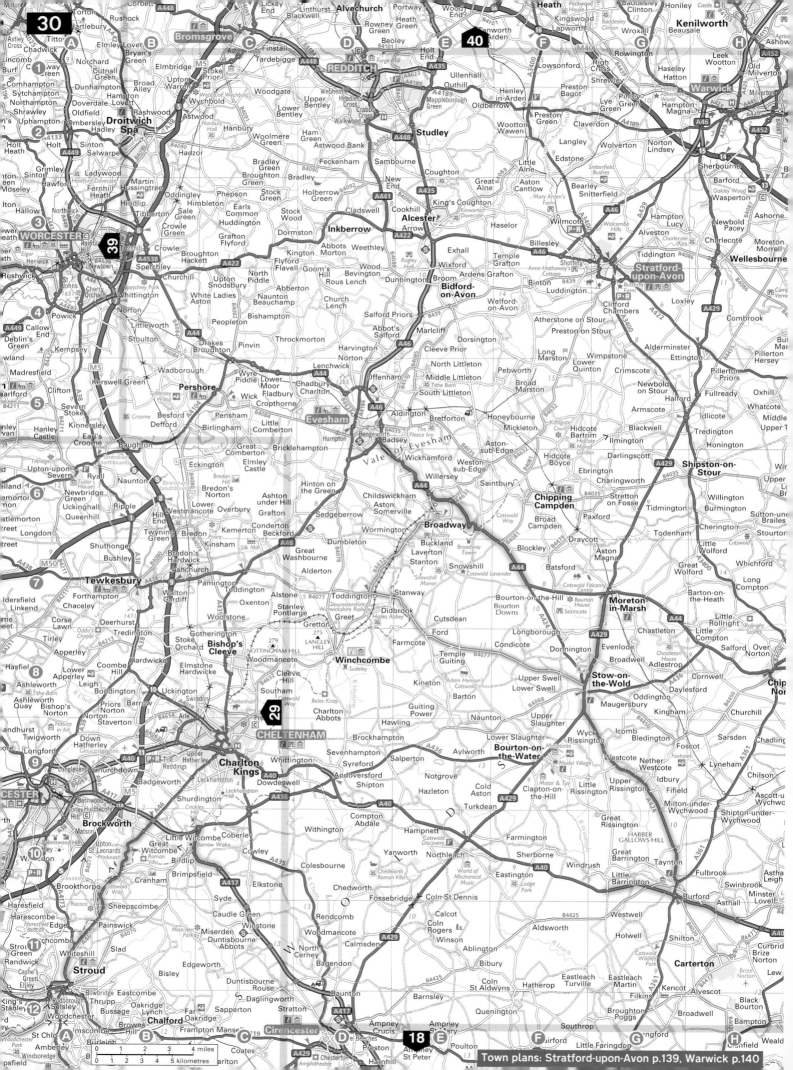

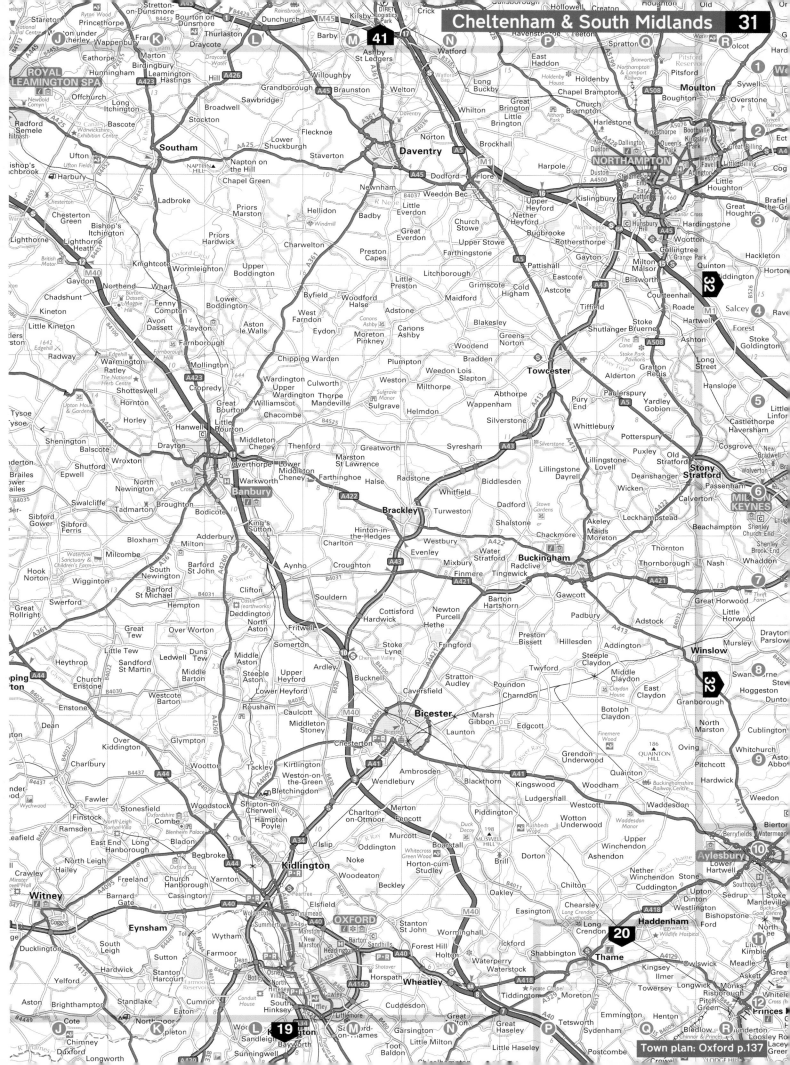

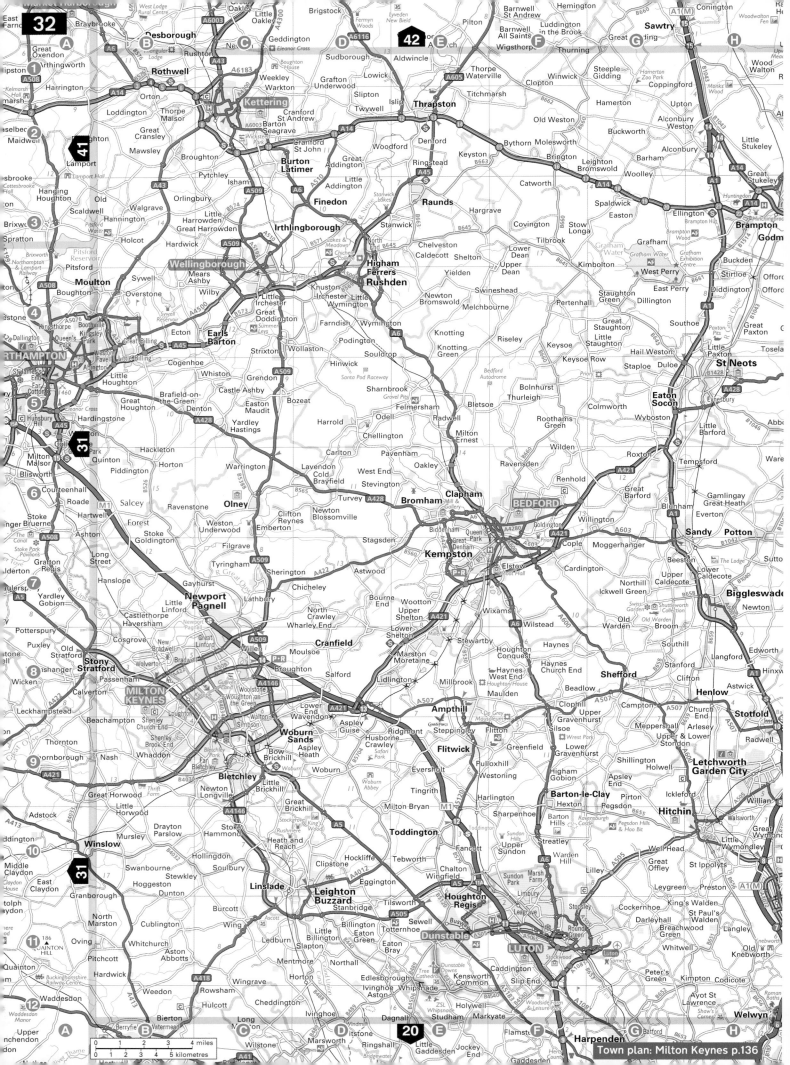

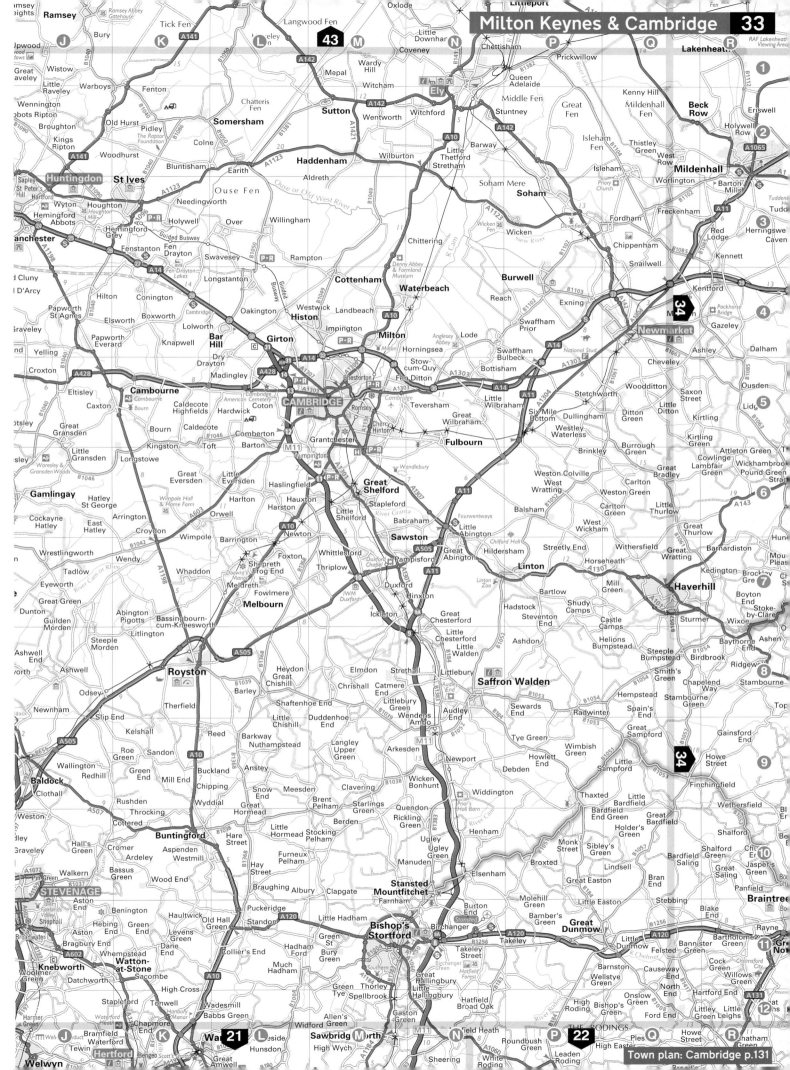

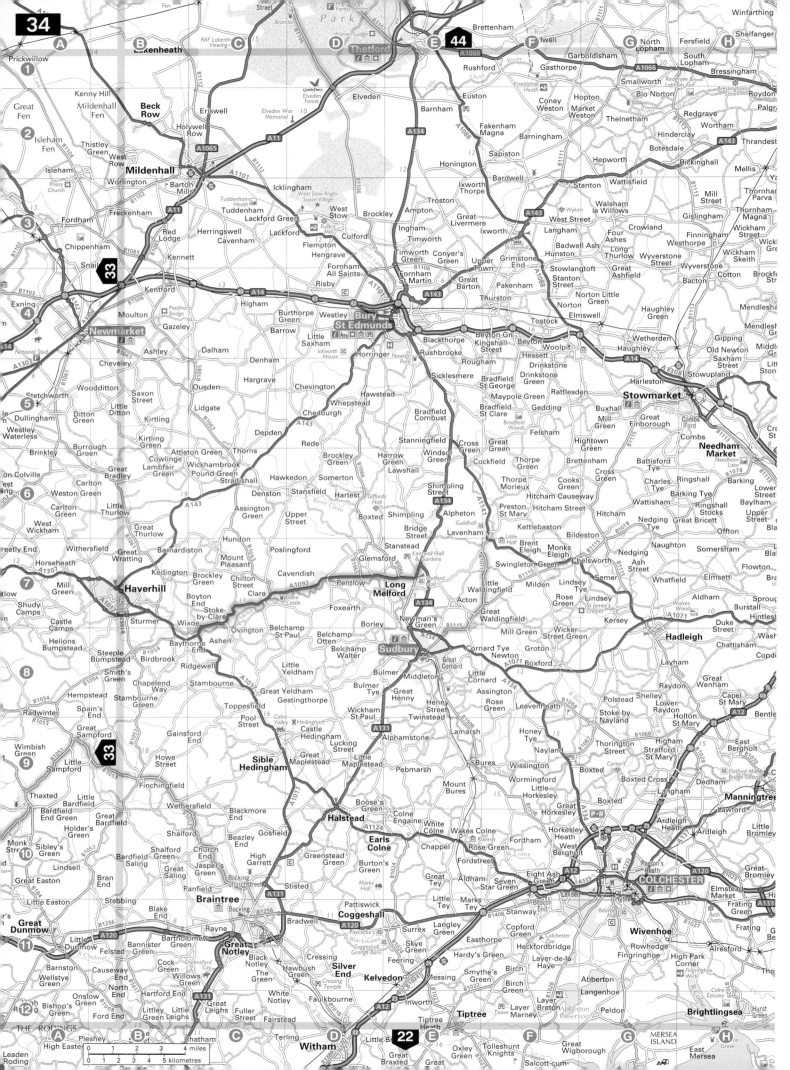

Town plan: Ipswich p.134

A B C D E F G H

1

Aberystwyth

0   200 m

2

*Cardigan
Bay*

Bandstand
St Paul Methodist
St David's URC
Aberystwyth North Beach
The Morlan Centre

Ceredigion
Surgery
Capel y Morfa

Royal Pier

CAB
Bethel

Coastguard Station
University (Old College)
NORTHGATE ST
A487

3
Clock Tower
St Michael's
Salvation Army
Holy Trinity

Monument
Aberystwyth Castle (ruins)
Castle
Market Hall
ALEXANDRA ROAD
Aberystwyth STATION

4
Eglwys y Santes Fair
Superstores
Ystwyth Retail Park
Rheidol

Trefechan Bridge
Vale of Rheidol Steam Railway Station

Slipway
Justice Centre
Park Avenue (Aberystwyth Town FC)

Ro-fawr
Fire Station
Police Station

5
Marina
TA Centre

Lifeboat Station
BLVD ST BRIEUC

TLT
CARDIGAN
Aqua Terra

6

C A R D I G A N

B A Y

7
Llanrhys
Llansantffraid
Llanon

Aberarth
Aberaeron

8
New Quay
(Ceinewydd)
Llanina
Llwyncelyn
Ceredigion Heritage Coast
Maen-y-groes
Gilfachreda
Llanarth
Oakford
Cwmtydu
Cross Inn
Dihewyd
Ystrad Aeron
Nanternis
Caerwedros
Mydroilyn
Ynys-Lochtyn
Pendinas Lochtyn
Llwyndafydd
Temple E
Llangrannog
Pontgarreg
Cae Hir

9
Penbryn
Plwmp
311
Ceredigion Heritage Coast
Sarnau
Pentregat
Gorsgoch
Cardigan Island
Tresaith
Brynhoffnant
Talgarreg
324
Aberporth
Cardigan Island Coastal Farm
Blaenannerch
Tan-y-groes
Rhydlewis
Cwrt-newydd
Y Ferwig
Glynarthen
Ffostrasol
Llanwnne
Poppit Sands
Penparc
Tremain
Blaenporth
Bettws Ifan
Hawen
Penrhiw-pal
Pontshaen

10
St Dogmaels Moylgrove Heritage Coast
St Dogmaels
Cardigan
(Aberteifi)
Beulah
Troedyraur
Maesllyn
Tre-groes
Prengwyn
Rhydowen
Drefach
Moylegrove
Pen-y-bryn
Llechryd
Ponthirwaun
Brongest
Croes-lan
Llanwenog
Llanybydder
Trwyn y bwa
Welsh Wildlife Centre
Llandygwydd
Cwm-cou
258
Capel Dewi
Newport
Teifi Marshes
Castle
TIVY SIDE
Penrhiwllan
Rock Mill Woollen & Water Mill
Llanllwni

11
Bryn-Henllan
Cilgerran
National Coracle Centre
Adpar
Llandyfriog
Pentre-cwrt
Llangeler
Pontwelly
Llanfihangel-ar-arth
Nevern
Felindre Farchog
Abercych
Genarth
Newcastle
Emlyn
(Castell Newydd Emlyn)
Henllan
Dinas Cross
Newport
Rhoshill
Pen-rhiw
Drefach
National Wool
Eglwyswrw
Newchapel
Felindre
Glynteg

12
MYNYDD CAREGOG
Crosswell
Boncath
25
Cwmhiraeth
Pentre-cwrt
311
Brynberian
Blaenffos
Capel Iwan
257
Pencader
369
New Inn
Pontfaen
Bwlch-y-groes
335
Cwmpengraig
314
Gwyddgrug
358
Gwerno

A B C D E F G H

0   1   2   3   4 miles
0 1 2 3 4 5 kilometres

PEMBROKESHIRE COAST
MYNYDD PRESELI

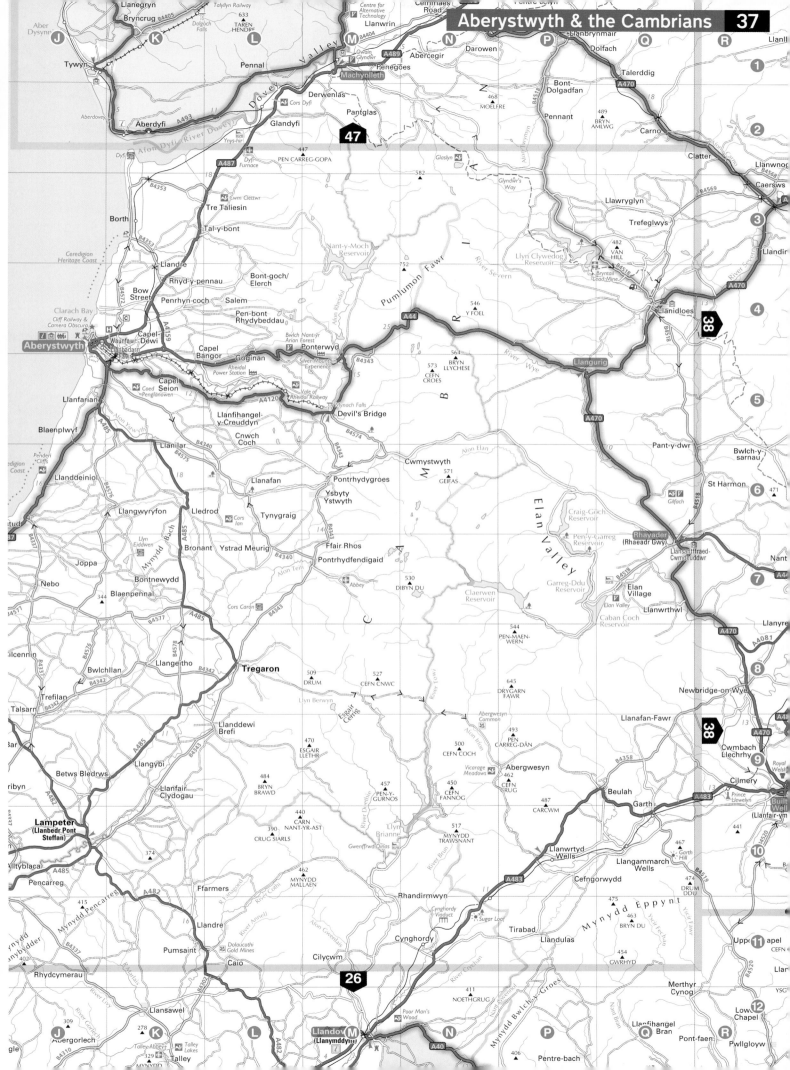

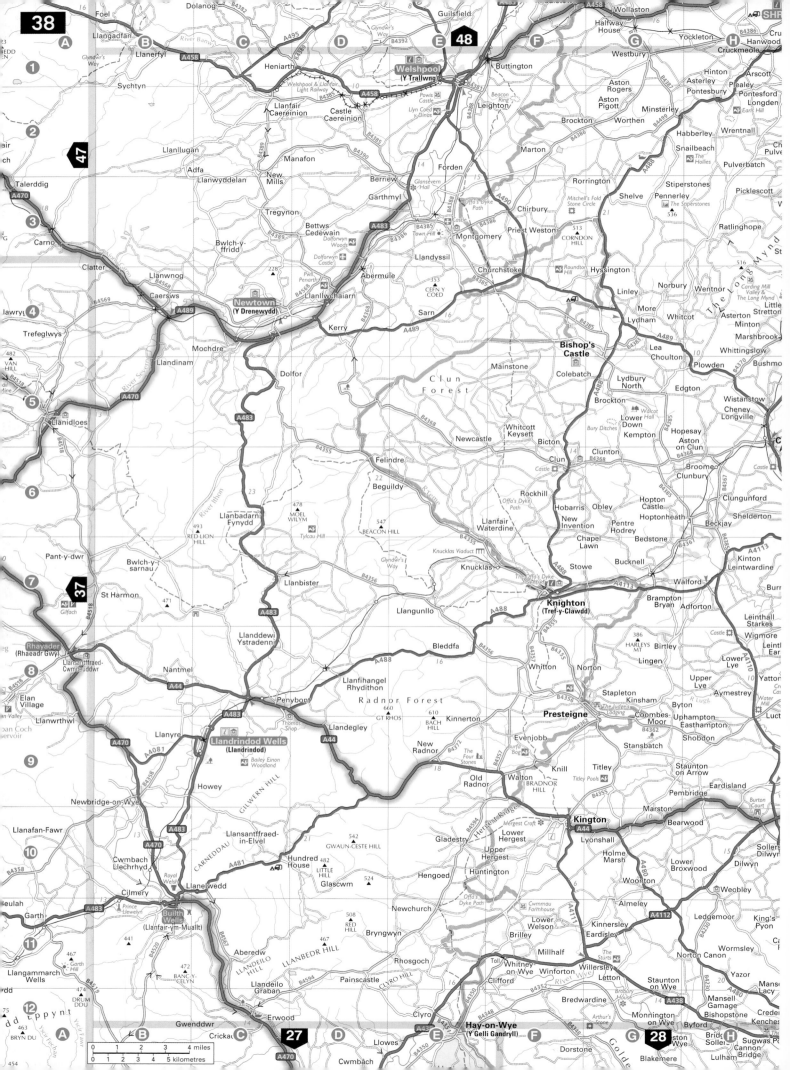

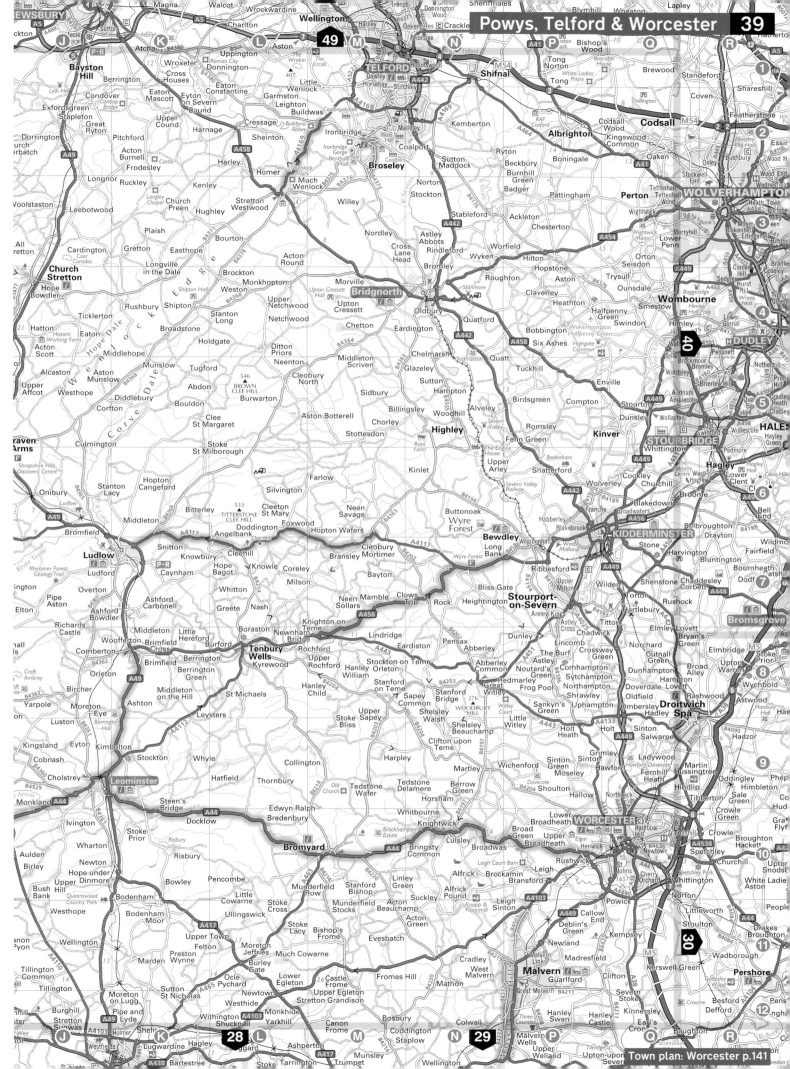

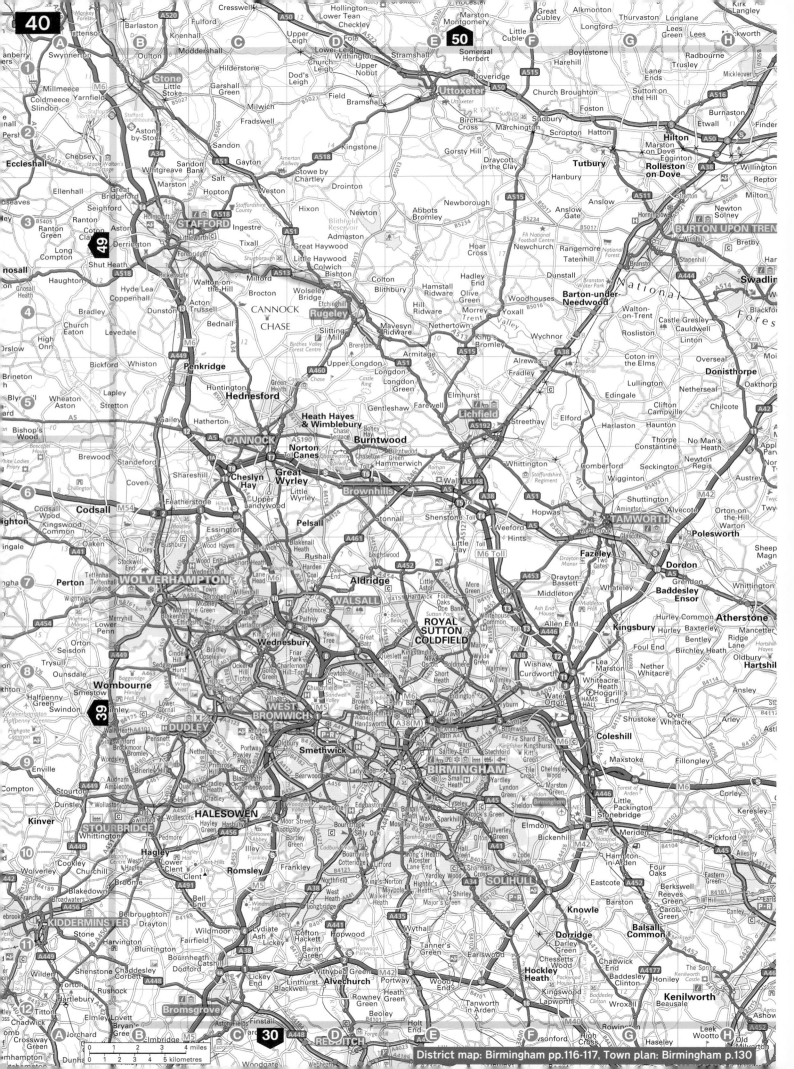

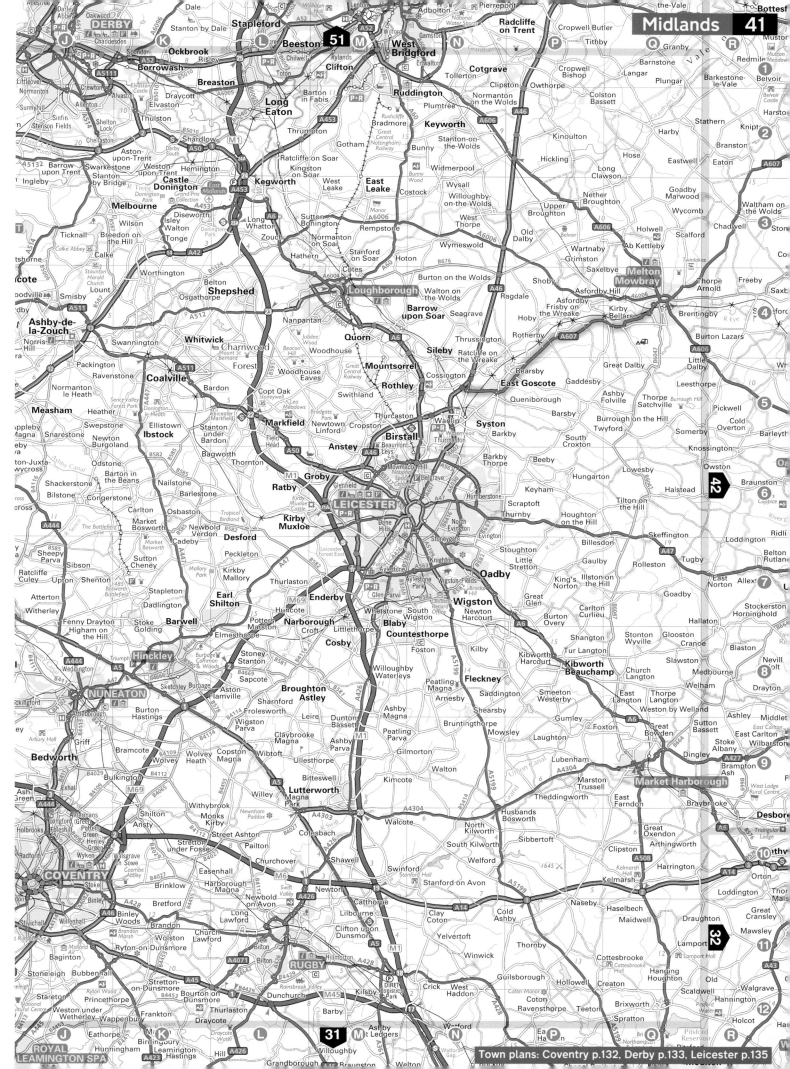

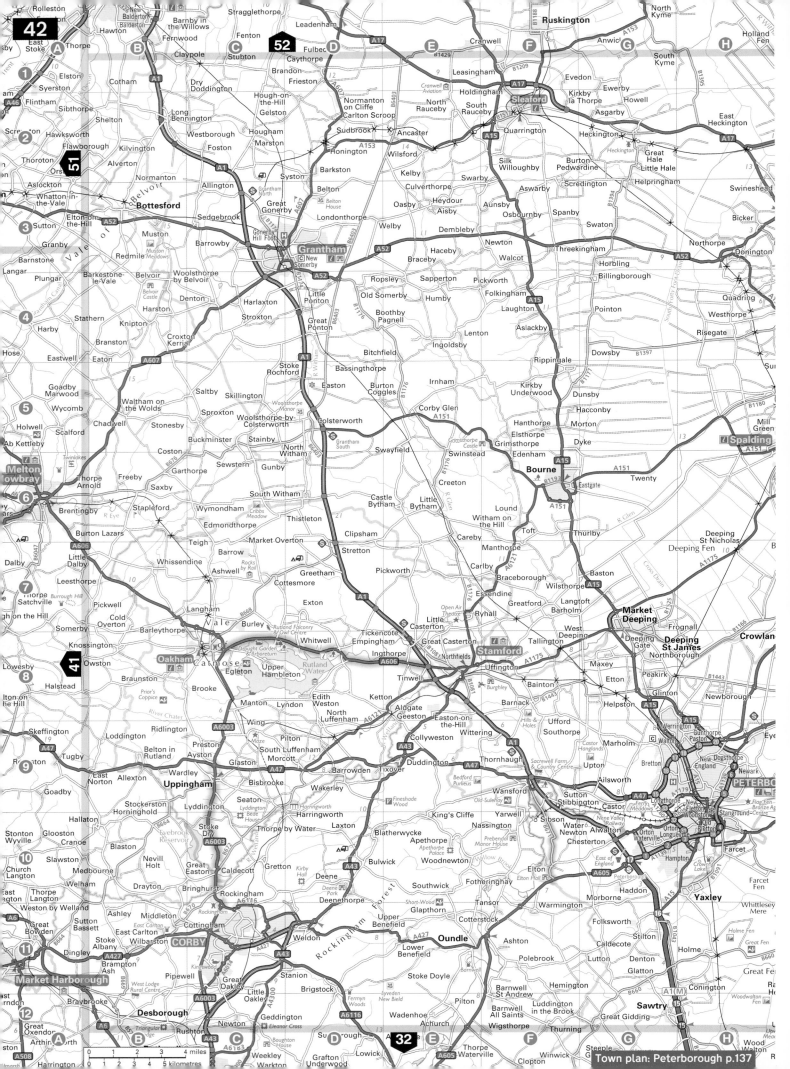

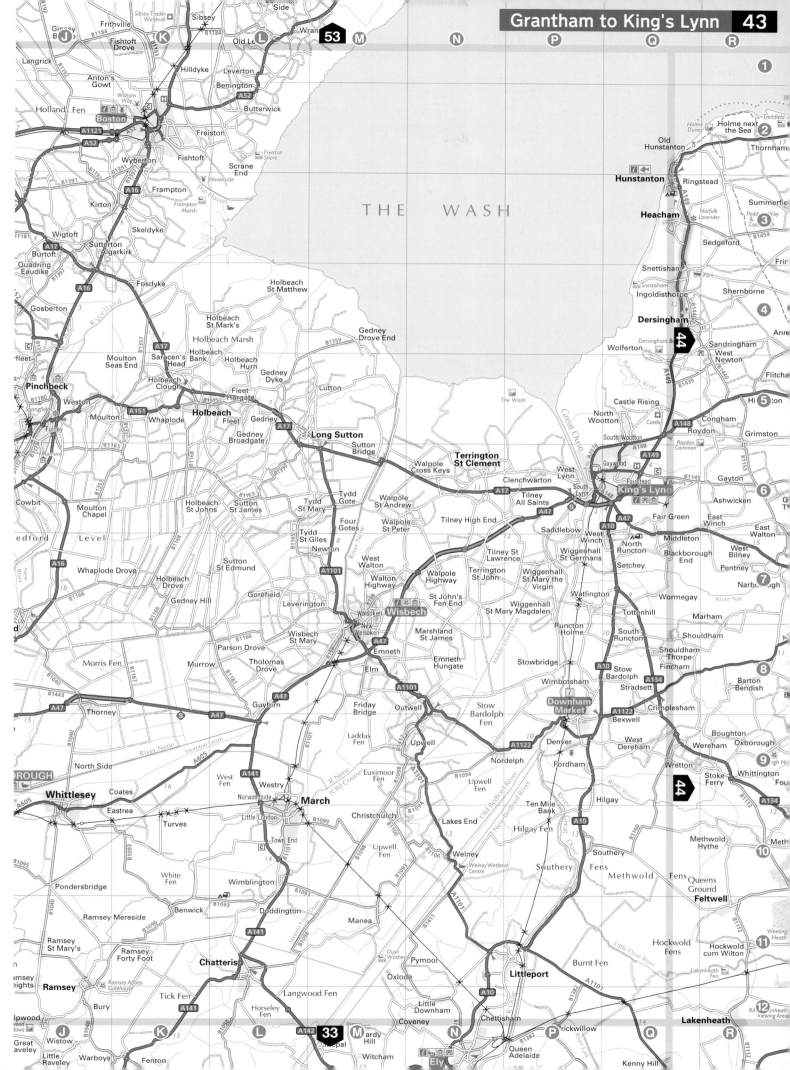

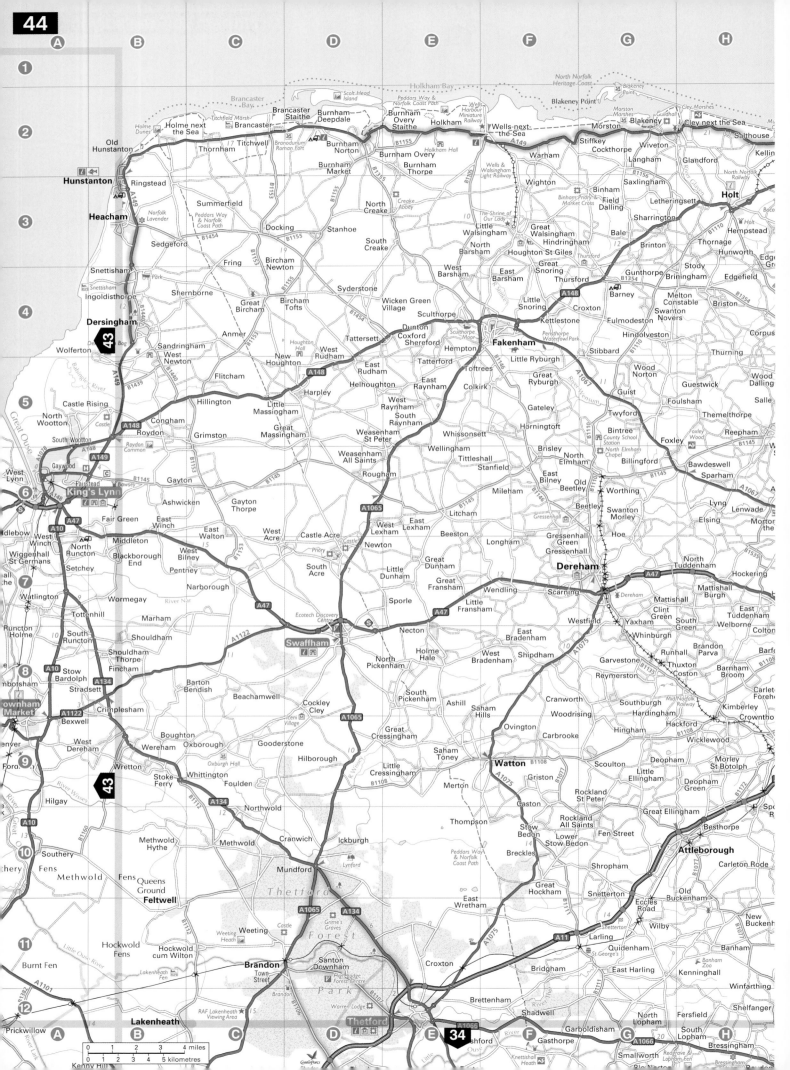

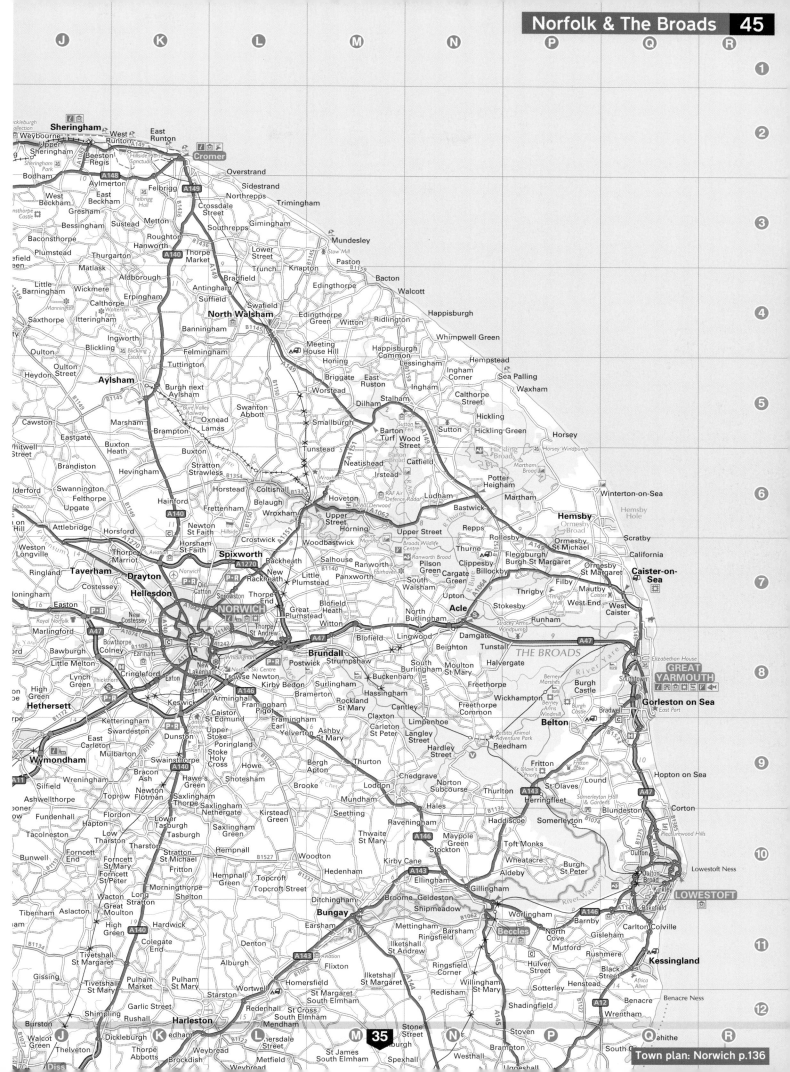

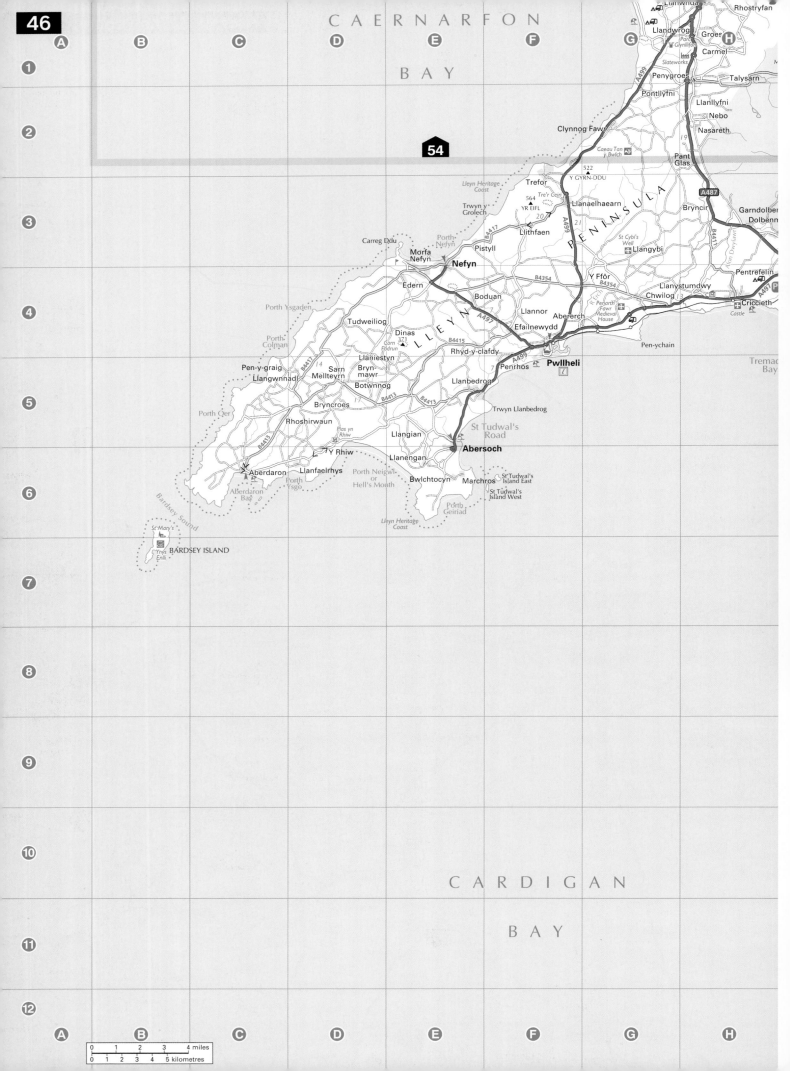

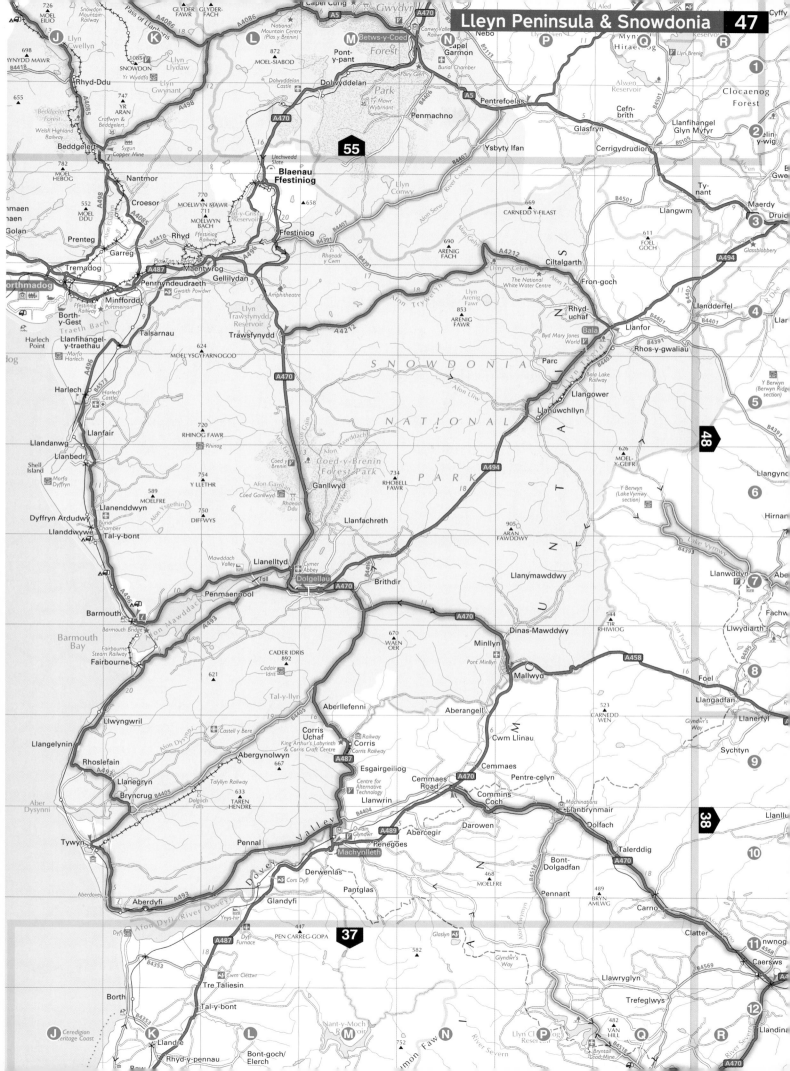

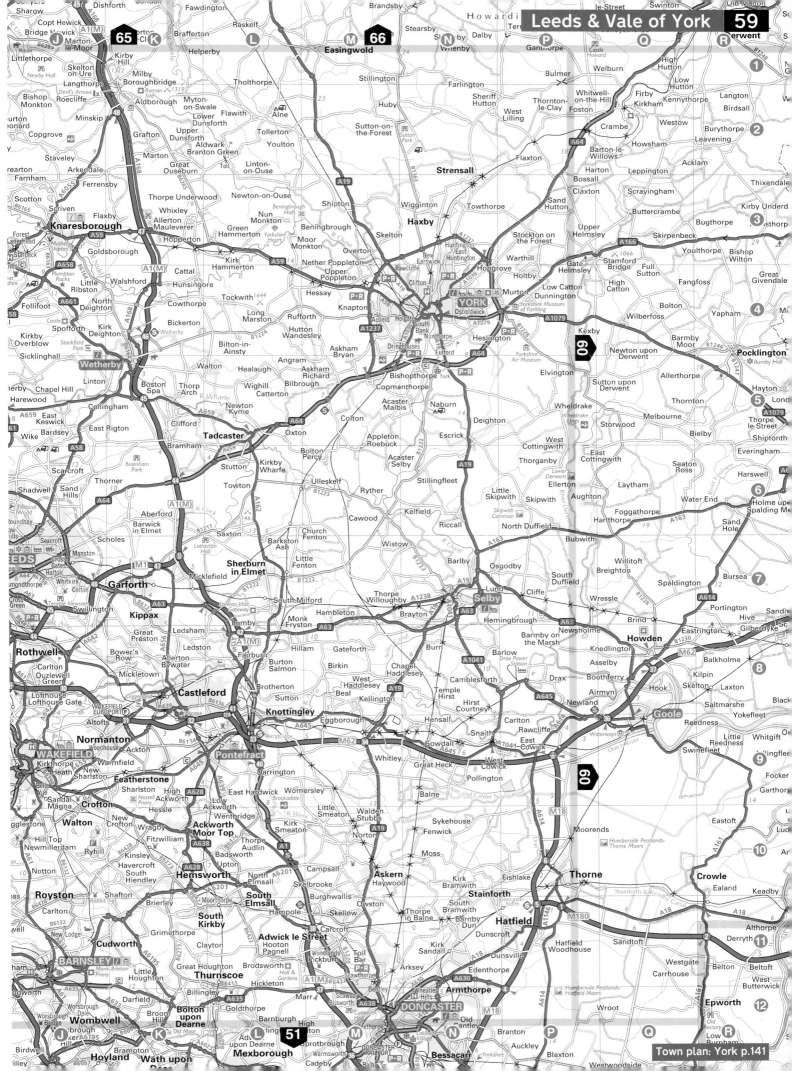

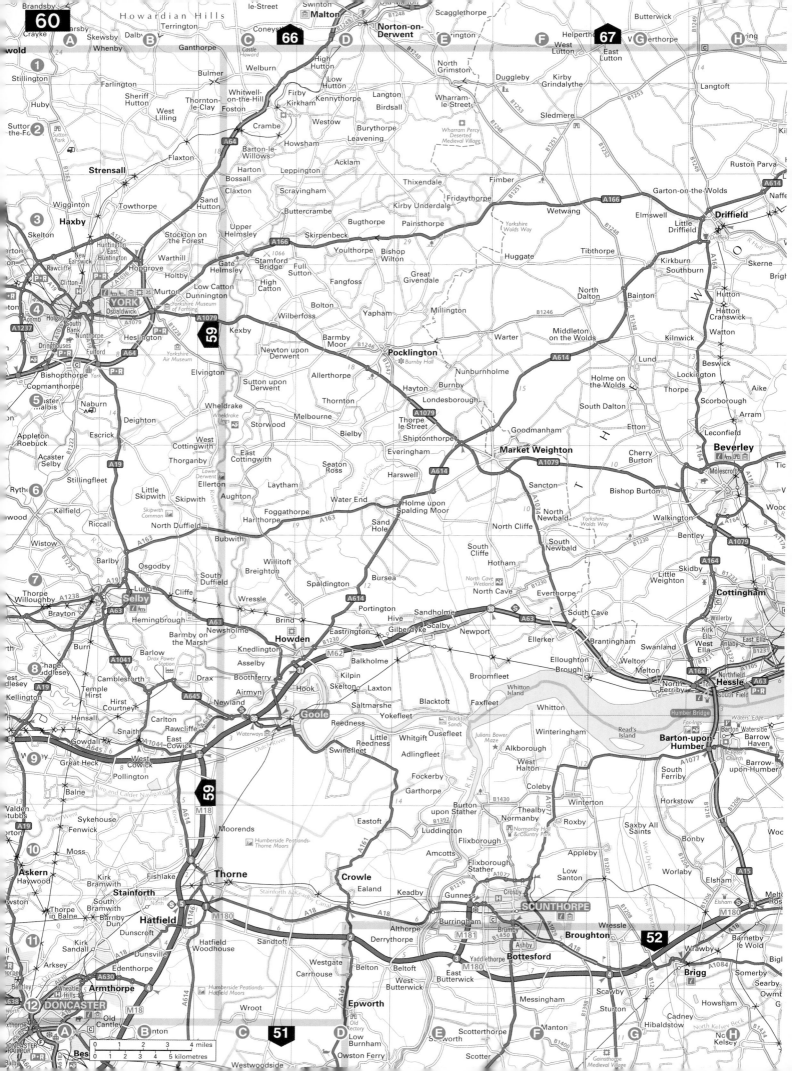

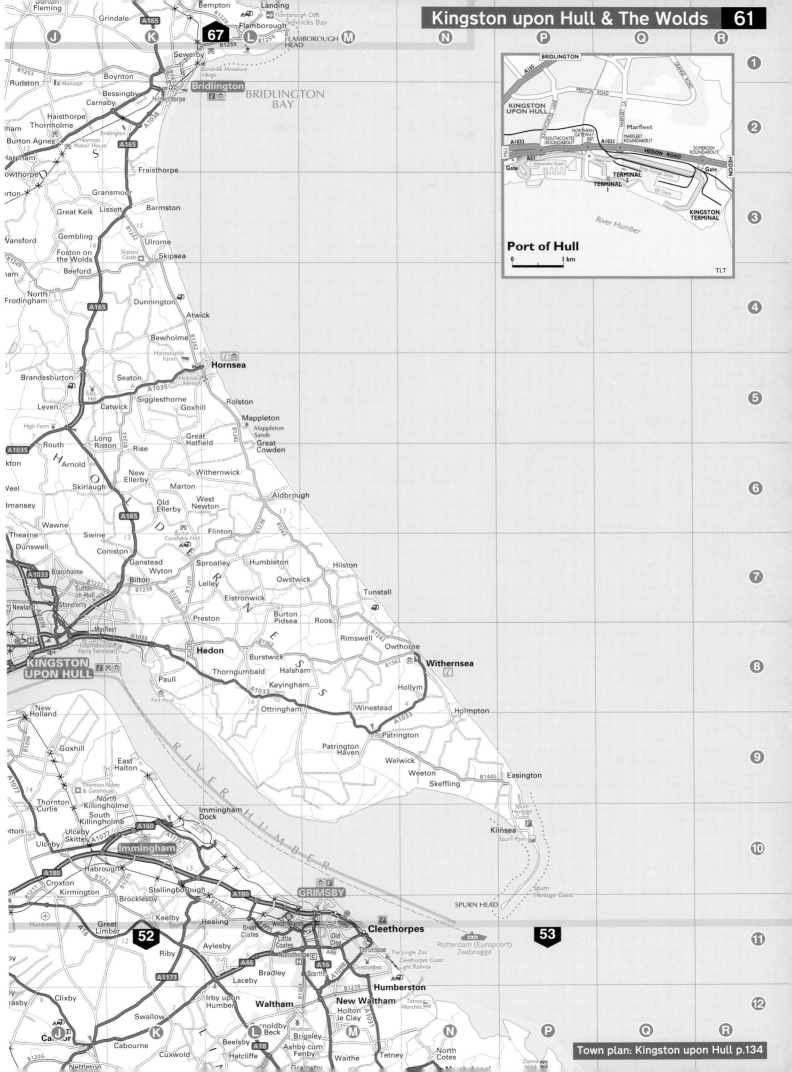

J   K   67   L   M   N   P   Q   R

①②③④⑤⑥⑦⑧⑨⑩⑪⑫

Port of Hull

BRIDLINGTON

A165

KINGSTON UPON HULL

PRESTON ROAD

SOUTHCOATES LANE

MARFLEET LA

GRANGE ROAD

Marfleet

NORTHERN GATEWAY RBT

MARFLEET ROUNDABOUT

SOMERDEN ROUNDABOUT

A1033   SOUTHCOATES ROUNDABOUT   A1033

M62   A63   HEDON ROAD   HEDON

Gate   Alexandra Dock   King George Dock   Gate

TERMINAL 1   TERMINAL 2   QE Dock

KINGSTON TERMINAL

River Humber

0   1 km

TLT

Burton Fleming   Bempton   Landing   Flamborough Cliffs
Grindale   Selwicks Bay
A165   B1229   Flamborough
Rudston   B1255   FLAMBOROUGH HEAD
B1253   Sewerby
Boynton   Bondville Miniature Village
Bridlington   BRIDLINGTON BAY
Haisthorpe   Bessingby   Hilderthorpe
Thornholme   Carnaby
Burton Agnes   Bridlington
Harpham   Norman Manor House   A165
Lowthorpe   Fraisthorpe
Gransmoor
Vansford   Great Kelk   Lissett   Barmston
Gembling   B1242   Ulrome
Foston on the Wolds   Skipsea Castle   Skipsea
B1249   Beeford
North Frodingham   A165
Dunnington   Atwick
Brandesburton   Bewholme   B1242
Seaton   Honeysuckle Farm
Hornsea
Leven   Sigglesthorne   Hornsea Mere
Catwick   A1035   Goxhill   Rolston
High Farm   Long Riston   Great Hatfield   Mappleton
A1035   Routh   Rise   B1242   Mappleton Sands
Arnold   Withernwick   Great Cowden
Veel   Skirlaugh   New Ellerby   Marton
HOLDERNESS
Wawne   Old Ellerby   West Newton   Aldbrough
Thearne   Swine   B1238   Flinton   B1241
Dunswell   A165   Coniston   Burton Constable Hall
Bransholme   Ganstead   Sproatley   Humbleton   Hilston
A1033   Wyton   Lelley   Owstwick
Sutton-on-Hull   Bilton   B1239   Elstronwick   Tunstall
Stoneferry   B1237   Preston   Burton Pidsea   Roos
Newland   B1238   Rimswell
KINGSTON UPON HULL   A1033   Marfleet   B1362   Owthorne
International Ferry Terminal   Hedon   Burstwick   Withernsea
Thorngumbald   Halsham   B1362   Hollym
Paull   Keyingham   Holmpton
Fort Paull   Ottringham   Winestead   A1033
New Holland   Patrington
Goxhill   B1206   Patrington Haven   Welwick
East Halton   Weeton   Skeffling   Easington   B1445
Thornton Abbey & Gatehouse
Thornton Curtis   North Killingholme   Immingham Dock   Spurn Heritage Coast
A1077   South Killingholme   Kilnsea   Spurn Point
Ulceby Skitter   A160   A1077   A1173
Ulceby   Immingham   Spurn Heritage Coast
A180   Habrough
Croxton   B1211   B1210
Kirmington   Keelby   Stallingborough   A180   SPURN HEAD
Brocklesby   B1210   GRIMSBY
Humberside   Healing   Great Coates   West Marsh   Rotterdam (Europoort) Zeebrugge
Great Limber   52   Riby   Little Coates   Cleethorpes
Aylesby   Nunsthorpe   Thrunscoe   The Jungle Zoo   53
Clixby   Swallow   A46   Old Clee   Cleethorpes Coast Light Railway
A1173   Laceby   A16   Scartho   A1098
Bradley   Humberston
Cadney   Irby upon Humber   B1219   New Waltham   Tetney Marshes
Cabourne   Waltham   Holton le Clay   A1031
B1205   Cuxwold   Arnoldby Beck   North Cotes
Nettleton   A18   Beelsby   Ashby cum Fenby   Waithe   Tetney
Brigsley   Hatcliffe   Grainsby

J   K   L   M   N   P   Q   R

Town plan: Kingston upon Hull p.134

RIVER HUMBER

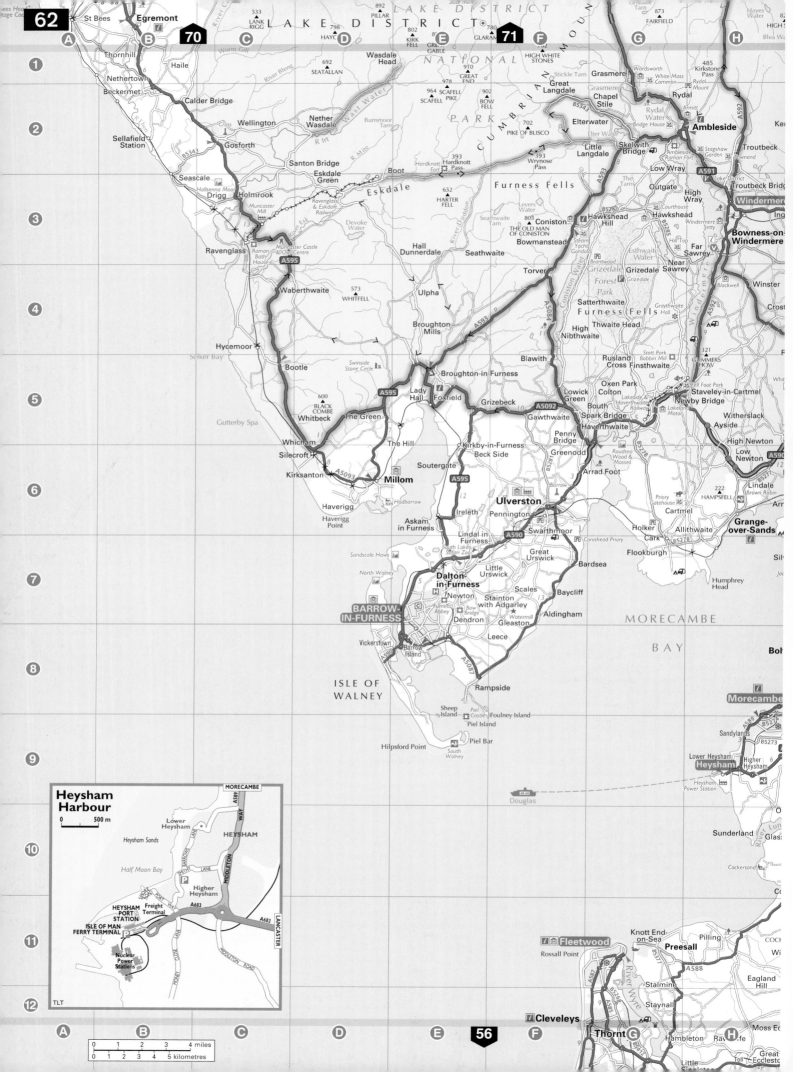

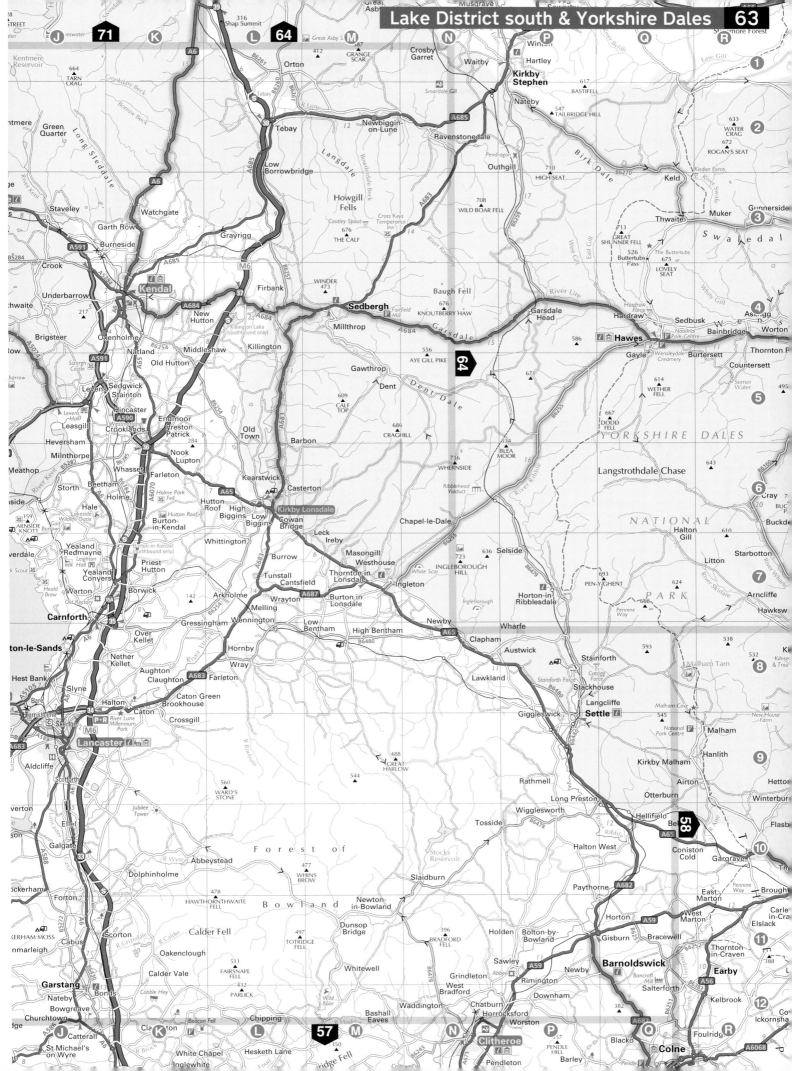

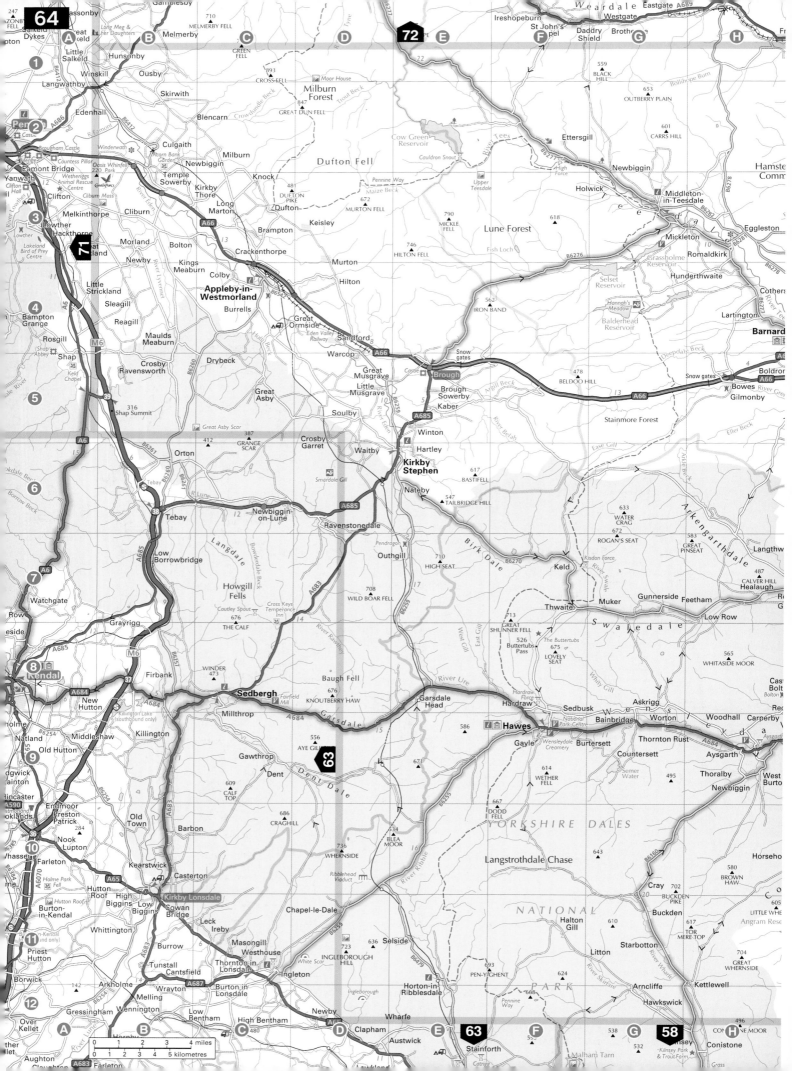

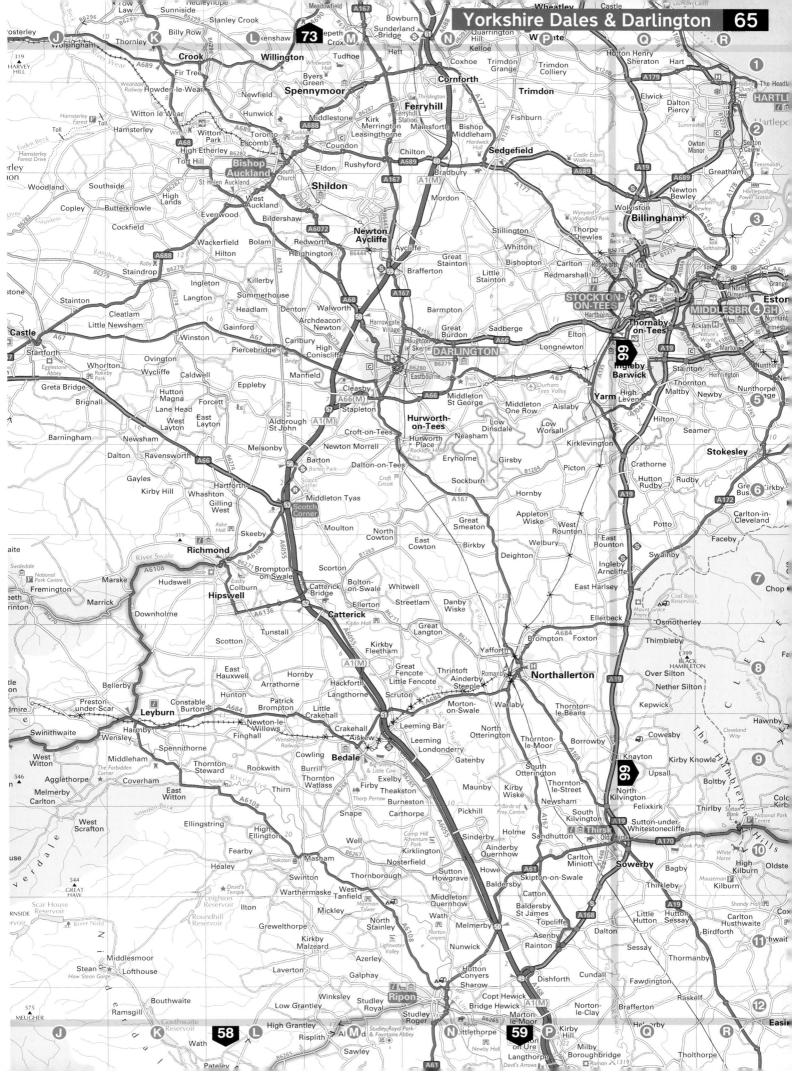

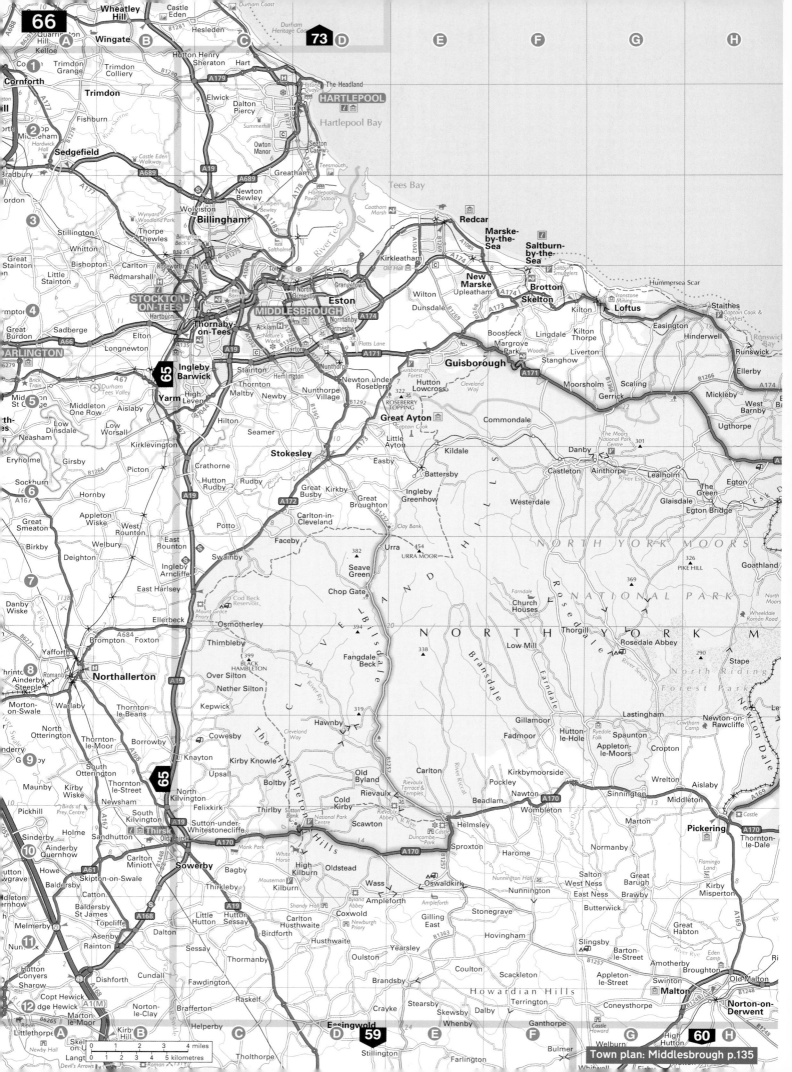

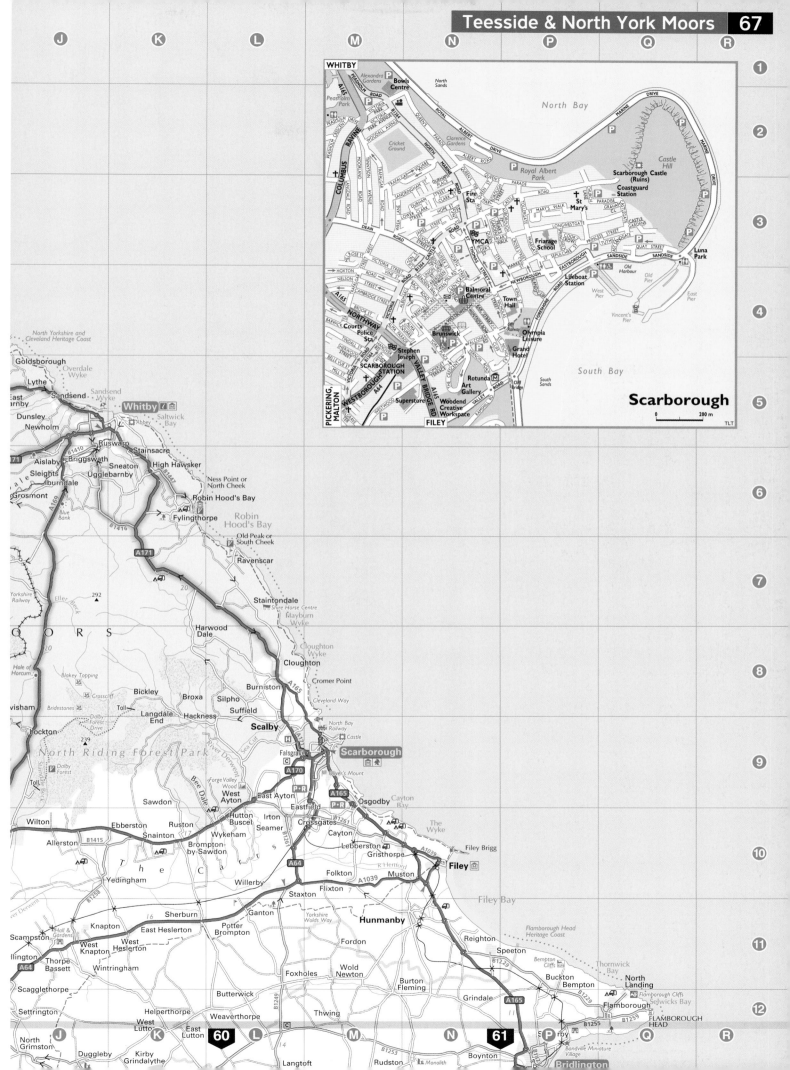

Scarborough

WHITBY

Alexandra Gardens
Bowls Centre
North Sands
North Bay
Peasholm Park
PEASHOLM ROAD
Victoria Park
Cricket Ground
Royal Albert Park
COLUMBUS RAVINE
A165
DRIVE
MARINE DRIVE
Castle Hill
Scarborough Castle (Ruins)
Coastguard Station
St Mary's
Fire Sta
YMCA
Friarage School
Balmoral Centre
Town Hall
Stephen Joseph
SCARBOROUGH STATION
Police Sta
Courts
Brunswick
Grand Hotel
Olympia Leisure
Railway
Rotunda Art Gallery
Superstore
Woodend Creative Workspace
WESTBOROUGH
NORTHWAY
VALLEY BRIDGE RD
PICKERING, MALTON
FILEY
Luna Park
Old Harbour
West Pier
Vincent's Pier
East Pier
Old Pier
Lifeboat Station
South Bay
South Sands
Cliff Bridge

0   200 m
TLT

North Yorkshire and Cleveland Heritage Coast
Goldsborough
Lythe
East Barnby
Sandsend
Sandsend Wyke
Overdale Wyke
Dunsley
Newholm
Whitby
Saltwick Bay
Abbey
Ruswarp
Stainsacre
Aislaby
Briggswath
Sneaton
High Hawsker
Sleights
Ugglebarnby
B1410
Iburndale
B1447
Grosmont
Blue Bank
Ness Point or North Cheek
B7416
Robin Hood's Bay
Fylingthorpe
Robin Hood's Bay
Old Peak or South Cheek
A171
Ravenscar
Staintondale
Shire Horse Centre
Hayburn Wyke
North Yorkshire Railway
292
MOORS
Harwood Dale
Cloughton Wyke
Cloughton
Hole of Horcum
Blakey Topping
Crosscliff
Bickley
Broxa
Silpho
Cromer Point
Bridestones
Burniston
Cleveland Way
Lockton
Langdale End
Hackness
Suffield
Scalby
Dalby Forest Drive
239
Toll
Sawdon
Bee Dale
Forge Valley Wood
West Ayton
East Ayton
Eastfield
North Bay Railway
Castle
Scarborough
Falsgrave
Oliver's Mount
North Riding Forest Park
Dalby Forest
Toll
River Derwent
Sea Cut
A170
A165
Osgodby
Cayton Bay
The Wyke
Wilton
Ebberston
Ruston
Wykeham
Irton
Seamer
Crossgates
Cayton
Filey Brigg
Allerston
Snainton
Brompton-by-Sawdon
Hutton Buscel
Lebberston
Gristhorpe
Filey
B1415
B1261
Yedingham
Willerby
Folkton
Muston
Filey Bay
B1258
Sherburn
Ganton
Potter Brompton
Staxton
Flixton
Yorkshire Wolds Way
Hunmanby
Scampston
Hall & Gardens
Knapton
East Heslerton
West Heslerton
Fordon
Reighton
Flamborough Head Heritage Coast
A64
Ilington
Thorpe Bassett
West Knapton
Wintringham
Foxholes
Wold Newton
Speeton
Thornwick Bay
North Landing
Scagglethorpe
Helperthorpe
Butterwick
Burton Fleming
Grindale
Bempton Cliffs
Buckton
Bempton
B1229
Flamborough
Flamborough Cliffs
Selwicks Bay
Settrington
West Lutton
Weaverthorpe
Thwing
A165
B1249
FLAMBOROUGH HEAD
North Grimston
Duggleby
East Lutton
Langtoft
Rudston
Monolith
Boynton
B1253
Bondville Miniature Village
Bridlington
Kirby Grindalythe

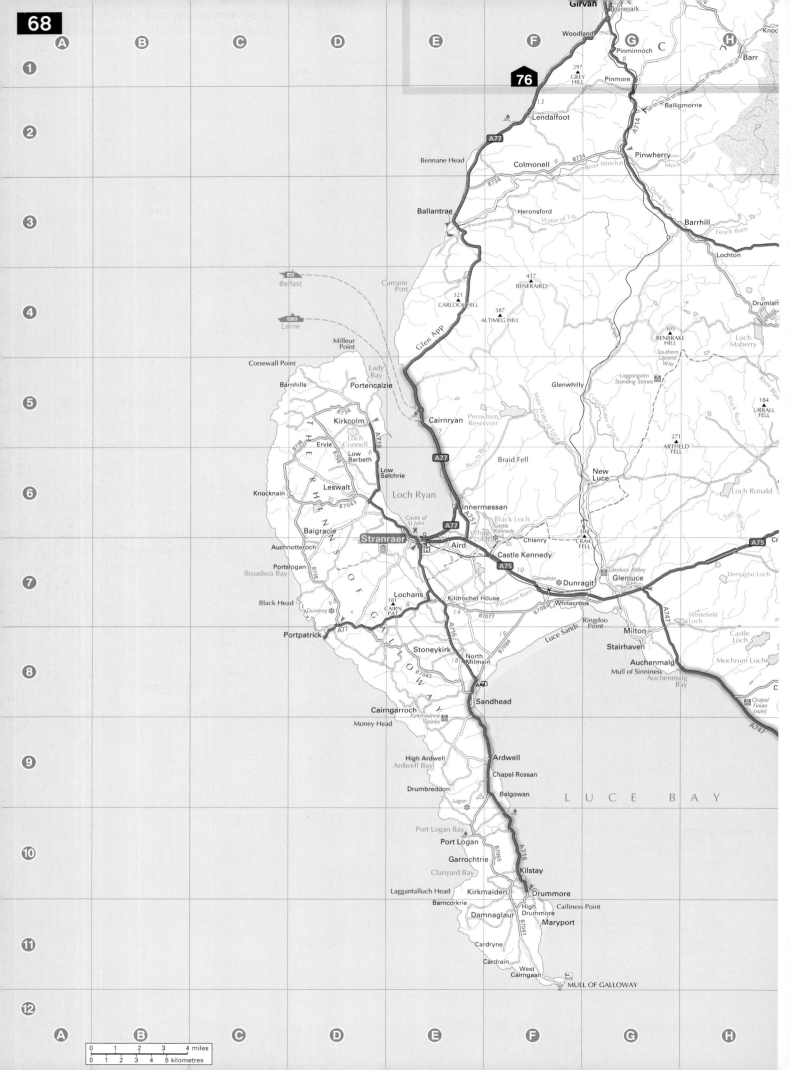

A B C D E F G H

1
2
3
4
5
6
7
8
9
10
11
12

A B C D E F G H

76

Girvan
Douhepark
Woodland
Pinminnoch
297 GREY HILL
Pinmore
Pinwherry
Barr
Knoc
A714
Balligmorrie
Lendalfoot
A77
Bennane Head
Colmonell
B734
River Stinchar
Muck Water
Dusk River
Ballantrae
Heronsford
Water of Tig
Barrhill
Feoch Burn
Lochton
Belfast
Currarie Port
437 BENERAIRD
Drumlan
Larne
321 CARLOCK HILL
387 ALTIMEG HILL
305 BENBRAKE HILL
Loch Maberry
Milleur Point
Lady Bay
Glen App
Southern Upland Way
River Bla
Corsewall Point
Portencalzie
Glenwhilly
Laggangairn Standing Stones
Cross Water of Luce
Barnhills
B738
Kirkcolm
Penwhirn Reservoir
184 URRALL FELL
Ervie
B798
Low Barbeth
Loch Connell
A718
Cairnryan
Braid Fell
271 ARTFIELD FELL
Knocknain
Leswalt
Low Salchrie
Beoch Burn
Main Water of Luce
New Luce
Loch Ronald
THE RHINS
B7043
Loch Ryan
Innermessan
A751
Black Loch
Castle Kennedy
CRAIG FELL
Tarf Water
Balgracie
Castle of St John
A77
White Loch
Chlenry
184
A75
Cr
Auchnotteroch
Stranraer
Aird
Castle Kennedy
Glenwhan
A75 10
Dunragit
Glenluce Abbey
Glenluce
Dernaglar Loch
Portslogan
B738
Broadsea Bay
Kildrochet House
Pillanton Burn
B7084
Whitecrook
Luce Sands
Ringdoo Point
Milton
A747
Whitefield Loch
Black Head
Dunskey
Lochans
181 CAIRN PAT
14
B7077
Ringdoo Point
Stairhaven
Castle Loch
Portpatrick
A77
Stoneykirk
A716
North Milmain
18
B7084
19
Auchenmalg
Mull of Sinniness
Auchenmalg Bay
Mochrum Loch
THE MACHARS OF GALLOWAY
Cairngarroch
Kirkmadrine Stones
Sandhead
Money Head
High Ardwell
Ardwell Bay
Ardwell
Chapel Rossan
L U C E   B A Y
Chapel Finian (ruin)
C
Drumbreddon
Balgowan
Logan
Port Logan Bay
Port Logan
B7065
A716
Kilstay
Garrochtrie
Clanyard Bay
Laggantalluch Head
Kirkmaiden
Drummore
Barncorkrie
High Drummore
Cailiness Point
Damnaglaur
Maryport
B7041
Cardryne
Cardrain
West Cairngaan
MULL OF GALLOWAY

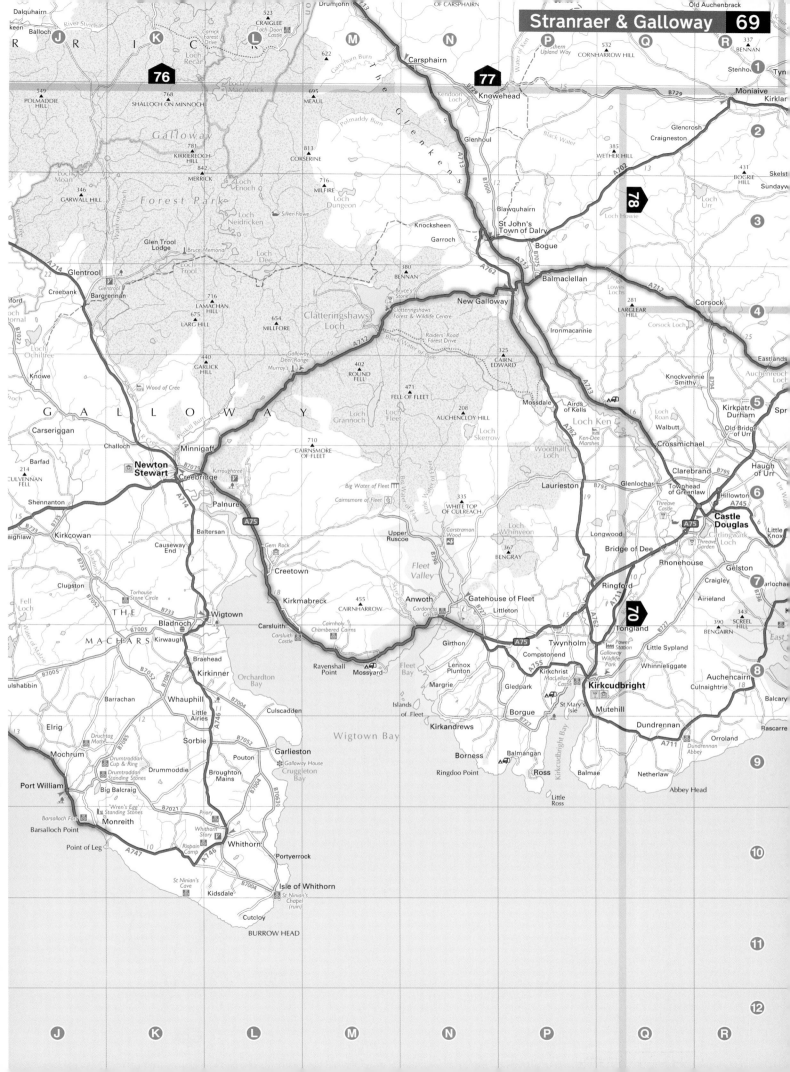

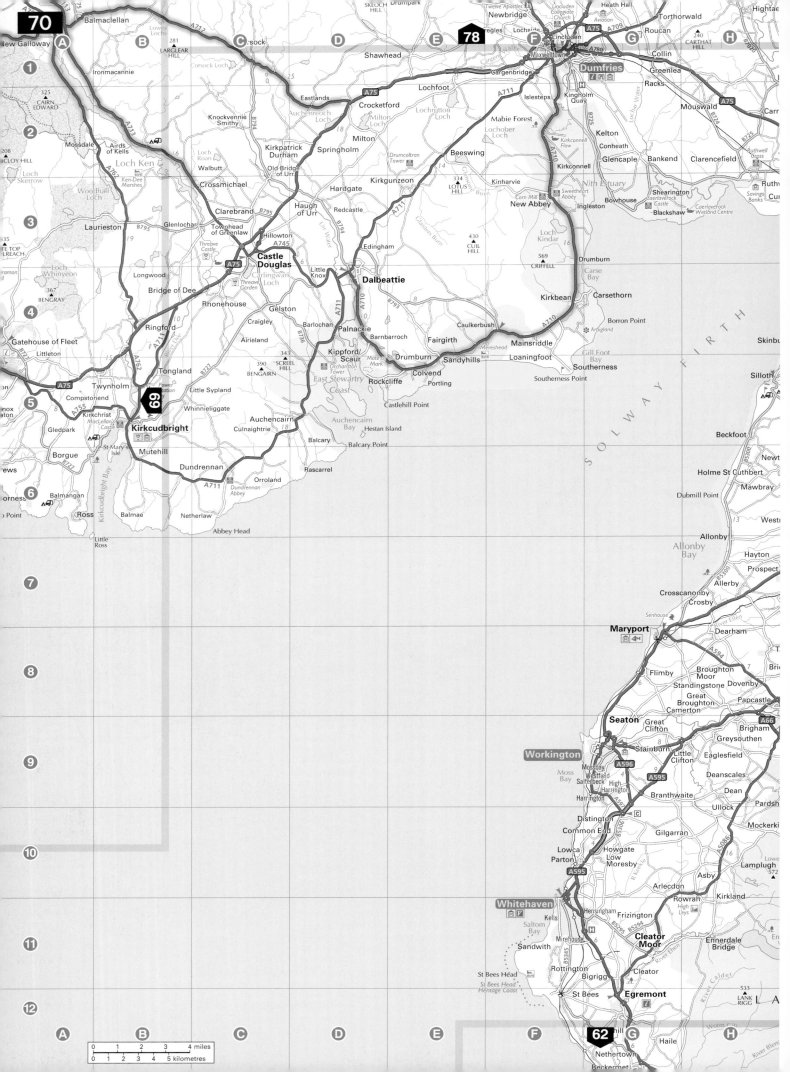

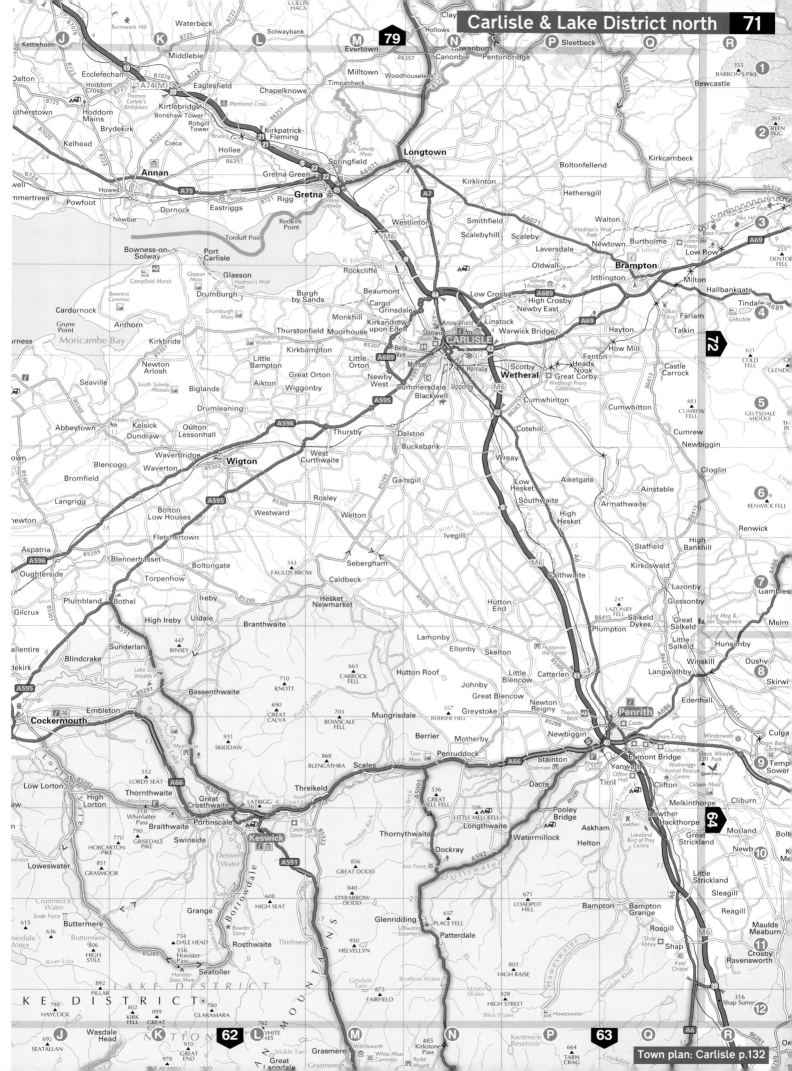

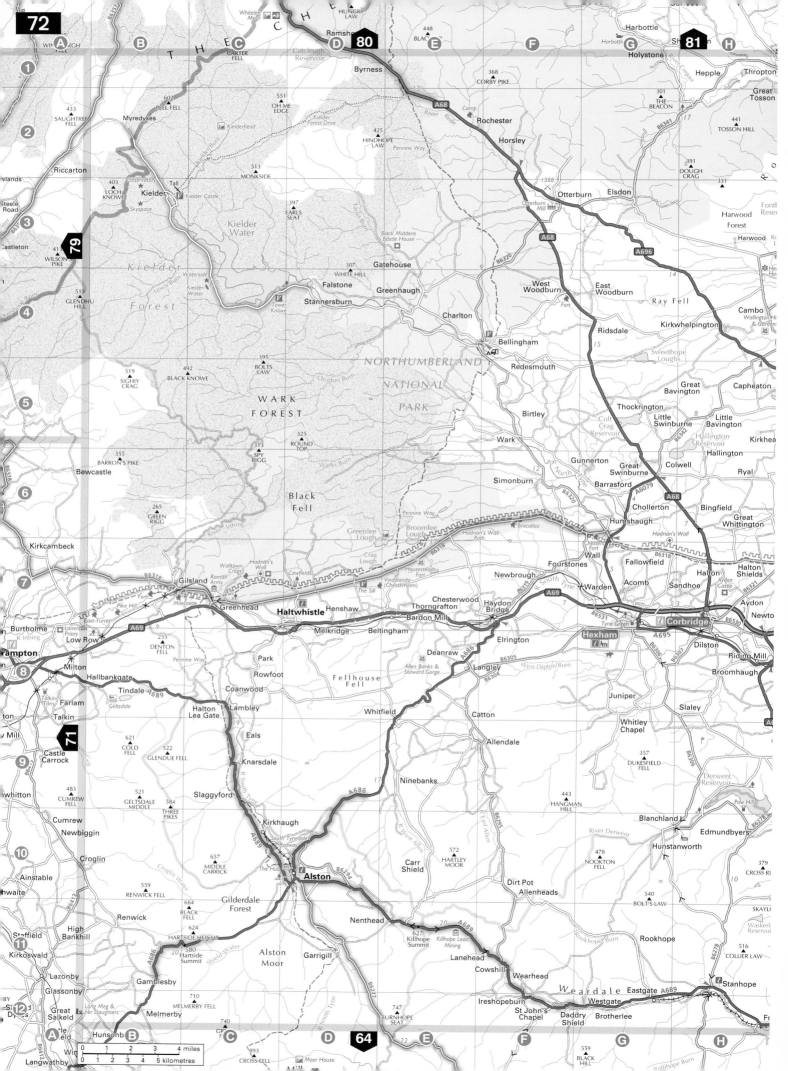

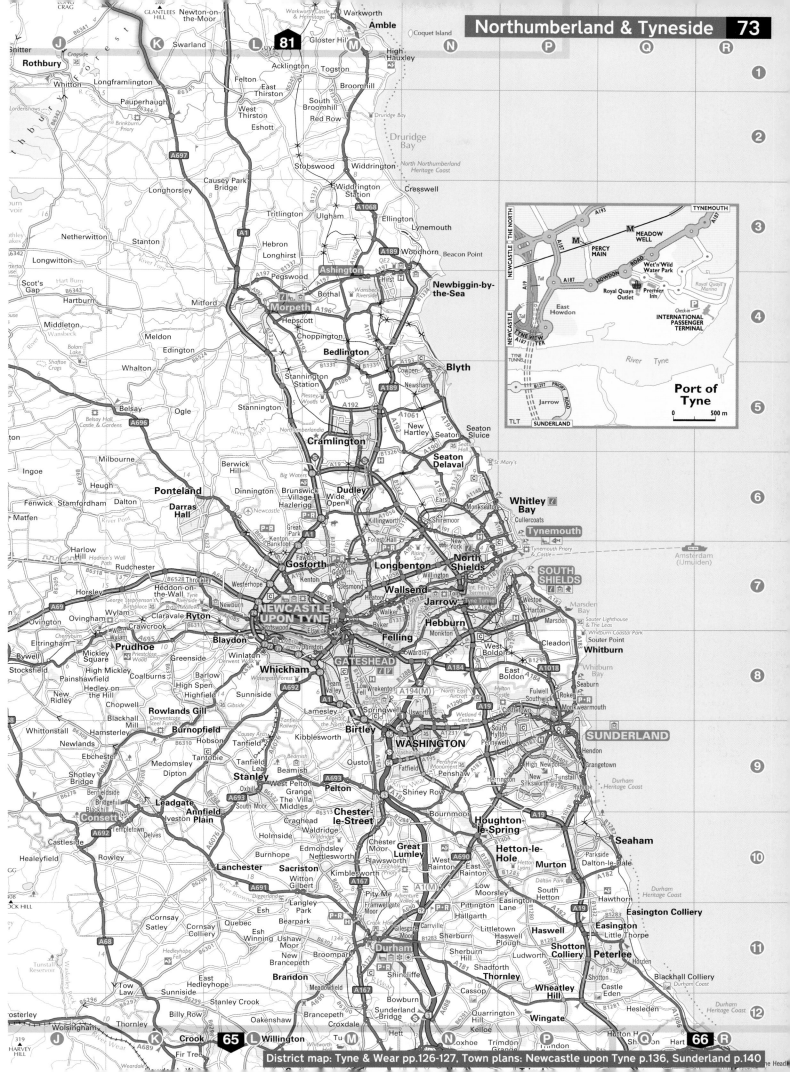

Port of Tyne

0   500 m

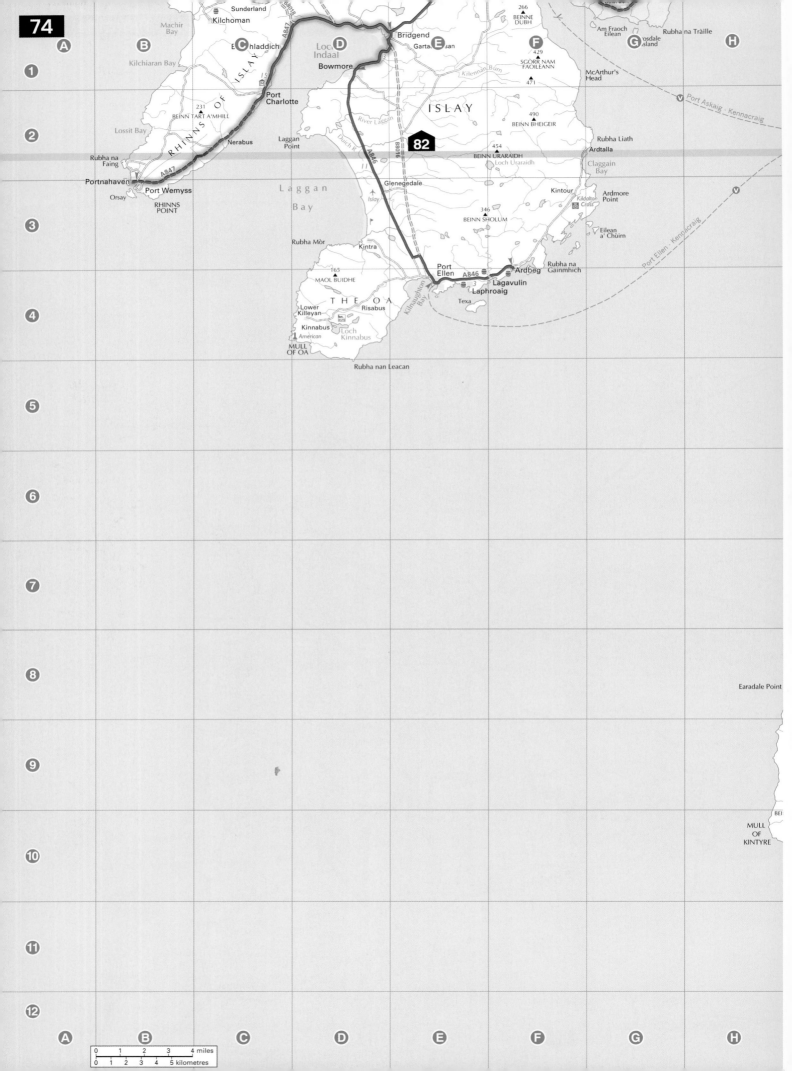

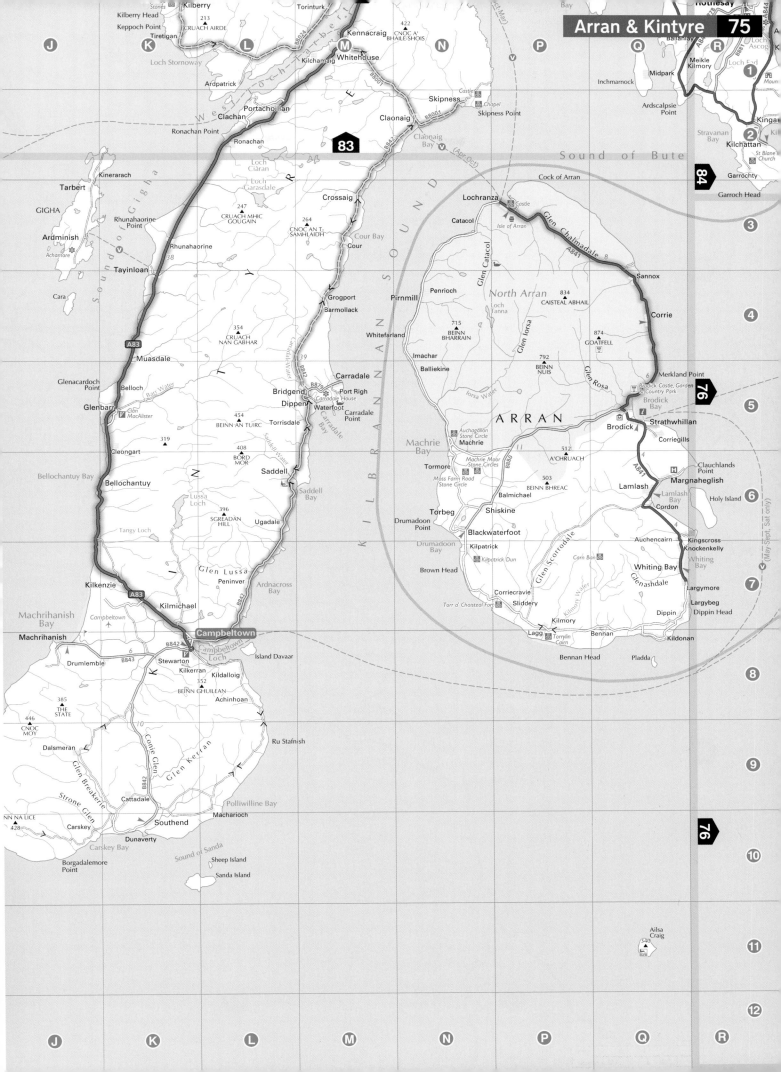

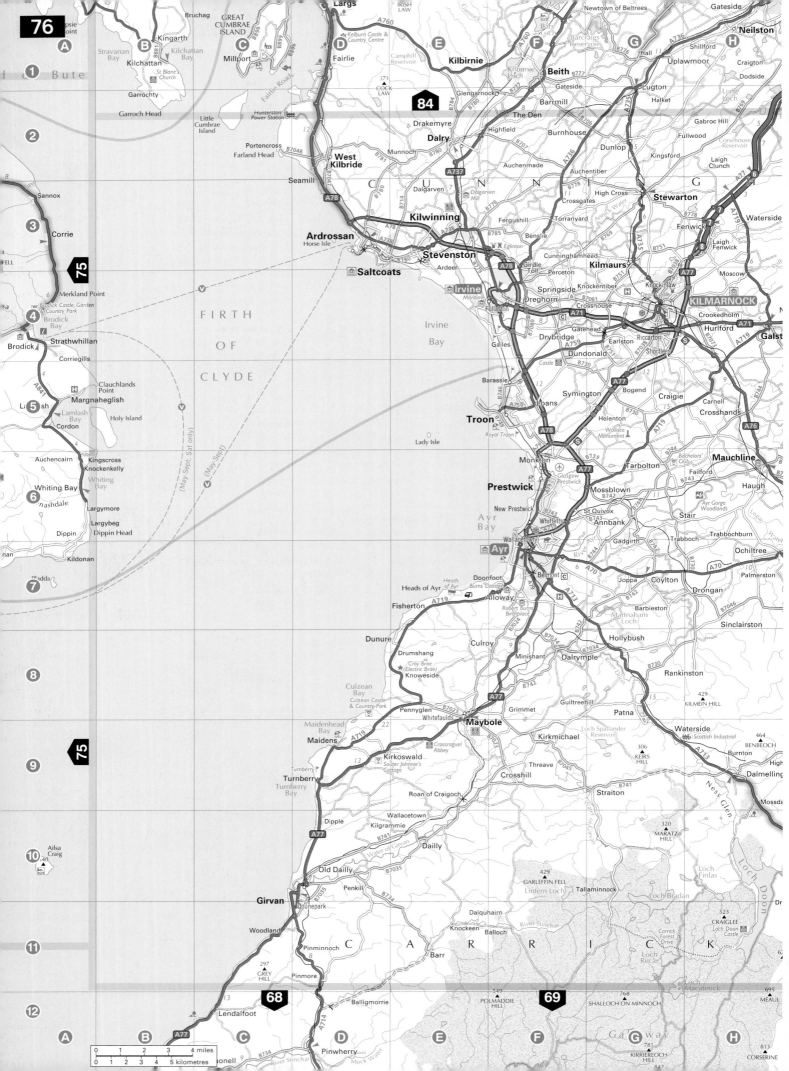

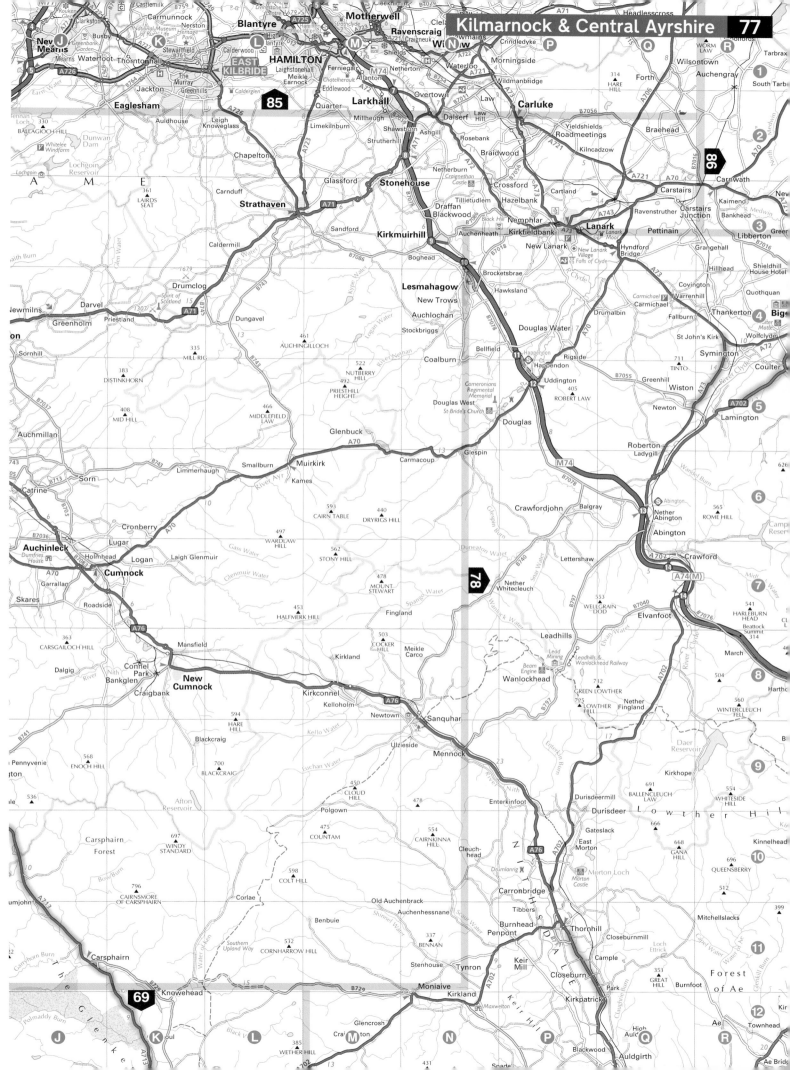

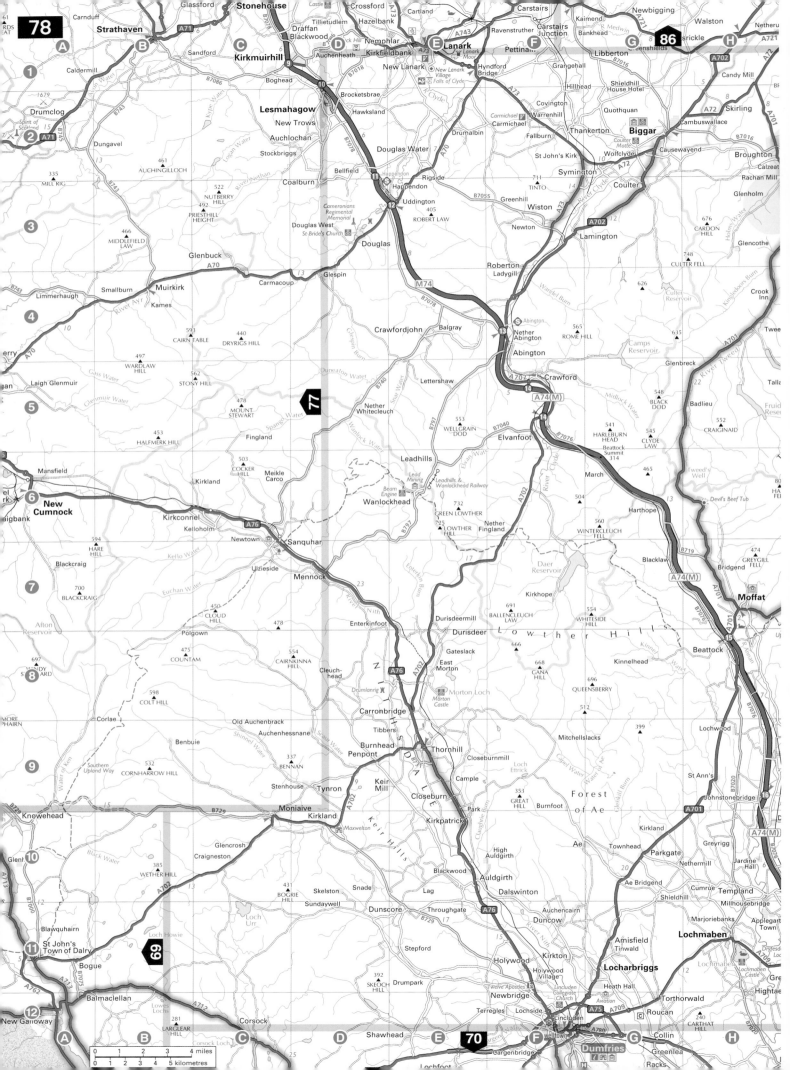

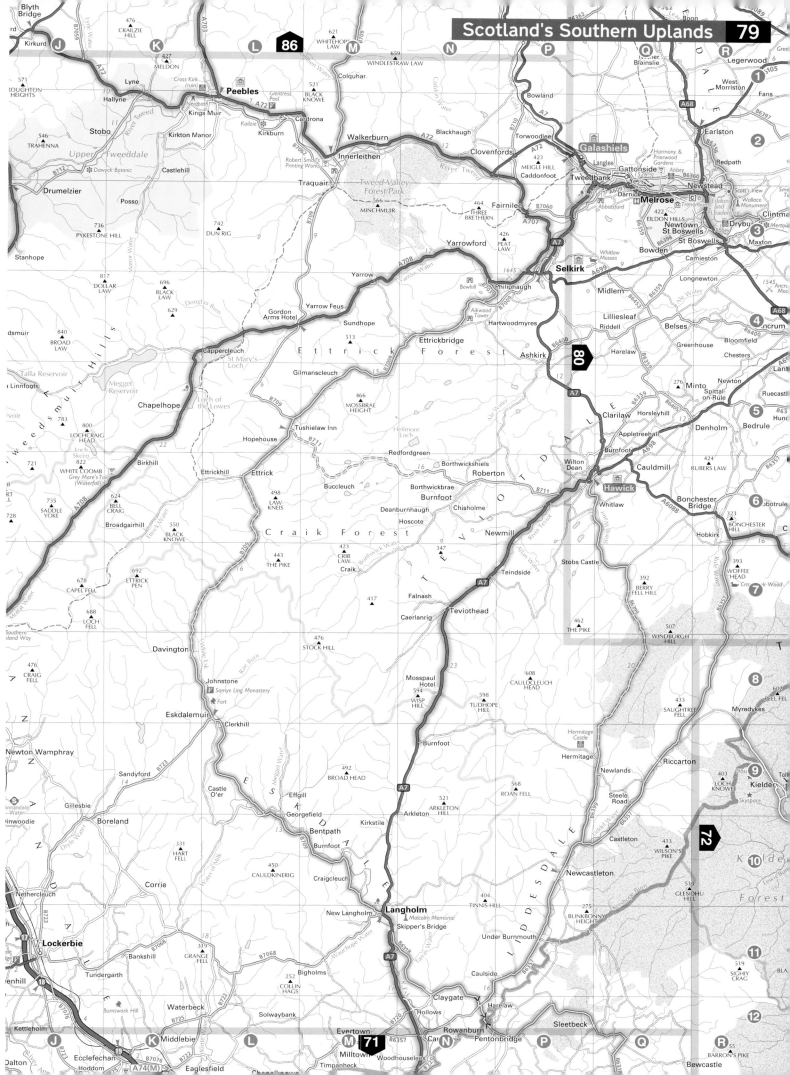

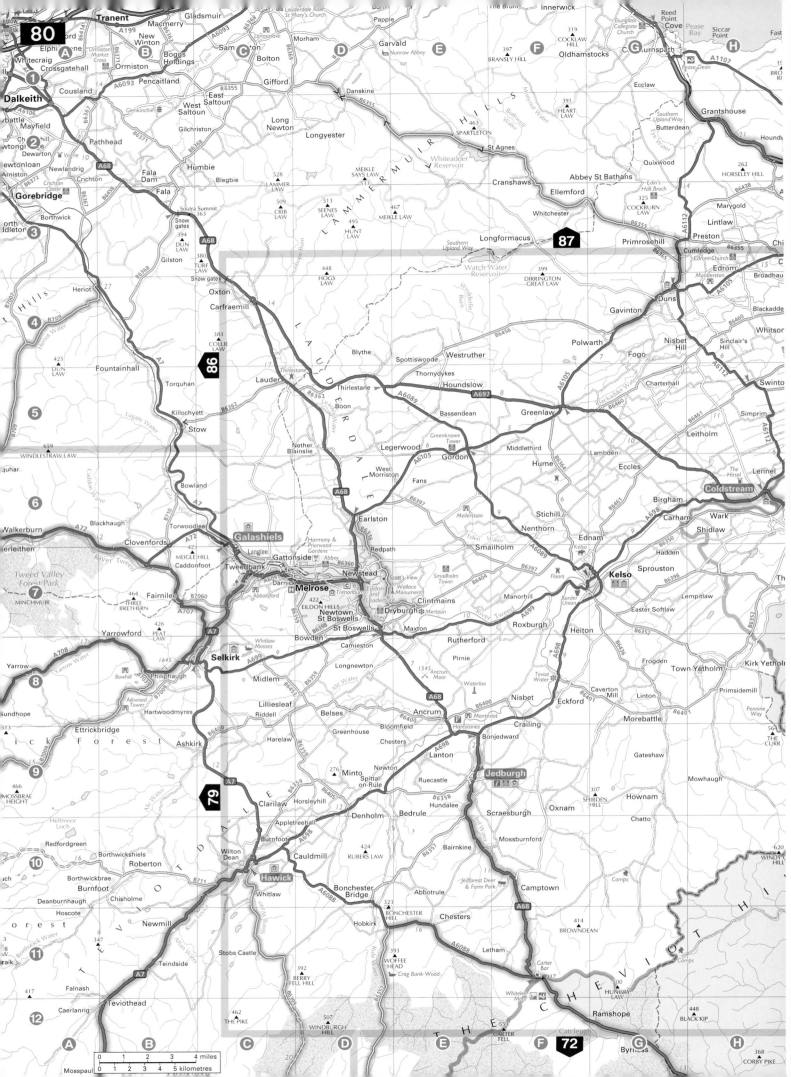

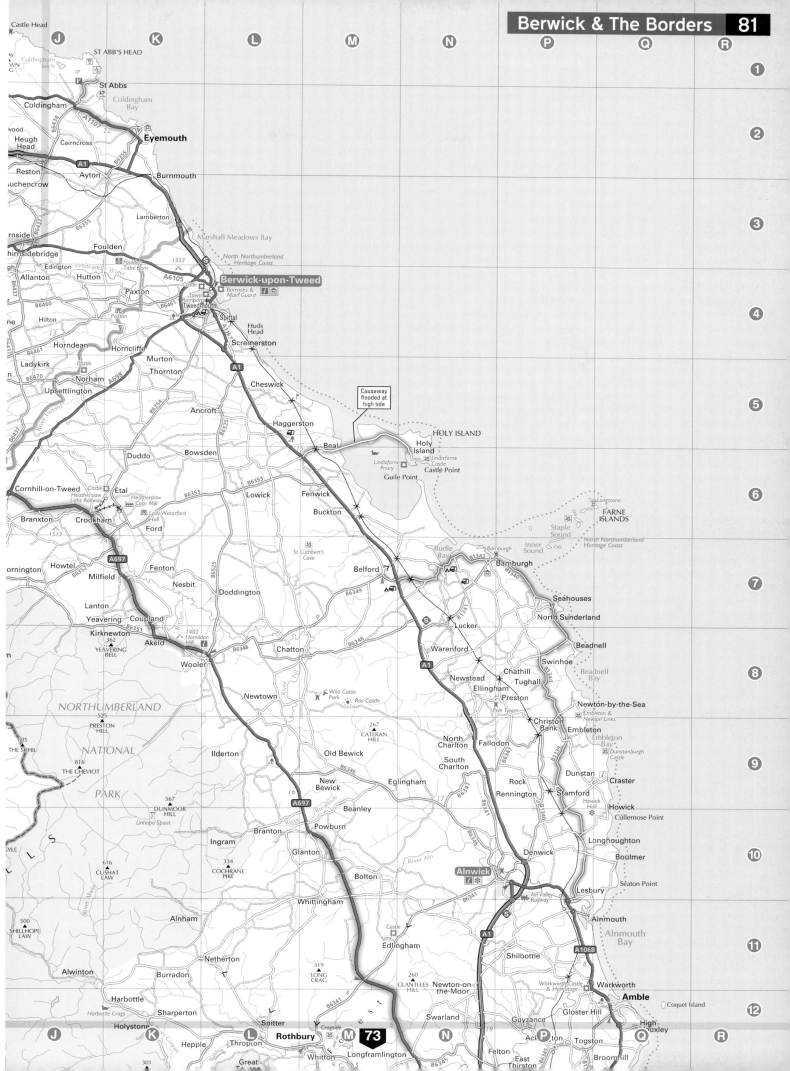

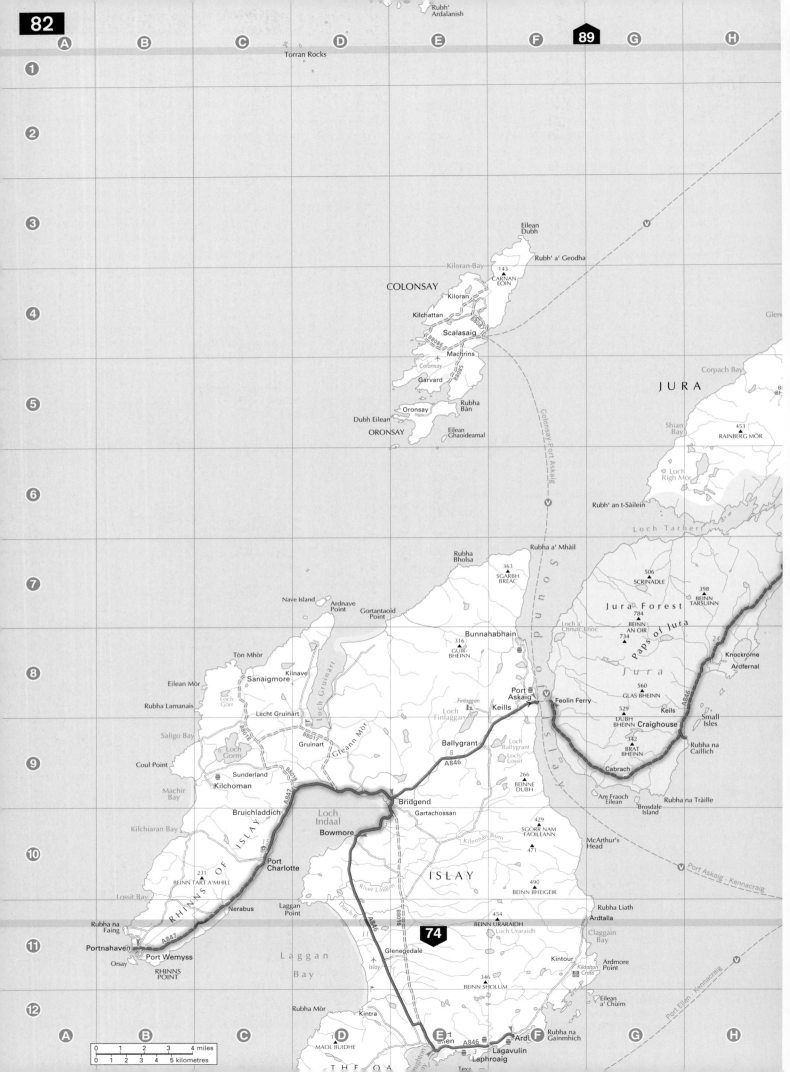

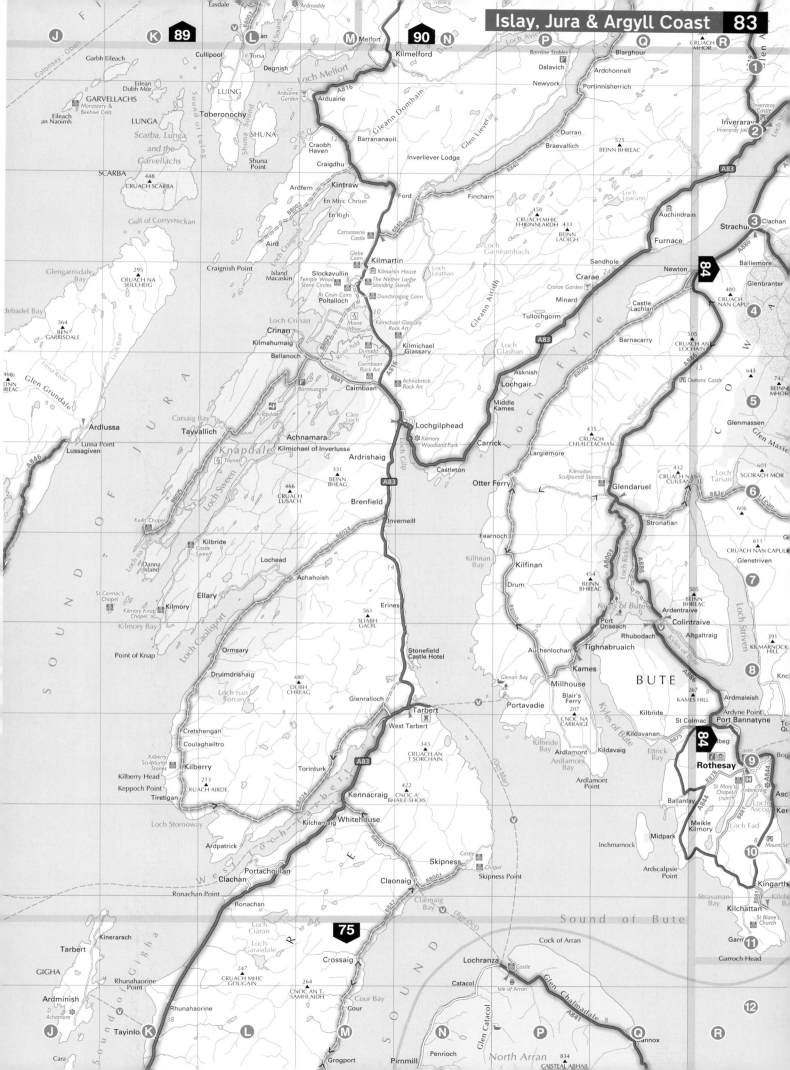

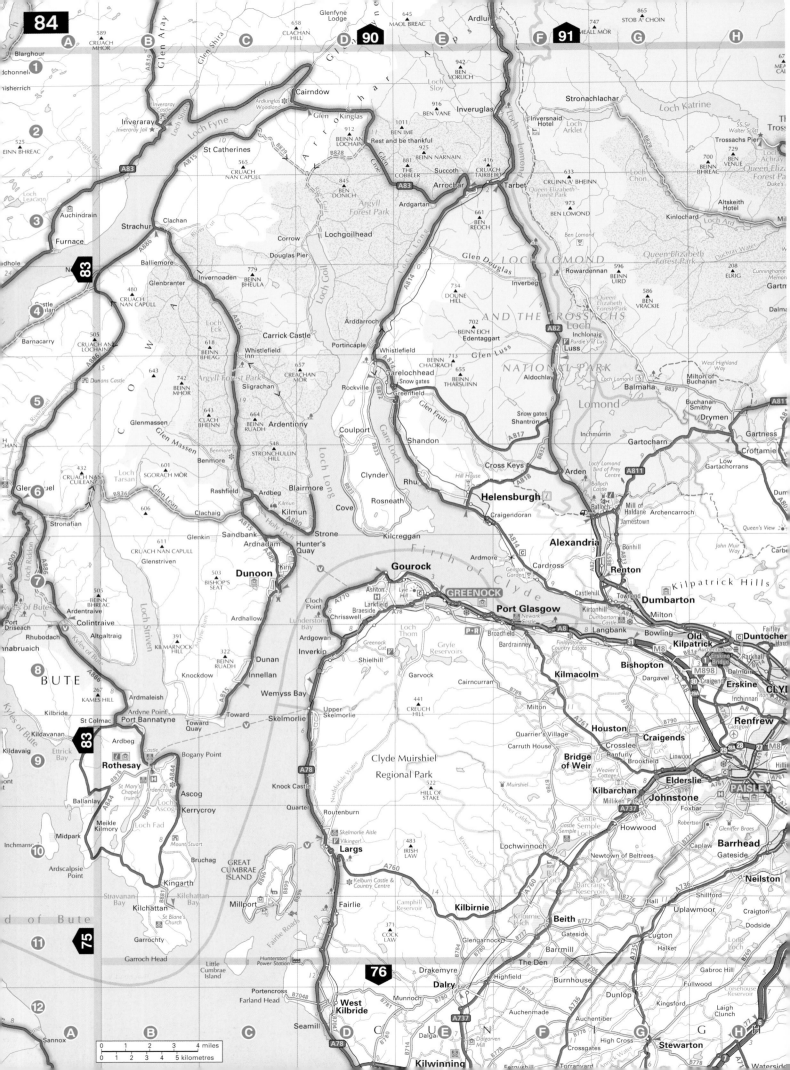

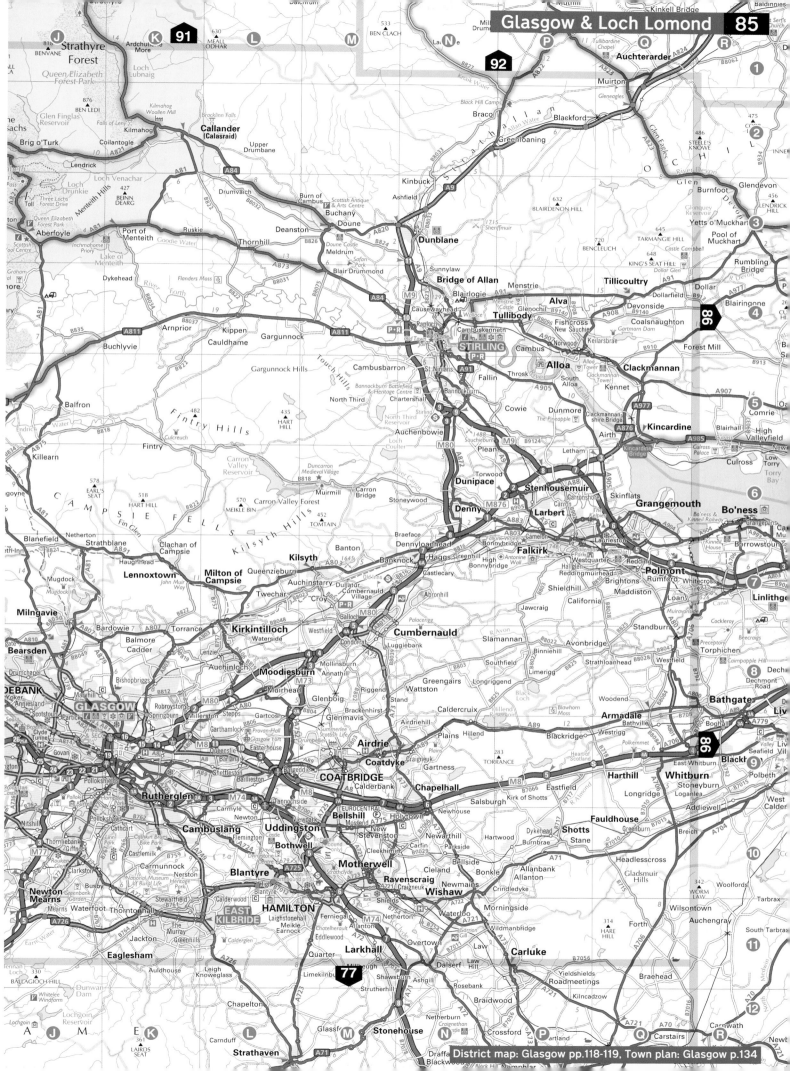

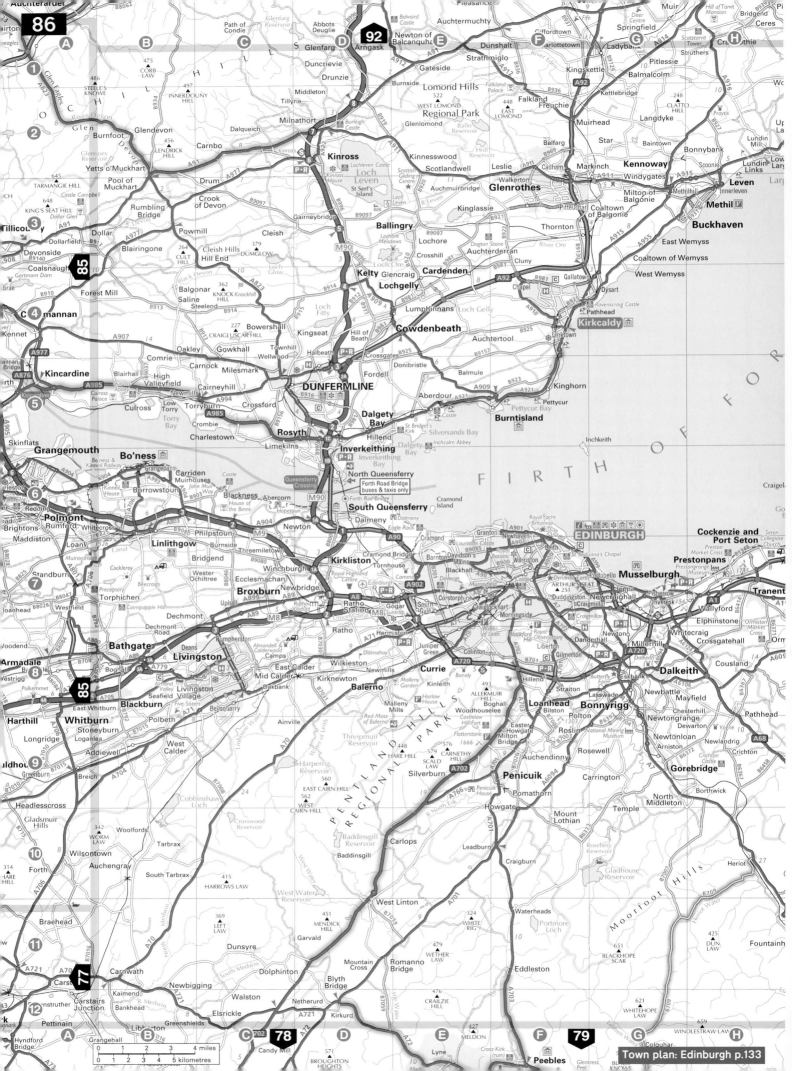

A   B   C   D   E   F   G   H

1

2

3

Eilean Mòr

Bàgh a' Chaisteil
(Castlebay)
Loch-Baghasdail
(Lochboisdale)
(Oct-Mar)

Rubha
Mòr
Rubha
Sgor-innis

Bousd   Sorisdale

4

Cliad
Bay

B8072

Arnabost

Grishipoll

Clabhach

Loch
Cliad

B8071

Hogh Bay   Ballyhaugh   **Arinagour**

COLL

Coll Oban

5

Bàgh a' Chaisteil
(Castlebay)

Totronald

Coll

Apr-Oct. Weds only)

Feall
Bay

Arileod   Acha

B8070

Caliach Point

Uig

Eilean
Ornsay

Calgar

Calgary Point

Crossapol
Bay

Rubha
Fàsachd

Calgary Bay

6

Rubha Port
Bhiosd

Clachan
Mor

Caoles

Rùbha Dubh

Loch Breachacha

Treshnish Point

Ensa

Balephetrish
Bay

Ruaig

Ballevullin   Cornoigmore

Loch
Bhasapoll

B8068

Gunna

Rubh' a' Chaoil

Hough
Bay

Kenovay

B8069

Fladda

7

Kilkenneth

Tiree

Gott
Bay

Moss   **Heylipoll**

B8065

Scarinish

Lunga

L

Middleton

Crossapol

B8065

TIREE

Barrapoll

Hynish Bay

TRESHNISH
ISLES

Gometra

Loch a'
Phuill

B8067

Balemartine

Mannal

8

Rinn
Thorbhais

Balephuil
Bay

Hynish

Bac Mòr or Dutchman's Cap

Bac Beag

Staffa   Little Colonsa

Loch

Fingal's

Isle o

9

10

IONA

Iona Abbey
& Nunnery

Rubha nan Cearc

Baile Mòr   **Kintra**

MacLean's
Cross

Loch
Lathaich

Fionnphort

Aridhglas

St Columba
Exhibition
Centre

Bun

ROSS O

11

Soa Island

Erraid

Arc

Ru
Ard

12

Torran Rocks

A   B   C   D   E   F   G   H

0   1   2   3   4 miles
0 1 2 3 4   5 kilometres

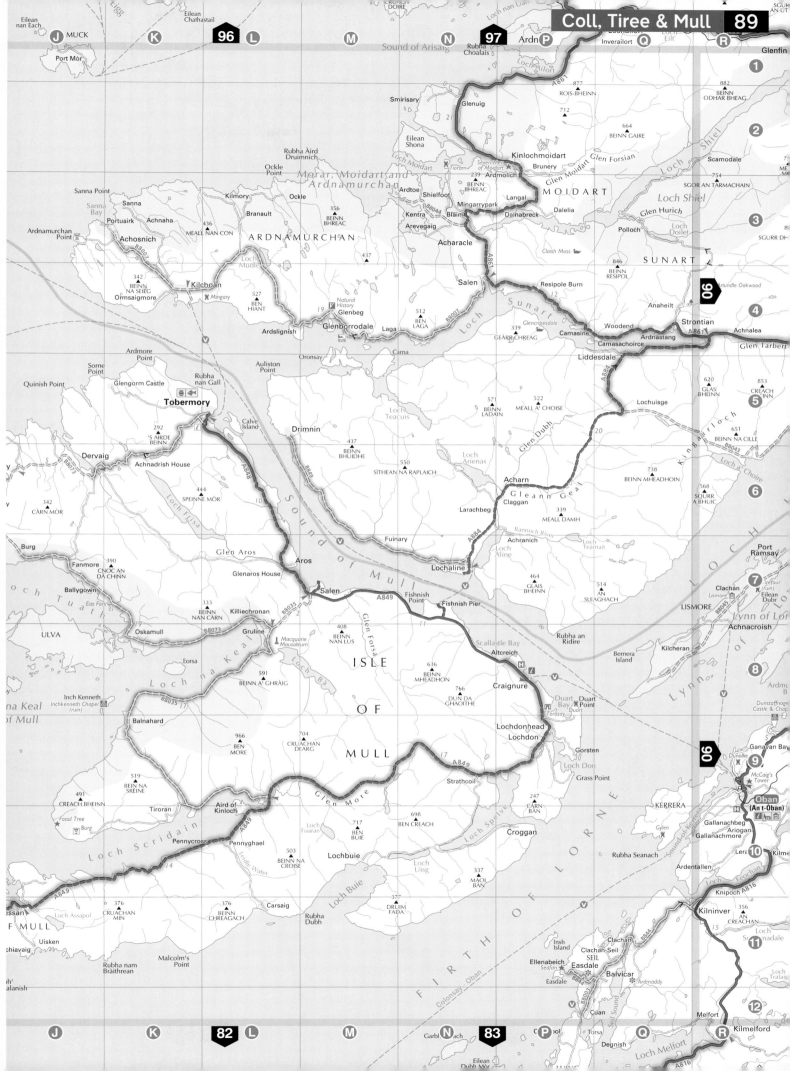

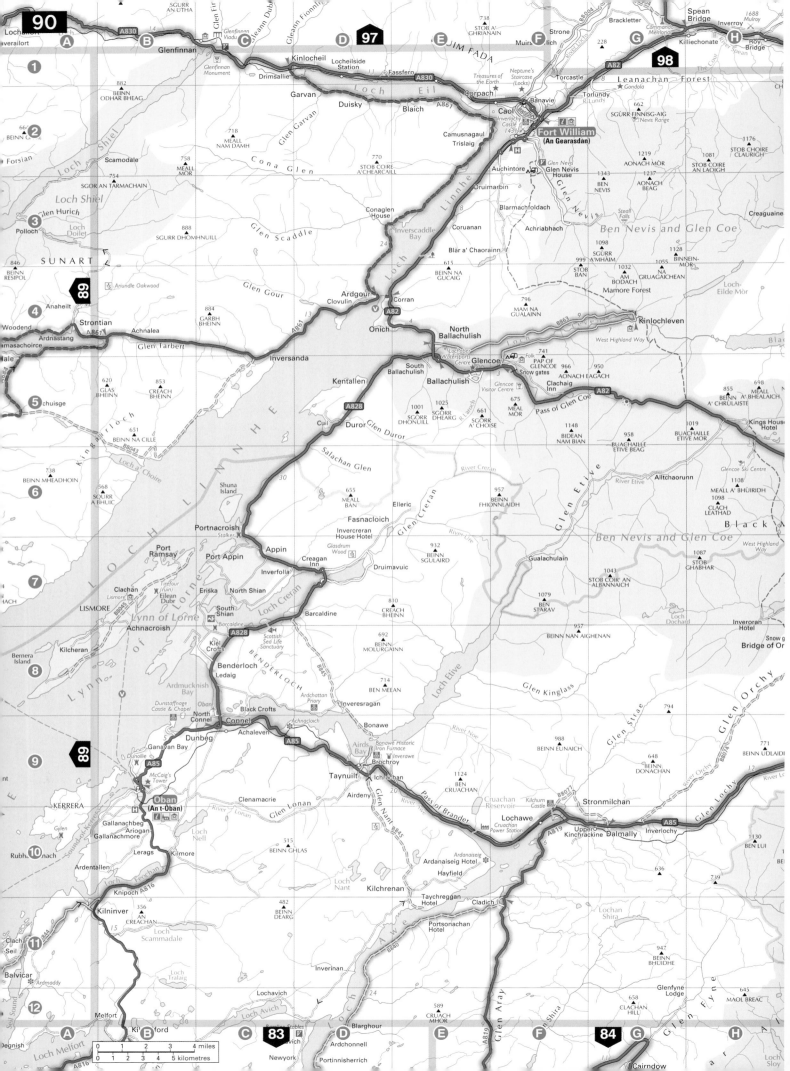

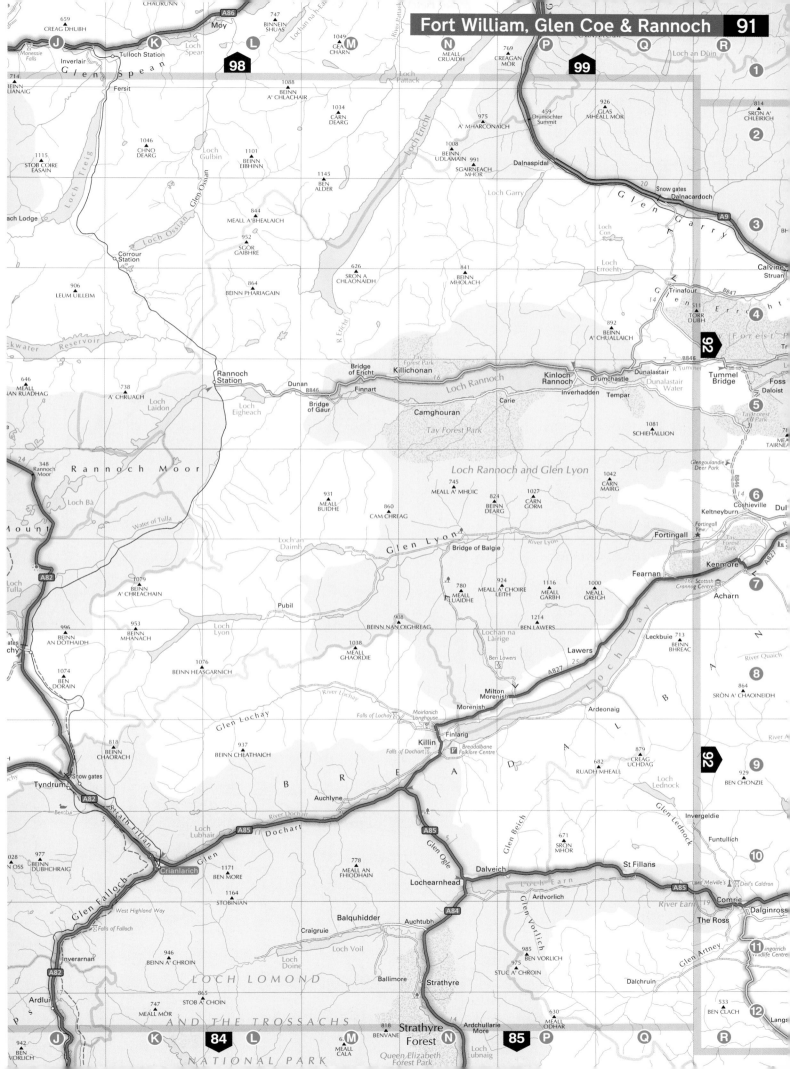

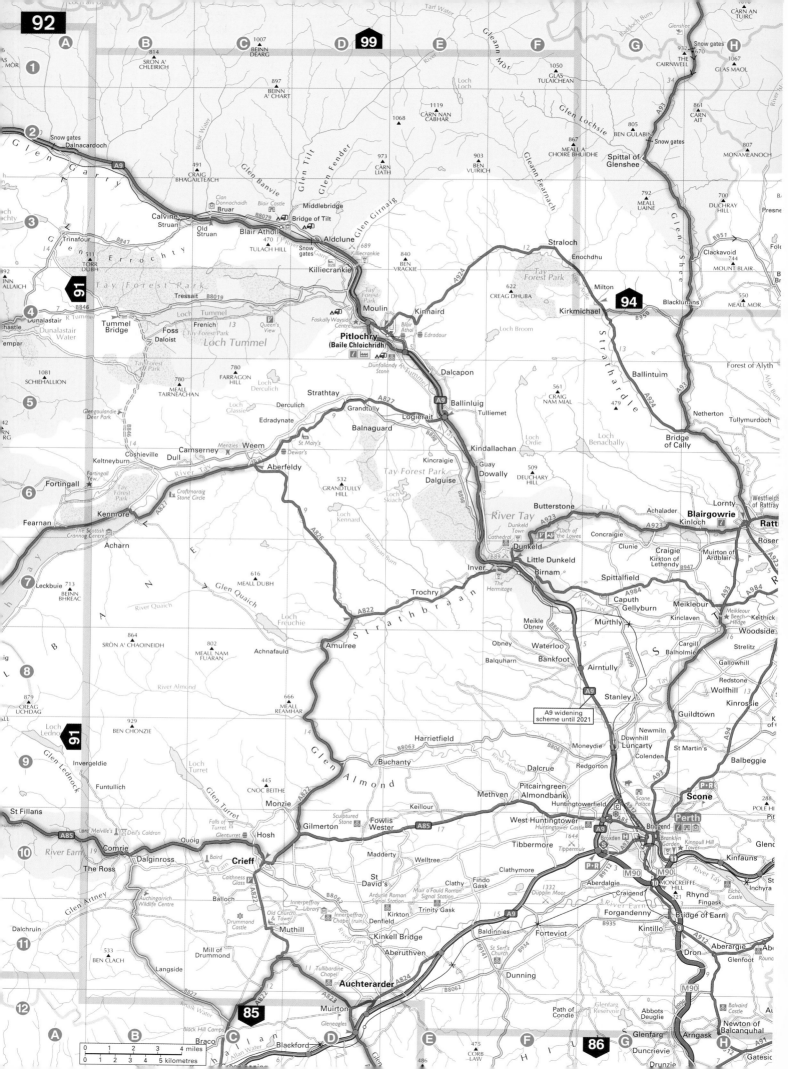

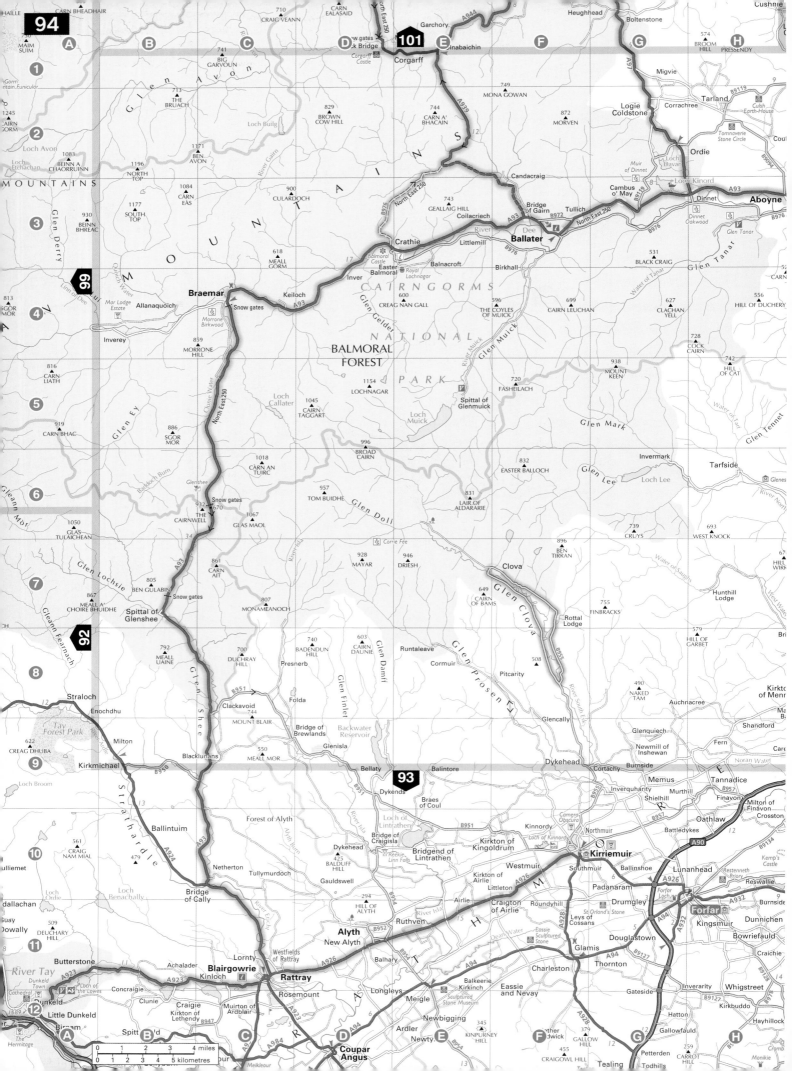

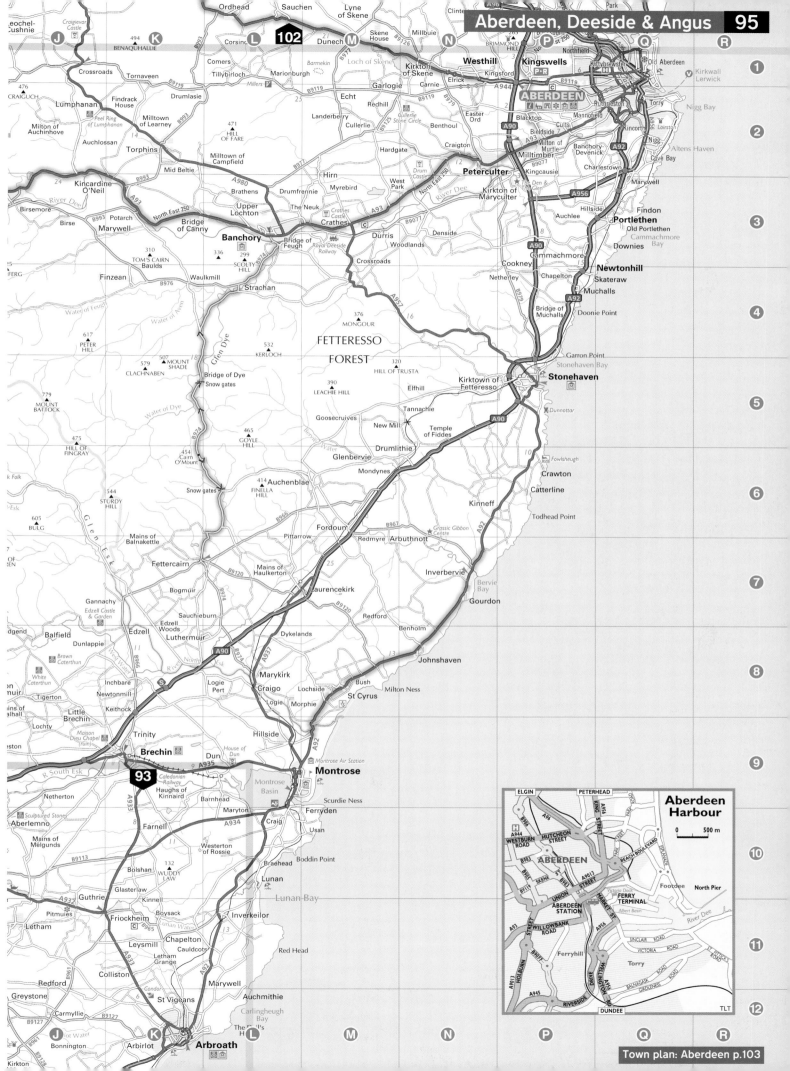

Aberdeen Harbour

ELGIN — PETERHEAD

ABERDEEN

ABERDEEN STATION

FERRY TERMINAL

North Pier

Footdee

Torry

Ferryhill

DUNDEE

0   500 m

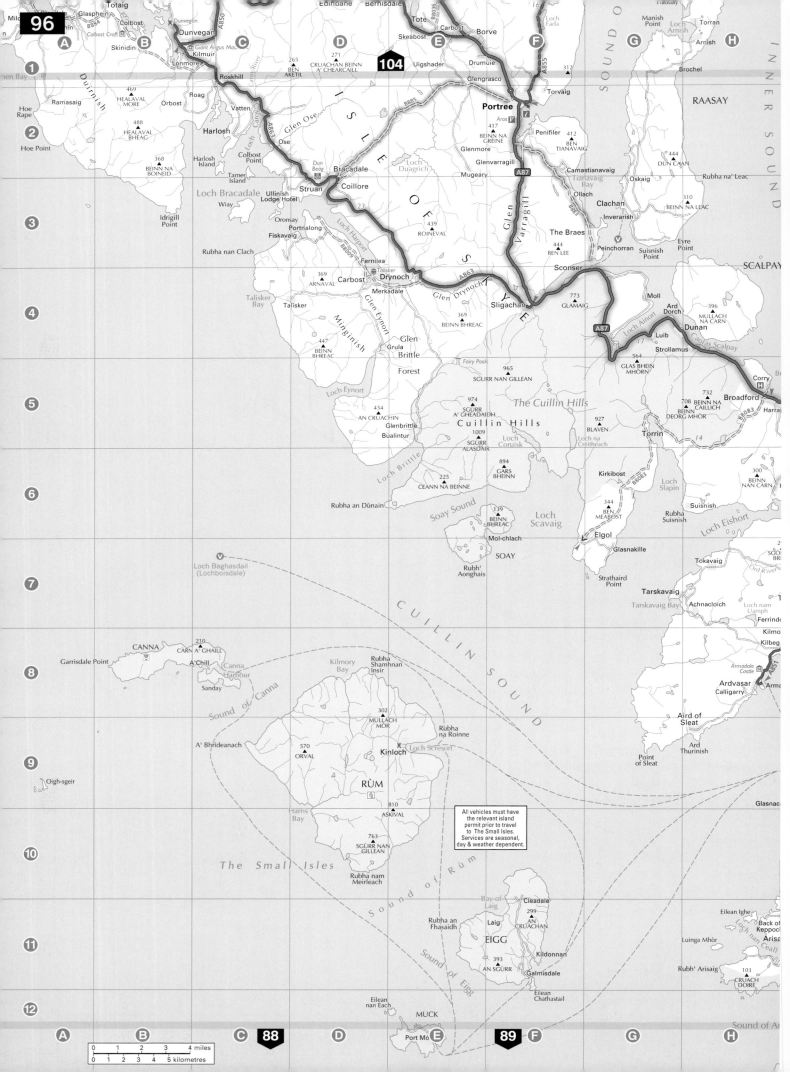

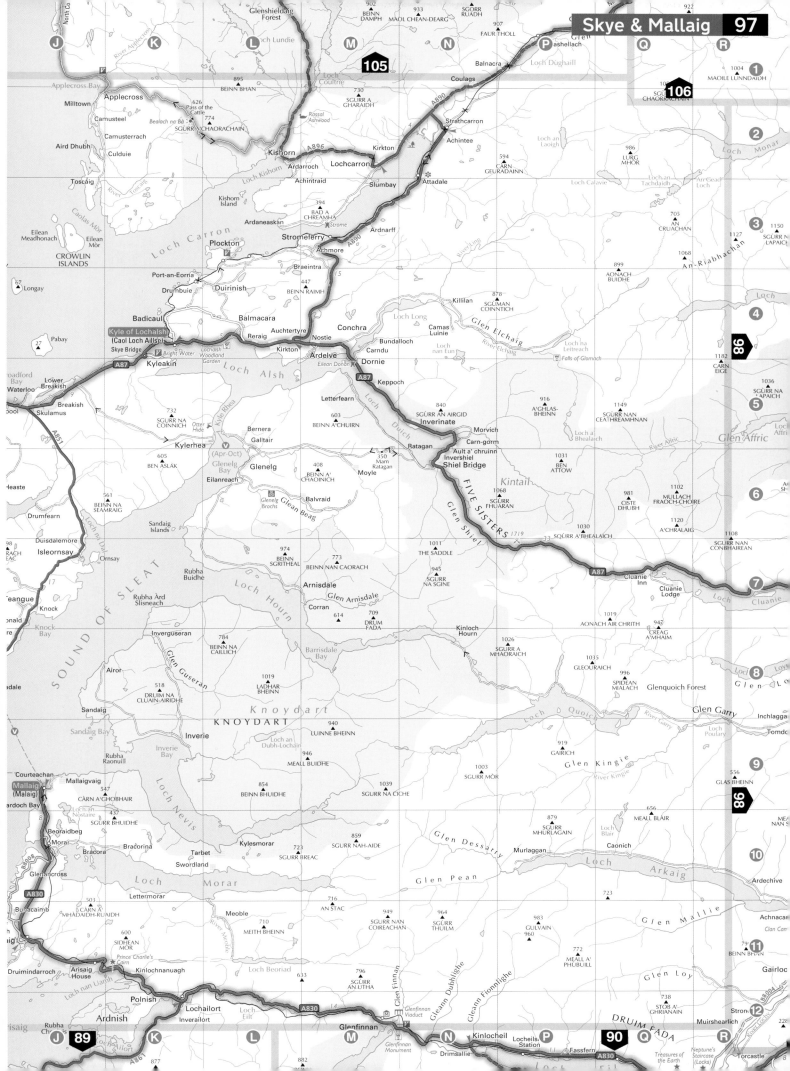

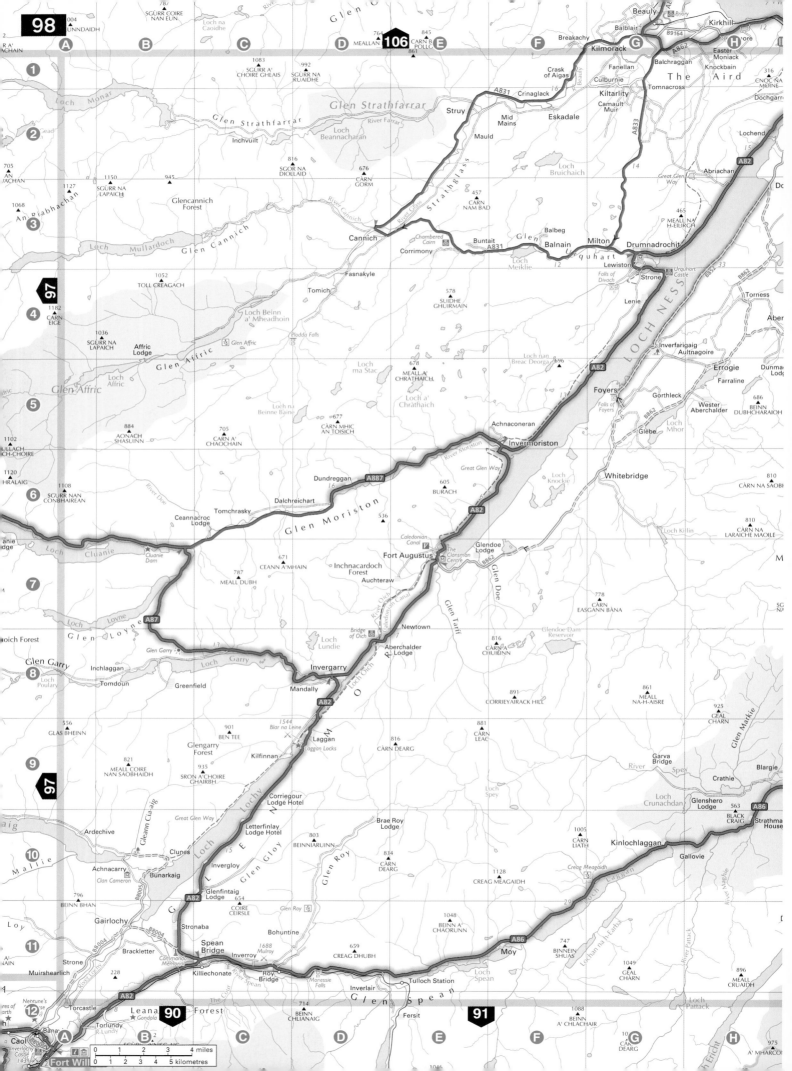

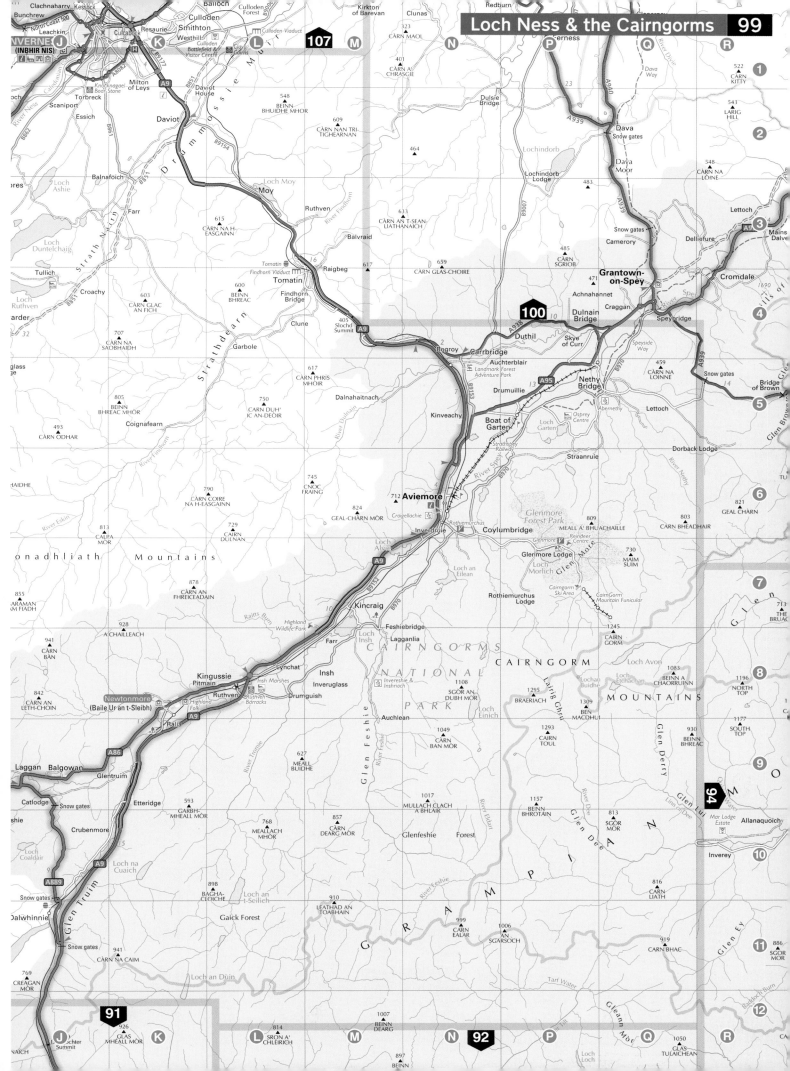

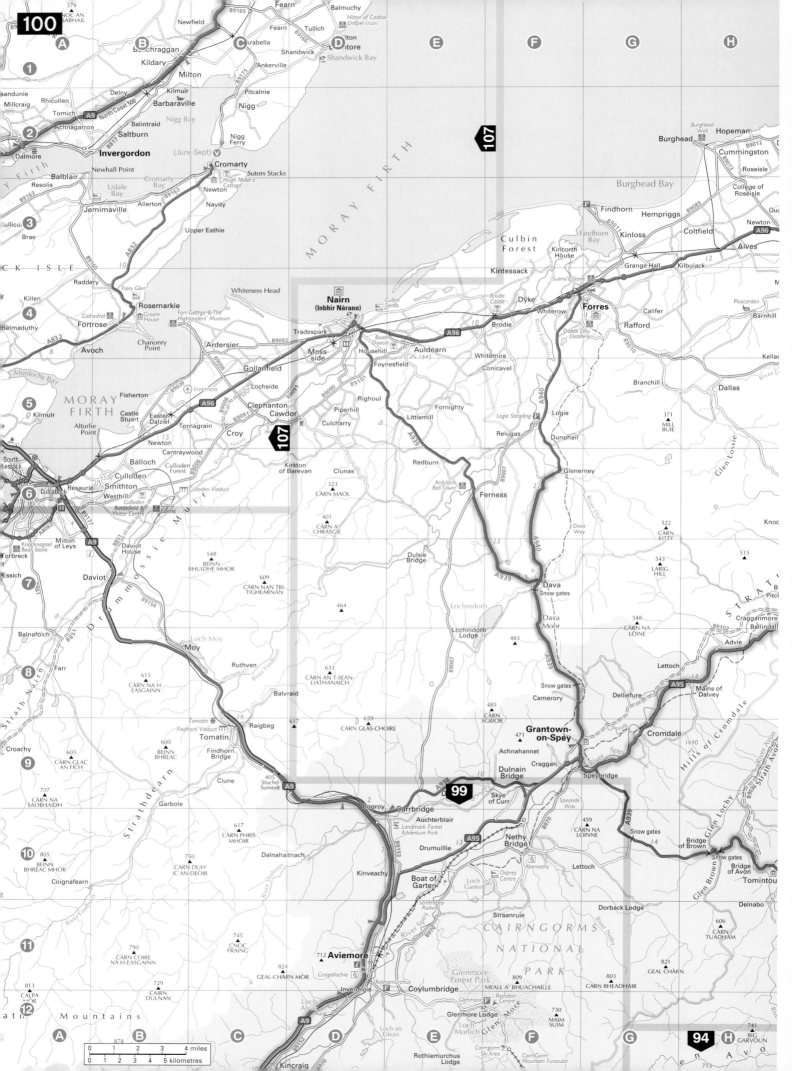

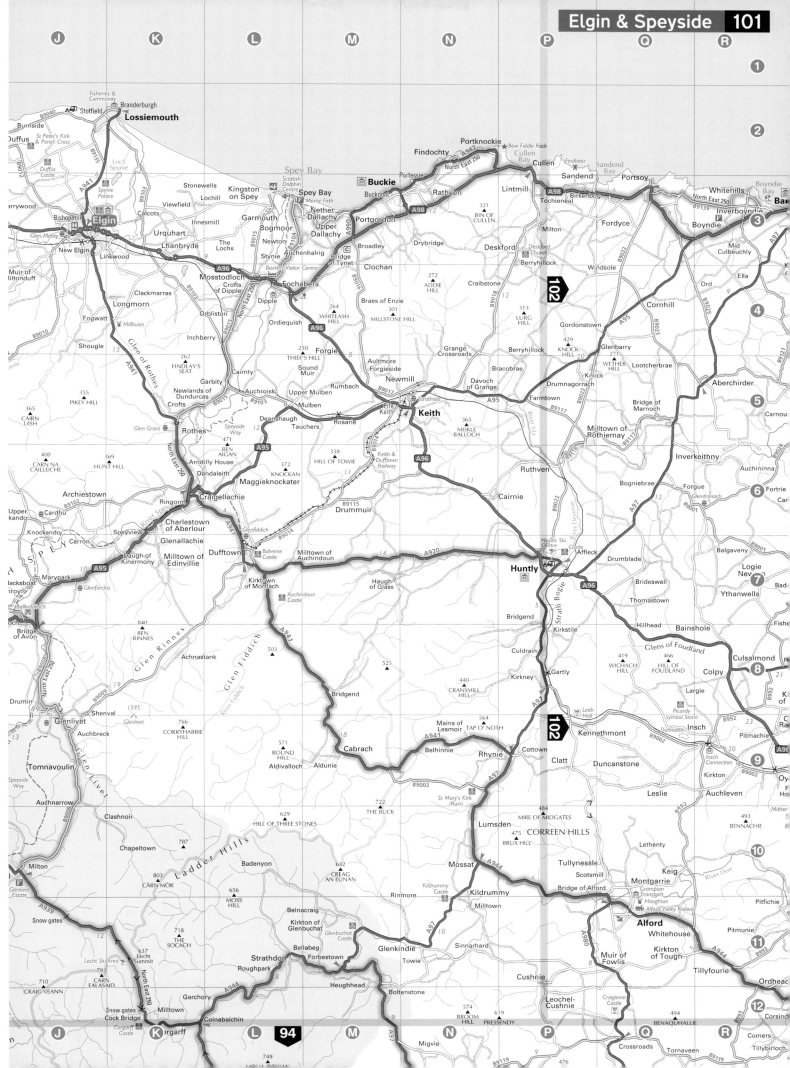

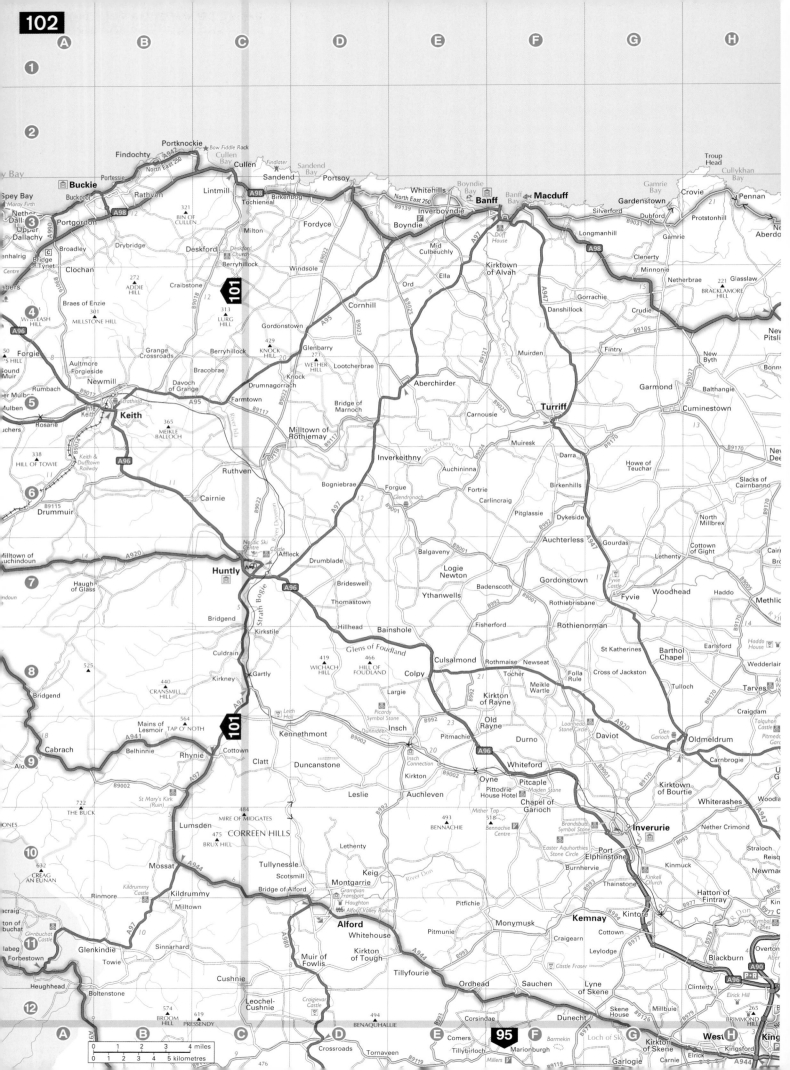

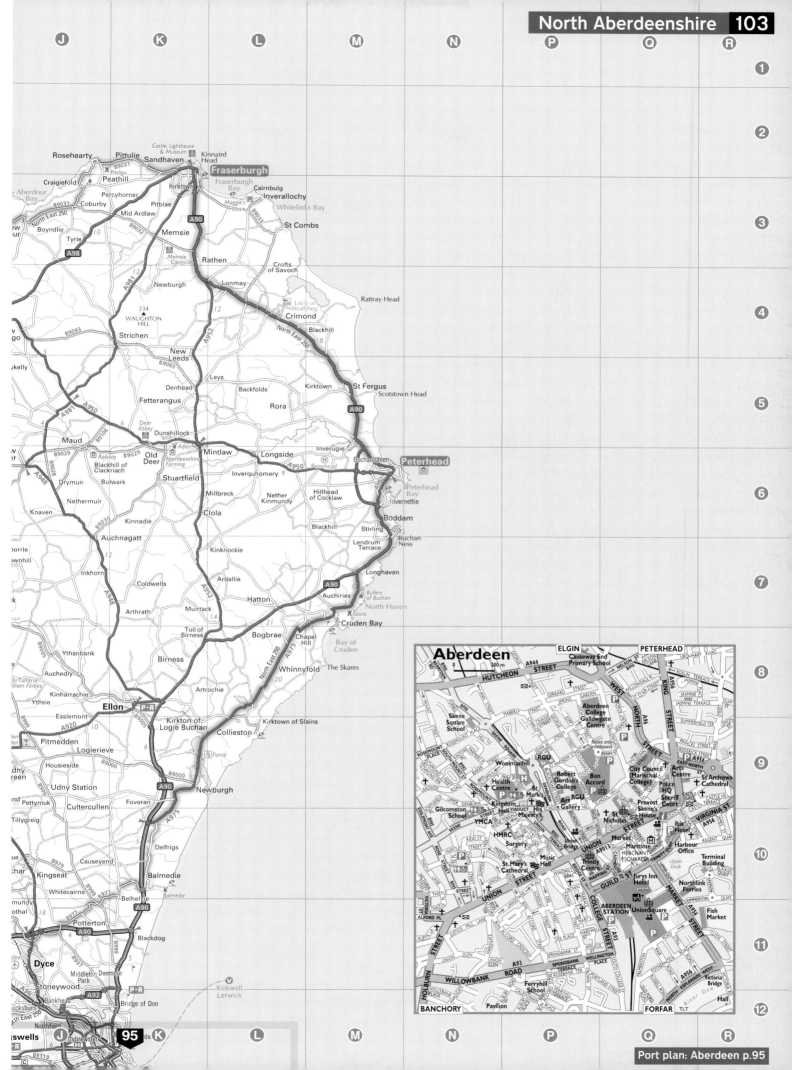

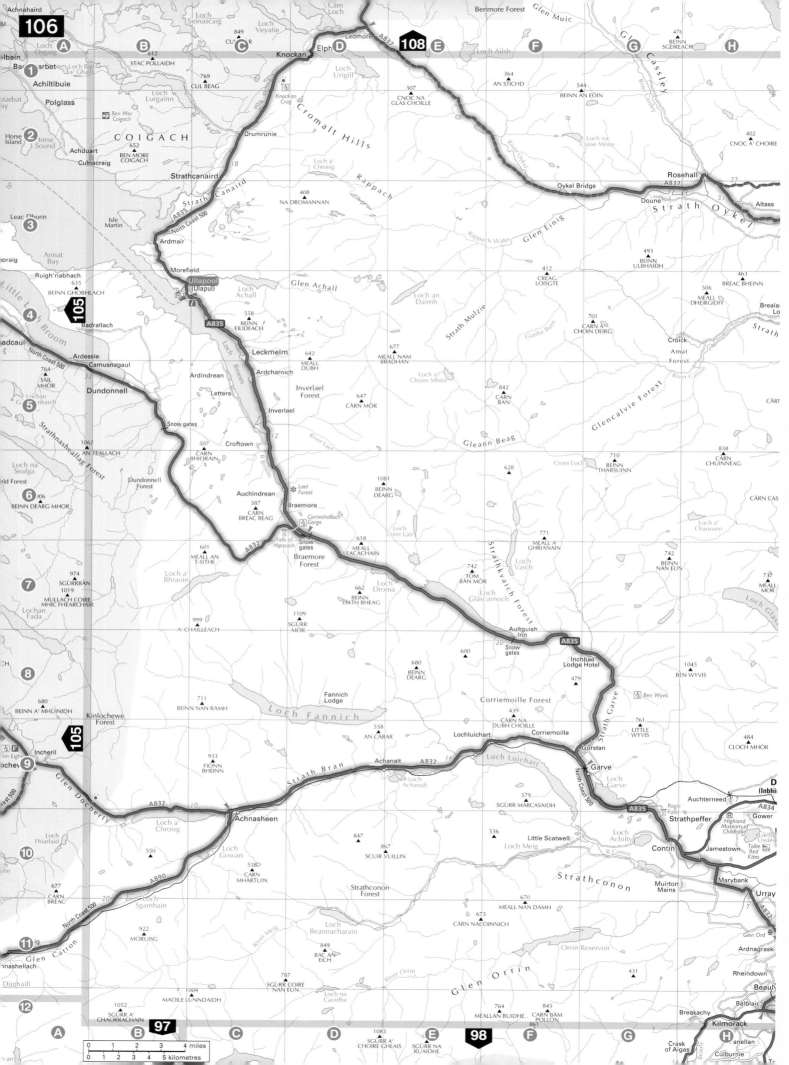

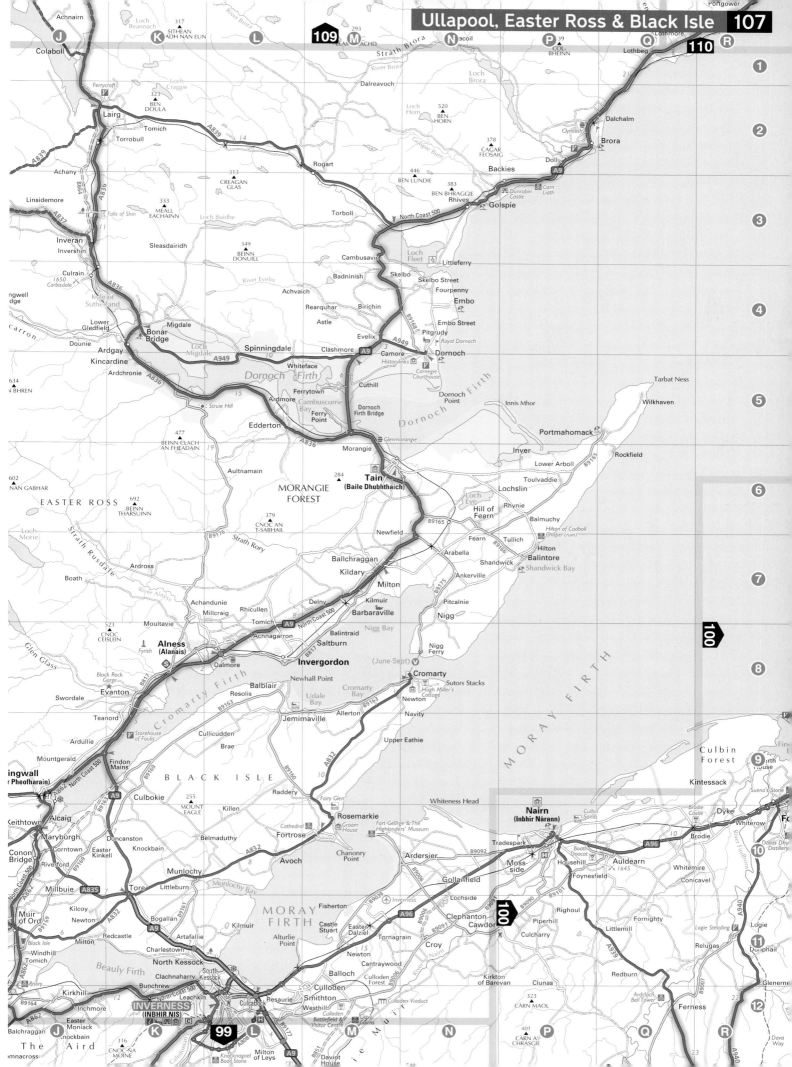

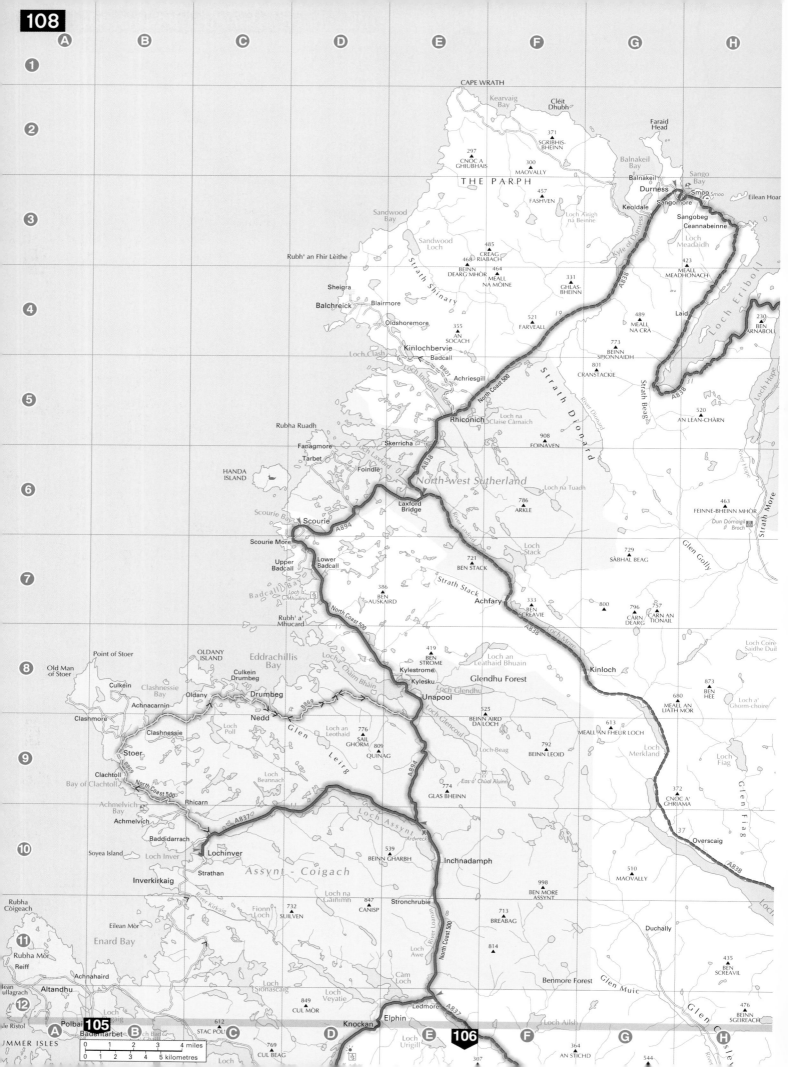

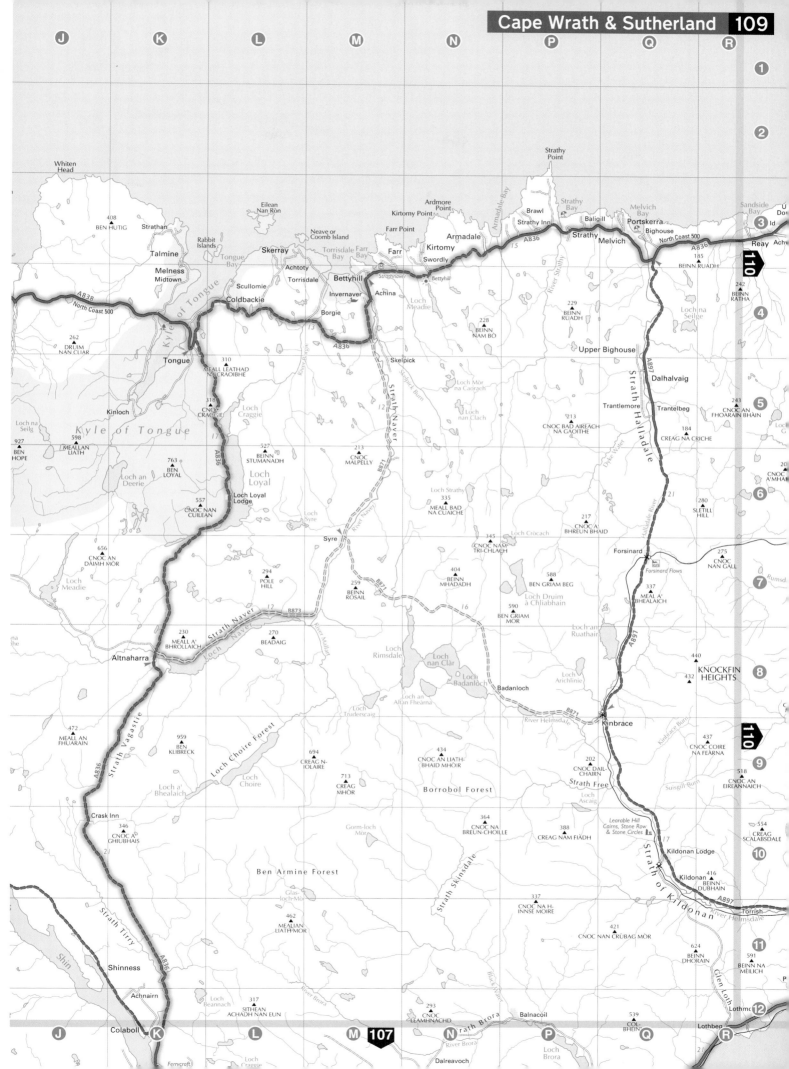

J · K · L · M · N · P · Q · R

1
2
3
4
5
6
7
8
9
10
11
12

Whiten
Head

408
BEN HUTIG
Strathan
Talmine
Melness
Midtown

Rabbit
Islands

Eilean
Nan Ròn
Skerray
Achtoty
Scullomie
Torrisdale

Neave or
Coomb Island

Torrisdale Farr
Bay
Bettyhill
Invernaver
Borgie

Farr Point
Farr
Swordly
Achina

Kirtomy Point
Kirtomy
Armadale

Ardmore
Point
Strathy Inn
Strathy

Strathy
Point
Strathy
Bay
Brawl
Melvich

Armadale Bay
Baligill
Portskerra
Bighouse
Melvich

Strathy
Bay

Sandside
Bay
Reay

North Coast 500
A836

Id
Do
Achy

185
BEINN RUADH
242
BEINN RATHA

262
DRUIM NAN CLIAR

A838
North Coast 500

Kyle of Tongue
Tongue

Coldbackie

A836

13

Strathnaver
Bettyhill

Loch
Meadie

229
BEINN RUADH

228
BEINN NAM BÒ

Upper Bighouse

Dalhalvaig

Strath Halladale

A897

310
MEALL LEATHAD
NA CRAOIBHE

318
CNOC CRAGGIE

Loch
Craggie

Skelpick

Skelpick Burn

Strath Naver

12

Trantlemore
Trantelbeg

213
CNOC BAD AIREACH
NA GAOITHE

243
CNOC AN
FHOARAIN BHÀIN

184
CREAG NA CRICHE

Kinloch

598
MEALLAN
LIATH

927
BEN
HOPE

763
BEN
LOYAL

Loch an
Deerie

527
BEINN
STUMANADH

Loch
Loyal

213
CNOC
MALPELLY

B871

Loch Mòr
na Caorach

Loch
nan Clach

20
CNOC
A'MHA

557
CNOC NAN
CUILEAN

Loch Loyal
Lodge

Loch
Syre

River Naver

Syre

335
MEALL BAD
NA CUAICHE

Loch Strathy

217
CNOC A'
BHREUN BHAID

280
SLETTILL
HILL

Lo

656
CNOC AN
DAIMH MÒR

Loch
Meadie

294
POLE
HILL

259
BEINN
ROSAIL

B871

404
BEINN
MHADADH

345
CNOC NAM
TRI-CHLACH

Loch Cròcach

588
BEN GRIAM BEG

Loch Druim
à Chliabhain

Forsinard

Forsinard Flows

275
CNOC
NAN GALL

230
MEALL A'
BHROLLAICH

270
BEADAIG

Strath Naver

B873

River Mallart

12

16

590
BEN GRIAM
MÒR

337
MEAL A'
BHEALAICH

Altnaharra

Loch Naver

Loch
Rimsdale

Loch
nan Clàr

Loch an
Allt an Fheàrna

Loch an
Ruathain

440

432

KNOCKFIN
HEIGHTS

472
MEALL AN
FHUARAIN

Strath Vagastie

A836

959
BEN
KLIBRECK

Loch Choire Forest

694
CREAG N-
IOLAIRE

Loch
Badanloch

Badanloch

River Helmsdale

B871

Kinbrace

437
CNOC COIRE
NA FEARNA

Crask Inn

346
CNOC A'
GHIUBHAIS

Loch a'
Bhealaich

Loch
Choire

713
CREAG
MHÒR

434
CNOC AN LIATH-
BHAID MHÒR

Borrobol Forest

202
CNOC DAIL-
CHAIRN

Strath Free

Loch
Ascaig

Kindrace Burn

518
CNOC AN
EIREANNAICH

554
CREAG
SCALABSDALE

Ben Armine Forest

Gorm-loch
Mòr

364
CNOC NA
BREUN-CHOILLE

388
CREAG NAM FIÀDH

Learable Hill
Cairns, Stone Row
& Stone Circles

17

Kildonan Lodge

Kildonan

416
BEINN
DUBHAIN

Glas-
loch-Mòr

462
MEALLAN
LIATH-MÒR

Strath Skinsdale

337
CNOC NA H-
INNSE MOIRE

421
CNOC NAN CRÙBAG MÒR

Strath of Kildonan

River Helmsdale

Torrish

624
BEINN
DHORAIN

591
BEINN NA
MÈILICH

Shinness

Achnairn

A836

Strath Tirry

Shin

317
SITHEAN
ACHADH NAN EUN

Loch
Beannach

River Brora

293
CNOC
LEAMHNACHD

Strath Brora

Balnacoil

539
COL-
BHEINN

Lothbeg

Lothmc

Colaboll

J · K · L · M · N · P · Q · R

Ferrycroft

Loch
Craggie

River Brora

Dalreavoch

Loch
Brora

21

110
110
110

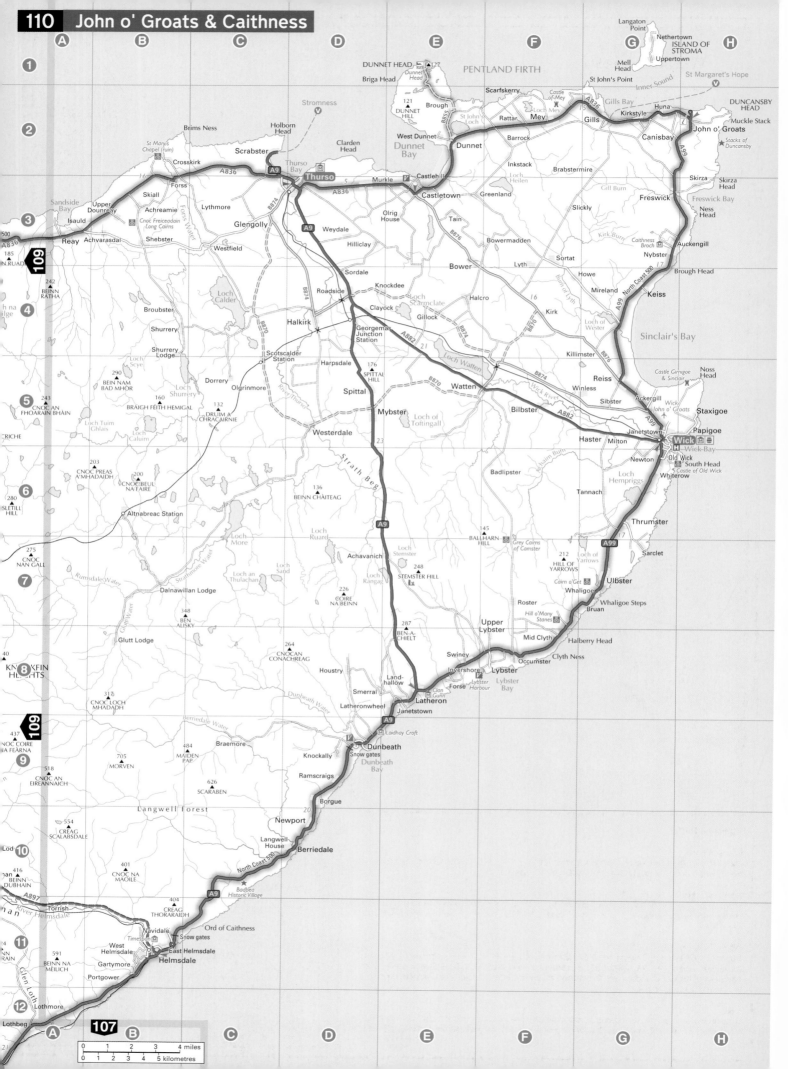

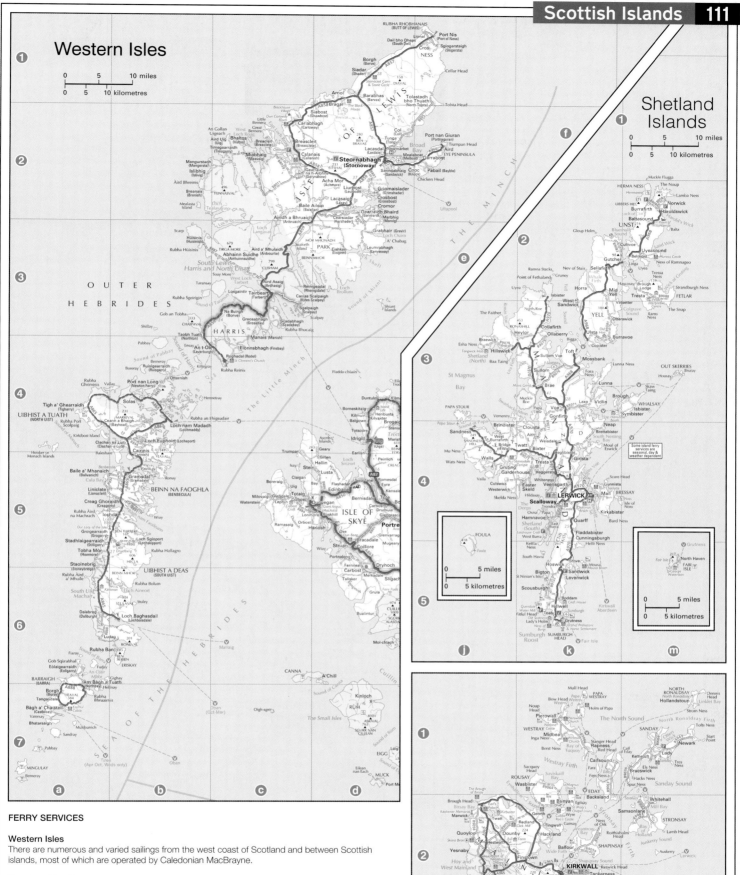

Western Isles

0 5 10 miles
0 5 10 kilometres

Shetland Islands

0 5 10 miles
0 5 10 kilometres

Orkney Islands

0 5 10 miles
0 5 10 kilometres

FERRY SERVICES

Western Isles

There are numerous and varied sailings from the west coast of Scotland and between Scottish islands, most of which are operated by Caledonian MacBrayne.

Shetland Islands

The main service is from Aberdeen on the mainland to the island port of Lerwick. A service from Kirkwall (Orkney) to Lerwick is also available. Shetland Islands Council operates an inter-island car ferry service.

Orkney Islands

The main service is from Scrabster on the Caithness coast to the island port of Stromness and there is a further service from Gills (Caithness) to St Margaret's Hope on South Ronaldsay. A service from Aberdeen to Kirkwall provides a link to Shetland at Lerwick. Inter-island car ferry services are also operated by Orkney Ferries.

Note

Some island services are day dependant and advance reservations are recommended. Before setting off on your journey, confirm and book sailings by contacting the ferry operator listed on page VII of this atlas.

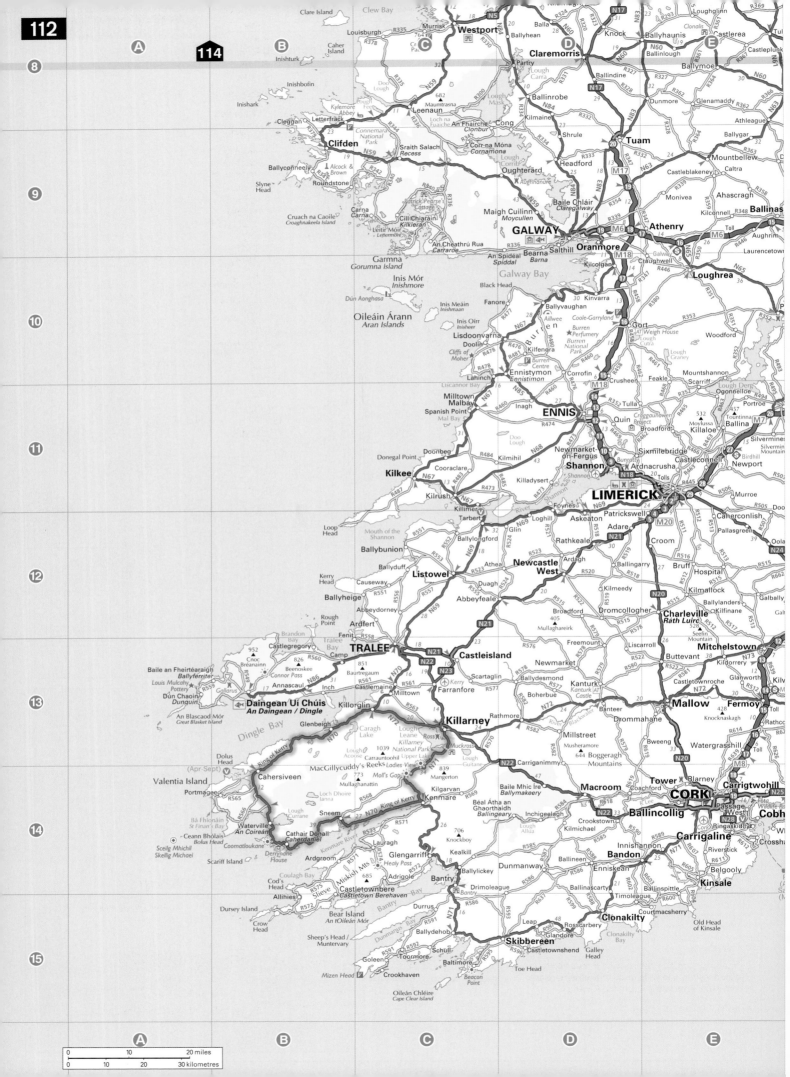

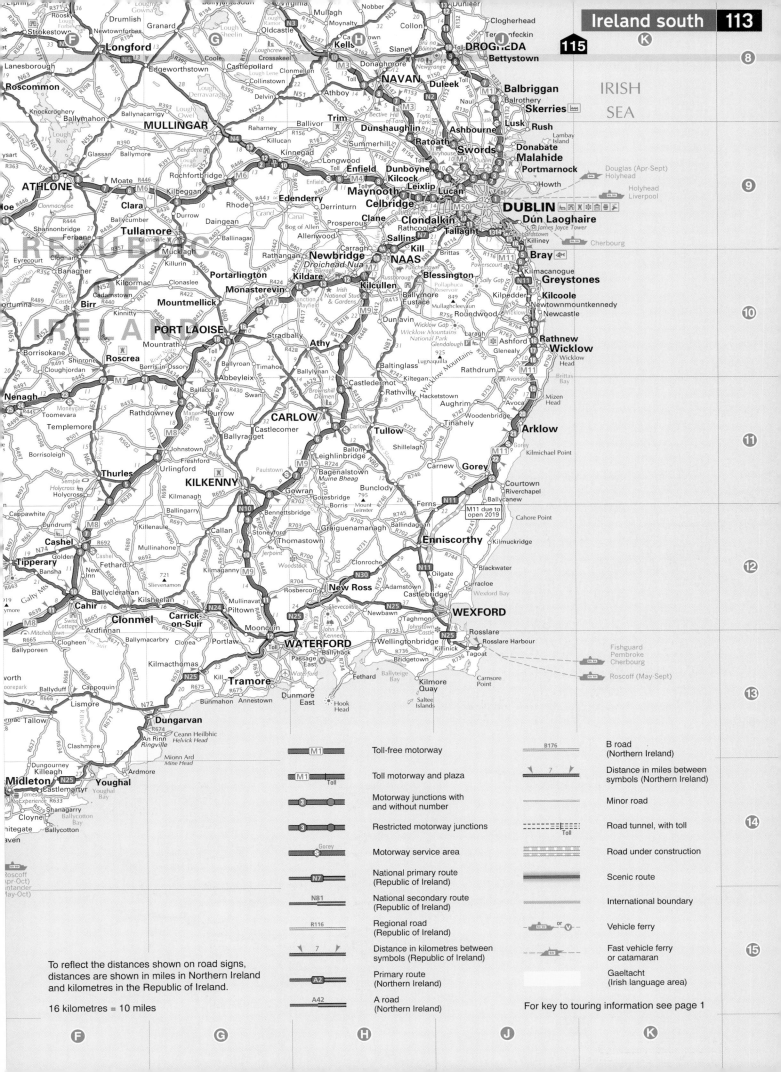

Ireland index

Abbeydorney....C12
Abbeyfeale....D12
Abbeyleix....G11
Adamstown....H12
Adare....D12
Adrigole....C14
Aghalee....J5
Ahascragh....E9
Ahoghill....J4
Allenwood....H9
Allihies....B15
An Bun Beag....E4
An Charraig....E5
An Cheathrú Rua....C9
An Clochán Liath....E4
An Coireán....B14
An Daingean....B13
An Fál Carrach....F3
An Fhairche....C9
Annahilt....J6
Annalong....J7
Annascaul....B13
Annestown....G13
An Rinn....G13
An Spidéal....D9
Antrim....J5
Ardagh....D12
Ardara....E5
Ardee....H8
Ardfert....C12
Ardfinnan....F12
Ardglass....K6
Ardgroom....B14
Ardmore....F14
Ardnacrusha....E11
Arklow....J11
Armagh....H6
Armoy....J3
Arvagh....G7
Ashbourne....J9
Ashford....J10
Askeaton....D12
Athboy....H8
Athea....D12
Athenry....E9
Athleague....E8
Athlone....F9
Athy....H10
Augher....G6
Aughnacloy....H6
Aughrim....E9
Aughrim....J11
Avoca....J11

Bagenalstown....H11
Baile an Fheirtéaraigh....B13
Baile Chláir....D9
Baile Mhic Íre....D14
Baile na Finne....F4
Bailieborough....H7
Balbriggan....J8
Balla....D8
Ballacolla....G11
Ballaghaderreen....E7
Ballina....D7
Ballina....E11
Ballinafad....E7
Ballinagar....G9
Ballinagh....G7
Ballinamallard....G6
Ballinamore....F7
Ballinascarty....D14
Ballinasloe....E9
Ballincollig....E14
Ballindaggan....H12
Ballindine....D8
Ballineen....D14
Ballingarry....D12
Ballingarry....G12
Ballingeary....D14
Ballinlough....E8
Ballinrobe....D8
Ballinspittle....E14
Ballintra....F5
Ballivor....H9
Ballon....H11
Ballybay....H7
Ballybofey....F5
Ballybunion....C12
Ballycanew....J11
Ballycarry....K5

Ballycastle....J3
Ballycastle....C6
Ballyclare....J5
Ballyclerahan....F12
Ballyconneely....B9
Ballyconnell....G7
Ballycotton....F14
Ballydehob....C15
Ballydesmond....D13
Ballyduff....C12
Ballyduff....F13
Ballyfarnon....E7
Ballyferriter....B13
Ballygally....J4
Ballygar....E9
Ballygawley....H6
Ballygawley....E6
Ballygowan....K5
Ballyhaise....G7
Ballyhalbert....K5
Ballyhaunis....E8
Ballyhean....D8
Ballyheige....C12
Ballyjamesduff....G8
Ballylanders....E12
Ballylickey....C14
Ballyliffin....G3
Ballylongford....C12
Ballylynan....H10
Ballymacarbry....F13
Ballymahon....F8
Ballymakeery....D14
Ballymena....J4
Ballymoe....E8
Ballymoney....H4
Ballymore....F9
Ballymore Eustace....H10
Ballymote....E7
Ballynacarrigy....G8
Ballynahinch....J6
Ballynure....J5
Ballyporeen....F13
Ballyragget....G11
Ballyroan....G10
Ballysadare....E6
Ballyshannon....F5
Ballyvaughan....D10
Ballywalter....K5
Balrothery....J8
Baltimore....C15
Baltinglass....H10
Banagher....F10
Banbridge....J6
Bandon....E14
Bangor....K5
Bangor Erris....C7
Bansha....F12
Banteer....D13
Bantry....C14
Barna....D9
Béal an Mhuirthead....B6
Béal Átha an Ghaorthaidh....D14
Bearna....D9
Belcoo....F6
Belfast....J5
Belgooly....E14
Bellaghy....H5
Belleek....F6
Belmullet....B6
Belturbet....G7
Benburb....H6
Bennettsbridge....G12
Beragh....G5
Bessbrook....J6
Bettystown....J8
Birr....F10
Blacklion....F6
Blackwater....J12
Blarney....E14
Blessington....H10
Boherbue....D13
Borris....H12
Borris-in-Ossory....F10
Borrisokane....F10
Borrisoleigh....F11
Boyle....E7
Bray....J10
Bridgetown....H13

Brittas....J9
Broadford....E11
Broadford....D12
Broughshane....J4
Bruff....E12
Bunbeg....E4
Bunclody....H11
Buncrana....G3
Bundoran....E6
Bunmahon....G13
Bunnyconnellan....D7
Bushmills....H3
Buttevant....E13
Bweeng....E13

Cadamstown....F10
Caherconlish....E12
Caherdaniel....B14
Cahersiveen....B14
Cahir....F12
Caledon....H6
Callan....G12
Caltra....E9
Camp....B13
Carndonagh....G3
Cappawhite....F12
Cappoquin....F13
Carlanstown....H8
Carlingford....J7
Carlow....H11
Carna....C9
Carnew....J11
Carnlough....J4
Carragh....K5
Carraig Airt....F3
Carraroe....C9
Carrick....E5
Carrickfergus....K5
Carrickmacross....H7
Carrickmore....H5
Carrick-on-Shannon....F7
Carrick-on-Suir....G12
Carrigaline....E14
Carrigallen....F7
Carriganimmy....D13
Carrigart....F3
Carrigtwohill....E14
Carryduff....J5
Cashel....F12
Castlebar....D8
Castlebellingham....J7
Castleblakeney....E9
Castlebridge....J12
Castlecomer....G11
Castleconnell....E11
Castlederg....G5
Castledermot....H11
Castlegregory....B13
Castleisland....C13
Castlemaine....C13
Castlemartyr....E14
Castleplunket....E8
Castlepollard....G8
Castlerea....E8
Castlerock....H3
Castletownbere....B15
Castletownroche....E13
Castletownshend....D15
Castlewellan....J6
Cathair Dónall....B14
Causeway....C12
Cavan....G7
Celbridge....H9
Charlestown....D7
Charleville....E12
Cill Charthaigh....E5
Cill Chiaráin....C9
Clady....G5
Clane....H9
Clara....G9
Claregalway....D9
Claremorris....D8
Clashmore....F13
Claudy....G4
Cleggan....B8
Clifden....B9
Cliffoney....E6
Cloghan....F10
Clogheen....F13
Clogher....G6

Clogherhead....J8
Clogh Mills....J4
Clonakilty....D15
Clonaslee....G10
Clonbur....C9
Clondalkin....J9
Clonea....G13
Clonmany....G3
Clonmel....F12
Clonmellon....H8
Clonroche....H12
Clough....K6
Cloughjordan....F10
Cloyne....F14
Coachford....D14
Coagh....H5
Coalisland....H5
Cobh....E14
Coleraine....H3
Collinstown....G8
Collon....H8
Collooney....E7
Comber....K5
Cong....D9
Convoy....F4
Cookstown....H5
Coole....G8
Cooraclare....C11
Cootehill....G7
Cork....E14
Cornamona....C9
Corr na Móna....C9
Corrofin....D10
Courtmacsherry....E15
Courtown....J11
Craughwell....E10
Creeslough....F4
Croithlí....E4
Crolly....E4
Crookhaven....C15
Crookstown....D14
Croom....E12
Crossakeel....H8
Crosshaven....E14
Crossmaglen....H7
Crossmolina....D7
Crumlin....J5
Crusheen....D10
Culdaff....G3
Cullybackey....J4
Culmore....G4
Curracloe....J12
Curry....E7
Cushendall....J4
Cushendun....J3

Daingean....G9
Daingean Uí Chúis....B13
Delvin....G8
Derrinturn....H9
Derry....G4
Derrygonnelly....F6
Derrylin....G7
Dervock....H3
Dingle....B13
Doagh....J5
Donabate....J9
Donaghadee....K5
Donaghmore....E8
Donaghmore....H8
Donegal....F5
Donemana....G4
Doolin....C10
Doon....E12
Doonbeg....C11
Downings....F3
Downpatrick....K6
Dowra....F6
Draperstown....H5
Drimoleague....D14
Drogheda....J8
Droichead Nua....H10
Dromahair....E6
Dromara....J6
Dromcolloger....D12
Dromiskin....J7
Dromod....F8
Dromore....J6

Dromore....G5
Dromore West....D6
Drumaness....K6
Drumfries....G3
Drumkeeran....F7
Drumlish....F8
Drumquin....G5
Drumshanbo....F7
Drumsna....F7
Duagh....C12
Dublin....J9
Duleek....J8
Dunboyne....J9
Dún Chaoin....A13
Dundalk....J7
Dundonald....K5
Dundrum....F12
Dunfanaghy....F3
Dungannon....H5
Dungarvan....G13
Dungiven....H4
Dunglow....E4
Dungourney....F14
Dunkineely....E5
Dunlavin....H10
Dunleer....J8
Dunloy....J4
Dunmanway....D14
Dunmore....E8
Dunmore East....H13
Dunquin....A13
Dunshaughlin....H9
Durrow....G9
Durrus....C15
Dysart....E9

Easky....D6
Edenderry....H9
Edgeworthstown....G8
Eglinton....G4
Elphin....E7
Emyvale....H6
Enfield....H9
Ennis....D11
Enniscorthy....H12
Enniscrone....D6
Enniskean....D14
Enniskillen....F6
Ennistymon....D10
Eyrecourt....F10

Fahan....G4
Falcarragh....F3
Fanore....C11
Farranfore....C13
Feakle....E11
Fenagh....F7
Fenit....B13
Ferbane....F9
Fermoy....E13
Ferns....J12
Fethard....F12
Fethard....H13
Fintona....G6
Fintown....F4
Fivemiletown....G6
Foxford....D7
Foynes....D12
Freemount....D13
Frenchpark....E8
Freshford....G11

Galbally....E12
Galway....D9
Garrison....F6
Garvagh....H4
Gilford....J6
Glandore....D15
Glanworth....E13
Glaslough....H6
Glasson....F9
Gleann Cholm Cille....E5
Glenamaddy....E8
Glenarm....J4
Glenavy....J5
Glenbeigh....B13
Glencolumbkille....E5
Glenealy....J10
Glengarriff....C14
Glenties....E5

Glin....D12
Golden....F12
Goleen....C15
Goresbridge....H11
Gorey....J11
Gort....D10
Gorteen....E7
Gortin....G5
Gowran....H11
Graiguenamanagh....H12
Granard....G8
Grange....E6
Greencastle....H3
Greencastle....G5
Greenore....J7
Greyabbey....K5
Greystones....J10
Gulladuff....H4

Hacketstown....H11
Headford....D9
Hillsborough....J6
Hilltown....J6
Holycross....F11
Holywood....K5
Hospital....E12
Howth....J9

Inagh....D11
Inch....B13
Inchigeelagh....D14
Inishcrone....D6
Innishannon....E14
Irvinestown....F6

Johnstown....G11

Kanturk....D13
Keadue....F7
Keady....H6
Kealkill....C14
Keel....B7
Kells....J4
Kells....H8
Kenmare....C14
Kesh....F5
Kilbeggan....G9
Kilcar....E5
Kilcock....H9
Kilcolgan....D10
Kilconnell....E9
Kilcoole....J10
Kilcormac....F10
Kilcullen....H10
Kildare....H10
Kildorrery....E13
Kilfenora....D10
Kilfinane....E12
Kilgarvan....C14
Kilkee....C11
Kilkeel....J7
Kilkenny....G11
Kilkieran....C9
Kill....H9
Kill....G13
Killadysert....D11
Killala....D6
Killaloe....E11
Killarney....C13
Killashandra....G7
Killeagh....F14
Killenaule....F12
Killimer....C11
Killiney....J9
Killinick....J13
Killorglin....C13
Killough....K6
Killucan....G9
Killurin....G10
Killybegs....E5
Killyleagh....K6
Kilmacanoge....J10
Kilmacrenan....F4
Kilmacthomas....G13
Kilmaganny....G12
Kilmaine....D8
Kilmallock....E12
Kilmanagh....G12
Kilmeedy....D12
Kilmichael....D14
Kilmihil....C11
Kilmore Quay....H13

Kilmuckridge....J12
Kilpedder....J10
Kilrea....H4
Kilrush....C11
Kilsheelan....G12
Kiltegan....H11
Kiltimagh....D8
Kilworth....E13
Kingscourt....H7
Kinlough....E6
Kinnegad....G9
Kinnitty....F10
Kinsale....E14
Kinvarra....D10
Kircubbin....K5
Knock....D8
Knockcroghery....F8

Lahinch....C10
Lanesborough....F8
Laragh....J10
Larne....K4
Lauragh....C14
Laurencetown....F10
Leap....D15
Leenaun....C8
Leighlinbridge....H11
Leitrim....B9
Leitrim....F7
Leixlip....H9
Letterfrack....B8

Letterkenny....F4
Lifford....G4
Limavady....H4
Limerick....E11
Lisbellaw....G6
Lisburn....J5
Liscarroll....D13
Lisdoonvarna....D10
Lismore....F13
Lisnaskea....G6
Listowel....C12
Loghill....D12
Londonderry....G4
Longford....F8
Longwood....H9
Loughbrickland....J6
Loughglinn....E8
Loughrea....E10
Louisburgh....C8
Lucan....J9
Lurgan....J6
Lusk....J9

Macroom....D14
Maghera....H4
Magherafelt....H5
Maguiresbridge....G6
Maigh Cuilinn....D9
Malahide....J9
Málainn Mhóir....E5
Malin....G3

112

0   10   20 miles
0   10   20   30 kilometres

Malin More	E5	Muine Bheag	H11	Newtownbutler	G7
Mallow	E13	Mullagh	H8	Newtown-	
Manorhamilton	F6	Mullaghmore	G4	cunningham	G4
Markethill	H6	Mullinavat	G12	Newtownforbes	F8
Martinstown	J4	Mullinavat	G12	Newtownhamilton	H6
Maynooth	H9	Mullingar	G9	Newtownmount-	
Mayobridge	J6	Mulranny	C8	kennedy	J10
Midleton	F14	Murrisk	C8	Newtownstewart	G5
Milford	F4	Murroe	E11	Nobber	H8
Millstreet	D13				
Milltown	C13	Naas	H10	Ogonnelloe	E11
Milltown Malbay	C11	Na Dúnaibh	F3	Oilgate	H12
Mitchelstown	E13	Naul	J8	Oldcastle	G8
Moate	F9	Navan	H8	Omagh	G5
Mohill	F7	Nenagh	E11	Omeath	J7
Monaghan	H6	Newbawn	H12	Oola	E12
Monasterevin	G10	Newbliss	G7	Oranmore	D9
Moneymore	H5	Newbridge	H10	Oughterard	D9
Monivea	E9	Newcastle	J6		
Mooncoin	G13	Newcastle	J10	Pallasgreen	E12
Mountbellew	E9	Newcastle West	D12	Partry	D8
Mountcharles	F5	New Inn	F12	Passage East	H13
Mountmellick	G10	Newmarket	D13	Passage West	H13
Mountrath	G10	Newmarket-on-		Patrickswell	E12
Mountshannon	E10	Fergus	D11	Pettigo	F5
Moville	G3	Newport	C7	Piltown	G12
Moy	H6	Newport	E11	Plumbridge	G5
Moycullen	D9	New Ross	H12	Pomeroy	H5
Moynalty	H8	Newry	J6	Portadown	H6
Mucklagh	G9	Newtownabbey	J5	Portaferry	K6
Muff	G4	Newtownards	K5	Portarlington	G10

Portavogie	K6	Rathmore	D13	Salthill	D9
Portballintrae	H3	Rathmullan	G4	Scarriff	E11
Portglenone	H4	Rathnew	J10	Scartaglin	C13
Port Laoise	G10	Rathvilly	H11	Schull	C15
Portlaw	G13	Ratoath	J9	Seskinore	G5
Portmagee	B14	Recess	C9	Shanagarry	F14
Portmarnock	J9	Rhode	G10	Shannon	D11
Portnablagh	F3	Ringaskiddy	E14	Shannonbridge	F9
Portnoo	E4	Ringville	G13	Shercock	H7
Portroe	E11	Riverchapel	J11	Shillelagh	H11
Portrush	H3	Riverstick	E14	Shinrone	F10
Portstewart	H3	Rochfortbridge	G9	Shrule	D9
Portumna	E10	Rockcorry	H7	Silvermines	E11
Poyntzpass	J6	Roosky	F8	Sion Mills	G5
Prosperous	H9	Rosbercon	H12	Sixmilebridge	D11
		Roscommon	F8	Skerries	J8
Raharney	G9	Roscrea	F10	Skibbereen	D15
Ramelton	F4	Rosscarbery	D15	Slane	H8
Randalstown	J5	Rosses Point	E6	Sligo	E6
Raphoe	G4	Rosslare	J13	Smithborough	G6
Rasharkin	H4	Rosslare Harbour	J13	Sneem	B14
Rathangan	H10	Rosslea	G6	Spanish Point	C11
Rathcoole	J9	Rossnowlagh	E5	Spiddal	D9
Rathcormac	E13	Rostrevor	J7	Sraith Salach	C9
Rathdowney	G11	Roundstone	B9	Stewartstown	H5
Rathdrum	J10	Roundwood	J10	Stoneyford	G12
Rathfriland	J6	Rush	J9	Strabane	G4
Rathkeale	D12			Stradbally	G10
Ráth Luirc	E12	Saintfield	K6	Stradone	G7
		St Johnston	G4	Strandhill	E6
		Sallins	H9	Strangford	K6

Stranorlar	F5	Tubbercurry	E7
Strokestown	F8	Tulla	D11
Summerhill	H9	Tullamore	G9
Swan	G11	Tullow	H11
Swanlinbar	F6	Tulsk	E8
Swinford	D7	Turlough	D7
Swords	J9		
		Urlingford	G11
Taghmon	H12		
Tagoat	J13	Virginia	G8
Tallaght	J9		
Tallow	F13	Warrenpoint	J7
Tandragee	J6	Waterford	G13
Tarbert	C12	Watergrasshill	E13
Templemore	F11	Waterville	B14
Termonfeckin	J8	Wellingtonbridge	H13
Thomastown	G12	Westport	C8
Thurles	F11	Wexford	J12
Timahoe	G10	Whitegate	E14
Timoleague	D15	Whitehead	K5
Tinahely	J11	Wicklow	J10
Tipperary	F12	Woodenbridge	J11
Tobercurry	E7	Woodford	E10
Tobermore	H4		
Toomevara	F11	Youghal	F14
Toormore	C15		
Tower	E14		
Tralee	C13		
Tramore	G13		
Trim	H8		
Tuam	D9		

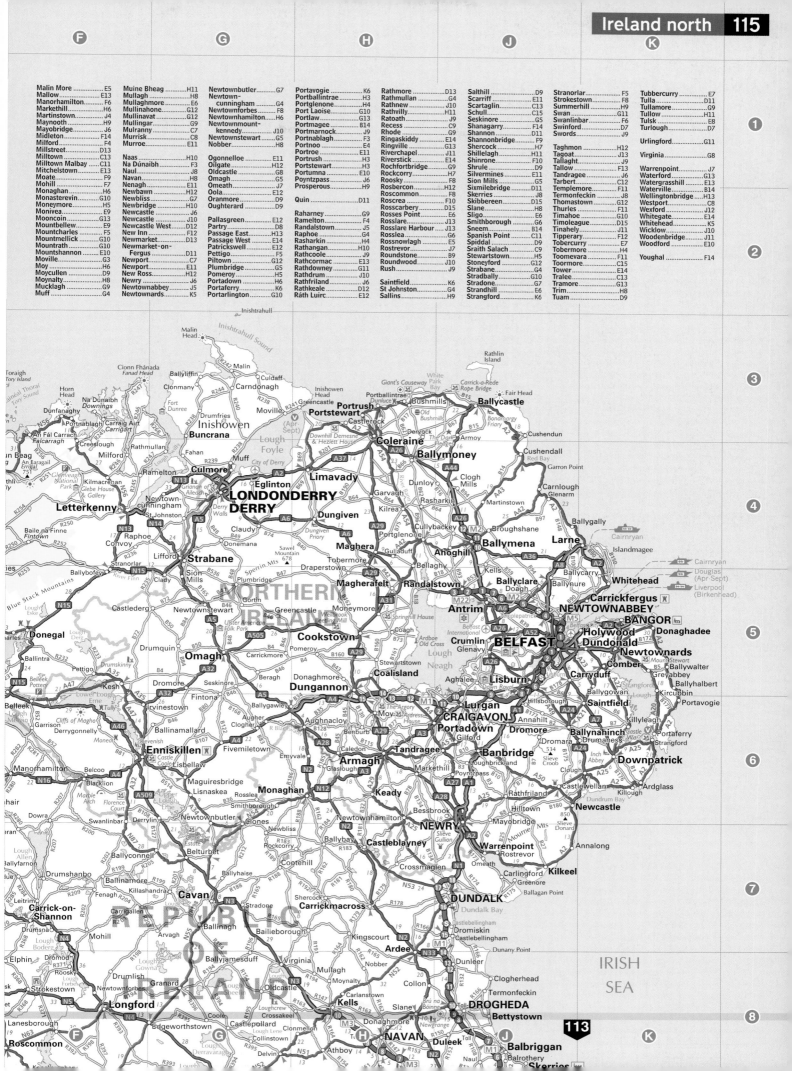

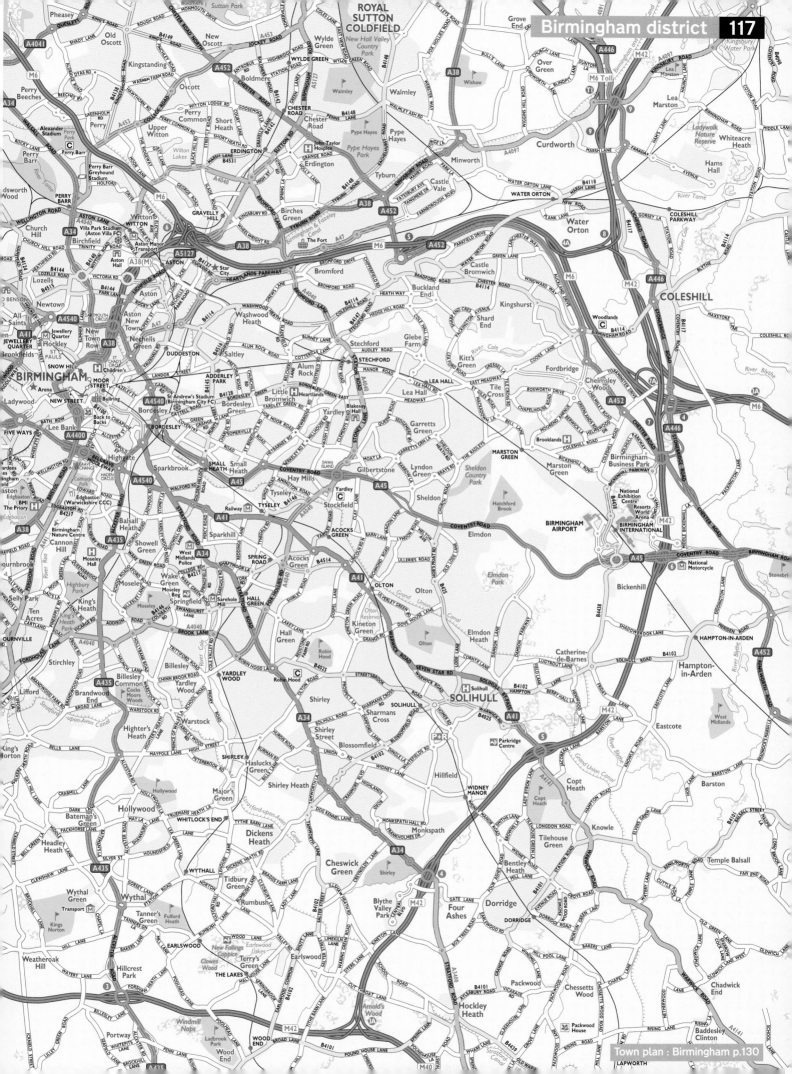

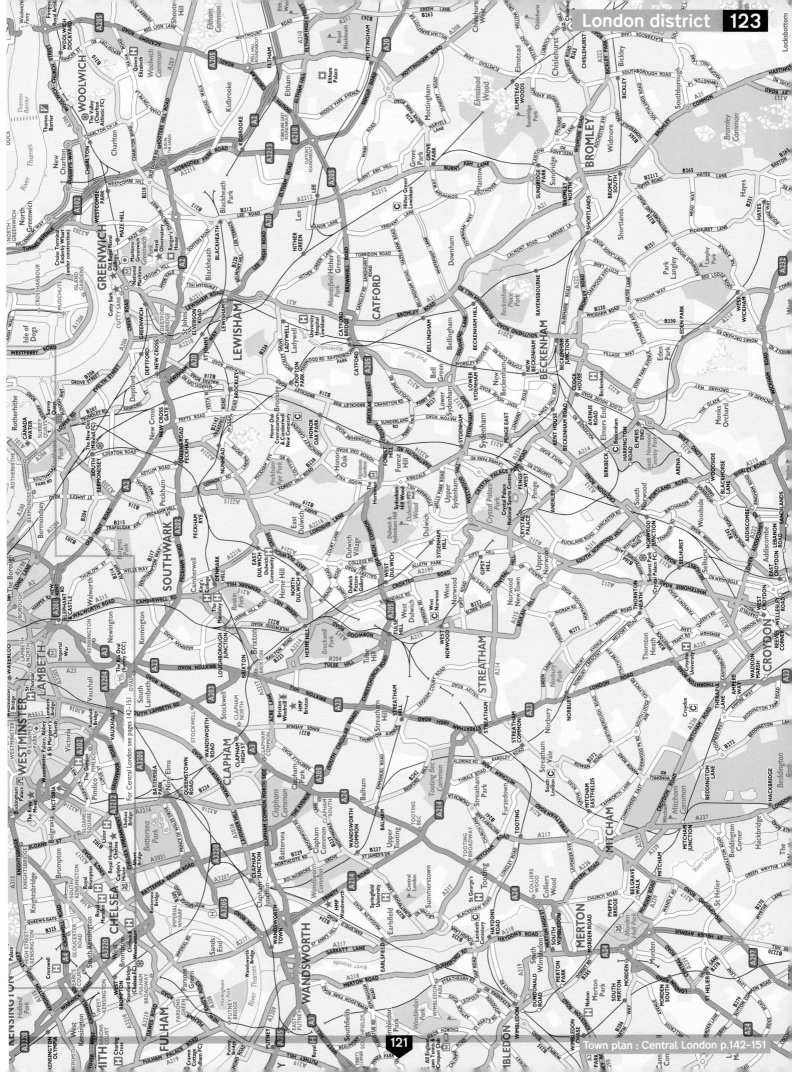

Town plan : Manchester p.135

NORTH

SEA

Amsterdam (IJmuiden)

WHITLEY BAY

Whitley Bay
Links Art Gallery
Whitley Bay
Cullercoats
Marden Park Nature Reserve
Marden
Blue Reef
Longsands South
Preston
TYNEMOUTH
Tynemouth
King Edwards Bay
Tynemouth Priory & Castle
NORTH SHIELDS
Stephenson Railway
West Chirton
North Tyneside Steam Railway
North Shields
Arbeia Roman Fort & Museum
The Lawe
Sandhaven
SOUTH SHIELDS
South Shields
Mill Dam
Chichester
Westoe
Cauldwell
Harton
Marsden Rock
Harton Nook
Marsden
Tyne Dock
Souter Lighthouse & The Leas
Whitburn Coastal Park
Marsden Bay
West Holywell
East Holywell
Earsdon
Monkseaton
West Monkseaton
Shiremoor
Murton
Northumberland Park
West Allotment
New York
Billy Mill
North Tyneside General
Benton Square
Willington Square
Willington
Holy Cross
Howdon
East Howdon
Willington Quay
Point Pleasant
Segedunum Roman Fort & Baths
WALLSEND
Wall's End
Tyne Tunnel
Royal Quays
International Passenger Terminal
Percy Main
Meadow Well
River Tyne
JARROW
Jarrow Hall
St Paul's Monastery
East Jarrow
Hebburn Colliery
Hebburn New Town
HEBBURN
Monkton
Primrose
Bede
Simonside
West Harton
Brockley Whins
South Tyneside General
Biddick Hall
Whiteleas
Cleadon Park
South Shields
Whitburn
Hedworth
Fellgate
Boldon Colliery
Cleadon
Wardley
West Boldon
East Boldon
Whitburn
Folingsby
Greyhound Stadium
South Bents
Boldon
Whitburn Bay
Seaburn
George Washington
Witherwack
Carley Hill
Fulwell
Seaburn
Downhill
Marley Pots
High Southwick
Roker
Usworth
North East Aircraft
Hylton Castle
Castletown
Southwick
Monkwearmouth
Stadium of Light
Sunderland Harbour
Concord
Sulgrave
Hylton Plantation
Northern Spire Bridge
Low Southwick
Queen Alexandra Bridge
Ayre's Quay
Stadium of Light (Sunderland AFC)
National Glass Centre
Albany
Hertburn
Washington Old Hall
South Hylton
Pallion
Deptford
St Peter's
Millfield
Bishopwearmouth
SUNDERLAND
Washington Wetland Centre
Washington Village
Barmston
Teal Farm
Pennywell
Ford
Sunderland Royal
University
Park Lane
Sunderland Eye Infirmary
Hillview
Columbia
Wearside
Sunderland
High Barnes
Barnes Park
Ashbrooke
Hendon
Grangetown
The Princess Anne Park
Biddick
Fatfield
Springwell
Humbledon
Mount Pleasant
Penshaw
Penshaw Monument
Herrington Country Park
Hastings Hill
Grindon
Plains Farm
Thorney Close
Silksworth Sports Complex & Ski Centre
New Silksworth
Middle Herrington
East Herrington
Silksworth
Shiney
Biddick Gill Wood
Rhope Colliery

Town plans : Newcastle upon Tyne p.136, Sunderland p.140

Town, port and airport plans

Motorway and junction	One-way, gated/closed road	Railway station	Car park, with electric charging point
Primary road single/dual carriageway and numbered junction	Restricted access road	Light rapid transit system station	Park and Ride (at least 6 days per week)
A road single/dual carriageway and numbered junction	Pedestrian area	Level crossing	Bus/coach station
B road single/dual carriageway	Footpath	Tramway	Hospital
Local road single/dual carriageway	Road under construction	Airport, heliport	24-hour Accident & Emergency hospital
Other road single/dual carriageway, minor road	Road tunnel	Railair terminal	Beach (award winning)
Building of interest	Lighthouse	Theatre or performing arts centre	City wall
Ruined building	Castle	Cinema	Escarpment
Tourist Information Centre	Castle mound	Abbey, chapel, church	Cliff lift
Visitor or heritage centre	Monument, statue	Synagogue	River/canal, lake
World Heritage Site (UNESCO)	Post Office	Mosque	Lock, weir
Museum	Public library	Golf course	Viewpoint
English Heritage site	Shopping centre	Racecourse	Park/sports ground
Historic Scotland site	Shopmobility	Nature reserve	Cemetery
Cadw (Welsh heritage) site	Football stadium	Aquarium	Woodland
National Trust site	Rugby stadium	Agricultural showground	Built-up area
National Trust Scotland site	County cricket ground	Toilet, with facilities for the less able	Beach

Central London street map (see pages 142–151)

London Underground station	London Overground station
Docklands Light Railway (DLR) station	Central London Congestion Charge and Ultra Low Emission boundary

Royal Parks

Green Park — Park open 5am–midnight. Constitution Hill and The Mall closed to traffic Sundays and public holidays 8am–dusk.

Grosvenor Square Garden — Park open 7:30am–dusk.

Hyde Park — Park open 5am–midnight. Park roads closed to traffic midnight–5am.

Kensington Gardens — Park open 6am–dusk.

Regent's Park — Park open 5am–dusk. Park roads closed to traffic midnight–7am, except for residents.

St James's Park — Park open 5am–midnight. The Mall closed to traffic Sundays and public holidays 8am–dusk.

Victoria Tower Gardens — Park open dawn–dusk.

Traffic regulations in the City of London include security checkpoints and restrict the number of entry and exit points.

Note: Oxford Street is closed to through-traffic (except buses & taxis) 7am–7pm Monday–Saturday.

Central London Congestion Charge Zone (CCZ)

The charge for driving or parking a vehicle on public roads in this Central London area, during operating hours, is £11.50 per vehicle per day in advance or on the day of travel. Alternatively you can pay £10.50 by registering with CC Auto Pay, an automated payment system. Drivers can also pay the next charging day after travelling in the zone but this will cost £14. Payment permits entry, travel within and exit from the CCZ by the vehicle as often as required on that day.

The CCZ operates between 7am and 6pm, Mon–Fri only. There is no charge at weekends, on public holidays or between 25th Dec and 1st Jan inclusive.

For up to date information on the CCZ, exemptions, discounts or ways to pay, visit *www.tfl.gov.uk/modes/driving/congestion-charge*

Ultra Low Emission Zone (ULEZ)

All vehicles in Central London need to meet minimum exhaust emission standards or pay a daily Emission Surcharge. It applies to the same area covered by the Congestion Charge and operates 24 hours a day, every day of the year. The surcharge is £12.50 for motorcycles, cars and vans and is in addition to the Congestion Charge.

For further information visit *www.tfl.gov.uk/ULEZ*

In addition the Low Emission Zone (LEZ) operates across Greater London, 24 hours every day of the year and is aimed at the most heavy-polluting vehicles. It does not apply to cars or motorcycles. For details visit *www.tfl.gov.uk/LEZ*

Town Plans

Aberdeen 103
Aberystwyth.........................36
Basingstoke.......................129
Bath...................................129
Birmingham 130
Blackpool 130
Bournemouth 130
Bradford 130
Brighton 131
Bristol 131
Cambridge 131
Canterbury 131
Cardiff 132
Carlisle 132
Chester 132
Coventry 132
Derby 133
Dundee 133
Edinburgh 133
Exeter 133
Glasgow 134
Ipswich 134
Kingston upon Hull 134
Leeds 134
Leicester 135
Liverpool 135
LONDON..................142–151
Manchester.........................135

Middlesbrough....................135
Milton Keynes 136
Newcastle upon Tyne 136
Newquay 3
Norwich 136
Nottingham........................136
Oxford 137
Peterborough 137
Plymouth 137
Portsmouth 137
Ramsgate 23
Reading 138
Royal Tunbridge Wells.............138
Salisbury 138
Scarborough 67
Sheffield 138
Shrewsbury 139
Southampton 139
Stoke-on-Trent (Hanley) 139
Stratford-upon-Avon 139
Sunderland.........................140
Swansea 140
Taunton 140
Warwick 140
Watford 141
Winchester 141
Worcester 141
York...................................141

Ferry Ports

Aberdeen Harbour 95
Dover, Port of.......................12
Fishguard Harbour 24
Harwich International Port 35
Heysham Harbour 62
Holyhead Harbour...............54
Hull, Port of 61
Liverpool Docks 56
Newhaven Harbour 11
Pembroke Dock....................24
Plymouth, Port of.......................4
Port of Tyne........................73
Portsmouth Harbour 10

Channel Tunnel

Folkestone Terminal 13
Calais / Coquelles Terminal 13

Central London

Basingstoke | Bath

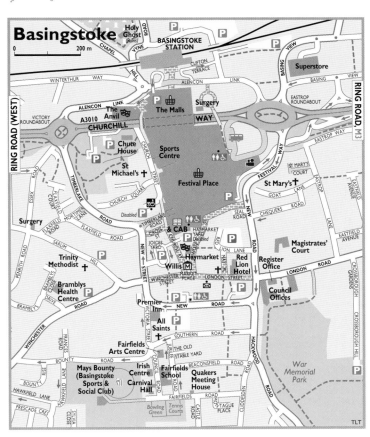

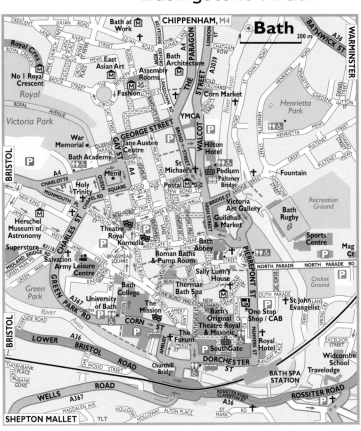

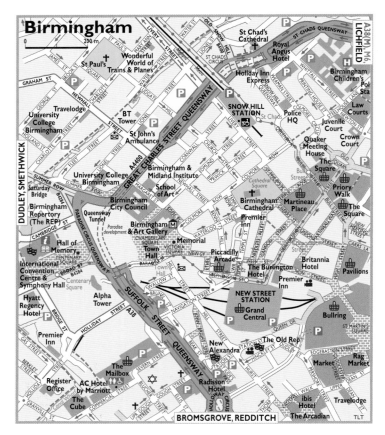

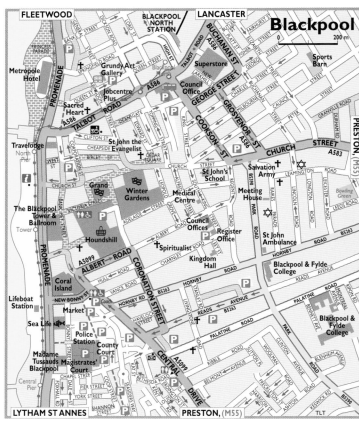

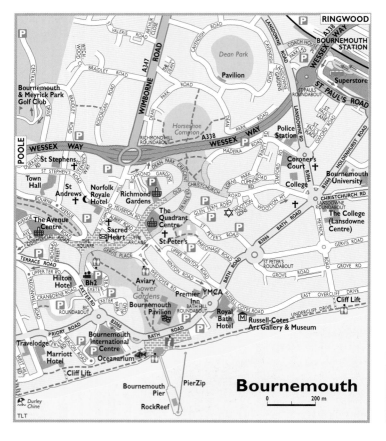

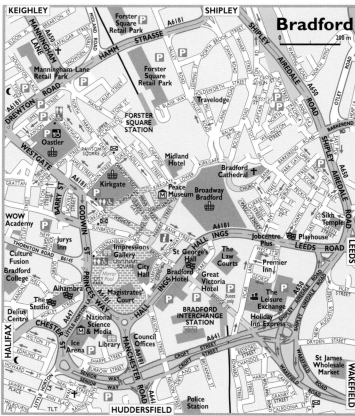

Brighton

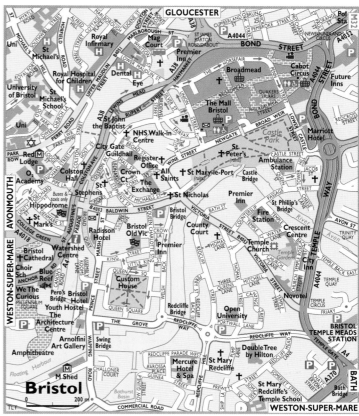

Bristol

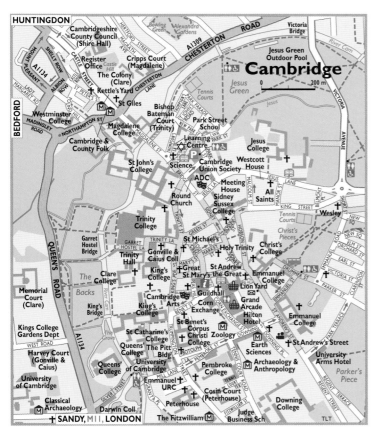

Cambridge

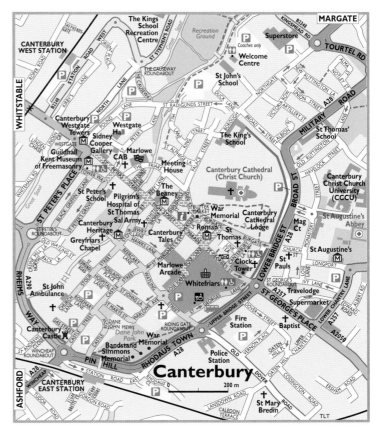

Canterbury

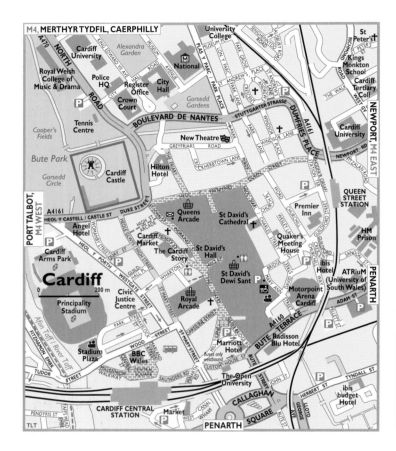

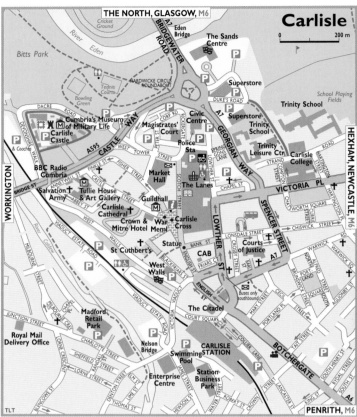

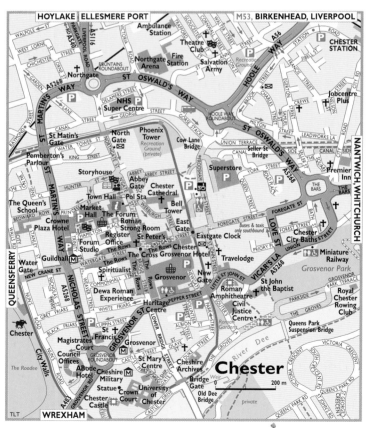

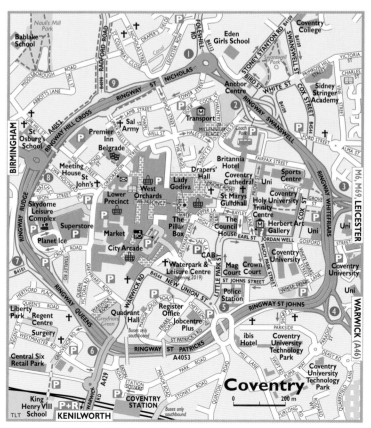

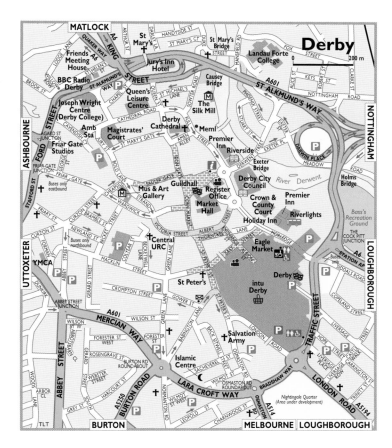

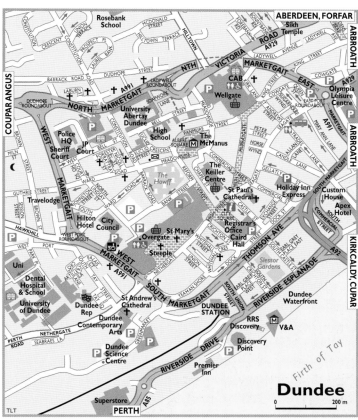

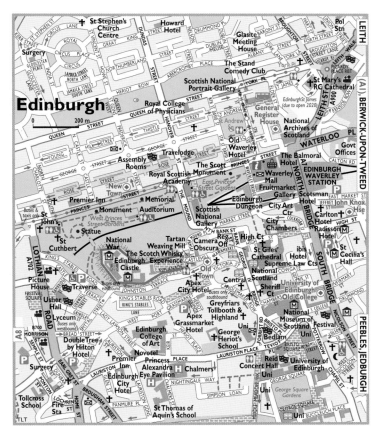

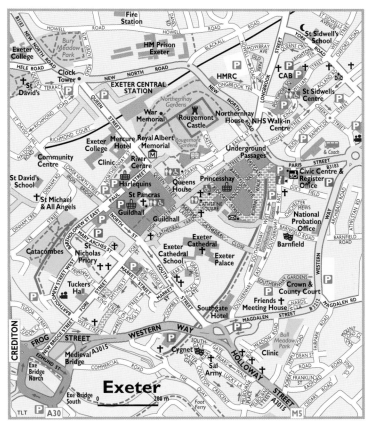

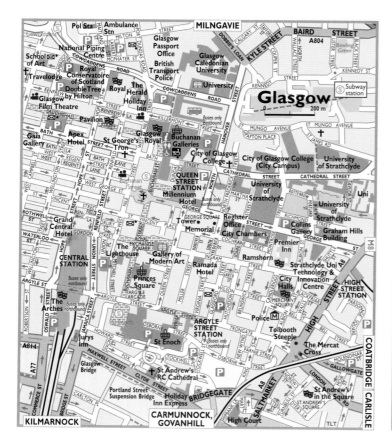

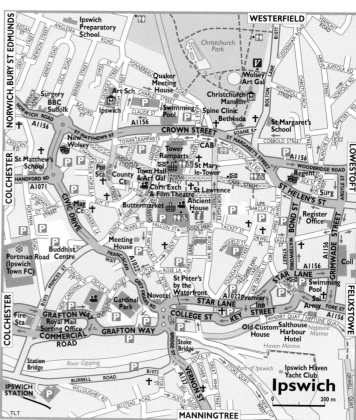

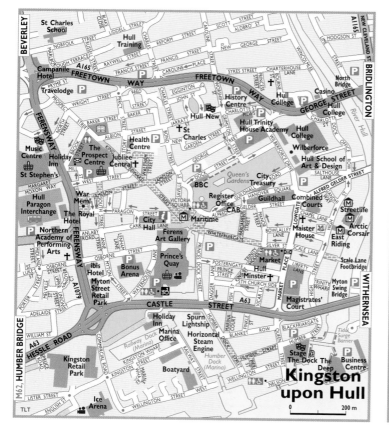

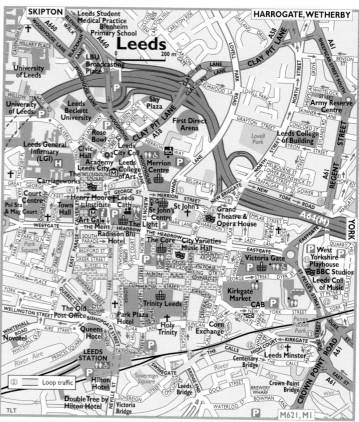

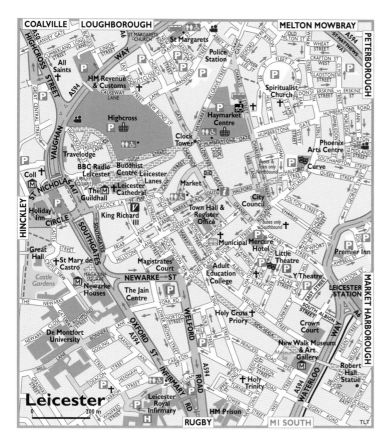

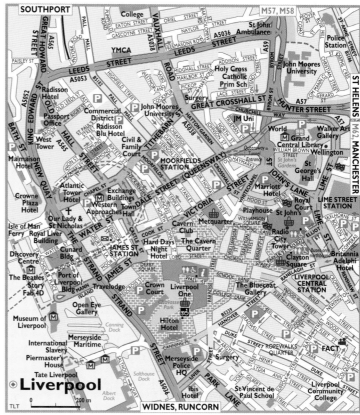

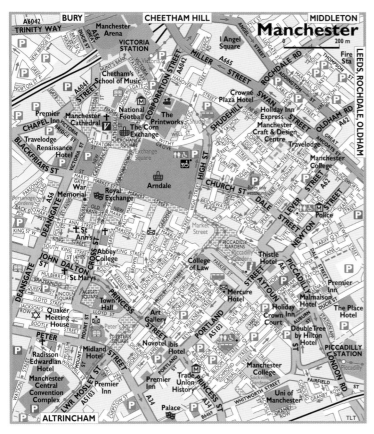

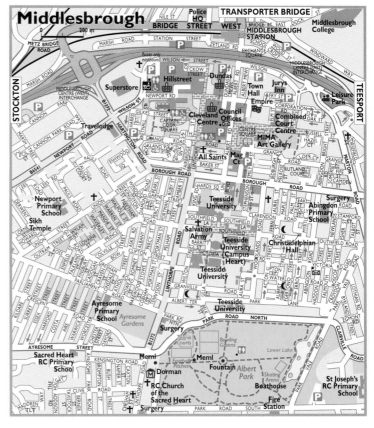

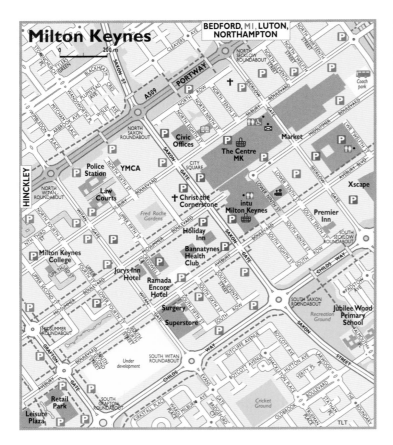

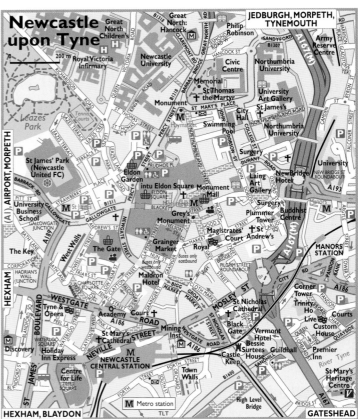

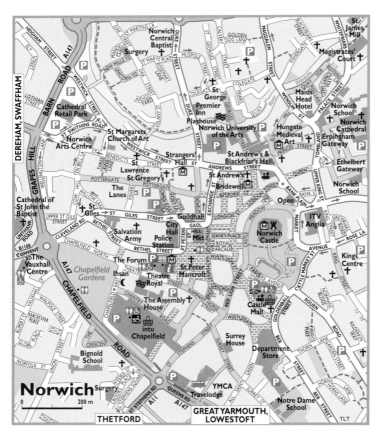

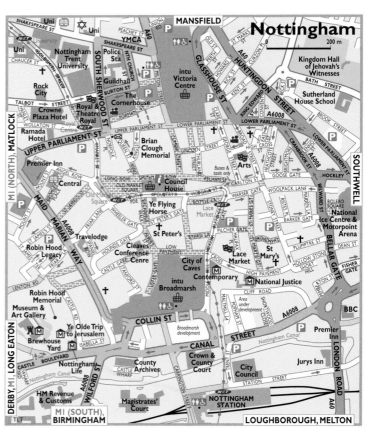

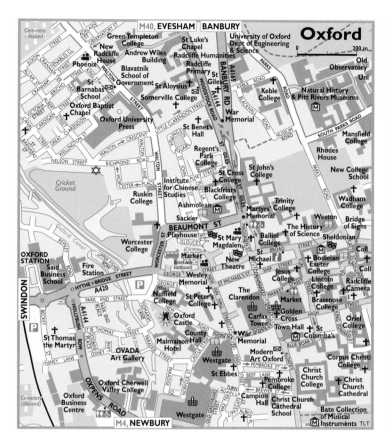

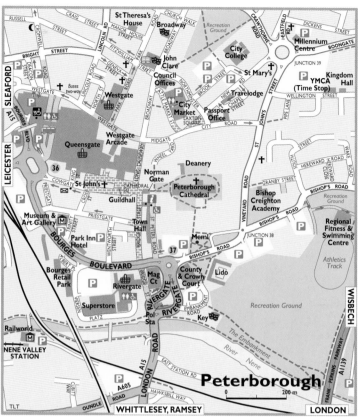

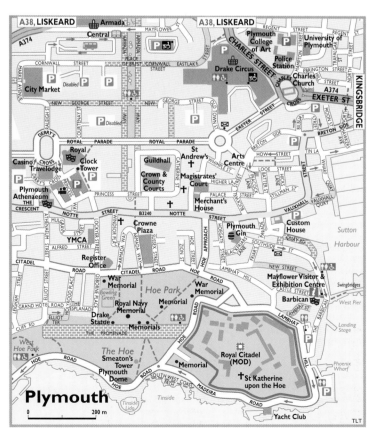

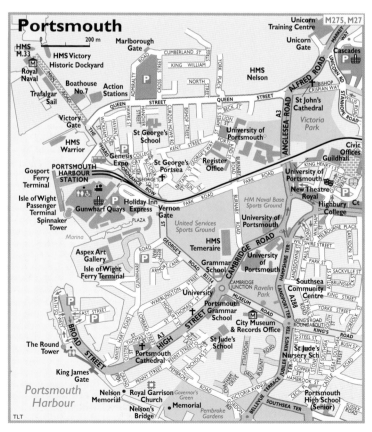

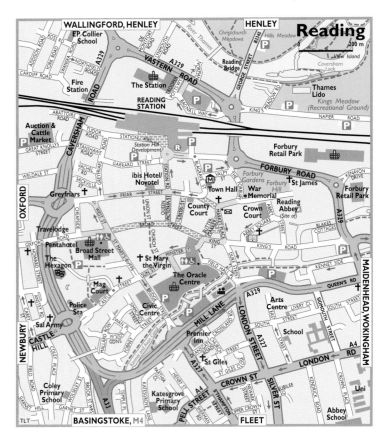

Reading

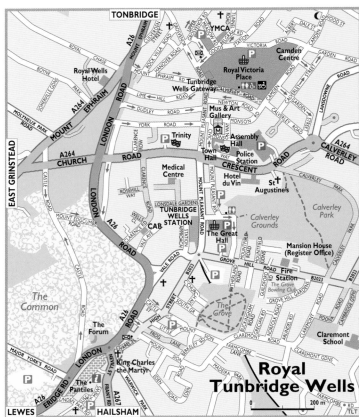

Royal Tunbridge Wells

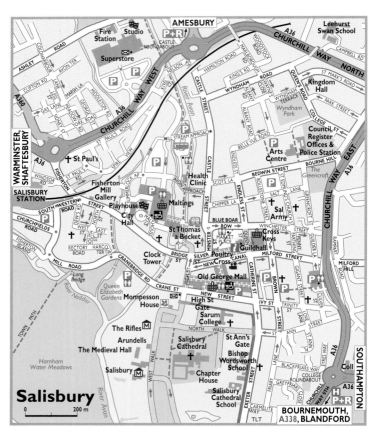

Salisbury

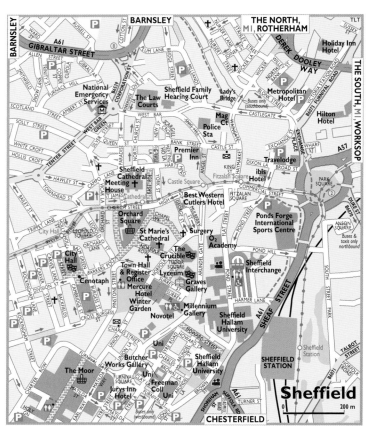

Sheffield

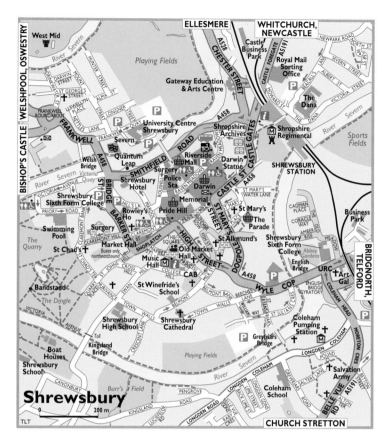

Shrewsbury

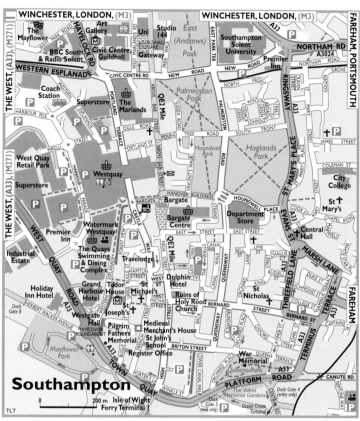

Southampton

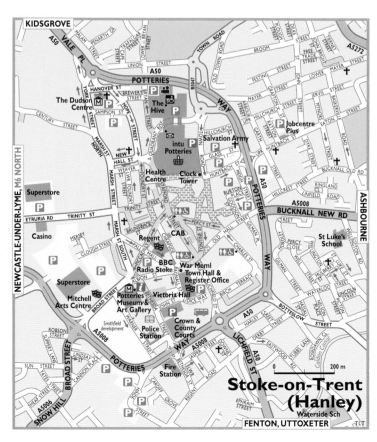

Stoke-on-Trent (Hanley)

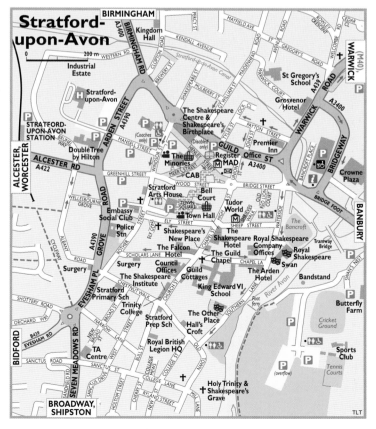

Stratford-upon-Avon

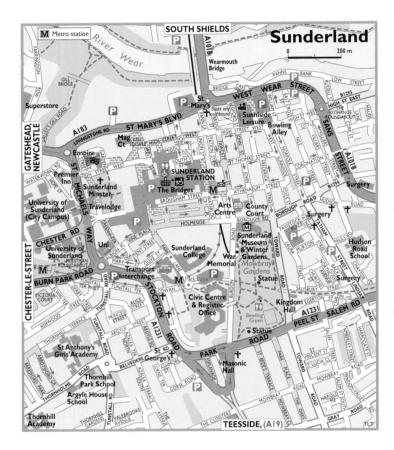

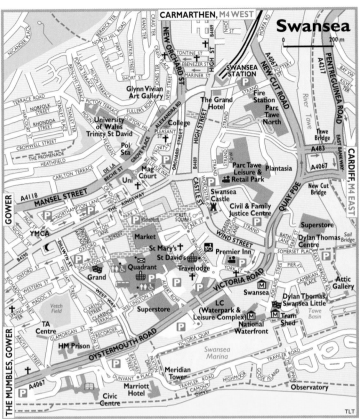

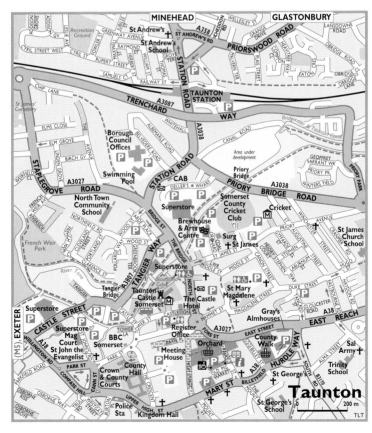

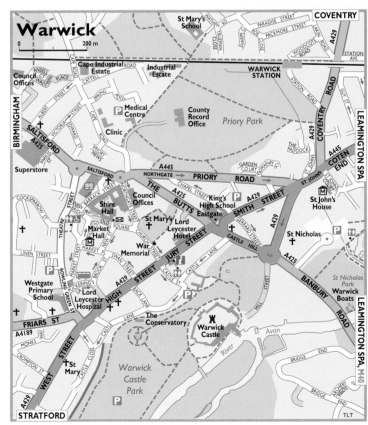

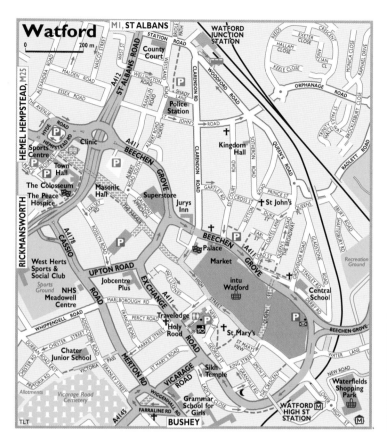

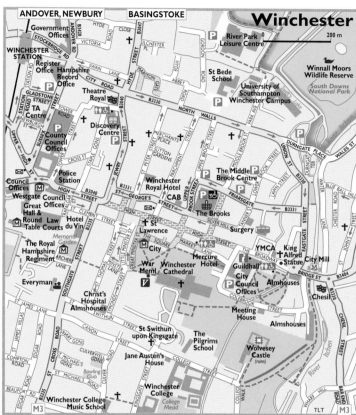

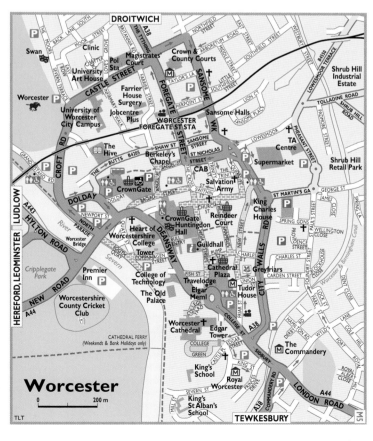

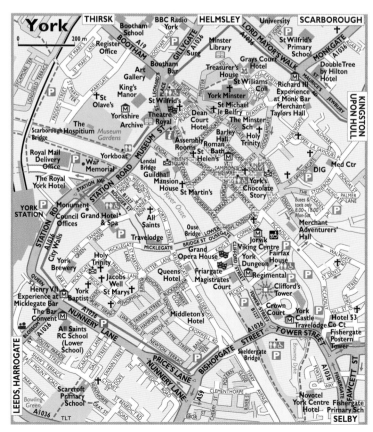

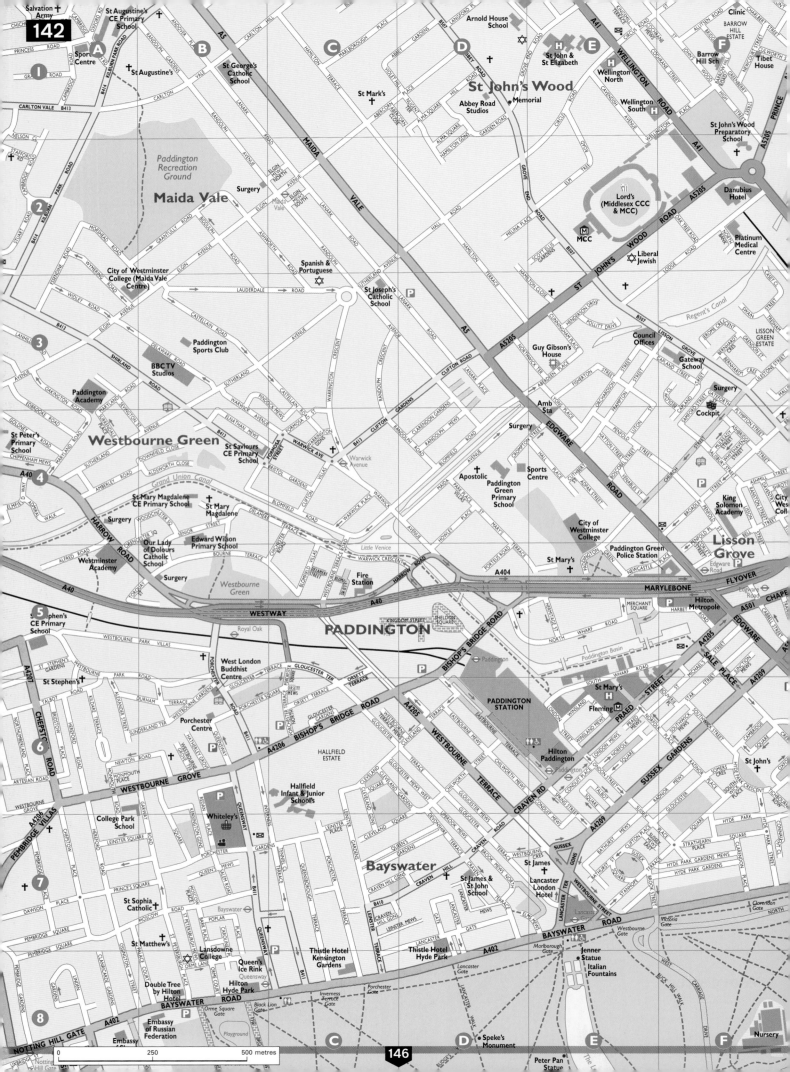

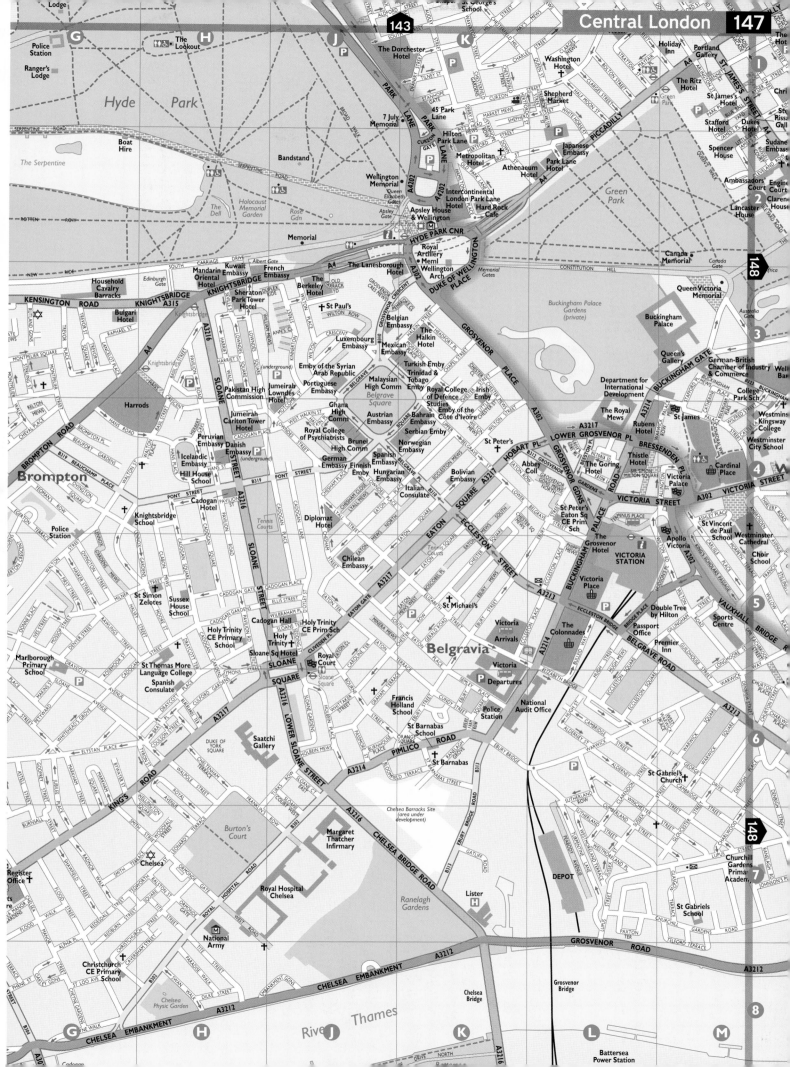

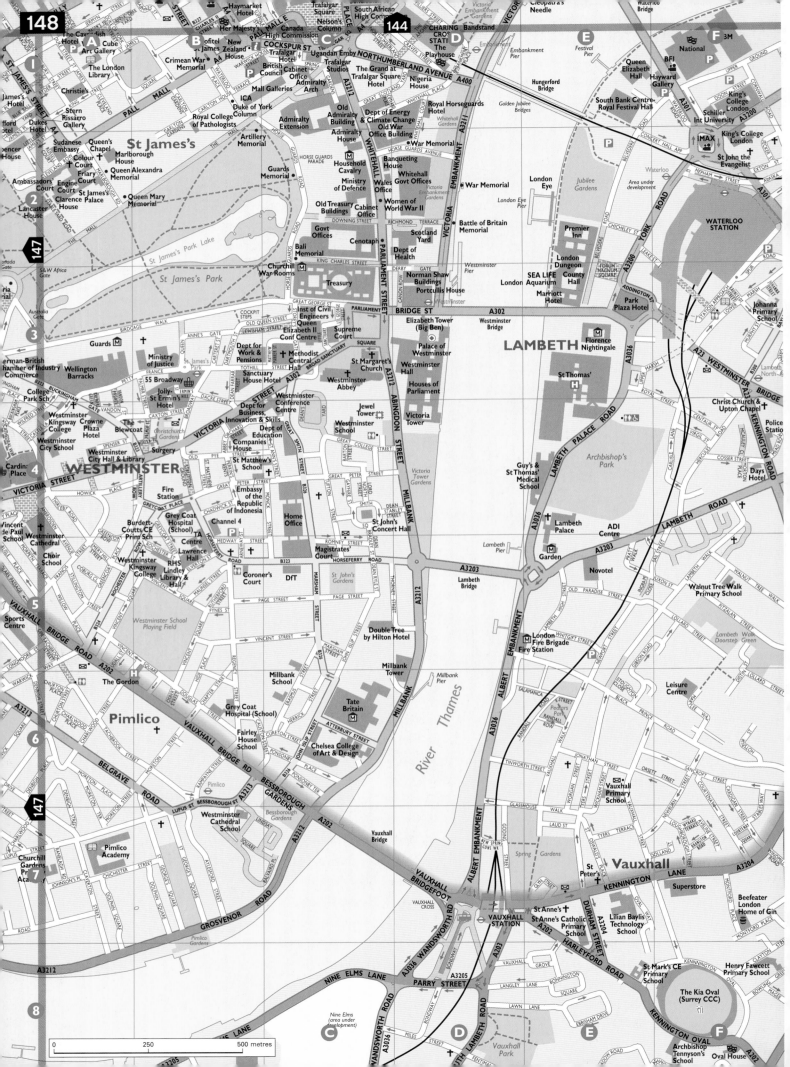

This index lists street and station names, and top places of tourist interest shown in red. Names are listed in alphabetical order and written in full, but may be abbreviated on the map. Each entry is followed by its Postcode District and then the page number and grid reference to the square in which the name is found. Names are asterisked (*) in the index where there is insufficient space to show them on the map.

A

Abbey Gardens NW8 ....142 C1
Abbey Orchard Street SW1P 148 B4
Abbey Road NW8 ....142 D1
Abbey Street SE1 ....150 B7
Abchurch Lane EC4N 145 L7
Abercorn Close NW8 ....142 C1
Abercorn Place NW8 ....142 C1
Aberdour Place SE1 ....142 E3
Aberdour Street SE1 ....149 M5
Abingdon Road W8 ....146 A4
Abingdon Street SW1P 148 C3
Abingdon Villas W8 ....146 A3
Ackroyd Drive E3 ....151 L1
Acorn Walk SE16 ....151 K5
Acton Street WC1X 144 E2
Adam and Eve Mews W8 ....146 A3
Adam's Row W1K 143 K8
Adam Street WC2N 144 D8
Addington Street SE1 ....148 E3
Addle Hill EC4V 145 H7
Adelina Grove E1 ....150 F1
Adeline Place WC1B 144 B5
Adler Street E1 ....150 D2
Admiral Place SE16 ....151 K5
Admiral Walk W9 ....142 A4
Adpar Street W2 ....142 E4
Agar Street WC2N 144 D8
Agdon Street EC1V 145 H3
Agnes Street E14 ....151 L2
Ainsty Street SE16 ....151 G6
Air Street W1B 144 A8
Alaska Street SE1 ....148 F2
Albany Road SE5 ....149 L8
Albany Street NW1 ....143 L1
Albemarle Street W1S 145 H4
Albermarle Way EC1V 149 H6
Alberta Street SE17 ....149 H6
Albert Bridge SW3 ....147 G8
Albert Embankment SE1 ....148 D7
Albert Gardens E1 ....151 H3
Albert Gate SW1X 147 H2
Albert Place W8 ....146 C3
Albion Gate W2 ....143 G7
Albion Place EC1M 145 H4
Albion Street SE16 ....151 G7
Albion Street W2 ....143 G7
Aldenham Street NW1 ....144 A1
Aldermanbury EC2V 145 K6
Alderney Mews SE1 ....149 K4
Alderney Street SW1V 147 L6
Aldersgate Street EC1A 145 J4
Aldford Street W1K 143 J8
Aldgate EC3M 150 B3
Aldgate ⊖ EC3N 150 B3
Aldgate East ⊖ E1 ....150 B3
Aldgate High Street EC3N 150 B3
Aldgate Square EC3N 150 B3
Aldsworth Close W9 ....142 B4
Aldwych WC2E 144 E7
Alexander Place SW7 ....146 E5
Alexander Street W2 ....142 A6
Alexandra Gate SW7 ....146 E3
Alfred Mews WC1E 144 B4
Alfred Place WC1E 144 B4
Alfred Road W2 ....142 A5
Alice Street SE1 ....149 M4
Alie Street E1 ....150 C3
Allen Street W8 ....146 A4
Allhallows Lane EC4R 145 L8
Allington Street SW1E 147 M4
Allitsen Road NW8 ....142 F1
Allsop Place NW1 ....143 H4
Alma Square NW8 ....142 D1
Alpha Place SW3 ....147 G8
Alsace Road SE17 ....149 M7
Alscot Road * SE1 ....150 C8
Alvey Street SE17 ....149 M6
Ambergate Street SE17 ....149 H7
Amberley Road W9 ....142 A4
Ambrosden Avenue SW1P 148 A4
Amelia Street SE17 ....149 J6
America Square EC3N 150 B3
America Street SE1 ....149 J2
Ampton Street WC1X 144 E2
Amwell Street EC1R 144 F2
Anchorage Point E14 ....151 M6
Andover Place NW6 ....142 B1
Angel ⊖ N1 ....145 G1
Angela Hooper Place * SW1E 148 A4
Angel Junction N1 ....145 G1
Angel Lane EC4R 145 L8
Angel Street EC1A 145 J6
Ann Moss Way SE16 ....151 G7
Ann's Close SW1X 147 J3
Ansdell Street W8 ....146 B4
Antill Terrace E1 ....151 H2
Antizan Street E1 ....150 B2
Apple Tree Yard SW1Y 144 A8
Appold Street EC2A 145 M4
Apsley Gate W1J 147 J2
Apsley House & Wellington Museum W1J 147 K2
Aquinas Street SE1 ....149 G1
Arbour Square E1 ....151 H2
Archangel Street SE16 ....151 J7
Archer Street W1B 144 B7
Arch Street SE1 ....149 J4
Arden Estate N1 ....145 M1
Argyle Square WC1H 144 D2
Argyle Street WC1H 144 D2
Argyll Road W8 ....146 A3
Argyll Street W1F 143 M6
Arlington Street SW1A 147 M1
Arlington Way EC1R 145 G2
Arne Street WC2H 144 D6
Arneway Street SW1P 148 B5
Arnhem Place E14 ....151 M8
Arnold Estate SE1 ....150 C7
Arnside Street SE17 ....149 K8
Artesian Road W11 ....142 A6
Arthur Street EC4V 145 L7
Artichoke Hill E1W 150 E4
Artillery Lane E1 ....150 A1
Artillery Row SW1P 148 B4
Arundel Street WC2R 144 F7

B

Babmaes Street SW1Y 144 B8
Bache's Street N1 ....145 L2
Back Church Lane E1 ....150 D3
Back Hill EC1R 145 G4
Bacon Grove SE1 ....150 B8
Bainbridge Street WC1A 144 C6
Bakers Mews W1U 143 J6
Baker's Row EC1R 145 G4
Baker Street NW1 ....143 H4
Baker Street W1U 143 J5
Baker Street ⊖ NW1 ....143 H4
Balcombe Street NW1 ....143 G3
Balderton Street W1K 143 J7
Baldwin's Gardens EC1N 144 F5
Baldwin Street EC1V 145 L2
Bale Road E1 ....151 J1
Balfe Street N1 ....144 D1
Balfour Mews W1K 143 K8
Balfour Place W1K 143 J8
Balfour Street SE17 ....149 K5
Baltic Street East EC1Y 145 J3
Baltic Street West EC1Y 145 J4
Balvaird Place SW1V 148 C7
Bank ⊖ EC2R 145 L6
Bank End SE1 ....149 K1
Bankside SE1 ....145 J8
Banner Street EC1Y 145 K3
Banyard Road SE16 ....150 E8
Barbican EC1A 145 J4
Barbican ⊖ EC1A 145 J5
Barbican Estate EC2Y 145 J5
Barge House Street SE1 ....149 G1
Bark Place W2 ....142 B7
Barkston Gardens SW5 ....146 B6
Barley Corn Way E14 ....151 L4
Barlow/Congreve Estate SE17 ....149 M5
Barlow Place W1J 143 L7
Barlow Street SE17 ....149 L5
Barnardo Street E1 ....151 H3
Barnby Street NW1 ....144 A1
Barnes Street E14 ....151 J2
Barnham Street SE1 ....150 A6
Baron's Place SE1 ....149 G3
Baron Street N1 ....145 G1
Barrett Street W1U 143 K6
Barrow Hill Estate NW8 ....142 F1
Barrow Hill Road NW8 ....142 F1
Barter Street WC1A 144 D5
Bartholomew Close EC1A 145 J5
Bartholomew Lane EC2R 145 L6
Bartholomew Street SE1 ....149 L5
Bartlett Court EC4A 145 G6
Barton Street SW1P 148 C4
Basil Street SW3 ....147 H4
Basin Approach E14 ....151 K3
Basinghall Avenue EC2V 145 K5
Basinghall Street EC2V 145 K5
Bastwick Street EC1V 145 J3
Bateman's Buildings W1D 144 B6
Bateman Street W1D 144 B6
Bath Court EC1V 145 G3
Bath Terrace SE1 ....149 J4
Bathurst Mews W2 ....142 E7
Bathurst Street W2 ....142 E7
Battle Bridge Lane SE1 ....149 M1
Batty Street E1 ....150 D2
Bayley Street WC1B 144 B5
Baylis Road SE1 ....148 F3
Bayswater ⊖ W2 ....142 B7
Bayswater Road W2 ....142 E7
Baythorne Street E3 ....151 L1
Beaconsfield Road SE17 ....149 M7
Beak Street W1F 144 A7
Bear Gardens SE1 ....145 J8
Bear Lane SE1 ....149 H1
Beauchamp Place SW3 ....147 G4
Beaufort Gardens SW3 ....147 G4
Beaufort Street SW3 ....146 E8
Beaumont Place W1T 144 A3
Beaumont Street W1G 143 K4
Beccles Street E14 ....151 M3
Beckett Street SE1 ....149 L3
Beckway Street SE17 ....149 M6
Bedale Street SE1 ....149 L1
Bedford Avenue WC1B 144 C5
Bedfordbury WC2N 144 C7
Bedford Gardens W8 ....146 A2
Bedford Place WC1N 144 D4

Bedford Row WC1R 144 E4
Bedford Square WC1B 144 B5
Bedford Street WC2E 144 D7
Bedford Way WC1H 144 C3
Bedlow Close NW8 ....142 F3
Beech Street EC2Y 145 J4
Beeston Place SW1W 147 L4
Belgrave Mews North * SW1X 147 J3
Belgrave Mews South * SW1X 147 K4
Belgrave Place SW1X 147 J4
Belgrave Road SW1V 147 L5
Belgrave Road SW1V 148 A6
Belgrave Square SW1X 147 J3
Belgrave Street E1 ....151 J2
Belgrove Street WC1H 144 D2
Bell Lane E1 ....150 B1
Bell Street NW1 ....142 F4
Bell Yard WC2A 144 F6
Belvedere Road SE1 ....148 E2
Benjamin Street EC1M 151 J1
Ben Jonson Road E1 ....147 M1
Bennett Street SW1A 147 M1
Ben Smith Way SE16 ....150 D7
Benson Quay E1W 150 F4
Bentinck Mews W1U 143 K6
Bentinck Street W1U 143 K6
Bere Street E1W 151 H3
Bergen Square SE16 ....151 K8
Berkeley Mews W1H 143 H6
Berkeley Square W1J 143 L8
Berkeley Street W1J 143 L8
Bermondsey ⊖ SE16 ....150 E7
Bermondsey Spa SE16 ....150 C8
Bermondsey Square SE1 ....150 A8
Bermondsey Street SE1 ....150 A6
Bermondsey Wall East SE16 ....150 E7
Bermondsey Wall Estate SE16 ....150 D7
Bermondsey Wall West SE16 ......150 C6
Bernard Street WC1N 144 D4
Berners Mews W1T 144 A5
Berners Place W1F 144 A6
Berners Street W1T 144 A5
Bernhardt Crescent NW8 ....142 F3
Berryfield Road SE17 ....149 J6
Berry Street EC1V 145 H3
Berwick Street W1F 144 A6
Bessborough Gardens SW1V 148 C6
Bessborough Street SW1V 148 B6
Betterton Street WC2H 144 D6
Bevenden Street N1 ....145 L2
Bevin Close SE16 ....151 J5
Bevington Street SE16 ....150 D7
Bevin Way WC1X 144 F1
Bevis Marks EC3A 150 A2
Bewley Street E1 ....150 F3
Bickenhall Street W1U 143 H4
Bidborough Street WC1H 144 C2
Biddulph Road W9 ....142 B2
Big Ben (Elizabeth Tower) SW1A .148 D3
Bigland Street E1 ....150 E3
Billiter Square EC3M 150 A3
Billiter Street EC3M 150 A3
Bina Gardens SW5 ....146 C6
Bingham Place W1U 143 J4
Binney Street W1K 143 K7
Birchfield Street E14 ....151 M3
Birchin Lane EC3V 145 L7
Birdcage Walk SW1H 148 A3
Birde Lane EC4Y 145 H6
Bird Street W1C 143 K6
Birkenhead Street N1 ....144 D1
Bishop's Bridge Road W2 ....142 C6
Bishopsgate EC2M 150 A2
Bishops Square E1 ....150 B1
Bishop's Terrace SE11 ....149 G5
Bittern Street SE1 ....149 J3
Blackall Street EC2A 145 M3
Blackburne's Mews W1K 143 J7
Blackfriars ⇌ EC4V 145 H7
Blackfriars Bridge SE1 ....145 H8
Blacklands Terrace SW3 ....147 H6
Black Friars Lane EC4V 145 H7
Blackfriars Road SE1 ....149 H3
Blackhorse Court SE1 ....149 L4
Black Lion Gate W2 ....142 B8
Black Prince Road SE1 ....148 E6
Blackwood Street SE17 ....149 K6
Blandford Street W1U 143 H5
Bleeding Heart Yard EC1N 145 G5
Blenheim Street W1S 143 L7
Bletchley Street N1 ....145 K1
Blomfield Mews W2 ....142 C5
Blomfield Road W9 ....142 C5
Blomfield Street EC2M 145 M5
Blomfield Villas W2 ....142 C5
Bloomfield Terrace SW1W 147 J6
Bloomsbury Square WC1A 144 D5
Bloomsbury Street WC1B 144 C5
Bloomsbury Way WC1A 144 C5
Blount Street E14 ....151 K2
Blue Ball Yard SW1A 147 M1
Bohn Road E1 ....151 J1
Bolsover Street W1W 143 L4
Bolton Gardens SW5 ....146 B6
Bolton Street W1J 147 L1
Bondway SW8 ....148 D8
Bonhill Street EC2A 145 L4
Bonnington Square SW8 ....148 E8
Boot Street N1 ....145 M2
Borough ⊖ SE1 ....149 K3
Borough High Street SE1 ....149 K3
Borough Road SE1 ....149 H3
Boscobel Place SW1W 147 K5
Boscobel Street NW8 ....142 E4
Boss Street SE1 ....150 B6
Boston Place NW1 ....143 G3
Botolph Lane EC3R 145 M7
Boundary Lane SE17 ....147 K8
Boundary Row SE1 ....149 G2
Bourdon Street W1K 143 L7
Bourlet Close W1W 143 M5
Bourne Estate EC1N 144 F4
Bourne Street SW1W 147 J6
Bourne Terrace W2 ....142 B5
Bournemouth Place * SE16 ....151 K6
Bouverie Place W2 ....142 F6
Bouverie Street EC4Y 145 G6
Bowland Yard * SW1X 147 J3
Bow Lane EC4M 145 K6

Bowling Green Lane EC1R 145 G3
Bowling Green Place SE1 ....149 L2
Bowling Green Street SE11 ....148 F8
Bowling Green Walk N1 ....145 M2
Bowsell Street WC1N 144 D4
Bow Street WC2E 144 D7
Boyd Street E1 ....150 D3
Boyfield Street SE1 ....149 H3
Boyle Street W1S 143 M7
Boyson Road SE17 ....149 K8
Brackley Street EC1Y 145 J4
Bradenham Close SE17 ....149 K8
Brad Street SE1 ....149 G2
Braganza Street SE17 ....149 H7
Braham Street E1 ....150 C3
Bramerton Street SW3 ....146 F7
Bramham Gardens SW5 ....146 B6
Branch Road E14 ....151 J3
Brandon Estate SE17 ....149 H8
Brandon Street SE17 ....149 K6
Brangton Road SE11 ....148 F7
Bray Crescent SE16 ....151 H6
Bray Place SW3 ....147 H6
Bread Street EC4M 145 K7
Bream's Buildings EC4A 144 F6
Brechin Place SW7 ....146 D6
Breezer's Hill E1W 150 D4
Brendon Street W1H 143 G5
Bressenden Place SW1W 147 L4
Brettell Street SE17 ....149 L7
Brewers Green SW1H 148 A3
Brewer Street W1F 144 A7
Brewhouse Lane E1W 150 F6
Brewhouse Walk SE16 ....151 J5
Brick Lane E1 ....150 C1
Brick Street W1J 147 K2
Bridewell Place EC4V 145 H7
Bridgeman Street NW8 ....142 F1
Bridge Place SW1V 147 L5
Bridgeport Place E1W 150 D4
Bridge Street SW1A 148 D3
Bridgewater Street EC2Y 145 J4
Bridgeway Street NW1 ....144 A1
Bridle Lane W1F 144 A7
Bridstow Place W2 ....142 A6
Brightlingsea Place E14 ....151 L4
Brill Place NW1 ....144 C1
Bristol Gardens W9 ....142 B4
Briset Street EC1M 145 H4
Britannia Street WC1X 144 E2
Britannia Walk N1 ....145 L2
Britannia Way N1 ....145 L1
Britten Street SW3 ....146 F7
Britton Street EC1M 145 H4
Broadbent Street W1K 143 L7
Broadgate Circle EC2M 145 M5
Broadley Street NW8 ....142 F4
Broadley Terrace NW1 ....142 F4
Broadstone Place W1U 143 J5
Broad Walk NW1 ....143 K1
Broad Walk W2 ....143 H7
Broadwall SE1 ....149 G1
Broadway SW1H 148 B4
Broadwick Street W1F 144 A7
Brockham Street SE1 ....149 K4
Brodlove Lane E1W 151 H3
Bromley Street E1 ....151 J2
Brompton Place SW3 ....147 G4
Brompton Road SW3 ....147 G4
Brompton Road SW7 ....146 F5
Brompton Square SW3 ....146 F4
Bronti Close SE17 ....149 K7
Brook Drive SE11 ....149 G5
Brooke Street EC1N 144 F5
Brook Gate W2 ....143 H8
Brook Mews North W2 ....142 D7
Brook's Mews W1K 143 K7
Brook Street W1K 143 K7
Brook Street W2 ....142 E7
Brown Heart Gardens W1K 143 K7
Browning Mews W1G 143 K5
Browning Street SE17 ....149 K6
Brownlow Mews WC1N 144 E3
Brownlow Street WC1V 144 E5
Brown Street W1H 143 G6
Brunel Road SE16 ....151 G6
Brune Street E1 ....150 B1
Brunswick Close SE1 ....150 A6
Brunswick Gardens W8 ....146 A1
Brunswick Place N1 ....145 L2
Brunswick Quay SE16 ....151 J8
Brunswick Square WC1N 144 D3
Brunswick Street WC1N 144 D3
Brunton Place E14 ....151 K3
Brushfield Street E1 ....150 B1
Bruton Lane W1J 143 L8
Bruton Place W1J 143 L8
Bruton Street W1J 143 L8
Bryan Road SE16 ....151 K6
Bryanstone Mews West W1H 143 G5
Bryanston Mews East W1H 143 H5
Bryanston Place W1H 143 H5
Bryanston Square W1H 143 H5
Bryanston Street W1C 143 H7
Buck Hill Walk W2 ....142 E8
Buckingham Gate SW1E 147 L3
Buckingham Mews SW1E 147 M3
Buckingham Palace SW1A 147 L3
Buckingham Palace Road SW1W ..147 L5
Buckingham Palace Road SW1W ..147 M4
Buckland Street N1 ....145 L1
Buckle Street E1 ....150 C2
Bucknall Street WC2H 144 C6
Bucknall Street WC2H 149 K5
Buckters Rents SE16 ....151 J5
Budge's Walk W2 ....146 D2
Bulleid Way SW1V 147 L5
Bunhill Row EC1Y 145 L3
Burbage Close SE1 ....149 K4
Burdett Estate E14 ....151 M1
Burdett Road E14 ....151 L2
Burdett Street SE1 ....148 F3
Burge Street SE1 ....149 L4
Burgess Street E14 ....151 M1
Burgon Street EC4V 143 M8
Burlington Arcade W1J 143 M8
Burlington Gardens W1S 143 M8
Burnhouse Place SW1W 147 J6
Burnsall Street SW3 ....147 G7

Burnside Close SE16 ....151 J5
Burrell Street SE1 ....149 H1
Burslem Street E1 ....150 D3
Burton Grove SE17 ....149 L7
Burton Street WC1H 144 C3
Burwood Place W2 ....143 G6
Bury Close SE16 ....151 H5
Bury Court EC3A 150 A2
Bury Place WC1A 144 D5
Bury Street EC3A 150 A2
Bury Street SW1Y 148 A1
Bury Walk SW3 ....146 F6
Bushell Street E1W 150 D5
Bush Lane EC4V 145 L7
Butcher Row E1 ....151 J3
Bute Street SW7 ....146 E5
Butler Place SW1H 148 B4
Butler's Wharf SE1 ....150 C6
Buttesland Street N1 ....145 L2
Byefield Close SE16 ....151 K6
Bylands Close SE16 ....151 J5
Byng Place WC1E 144 B4
Byng Street E14 ....151 M6
Byward Street EC3R 150 A4
Bywater Place SE16 ....151 K5
Bywater Street SW3 ....147 G6

C

Cabbell Street NW1 ....142 F5
Cable Street E1 ....150 F3
Cadiz Street SE17 ....149 K7
Cadogan Gardens SW3 ....147 H5
Cadogan Gate SW1X 147 H5
Cadogan Lane SW1X 147 J4
Cadogan Place SW1X 147 J4
Cadogan Square SW1X 147 H5
Cadogan Street SW3 ....147 G6
Caledonian Road N1 ....144 D1
Caledonia Street N1 ....144 D1
Cale Street SW3 ....146 F6
Callow Street SW3 ....146 D7
Calshot Street N1 ....144 E1
Calthorpe Street WC1X 144 E3
Cambridge Circus WC2H 144 C7
Cambridge Gardens NW6 ....142 A1
Cambridge Gate NW1 ....143 L3
Cambridge Road NW6 ....142 A1
Cambridge Road NW6 ....142 A2
Cambridge Square W2 ....142 F6
Cambridge Street SW1V 147 L6
Cambridge Terrace NW1 ....143 L2
Cambridge Terrace Mews NW1 ...143 L3
Camdenhurst Street E14 ....151 K2
Camera Place SW10 ....146 D8
Camomile Street EC3A 150 A2
Campden Grove W8 ....146 A2
Campden Hill Road W8 ....146 A2
Campden Street W8 ....146 A1
Camperdown Street E1 ....150 C3
Canada Estate SE16 ....151 G7
Canada Gate SW1A 147 M3
Canada Street SE16 ....151 H7
Canada Water ⊖ SE16 ....151 G7
Canada Wharf SE16 ....151 L5
Canal Street SE5 ....149 L8
Canary Riverside E14 ....151 L4
Candle Street E1 ....151 K1
Canning Place W8 ....146 C4
Cannon Drive E14 ....151 M4
Cannon Street EC4N 145 K7
Cannon Street ⇌ ⊖ EC4R 145 K7
Cannon Street Road E1 ....150 E3
Canon Beck Road SE16 ....151 G6
Canon Row SW1A 148 D3
Canton Street E14 ....151 M3
Capeners Close * SW1X 147 J3
Capland Street NW8 ....142 E3
Capper Street WC1E 144 A4
Capstan Way E16 ....151 K5
Carbis Road E14 ....151 L2
Carburton Street W1W 143 L4
Cardigan Street SE11 ....148 F6
Cardington Street NW1 ....144 A2
Carey Street WC2A 144 F6
Carlisle Avenue EC3N 150 B3
Carlisle Lane SE1 ....148 F4
Carlisle Place SW1P 147 M5
Carlisle Street W1D 144 B6
Carlos Place W1K 143 K7
Carlton Gardens SW1Y 148 B2
Carlton Hill NW6 ....142 B1
Carlton House Terrace SW1Y 148 B1
Carlton Street SW1Y 147 L1
Carlton Vale NW6 ....142 A1
Carlton Vale NW6 ....142 B1
Carlyle Square SW3 ....146 F7
Carmelite Street EC4Y 145 G7
Carnaby Street W1F 143 M7
Caroline Place W2 ....142 B7
Caroline Street E1 ....151 H3
Caroline Terrace SW1W 147 J5
Carpenter Street W1K 143 K7
Carrington Street W1J 147 L1
Carr Street E14 ....151 K1
Carteret Street SW1H 148 B3
Carter Lane EC4V 145 H7
Carter Place SE17 ....149 K7
Carter Street SE17 ....149 J7
Carthusian Street EC1M 145 J4
Carting Lane WC2R 144 D8
Cartwright Gardens WC1H 144 C2
Cartwright Street E1 ....150 C4
Casey Close NW8 ....142 F3
Casson Street E1 ....150 C1
Castellain Road W9 ....142 B3
Castlebrook Close SE11 ....149 G5
Castle Lane SW1E 147 M4
Catesby Street SE17 ....149 L6
Cathay Street SE16 ....150 F7
Cathcart Road SW10 ....146 C8
Cathedral Walk SW1E 147 M4
Catherine Place SW1E 147 M4
Catherine Street WC2E 144 D7
Cato Street W1H 143 G5
Causton Street SW1P 148 B6

Cavell Street – Farringdon Road

153

Cavell Street E1 150 F1
Cavendish Avenue NW8 142 E1
Cavendish Place W1G 143 L6
Cavendish Square W1G 143 L6
Cavendish Street N1 145 L1
Caversham Street SW3 147 G8
Caxton Street SW1H 148 B4
Cayton Street EC1V 145 K2
Centaur Street SE1 148 F4
Central Street EC1V 145 J2
Chadwell Street EC1R 145 G1
Chadwick Street SW1P 148 B4
Chagford Street NW1 143 H4
Chalton Street NW1 144 B1
Chambers Street SE16 150 D7
Chamber Street E1 150 C3
Chambers Wharf SE16 150 D6
Chancel Street SE1 149 H1
Chancery Lane WC2A 144 F5
Chancery Lane ⊖ WC1V 144 F5
Chandos Place WC2N 144 C8
Chandos Street W1G 143 L5
Chantry Square W8 146 B4
Chapel Market * N1 144 F1
Chapel Street NW1 142 F5
Chapel Street SW1X 147 K3
Chaplin Close SE1 149 G3
Chapman Street E1 150 E3
Chapter Road SE17 149 H7
Chapter Street SW1P 148 B6
Chargrove Close SE16 151 H6
Charing Cross ⇌ ⊖ WC2N 148 D1
Charing Cross Road WC2H 144 B6
Charing Cross Road WC2N 144 C7
Charlbert Street NW8 142 F1
Charles II Street SW1Y 144 B8
Charles Square N1 145 M2
Charles Street W1J 147 K1
Charleston Street SE17 149 K6
Charlotte Road EC2A 145 M3
Charlotte Street W1T 144 A4
Charlwood Place SW1V 148 A6
Charlwood Street SW1V 147 M7
Charlwood Street SW1V 148 A6
Charrington Street NW1 144 B1
Charterhouse Square EC1M 145 H4
Charterhouse Street EC1M 145 G5
Chart Street N1 145 L2
Chaseley Street E14 151 J2
Chatham Street SE17 149 L5
Cheapside EC2V 145 K6
Chelsea Bridge SW1W 147 K8
Chelsea Bridge Road SW1W 147 J7
Chelsea Embankment SW3 147 G8
Chelsea Manor Gardens SW3 146 F7
Chelsea Manor Street SW3 147 G7
Chelsea Park Gardens SW3 146 E8
Chelsea Physic Garden SW3 147 H8
Chelsea Square SW3 146 E7
Cheltenham Terrace SW3 147 H6
Chenies Mews WC1E 144 B4
Chenies Street WC1E 144 B4
Cheniston Gardens W8 146 A4
Chepstow Place W2 142 A7
Chepstow Road W2 142 A6
Chequer Street EC1Y 145 K3
Cherbury Street N1 145 L1
Cherry Garden Street SE16 150 E7
Chesham Close SW1X 147 J4
Chesham Place SW1X 147 J4
Chesham Street SW1X 147 J4
Chester Close SW1X 147 K3
Chester Close North NW1 143 L2
Chester Close South NW1 143 L2
Chesterfield Gardens W1J 147 K1
Chesterfield Hill W1J 143 K8
Chesterfield Street W1J 147 K1
Chester Gate NW1 143 L2
Chester Mews SW1X 147 K3
Chester Place NW1 143 L1
Chester Road NW1 143 K2
Chester Row SW1W 147 K5
Chester Square SW1W 147 K5
Chester Square Mews SW1W 147 K4
Chester Street SW1X 147 K4
Chester Terrace NW1 143 L2
Chester Way SE11 149 G6
Cheval Place SW7 147 G4
Cheval Street E14 151 M7
Cheyne Gardens SW3 147 G8
Cheyne Row SW3 146 F8
Cheyne Walk SW3 146 F8
Chicheley Street SE1 148 E2
Chichester Road NW6 142 A1
Chichester Road W2 142 C5
Chichester Street SW1V 148 A7
Chicksand Street E1 150 C1
Chigwell Hill E1W 150 E4
Child's Place SW5 146 A5
Child's Street SW5 146 A5
Chiltern Street W1U 143 J4
Chilworth Mews W2 142 D6
Chilworth Street W2 142 D6
China Hall Mews SE16 151 G8
Chinatown W1D 144 B7
Chippenham Mews W9 142 A4
Chiswell Street EC1Y 145 K4
Chitty Street W1T 144 A4
Christchurch Street SW3 147 G8
Christian Street E1 150 D3
Christina Street EC2A 145 M3
Christopher Close SE16 151 H6
Christopher Street EC2A 145 L4
Chudleigh Street E1 151 H2
Chumleigh Street SE5 149 M8
Churchill Gardens Road SW1V 147 L7
Churchill War Rooms SW1A 148 C3
Church Street NW8 142 F4
Church Way NW1 144 B2
Churchyard Row SE1 149 H5
Churton Place SW1V 148 A6
Churton Street SW1V 148 A6
Circus Road NW8 142 E1
Cirencester Square W2 142 A5
City Garden Row N1 145 J1
City Road EC1V 145 J1
City Road EC1Y 145 L3
City Thameslink ⇌ EC4M 145 H6
Clabon Mews SW1X 147 H5
Clack Street SE16 151 G7
Clanricarde Gardens W2 142 A8
Clarkson Row NW1 143 M1
Claremont Square N1 144 F1
Clarence Gardens NW1 143 L2
Clarence Mews SE16 151 G6
Clarendon Gardens W9 142 D4
Clarendon Gate W2 142 F7
Clarendon Place W2 142 F7
Clarendon Street SW1V 147 L6
Clareville Grove SW7 146 D6
Clareville Street SW7 146 D6
Clarges Mews W1J 147 L1
Clarges Street W1J 147 L1
Clark Street E1 150 F2
Clarkson Row NW1 143 M1
Claverton Street SW1V 148 A7
Clave Street E1W 150 F5
Clay Street W1U 143 H5
Clayton Street SE11 148 F8
Cleaver Square SE11 149 G7
Cleaver Street SE11 149 G7
Clegg Street E1W 150 F5
Clemence Street E14 151 L2
Clements Lane EC4N 145 L7
Clement's Road SE16 150 E8
Clenston Mews W1H 143 H6
Clere Street EC2A 145 L3
Clerkenwell Close EC1R 145 G3
Clerkenwell Green EC1R 145 G4
Clerkenwell Road EC1M 145 G4
Cleveland Gardens W2 142 C6
Cleveland Mews W1T 143 M4
Cleveland Place SW1Y 148 A1
Cleveland Row SW1A 148 A2
Cleveland Square W2 142 C6
Cleveland Street W1T 143 M4
Cleveland Terrace W2 142 D6
Clifford Street W1S 143 M7
Clifton Gardens W9 142 C4
Clifton Place SE16 151 G6
Clifton Place W2 142 E7
Clifton Road W9 142 D3
Clifton Street EC2A 145 M3
Clifton Villas W9 142 C4
Clink Street SE1 149 K1
Clipper Close SE16 151 H6
Clipstone Mews W1W 143 M4
Clipstone Street W1W 143 L4
Cliveden Place SW1W 147 J5
Cloak Lane EC4R 145 K7
Cloth Fair EC1A 145 J5
Cloth Street EC1A 145 J5
Cluny Place SE1 150 A8
Cobb Street E1 150 B2
Cobourg Street NW1 144 A2
Coburg Close SW1P 148 A5
Cochrane Mews NW8 142 E1
Cochrane Street NW8 142 E1
Cock Lane EC1A 145 H5
Cockspur Street SW1Y 148 C1
Codling Close * E1W 150 D5
Coin Street SE1 149 G1
Coke Street E1 150 D2
Colbeck Mews SW7 146 C6
Colebrook Row N1 145 H1
Coleherne Road SW10 146 B7
Coleman Street EC2R 145 L6
Cole Street SE1 149 K3
Coley Street WC1X 144 F3
College Hill EC4R 145 K7
College Street EC4R 145 K7
Collett Road SE16 150 D8
Collier Street N1 144 E1
Collingham Gardens SW5 146 B6
Collingham Place SW5 146 B5
Collingham Road SW5 146 B5
Colnbrook Street SE1 149 H4
Colombo Street SE1 149 H1
Colonnade WC1N 144 D4
Coltman Street E14 151 K2
Commercial Road E1 150 D2
Commercial Road E14 151 K3
Commercial Street E1 150 B1
Compton Street EC1V 145 H3
Concert Hall Approach SE1 148 E2
Conder Street E14 151 K2
Conduit Mews W2 142 E6
Conduit Place W2 142 E6
Conduit Street W1S 143 L7
Congreve Street SE17 149 M5
Connaught Close W2 142 F7
Connaught Place W2 143 G7
Connaught Square W2 143 G6
Connaught Street W2 143 G6
Cons Street SE1 149 G2
Constitution Hill SW1A 147 L3
Content Street SE17 149 K5
Conway Street W1T 143 M4
Cookham Crescent SE16 151 H6
Cook's Road SE17 149 H8
Coombs Street N1 145 J1
Cooper's Lane Estate NW1 144 B1
Cooper's Row EC3N 150 B3
Copenhagen Place E14 151 L2
Cope Place W8 146 A4
Copley Court SE17 149 J8
Copley Street E1 151 H2
Copperfield Road E3 151 K1
Copperfield Street SE1 149 J2
Copthall Avenue EC2R 145 L6
Coptic Street WC1A 144 C5
Coral Street SE1 149 G3
Coram Street WC1H 144 C3
Cork Square E1W 150 E4
Cork Street W1S 143 M8
Corlett Street NW1 142 F5
Cornhill EC3V 145 L6
Cornwall Gardens SW7 146 C4
Cornwall Mews South SW7 146 C5
Cornwall Road SE1 148 F1
Cornwall Road SE1 149 G2
Cornwall Street E1 150 E3
Cornwall Terrace Mews NW1 143 H4
Cornwood Drive E1 151 G2
Coronet Street N1 145 M2
Corporation Row EC1R 145 G3
Corsham Street N1 145 L2
Cosser Street SE1 148 F4
Cosway Street NW1 143 G4
Cottage Place SW3 146 F4
Cottesmore Gardens W8 146 B4
Cottons Lane SE1 149 M1
Coulson Street SW3 147 H6
Counter Street SE1 149 M1
County Street SE1 149 K5
Courtenay Square SE11 148 F7
Courtenay Street SE11 148 F7
Courtfield Gardens SW5 146 B5
Courtfield Mews * SW5 146 C5
Courtfield Road SW7 146 C5
Court Street E1 150 E1
Cousin Lane SE1 145 K8
Covent Garden ⊖ WC2E 144 D7
Covent Garden WC2E 144 D7
Coventry Street W1D 144 B8
Cowcross Street EC1M 145 H4
Cowper Street EC2A 145 L3
Crail Row SE17 149 L5
Cramer Street W1U 143 J5
Crampton Street SE17 149 J6
Cranbourn Street WC2H 144 C7
Cranleigh Street NW1 144 A1
Cranley Gardens SW7 146 D6
Cranley Mews SW7 146 D6
Cranley Place SW7 146 E6
Cranston Estate N1 145 L1
Cranwood Street EC1V 145 L2
Craven Hill W2 142 D7
Craven Hill Gardens W2 142 C7
Craven Road W2 142 D7
Craven Street WC2N 148 D1
Craven Terrace W2 142 D7
Crawford Passage EC1R 145 G3
Crawford Place W1H 143 G5
Crawford Street W1H 143 G5
Creechurch Lane EC3A 150 A3
Creed Lane EC4V 145 H7
Cresswell Place SW10 146 D6
Cressy Place E1 151 G1
Crestfield Street WC1H 144 D2
Crimscott Street SE1 150 A8
Crispin Street E1 150 B1
Cromer Street WC1H 144 D2
Crompton Street W2 142 D4
Cromwell Mews * SW7 146 E5
Cromwell Place SW7 146 E5
Cromwell Road SW5 146 B5
Cromwell Road SW7 146 E5
Crondall Court N1 145 M1
Crondall Street N1 145 L1
Cropley Street N1 145 K1
Crosby Row SE1 149 L3
Cross Lane EC3R 150 A4
Crosswall EC3N 150 B3
Crowder Street E1 150 E3
Crucifix Lane SE1 150 A6
Cruikshank Street WC1X 144 F1
Crutched Friars EC3N 150 A3
Cuba Street E14 151 M6
Cubitt Street WC1X 144 E2
Culford Gardens SW3 147 H6
Culling Road SE16 150 F7
Cullum Street EC3M 145 M7
Culross Street W1K 143 J8
Culworth Street NW8 142 F1
Cumberland Gardens WC1X 144 F2
Cumberland Gate W2 143 H7
Cumberland Market NW1 143 L2
Cumberland Street SW1V 147 L6
Cumberland Terrace NW1 143 L1
Cumberland Terrace Mews NW1 143 L1
Cumberland Wharf SE16 151 G6
Cumming Street N1 144 E1
Cundy Street SW1W 147 K6
Cunningham Place NW8 142 E3
Cureton Street SW1P 148 C6
Curlew Street SE1 150 B6
Cursitor Street EC4A 144 F6
Curtain Road EC2A 145 M3
Curtain Road EC2A 145 M4
Curzon Gate W2 147 K2
Curzon Street W1J 147 K1
Cuthbert Street W2 142 E4
Cutler Street EC3A 150 A2
Cynthia Street N1 144 F1
Cypress Place W1T 144 A4
Cyrus Street EC1V 145 H3

D

Dacre Street SW1H 148 B3
Dakin Place E1 151 J1
Dallington Street EC1V 145 H3
Damien Street E1 150 F2
Dane Street WC1R 144 E5
Dansey Place W1D 144 B7
Dante Road SE11 149 H5
Danvers Street SW3 146 F8
D'Arblay Street W1F 144 A6
Dartford Street SE17 149 K8
Dartmouth Street SW1H 148 B3
Darwin Street SE17 149 L5
Date Street SE17 149 K7
Davenant Street E1 150 D1
Daventry Street NW1 142 F4
Davidge Street SE1 149 H3
Davies Mews W1K 143 K7
Davies Street W1K 143 K7
Dawes Street SE17 149 L6
Dawson Place W2 142 A7
Deal Porters Way SE16 151 G8
Deal Street E1 150 D1
Dean Bradley Street SW1P 148 C5
Dean Close SE16 151 H6
Deancross Street E1 150 F3
Deanery Street W1K 147 K1
Dean Farrar Street SW1H 148 B3
Dean Ryle Street SW1P 148 C5
Dean's Buildings SE17 149 L6
Dean Stanley Street SW1P 148 C4
Dean Street W1D 144 B6
Dean's Yard SW1P 148 C4
Decima Street SE1 149 M4
Deck Close SE16 151 J6
Defoe Close SE16 151 K7
Delamere Street W2 142 C5
Delamere Terrace W2 142 B4
De Laune Street SE17 149 H7
Delaware Road W9 142 B3
Dellow Street E1 150 F3
Delverton Road SE17 149 H7
Denbigh Place SW1V 147 M6
Denbigh Street SW1V 147 M6
Denbigh Street SW1V 148 A6
Denman Street W1D 144 B7
Denmark Street WC2H 144 C6
Denny Close SE11 149 G6
Denny Street SE11 149 G6
Denyer Street SW3 147 G5
Derby Gate SW1A 148 D3
Derby Street W1J 147 K1
Dering Street W1S 143 L6
Derry Street W8 146 B3
De Vere Gardens W8 146 C3
Deverell Street SE1 149 L4
Devonport Street E1 151 G3
Devonshire Close W1G 143 K4
Devonshire Mews South W1G 143 K4
Devonshire Mews West W1G 143 K4
Devonshire Place W1G 143 K4
Devonshire Place Mews W1G 143 K4
Devonshire Row EC2M 150 A2
Devonshire Square EC2M 150 A2
Devonshire Street W1G 143 K4
Devonshire Terrace W2 142 D7
De Walden Street W1G 143 K5
Dickens Estate SE16 150 D7
Dickens Square SE1 149 K4
Dilke Street SW3 147 H8
Dingley Place EC1V 145 K2
Dingley Road EC1V 145 J2
Disney Place SE1 149 K2
Distaff Lane EC4V 145 J7
Distin Street SE11 148 F6
Dockhead SE1 150 C7
Dockley Road SE16 150 D8
Dock Street E1 150 D4
Doddington Grove SE17 149 H7
Doddington Place SE17 149 H8
Dodson Street SE1 149 G3
Dod Street E14 151 M2
Dolben Street SE1 149 H2
Dolland Street SE11 148 E7
Dolphin Square SW1V 148 A7
Dolphin Square SW1V 148 B7
Dombey Street WC1N 144 E4
Dominion Drive SE16 151 H7
Dominion Street EC2A 145 L5
Donegal Street N1 144 F1
Dongola Road E1 151 J1
Donne Place SW3 147 G5
Doon Street SE1 148 F1
Dora Street E14 151 L2
Doric Way NW1 144 B2
Dorset Rise EC4Y 145 G7
Dorset Square NW1 143 H4
Dorset Street W1U 143 H5
Doughty Mews WC1N 144 E3
Doughty Street WC1N 144 E3
Douglas Street SW1P 148 B6
Douro Place W8 146 C3
Douthwaite Square * E1W 150 D5
Dovehouse Street SW3 146 E6
Dover Street W1J 147 L1
Dover Street W1S 143 L8
Dowgate Hill EC4R 145 K7
Downfield Close W9 142 B4
Downing Street SW1A 148 C2
Down Street W1J 147 K2
Downtown Road SE16 151 K6
D'Oyley Street SW1X 147 J5
Draco Street SE17 149 J8
Drake Close SE16 151 H6
Draycott Avenue SW3 147 G5
Draycott Place SW3 147 H6
Draycott Terrace SW3 147 H5
Drayson Mews W8 146 A3
Drayton Gardens SW10 146 D6
Druid Street SE1 150 A6
Druid Street SE1 150 B6
Drummond Crescent NW1 144 B2
Drummond Gate * SW1V 148 B6
Drummond Road SE16 150 E8
Drummond Street NW1 144 A3
Drury Lane WC2B 144 D6
Dryden Court SE11 149 G5
Dryden Street WC2B 144 D6
Duchess Mews W1G 143 L5
Duchess Street W1B 143 L5
Duchy Street SE1 149 G1
Duckett Street E1 151 J1
Duck Lane W1F 144 B6
Dufferin Street EC1Y 145 K4
Duke of Wellington Place SW1W 147 K3
Duke of York Square SW3 147 H6
Duke of York Street SW1Y 148 A1
Duke Shore Wharf E14 151 K4
Duke's Lane W8 146 A2
Duke's Place EC3A 150 B2
Duke's Road WC1H 144 C2
Duke Street W1K 143 K7
Duke Street W1U 143 J6
Duke Street Hill SE1 149 L1
Duke Street St James's SW1Y 148 A1
Dunbar Wharf E14 151 L4
Duncannon Street WC2N 144 C8
Duncan Terrace N1 145 H1
Dundee Street E1W 150 E5
Dundee Wharf E14 151 L4
Dunelm Street E1 151 H2
Dunlop Place SE16 150 C8
Dunraven Street W1K 143 H7
Dunster Court EC3R 150 A3
Duplex Ride SW1X 147 H3
Durand's Wharf SE16 151 L6
Durham Row E1 151 J1
Durham Street SE11 148 E7
Durham Terrace W2 142 A6
Dyott Street WC1A 144 C6
Dysart Street EC2A 145 M4

E

Eagle Court EC1M 145 H4
Eagle Street WC1R 144 E5
Eamont Street * NW8 143 G1
Eardley Crescent SW5 146 A7
Earlham Street WC2H 144 C7
Earl's Court ⇌ ⊖ SW5 146 A6
Earl's Court Gardens SW5 146 B6
Earl's Court Road SW5 146 A6
Earl's Court Square SW5 146 A6
Earlstoke Street EC1V 145 H2
Earl Street EC2A 145 M4
Earnshaw Street WC2H 144 C6
East Arbour Street E1 151 H2
Eastbourne Mews W2 142 D6
Eastbourne Terrace W2 142 D6
Eastcastle Street W1W 144 A6
Eastcheap EC3M 145 M7
Eastfield Street E14 151 K1
East India Dock Road E14 151 M3
East Lane SE16 150 D6
Easton Street WC1X 144 F3
East Poultry Avenue EC1A 145 H5
East Road N1 145 L2
East Smithfield E1W 150 C4
East Street SE17 149 L6
East Tenter Street E1 150 C3
Eaton Close SW1W 147 J5
Eaton Gate SW1W 147 J5
Eaton Lane SW1W 147 L4
Eaton Mews North SW1W 147 J5
Eaton Mews South SW1W 147 K5
Eaton Mews West SW1W 147 K5
Eaton Place SW1X 147 J4
Eaton Row SW1W 147 K4
Eaton Square SW1W 147 K5
Eaton Terrace SW1W 147 J5
Ebbisham Drive SW8 148 E8
Ebury Bridge SW1W 147 K6
Ebury Bridge Road SW1W 147 K7
Ebury Mews SW1W 147 K5
Ebury Square SW1W 147 K6
Ebury Street SW1W 147 K5
Eccleston Bridge SW1W 147 L5
Eccleston Mews SW1X 147 K4
Eccleston Place SW1W 147 L5
Eccleston Square SW1V 147 L6
Eccleston Street SW1X 147 K4
Edbrooke Road W9 142 A3
Edge Street W8 146 A1
Edgware Road W2 142 F5
Edgware Road ⊖ NW1 142 F5
Edinburgh Gate SW1X 147 H3
Edith Grove SW10 146 C8
Edwards Mews W1H 143 J6
Egerton Crescent SW3 146 F5
Egerton Gardens SW3 146 F5
Egerton Terrace SW3 147 G4
Eglington Court SE17 149 J7
Elba Place SE17 149 K5
Eldon Road W8 146 B4
Eldon Street EC2M 145 L5
Eleanor Close SE16 151 H6
Elephant & Castle SE1 149 J4
Elephant & Castle ⇌ ⊖ SE1 149 J5
Elephant Lane SE16 150 F6
Elephant Road SE17 149 J5
Elf Row E1W 151 G3
Elgar Street SE16 151 K7
Elgin Avenue W9 142 B2
Elgin Mews North W9 142 C2
Elgin Mews South W9 142 C2
Elia Mews N1 145 H1
Elia Street N1 145 H1
Elim Estate SE1 149 M3
Elim Street SE1 149 M3
Elizabeth Bridge SW1V 147 L6
Elizabeth Street SW1W 147 K5
Ellen Street E1 150 D3
Elliott's Row SE11 149 H5
Ellis Street SW1X 147 J5
Elmfield Way W9 142 A4
Elm Park Gardens SW10 146 E7
Elm Park Lane SW3 146 E7
Elm Park Road SW3 146 E8
Elm Place SW7 146 E7
Elms Mews W2 142 D7
Elm Street WC1X 144 F4
Elm Tree Road NW8 142 E2
Elnathan Mews W9 142 B4
Elsa Street E1 151 J1
Elsted Street SE17 149 L6
Elvaston Mews SW7 146 D4
Elvaston Place SW7 146 D4
Elverton Street SW1P 148 B5
Ely Place EC1N 145 G5
Elystan Place SW3 147 G6
Elystan Street SW3 146 F6
Embankment ⊖ WC2N 148 D1
Embankment Gardens SW3 147 H8
Embankment Place WC2N 148 D1
Emba Street SE16 150 D7
Emerald Street WC1N 144 E4
Emerson Street SE1 149 J1
Emery Hill Street SW1P 148 A5
Emery Street SE1 149 G3
Emperor's Gate SW7 146 C5
Empire Square SE1 149 L3
Empress Place SW6 146 A7
Endell Street WC2H 144 C6
Endsleigh Gardens WC1H 144 B3
Endsleigh Place WC1H 144 B3
Endsleigh Street WC1H 144 B3
Enford Street W1H 143 G5
English Grounds SE1 149 M1
Enid Street SE16 150 C8
Ennismore Gardens SW7 146 F3
Ennismore Gardens Mews SW7 146 F3
Ennismore Mews SW7 146 F3
Ennismore Street SW7 146 F4
Ensign Street E1 150 D4
Epworth Street EC2A 145 L3
Erasmus Street SW1P 148 C6
Errol Street EC1Y 145 K4
Essendine Road W9 142 A3
Essex Street WC2R 144 F7
Essex Villas W8 146 A3
Europa Place EC1V 145 J2
Euston ⇌ ⊖ ⊖ NW1 144 B2
Euston Road NW1 144 B3
Euston Square NW1 144 B2
Euston Square ⊖ NW1 144 A3
Euston Street NW1 144 A3
Evelyn Gardens SW7 146 D7
Evelyn Walk N1 145 L1
Eversholt Street NW1 144 A1
Everton Mews NW1 143 M2
Ewer Street SE1 149 J2
Ewhurst Close E1 151 G1
Exchange Square EC2A 145 M4
Exeter Street WC2E 144 D7
Exhibition Road SW7 146 E3
Exmouth Market EC1R 145 G3
Exon Street SE17 149 M6
Exton Street SE1 148 F2
Eyre Street Hill EC1R 144 F4

F

Fairclough Street E1 150 D3
Fair Street SE1 150 B6
Falmouth Road SE1 149 K4
Fann Street EC1M 145 J4
Fanshaw Street N1 145 M1
Farmer Street W8 146 A1
Farm Lane SW6 146 A8
Farm Street W1K 143 K8
Farnham Place SE1 149 J1
Farrance Street E14 151 M3
Farringdon ⇌ ⊖ EC1M 145 G4
Farringdon Lane EC1R 145 G4
Farringdon Road EC1R 144 F3

Farringdon Street EC1M 145 H5
Farrins Rents SE16 .... 151 J5
Farrow Place SE16 .... 151 K7
Farthing Fields * E1W 150 F5
Fashion Street E1 .... 150 B1
Faunce Street SE17 .... 149 H7
Fawcett Street SW10 .... 146 C8
Featherstone Street EC1Y 145 L3
Fenchurch Avenue EC3M 150 A3
Fenchurch Buildings EC3M 150 A3
Fenchurch Place EC3M 150 A3
Fenchurch Street EC3M 150 A3
Fenchurch Street ⇌ EC3M 150 A3
Fendall Street SE1 .... 150 B8
Fenning Street SE1 .... 149 M2
Fentiman Road SW8 .... 148 D8
Fernsbury Street WC1 .... 144 F2
Fetter Lane EC4A 145 G6
Fieldgate Street E1 .... 150 D2
Fielding Street SE17 .... 149 J7
Field Street WC1X 144 D1
Finborough Road SW10 .... 146 B8
Finch Lane EC3V 145 L6
Finland Street SE16 .... 151 K8
Finsbury Circus EC2M 145 L5
Finsbury Estate EC1R 145 G3
Finsbury Market EC2A 145 M4
Finsbury Square EC2A 145 L4
Finsbury Street EC2Y 145 L4
First Street SW3 .... 147 G5
Fishermans Drive SE16 .... 151 J6
Fisher Street WC1R 144 D5
Fisherton Street NW8 .... 142 E3
Fish Street Hill EC3R 145 L7
Fitzalan Street SE11 .... 148 F5
Fitzhardinge Street W1H 143 J6
Fitzroy Square W1T 143 M4
Fitzroy Street W1T 143 M4
Flamborough Street E14 .... 151 J3
Flank Street E1 .... 150 C4
Flaxman Terrace WC1H 144 C3
Fleet Street EC4A 145 G6
Fleming Road SE17 .... 149 H8
Fletcher Street E1 .... 150 D3
Flint Street SE17 .... 149 L6
Flitcroft Street WC2H 144 C6
Flockton Street SE16 .... 150 D7
Flood Street SW3 .... 147 G7
Flood Walk SW3 .... 147 G7
Floral Street WC2E 144 D7
Foley Street W1W 143 M5
Forbes Street E1 .... 150 D3
Fordham Street E1 .... 150 D2
Ford Square E1 .... 150 F2
Fore Street EC2Y 145 K5
Formosa Street W9 .... 142 C4
Forset Street W1H 143 G6
Forsyth Gardens SE17 .... 149 H8
Foster Lane EC2V 145 J6
Foulis Terrace SW7 .... 146 E6
Foundry Close SE16 .... 151 J5
Fournier Street E1 .... 150 B1
Fowey Close E1W 150 E5
Frampton Street NW8 .... 142 E4
Francis Street SW1P 148 A5
Franklin's Row SW3 .... 147 H6
Frazier Street SE1 .... 149 G3
Frean Street SE16 .... 150 C8
Frederick Close W2 .... 143 G7
Frederick Street WC1X 144 E2
Frederic Mews * SW1X 147 J3
Freemantle Street SE17 .... 149 M6
Friday Street EC4V 145 J7
Friend Street EC1V 145 H2
Frith Street W1D 144 B6
Fulbourne Street E1 .... 150 E1
Fulford Street SE16 .... 150 F7
Fulham Road SW10 .... 146 D8
Fulham Road SW3 .... 146 F6
Furnival Street EC4A 144 F5
Fynes Street SW1P 148 B5

G

Gabriel's Wharf SE1 .... 149 G1
Gainsford Street SE1 .... 150 B6
Galleon Close SE16 .... 151 G6
Galsworthy Avenue E14 .... 151 K2
Galway Street EC1V 145 K2
Gambia Street SE1 .... 149 H2
Garden Road NW8 .... 142 D1
Garden Row SE1 .... 149 H4
Garden Street E1 .... 151 H1
Garden Terrace * SW1V 148 B6
Garden Walk EC2A 145 M3
Gard Street EC1V 145 J2
Garford Street E14 .... 151 M4
Garnault Place EC1R 145 G3
Garnet Street E1W 150 F4
Garrett Street EC1Y 145 K3
Garrick Street WC2E 144 C7
Garterway SE16 .... 151 H7
Garway Road W2 .... 142 B6
Gaspar Mews SW7 .... 146 C5
Gataker Street * SE16 .... 150 E8
Gate Mews SW7 .... 146 F3
Gateforth Street NW8 .... 142 F3
Gate Mews NW1 .... 143 L3
Gatesborough Street * EC2A 145 M3
Gate Street WC2A 144 E5
Gatliff Road SW1W 147 K7
Gaunt Street SE1 .... 149 J4
Gayfere Street SW1P 148 C4
Gaywood Street SE1 .... 149 H4
Gaza Street SE17 .... 149 H7
Gedling Place SE1 .... 150 C7
Gee Street EC1V 145 J3
George Mathers Road SE11 .... 149 H5
George Row SE16 .... 150 C7
George Street W1H 143 H6
George Yard W1K 143 K7
Geraldine Street SE1 .... 149 H4
Gerald Road SW1W 147 K5
Gerrard Street W1D 144 B7
Gerridge Street SE1 .... 149 G3
Gertrude Street SW10 .... 146 D8
Gibson Road SE11 .... 148 E6
Gilbert Place WC1A 144 C5
Gilbert Road SE11 .... 149 G5
Gilbert Street W1K 143 K7
Gildea Street W1W 143 L5

Gillingham Street SW1V 147 M5
Gill Street E14 .... 151 L3
Gilston Road SW10 .... 146 D7
Giltspur Street EC1A 145 H5
Gladstone Street SE1 .... 149 H4
Glamis Place E1W 151 G4
Glamis Road E1W 151 G4
Glasgow Terrace SW1V 147 M7
Glasshill Street SE1 .... 149 J3
Glasshouse Street W1B 144 A8
Glasshouse Walk SE11 .... 148 D7
Glasshouse Yard EC1 .... 145 J4
Glebe Place SW3 .... 146 F7
Gledhow Road SW5 .... 146 C6
Glentworth Street NW1 .... 143 H4
Globe Pond Road SE16 .... 151 J5
Globe Street SE1 .... 149 K3
Gloucester Court * EC3R 150 A4
Gloucester Gardens W2 .... 142 C6
Gloucester Mews W2 .... 142 D6
Gloucester Mews West W2 .... 142 C6
Gloucester Place W1U 143 H3
Gloucester Place NW1 .... 143 H5
Gloucester Place Mews W1U 143 H5
Gloucester Road SW7 .... 146 C4
Gloucester Road SW7 .... 146 C4
Gloucester Road ⊖ SW7 .... 146 C5
Gloucester Square W2 .... 142 E6
Gloucester Street SW1V 147 M7
Gloucester Terrace W2 .... 142 B5
Gloucester Terrace W2 .... 142 D6
Gloucester Walk W8 .... 146 A4
Gloucester Way EC1R 145 G2
Glyn Street SE11 .... 148 E7
Godfrey Street SW3 .... 147 G6
Goding Street SE11 .... 148 D7
Godliman Street EC4V 145 J7
Godwin Close * N1 .... 145 K1
Golden Hinde II SE1 .... 149 L1
Golden Jubilee Bridge WC2N 148 D1
Golden Lane EC1Y 145 J4
Golden Square W1F 144 A7
Golding Street E1 .... 150 E3
Goldney Road W9 .... 142 A4
Goldsmith Street EC2V 145 K6
Gomm Road SE16 .... 151 G8
Goodge Place W1T 144 A5
Goodge Street W1T 144 A5
Goodge Street ⊖ W1T 144 B5
Goodwin Close SE16 .... 150 C8
Gordon Place W8 .... 146 A2
Gordon Square WC1H 144 B3
Gordon Street WC1H 144 B3
Gore Street SW7 .... 146 D4
Goring Street * EC3A 150 A2
Gosfield Street W1W 143 L5
Goslett Yard WC2H 144 B6
Goswell Road EC1V 145 H1
Gough Street WC1X 144 F3
Goulston Street E1 .... 150 B2
Gower Mews WC1E 144 B5
Gower Place NW1 .... 144 A3
Gower Street WC1E 144 B3
Gower's Walk E1 .... 150 D2
Gracechurch Street EC3V 145 M7
Grafton Place NW1 .... 144 B2
Grafton Street W1S 143 L8
Grafton Way W1T 144 A4
Graham Street N1 .... 145 J1
Graham Terrace SW1W 147 J6
Granby Terrace NW1 .... 143 M1
Grand Avenue EC1A 145 H5
Grange Road SE1 .... 150 B8
Grange Walk SE1 .... 150 A8
Grange Yard SE1 .... 150 B8
Grantully Road W9 .... 142 B2
Granville Place W1H 143 J6
Granville Road NW6 .... 142 A1
Granville Square WC1X 144 F2
Grape Street WC2H 144 C6
Gravel Lane E1 .... 150 B2
Gray's Inn Road WC1X 144 D2
Gray's Inn Square WC1R 144 F5
Gray Street SE1 .... 149 G3
Great Castle Street W1G 143 L6
Great Central Street NW1 .... 143 G4
Great Chapel Street W1D 144 B6
Great College Street SW1P 148 C4
Great Cumberland Place W1H 143 H6
Great Dover Street SE1 .... 149 K3
Great Eastern Street EC2A 145 M3
Great George Street SW1P 148 C3
Great Guildford Street SE1 .... 149 J1
Great James Street WC1N 144 E4
Great Marlborough Street W1F 143 M7
Great Maze Pond SE1 .... 149 L2
Great New Portland Street WC2H 144 C7
Greatorex Street E1 .... 150 D1
Great Ormond Street WC1N 144 D4
Great Percy Street WC1X 144 F2
Great Peter Street SW1P 148 B4
Great Portland Street W1W 143 L4
Great Portland Street ⊖ W1W 143 L4
Great Pulteney Street W1F 144 A7
Great Queen Street WC2B 144 D6
Great Russell Street WC1B 144 C5
Great Scotland Yard SW1A 148 C1
Great Smith Street SW1P 148 C4
Great Suffolk Street SE1 .... 149 H2
Great Sutton Street EC1V 145 H4
Great Swan Alley EC2R 145 L6
Great Titchfield Street W1W 143 M4
Great Tower Street EC3M 145 M7
Great Tower Street EC3R 150 A4
Great Winchester Street EC2N 145 L6
Great Windmill Street W1D 144 B7
Greek Street W1D 144 B6
Greenacre Square SE16 .... 151 J6
Green Bank E1W 150 E5
Greenberry Street NW8 .... 142 F1
Greencoat Place SW1P 148 A5
Greenfield Road E1 .... 150 D2
Greenham Close SE1 .... 149 G3
Green Park ⊖ W1J 147 M1
Green Street W1K 143 J7
Greenwell Street W1W 143 L4
Greet Street SE1 .... 149 G2
Grenade Street E14 .... 151 L4
Grendon Street NW8 .... 142 F3
Grenville Place SW7 .... 146 C5
Gresham Street EC2V 145 J6
Gresse Street W1T 144 B5
Greville Street EC1N 145 G5
Greycoat Place SW1P 148 B4

Greycoat Street SW1P 148 B4
Grigg's Place SE1 .... 150 A8
Grosvenor Bridge SW8 .... 147 L8
Grosvenor Crescent SW1X 147 J3
Grosvenor Crescent Mews SW1X 147 J3
Grosvenor Gardens SW1W 147 L4
Grosvenor Gardens Mews East SW1W 147 L4
Grosvenor Gardens Mews North SW1W 147 L4
Grosvenor Gardens Mews South * SW1W 147 L4
Grosvenor Gate W2 .... 143 H8
Grosvenor Hill W1K 143 L7
Grosvenor Place SW1X 147 K3
Grosvenor Road SW1V 147 L8
Grosvenor Square W1K 143 J7
Grosvenor Street W1K 143 K7
Grosvenor Terrace SE5 .... 149 J8
Grove End Road NW8 .... 142 D2
Guildhouse Street SW1V 147 M5
Guildford Street WC1N 144 D4
Guinness Square SE1 .... 149 M5
Gulliver Street SE16 .... 151 K8
Gunpowder Square EC4A 145 G6
Gun Street E1 .... 150 B1
Gunthorpe Street E1 .... 150 C2
Gutter Lane EC2V 145 J6
Guy Street SE1 .... 149 L3

H

Haberdasher Street N1 .... 145 L2
Haddonhall Estate SE1 .... 149 M4
Hainton Close E1 .... 150 F3
Halcrow Street * E1 .... 150 F2
Half Moon Street W1J 147 L1
Halford Road SW6 .... 146 A8
Halkin Place SW1X 147 J4
Halkin Street SW1X 147 K3
Hallam Street W1W 143 L5
Halley Street E14 .... 151 K1
Hallfield Estate W2 .... 142 C6
Hall Place W2 .... 142 E4
Hall Road NW8 .... 142 D2
Hall Street EC1V 145 H2
Halpin Place SE17 .... 149 M6
Halsey Street SW3 .... 147 G5
Hamilton Close NW8 .... 142 D2
Hamilton Close SE16 .... 151 K7
Hamilton Gardens NW8 .... 142 D2
Hamilton Place W1J 147 K2
Hamilton Terrace NW8 .... 142 C1
Hamlet Way SE1 .... 149 L3
Hammett Street EC3N 150 B4
Hampden Close NW1 .... 144 B1
Hampden Gurney Street W2 .... 143 H6
Hampstead Road NW1 .... 143 M2
Hampton Street SE17 .... 149 J6
Hanbury Street E1 .... 150 C1
Hand Court WC1V 144 E5
Handel Street WC1N 144 D3
Hankey Place SE1 .... 149 L3
Hannibal Road E1 .... 151 G1
Hanover Square W1S 143 L6
Hanover Street W1S 143 L7
Hans Crescent SW3 .... 147 H3
Hanson Street W1W 143 M4
Hans Place SW1X 147 H4
Hans Road SW3 .... 147 G4
Hans Street SW1X 147 H4
Hanway Place W1T 144 B6
Hanway Street W1T 144 B6
Harbet Road W2 .... 142 F5
Harcourt Street W1H 143 G5
Harcourt Terrace SW10 .... 146 C7
Hardinge Street E1W 151 G3
Hardwick Street EC1R 145 G2
Hardwidge Street SE1 .... 149 M2
Hardy Close SE16 .... 151 H6
Harewood Place W1G 143 L6
Harewood Row NW1 .... 143 G4
Harewood Avenue NW1 .... 143 G4
Harford Street E1 .... 151 J1
Harleyford Road SE11 .... 148 E8
Harley Gardens SW10 .... 146 D7
Harley Place W1G 143 K5
Harley Street W1G 143 K5
Harmsworth Street SE17 .... 149 G7
Harold Estate SE1 .... 150 A8
Harper Road SE1 .... 149 K4
Harpour Street WC1N 144 E4
Harriet Street SW1X 147 H3
Harriet Walk SW1X 147 H3
Harrington Gardens SW7 .... 146 C6
Harrington Road SW7 .... 146 E5
Harrington Square NW1 .... 143 M1
Harrington Street NW1 .... 143 M2
Harrison Street WC1H 144 D2
Harrods SW1X 147 G4
Harrowby Street W1H 143 G6
Harrow Place E1 .... 150 B2
Harrow Road W2 .... 142 A4
Hart Street EC3R 150 A3
Hasker Street SW3 .... 147 G5
Hastings Street WC1H 144 C2
Hatfields SE1 .... 149 G1
Hatherley Grove W2 .... 142 B6
Hatteraick Road SE16 .... 151 G6
Hatton Garden EC1N 145 G4
Hatton Street W2 .... 142 E4
Hatton Wall EC1N 145 G4
Havering Street E1 .... 151 H3
Haverstock Street N1 .... 145 J1
Hawke Place * SE16 .... 151 H6
Haydon Street EC3N 150 B3
Hayes Place NW1 .... 143 G4
Hay Hill W1J 143 L8
Hayles Street SE11 .... 149 H5
Haymarket SW1Y 144 B8
Hayne Street EC1A 145 J4
Hay's Lane SE1 .... 149 M1
Hay's Mews W1J 143 L8
Haywood Place EC1R 145 H3
Headfort Place SW1X 147 K3
Head Street E1 .... 151 H2
Hearnshaw Street E14 .... 151 K2
Hearn Street EC2A 145 M4
Heathcote Street WC1N 144 E3
Heddon Street W1B 143 M7
Heddon Street W1S 144 A7
Hedger Street SE11 .... 149 H5
Heiron Street SE17 .... 149 J8
Hellings Street E1W 150 D5

Helmet Row EC1V 145 K3
Helsinki Square SE16 .... 151 L8
Henderson Drive NW8 .... 142 E3
Heneage Lane EC3A 150 A3
Heneage Street E1 .... 150 C1
Henrietta Place W1G 143 L6
Henrietta Street WC2E 144 D7
Henriques Street E1 .... 150 D2
Henshaw Street SE17 .... 149 L5
Herbal Hill EC1R 145 G4
Herbert Crescent SW1X 147 H4
Herbrand Street WC1H 144 C3
Hercules Road SE1 .... 148 F4
Hereford Road W2 .... 142 A6
Hereford Square SW7 .... 146 D6
Hermitage Street W2 .... 142 E5
Hermitage Wall E1W 150 D5
Hermit Street EC1V 145 H2
Heron Place SE16 .... 151 K5
Heron Quay E14 .... 151 M5
Herrick Street SW1P 148 C6
Hertford Street W1J 147 K2
Hertsmere Road E14 .... 151 M4
Hesper Mews SW5 .... 146 B6
Hessel Street E1 .... 150 E3
Heygate Street SE17 .... 149 J5
Hide Place SW1P 148 B6
High Holborn WC1V 144 E5
High Street Kensington ⊖ W8 .... 146 A3
Hildyard Road SW6 .... 146 A8
Hilliards Court E1W 151 G4
Hillingdon Street SE17 .... 149 J8
Hill Road NW8 .... 142 D1
Hills Place W1F 143 M6
Hill Street W1J 143 K8
Hinde Street W1U 143 K6
Hind Grove E14 .... 151 M3
Hindgrove Area E14 .... 151 M3
Hithe Grove SE16 .... 151 G8
HMS Belfast SE1 .... 150 A5
Hobart Place SW1W 147 K4
Hobury Street SW10 .... 146 D8
Hogarth Road SW5 .... 146 B6
Holbein Mews SW1W 147 J6
Holbein Place SW1W 147 J6
Holborn EC1N 145 G5
Holborn ⊖ WC2B 144 E5
Holborn Circus EC1N 145 G5
Holborn Viaduct EC1A 145 G5
Holford Street WC1X 144 F2
Holland Street SE1 .... 149 H1
Holland Street W8 .... 146 A3
Hollen Street W1F 144 A6
Holles Street W1C 143 L6
Hollywood Road SW10 .... 146 C8
Holyoak Road SE11 .... 149 H5
Holyrood Street SE1 .... 149 M2
Holyrood Street SE1 .... 150 A6
Holywell Row EC2A 145 M4
Homefield Street * N1 .... 145 M1
Homer Row W1H 143 G5
Homer Street W1H 143 G5
Hooper Street E1 .... 150 D3
Hopetown Street E1 .... 150 C1
Hopkins Street W1F 144 A6
Hopton Street SE1 .... 149 H1
Hopwood Road SE17 .... 149 L8
Hornton Place W8 .... 146 A3
Hornton Street W8 .... 146 A2
Horse & Dolphin Yard W1D 144 B7
Horseferry Road E14 .... 151 J3
Horseferry Road SW1P 148 B4
Horse Guards Avenue SW1A 148 C2
Horse Guards Parade SW1A 148 C2
Horse Guards Road SW1A 148 C2
Horselydown Lane SE1 .... 150 B6
Horsley Street SE17 .... 149 K8
Hosier Lane EC1A 145 H5
Hothfield Place SE16 .... 151 G8
Hotspur Street SE11 .... 148 F6
Houghton Street WC2A 144 E6
Houndsditch EC3A 150 A2
Houses of Parliament SW1A 148 D3
Howick Place SW1E 148 A4
Howland Street W1T 144 A4
Howland Way SE16 .... 151 K7
Howley Place W2 .... 142 D4
Hoxton Square N1 .... 145 M2
Hoxton Street N1 .... 145 M1
Hudson's Place SW1V 147 M5
Hugh Mews SW1V 147 L6
Hugh Street SW1V 147 L6
Hugh Street SW1V 147 L6
Hull Close SE16 .... 151 J6
Hull Street EC1V 145 J2
Hungerford Bridge SE1 .... 148 E1
Hunter Close SE1 .... 149 M4
Hunter Street WC1N 144 D3
Huntley Street WC1E 144 A4
Huntsman Street SE17 .... 149 M6
Huntsworth Mews NW1 .... 143 H3
Hurley Crescent SE16 .... 151 H6
Hutching's Street E14 .... 151 M7
Hutton Street EC4Y 145 G7
Hyde Park W2 .... 147 G1
Hyde Park Corner W1J 147 K2
Hyde Park Corner ⊖ W1J 147 K2
Hyde Park Court SW7 .... 146 D3
Hyde Park Crescent W2 .... 142 F6
Hyde Park Gardens Mews W2 .... 142 F7
Hyde Park Gardens W2 .... 142 F7
Hyde Park Gate SW7 .... 146 C3
Hyde Park Gate SW7 .... 146 D3
Hyde Park Square W2 .... 142 F7
Hyde Park Street W2 .... 142 F7

I

Idol Lane EC3R 145 M7
Ifield Road SW10 .... 146 B8
Iliffe Street SE17 .... 149 J6
Iliffe Yard SE17 .... 149 J6
Imperial College Road SW7 .... 146 D4
Imperial War Museum SE1 .... 149 G4
India Street EC3N 150 B3
Ingestre Place W1F 144 A7
Inglebert Street EC1R 144 F2
Ingram Close SE11 .... 148 E5
Inner Circle NW1 .... 143 J2
Inverness Terrace W2 .... 142 B6
Inverness Terrace Gate W2 .... 142 C8
Invicta Plaza SE1 .... 149 H1
Inville Road SE17 .... 149 L7

Ironmonger Lane EC2V 145 K6
Ironmonger Row EC1V 145 K2
Irving Street WC2N 144 C8
Isambard Place SE16 .... 151 G6
Island Row E14 .... 151 K3
Iverna Court W8 .... 146 A4
Iverna Gardens W8 .... 146 A4
Ives Street SW3 .... 147 G5
Ivor Place NW1 .... 143 G4
Ixworth Place SW3 .... 146 F6

J

Jacob Street SE1 .... 150 C6
Jamaica Gate SE16 .... 150 F8
Jamaica Road SE1 .... 150 C7
Jamaica Road SE16 .... 150 E7
Jamaica Street E1 .... 151 G2
Jamaica Wharf SE1 .... 150 C6
James Street W1U 143 K6
James Street WC2E 144 D7
Jameson Street W8 .... 146 A1
Jamuna Close E14 .... 151 K1
Janeway Street SE16 .... 150 D7
Jardine Road E1W 151 J4
Java Wharf SE1 .... 150 C6
Jay Mews SW7 .... 146 D3
Jermyn Street SW1Y 144 A8
Jerome Crescent NW8 .... 142 F3
Jewery Street EC3N 150 B3
Joan Street SE1 .... 149 G2
Jockey's Fields WC1R 144 E4
Johanna Street SE1 .... 148 F3
John Adam Street WC2N 144 D8
John Carpenter Street EC4Y 145 G7
John Fisher Street E1 .... 150 C4
John Islip Street SW1P 148 C5
John Prince's Street W1G 143 L6
John Roll Way SE16 .... 150 D7
John Ruskin Street SE5 .... 149 J8
John's Mews WC1N 144 E4
Johnson's Place SW1V 148 A7
Johnson Street E1 .... 151 G3
John Street WC1N 144 E4
Joiner Street SE1 .... 149 L1
Jonathan Street SE11 .... 148 E6
Jubilee Place SW3 .... 147 G6
Jubilee Street E1 .... 151 G2
Jubilee Walk SE1 .... 146 B1
Judd Street WC1H 144 C2
Junction Mews W2 .... 142 F5
Juxon Street SE11 .... 148 E5

K

Katherine Close SE16 .... 151 H5
Kean Street WC2B 144 E6
Keel Close SE16 .... 151 J6
Keeley Street WC2B 144 E6
Keeton's Road SE16 .... 150 E7
Kell Street SE1 .... 149 H3
Kelso Place W8 .... 146 B4
Kemble Street WC2B 144 E6
Kempsford Gardens SW5 .... 146 A7
Kempsford Road SE11 .... 149 G6
Kendall Place W1U 143 J5
Kendal Street W2 .... 143 G6
Kennet Street E1W 150 D5
Kenning Street SE16 .... 151 G6
Kennings Way SE11 .... 149 G7
Kennington ⊖ SE11 .... 149 H7
Kennington Lane SE11 .... 148 E7
Kennington Oval SE11 .... 148 E8
Kennington Park Gardens SE11 .... 149 G8
Kennington Park Place SE11 .... 149 G7
Kennington Park Road SE11 .... 149 G7
Kennington Road SE1 .... 148 F4
Kennington Road SE11 .... 149 G5
Kennington Oval SE11 .... 148 F8
Kenrick Place W1U 143 J5
Kensington Church Street W8 .... 146 A1
Kensington Court W8 .... 146 B3
Kensington Gardens W2 .... 146 C1
Kensington Gardens Square W2 .... 142 B6
Kensington Gate W8 .... 146 C4
Kensington Gore SW7 .... 146 D3
Kensington High Street W8 .... 146 A4
Kensington Palace W8 .... 146 B2
Kensington Palace Gardens W8 .... 146 B1
Kensington Palace Gardens W8 .... 146 B2
Kensington Place W8 .... 146 A1
Kensington Road SW7 .... 147 G3
Kensington Road W8 .... 146 B3
Kensington Square W8 .... 146 B3
Kenton Street WC1H 144 C3
Kenway Road SW5 .... 146 A6
Keystone Close N1 .... 144 D1
Keyworth Street SE1 .... 149 H4
Kia Oval (Surrey County Cricket Ground) 148 F8
Kilburn Park Road NW6 .... 142 A2
Kildare Terrace W2 .... 142 A6
Killick Street N1 .... 144 E1
Kinburn Street SE16 .... 151 H6
Kinder Street E1 .... 150 E2
King & Queen Wharf SE16 .... 151 H5
King and Queen Street SE17 .... 149 K6
King Charles Street SW1A 148 C2
King David Lane E1 .... 151 G3
Kingdom Street W2 .... 142 C5
King Edward Street EC1A 145 J6
King Edward Walk SE1 .... 149 G4
King James Street SE1 .... 149 H3
Kingly Street W1F 143 M7
King's Arms Yard EC2R 145 L6
King's Bench Street SE1 .... 149 H2
Kingscote Street EC4V 145 H7
King's Cross ⇌ N1C 144 C1
King's Cross Road WC1X 144 E2
King's Cross Square N1C 144 D1
King's Cross St Pancras ⊖ N1C 144 D1
Kingsgate Walk * SW1E 148 A4
King's Head Yard SE1 .... 149 L1
King's Mews WC1N 144 F4
Kingsmill Terrace NW8 .... 142 E1
King Square EC1V 145 J2
King's Road SW3 .... 146 E8
King's Scholars Passage SW1P 147 M5
King's Stairs Close SE16 .... 150 F6
King Street WC2E 144 D7
King Street SW1Y 148 A1
King Street EC2V 145 K6

Oval Way SE11 .... 148 E7
Ovington Square SW3 .... 147 G4
Ovington Street SW3 .... 147 G5
Owen Street EC1V 145 G1
Oxendon Street SW1Y 144 B8
Oxford Circus W1B 143 M6
Oxford Road NW6 .... 142 A1
Oxford Square W2 .... 142 F6
Oxford Street W1C 143 L6
Oxford Street WC1A 144 A6

P

Pace Place E1 .... 150 E3
Pacific Wharf SE16 .... 151 H5
Paddington ⇌ W2 .... 142 D6
Paddington Green W2 .... 142 E6
Paddington Street W1U 143 J5
Pageant Crescent SE16 .... 151 J5
Page Street SW1P 148 B5
Paget Street EC1V 145 H1
Pakenham Street WC1X 144 E3
Palace Avenue W8 .... 146 B2
Palace Court W2 .... 142 A7
Palace Gardens Terrace W8 .... 146 C3
Palace Gate W8 .... 146 D3
Palace Green W8 .... 146 B2
Palace of Westminster SW1A 148 D3
Palace Place SW1E 147 M4
Palace Street SW1E 147 M4
Pall Mall SW1Y 148 A1
Pall Mall East SW1Y 148 B1
Palmer Street SW1H 148 B3
Pancras Lane EC4N 145 K6
Pancras Road N1C 144 C1
Panton Street SW1Y 144 B8
Paradise Street SE16 .... 150 E7
Paradise Walk SW3 .... 147 H8
Pardoner Street SE1 .... 149 L4
Pardon Street EC1V 145 H3
Parfett Street E1 .... 150 D2
Paris Garden SE1 .... 149 H8
Park Crescent W1B 143 K4
Park Crescent Mews West W1G 143 K4
Parker's Row SE1 .... 150 C7
Parker Street WC2B 144 D6
Park Lane W1K 143 H7
Park Lane W2 .... 147 J1
Park Place SW1A 147 M1
Park Place Villas W2 .... 142 D4
Park Road NW1 .... 143 H3
Park Square East NW1 .... 143 L3
Park Square Mews NW1 .... 143 K3
Park Square West NW1 .... 143 K3
Park Street SE1 .... 149 K1
Park Street W1K 143 J7
Park Village East NW1 .... 143 L1
Park Walk SW10 .... 146 D8
Park West Place W2 .... 143 G6
Parliament Street SW1A 148 C2
Parry Street SW8 .... 148 D8
Passmore Street SW1W 147 J6
Pater Street W8 .... 146 A4
Paternoster Square EC4 .... 145 J6
Paul Street EC2A 145 M3
Paultons Square SW3 .... 146 E8
Paveley Street NW1 .... 143 G3
Pavilion Road SW1X 147 H3
Pavilion Street SW1X 147 H4
Paxton Terrace SW1V 147 L7
Peabody Avenue SW1V 147 L7
Peabody Estate SE1 .... 149 J1
Peacock Street SE17 .... 149 H6
Pearl Street E1W 150 F5
Pearman Street SE1 .... 149 G3
Peartree Lane E1W 151 G4
Pear Tree Street EC1V 145 J3
Peel Street W8 .... 146 A1
Peerless Street EC1V 145 L2
Pelham Crescent SW7 .... 146 F6
Pelham Place SW7 .... 146 F5
Pelham Street SW7 .... 146 F5
Pelier Street SE17 .... 149 K8
Pemberton Row EC4A 145 G6
Pembridge Gardens W2 .... 142 A8
Pembridge Place W2 .... 142 A7
Pembridge Square W2 .... 142 A8
Pembridge Villas W11 .... 142 A7
Pembroke Close SW1X 147 J3
Penang Street E1W 150 F5
Penfold Place NW8 .... 142 F5
Penfold Street NW8 .... 142 E4
Pennant Mews W8 .... 146 B5
Pennington Street E1W 150 D4
Pennyfields E14 .... 151 M4
Penrose Grove SE17 .... 149 J7
Penrose Street SE17 .... 149 J7
Penton Place SE17 .... 149 H6
Penton Rise WC1X 144 E2
Penton Street N1 .... 144 F1
Pentonville Road N1 .... 144 E1
Penywern Road SW5 .... 146 A6
Pepper Street SE1 .... 149 J2
Pepys Street EC3N 150 A4
Percival Street EC1V 145 H3
Percy Circus WC1X 144 F2
Percy Street W1T 144 B5
Perkin's Rents SW1P 148 B4
Perryn Road SE16 .... 150 E7
Petersham Mews SW7 .... 146 D4
Petersham Place SW7 .... 146 C4
Peter Street W1F 144 B7
Peto Place NW1 .... 143 L3
Petticoat Lane E1 .... 150 B2
Petty France SW1H 148 A3
Petty Wales EC3R 150 A4
Petyward SW3 .... 147 G6
Phelp Street SE17 .... 149 L7
Phene Street SW3 .... 147 G8
Phillimore Walk W8 .... 146 A3
Philpot Lane EC3M 145 M7
Philpot Street E1 .... 150 E2
Phipp's Mews SW1W 147 L5
Phipp Street EC2A 145 M3
Phoenix Place WC1X 144 E3
Phoenix Road NW1 .... 144 B2
Phoenix Street WC2H 144 C6
Piccadilly W1J 147 L2
Piccadilly Arcade SW1Y 147 M1
Piccadilly Circus W1B 144 B8
Piccadilly Circus ⊖ W1J 144 B8
Pickard Street EC1V 145 J2

Picton Place W1U 143 K6
Pier Head E1W 150 E6
Pigott Street E14 .... 151 M3
Pilgrimage Street SE1 .... 149 L3
Pimlico ⊖ SW1V 148 B6
Pimlico Road SW1W 147 J6
Pinchin Street E1 .... 150 D3
Pindar Street EC2A 145 M4
Pindock Mews W9 .... 142 B3
Pine Street EC1R 144 F3
Pitfield Street N1 .... 145 M1
Pitsea Street E1 .... 151 H3
Pitt's Head Mews W1J 147 K2
Pitt Street W8 .... 146 A2
Pixley Street E14 .... 151 L2
Platina Street * EC2A 145 L3
Plover Way SE16 .... 151 K8
Plumbers Row E1 .... 150 D2
Plumtree Court EC4A 145 G5
Plympton Street NW8 .... 142 F4
Pocock Street SE1 .... 149 H2
Poland Street W1F 144 A6
Pollen Street W1S 143 L7
Pollitt Drive NW8 .... 142 E3
Polperro Mews SE11 .... 149 G5
Polygon Road NW1 .... 144 B1
Pond Place SW3 .... 146 F6
Ponler Street E1 .... 150 E3
Ponsonby Place SW1P 148 C6
Ponsonby Terrace SW1P 148 C6
Ponton Road * SW1V 148 B8
Pont Street SW1X 147 H4
Poolmans Street SE16 .... 151 H6
Pope Street SE1 .... 150 B7
Poplar Place W2 .... 142 B7
Poppin's Court EC4A 145 H6
Porchester Gardens W2 .... 142 B7
Porchester Gate W2 .... 142 C8
Porchester Place W2 .... 143 G6
Porchester Road W2 .... 142 B5
Porchester Square W2 .... 142 B6
Porchester Terrace W2 .... 142 C7
Porchester Terrace
    North W2 .... 142 C6
Porlock Street SE1 .... 149 L3
Porter Street NW1 .... 143 H4
Porteus Road W2 .... 142 D5
Portland Place W1B 143 L4
Portland Place W1B 143 L5
Portland Square E1W 150 E5
Portland Street SE17 .... 149 L7
Portman Close W1H 143 J6
Portman Mews South W1H 143 J6
Portman Square W1H 143 J6
Portman Street W1H 143 J6
Portpool Lane EC1N 144 F4
Portsea Place W2 .... 143 G6
Portsmouth Street WC2A 144 E6
Portsoken Street E1 .... 150 B3
Portugal Street WC2A 144 E6
Potier Street SE1 .... 149 L4
Potters Fields SE1 .... 150 B6
Pottery Street SE16 .... 150 E7
Poultry EC2V 145 K6
Powis Place WC1N 144 D4
Praed Mews W2 .... 142 E6
Praed Street W2 .... 142 E6
Pratt Walk SE1 .... 148 E5
Premier Place E14 .... 151 M4
Prescot Street E1 .... 150 C3
Preston Close SE1 .... 149 M5
Price's Street SE1 .... 149 H1
Prideaux Place WC1X 144 F2
Primrose Street EC2A 150 A1
Prince Albert Road NW8 .... 142 F1
Prince Consort Road SW7 .... 146 D3
Princelet Street E1 .... 150 C1
Prince of Wales Gate SW7 .... 146 F3
Princes Arcade SW1Y 144 A8
Prince's Gardens SW7 .... 146 E3
Prince's Gate Mews SW7 .... 146 E4
Princes Riverside
    Road SE16 .... 151 H5
Prince's Square W2 .... 142 A7
Princess Road NW6 .... 142 A1
Princess Street SE1 .... 149 H4
Princess Street W1B 143 L6
Prince's Street EC2R 145 L6
Princeton Street WC1R 144 E5
Prioress Street SE1 .... 149 L4
Priory Green Estate N1 .... 144 E1
Priory Walk SW10 .... 146 D7
Proctor Street WC1V 144 E5
Prospect Place E1W 151 G5
Prospect Street SE16 .... 150 E7
Provident Court W1K 143 J7
Provost Street N1 .... 145 L1
Prusom Street E1W 150 F5
Pudding Lane EC3R 145 M7
Pumphouse Mews E1 .... 150 D3
Purbrook Street SE1 .... 150 A7
Purcell Street N1 .... 145 M1
Purchese Street NW1 .... 144 B1

Q

Quebec Way SE16 .... 151 J7
Queen Anne's Gate SW1H 148 B3
Queen Anne Street W1G 143 K5
Queen Elizabeth Street SE1 .... 150 B6
Queen Mother Gate W2 .... 147 J2
Queensborough Terrace W2 .... 142 C7
Queensbury Place SW7 .... 146 E5
Queen's Gardens W2 .... 142 C7
Queen's Gate SW7 .... 146 D3
Queen's Gate SW7 .... 146 D4
Queen's Gate Gardens SW7 .... 146 D5
Queen's Gate Mews SW7 .... 146 D4
Queen's Gate Place SW7 .... 146 D4
Queen's
    Place Mews SW7 .... 146 D4
Queen's Gate Terrace SW7 .... 146 C4
Queen's Mews W2 .... 142 B7
Queen Square WC1N 144 D4
Queen's Row SE17 .... 149 K7
Queen Street EC4N 145 K7
Queen Street W1J 147 L1
Queen Street Place EC4R 145 K7
Queen's Walk SE1 .... 150 A5
Queen's Walk SW1A 147 M2
Queensway W2 .... 142 B6
Queensway ⊖ W2 .... 142 B8
Queen Victoria Street EC4V 145 J7
Quick Street N1 .... 145 H1

R

Raby Street E14 .... 151 K2
Radcliffe Road SE1 .... 150 B8
Radcot Street SE11 .... 149 G7
Radnor Mews W2 .... 142 E6
Radnor Place W2 .... 142 F6
Radnor Street EC1V 145 K3
Radnor Walk SW3 .... 147 G7
Railway Approach SE1 .... 149 L1
Railway Avenue SE16 .... 151 G6
Railway Street N1 .... 144 D1
Raine Street E1W 150 F5
Ralston Street SW3 .... 147 H7
Ramillies Place W1F 143 M6
Ramillies Street W1F 143 M6
Rampart Street E1 .... 150 E2
Rampayne Street SW1V 148 B6
Randall Road SE11 .... 148 D6
Randall Row SE11 .... 148 E6
Randolph Avenue W9 .... 142 B1
Randolph Crescent W9 .... 142 C3
Randolph Gardens NW6 .... 142 B1
Randolph Mews W9 .... 142 D4
Randolph Road W9 .... 142 C4
Ranelagh Grove SW1W 147 K6
Ranelagh Road SW1V 148 A7
Rangoon Street * EC3N 150 B3
Ranston Street NW8 .... 142 F4
Raphael Street SW7 .... 147 G3
Ratcliffe Cross Street E1W 151 J3
Ratcliffe Lane E14 .... 151 J3
Rathbone Place W1T 144 B5
Rathbone Street W1T 144 A5
Raven Row E1 .... 150 F1
Ravensdon Street SE11 .... 149 G7
Ravey Street EC2A 145 M3
Rawlings Street SW3 .... 147 G5
Rawstorne Street EC1V 145 H2
Ray Street EC1R 145 G4
Reardon Place E1W 150 F5
Reardon Street E1W 150 E5
Redan Place W2 .... 142 B6
Redburn Street SW3 .... 147 G7
Redcastle Close E1W 151 G4
Redcliffe Gardens SW10 .... 146 B7
Redcliffe Mews SW10 .... 146 C7
Redcliffe Place SW10 .... 146 C8
Redcliffe Road SW10 .... 146 D7
Redcliffe Square SW10 .... 146 B7
Redcliffe Street SW10 .... 146 B8
Redcross Way SE1 .... 149 K2
Redesdale Street SW3 .... 147 G7
Redfield Lane SW5 .... 146 A5
Redhill Street NW1 .... 143 L1
Red Lion Row SE5 .... 149 K8
Red Lion Square WC1R 144 E5
Red Lion Street WC2B 144 E5
Redman's Road E1 .... 151 G1
Red Place W1K 143 J7
Redriff Road SE16 .... 151 J8
Reedworth Street SE11 .... 149 G6
Reeves Mews W1K 143 J8
Regal Close E1 .... 150 D1
Regan Way N1 .... 145 M1
Regency Street SW1P 148 B5
Regent Place W1B 144 A7
Regent's Park ⊖ W1B 143 L4
Regent's Park NW1 .... 143 J1
Regent's Park Estate NW1 .... 143 L2
Regent Square WC1H 144 D2
Regent Street SW1Y 144 B8
Regent Street W1S 143 M7
Relton Mews SW7 .... 147 G4
Remington Street N1 .... 145 H1
Remnant Street WC2A 144 E6
Renforth Street SE16 .... 151 G7
Renfrew Road SE11 .... 149 H5
Rennie Street SE1 .... 149 H1
Rephidim Street SE1 .... 149 M4
Repton Street E14 .... 151 K2
Reveley Square SE16 .... 151 K7
Rex Place W1K 143 J8
Rhodeswell Road E14 .... 151 L2
Rich Street E14 .... 151 M3
Rickett Street SW6 .... 146 A8
Ridgemount Street WC1E 144 B4
Ridgemount Gardens WC1E 144 B4
Riding House Street W1W 143 M5
Riley Road SE1 .... 150 B7
Ripley's Believe It or Not! W1J 144 B8
Risborough Street SE1 .... 149 J2
Risdon Street SE16 .... 151 G7
Rissinghill Street N1 .... 144 F1
River Street EC1R 144 F2
Rivington Street EC2A 145 M3
Robert Adam Street W1U 143 J6
Roberts Close SE16 .... 151 J7
Robert Street NW1 .... 143 L2
Rochester Row SW1P 148 B5
Rochester Street SW1P 148 B4
Rockingham Street SE1 .... 149 J4
Rocliffe Street N1 .... 145 H1
Roding Mews E1W 150 D5
Rodmarton Street W1U 143 H5
Rodney Place SE17 .... 149 K5
Rodney Road SE17 .... 149 K5
Rodney Street N1 .... 144 E1
Roger Street WC1N 144 E4
Roland Gardens SW7 .... 146 D6
Roland Way SE17 .... 149 L7
Romford Street E1 .... 150 E2
Romilly Street W1D 144 B7
Romney Street SW1P 148 C5
Rood Lane EC3M 145 M7
Ropemaker Road SE16 .... 151 K7
Ropemaker Street EC2Y 145 L4
Roper Lane SE1 .... 150 B7
Rope Street SE16 .... 151 K8
Rope Walk Gardens E1 .... 150 E2
Rosary Gardens SW7 .... 146 D6
Roscoe Street EC1Y 145 K3
Rose Alley SE1 .... 145 K8
Rosebery Avenue EC1R 144 F3
Rosemoor Street SW3 .... 147 G6
Rose Street WC2E 144 C7
Rossmore Road NW1 .... 143 G3
Rotherhithe ⊖ SE16 .... 151 H6
Rotherhithe Street SE16 .... 151 G6
Rotherhithe Street SE16 .... 151 J4
Rotherhithe Tunnel SE16 .... 151 H5
Rothsay Street SE1 .... 149 M4
Rotten Row W2 .... 146 F2

Rouel Road SE16 .... 150 C8
Roupell Street SE1 .... 149 G2
Royal Albert Hall SW7 .... 146 E3
Royal Avenue SW3 .... 147 H6
Royal Hospital Road SW3 .... 147 H7
Royal Mint Street E1 .... 150 C4
Royal Oak ⊖ W2 .... 142 B5
Royal Oak Yard SE1 .... 150 A7
Royal Opera House WC2E 144 D7
Royal Road SE17 .... 149 H8
Royal Street SE1 .... 148 E3
Rudolph Road NW6 .... 142 A1
Rugby Street WC1N 144 E4
Rum Close E1W 150 F4
Rupack Street SE16 .... 150 F7
Rupert Street W1D 144 B7
Rushworth Street SE1 .... 149 H2
Russell Court SW1A 148 A2
Russell Square WC1B 144 C4
Russell Square ⊖ WC1B 144 D4
Russell Street WC2B 144 D7
Russia Dock Road SE16 .... 151 K6
Rutherford Street SW1P 148 B5
Rutland Gardens SW7 .... 147 G3
Rutland Gate SW7 .... 146 F3
Rutland Mews SW7 .... 146 F4
Rutland Street SW7 .... 146 F4
Ryder Street SW1Y 148 A1

S

Sackville Street W1S 144 A8
Saffron Hill EC1N 145 G4
Saffron Street EC1N 145 G4
Sail Street SE11 .... 148 F5
St Agnes Place SE11 .... 149 G8
St Alban's Grove W8 .... 146 B4
St Alban's Street SW1Y 144 B8
St Alphage Garden EC2Y 145 K5
St Andrews Hill EC4V 145 H7
St Andrew's Place NW1 .... 143 L3
St Andrew Street EC4A 145 G5
St Anne's Court W1F 144 B6
St Ann's Street SW1P 148 C4
St Anselm's Place W1K 143 K7
St Barnabas Street SW1W 147 K6
St Botolph Street EC3N 150 B2
St Bride Street EC4A 145 G6
St Chad's Street WC1H 144 D2
St Clare Street EC3N 150 B3
St Clements Lane WC2A 144 E6
St Cross Street EC1N 145 G4
St Dunstan's Hill EC3R 145 M8
St Dunstan's Lane EC3R 145 M7
St Elmos Road SE16 .... 151 J7
St Ermin's Hill SW1H 148 B3
St George's Circus SE1 .... 149 H3
St George's Drive SW1V 147 M6
St George's Estate E1 .... 150 D3
St George's Lane * EC3R 145 M7
St George's Road SE1 .... 149 G4
St George's Square SW1V 148 B7
St George Street W1S 143 L7
St Giles High Street WC2H 144 C6
St Helen's Place EC3A 145 M6
St James Market * SW1Y 144 B8
St James's Park ⊖ SW1H 148 B3
St James's Park SW1A 148 B3
St James's Place SW1A 147 M2
St James's Road SE16 .... 150 D8
St James's Square SW1Y 148 A1
St James's Street SW1A 147 M1
St James Walk EC1R 145 G3
St John's Lane EC1M 145 H4
St John's Place EC1M 145 H4
St John's Square EC1V 145 H4
St John Street EC1V 145 H2
St John's Wood High Street NW8 .... 142 F1
St John's Wood Road NW8 .... 142 E3
St Katharine's Way E1W 150 C5
St Leonard's Terrace SW3 .... 147 H7
St Loo Avenue SW3 .... 147 G8
St Luke's Close EC1V 145 K3
St Luke's Street SW3 .... 146 F6
St Manningtree E1 .... 150 C2
St Mark Street E1 .... 150 C3
St Martin's Lane WC2N 144 C7
St Martin's le Grand EC1A 145 J6
St Martin's Street WC2N 144 C8
St Mary at Hill EC3R 145 M8
St Mary Axe EC3A 150 A3
St Marychurch Street SE16 .... 150 F7
St Mary's Gardens SE11 .... 149 G5
St Mary's Terrace W2 .... 142 D4
St Mary's Walk SE11 .... 149 G5
St Matthew Street SW1P 148 B4
St Michael's Street W2 .... 142 F6
St Olav's Square SE16 .... 150 F7
St Oswald's Place SE11 .... 148 E7
St Oswulf Street * SW1P 148 C6
St Pancras International ⇌ N1C 144 C1
St Paul's ⊖ EC1A 145 J6
St Paul's Avenue SE16 .... 151 J5
St Paul's Cathedral EC4M 145 J6
St Paul's Churchyard EC4M 145 J6
St Paul's Way E1 .... 151 L1
St Petersburgh Mews W2 .... 142 B7
St Petersburgh Place W2 .... 142 B7
St Saviours Wharf SE1 .... 150 C6
St Stephen's Gardens W2 .... 142 A5
St Swithin's Lane EC4N 145 L7
St Thomas Street SE1 .... 149 L2
St Vincent Street W1U 143 J5
Salamanca Street SE11 .... 148 D6
Salem Road W2 .... 142 B7
Sale Place W2 .... 142 F6
Salisbury Court EC4Y 145 G6
Salisbury Place W1H 143 H4
Salisbury Street NW8 .... 142 F4
Salmon Lane E14 .... 151 J2
Salter Road SE16 .... 151 J5
Salter Street E14 .... 151 M4
Samford Street NW8 .... 142 F4
Sampson Street E1W 150 D5
Sancroft Street SE11 .... 148 F6
Sandland Street WC1R 144 E5
Sandpiper Close SE16 .... 151 L6
Sandwich Street WC1H 144 C2
Sandy's Row E1 .... 150 B1
Sans Walk EC1R 145 G3
Sardinia Street WC2A 144 E6
Savage Gardens EC3N 150 B3
Savile Row W1S 143 M7
Savoy Hill WC2R 144 E8

Savoy Place WC2R 144 D8
Savoy Street WC2E 144 E7
Sawyer Street SE1 .... 149 J2
Scala Street W1T 144 A5
Scandrett Street E1W 150 E5
Scarborough Street E1 .... 150 C3
Scarsdale Villas W8 .... 146 A4
Schooner Close * SE16 .... 151 H6
Science Museum SW7 .... 146 E4
Scoresby Street SE1 .... 149 H2
Scotch House Junction SW1X 147 H3
Scotland Place SW1A 148 C1
Scott Ellis Gardens NW8 .... 142 E2
Scott Lidgett Crescent SE16 .... 150 D7
Scrutton Street EC2A 145 M3
Seaford Street WC1H 144 D2
Seagrave Road SW6 .... 146 A8
Sea Life London Aquarium SE1 .... 148 E3
Searles Road SE1 .... 149 L5
Sebastian Street EC1V 145 H2
Secker Street SE1 .... 148 F2
Sedan Way SE17 .... 149 M6
Sedding Street SW1X 147 J5
Seddon Street WC1X 144 E3
Seething Lane EC3N 150 A4
Sekforde Street EC1R 145 H3
Selfridges W1A 143 J6
Selsey Street E14 .... 151 M1
Selwood Place SW7 .... 146 E6
Semley Place SW1W 147 K6
Senior Street W2 .... 142 B4
Senrab Street E1 .... 151 H2
Serle Street WC2A 144 F5
Serpentine Bridge W2 .... 146 E1
Serpentine Road W2 .... 146 F1
Seth Street SE16 .... 151 G7
Settles Street E1 .... 150 D2
Seven Dials WC2H 144 C6
Seville Street SW1X 147 H3
Sevington Street W9 .... 142 A3
Seward Street EC1V 145 J3
Seymour Mews W1H 143 J6
Seymour Place W1H 143 G5
Seymour Street W2 .... 143 G6
Seymour Street W2 .... 143 G7
Seymour Walk SW10 .... 146 C7
Shad Thames SE1 .... 150 B6
Shad Thames SE1 .... 150 C6
Shadwell ⊖ E1 .... 150 F3
Shadwell Gardens E1 .... 150 F3
Shaftesbury Avenue W1D 144 B7
Shaftesbury Avenue WC2H 144 C6
Shaftesbury Street N1 .... 145 K1
Shakespeare's Globe SE1 .... 145 J8
Shand Street SE1 .... 150 A6
Sharsted Street SE17 .... 149 H7
Shaw Crescent E14 .... 151 K2
Shawfield Street SW3 .... 147 G7
Sheffield Terrace W8 .... 146 A2
Sheldon Square W2 .... 142 D5
Shelmerdine Close E3 .... 151 M1
Shelton Street WC2H 144 D6
Shepherdess Walk N1 .... 145 K1
Shepherd Street W1J 147 K1
Sheraton Street W1F 144 B6
Sherborne Lane EC4N 145 L7
Sherwood Street W1D 144 A7
Ship and Mermaid Row SE1 .... 149 M2
Shipwright Road SE16 .... 151 K7
Shirland Road W9 .... 142 A3
Shoe Lane EC4A 145 G5
Shorter Street EC3N 150 B4
Shorts Gardens WC2H 144 C6
Short Street SE1 .... 149 G2
Shoulder of Mutton Alley E14 .... 151 K3
Shouldham Street W1H 143 G5
Shroton Street NW1 .... 142 F4
Siddons Lane W1H 143 H4
Sidmouth Street WC1N 144 D3
Sidney Square E1 .... 150 F2
Sidney Street E1 .... 150 F1
Silex Street SE1 .... 149 H3
Silk Street EC2Y 145 K4
Silver Walk SE16 .... 151 K5
Silvester Street SE1 .... 149 K3
Singer Street EC2A 145 L2
Sir John Soane's Museum WC2A 144 E5
Sir Simon Milton Square SW1V 147 L4
Skinner Place * SW1W 147 J6
Skinners Lane EC4V 145 K7
Skinner Street EC1R 145 G3
Slippers Place SE16 .... 150 F8
Sloane Avenue SW3 .... 147 G6
Sloane Court East SW3 .... 147 J6
Sloane Court West SW3 .... 147 J6
Sloane Gardens SW1W 147 J6
Sloane Square ⊖ SW1W 147 J6
Sloane Street SW1X 147 H3
Sloane Terrace SW1X 147 J5
Smeaton Street E1W 150 E5
Smithfield Street EC1A 145 H5
Smith Square SW1P 148 C4
Smith Street SW3 .... 147 G7
Smith Terrace SW3 .... 147 G7
Smithy Street E1 .... 151 G1
Snowden Street EC2A 145 M4
Snow Hill EC1A 145 H5
Snowsfields SE1 .... 149 L2
Soho Square W1D 144 B6
Soho Street W1D 144 B6
Somerford Way SE16 .... 151 K7
Somers Crescent W2 .... 142 F6
Somerset House WC2R 144 E7
Somerstown Estate NW1 .... 144 A1
Sondes Street SE17 .... 149 L7
South & West Africa Gate SW1A 148 A3
Southall Place SE1 .... 149 L3
Southampton Buildings WC2A 144 F5
Southampton Place WC1A 144 D5
Southampton Row WC1B 144 D4
Southampton Street WC2E 144 D7
South Audley Street W1K 143 K8
South Carriage Drive SW1X 147 H3
South Carriage Drive SW7 .... 146 F3
South Eaton Place SW1W 147 J5
Southern Street N1 .... 144 E1
South Kensington ⊖ SW7 .... 146 E6
South Kensington ⊖ SW7 .... 146 E5
South Lambeth Road SW8 .... 148 D8
South Molton Lane W1K 143 K7
South Molton Street W1K 143 K7
South Parade SW3 .... 146 E7
South Place EC2M 145 L4
South Sea Street SE16 .... 151 L8
South Square WC1R 144 F5

South Street W1K...............147 J1
South Tenter Street E1...........150 C3
South Terrace SW7..............146 F5
Southwark SE1.................149 H2
Southwark Bridge SE1...........145 K8
Southwark Bridge Road SE1......149 J3
Southwark Street SE1...........149 H1
Southwell Gardens SW7.........146 C5
South Wharf Road W2...........142 E6
Southwick Mews W2.............142 F6
Southwick Place W2.............142 F6
Southwick Street W2............142 F6
Sovereign Close E1W............150 F4
Sovereign Crescent SE16........151 J4
Spanish Place W1U.............143 J5
Spa Road SE1..................150 C8
Spear Mews SW5...............146 A6
Spelman Street E1..............150 C1
Spence Close SE16.............151 K7
Spencer Street EC1V............145 H2
Spenser Street SW1E............148 A4
Spert Street E14...............151 J4
Spital Square E1...............150 A1
Spring Gardens SW1A...........148 C1
Spring Street W2...............142 E6
Spurgeon Street SE1............149 L4
Spur Road SE1.................148 F3
Stables Way SE11..............148 F7
Stable Yard Road SW1A.........148 A2
Stacey Street WC2H............144 C6
Stafford Place SW1E............147 M3
Stafford Road NW6.............142 A2
Stafford Street W1S............143 M8
Stafford Terrace W8............146 A3
Stainer Street SE1..............149 L2
Staining Lane EC2V............145 K6
Stainsby Road E14.............151 M2
Stalham Street SE16............150 F8
Stamford Street SE1............149 G1
Stanford Place SE1.............149 M6
Stanford Road W8..............146 B4
Stanhope Close * SE16..........151 H6
Stanhope Gardens SW7.........146 C5
Stanhope Gate W1K............147 K1
Stanhope Mews SW7............146 C5
Stanhope Mews East SW7.......146 D5
Stanhope Mews West SW7.......146 C5
Stanhope Place W2.............143 G7
Stanhope Place Gate W2.........143 G7
Stanhope Row W1J.............147 K1
Stanhope Street NW1...........143 M1
Stanhope Terrace W2...........142 E7
Stannary Street SE11...........149 G7
Staples Close SE16.............151 J5
Staple Street SE1..............149 L3
Starcross Street NW1...........144 A2
Star Street W2.................142 F6
Station Approach SE1...........148 F3
Stave Yard Road SE16...........151 J5
Stead Street SE17..............149 K6
Steedman Street SE17...........149 J5
Steel's Lane E1................151 G3
Steeres Way SE16..............151 K7
Stephenson Way NW1...........144 A3
Stephen Street W1T............144 B5
Stepney Green E1..............151 H1
Stepney High Street E1.........151 J1
Stepney Way E1................150 E1
Sterling Street SW7............147 G3
Stevedore Street E1W..........150 E5
Stevens Street SE1.............150 A7
Steward Street * E1.............150 B1
Stewart's Grove SW3...........146 F6
Stew Lane EC4V...............145 J7
Stillington Street SW1P.........148 A5
Stockholm Way E1W...........150 D5
Stocks Place E14..............151 M3
Stone Buildings WC2A..........144 F5
Stonecutter Street EC4A........145 G6
Stoney Lane E1................150 B2
Stoney Street SE1.............149 K1
Stopford Road SE17............149 J7
Store Street WC1E.............144 B5
Storey's Gate SW1H............148 C3
Storks Road SE16..............150 D8
Stoughton Close SE11..........148 E6
Stourcliffe Street W1H..........143 G6
Strafford Street E14............151 M6
Strand WC2R.................144 D8
Stratford Place W1C............143 K6
Stratford Road W8.............146 A5
Strathearn Place W2............142 F7
Stratton Street W1J............147 L1
Strutton Ground SW1P.........148 B4
Strype Street E1...............150 B2
Stuart Road NW6..............142 A2
Stukeley Street WC2B..........144 D6
Sturgeon Street SE17..........149 J7
Sturge Street SE1.............149 J3
Sturt Street N1...............145 K1
Stutfield Street E1.............150 D3
Sudley Street N1..............145 H1
Sudrey Street SE1.............149 J3
Suffolk Lane EC4V.............145 L7
Suffolk Street SW1Y...........144 B8
Sugar Lane SE16..............150 D7
Sugar Quay Walk EC3R.........150 A4
Sullivan Road SE11............149 G5
Summercourt Road E1..........151 G2
Summers Street EC1R..........144 F4
Sumner Place SW7.............146 E6
Sumner Street SE1............149 J1
Sunderland Terrace W2.........142 A6
Sun Passage SE16.............150 D8
Sun Street EC2M..............145 M4
Sun Street Passage EC2M.......145 M5
Surrendale Place W9............142 A4
Surrey Quays Road SE16........151 H7
Surrey Row SE1...............149 H2
Surrey Square SE17............149 M6
Surrey Street WC2E............144 E7
Surrey Water Road SE16........151 H6
Sussex Gardens W2............142 E6
Sussex Mews East W2..........142 E7
Sussex Place NW1.............143 H3
Sussex Place W2..............142 E6
Sussex Square W2.............142 E7
Sussex Street SW1V............147 L7
Sutherland Avenue W9.........142 A4
Sutherland Row SW1V..........147 L6
Sutherland Square SE17........149 J7
Sutherland Street SW1V........147 L7
Sutton Row W1D..............144 B6
Sutton Street E1...............151 G3

Suttons Way EC1Y.............145 K4
Swain Street NW8.............142 F3
Swallow Place W1B............143 L6
Swallow Street W1B............144 A8
Swan Lane EC4R..............145 L8
Swan Mead SE1...............149 M4
Swan Road SE16..............151 G6
Swan Street SE1..............149 L2
Swan Walk SW3...............147 H8
Swedenborg Gardens E1........150 E4
Sweeney Crescent SE1.........150 C7
Swinton Street WC1X..........144 E2
Sydney Place SW7.............146 F6
Sydney Street SW3............146 F6
Symons Street SW3............147 H6

T

Tabard Gardens Estate SE1......149 L3
Tabard Street SE1.............149 L3
Tabernacle Street EC2A.........145 L3
Tachbrook Street SW1V........148 A6
Talbot Road W2...............142 A6
Talbot Square W2.............142 E6
Talbot Yard SE1..............149 L2
Tallis Street EC4Y.............145 G7
Tamworth Street SW6..........146 A8
Tanner Street SE1.............150 A7
Taplow Street N1..............145 K1
Tarling Street E1..............150 F3
Tarver Road SE17.............149 H7
Tatum Street SE17............149 M6
Taunton Place NW1............143 G3
Tavistock Place WC1H.........144 C3
Tavistock Square WC1H........144 C3
Tavistock Street WC2E.........144 D7
Taviton Street WC1H...........144 B3
Teak Close SE16..............151 K6
Tedworth Square SW3.........147 G7
Telford Terrace SW1V..........147 M7
Temeraire Street SE16.........151 G6
Temple ⊖ WC2R..............144 F7
Temple Avenue EC4Y..........145 G7
Temple Lane EC4Y............145 G7
Temple Place WC2R...........144 F7
Templeton Place SW5..........146 A5
Tench Street E1W.............150 E5
Tenniel Close W2.............142 C7
Tennis Street SE1.............149 L2
Tenterden Street W1S..........143 L6
Teredo Street SE16............151 J8
Terminus Place SW1V..........147 L4
Thame Road SE16.............151 H6
Thanet Street WC1H...........144 C2
Thavies Inn EC4A.............145 G6
Thayer Street W1U............143 K5
The Arches WC2N.............144 D8
The Boltons SW10.............146 C7
The Broad Walk W2............142 B8
The Broad Walk W8............146 C2
The Cut SE1.................149 G2
The Flower Walk W2...........146 D3
The Grange SE1...............150 B8
The Highway E1W.............150 E4
The Little Boltons SW10........146 C7
The Mall SW1A...............148 B2
The Mitre E14................151 L3
The Vale SW3................146 E8
Thirleby Road SW1P...........148 A4
Thomas More Street E1W.......150 D4
Thomas Road E14.............151 M2
Thoresby Street N1............145 K1
Thorney Street SW1P..........148 C5
Thornton Place W1H...........143 H4
Thrale Street SE1.............149 K1
Thrawl Street E1..............150 C1
Threadneedle Street EC2R......145 L6
Three Colt Street E14..........151 L3
Three Oak Lane SE1...........150 B6
Throgmorton Avenue EC2N.....145 L6
Throgmorton Street EC2N......145 L6
Thurland Road SE16...........150 D8
Thurloe Place SW7............146 F5
Thurloe Square SW7...........146 F5
Thurloe Street SW7............146 E5
Thurlow Street SE17...........149 M7
Tichbourne Row W2...........142 F6
Tiller Road E14...............151 M8
Tillman Street E1.............150 E3
Tilney Street W1J.............147 K1
Timber Pond Road SE16........151 J6
Tinsley Road E1...............151 G1
Tinworth Street SE11..........148 D6
Tisdall Place SE17.............149 L6
Tite Street SW3...............147 H8
Tiverton Street SE1............149 J4
Token House Yard EC2R........145 L6
Tolmer's Square NW1..........144 A3
Tomlin's Terrace E14...........151 K2
Tonbridge Street WC1H........144 D2
Tooley Street SE1.............149 L1
Tooley Street SE1.............150 B6
Tor Gardens W8..............146 A2
Torquay Street W2............142 A5
Torrens Street EC1V...........145 G1
Torrington Place SE1...........150 D5
Torrington Place WC1E.........144 B4
Tothill Street SW1H............148 B3
Tottenham Court Road ⊖ W1T..144 A4
Tottenham Court Road ⊖ W1D..144 B6
Tottenham Street W1T.........144 A5
Toulmin Street SE1............149 J3
Tower Bridge EC3N............150 B5
Tower Bridge Approach EC3N....150 B5
Tower Bridge Road SE1.........150 A7
Tower Bridge Wharf E1W.......150 C5
Tower Gateway ⊖ EC3N........150 B4
Tower Hill EC3N..............150 B4
Tower Hill ⊖ EC3N............150 B4
Tower of London EC3N.........150 B4

Tower Place EC3R.............150 A4
Tower Street WC2H............144 C7
Townsend Street SE17.........149 M5
Toynbee Street E1.............150 B1
Trafalgar Gardens E1..........151 H1
Trafalgar Square WC2N........144 C8
Trafalgar Street SE17..........149 L7
Transept Street NW1...........142 F5
Trebeck Street W1J............147 L1
Trebovir Road SW5............146 A6
Tregunter Road SW10..........146 C7
Trenton Road SE16............150 E8
Tresham Crescent NW8........142 F3
Trevor Place SW7.............147 G3
Trevor Square SW7............147 G3
Trevor Street SW7............147 G3
Trinidad Street E14............151 M4
Trinity Church Square SE1......149 K3
Trinity Square EC3N...........150 B4
Trinity Street SE1.............149 K3
Trump Street EC2V............145 K6
Tudor Street EC4Y............145 G7
Tufton Street SW1P...........148 C4
Tunnel Road SE16............151 G6
Turks Row SW3...............147 J6
Turner's Road E3.............151 L2
Turner Street E1..............150 E2
Turnmill Street EC1N..........145 G4
Turpentine Lane SW1V........147 L7
Turquand Street SE17..........149 K6
Tyers Gate SE1...............149 M3
Tyers Street SE11............148 E7
Tyers Terrace SE11...........148 E7
Tyron Street SW3.............147 H6
Tysoe Street EC1R............145 G3

U

Udall Street SW1P.............148 A5
Ufford Street SE1.............149 G2
Ulster Place NW1.............143 K4
Umberston Street E1...........150 E2
Undershaft EC3A..............150 A2
Underwood Road N1...........145 K2
Underwood Street N1..........145 K1
Union Street SE1..............149 H2
University Street WC1E.........144 A4
Upbrook Mews W2............142 D6
Upper Belgrave Street SW1X....147 K4
Upper Berkeley Street W1H.....143 H6
Upper Brook Street W1K.......143 J7
Upper Cheyne Row SW3........146 F8
Upper Grosvenor Street W1K....143 J8
Upper Ground SE1............148 F1
Upper Harley Street NW1.......143 K3
Upper James Street W1F.......144 A7
Upper John Street W1F........144 A7
Upper Marsh SE1.............148 E3
Upper Montagu Street W1H.....143 H5
Upper St Martin's WC2H........144 C7
Upper Tachbrook Street SW1V..148 A5
Upper Thames Street EC4V.....145 J7
Upper Wimpole Street W1G....143 K4
Upper Woburn Place WC1H.....144 B2
Urlwin Street SE5.............149 J8
Uxbridge Street W8...........146 A1

V

Valentine Place SE1...........149 G3
Vandon Passage SW1H.........148 A3
Vandon Street SW1H...........148 A3
Varden Street E1..............150 E2
Varndell Street NW1...........143 M2
Vauban Street SE16...........150 C8
Vaughan Street SE16..........151 J6
Vaughan Way E1W............150 D5
Vauxhall ⊖ E1W..............148 D7
Vauxhall Bridge SW1V.........148 C7
Vauxhall Bridgefoot SE1........148 D7
Vauxhall Bridge Road SW1V....147 M5
Vauxhall Cross SW1V..........148 D7
Vauxhall Grove SW8...........148 D8
Vauxhall Street SE11..........148 E6
Vauxhall Walk SE11...........148 E6
Venables Street W2............142 E4
Vere Street W1G..............143 K6
Vernon Place WC1A............144 D5
Vernon Rise WC1X............144 E2
Verulam Street WC1X..........144 F4
Vestry Street N1..............145 L2
Victoria ⊖ ⇌ SW1Y...........147 L5
Victoria & Albert Museum SW7..146 F4
Victoria Embankment SE1.......148 D2
Victoria Embankment WC2R....144 F7
Victoria Gate W2.............142 F7
Victoria Road W8.............146 C4
Victoria Square SW1W.........147 L4
Victoria Street SW1E..........147 L4
Victory Place SE17............149 K5
Victory Way SE16.............151 K7
Vigo Street W1S..............143 M8
Villa Street SE17..............149 L7
Villiers Street WC2N...........144 D8
Vincent Close SE16............151 K7
Vincent Square SW1P..........148 B5
Vincent Street SW1P...........148 B5
Vincent Terrace N1............145 H1
Vince Street EC1V.............145 L2
Vine Court E1................150 D1
Vinegar Street E1W...........150 E5
Vine Hill EC1R...............144 F4
Vine Lane SE1...............150 A6
Vine Street EC3N.............150 B3
Violet Hill NW8..............142 C1
Virgil Street SE1.............148 E4
Virginia Street E1W...........150 D4
Viscount Street EC2Y..........145 J4

W

Wadding Street SE17..........149 K6
Wakefield Street WC1H.........144 D3
Wakeling Street E14...........151 J3
Wakley Street EC1V...........145 H2
Walbrook EC4N...............145 L7
Walcorde Avenue SE17.........149 K6
Walcot Square SE11...........149 G5
Walden Street E1.............150 E2
Waley Street E1..............151 J1

Wallwood Street E14...........151 M1
Walnut Tree Walk SE11.........148 F5
Walpole Street SW3............147 H6
Walter Terrace E1.............151 H2
Walton Place SW3.............147 H4
Walton Street SW3............147 G4
Walworth Place SE17...........149 K7
Walworth Road SE17...........149 J5
Wandsworth Road SW8.........148 C8
Wansey Street SE17...........149 J6
Wapping ⊖ E1W..............150 F5
Wapping High Street E1W......150 E6
Wapping Lane E1W............150 F4
Wapping Wall E1W............151 G5
Warden's Grove SE1...........149 J2
Wardour Street W1F..........144 B6
Warner Street EC1R...........144 F4
Warren Street W1T............143 M4
Warren Street ⊖ NW1.........143 M3
Warrington Crescent W9........142 C3
Warrington Gardens W9........142 C4
Warwick Avenue W9...........142 B3
Warwick Avenue ⊖ W9........142 C4
Warwick Crescent W2..........142 C5
Warwick House Street SW1Y....148 B1
Warwick Lane EC4M...........145 H6
Warwick Place W9.............142 C4
Warwick Road SW5............146 A6
Warwick Row SW1E...........147 L4
Warwick Square SW1V.........147 M6
Warwick Street W1B...........144 A7
Warwick Way SW1V...........147 L6
Waterhouse Square EC1N......145 G5
Waterloo ⊖ SE1..............148 F2
Waterloo Bridge SE1...........148 E1
Waterloo Bridge WC2R........144 E8
Waterloo East ⇌ SE1..........149 G2
Waterloo Place SW1Y..........148 B1
Waterloo Road SE1............148 F1
Waterloo Road SE1............149 G2
Waterman Way E1W...........150 E5
Waterside Close SE16..........150 D7
Watling Street EC4N...........145 K7
Watney Street E1.............150 F3
Watts Street E1W.............150 E5
Waveney Close E1W...........150 D5
Waverton Street W1J...........143 K8
Weavers Lane SE1.............150 A6
Webber Row SE1..............149 G3
Webber Street SE1............149 H3
Webb Street SE1..............150 A8
Webster Road SE16...........150 D8
Weigh House Street W1K.......143 K7
Welbeck Street W1G...........143 K5
Welbeck Way W1G............143 K6
Welland Mews E1W...........150 E5
Wellclose Square E1...........150 D4
Wellesley Street E1............151 H2
Wellesley Terrace N1..........145 K2
Wellington Arch W1J...........147 K2
Wellington Square SW3........147 H6
Wellington Place NW8.........142 E2
Wellington Road NW8.........142 E1
Wellington Street WC2E........144 D7
Wells Mews W1T.............144 A5
Wells Street W1T.............144 A5
Wells Way SE5...............149 M8
Wenlock Road N1.............145 K1
Wenlock Street N1............145 K1
Wentworth Street E1..........150 B2
Werrington Street NW1........144 A1
Wesley Street W1G...........143 K5
West Arbour Street E1.........151 G2
Westbourne Crescent W2......142 D7
Westbourne Gardens W2.......142 B6
Westbourne Gate W2..........142 E7
Westbourne Grove W2.........142 A6
Westbourne Grove Terrace W2..142 B6
Westbourne Park Road W2.....142 A5
Westbourne Park Villas W2.....142 A5
Westbourne Street W2.........142 E7
Westbourne Terrace W2........142 D6
Westbourne Terrace Mews W2..142 C6
Westbourne Terrace Road W2...142 C5
West Brompton ⊖ ⇌ SW5.....146 A7
West Carriage Drive W2.......146 E2
Westcott Road SE17...........149 H8
West Cromwell Road SW5......146 A5
Western Place SE16............151 G6
Westferry ⊖ E14.............151 M4
Westferry Circus E14..........151 M5
Westferry Road E14...........151 M5
West Gardens E1W............150 F4
Westgate Terrace SW10........146 B7
West Halkin Street SW1X.......147 J4
West Harding Street EC4A......145 G6
West India Avenue E14.........151 M5
West India Dock Road E14......151 M3
Westland Place N1............145 K2
West Lane SE16..............150 E7
Westminster ⊖ SW1A.........148 D3
Westminster Abbey SW1P......148 C3
Westminster Bridge SE1........148 D3
Westminster Bridge Road SE1...148 F3
Westmoreland Place SW1V.....147 L7
Westmoreland Road SE17.......149 K8
Westmoreland Street W1G.....143 K5
Westmoreland Terrace SW1V...147 L7
Weston Rise WC1X............144 E1
Weston Street SE1............149 M2
Weston Street SE1............149 M3
Westport Street E1............151 H2
West Poultry Avenue EC1A.....145 H5
West Road SW3..............147 H7
West Smithfield EC1A..........145 H5
West Street WC2H............144 C7
West Tenter Street E1.........150 C3
West Warwick Place SW1V.....147 M6
Westway W2.................142 B5
Wetherby Gardens SW5........146 C6
Weyhill Road E1..............150 D2
Weymouth Mews W1G........143 L5
Weymouth Street W1G........143 K5
Wharfdale Road * N1..........144 D1
Wharf Road N1...............145 J1
Wharton Street WC1X.........144 F2
Wheatley Street W1G..........143 K5
Whetstone Park WC2A.........144 E5
Whidborne Street WC1H.......144 D2
Whiskin Street EC1R..........145 G2
Whitcomb Street WC2H........144 B8
Whitechapel ⊖ ⇌ E1.........150 E1
Whitechapel Estate E1.........150 C4
Whitechapel High Street E1.....150 C2

Whitechapel Road E1..........150 D1
Whitecross Street EC1Y........145 K3
Whitefriars Street EC4Y........145 G6
Whitehall SW1A..............148 C2
Whitehall Court SW1A.........148 D2
Whitehall Place SW1A.........148 D1
White Hart Street SE11.........149 G6
White Hart Yard SE1..........149 L2
Whitehaven Street NW8.......142 F4
Whitehead's Grove SW3........147 G6
White Horse Lane E1..........151 H1
Whitehorse Road E1...........151 H2
Whitehorse Road E1...........151 J3
White Horse Street W1J........147 L1
White Kennett Street E1........150 B2
White Lion Hill EC4V..........145 H7
White Lion Street N1..........144 F1
White's Grounds SE1..........150 A7
White's Row E1..............150 B1
White Tower Way E1..........151 J1
Whitfield Place W1T...........144 A4
Whitfield Street W1T..........144 A4
Whitgift Street SE11..........148 E5
Whittaker Street SW1W........147 J6
Whittlesey Street SE1.........149 G2
Wicker Street E1.............150 E3
Wickham Close E1............151 G1
Wickham Street SE11..........148 E7
Wicklow Street WC1X.........144 E2
Widegate Street E1...........150 A1
Widley Road W9.............142 A3
Wigmore Place W1G..........143 K5
Wigmore Street W1U..........143 J6
Wigton Place SE11............149 G7
Wilbraham Place SW1X........147 J5
Wilcox Place * SW1E..........148 A4
Wild Court WC2B.............144 D6
Wild's Rents SE1.............149 M4
Wild Street WC2B.............144 D6
Wilfred Street SW1E..........147 M4
Wilkes Street E1.............150 B1
William IV Street WC2N........144 C8
William Mews SW1X...........147 H3
William Road NW1............143 M3
Willow Place SW1P............148 A5
Willow Street EC2A...........145 M3
Wilmington Square WC1X......144 F3
Wilmington Street WC1X.......144 F2
Wilson Grove SE16............150 E7
Wilson Street EC2A...........145 L4
Wilton Crescent SW1X.........147 J3
Wilton Mews SW1X...........147 K4
Wilton Place SW1X............147 J3
Wilton Road SW1V............147 M5
Wilton Row SW1X............147 J3
Wilton Street SW1X...........147 K4
Wimpole Mews W1G..........143 K5
Wimpole Street W1G..........143 K5
Winchester Street SW1V.......147 L6
Winchester Walk SE1..........149 K1
Wincott Street SE11...........149 G5
Windmill Road SE11...........148 F7
Windmill Street W1T..........144 B5
Windrose Close SE16..........151 H6
Windsor Terrace N1...........145 K1
Wine Close E1W..............150 F5
Winnett Street W1D...........144 B7
Winsland Mews W2...........142 E6
Winsland Street W2...........142 E6
Winsley Street W1W..........144 A6
Winthrop Street E1...........150 E1
Woburn Place WC1H..........144 C3
Woburn Square WC1H.........144 C4
Wodeham Gardens E1.........150 E1
Wolfe Crescent SE16..........151 H7
Wolseley Street SE1...........150 C6
Woodbridge Street EC1R.......145 G3
Woodchester Square W9.......142 A4
Woodfall Street SW3...........147 H7
Woodland Crescent SE16.......151 H7
Woodseer Street E1...........150 C1
Woods Mews W1K............143 J7
Woods Place SE1.............150 A8
Woodstock Street W1C........143 K6
Wood Street EC2V............145 K6
Woolaston Close SE1..........149 J5
Wooler Street SE17...........149 L7
Wootton Street SE1...........149 G2
Worgan Street SE11...........148 E6
Worgan Street * SE11.........151 H8
Wormwood Street EC2M.......145 M5
Worship Street EC2A..........145 M4
Wren Street WC1X............144 E3
Wright's Lane W8.............146 A3
Wyatt Close SE16............151 L7
Wyclif Street EC1V............145 H2
Wymering Road W9...........142 A2
Wynard Terrace SE11..........148 F7
Wyndham Place W1H..........143 H5
Wyndham Street W1H.........143 G4
Wynnstay Gardens W8........146 A4
Wynyatt Street EC1V..........145 H2
Wythburn Place W1H.........143 H6

Y

Yalding Road * SE16..........150 C8
Yardley Street WC1X..........144 F2
Yeoman's Row SW3...........147 G4
York Boulevard WC2N.........144 D8
York Bridge NW1.............143 J3
York Gate NW1..............143 J4
York Road SE1..............148 E2
Yorkshire Road E14...........151 K3
York Square E14.............151 J2
York Street W1H.............143 G5
York Street W1H.............143 H5
York Terrace East NW1........143 J4
York Terrace West NW1........143 J4
York Way N1................144 D1
Young Street W8.............146 B3

Z

Zoar Street SE1..............149 J1
ZSL London Zoo NW1.........143 J1

This index lists places appearing in the main map section of the atlas in alphabetical order. The reference following each name gives the atlas page number and grid reference of the square in which the place appears. The map shows counties, unitary authorities and administrative areas, together with a list of the abbreviated name forms used in the index. The top 100 places of tourist interest are indexed in red, World Heritage sites in green, motorway service areas in blue, airports in blue *italic* and National Parks in green *italic*.

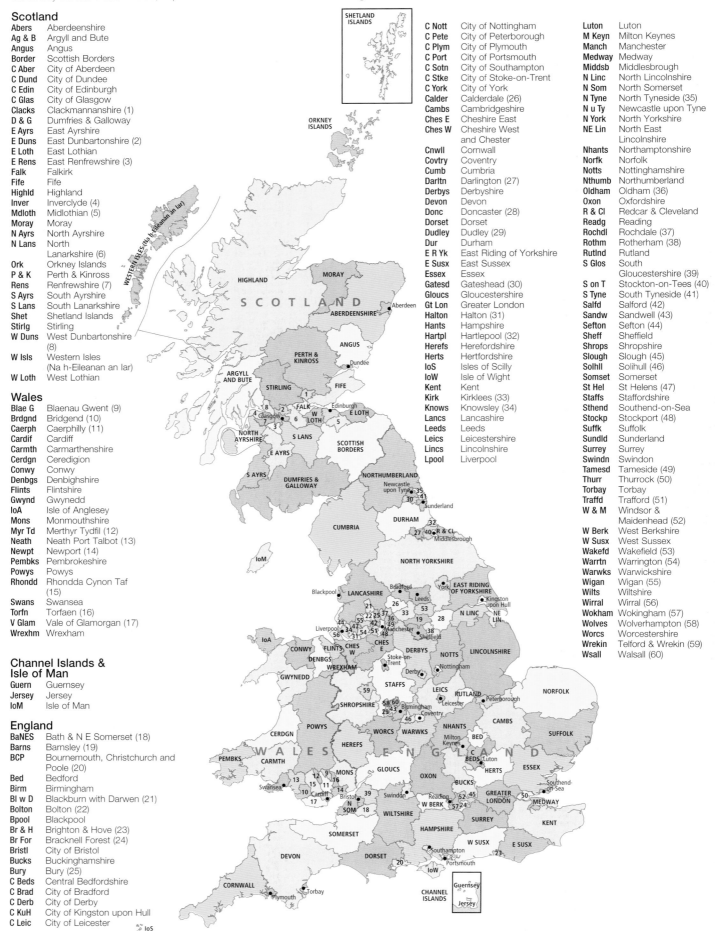

Scotland

Abers	Aberdeenshire
Ag & B	Argyll and Bute
Angus	Angus
Border	Scottish Borders
C Aber	City of Aberdeen
C Dund	City of Dundee
C Edin	City of Edinburgh
C Glas	City of Glasgow
Clacks	Clackmannanshire (1)
D & G	Dumfries & Galloway
E Ayrs	East Ayrshire
E Duns	East Dunbartonshire (2)
E Loth	East Lothian
E Rens	East Renfrewshire (3)
Falk	Falkirk
Fife	Fife
Highld	Highland
Inver	Inverclyde (4)
Mdloth	Midlothian (5)
Moray	Moray
N Ayrs	North Ayrshire
N Lans	North Lanarkshire (6)
Ork	Orkney Islands
P & K	Perth & Kinross
Rens	Renfrewshire (7)
S Ayrs	South Ayrshire
S Lans	South Lanarkshire
Shet	Shetland Islands
Stirlg	Stirling
W Duns	West Dunbartonshire (8)
W Isls	Western Isles (Na h-Eileanan an Iar)
W Loth	West Lothian

Wales

Blae G	Blaenau Gwent (9)
Brdgnd	Bridgend (10)
Caerph	Caerphilly (11)
Cardif	Cardiff
Carmth	Carmarthenshire
Cerdgn	Ceredigion
Conwy	Conwy
Denbgs	Denbighshire
Flints	Flintshire
Gwynd	Gwynedd
IoA	Isle of Anglesey
Mons	Monmouthshire
Myr Td	Merthyr Tydfil (12)
Neath	Neath Port Talbot (13)
Newpt	Newport (14)
Pembks	Pembrokeshire
Powys	Powys
Rhondd	Rhondda Cynon Taf (15)
Swans	Swansea
Torfn	Torfaen (16)
V Glam	Vale of Glamorgan (17)
Wrexhm	Wrexham

Channel Islands & Isle of Man

Guern	Guernsey
Jersey	Jersey
IoM	Isle of Man

England

BaNES	Bath & N E Somerset (18)
Barns	Barnsley (19)
BCP	Bournemouth, Christchurch and Poole (20)
Bed	Bedford
Birm	Birmingham
Bl w D	Blackburn with Darwen (21)
Bolton	Bolton (22)
Bpool	Blackpool
Br & H	Brighton & Hove (23)
Br For	Bracknell Forest (24)
Bristl	City of Bristol
Bucks	Buckinghamshire
Bury	Bury (25)
C Beds	Central Bedfordshire
C Brad	City of Bradford
C Derb	City of Derby
C KuH	City of Kingston upon Hull
C Leic	City of Leicester

C Nott	City of Nottingham
C Pete	City of Peterborough
C Plym	City of Plymouth
C Port	City of Portsmouth
C Sotn	City of Southampton
C Stke	City of Stoke-on-Trent
C York	City of York
Calder	Calderdale (26)
Cambs	Cambridgeshire
Ches E	Cheshire East
Ches W	Cheshire West and Chester
Cnwll	Cornwall
Covtry	Coventry
Cumb	Cumbria
Darltn	Darlington (27)
Derbys	Derbyshire
Devon	Devon
Donc	Doncaster (28)
Dorset	Dorset
Dudley	Dudley (29)
Dur	Durham
E R Yk	East Riding of Yorkshire
E Susx	East Sussex
Essex	Essex
Gatesd	Gateshead (30)
Gloucs	Gloucestershire
Gt Lon	Greater London
Halton	Halton (31)
Hants	Hampshire
Hartpl	Hartlepool (32)
Herefs	Herefordshire
Herts	Hertfordshire
IoS	Isles of Scilly
IoW	Isle of Wight
Kent	Kent
Kirk	Kirklees (33)
Knows	Knowsley (34)
Lancs	Lancashire
Leeds	Leeds
Leics	Leicestershire
Lincs	Lincolnshire
Lpool	Liverpool

Luton	Luton
M Keyn	Milton Keynes
Manch	Manchester
Medway	Medway
Middsb	Middlesbrough
N Linc	North Lincolnshire
N Som	North Somerset
N Tyne	North Tyneside (35)
N u Ty	Newcastle upon Tyne
N York	North Yorkshire
NE Lin	North East Lincolnshire
Nhants	Northamptonshire
Norfk	Norfolk
Notts	Nottinghamshire
Nthumb	Northumberland
Oldham	Oldham (36)
Oxon	Oxfordshire
R & Cl	Redcar & Cleveland
Readg	Reading
Rochdl	Rochdale (37)
Rothm	Rotherham (38)
Rutlnd	Rutland
S Glos	South Gloucestershire (39)
S on T	Stockton-on-Tees (40)
S Tyne	South Tyneside (41)
Salfd	Salford (42)
Sandw	Sandwell (43)
Sefton	Sefton (44)
Sheff	Sheffield
Shrops	Shropshire
Slough	Slough (45)
Solhll	Solihull (46)
Somset	Somerset
St Hel	St Helens (47)
Staffs	Staffordshire
Sthend	Southend-on-Sea
Stockp	Stockport (48)
Suffk	Suffolk
Sundld	Sunderland
Surrey	Surrey
Swindn	Swindon
Tamesd	Tameside (49)
Thurr	Thurrock (50)
Torbay	Torbay
Traffd	Trafford (51)
W & M	Windsor & Maidenhead (52)
W Berk	West Berkshire
W Susx	West Sussex
Wakefd	Wakefield (53)
Warrtn	Warrington (54)
Warwks	Warwickshire
Wigan	Wigan (55)
Wilts	Wiltshire
Wirral	Wirral (56)
Wokham	Wokingham (57)
Wolves	Wolverhampton (58)
Worcs	Worcestershire
Wrekin	Telford & Wrekin (59)
Wsall	Walsall (60)

A

Place	County	Page	Grid
Abbas Combe	Somset	17	Q10
Abberley	Worcs	39	N8
Abberley Common	Worcs	39	N8
Abberton	Essex	34	G11
Abberton	Worcs	30	C4
Abbess Roding	Essex	22	C2
Abbeydale	Sheff	50	H4
Abbey Dore	Herefs	28	D3
Abbey Green	Staffs	50	C8
Abbey St Bathans	Border	87	P9
Abbeystead	Lancs	63	K10
Abbeytown	Cumb	71	J5
Abbey Village	Lancs	57	M4
Abbey Wood	Gt Lon	21	P7
Abbotrule	Border	80	E10
Abbots Bickington	Devon	14	G9
Abbots Bromley	Staffs	40	E3
Abbotsbury	Dorset	7	N6
Abbots Deuglie	P & K	92	G12
Abbotsham	Devon	14	H6
Abbotskerswell	Devon	6	B8
Abbots Langley	Herts	20	H3
Abbots Leigh	N Som	17	M2
Abbotsley	Cambs	32	H5
Abbots Morton	Worcs	30	D3
Abbots Ripton	Cambs	32	H2
Abbot's Salford	Warwks	30	E4
Abbot's Worthy	Hants	9	N2
Abbotts Ann	Hants	19	K11
Abbott Street	Dorset	8	E7
Abdon	Shrops	39	L5
Aberaeron	Cerdgn	36	G7
Aberaman	Rhondd	27	L8
Aberangell	Gwynd	47	N8
Aberarder	Highld	99	J4
Aberargie	P & K	92	H11
Aberarth	Cerdgn	36	H7
Aberavon	Neath	26	G10
Abercanaid	Myr Td	27	M7
Abercarn	Caerph	27	P9
Abercastle	Pembks	24	F3
Abercegir	Powys	47	N10
Aberchalder Lodge	Highld	98	D8
Aberchirder	Abers	102	E5
Abercorn	W Loth	86	C6
Abercraf	Powys	26	H6
Abercregan	Neath	26	H9
Abercwmboi	Rhondd	27	L8
Abercych	Pembks	36	D11
Abercynon	Rhondd	27	M9
Aberdalgie	P & K	92	G10
Aberdare	Rhondd	27	L8
Aberdaron	Gwynd	46	C6
Aberdeen	C Aber	95	Q1
Aberdeen Airport	C Aber	103	J11
Aberdour	Fife	86	E5
Aberdulais	Neath	26	G8
Aberdyfi	Gwynd	47	K11
Abereiddy	Pembks	24	E3
Abererch	Gwynd	46	G4
Aberfan	Myr Td	27	M8
Aberfeldy	P & K	92	C6
Aberffraw	IoA	54	E7
Aberford	Leeds	59	K6
Aberfoyle	Stirlg	85	J3
Abergavenny	Mons	28	C6
Abergele	Conwy	55	P6
Abergorlech	Carmth	26	D3
Abergwesyn	Powys	37	P9
Abergwili	Carmth	25	Q5
Abergwynfi	Neath	27	J9
Abergwyngregyn	Gwynd	55	J7
Abergynolwyn	Gwynd	47	L9
Aberkenfig	Brdgnd	27	J11
Aberlady	E Loth	87	J6
Aberlemno	Angus	93	N5
Aberllefenni	Gwynd	47	M8
Aberllynfi	Powys	27	N2
Aberlour, Charlestown of	Moray	101	K6
Abermule	Powys	38	D4
Abernant	Carmth	25	N4
Abernant	Rhondd	27	L7
Abernethy	P & K	92	H11
Abernyte	P & K	93	J8
Aberporth	Cerdgn	36	C10
Abersoch	Gwynd	46	E6
Abersychan	Torfn	28	B7
Aberthin	V Glam	16	D2
Abertillery	Blae G	27	P7
Abertridwr	Caerph	27	N10
Abertridwr	Powys	48	B10
Aberuthven	P & K	92	E11
Aberystwyth	Cerdgn	37	J4
Abingdon-on-Thames	Oxon	19	N2
Abinger Common	Surrey	10	H2
Abinger Hammer	Surrey	10	H1
Abington	Nhants	32	A5
Abington	S Lans	78	F4
Abington Pigotts	Cambs	33	K7
Abington Services	S Lans	78	F4
Abingworth	W Susx	10	H6
Ab Kettleby	Leics	41	Q3
Ablington	Gloucs	30	E11
Abney	Derbys	50	G5
Aboyne	Abers	95	J3
Abhainn Suidhe	W Isls	111	c3
Abram	Wigan	57	L8
Abriachan	Highld	98	H2
Abridge	Essex	21	P4
Abronhill	N Lans	85	N7
Abson	S Glos	17	P2
Abthorpe	Nhants	31	N5
Aby	Lincs	53	L7
Acaster Malbis	C York	59	N5
Acaster Selby	N York	59	M6
Accrington	Lancs	57	N3
Acha	Ag & B	88	F5
Achahoish	Ag & B	83	L7
Achalader	P & K	92	G6
Achaleven	Ag & B	90	C9
Acha Mor	W Isls	111	d2
Achanalt	Highld	106	D9
Achandunie	Highld	107	K7
Achany	Highld	107	J3
Acharacle	Highld	89	N3
Acharn	Highld	89	P6
Acharn	P & K	92	B6
Achavanich	Highld	110	E7
Achduart	Highld	105	Q2
Achfary	Highld	108	F7
A'Chill	Highld	96	C8
Achiltibuie	Highld	105	Q1
Achina	Highld	109	M4
Achinhoan	Ag & B	75	L8
Achintee	Highld	97	N2
Achintraid	Highld	97	L2
Achmelvich	Highld	108	B10
Achmore	Highld	97	M3
Achmore	W Isls	111	d2
Achnacarnin	Highld	108	B8
Achnacarry	Highld	98	B10
Achnacloich	Highld	96	H7
Achnaconeran	Highld	98	F5
Achnacroish	Ag & B	90	B7
Achnadrish House	Ag & B	89	K6
Achnafauld	P & K	92	D8
Achnagarron	Highld	107	L8
Achnaha	Highld	89	K3
Achnahaird	Highld	108	A11
Achnahannet	Highld	100	F9
Achnairn	Highld	109	K12
Achnalea	Highld	90	B4
Achnamara	Ag & B	83	L5
Achnasheen	Highld	106	C10
Achnashellach	Highld	105	Q11
Achnastank	Moray	101	K8
Achosnich	Highld	89	K3
Achranich	Highld	89	P6
Achreamie	Highld	110	B3
Achriabhach	Highld	90	F3
Achriesgill	Highld	108	E5
Achtoty	Highld	109	M3
Achurch	Nhants	42	E12
Achvaich	Highld	107	L4
Achvarasdal	Highld	110	B3
Ackergill	Highld	110	G5
Acklam	Middsb	66	C4
Acklam	N York	60	D2
Ackleton	Shrops	39	P3
Acklington	Nthumb	73	M1
Ackton	Wakefd	59	K9
Ackworth Moor Top	Wakefd	59	K10
Acle	Norfk	45	N7
Acock's Green	Birm	40	E10
Acol	Kent	23	P9
Acomb	C York	59	M4
Acomb	Nthumb	72	G7
Aconbury	Herefs	28	F3
Acton	Ches E	49	L5
Acton	Gt Lon	21	K7
Acton	Staffs	49	P7
Acton	Suffk	34	E7
Acton	Wrexhm	48	G5
Acton Beauchamp	Herefs	39	M11
Acton Bridge	Ches W	49	L1
Acton Burnell	Shrops	39	K2
Acton Green	Herefs	39	M11
Acton Round	Shrops	39	L3
Acton Scott	Shrops	39	J4
Acton Trussell	Staffs	40	C4
Acton Turville	S Glos	18	B5
Adbaston	Staffs	49	N9
Adber	Dorset	17	N11
Adbolton	Notts	51	N12
Adderbury	Oxon	31	L7
Adderley	Shrops	49	M7
Addiewell	W Loth	86	B9
Addingham	C Brad	58	E4
Addington	Bucks	31	Q8
Addington	Gt Lon	21	M9
Addington	Kent	22	D10
Addiscombe	Gt Lon	21	M9
Addlestone	Surrey	20	G9
Addlethorpe	Lincs	53	N9
Adeyfield	Herts	20	H2
Adfa	Powys	38	C2
Adforton	Herefs	38	H7
Adisham	Kent	23	N11
Adlestrop	Gloucs	30	G8
Adlingfleet	E R Yk	60	E9
Adlington	Lancs	57	L6
Admaston	Staffs	40	D3
Admaston	Wrekin	49	L11
Adpar	Cerdgn	36	E11
Adsborough	Somset	16	H9
Adscombe	Somset	16	G8
Adstock	Bucks	31	Q7
Adstone	Nhants	31	N4
Adversane	W Susx	10	H5
Advie	Highld	100	H8
Adwick le Street	Donc	59	M11
Adwick upon Dearne	Donc	51	L1
Ae	D & G	78	G10
Ae Bridgend	D & G	78	G10
Afan Forest Park	Neath	26	H8
Affleck	Abers	102	D7
Affpuddle	Dorset	8	B8
Affric Lodge	Highld	98	B5
Afon-wen	Flints	48	D2
Afton	IoW	9	L9
Agglethorpe	N York	65	J9
Aigburth	Lpool	56	H10
Aike	E R Yk	60	H5
Aiketgate	Cumb	71	P6
Aikton	Cumb	71	L5
Ailsworth	C Pete	42	G9
Ainderby Quernhow	N York	65	N10
Ainderby Steeple	N York	65	N8
Aingers Green	Essex	35	J11
Ainsdale	Sefton	56	F6
Ainstable	Cumb	71	Q6
Ainsworth	Bury	57	N6
Ainthorpe	N York	66	G6
Aintree	Sefton	56	H8
Ainville	W Loth	86	D9
Aird	Ag & B	83	L3
Aird	D & G	68	E7
Aird	W Isls	111	e2
Àird a' Mhulaidh	W Isls	111	c3
Aird Asaig	W Isls	111	c3
Aird Dhubh	Highld	97	J2
Airdeny	Ag & B	90	C9
Aird of Kinloch	Ag & B	89	L9
Aird of Sleat	Highld	96	H7
Airdrie	N Lans	85	M9
Airdriehill	N Lans	85	N9
Airds of Kells	D & G	69	P5
Àird Uig	W Isls	111	c2
Airidh a bhruaich	W Isls	111	c3
Airieland	D & G	70	C4
Airlie	Angus	93	K5
Airmyn	E R Yk	60	C8
Airntully	P & K	92	G8
Airor	Highld	97	J8
Airth	Falk	85	Q5
Airton	N York	58	B3
Aisby	Lincs	42	E3
Aisby	Lincs	52	C5
Aish	Devon	5	N7
Aish	Devon	6	A10
Aisholt	Somset	16	G8
Aiskew	N York	65	M9
Aislaby	N York	66	H9
Aislaby	N York	67	J6
Aislaby	S on T	65	P5
Aisthorpe	Lincs	52	D7
Aith	Shet	111	k4
Akeld	Nthumb	81	K8
Akeley	Bucks	31	P6
Akenham	Suffk	35	J7
Albaston	Cnwll	5	K6
Alberbury	Shrops	48	G11
Albourne	W Susx	11	M6
Albrighton	Shrops	39	P2
Albrighton	Shrops	49	J10
Alburgh	Norfk	45	L11
Albury	Herts	33	M10
Albury	Surrey	10	H1
Albury Heath	Surrey	10	G2
Alcaig	Highld	107	J10
Alcaston	Shrops	39	J5
Alcester	Warwks	30	E3
Alcester Lane End	Birm	40	E10
Alciston	E Susx	11	P8
Alcombe	Somset	16	C7
Alconbury	Cambs	32	H2
Alconbury Weston	Cambs	32	H2
Aldborough	N York	59	K2
Aldborough	Norfk	45	K4
Aldbourne	Wilts	19	J5
Aldbrough	E R Yk	61	L6
Aldbrough St John	N York	65	L5
Aldbury	Herts	20	F2
Aldcliffe	Lancs	63	J9
Aldclune	P & K	92	D3
Aldeburgh	Suffk	35	P5
Aldeby	Norfk	45	P10
Aldenham	Herts	21	J4
Alderbury	Wilts	8	H3
Alderford	Norfk	45	J6
Alderholt	Dorset	8	H5
Alderley	Gloucs	29	K10
Alderley Edge	Ches E	57	Q12
Aldermans Green	Covtry	41	J10
Aldermaston	W Berk	19	P7
Alderminster	Warwks	30	G4
Aldershot	Hants	20	D12
Alderton	Gloucs	30	D7
Alderton	Nhants	31	Q5
Alderton	Suffk	35	M8
Alderton	Wilts	18	C4
Aldfield	N York	58	H1
Aldford	Ches W	48	H4
Aldgate	Rutlnd	42	E8
Aldham	Essex	34	F10
Aldham	Suffk	34	H7
Aldingbourne	W Susx	10	E8
Aldingham	Cumb	62	F7
Aldington	Kent	13	K3
Aldington	Worcs	30	E5
Aldington Corner	Kent	13	K3
Aldivalloch	Moray	101	M9
Aldochlay	Ag & B	84	F5
Aldreth	Cambs	33	M3
Aldridge	Wsall	40	D7
Aldringham	Suffk	35	P5
Aldsworth	Gloucs	30	F11
Aldunie	Moray	101	M9
Aldwark	Derbys	50	G8
Aldwark	N York	59	L2
Aldwick	W Susx	10	E9
Aldwincle	Nhants	32	E1
Aldworth	W Berk	19	P5
Alexandria	W Duns	84	G7
Aley	Somset	16	G8
Alfington	Devon	6	F4
Alfold	Surrey	10	G4
Alfold Crossways	Surrey	10	G3
Alford	Abers	102	D11
Alford	Lincs	53	L8
Alford	Somset	17	N9
Alfreton	Derbys	51	K9
Alfrick	Worcs	39	N10
Alfrick Pound	Worcs	39	N10
Alfriston	E Susx	11	P8
Algarkirk	Lincs	43	J3
Alhampton	Somset	17	P8
Alkborough	N Linc	60	F9
Alkham	Kent	13	N2
Alkmonton	Derbys	50	F12
Allaleigh	Devon	5	Q8
Allanaquoich	Abers	94	B4
Allanbank	N Lans	85	N10
Allanton	Border	81	J4
Allanton	N Lans	85	N10
Allanton	S Lans	85	M11
Allaston	Gloucs	28	H7
Allbrook	Hants	9	M4
All Cannings	Wilts	18	F8
Allendale	Nthumb	72	F9
Allen End	Warwks	40	F7
Allenheads	Nthumb	72	F11
Allen's Green	Herts	33	M12
Allensmore	Herefs	28	E2
Allenton	C Derb	41	J2
Aller	Devon	15	N4
Aller	Somset	17	K9
Allerby	Cumb	70	H7
Allercombe	Devon	6	E4
Allerford	Somset	16	B6
Allerston	N York	67	J10
Allerthorpe	E R Yk	60	D5
Allerton	C Brad	58	E7
Allerton	Highld	107	M8
Allerton	Lpool	56	H10
Allerton Bywater	Leeds	59	K8
Allerton Mauleverer	N York	59	K3
Allesley	Covtry	40	H10
Allestree	C Derb	51	J11
Allexton	Leics	42	B9
Allgreave	Ches E	50	C7
Allhallows	Medway	22	G7
Alligin Shuas	Highld	105	M10
Allington	Dorset	7	L4
Allington	Lincs	42	C3
Allington	Wilts	18	D5
Allington	Wilts	18	F8
Allington	Wilts	18	H11
Allithwaite	Cumb	62	H6
Alloa	Clacks	85	P4
Allonby	Cumb	70	H7
Alloway	S Ayrs	76	F7
Allowenshay	Somset	17	K12
All Stretton	Shrops	39	J3
Alltchaorunn	Highld	90	G6
Alltwalis	Carmth	25	Q3
Alltwen	Neath	26	G7
Alltyblaca	Cerdgn	36	H10
Allweston	Dorset	17	P12
Almeley	Herefs	38	G11
Almington	Staffs	49	N8
Almodington	W Susx	10	D9
Almondbank	P & K	92	F9
Almondbury	Kirk	58	F10
Almondsbury	S Glos	28	H11
Alne	N York	59	L2
Alness	Highld	107	L8
Alnham	Nthumb	81	L11
Alnmouth	Nthumb	81	P11
Alnwick	Nthumb	81	P10
Alperton	Gt Lon	21	J6
Alphamstone	Essex	34	E9
Alpheton	Suffk	34	E6
Alphington	Devon	6	C5
Alport	Derbys	50	G7
Alpraham	Ches E	49	L4
Alresford	Essex	34	H11
Alrewas	Staffs	40	F5
Alsager	Ches E	49	P4
Alsop en le Dale	Derbys	50	F9
Alston	Cumb	72	D10
Alston	Devon	7	J3
Alstone	Gloucs	29	N3
Alstonefield	Staffs	50	F9
Alston Sutton	Somset	17	K6
Alswear	Devon	15	M7
Altandhu	Highld	108	A12
Altarnun	Cnwll	4	F4
Altass	Highld	106	H3
Altcreich	Ag & B	89	N8
Altgaltraig	Ag & B	83	Q8
Althorne	Essex	22	H4
Althorpe	N Linc	60	E11
Altnabreac Station	Highld	110	B6
Altnaharra	Highld	109	K8
Altofts	Wakefd	59	J9
Alton	Derbys	51	J7
Alton	Hants	10	B3
Alton	Staffs	50	E11
Alton Barnes	Wilts	18	G8
Alton Pancras	Dorset	7	Q3
Alton Priors	Wilts	18	G8
Alton Towers	Staffs	50	E11
Altrincham	Traffd	57	P10
Altskeith Hotel	Stirlg	84	H3
Alva	Clacks	85	P4
Alvanley	Ches W	49	J1
Alvaston	C Derb	41	K2
Alvechurch	Worcs	40	D11
Alvecote	Warwks	40	G6
Alvediston	Wilts	8	E3
Alveley	Shrops	39	N5
Alverdiscott	Devon	15	J7
Alverstoke	Hants	9	P7
Alverstone	IoW	9	P9
Alverthorpe	Wakefd	58	H9
Alverton	Notts	42	B2
Alves	Moray	100	H3
Alvescot	Oxon	30	H12
Alveston	S Glos	28	H10
Alveston	Warwks	30	G3
Alvingham	Lincs	53	K5
Alvington	Gloucs	28	H8
Alwalton	C Pete	42	G10
Alwinton	Nthumb	81	J11
Alwoodley	Leeds	58	H6
Alyth	P & K	93	J6
Am Bàgh a Tuath	W Isls	111	a7
Ambergate	Derbys	51	J9
Amberley	Gloucs	29	L8
Amberley	W Susx	10	G7
Amble	Nthumb	81	Q12
Amblecote	Dudley	40	B9
Ambler Thorn	C Brad	58	E8
Ambleside	Cumb	62	G2
Ambleston	Pembks	24	H4
Ambrosden	Oxon	31	N9
Amcotts	N Linc	60	E10
Amersham	Bucks	20	F4
Amersham Common	Bucks	20	F4
Amersham Old Town	Bucks	20	F4
Amersham on the Hill	Bucks	20	F4
Amesbury	Wilts	18	H11
Amhuinnsuidhe	W Isls	111	c3
Amington	Staffs	40	G6
Amisfield	D & G	78	G11
Amlwch	IoA	54	F3
Ammanford	Carmth	26	E6
Amotherby	N York	66	G11
Ampfield	Hants	9	L3
Ampleforth	N York	66	E10
Ampney Crucis	Gloucs	30	E12
Ampney St Mary	Gloucs	18	G1
Ampney St Peter	Gloucs	18	F1
Amport	Hants	19	K11
Ampthill	C Beds	32	E8
Ampton	Suffk	34	E3
Amroth	Pembks	25	K7
Amulree	P & K	92	D8
Amwell	Herts	21	J2
Anaheilt	Highld	89	Q4
Ancaster	Lincs	42	E2
Ancells Farm	Hants	20	D11
Ancroft	Nthumb	81	L5
Ancrum	Border	80	E8
Ancton	W Susx	10	F9
Anderby	Lincs	53	N8
Andover	Hants	19	L10
Andoversford	Gloucs	30	D9
Andreas	IoM	56	d2
Anerley	Gt Lon	21	M9
Anfield	Lpool	56	G9
Angarrack	Cnwll	2	E7
Angelbank	Shrops	39	L7
Angle	Pembks	24	F8
Anglesey	IoA	54	F5
Anglesey Abbey	Cambs	33	N4
Angmering	W Susx	10	H8
Angram	N York	59	M5
Ankerville	Highld	107	N7
Anlaby	E R Yk	60	H8
Anmer	Norfk	44	C4
Anmore	Hants	9	Q5
Annan	D & G	71	K3
Annandale Water Services	D & G	78	H9
Annat	Highld	105	N10
Annathill	N Lans	85	M8
Anna Valley	Hants	19	L11
Annbank	S Ayrs	76	G6
Anne Hathaway's Cottage	Warwks	30	F3
Annfield Plain	Dur	73	L9
Anniesland	C Glas	85	J8
Ansdell	Lancs	56	G3
Ansford	Somset	17	P9
Ansley	Warwks	40	H8
Anslow	Staffs	40	G3
Anslow Gate	Staffs	40	G3
Anstey	Herts	33	L9
Anstey	Leics	41	M6
Anstruther	Fife	87	L2
Ansty	W Susx	11	L5
Ansty	Warwks	41	K10
Ansty	Wilts	8	E3
Anthorn	Cumb	71	K4
Antingham	Norfk	45	L4
An t-Ob	W Isls	111	c4
Antonine Wall		85	P7
Anton's Gowt	Lincs	43	J1
Antony	Cnwll	5	J8
Antrobus	Ches W	57	M11
Anwick	Lincs	52	G12
Anwoth	D & G	69	N7
Aperfield	Gt Lon	21	N10
Apethorpe	Nhants	42	E10
Apley	Lincs	52	G8
Apperknowle	Derbys	51	J5
Apperley	Gloucs	29	M3
Appin	Ag & B	90	C7
Appleby	N Linc	60	G10
Appleby-in-Westmorland	Cumb	64	C4
Appleby Magna	Leics	40	H5
Appleby Parva	Leics	40	H6
Applecross	Highld	97	J2
Appledore	Devon	14	H6
Appledore	Devon	16	E12
Appledore	Kent	13	J4
Appleford	Oxon	19	N3
Applegarth Town	D & G	78	H11
Appleshaw	Hants	19	K10
Appleton	Halton	57	K10
Appleton	Oxon	19	M1
Appleton Roebuck	N York	59	M6
Appleton Thorn	Warrtn	57	M11
Appleton Wiske	N York	65	P6
Appletreehall	Border	80	C10
Appletreewick	N York	58	D3
Appley	Somset	16	E10
Appley Bridge	Lancs	57	K7
Apse Heath	IoW	9	P10
Apsley End	C Beds	32	G9
Apuldram	W Susx	10	D9
Arabella	Highld	107	N7
Arbirlot	Angus	93	Q7
Arborfield	Wokham	20	C9
Arborfield Cross	Wokham	20	C9
Arbourthorne	Sheff	51	J4
Arbroath	Angus	93	Q7
Arbuthnott	Abers	95	N6
Archddu	Carmth	25	Q8
Archdeacon Newton	Darltn	65	M4
Archencarroch	W Duns	84	G6
Archiestown	Moray	101	J6
Arclid	Ches E	49	P3
Ardallie	Abers	103	L7
Ardanaiseig Hotel	Ag & B	90	E10
Ardaneaskan	Highld	97	L3
Ardarroch	Highld	97	L2
Ardbeg	Ag & B	74	F4
Ardbeg	Ag & B	84	D9
Ardbeg	Ag & B	84	C6
Ardcharnich	Highld	106	C5
Ardchiavaig	Ag & B	89	J11
Ardchonnell	Ag & B	83	P1
Ardchronie	Highld	107	K5
Ardchullarie More	Stirlg	91	N12
Arddarroch	Ag & B	84	D4
Arddleen	Powys	48	F11
Ard Dorch	Highld	96	G4
Ardechive	Highld	98	A10
Ardeer	N Ayrs	76	E4
Ardeley	Herts	33	K10
Ardelve	Highld	97	M4
Arden	Ag & B	84	F6
Ardens Grafton	Warwks	30	E4
Ardentallen	Ag & B	90	B10
Ardentinny	Ag & B	84	D5
Ardentraive	Ag & B	83	Q7
Ardeonaig	Stirlg	91	P8
Ardersier	Highld	107	N10
Ardessie	Highld	105	Q5
Ardfern	Ag & B	83	M3
Ardfernal	Ag & B	82	H8
Ardgartan	Ag & B	84	E3
Ardgay	Highld	107	K4
Ardgour	Highld	90	D4
Ardgowan	Inver	84	D8
Ardhallow	Ag & B	84	C7
Ardhasig	W Isls	111	c3
Ardheslaig	Highld	105	L10
Ardindrean	Highld	106	C5
Ardingly	W Susx	11	M4
Ardington	Oxon	19	M3
Ardlamont	Ag & B	83	P9
Ardleigh	Essex	34	H10
Ardleigh Heath	Essex	34	H10
Ardler	P & K	93	J7
Ardley	Oxon	31	M8
Ardlui	Ag & B	91	J12
Ardlussa	Ag & B	83	J5
Ardmair	Highld	106	B3
Ardmaleish	Ag & B	84	B8

160 Ardminish – Bangor

Ardminish Ag & B 75 J3
Ardmolich Highld 89 P2
Ardmore Ag & B 83 F7
Ardmore Highld 107 L5
Ardnadam Ag & B 84 C7
Ardnagrask Highld 106 H11
Ardnamurchan Highld 89 L3
Ardnarff Highld 97 M3
Ardnastang Highld 89 Q4
Ardpatrick Ag & B 83 L10
Ardrishaig Ag & B 83 M6
Ardross Highld 107 K7
Ardrossan N Ayrs 76 D3
Ardsley East Leeds 58 H8
Ardslignish Highld 89 L4
Ardtalla Ag & B 82 G11
Ardtoe Highld 89 M3
Arduaine Ag & B 83 M2
Ardullie Highld 107 J9
Ardvasar Highld 96 H8
Ardvorlich P & K 91 P10
Ardvourlie W Isls 111 c3
Ardwell D & G 68 F9
Ardwick Manch 57 Q9
Areley Kings Worcs 39 P7
Arevegaig Highld 89 N3
Arford Hants 10 D3
Argoed Caerph 27 N8
Argyll Forest Park Ag & B 84 D3
Aribruach W Isls 111 c3
Aridhglas Ag & B 88 H10
Arileod Ag & B 88 E5
Arinagour Ag & B 88 F5
Ariogan Ag & B 90 B10
Arisaig Highld 97 J11
Arisaig House Highld 97 J11
Arkendale N York 59 K2
Arkesden Essex 33 M9
Arkholme Lancs 63 L7
Arkleton D & G 79 N10
Arkley Gt Lon 21 K4
Arksey Donc 59 M11
Arkwright Town Derbys 51 K6
Arle Gloucs 29 N4
Arlecdon Cumb 70 G10
Arlesey C Beds 32 H9
Arleston Wrekin 49 M12
Arley Ches E 57 M11
Arley Warwks 40 H8
Arlingham Gloucs 29 J6
Arlington Devon 15 K4
Arlington E Susx 12 B8
Armadale Highld 96 H8
Armadale Highld 109 N3
Armadale W Loth 85 Q8
Armathwaite Cumb 71 Q6
Arminghall Norfk 45 L8
Armitage Staffs 40 E4
Armley Leeds 58 H7
Armscote Warwks 30 G5
Armthorpe Donc 59 N12
Arnabost Ag & B 88 F4
Arncliffe N York 64 G12
Arncroach Fife 87 K2
Arndilly House Moray 101 K6
Arne Dorset 8 E9
Arnesby Leics 41 N8
Arngask P & K 92 H12
Arnisdale Highld 97 L7
Arnish Highld 104 H11
Arniston Mdloth 86 G9
Arnol W Isls 111 d1
Arnold E R Yk 61 J6
Arnold Notts 51 N10
Arnprior Stirlg 85 K4
Arnside Cumb 63 J6
Aros Ag & B 89 L7
Arrad Foot Cumb 62 F6
Arram E R Yk 60 H5
Arran N Ayrs 75 P5
Arrathorne N York 65 L8
Arreton IoW 9 N9
Arrina Highld 105 L10
Arrington Cambs 33 K6
Arrochar Ag & B 84 E3
Arrow Warwks 30 E3
Arscott Shrops 38 H1
Artafallie Highld 107 K11
Arthington Leeds 58 H5
Arthingworth Nhants 41 Q10
Arthrath Abers 103 K7
Artrochie Abers 103 L8
Arundel W Susx 10 G8
Asby Cumb 70 H10
Ascog Ag & B 84 B9
Ascot W & M 20 E9
Ascott-under-Wychwood Oxon 30 H9
Asenby N York 65 P11
Asfordby Leics 41 P4
Asfordby Hill Leics 41 Q4
Asgarby Lincs 42 G2
Ash Kent 22 C9
Ash Kent 23 P10
Ash Somset 17 L11
Ash Surrey 20 E12
Ashampstead W Berk 19 P5
Ashbocking Suffk 35 K6
Ashbourne Derbys 50 F10
Ashbrittle Somset 16 E11
Ashburton Devon 5 P6
Ashbury Devon 15 J11
Ashbury Oxon 19 J4
Ashby N Linc 52 C2
Ashby by Partney Lincs 53 L9
Ashby cum Fenby NE Lin 53 J4
Ashby de la Launde Lincs 52 F11
Ashby-de-la-Zouch Leics 41 J4
Ashby Folville Leics 41 P5
Ashby Magna Leics 41 M9
Ashby Parva Leics 41 M9
Ashby Puerorum Lincs 53 K8
Ashby St Ledgers Nhants 31 M1
Ashby St Mary Norfk 45 M9
Ashchurch Gloucs 29 N3
Ashcombe Devon 6 C6
Ashcombe N Som 17 J4
Ashcott Somset 17 L8
Ashdon Essex 33 P8
Ashdown Forest E Susx 11 P4
Ashe Hants 19 N10
Asheldham Essex 23 J3
Ashen Essex 34 C8
Ashendon Bucks 31 P10
Asheridge Bucks 20 F3
Ashfield Stirlg 85 N3
Ashfield cum Thorpe Suffk 35 K4
Ashfield Green Suffk 35 L3
Ashford Devon 5 N9
Ashford Devon 15 J5
Ashford Kent 13 J2
Ashford Surrey 20 H8
Ashford Bowdler Shrops 39 K7
Ashford Carbonell Shrops 39 K7
Ashford Hill Hants 19 P8
Ashford in the Water Derbys 50 G6
Ashgill S Lans 77 N2
Ash Green Surrey 20 E12
Ash Green Warwks 41 J9
Ashill Devon 6 E1
Ashill Norfk 44 E8
Ashill Somset 17 J11
Ashingdon Essex 22 G5
Ashington Nthumb 73 M4
Ashington Somset 17 N11
Ashington W Susx 11 J7
Ashkirk Border 79 P4
Ashleworth Gloucs 29 L4
Ashleworth Quay Gloucs 29 L4
Ashley Cambs 34 B5
Ashley Ches E 57 P11
Ashley Devon 15 L9
Ashley Gloucs 29 N9
Ashley Hants 9 J8
Ashley Hants 9 L2
Ashley Kent 13 P1
Ashley Nhants 42 B11
Ashley Staffs 49 N7
Ashley Wilts 18 B7
Ashley Green Bucks 20 F3
Ash Magna Shrops 49 K7
Ashmansworth Hants 19 M8
Ashmansworthy Devon 14 F8
Ash Mill Devon 15 N7
Ashmore Dorset 8 D4
Ashmore Green W Berk 19 N6
Ashorne Warwks 30 H3
Ashover Derbys 51 J8
Ashow Warwks 40 H12
Ashperton Herefs 28 H1
Ashprington Devon 5 Q8
Ash Priors Somset 16 F9
Ashreigney Devon 15 L9
Ash Street Suffk 34 G7
Ashtead Surrey 21 J10
Ash Thomas Devon 6 D1
Ashton Ches W 49 J2
Ashton Cnwll 2 F9
Ashton Devon 6 B6
Ashton Herefs 39 K8
Ashton Inver 84 D7
Ashton Nhants 31 Q4
Ashton Nhants 42 F11
Ashton Common Wilts 18 D8
Ashton-in-Makerfield Wigan 57 L8
Ashton Keynes Wilts 18 F2
Ashton under Hill Worcs 30 C6
Ashton-under-Lyne Tamesd 50 C2
Ashton Vale Bristl 17 N3
Ashurst Hants 9 K5
Ashurst Kent 11 P3
Ashurst Lancs 57 J7
Ashurst W Susx 11 J6
Ashurstwood W Susx 11 N3
Ash Vale Surrey 20 E11
Ashwater Devon 5 J2
Ashwell Herts 33 J8
Ashwell Rutlnd 42 C7
Ashwell End Herts 33 J8
Ashwellthorpe Norfk 45 J9
Ashwick Somset 17 P6
Ashwicken Norfk 44 B6
Askam in Furness Cumb 62 E6
Askern Donc 59 M10
Askerswell Dorset 7 M4
Askett Bucks 20 D3
Askham Cumb 71 Q10
Askham Notts 51 Q6
Askham Bryan C York 59 M5
Askham Richard C York 59 M5
Asknish Ag & B 83 P5
Askrigg N York 64 G8
Askwith N York 58 F5
Aslackby Lincs 42 F4
Aslacton Norfk 45 J11
Aslockton Notts 51 Q11
Aspatria Cumb 71 J7
Aspenden Herts 33 K10
Aspley Guise C Beds 32 D9
Aspley Heath C Beds 32 D9
Aspull Wigan 57 L7
Asselby E R Yk 60 C8
Assington Suffk 34 F8
Assington Green Suffk 34 C6
Astbury Ches E 49 Q3
Astcote Nhants 31 P4
Asterby Lincs 53 J7
Asterley Shrops 38 G1
Asterton Shrops 38 H4
Asthall Oxon 30 H10
Asthall Leigh Oxon 30 H10
Astle Highld 107 M4
Astley Shrops 49 K10
Astley Warwks 40 H9
Astley Wigan 57 M8
Astley Worcs 39 P8
Astley Abbots Shrops 39 N3
Astley Bridge Bolton 57 N6
Astley Cross Worcs 39 P8
Aston Birm 40 E9
Aston Ches E 49 L6
Aston Ches W 57 K12
Aston Derbys 50 F4
Aston Flints 48 F3
Aston Herts 33 J11
Aston Oxon 31 J12
Aston Rothm 51 L4
Aston Shrops 39 P4
Aston Shrops 49 K9
Aston Staffs 40 B3
Aston Staffs 49 N7
Aston Wokham 20 C6
Aston Wrekin 49 L12
Aston Abbotts Bucks 32 C11
Aston Botterell Shrops 39 L5
Aston-by-Stone Staffs 40 B2
Aston Cantlow Warwks 30 F3
Aston Clinton Bucks 20 E2
Aston Crews Herefs 29 J4
Aston End Herts 33 J11
Aston Fields Worcs 40 C12
Aston Flamville Leics 41 L8
Aston Ingham Herefs 29 J4
Aston le Walls Nhants 31 L4
Aston Magna Gloucs 30 G7
Aston Munslow Shrops 39 K5
Aston on Clun Shrops 38 H6
Aston Pigott Shrops 38 G2
Aston Rogers Shrops 38 G2
Aston Rowant Oxon 20 B4
Aston Somerville Worcs 30 D6
Aston-sub-Edge Gloucs 30 F6
Aston Tirrold Oxon 19 P4
Aston-upon-Trent Derbys 41 K2
Aston Upthorpe Oxon 19 P4
Astwick C Beds 32 H8
Astwood M Keyn 32 D7
Astwood Worcs 30 C2
Astwood Bank Worcs 30 D2
Aswarby Lincs 42 F3
Aswardby Lincs 53 L9
Atcham Shrops 39 K1
Athelhampton Dorset 8 B8
Athelington Suffk 35 K3
Athelney Somset 17 J9
Athelstaneford E Loth 87 K6
Atherington Devon 15 K7
Atherstone Warwks 40 H7
Atherstone on Stour Warwks 30 G4
Atherton Wigan 57 M8
Atlow Derbys 50 G10
Attadale Highld 97 N3
Atterby Lincs 52 E5
Attercliffe Sheff 51 J3
Atterton Leics 41 J7
Attingham Park Shrops 49 K12
Attleborough Norfk 44 H10
Attleborough Warwks 41 J8
Attlebridge Norfk 45 J6
Attleton Green Suffk 34 C6
Atwick E R Yk 61 K4
Atworth Wilts 18 C7
Aubourn Lincs 52 D10
Auchbreck Moray 101 J9
Auchedly Abers 103 J8
Auchenblae Abers 95 M6
Auchenbowie Stirlg 85 N5
Auchencairn D & G 70 D5
Auchencairn D & G 78 F11
Auchencairn N Ayrs 75 Q6
Auchencrow Border 87 Q9
Auchendinny Mdloth 86 F9
Auchengray S Lans 86 B10
Auchenhalrig Moray 101 M3
Auchenheath S Lans 77 N3
Auchenhessnane D & G 77 N11
Auchenlochan Ag & B 83 P8
Auchenmade N Ayrs 76 F2
Auchenmalg D & G 68 G8
Auchentiber N Ayrs 76 F2
Auchindrain Ag & B 83 Q3
Auchindrean Highld 106 C6
Auchininna Abers 102 E6
Auchinleck E Ayrs 77 J7
Auchinloch N Lans 85 L8
Auchinstarry N Lans 85 M7
Auchintore Highld 90 F2
Auchiries Abers 103 M7
Auchlean Highld 99 M9
Auchlee Abers 95 P3
Auchleven Abers 102 E9
Auchlochan S Lans 77 N4
Auchlossan Abers 95 J2
Auchlyne Stirlg 91 M9
Auchmillan E Ayrs 77 J5
Auchmithie Angus 93 R6
Auchmuirbridge Fife 86 E3
Auchnacree Angus 94 H8
Auchnagatt Abers 103 J7
Auchnarrow Moray 101 J9
Auchnotteroch D & G 68 D7
Auchroisk Moray 101 L5
Auchterarder P & K 92 E12
Auchteraw Highld 98 E7
Auchterblair Highld 99 N5
Auchtercairn Highld 105 M7
Auchterderran Fife 86 E3
Auchterhouse Angus 93 L8
Auchterless Abers 102 F7
Auchtermuchty Fife 93 J12
Auchterneed Highld 106 H9
Auchtertool Fife 86 E4
Auchtertyre Highld 97 L4
Auchtubh Stirlg 91 N11
Auckengill Highld 110 G3
Auckley Donc 51 P1
Audenshaw Tamesd 50 B2
Audlem Ches E 49 M6
Audley Staffs 49 P5
Audley End Essex 33 N8
Audley End House & Gardens Essex 33 N8
Audnam Dudley 40 B9
Aughton E R Yk 60 C6
Aughton Lancs 56 H7
Aughton Lancs 63 K8
Aughton Rothm 51 L4
Aughton Wilts 19 J9
Aughton Park Lancs 56 H7
Auldearn Highld 100 E4
Aulden Herefs 39 J10
Auldgirth D & G 78 E10
Auldhouse S Lans 77 K2
Ault a' chruinn Highld 97 N5
Aultbea Highld 105 N5
Aultgrishin Highld 105 L5
Aultguish Inn Highld 106 F8
Ault Hucknall Derbys 51 L7
Aultmore Moray 101 M5
Aultnagoire Highld 98 H4
Aultnamain Highld 107 L6
Aunsby Lincs 42 F3
Aust S Glos 28 G10
Austerfield Donc 51 P2
Austrey Warwks 40 H6
Austwick N York 63 N8
Authorpe Lincs 53 L7
Avebury Wilts 18 G6
Avebury Wilts 18 G6
Aveley Thurr 22 C7
Avening Gloucs 29 M8
Averham Notts 51 Q9
Aveton Gifford Devon 5 N10
Aviemore Highld 99 N6
Avington W Berk 19 L7
Avoch Highld 107 L10
Avon Hants 8 G7
Avonbridge Falk 85 Q8
Avon Dassett Warwks 31 K4
Avonmouth Bristl 28 F12
Avonwick Devon 5 P8
Awbridge Hants 9 K3
Awliscombe Devon 6 F3
Awre Gloucs 29 J7
Awsworth Notts 51 L11
Axbridge Somset 17 L5
Axford Hants 19 Q11
Axford Wilts 19 J6
Axminster Devon 6 H3
Axmouth Devon 6 H5
Aycliffe Dur 65 M3
Aydon Nthumb 72 H7
Aylburton Gloucs 28 H8
Aylesbeare Devon 6 D4
Aylesbury Bucks 20 D1
Aylesby NE Lin 52 H3
Aylesford Kent 22 E10
Aylesham Kent 23 N11
Aylestone C Leic 41 M7
Aylestone Park C Leic 41 N7
Aylmerton Norfk 45 K3
Aylsham Norfk 45 K5
Aylton Herefs 28 H2
Aylworth Gloucs 30 E9
Aymestrey Herefs 38 H8
Aynho Nhants 31 L7
Ayot St Lawrence Herts 32 H12
Ayr S Ayrs 76 F7
Aysgarth N York 64 H9
Ayshford Devon 16 E11
Ayside Cumb 62 H5
Ayston Rutlnd 42 C9
Ayton Border 81 J3
Azerley N York 65 M11

B

Babbacombe Torbay 6 C9
Babbs Green Herts 33 L12
Babcary Somset 17 N9
Babraham Cambs 33 N6
Babworth Notts 51 P5
Backaland Ork 111 h1
Backfolds Abers 103 L5
Backford Ches W 48 H2
Backies Highld 107 N3
Back of Keppoch Highld 97 J11
Backwell N Som 17 L3
Baconsthorpe Norfk 45 J3
Bacton Herefs 28 D3
Bacton Norfk 45 M4
Bacton Suffk 34 H4
Bacup Lancs 57 Q4
Badachro Highld 105 L7
Badanloch Highld 109 N8
Badbury Swindn 18 H5
Badby Nhants 31 M3
Badcall Highld 108 E5
Badcaul Highld 105 Q4
Baddeley Edge C Stke 50 B9
Baddeley Green C Stke 50 B9
Baddesley Clinton Warwks 40 G11
Baddesley Ensor Warwks 40 H7
Baddidarrach Highld 108 C10
Baddinsgill Border 86 D10
Badenscoth Abers 102 F7
Badentarbet Highld 105 Q1
Badenyon Abers 101 L10
Badger Shrops 39 N3
Badgeworth Gloucs 29 M5
Badgworth Somset 17 K5
Badicaul Highld 97 K4
Badingham Suffk 35 M3
Badlesmere Kent 23 J11
Badlieu Border 78 H5
Badlipster Highld 110 F6
Badluarach Highld 105 P4
Badninish Highld 107 M4
Badrallach Highld 105 Q4
Badsey Worcs 30 E5
Badshot Lea Surrey 10 D1
Badsworth Wakefd 59 L10
Badwell Ash Suffk 34 G3
Bagber Dorset 17 Q12
Bagby N York 66 C10
Bag Enderby Lincs 53 K8
Bagendon Gloucs 30 D11
Bàgh a' Chaisteil W Isls 111 a7
Bagillt Flints 48 E1
Baginton Warwks 41 J11
Baglan Neath 26 G9
Bagley Shrops 48 H9
Bagley Somset 17 L7
Bagnall Staffs 50 B10
Bagshot Surrey 20 E10
Bagstone S Glos 29 J10
Bagworth Leics 41 K6
Bagwy Llydiart Herefs 28 E4
Baildon C Brad 58 F6
Baildon Green C Brad 58 F6
Baile Ailein W Isls 111 d2
Baile a' Mhanaich W Isls 111 b5
Baile Mòr Ag & B 88 G10
Baillieston C Glas 85 L9
Bainbridge N York 64 G9
Bainshole Abers 102 D8
Bainton C Pete 42 F8
Bainton E R Yk 60 G4
Baintown Fife 86 G2
Bairnkine Border 80 E10
Bakewell Derbys 50 G7
Bala Gwynd 47 Q4
Balallan W Isls 111 d2
Balbeg Highld 98 F3
Balbeggie P & K 92 H9
Balblair Highld 106 H12
Balblair Highld 107 L8
Balby Donc 51 M1
Balcary D & G 70 D5
Balchraggan Highld 98 G1
Balchreick Highld 108 D4
Balcombe W Susx 11 L4
Balcomie Links Fife 87 M1
Baldersby N York 65 N10
Baldersby St James N York 65 P11
Balderstone Lancs 57 L3
Balderton Notts 52 B12
Baldinnie Fife 93 M12
Baldinnies P & K 92 F11
Baldock Herts 33 J9
Baldock Services Herts 32 H9
Baldovie C Dund 93 M8
Baldrine IoM 56 d5
Baldslow E Susx 12 F7
Bale Norfk 44 G3
Baledgarno P & K 93 K9
Balemartine Ag & B 88 C7
Balerno C Edin 86 D8
Balfarg Fife 86 F2
Balfield Angus 95 J8
Balfour Ork 111 h2
Balfron Stirlg 85 J5
Balgaveny Abers 102 E7
Balgonar Fife 86 B4
Balgowan D & G 68 F9
Balgowan Highld 99 J9
Balgown Highld 104 E8
Balgracie D & G 68 D7
Balgray S Lans 78 E4
Balham Gt Lon 21 L8
Balhary P & K 93 J6
Balholmie P & K 92 H8
Baligill Highld 109 P3
Balintore Angus 93 K4
Balintore Highld 107 P7
Balintraid Highld 107 M8
Balivanich W Isls 111 b5
Balkeerie Angus 93 K6
Balkholme E R Yk 60 D8
Ballachulish Highld 90 E5
Ballajora IoM 56 e4
Ballanlay Ag & B 83 Q9
Ballantrae S Ayrs 68 E3
Ballasalla IoM 56 b6
Ballater Abers 94 F3
Ballaugh IoM 56 c3
Ballchraggan Highld 107 M7
Ballencrieff E Loth 87 J6
Ballevullin Ag & B 88 B7
Ball Green C Stke 50 B9
Ball Hill Hants 19 M8
Ballidon Derbys 50 G9
Balliekine N Ayrs 75 N5
Balliemore Ag & B 84 B3
Balligmorrie S Ayrs 68 G2
Ballimore Stirlg 91 M11
Ballindalloch Moray 101 J7
Ballindean P & K 93 J9
Ballinger Common Bucks 20 E3
Ballingham Herefs 28 G3
Ballingry Fife 86 E3
Ballinluig P & K 92 E5
Ballinshoe Angus 93 M5
Ballintuim P & K 92 G5
Balloch Highld 107 M11
Balloch N Lans 85 M7
Balloch P & K 92 C10
Balloch S Ayrs 76 F11
Balloch W Duns 84 G6
Balls Cross W Susx 10 F5
Balls Green E Susx 11 P3
Ballygown Ag & B 89 J7
Ballygrant Ag & B 82 E9
Ballyhaugh Ag & B 88 E5
Balmacara Highld 97 L4
Balmaclellan D & G 69 P4
Balmae D & G 69 P9
Balmaha Stirlg 84 G5
Balmalcolm Fife 86 G1
Balmangan D & G 69 P9
Balmedie Abers 103 K10
Balmerino Fife 93 L10
Balmichael N Ayrs 75 P6
Balmore E Duns 85 K8
Balmuchy Highld 107 P6
Balmule Fife 86 E5
Balmullo Fife 93 M10
Balnacoil Highld 109 P12
Balnacra Highld 105 P12
Balnacroft Abers 94 E3
Balnafoich Highld 99 K2
Balnaguard P & K 92 E5
Balnahard Ag & B 89 K9
Balnain Highld 98 F3
Balnakeil Highld 108 G3
Balne N York 59 N9
Balquharn P & K 92 F8
Balquhidder Stirlg 91 M11
Balsall Common Solhll 40 G11
Balsall Heath Birm 40 E9
Balscote Oxon 31 K6
Balsham Cambs 33 P6
Baltasound Shet 111 m2
Baltersan D & G 69 K6
Balthangie Abers 102 H5
Baltonsborough Somset 17 M8
Balvicar Ag & B 89 Q11
Balvraid Highld 97 M6
Balvraid Highld 99 M3
Bamber Bridge Lancs 57 K4
Bamber's Green Essex 33 P11
Bamburgh Nthumb 81 N7
Bamburgh Castle Nthumb 81 N7
Bamford Derbys 50 G4
Bampton Cumb 71 Q11
Bampton Devon 16 C10
Bampton Oxon 30 H12
Bampton Grange Cumb 71 Q11
Banavie Highld 90 F2
Banbury Oxon 31 L6
Bancffosfelen Carmth 26 C6
Banchory Abers 95 L3
Banchory-Devenick Abers 95 P2
Bancycapel Carmth 25 P6
Bancyfelin Carmth 25 N5
Bandirran P & K 93 J9
Banff Abers 102 F3
Bangor Gwynd 54 H7

Bangor-on-Dee Wrexhm 48 H6
Bangors Cnwll 14 D11
Banham Norfk 44 H11
Bank Hants 9 K6
Bankend D & G 70 G2
Bankfoot P & K 92 F8
Bankglen E Ayrs 77 K8
Bankhead C Aber 103 J12
Bankhead S Lans 86 B12
Banknock Falk 85 N7
Banks Lancs 56 H5
Bankshill D & G 79 K11
Banningham Norfk 45 K4
Bannister Green Essex 34 B11
Bannockburn Stirlg 85 N5
Banstead Surrey 21 K10
Bantham Devon 5 N10
Banton N Lans 85 M7
Banwell N Som 17 K4
Bapchild Kent 22 H10
Bapton Wilts 18 E12
Barabhas W Isls 111 d1
Barassie S Ayrs 76 F5
Barbaraville Highld 107 M7
Barbon Cumb 63 L6
Barbrook Devon 15 M3
Barby Nhants 41 M12
Barcaldine Ag & B 90 D7
Barcombe E Susx 11 N7
Barcombe Cross E Susx 11 N6
Barden Park Kent 12 C2
Bardfield End Green Essex 33 Q9
Bardfield Saling Essex 34 B10
Bardney Lincs 52 G9
Bardon Leics 41 K5
Bardon Mill Nthumb 72 E7
Bardowie E Duns 85 K8
Bardrainney Inver 84 F8
Bardsea Cumb 62 F7
Bardsey Leeds 59 J5
Bardsey Island Gwynd 46 B7
Bardwell Suffk 34 F3
Bare Lancs 63 J8
Barfad D & G 69 J4
Barford Norfk 45 J8
Barford Warwks 30 H2
Barford St John Oxon 31 K7
Barford St Martin Wilts 8 F2
Barford St Michael Oxon 31 K7
Barfrestone Kent 23 N12
Bargeddie N Lans 85 L9
Bargoed Caerph 27 N8
Bargrennan D & G 69 J4
Barham Cambs 32 G2
Barham Kent 23 N12
Barham Suffk 35 J6
Bar Hill Cambs 33 L4
Barholm Lincs 42 F7
Barkby Leics 41 N5
Barkby Thorpe Leics 41 N5
Barkestone-le-Vale Leics 41 R1
Barkham Wokham 20 C9
Barking Gt Lon 21 N6
Barking Suffk 34 H6
Barkingside Gt Lon 21 N5
Barking Tye Suffk 34 H6
Barkisland Calder 58 D9
Barkla Shop Cnwll 2 H6
Barkston Lincs 42 D2
Barkston Ash N York 59 L7
Barkway Herts 33 L9
Barlanark C Glas 85 L9
Barlaston Staffs 50 B12
Barlavington W Susx 10 F6
Barlborough Derbys 51 L5
Barlby N York 59 N7
Barlestone Leics 41 K6
Barley Herts 33 L8
Barley Lancs 57 P1
Barleythorpe Rutlnd 42 C8
Barling Essex 22 H5
Barlings Lincs 52 F9
Barlochan D & G 70 D4
Barlow Derbys 51 J6
Barlow Gatesd 73 K8
Barlow N York 59 N8
Barmby Moor E R Yk 60 D4
Barmby on the Marsh E R Yk 59 P8
Barmollack Ag & B 75 M4
Barmouth Gwynd 47 K7
Barmpton Darltn 65 N4
Barmston E R Yk 61 K3
Barnacarry Ag & B 83 Q4
Barnack C Pete 42 F8
Barnard Castle Dur 65 J4
Barnard Gate Oxon 31 K11
Barnardiston Suffk 34 B7
Barnbarroch D & G 70 D4
Barnby Suffk 45 P11
Barnby Dun Donc 59 N11
Barnby in the Willows Notts 52 C11
Barnby Moor Notts 51 P4
Barncorkrie D & G 68 E11
Barnes Gt Lon 21 K7
Barnes Street Kent 12 D1
Barnet Gt Lon 21 K4
Barnetby le Wold N Linc 52 F2
Barney Norfk 44 G4
Barnham Suffk 34 E2
Barnham W Susx 10 F8
Barnham Broom Norfk 44 H8
Barnhead Angus 93 R4
Barnhill C Dund 93 N8
Barnhill Moray 100 H4
Barnhills D & G 68 D5
Barningham Dur 65 J5
Barningham Suffk 34 F2
Barnoldby le Beck NE Lin 52 H3
Barnoldswick Lancs 63 Q11
Barns Green W Susx 10 H5
Barnsley Barns 59 J11
Barnsley Gloucs 30 E12
Barnstaple Devon 15 K5
Barnston Essex 33 Q11
Barnston Wirral 56 F11
Barnstone Notts 41 Q1
Barnt Green Worcs 40 D10
Barnton C Edin 86 E7
Barnton Ches W 49 L1
Barnwell All Saints Nhants 42 F12

Barnwell St Andrew Nhants 42 F12
Barnwood Gloucs 29 M5
Barr S Ayrs 76 E11
Barra W Isls 111 a7
Barra Airport W Isls 111 a6
Barrachan D & G 69 J8
Barraigh W Isls 111 a7
Barrananaoil Ag & B 83 M2
Barrapoll Ag & B 88 B7
Barrasford Nthumb 72 G6
Barrhead E Rens 84 H10
Barrhill S Ayrs 68 H3
Barrington Cambs 33 L6
Barrington Somset 17 K11
Barripper Cnwll 2 F7
Barrmill N Ayrs 84 F11
Barrock Highld 110 F2
Barrow Gloucs 29 M4
Barrow Lancs 57 N2
Barrow Rutlnd 42 C7
Barrow Somset 17 Q9
Barrow Suffk 34 C4
Barrowby Lincs 42 C3
Barrowden Rutlnd 42 D9
Barrowford Lancs 57 Q2
Barrow Gurney N Som 17 M3
Barrow Haven N Linc 60 H9
Barrow-in-Furness Cumb 62 E8
Barrow Island Cumb 62 E8
Barrow-upon-Humber N Linc 60 H9
Barrow upon Soar Leics 41 M4
Barrow upon Trent Derbys 41 J2
Barry Angus 93 P8
Barry V Glam 16 F3
Barry Island V Glam 16 F3
Barsby Leics 41 P5
Barsham Suffk 45 N11
Barston Solhll 40 G10
Bartestree Herefs 28 G1
Barthol Chapel Abers 102 H8
Bartholomew Green Essex 34 C11
Barthomley Ches E 49 N5
Bartley Hants 9 K5
Bartley Green Birm 40 D10
Bartlow Cambs 33 P7
Barton Cambs 33 L5
Barton Ches W 49 J5
Barton Gloucs 30 E8
Barton Lancs 56 G7
Barton Lancs 57 K2
Barton N York 65 M6
Barton Oxon 31 M11
Barton Torbay 6 C8
Barton Bendish Norfk 44 B8
Barton End Gloucs 29 L8
Barton Hartshorn Bucks 31 N7
Barton in Fabis Notts 41 M2
Barton in the Beans Leics 41 K6
Barton-le-Clay C Beds 32 F9
Barton-le-Street N York 66 G11
Barton-le-Willows N York 60 C2
Barton Mills Suffk 34 C3
Barton-on-Sea Hants 9 J8
Barton-on-the-Heath Warwks 30 G7
Barton Park Services N York 65 L6
Barton St David Somset 17 M9
Barton Seagrave Nhants 32 C2
Barton Stacey Hants 19 M11
Barton Town Devon 15 L4
Barton Turf Norfk 45 M5
Barton-under-Needwood Staffs 40 F4
Barton-upon-Humber N Linc 60 H9
Barton Waterside N Linc 60 H9
Barvas W Isls 111 d1
Barway Cambs 33 N2
Barwell Leics 41 K8
Barwick Devon 15 K10
Barwick Somset 17 M12
Barwick in Elmet Leeds 59 K6
Baschurch Shrops 48 H10
Bascote Warwks 31 K2
Bashall Eaves Lancs 63 M12
Basildon Essex 22 E5
Basingstoke Hants 19 Q9
Baslow Derbys 50 G6
Bason Bridge Somset 17 J7
Bassaleg Newpt 28 C10
Bassendean Border 80 E5
Bassenthwaite Cumb 71 K8
Bassett C Sotn 9 M4
Bassingbourn-cum-Kneesworth Cambs 33 K7
Bassingham Lincs 52 C10
Bassingthorpe Lincs 42 D5
Bassus Green Herts 33 K10
Baston Lincs 42 G7
Bastwick Norfk 45 N6
Batchworth Herts 20 G5
Batcombe Dorset 7 N3
Batcombe Somset 17 Q8
Batford Herts 21 J1
Bath BaNES 17 Q3
Bath BaNES 17 Q4
Bathampton BaNES 18 B7
Bathealton Somset 16 E10
Batheaston BaNES 18 B7
Bathford BaNES 18 B7
Bathgate W Loth 86 B8
Bathley Notts 51 Q8
Bathpool Cnwll 4 G5
Bathpool Somset 16 H10
Bath Side Essex 35 L9
Bathville W Loth 85 Q9
Bathway Somset 17 N6
Batley Kirk 58 G9
Batsford Gloucs 30 F7
Battersby N York 66 E6
Battersea Gt Lon 21 L7
Battisford Tye Suffk 34 G6
Battle E Susx 12 E7
Battle Powys 27 L3
Battledykes Angus 93 M5
Battlesbridge Essex 22 F5
Battleton Somset 16 C10
Baughton Worcs 29 M1
Baughurst Hants 19 P8
Baulds Abers 95 K4
Baulking Oxon 19 K3
Baumber Lincs 52 H8
Baunton Gloucs 30 D12

Baverstock Wilts 8 F2
Bawburgh Norfk 45 J8
Bawdeswell Norfk 44 H6
Bawdrip Somset 17 J8
Bawdsey Suffk 35 M8
Bawtry Donc 51 P3
Baxenden Lancs 57 P4
Baxterley Warwks 40 H7
Baybridge Hants 9 N3
Baycliff Cumb 62 F7
Baydon Wilts 19 K5
Bayford Herts 21 L2
Bayford Somset 17 Q9
Bayhead W Isls 111 a4
Baylham Suffk 34 H6
Baysham Herefs 28 G4
Bayston Hill Shrops 39 J1
Baythorne End Essex 34 C8
Bayton Worcs 39 M7
Bayworth Oxon 19 N1
Beachampton Bucks 31 Q6
Beachamwell Norfk 44 C8
Beachy Head E Susx 12 C10
Beacon Devon 6 G2
Beacon End Essex 34 F10
Beacon Hill Notts 52 B11
Beacon Hill Surrey 10 E3
Beacon's Bottom Bucks 20 C4
Beaconsfield Bucks 20 F5
Beaconsfield Services Bucks 20 F5
Beadlam N York 66 F9
Beadlow C Beds 32 F8
Beadnell Nthumb 81 P8
Beaford Devon 15 K8
Beal N York 59 M8
Beal Nthumb 81 M6
Bealsmill Cnwll 4 H5
Beaminster Dorset 7 L3
Beamish Dur 73 M9
Beamish Museum Dur 73 L9
Beamsley N York 58 E4
Beanacre Wilts 18 D7
Beanley Nthumb 81 M9
Beardon Devon 5 L4
Beare Green Surrey 11 J2
Bearley Warwks 30 F3
Bearpark Dur 73 M11
Bearsden E Duns 85 J8
Bearsted Kent 22 F11
Bearstone Shrops 49 N7
Bearwood BCP 8 F7
Bearwood Birm 40 D9
Bearwood Herefs 38 H10
Beattock D & G 78 H8
Beauchamp Roding Essex 22 C2
Beauchief Sheff 51 J5
Beaufort Blae G 27 N6
Beaulieu Hants 9 L7
Beauly Highld 107 J11
Beaumaris IoA 54 H6
Beaumaris Castle IoA 54 H6
Beaumont Cumb 71 M4
Beaumont Essex 35 J10
Beaumont Jersey 7 b2
Beaumont Leys C Leic 41 M6
Beausale Warwks 40 G12
Beauworth Hants 9 P3
Beaworthy Devon 14 H11
Beazley End Essex 34 C10
Bebington Wirral 56 G11
Bebside Nthumb 73 M5
Beccles Suffk 45 N11
Becconsall Lancs 57 J4
Beckbury Shrops 39 N2
Beckenham Gt Lon 21 M9
Beckermet Cumb 62 B2
Beckfoot Cumb 70 H5
Beckford Worcs 29 N2
Beckhampton Wilts 18 G7
Beckingham Lincs 52 C11
Beckingham Notts 51 R3
Beckington Somset 18 B9
Beckjay Shrops 38 H6
Beckley E Susx 12 G5
Beckley Oxon 31 M10
Beck Row Suffk 34 B2
Beck Side Cumb 62 E6
Beckton Gt Lon 21 N7
Beckwithshaw N York 58 H4
Becontree Gt Lon 21 P6
Bedale N York 65 M9
Bedchester Dorset 8 C4
Beddau Rhondd 27 M10
Beddgelert Gwynd 54 H11
Beddingham E Susx 11 N8
Beddington Gt Lon 21 L9
Beddington Corner Gt Lon 21 L9
Bedfield Suffk 35 K4
Bedford Bed 32 F6
Bedgrove Bucks 20 D2
Bedhampton Hants 10 B8
Bedingfield Suffk 35 K3
Bedlam N York 58 H2
Bedlington Nthumb 73 M5
Bedlinog Myr Td 27 M8
Bedminster Bristl 17 N2
Bedminster Down Bristl 17 N3
Bedmond Herts 20 H3
Bednall Staffs 40 C4
Bedrule Border 80 E10
Bedstone Shrops 38 G7
Bedwas Caerph 27 N10
Bedwellty Caerph 27 N8
Bedworth Warwks 41 J9
Beeby Leics 41 P6
Beech Hants 10 B3
Beech Staffs 49 Q7
Beech Hill W Berk 20 B9
Beechingstoke Wilts 18 G8
Beedon W Berk 19 M5
Beeford E R Yk 61 J4
Beeley Derbys 50 H7
Beelsby NE Lin 52 H3
Beenham W Berk 19 P7
Beer Devon 6 G5
Beer Somset 17 K9
Beercrocombe Somset 17 J11
Beer Hackett Dorset 7 N1
Beesands Devon 5 Q11
Beesby Lincs 53 M7
Beeson Devon 5 Q11

Beeston C Beds 32 G7
Beeston Ches W 49 K4
Beeston Leeds 58 H7
Beeston Norfk 44 F7
Beeston Notts 51 M12
Beeston Regis Norfk 45 J2
Beeswing D & G 70 E2
Beetham Cumb 63 J6
Beetham Somset 6 H1
Beetley Norfk 44 F6
Begbroke Oxon 31 L10
Begelly Pembks 25 K7
Beguildy Powys 38 E6
Beighton Norfk 45 N8
Beighton Sheff 51 K4
Beinn Na Faoghla W Isls 111 b5
Beith N Ayrs 84 F11
Bekesbourne Kent 23 M11
Belaugh Norfk 45 L6
Belbroughton Worcs 40 B11
Belchalwell Dorset 8 B5
Belchamp Otten Essex 34 D8
Belchamp St Paul Essex 34 D8
Belchamp Walter Essex 34 D8
Belchford Lincs 53 J8
Belford Nthumb 81 N7
Belgrave C Leic 41 N6
Belhaven E Loth 87 M6
Belhelvie Abers 103 K10
Belhinnie Abers 101 N9
Bellabeg Abers 101 L11
Bellanoch Ag & B 83 M5
Bellaty Angus 93 J4
Bell Busk N York 58 B3
Belleau Lincs 53 L7
Bell End Worcs 40 C11
Bellerby N York 65 K8
Belle Vue Cumb 71 M4
Belle Vue Wakefd 59 J9
Bellfield S Lans 78 D2
Bellingdon Bucks 20 F3
Bellingham Nthumb 72 F4
Belloch Ag & B 75 K5
Bellochantuy Ag & B 75 K6
Bell o' th' Hill Ches W 49 K6
Bellshill N Lans 85 M10
Bellside N Lans 85 M10
Bellsquarry W Loth 86 C8
Belluton BaNES 17 N4
Belmaduthy Highld 107 K10
Belmont Bl w D 57 M6
Belmont Gt Lon 21 K10
Belmont S Ayrs 76 F7
Belmont Shet 111 m2
Belnacraig Abers 101 M11
Belper Derbys 51 J10
Belsay Nthumb 73 K5
Belses Border 80 D8
Belsford Devon 5 P8
Belsize Herts 20 G4
Belstead Suffk 35 J8
Belstone Devon 5 M2
Belthorn Bl w D 57 N4
Beltinge Kent 23 M9
Beltingham Nthumb 72 E7
Beltoft N Linc 52 B3
Belton Leics 41 K4
Belton Lincs 42 D3
Belton N Linc 52 B3
Belton Norfk 45 P9
Belton Rutlnd 42 B9
Belton House Lincs 42 D3
Belton in Rutland Rutlnd 42 B9
Belvedere Gt Lon 21 P7
Belvoir Leics 42 B4
Bembridge IoW 9 Q9
Bemerton Wilts 8 G2
Bempton E R Yk 67 P12
Benacre Suffk 45 Q12
Benbecula W Isls 111 b5
Benbecula Airport W Isls 111 b5
Benbuie D & G 77 M11
Benderloch Ag & B 90 C8
Benenden Kent 12 F4
Benfieldside Dur 73 J9
Bengeo Herts 21 L1
Bengeworth Worcs 30 D5
Benhall Green Suffk 35 M5
Benhall Street Suffk 35 M5
Benholm Abers 95 N7
Beningbrough N York 59 M3
Benington Herts 33 J11
Benington Lincs 43 L2
Benllech IoA 54 G5
Benmore Ag & B 84 C6
Bennan N Ayrs 75 Q7
Ben Nevis Highld 90 G3
Benniworth Lincs 52 H7
Benover Kent 12 E1
Ben Rhydding C Brad 58 F5
Benslie N Ayrs 76 F3
Benson Oxon 19 Q3
Benthoul C Aber 95 N2
Bentley Donc 59 M11
Bentley E R Yk 60 H6
Bentley Hants 10 C2
Bentley Suffk 35 J8
Bentley Warwks 40 H8
Bentpath D & G 79 M10
Bentwichen Devon 15 M6
Bentworth Hants 19 Q11
Benvie Angus 93 M8
Benville Dorset 7 M3
Benwick Cambs 43 K11
Beoley Worcs 40 E12
Beoraidbeg Highld 97 J10
Bepton W Susx 10 D6
Berden Essex 33 N10
Berea Pembks 24 E3
Bere Alston Devon 5 J6
Bere Ferrers Devon 5 K7
Bere Regis Dorset 8 C8
Bergh Apton Norfk 45 M9
Berinsfield Oxon 19 P2
Berkeley Gloucs 29 J8
Berkhamsted Herts 20 F2
Berkley Somset 18 B10
Berkswell Solhll 40 G10
Bermondsey Gt Lon 21 M7
Bernera Highld 97 L5
Bernisdale Highld 104 E10
Berrick Prior Oxon 19 Q2

Berrick Salome Oxon 19 Q3
Berriedale Highld 110 D10
Berrier Cumb 71 N9
Berriew Powys 38 E2
Berrington Shrops 39 K2
Berrington Worcs 39 L8
Berrington Green Worcs 39 L8
Berrow Somset 16 H6
Berrow Green Worcs 39 N9
Berryfields Bucks 20 C1
Berryhillock Moray 101 P3
Berryhillock Moray 101 P5
Berrynarbor Devon 15 K3
Berry Pomeroy Devon 5 Q7
Bersham Wrexhm 48 F5
Bersted W Susx 10 E9
Berwick E Susx 11 P8
Berwick Bassett Wilts 18 G6
Berwick Hill Nthumb 73 L6
Berwick St James Wilts 18 F11
Berwick St John Wilts 8 D3
Berwick St Leonard Wilts 8 D2
Berwick-upon-Tweed Nthumb 81 L4
Bescar Lancs 56 H6
Besford Worcs 30 B5
Bessacarr Donc 51 N1
Bessingby E R Yk 61 K2
Bessingham Norfk 45 J3
Besthorpe Norfk 44 H10
Besthorpe Notts 52 B9
Bestwood Village Notts 51 M10
Beswick E R Yk 60 H5
Betchworth Surrey 21 K12
Bethel Gwynd 54 G8
Bethel IoA 54 E7
Bethersden Kent 12 H3
Bethesda Gwynd 55 J8
Bethesda Pembks 25 J5
Bethlehem Carmth 26 F4
Bethnal Green Gt Lon 21 M6
Betley Staffs 49 N6
Betsham Kent 22 C8
Betteshanger Kent 23 P11
Bettiscombe Dorset 7 K3
Bettisfield Wrexhm 49 J8
Bettws Brdgnd 27 J10
Bettws Newpt 28 C10
Bettws Cedewain Powys 38 D3
Bettws Ifan Cerdgn 36 E10
Bettws-Newydd Mons 28 D7
Bettyhill Highld 109 M4
Betws Bledrws Cerdgn 37 K9
Betws Gwerfil Goch Denbgs 48 B6
Betws-y-Coed Conwy 55 L9
Betws-yn-Rhos Conwy 55 N6
Beulah Cerdgn 36 E10
Beulah Powys 37 Q9
Bevercotes Notts 51 P6
Beverley E R Yk 60 H6
Beverston Gloucs 29 M9
Bewcastle Cumb 71 Q1
Bewdley Worcs 39 P7
Bewerley N York 58 F2
Bewholme E R Yk 61 K4
Bexhill-on-Sea E Susx 12 E8
Bexley Gt Lon 21 P8
Bexleyheath Gt Lon 21 P8
Bexwell Norfk 43 Q9
Beyton Suffk 34 F4
Beyton Green Suffk 34 F4
Bhaltos W Isls 111 c2
Bhatarsaigh W Isls 111 a7
Bibury Gloucs 30 E11
Bicester Oxon 31 N9
Bickenhill Solhll 40 F10
Bicker Lincs 42 H3
Bickerstaffe Lancs 57 J7
Bickerton N York 59 K4
Bickford Staffs 40 B5
Bickington Devon 5 Q6
Bickington Devon 15 J6
Bickleigh Devon 5 L7
Bickleigh Devon 6 C2
Bickley Ches W 49 K6
Bickley Gt Lon 21 N9
Bickley N York 67 K8
Bicknacre Essex 22 F3
Bicknoller Somset 16 G8
Bicknor Kent 22 G10
Bickton Hants 8 H4
Bicton Shrops 38 H5
Bicton Shrops 49 J11
Bidborough Kent 12 C2
Biddenden Kent 12 G3
Biddenham Bed 32 E6
Biddestone Wilts 18 C6
Biddisham Somset 17 K5
Biddlesden Bucks 31 N6
Biddulph Staffs 50 B8
Biddulph Moor Staffs 50 B8
Bideford Devon 14 H6
Bidford-on-Avon Warwks 30 E4
Bielby E R Yk 60 D5
Bieldside C Aber 95 P2
Bierley IoW 9 N10
Bierton Bucks 32 B12
Big Balcraig D & G 69 K9
Bigbury Devon 5 N10
Bigbury-on-Sea Devon 5 N10
Bigby Lincs 52 F3
Biggar S Lans 78 G2
Biggin Derbys 50 F8
Biggin Hill Gt Lon 21 N10
Biggleswade C Beds 32 H7
Bigholms D & G 79 M11
Bighouse Highld 109 Q3
Bighton Hants 9 Q1
Biglands Cumb 71 L5
Bignor W Susx 10 F6
Bigrigg Cumb 70 G11
Big Sand Highld 105 L6
Bigton Shet 111 k5
Bilborough C Nott 51 M11
Bilbrook Somset 16 D7
Bilbrough N York 59 M5
Bilbster Highld 110 F5
Bildershaw Dur 65 L3
Bildeston Suffk 34 G6
Billericay Essex 22 D5
Billesdon Leics 41 Q7
Billesley Warwks 30 F3
Billingborough Lincs 42 G4

162 Billinge – Boxford

Billinge St Hel 57 K8
Billingford Norfk 35 J2
Billingford Norfk 44 G6
Billingham S on T 66 C3
Billinghay Lincs 52 G11
Billingley Barns 59 K12
Billingshurst W Susx 10 H5
Billingsley Shrops 39 N5
Billington C Beds 32 D11
Billington Lancs 57 N2
Billockby Norfk 45 N7
Billy Row Dur 73 L12
Bilsborrow Lancs 57 K2
Bilsby Lincs 53 M8
Bilsham W Susx 10 F9
Bilsington Kent 13 K3
Bilsthorpe Notts 51 N8
Bilston Mdloth 86 F8
Bilston Wolves 40 C8
Bilstone Leics 41 J6
Bilton E R Yk 61 K7
Bilton N York 58 H3
Bilton Warwks 41 L11
Bilton-in-Ainsty N York 59 L4
Binbrook Lincs 52 H5
Bincombe Dorset 7 P6
Binegar Somset 17 N6
Binfield Br For 20 D8
Binfield Heath Oxon 20 C7
Bingfield Nthumb 72 H6
Bingham Notts 51 P11
Bingley C Brad 58 E6
Binham Norfk 44 G3
Binley Covtry 41 J10
Binley Hants 19 M9
Binley Woods Warwks 41 K11
Binnegar Dorset 8 C9
Binniehill Falk 85 P8
Binscombe Surrey 10 F2
Binstead IoW 9 P8
Binsted Hants 10 C2
Binsted W Susx 10 F8
Binton Warwks 30 F4
Bintree Norfk 44 G5
Birch Essex 34 F11
Bircham Newton Norfk 44 C4
Bircham Tofts Norfk 44 C4
Birchanger Essex 33 N11
Birchanger Green Services Essex 33 N11
Birch Cross Staffs 40 E2
Bircher Herefs 39 J8
Birchfield Birm 40 E8
Birch Green Essex 34 F11
Birchgrove Cardif 27 N11
Birchgrove Swans 26 F8
Birchgrove W Susx 11 N4
Birchington Kent 23 P9
Birchley Heath Warwks 40 H8
Birchover Derbys 50 G8
Birch Services Rochdl 57 Q7
Birch Vale Derbys 50 D4
Birchwood Lincs 52 D9
Birch Wood Somset 16 H12
Birchwood Warrtn 57 M9
Bircotes Notts 51 N3
Birdbrook Essex 34 B8
Birdforth N York 66 C11
Birdham W Susx 10 D9
Birdingbury Warwks 31 K1
Birdlip Gloucs 29 N6
Birdsall N York 60 E2
Birds Edge Kirk 58 G11
Birds Green Essex 22 C2
Birdsgreen Shrops 39 P5
Birdsmoorgate Dorset 7 K3
Birdwell Barns 51 J1
Birgham Border 80 G6
Birichin Highld 107 M4
Birkby N York 65 N7
Birkdale Sefton 56 G6
Birkenbog Abers 102 C3
Birkenhead Wirral 56 G10
Birkenhead (Queensway) Tunnel Lpool 56 G10
Birkenhills Abers 102 F6
Birkenshaw Kirk 58 G8
Birkhall Abers 94 F4
Birkhill Angus 93 L8
Birkhill D & G 79 K6
Birkin N York 59 M8
Birley Herefs 39 J10
Birley Carr Sheff 51 J3
Birling Kent 22 D10
Birlingham Worcs 30 C5
Birmingham Birm 40 E9
Birmingham Airport Solhll 40 F10
Birnam P & K 92 F7
Birness Abers 103 K8
Birse Abers 95 J3
Birsemore Abers 95 J3
Birstall Kirk 58 G8
Birstall Leics 41 N5
Birstwith N York 58 G3
Birtley Gatesd 73 M9
Birtley Herefs 38 G8
Birtley Nthumb 72 F5
Birts Street Worcs 29 K2
Bisbrooke Rutlnd 42 C9
Biscathorpe Lincs 52 H6
Bisham W & M 20 D6
Bishampton Worcs 30 C4
Bish Mill Devon 15 M7
Bishop Auckland Dur 65 L2
Bishopbridge Lincs 52 E5
Bishopbriggs E Duns 85 K8
Bishop Burton E R Yk 60 G6
Bishop Middleham Dur 65 N2
Bishopmill Moray 101 J3
Bishop Monkton N York 59 J2
Bishop Norton Lincs 52 E5
Bishopsbourne Kent 23 M11
Bishops Cannings Wilts 18 F7
Bishop's Castle Shrops 38 G4
Bishop's Caundle Dorset 17 Q12
Bishop's Cleeve Gloucs 29 N4
Bishop's Frome Herefs 39 M11
Bishop's Green Essex 33 Q12
Bishop's Hull Somset 16 G10
Bishop's Itchington Warwks 31 K3
Bishops Lydeard Somset 16 G9
Bishop's Norton Gloucs 29 L4
Bishop's Nympton Devon 15 N7
Bishop's Offley Staffs 49 P9
Bishop's Stortford Herts 33 M11
Bishop's Sutton Hants 9 Q2
Bishop's Tachbrook Warwks 30 H2
Bishop's Tawton Devon 15 K6
Bishopsteignton Devon 6 B7
Bishopstoke Hants 9 M4
Bishopston Swans 26 D10
Bishopstone Bucks 20 C2
Bishopstone E Susx 11 P9
Bishopstone Herefs 38 H12
Bishopstone Kent 23 N9
Bishopstone Swindn 19 J4
Bishopstone Wilts 8 F3
Bishopstrow Wilts 18 D11
Bishop Sutton BaNES 17 N4
Bishop's Waltham Hants 9 P4
Bishopswood Somset 6 H1
Bishop's Wood Staffs 49 Q12
Bishopsworth Bristl 17 N3
Bishop Thornton N York 58 H2
Bishopthorpe C York 59 N5
Bishopton Darltn 65 P4
Bishopton Rens 84 G8
Bishop Wilton E R Yk 60 D3
Bishton Newpt 28 D10
Bishton Staffs 40 D4
Bisley Gloucs 29 M7
Bisley Surrey 20 F10
Bissoe Cnwll 2 H7
Bisterne Hants 8 G7
Bitchfield Lincs 42 E4
Bittadon Devon 15 J4
Bittaford Devon 5 N8
Bitterley Shrops 39 K6
Bitterne C Sotn 9 M5
Bitteswell Leics 41 M9
Bitton S Glos 17 P3
Bix Oxon 20 B6
Bixter Shet 111 k4
Blaby Leics 41 M7
Blackadder Border 80 H4
Blackawton Devon 5 Q9
Blackborough Devon 6 E2
Blackborough End Norfk 43 Q7
Black Bourton Oxon 30 H12
Blackboys E Susx 11 Q6
Blackbrook Derbys 51 J10
Blackbrook St Hel 57 K9
Blackbrook Staffs 49 N7
Blackburn Abers 102 H11
Blackburn Bl w D 57 M4
Blackburn W Loth 86 B8
Blackburn with Darwen Services Bl w D 57 M4
Blackcraig E Ayrs 77 K9
Black Crofts Ag & B 90 C8
Blackdog Abers 103 K11
Black Dog Devon 15 N9
Blackdown Dorset 7 K3
Blacker Hill Barns 51 J1
Blackfen Gt Lon 21 P8
Blackfield Hants 9 M7
Blackford P & K 85 P2
Blackford Somset 17 K6
Blackford Somset 17 P10
Blackfordby Leics 41 J4
Blackhall C Edin 86 E7
Blackhall Colliery Dur 73 Q11
Blackhall Mill Gatesd 73 K9
Blackhaugh Border 79 N2
Blackheath Gt Lon 21 M7
Blackheath Sandw 40 C9
Blackheath Suffk 35 N2
Blackheath Surrey 10 G2
Blackhill Abers 103 M4
Blackhill Abers 103 M6
Blackhill Dur 73 J9
Blackhill of Clackriach Abers 103 J6
Blackhorse Devon 6 D4
Blacklaw D & G 78 G7
Blackley Manch 57 Q8
Blacklunans P & K 94 C9
Blackmarstone Herefs 28 F2
Blackmill Brdgnd 27 K10
Blackmoor Hants 10 C4
Blackmoor N Som 17 L4
Blackmoorfoot Kirk 58 E10
Blackmore Essex 22 C3
Blackmore End Essex 34 C9
Black Mountains 27 Q4
Blackness Falk 86 C6
Blacknest Hants 10 C2
Black Notley Essex 34 C11
Blacko Lancs 57 Q1
Black Pill Swans 26 E10
Blackpool Bpool 56 F2
Blackpool Devon 6 B12
Blackpool Zoo Bpool 56 G2
Blackridge W Loth 85 P9
Blackrod Bolton 57 L6
Blacksboat Moray 101 J7
Blackshaw D & G 70 G3
Blackshaw Head Calder 58 C8
Blackstone W Susx 11 K6
Black Street Suffk 45 Q11
Blackthorn Oxon 31 N9
Blackthorpe Suffk 34 E4
Blacktoft E R Yk 60 E8
Blacktop C Aber 95 P2
Black Torrington Devon 14 H10
Blackwall Derbys 50 G10
Blackwall Tunnel Gt Lon 21 M7
Blackwater Cnwll 2 H6
Blackwater Hants 20 D10
Blackwater IoW 9 N9
Blackwater Somset 16 H11
Blackwaterfoot N Ayrs 75 N6
Blackwell Cumb 71 N5
Blackwell Derbys 50 E6
Blackwell Derbys 51 K8
Blackwell Warwks 30 G5
Blackwell Worcs 40 C11
Blackwood Caerph 27 N8
Blackwood D & G 78 E10
Blackwood S Lans 77 N3
Blacon Ches W 48 H2
Bladnoch D & G 69 K8
Bladon Oxon 31 K10
Blaenannerch Cerdgn 36 D10
Blaenau Ffestiniog Gwynd 47 L3
Blaenavon Torfn 27 Q7
Blaenavon Industrial Landscape Torfn 27 P7
Blaencwm Rhondd 27 K8
Blaenffos Pembks 25 L2
Blaengarw Brdgnd 27 J9
Blaengwrach Neath 27 J7
Blaengwynfi Neath 27 J9
Blaenpennal Cerdgn 37 K7
Blaenplwyf Cerdgn 37 J5
Blaenporth Cerdgn 36 D10
Blaenrhondda Rhondd 27 K8
Blaenwaun Carmth 25 L4
Blaen-y-coed Carmth 25 N4
Blagdon N Som 17 M4
Blagdon Somset 16 G11
Blagdon Torbay 6 B9
Blagdon Hill Somset 16 G11
Blaich Highld 90 E2
Blain Highld 89 N3
Blaina Blae G 27 P7
Blair Atholl P & K 92 C3
Blair Drummond Stirlg 85 M3
Blairgowrie P & K 92 H6
Blairhall Fife 86 B5
Blairingone P & K 86 B3
Blairlogie Stirlg 85 N4
Blairmore Ag & B 84 D6
Blairmore Highld 108 D4
Blair's Ferry Ag & B 83 P8
Blaisdon Gloucs 29 J5
Blakebrook Worcs 39 P6
Blakedown Worcs 39 Q6
Blake End Essex 34 B11
Blakemere Ches W 49 K2
Blakemere Herefs 28 D1
Blakenall Heath Wsall 40 D7
Blakeney Gloucs 29 J7
Blakeney Norfk 44 G2
Blakenhall Ches E 49 N6
Blakenhall Wolves 40 B7
Blakesley Nhants 31 N4
Blanchland Nthumb 72 H10
Blandford Forum Dorset 8 C6
Blandford St Mary Dorset 8 C6
Blanefield Stirlg 85 J7
Blankney Lincs 52 F10
Blantyre S Lans 85 L10
Blàr a' Chaorainn Highld 90 F3
Blargie Highld 98 H9
Blarghour Ag & B 83 Q1
Blarmachfoldach Highld 90 F3
Blaston Leics 42 B10
Blatherwycke Nhants 42 D10
Blawith Cumb 62 F5
Blawquhairn D & G 69 N3
Blaxhall Suffk 35 M5
Blaxton Donc 51 P2
Blaydon Gatesd 73 L8
Bleadney Somset 17 L7
Bleadon N Som 17 J5
Blean Kent 23 L10
Bleasby Notts 51 Q10
Blebocraigs Fife 93 M11
Bleddfa Powys 38 E8
Bledington Gloucs 30 G9
Bledlow Bucks 20 C3
Bledlow Ridge Bucks 20 C4
Blegbie E Loth 87 J9
Blencarn Cumb 64 B2
Blencogo Cumb 71 K6
Blendworth Hants 10 B7
Blenheim Palace Oxon 31 K10
Blennerhasset Cumb 71 J7
Bletchingdon Oxon 31 L9
Bletchingley Surrey 21 M12
Bletchley M Keyn 32 C9
Bletchley Shrops 49 L8
Bletchley Park Museum M Keyn 32 C9
Bletherston Pembks 25 J5
Bletsoe Bed 32 E5
Blewbury Oxon 19 N4
Blickling Norfk 45 K4
Blidworth Notts 51 N9
Blidworth Bottoms Notts 51 N9
Blindcrake Cumb 71 J8
Blindley Heath Surrey 11 M2
Blisland Cnwll 4 D5
Blissford Hants 8 H5
Bliss Gate Worcs 39 N7
Blisworth Nhants 31 Q4
Blithbury Staffs 40 E4
Blockley Gloucs 30 F7
Blofield Norfk 45 M8
Blofield Heath Norfk 45 M7
Blo Norton Norfk 34 G2
Bloomfield Border 80 D8
Blore Staffs 50 F10
Bloxham Oxon 31 K7
Bloxholm Lincs 52 F11
Bloxwich Wsall 40 D7
Bloxworth Dorset 8 C8
Blubberhouses N York 58 F3
Blue Anchor Somset 16 D7
Blue Bell Hill Kent 22 E10
Blue John Cavern Derbys 50 F4
Blundellsands Sefton 56 F8
Blundeston Suffk 45 Q10
Blunham C Beds 32 G6
Blunsdon St Andrew Swindn 18 G3
Bluntington Worcs 40 B11
Bluntisham Cambs 33 K2
Blurton C Stke 50 B11
Blyborough Lincs 52 D5
Blyford Suffk 35 N2
Blymhill Staffs 49 P11
Blyth Notts 51 N4
Blyth Nthumb 73 N5
Blyth Bridge Border 86 D12
Blythburgh Suffk 35 P2
Blythe Border 80 D4
Blythe Bridge Staffs 50 C11
Blyth Services Notts 51 N3
Blyton Lincs 52 C5
Boarhills Fife 93 P11
Boarhunt Hants 9 P6
Boarstall Bucks 31 N10
Boath Highld 107 J7
Boat of Garten Highld 99 P5
Bobbing Kent 22 H9
Bobbington Staffs 39 P4
Bocking Essex 34 C11
Bocking Churchstreet Essex 34 C10
Boddam Abers 103 M6
Boddam Shet 111 k5
Boddington Gloucs 29 M4
Bodedern IoA 54 D5
Bodelwyddan Denbgs 55 Q6
Bodenham Herefs 39 K11
Bodenham Wilts 8 H3
Bodenham Moor Herefs 39 K11
Bodewryd IoA 54 E4
Bodfari Denbgs 48 C2
Bodffordd IoA 54 F6
Bodham Norfk 45 J3
Bodiam E Susx 12 F5
Bodicote Oxon 31 L6
Bodinnick Cnwll 4 E9
Bodle Street Green E Susx 12 D7
Bodmin Cnwll 3 N3
Bodmin Moor Cnwll 4 F5
Bodsham Kent 13 L2
Boduan Gwynd 46 E4
Bodwen Cnwll 3 M4
Bogallan Highld 107 K11
Bogbrae Abers 103 L8
Bogend S Ayrs 76 G5
Boggs Holdings E Loth 87 J7
Boghall Mdloth 86 F8
Boghall W Loth 86 B8
Boghead S Lans 77 N3
Bogmoor Moray 101 L3
Bogmuir Abers 95 K7
Bogniebrae Abers 102 D6
Bognor Regis W Susx 10 E9
Bogroy Highld 99 N4
Bogue D & G 69 P3
Bohortha Cnwll 3 J8
Bohuntine Highld 98 D11
Bolam Dur 65 L3
Bolberry Devon 5 N11
Boldmere Birm 40 E8
Boldre Hants 9 K7
Boldron Dur 65 J5
Bole Notts 52 B6
Bolehill Derbys 50 H9
Bolham Devon 16 C12
Bolham Water Devon 6 F1
Bolingey Cnwll 2 H5
Bollington Ches E 50 C5
Bolney W Susx 11 L5
Bolnhurst Bed 32 F5
Bolnore W Susx 11 M5
Bolshan Angus 93 Q5
Bolsover Derbys 51 L6
Bolsterstone Sheff 50 H2
Boltby N York 66 C9
Boltenstone Abers 101 M12
Bolton Bolton 57 N7
Bolton Cumb 64 B3
Bolton E Loth 87 K8
Bolton E R Yk 60 D4
Bolton Nthumb 81 M10
Bolton Abbey N York 58 E4
Bolton-by-Bowland Lancs 63 P11
Boltonfellend Cumb 71 P2
Boltongate Cumb 71 K7
Bolton-le-Sands Lancs 63 J8
Bolton Low Houses Cumb 71 K6
Bolton-on-Swale N York 65 M7
Bolton Percy N York 59 M6
Bolton upon Dearne Barns 51 L1
Bolventor Cnwll 4 E5
Bomere Heath Shrops 49 J10
Bonar Bridge Highld 107 K4
Bonawe Ag & B 90 D9
Bonby N Linc 60 G10
Boncath Pembks 25 L2
Bonchester Bridge Border 80 D10
Bondleigh Devon 15 L10
Bonds Lancs 63 J12
Bo'ness Falk 86 B6
Boney Hay Staffs 40 D5
Bonhill W Duns 84 G7
Boningale Shrops 39 P2
Bonjedward Border 80 E9
Bonkle N Lans 85 P10
Bonnington Angus 93 P7
Bonnington Kent 13 K3
Bonnybank Fife 86 G2
Bonnybridge Falk 85 N7
Bonnykelly Abers 102 H5
Bonnyrigg Mdloth 86 G8
Bonnyton Angus 93 L7
Bonsall Derbys 50 H8
Bonshaw Tower D & G 71 K2
Bont-Dolgadfan Powys 47 P10
Bont-goch Cerdgn 37 L4
Bontnewydd Cerdgn 37 K7
Bontnewydd Gwynd 54 G9
Bontuchel Denbgs 48 C4
Bonvilston V Glam 16 E2
Boode Devon 15 J5
Booker Bucks 20 D5
Boon Border 80 D5
Boosbeck R & Cl 66 F4
Boose's Green Essex 34 E9
Boot Cumb 62 D3
Booth Calder 58 D8
Boothby Graffoe Lincs 52 E10
Boothby Pagnell Lincs 42 D4
Boothferry E R Yk 60 C8
Boothstown Salfd 57 N8
Boothville Nhants 32 B4
Bootle Cumb 62 C5
Bootle Sefton 56 G9
Boraston Shrops 39 L8
Bordeaux Guern 6 c1
Borden Kent 22 G10
Boreham Essex 22 F2
Boreham Street E Susx 12 D7
Borehamwood Herts 21 J4
Boreland D & G 79 J10
Boreraig Highld 104 B10
Borgh W Isls 111 a7
Borgh W Isls 111 d1
Borgie Highld 109 M4
Borgue D & G 69 P9
Borgue Highld 110 D9
Borley Essex 34 E7
Borneskitaig Highld 104 E7
Borness D & G 69 N9
Boroughbridge N York 59 K2
Borough Green Kent 22 C11
Borrowash Derbys 41 K1
Borrowby N York 65 Q9
Borrowdale Cumb 71 L11
Borrowstoun Falk 86 B6
Borstal Medway 22 E9
Borth Cerdgn 37 K3
Borthwick Mdloth 86 H9
Borthwickbrae Border 79 N6
Borthwickshiels Border 79 N6
Borth-y-Gest Gwynd 47 J4
Borve Highld 104 F11
Borve W Isls 111 a7
Borve W Isls 111 c3
Borve W Isls 111 d1
Borwick Lancs 63 K7
Bosbury Herefs 39 M12
Boscastle Cnwll 4 D3
Boscombe BCP 8 G8
Boscombe Wilts 18 H11
Bosham W Susx 10 D8
Bosherston Pembks 24 G9
Bosley Ches E 50 B7
Bossall N York 60 C3
Bossiney Cnwll 4 D3
Bossingham Kent 13 M1
Bossington Somset 16 B6
Bostock Green Ches W 49 M2
Boston Lincs 43 K2
Boston Spa Leeds 59 K5
Boswinger Cnwll 3 L7
Botallack Cnwll 2 B8
Botany Bay Gt Lon 21 L4
Botesdale Suffk 34 H2
Bothal Nthumb 73 M4
Bothamsall Notts 51 P6
Bothel Cumb 71 J7
Bothenhampton Dorset 7 L5
Bothwell S Lans 85 L10
Bothwell Services S Lans 85 M10
Botley Bucks 20 F3
Botley Hants 9 N5
Botley Oxon 31 L11
Botolph Claydon Bucks 31 Q8
Botolphs W Susx 11 J8
Bottesford Leics 42 B3
Bottesford N Linc 52 C3
Bottisham Cambs 33 N5
Bottomcraig Fife 93 L10
Bottoms Calder 58 B9
Botusfleming Cnwll 5 J7
Botwnnog Gwynd 46 D5
Bough Beech Kent 11 P1
Boughrood Powys 27 N2
Boughton Nhants 31 Q2
Boughton Norfk 44 B9
Boughton Notts 51 P7
Boughton Aluph Kent 13 K1
Boughton Green Kent 22 F12
Boughton Monchelsea Kent 22 F12
Boughton Street Kent 23 K10
Bouldon Shrops 39 K5
Boulmer Nthumb 81 Q10
Boultham Lincs 52 D9
Bourn Cambs 33 K5
Bournbrook Birm 40 D10
Bourne Lincs 42 F6
Bournebridge Essex 21 P5
Bourne End Bucks 20 E6
Bourne End C Beds 32 D7
Bourne End Herts 20 G3
Bournemouth BCP 8 G8
Bournemouth Airport BCP 8 G7
Bournes Green Sthend 22 H6
Bournheath Worcs 40 C11
Bournmoor Dur 73 N9
Bournville Birm 40 D10
Bourton Dorset 8 B2
Bourton Oxon 19 J4
Bourton Shrops 39 L3
Bourton Wilts 18 F7
Bourton on Dunsmore Warwks 41 K12
Bourton-on-the-Hill Gloucs 30 F7
Bourton-on-the-Water Gloucs 30 F9
Bousd Ag & B 88 G4
Bouth Cumb 62 G5
Bouthwaite N York 65 K12
Boveridge Dorset 8 F4
Bovey Tracey Devon 5 Q5
Bovingdon Herts 20 G3
Bow Devon 15 M10
Bow Gt Lon 21 M6
Bow Ork 111 h3
Bow Brickhill M Keyn 32 C9
Bowbridge Gloucs 29 M7
Bowburn Dur 73 N12
Bowcombe IoW 9 M9
Bowd Devon 6 F5
Bowden Border 80 D7
Bowden Hill Wilts 18 D7
Bowdon Traffd 57 N10
Bower Highld 110 E3
Bowerchalke Wilts 8 F3
Bowermadden Highld 110 F3
Bowers Staffs 49 P8
Bowers Gifford Essex 22 E6
Bowershall Fife 86 C4
Bower's Row Leeds 59 K8
Bowes Dur 64 H5
Bowgreave Lancs 63 J12
Bowhouse D & G 70 G3
Bowland Border 79 P2
Bowley Herefs 39 K10
Bowlhead Green Surrey 10 E3
Bowling C Brad 58 F7
Bowling W Duns 84 G8
Bowmanstead Cumb 62 F3
Bowmore Ag & B 82 D10
Bowness-on-Solway Cumb 71 K3
Bowness-on-Windermere Cumb 62 H3
Bow of Fife Fife 93 K12
Bowriefauld Angus 93 N6
Bowsden Nthumb 81 L6
Bow Street Cerdgn 37 K4
Bowthorpe Norfk 45 K8
Box Gloucs 29 M8
Box Wilts 18 C7
Boxford Suffk 34 F8
Boxford W Berk 19 M6

Place	Page	Ref
Boxgrove W Susx	10	E8
Boxley Kent	22	F10
Boxmoor Herts	20	G3
Boxted Essex	34	G9
Boxted Essex	34	G9
Boxted Suffk	34	D6
Boxted Cross Essex	34	G9
Boxworth Cambs	33	K4
Boyden Gate Kent	23	N9
Boylestone Derbys	40	F1
Boyndie Abers	102	E3
Boyndlie Abers	103	J3
Boynton E R Yk	61	K1
Boysack Angus	93	Q6
Boyton Cnwll	4	H2
Boyton Suffk	35	N7
Boyton Wilts	18	D11
Boyton Cross Essex	22	D2
Boyton End Suffk	34	C7
Bozeat Nhants	32	C5
Brabourne Kent	13	L2
Brabourne Lees Kent	13	L3
Brabstermire Highld	110	G2
Bracadale Highld	96	D2
Braceborough Lincs	42	F7
Bracebridge Heath Lincs	52	E9
Bracebridge Low Fields Lincs	52	D9
Braceby Lincs	42	E3
Bracewell Lancs	63	Q11
Brackenfield Derbys	51	J8
Brackenhirst N Lans	85	M8
Brackla Brdgnd	27	K11
Bracklesham W Susx	10	D10
Brackletter Highld	98	B11
Brackley Nhants	31	N6
Bracknell Br For	20	E9
Braco P & K	85	N2
Bracobrae Moray	101	P5
Bracon Ash Norfk	45	K9
Bracora Highld	97	K10
Bracorina Highld	97	K10
Bradbourne Derbys	50	G9
Bradbury Dur	65	N2
Bradden Nhants	31	N5
Bradeley C Stke	49	Q5
Bradenham Bucks	20	D4
Bradenstoke Wilts	18	E5
Bradfield Devon	6	E2
Bradfield Essex	35	J9
Bradfield Norfk	45	L4
Bradfield Sheff	50	H3
Bradfield W Berk	19	P6
Bradfield Combust Suffk	34	E5
Bradfield Green Ches E	49	M4
Bradfield Heath Essex	35	J10
Bradfield St Clare Suffk	34	E5
Bradfield St George Suffk	34	E5
Bradford C Brad	58	F7
Bradford Devon	14	G10
Bradford Abbas Dorset	17	N12
Bradford Leigh Wilts	18	C8
Bradford-on-Avon Wilts	18	C8
Bradford-on-Tone Somset	16	G10
Bradford Peverell Dorset	7	P4
Bradiford Devon	15	K5
Brading IoW	9	Q9
Bradley Derbys	50	G10
Bradley Hants	19	Q11
Bradley NE Lin	53	J3
Bradley Staffs	49	Q11
Bradley Wolves	40	C8
Bradley Worcs	30	C2
Bradley Green Worcs	30	C2
Bradley in the Moors Staffs	50	D11
Bradley Stoke S Glos	28	H11
Bradmore Notts	41	N2
Bradnop Staffs	50	D9
Bradpole Dorset	7	L4
Bradshaw Calder	58	E8
Bradstone Devon	4	H4
Bradwall Green Ches E	49	N3
Bradwell Derbys	50	F5
Bradwell Essex	34	D11
Bradwell M Keyn	32	B8
Bradwell Norfk	45	Q8
Bradwell-on-Sea Essex	23	J3
Bradwell Waterside Essex	23	J2
Bradworthy Devon	14	F8
Brae Highld	107	L9
Brae Shet	111	k3
Braeface Falk	85	N7
Braehead Angus	95	L10
Braehead D & G	69	K8
Braehead S Lans	77	Q2
Braeintra Highld	97	M3
Braemar Abers	94	C4
Braemore Highld	106	C6
Braemore Highld	110	C9
Brae Roy Lodge Highld	98	D10
Braeside Inver	84	D7
Braes of Coul Angus	93	K4
Braes of Enzie Moray	101	M4
Braeswick Ork	111	i1
Braevallich Ag & B	83	P2
Braewick Shet	111	j3
Brafferton Darltn	65	N4
Brafferton N York	66	B12
Brafield-on-the-Green Nhants	32	B5
Bragar W Isls	111	d1
Bragbury End Herts	33	J11
Braidwood S Lans	77	P2
Brailsford Derbys	50	G11
Braintree Essex	34	C11
Braiseworth Suffk	35	J3
Braishfield Hants	9	L3
Braithwaite Cumb	71	K10
Braithwaite Donc	59	M2
Bramber W Susx	11	J7
Bramcote Warwks	41	K9
Bramdean Hants	9	Q2
Bramerton Norfk	45	L8
Bramfield Herts	33	J12
Bramfield Suffk	35	N3
Bramford Suffk	35	J7
Bramhall Stockp	50	B4
Bramham Leeds	59	K6
Bramhope Leeds	58	G5
Bramley Hants	19	Q8
Bramley Leeds	58	G7
Bramley Rothm	51	L3
Bramley Surrey	10	G2
Bramling Kent	23	N11
Brampford Speke Devon	6	C3
Brampton Cambs	32	H3
Brampton Cumb	64	C3
Brampton Cumb	71	Q4
Brampton Lincs	52	B7
Brampton Norfk	45	K5
Brampton Rothm	51	K1
Brampton Suffk	35	P1
Brampton Abbotts Herefs	28	H4
Brampton Ash Nhants	42	B11
Brampton Bryan Herefs	38	G7
Brampton-en-le-Morthen Rothm	51	L4
Bramshall Staffs	40	D2
Bramshaw Hants	9	J4
Bramshott Hants	10	D4
Bramwell Somset	17	L9
Branault Highld	89	L3
Brancaster Norfk	44	C2
Brancaster Staithe Norfk	44	D2
Brancepeth Dur	73	L12
Branchill Moray	100	G5
Branderburgh Moray	101	K2
Brandesburton E R Yk	61	J5
Brandeston Suffk	35	L5
Brandiston Norfk	45	J6
Brandon Dur	73	M11
Brandon Lincs	42	C1
Brandon Suffk	44	D11
Brandon Warwks	41	K11
Brandon Parva Norfk	44	H8
Brandsby N York	66	E11
Brandy Wharf Lincs	52	G4
Bran End Essex	33	Q10
Branksome BCP	8	F8
Branksome Park BCP	8	F8
Bransbury Hants	19	M11
Bransby Lincs	52	C7
Branscombe Devon	6	G5
Bransford Worcs	39	P10
Bransgore Hants	8	H7
Bransholme C KuH	61	J7
Bransley Shrops	39	M7
Branston Leics	42	B4
Branston Lincs	52	E9
Branston Staffs	40	G4
Branston Booths Lincs	52	F9
Branstone IoW	9	Q10
Brant Broughton Lincs	52	D11
Brantham Suffk	35	J9
Branthwaite Cumb	70	H9
Branthwaite Cumb	71	L7
Brantingham E R Yk	60	G8
Branton Donc	51	N1
Branton Nthumb	81	L10
Branton Green N York	59	K2
Branxton Nthumb	81	J6
Brassington Derbys	50	G9
Brasted Kent	21	P11
Brasted Chart Kent	21	P11
Brathens Abers	95	L3
Bratoft Lincs	53	M9
Brattleby Lincs	52	D7
Bratton Wilts	18	D9
Bratton Wrekin	49	L11
Bratton Clovelly Devon	5	K2
Bratton Fleming Devon	15	L4
Bratton Seymour Somset	17	P9
Braughing Herts	33	L10
Braunston Nhants	31	M2
Braunston Rutlnd	42	B8
Braunton Devon	14	H5
Brawby N York	66	G11
Brawl Highld	109	P3
Bray W & M	20	E7
Braybrooke Nhants	41	Q11
Brayford Devon	15	M5
Bray Shop Cnwll	4	H5
Brayton N York	59	N7
Braywick W & M	20	E7
Breachwood Green Herts	32	G11
Breacleit W Isls	111	c2
Breaclete W Isls	111	c2
Breadsall Derbys	51	J11
Breadstone Gloucs	29	J8
Breage Cnwll	2	G9
Breakachy Highld	106	H12
Breakish Highld	97	L3
Brealangwell Lodge Highld	106	H4
Bream Gloucs	28	H7
Breamore Hants	8	H4
Brean Somset	16	H5
Breanais W Isls	111	b2
Brearton N York	58	H3
Breascleit W Isls	111	c2
Breasclete W Isls	111	c2
Breaston Derbys	41	L2
Brechfa Carmth	26	C3
Brechin Angus	95	K9
Breckles Norfk	44	F10
Brecon Powys	27	L3
Brecon Beacons National Park	27	L4
Bredbury Stockp	50	B3
Brede E Susx	12	G6
Bredenbury Herefs	39	L10
Bredfield Suffk	35	L6
Bredgar Kent	22	G10
Bredhurst Kent	22	F10
Bredon Worcs	29	N2
Bredon's Hardwick Worcs	29	M2
Bredon's Norton Worcs	29	N2
Bredwardine Herefs	38	G12
Breedon on the Hill Leics	41	K3
Breich W Loth	85	Q10
Breightmet Bolton	57	N7
Breighton E R Yk	60	C7
Breinton Herefs	28	F2
Bremhill Wilts	18	E6
Brenchley Kent	12	D2
Brendon Devon	15	N3
Brenfield Ag & B	83	M6
Brenish W Isls	111	b2
Brent Cross Gt Lon	21	K6
Brent Eleigh Suffk	34	F7
Brentford Gt Lon	21	J7
Brentingby Leics	42	B6
Brent Knoll Somset	17	J6
Brent Mill Devon	5	N8
Brent Pelham Herts	33	M10
Brentwood Essex	22	C5
Brenzett Kent	13	J4
Brenzett Green Kent	13	J4
Brereton Staffs	40	D4
Brereton Green Ches E	49	P3
Bressay Shet	111	k4
Bressingham Norfk	34	H1
Bretby Derbys	40	H3
Bretford Warwks	41	K11
Bretforton Worcs	30	E5
Bretherton Lancs	57	J5
Brettabister Shet	111	k4
Brettenham Norfk	44	F12
Brettenham Suffk	34	F6
Bretton C Pete	42	G9
Bretton Flints	48	G3
Brewood Staffs	40	B6
Briantspuddle Dorset	8	B8
Brickendon Herts	21	L2
Bricket Wood Herts	20	H3
Brick Houses Sheff	50	H5
Bricklehampton Worcs	29	N1
Bride IoM	56	e2
Bridekirk Cumb	71	J8
Bridestowe Devon	5	L3
Brideswell Abers	102	D7
Bridford Devon	5	N3
Bridge Kent	23	M11
Bridgefoot Angus	93	L8
Bridgehampton Somset	17	N10
Bridge Hewick N York	65	N12
Bridgehill Dur	73	K9
Bridgemary Hants	9	P6
Bridgend Abers	101	P7
Bridgend Ag & B	75	J8
Bridgend Ag & B	82	E9
Bridgend Angus	95	J8
Bridgend Brdgnd	27	J11
Bridgend Cerdgn	36	C10
Bridgend D & G	78	H7
Bridgend Fife	93	L12
Bridgend Moray	101	M8
Bridgend P & K	92	G10
Bridgend W Loth	86	C7
Bridgend of Lintrathen Angus	93	K5
Bridge of Alford Abers	102	D10
Bridge of Allan Stirlg	85	N4
Bridge of Avon Moray	100	H10
Bridge of Avon Moray	101	J7
Bridge of Balgie P & K	91	N7
Bridge of Brewlands Angus	94	C9
Bridge of Brown Highld	100	H10
Bridge of Cally P & K	92	H5
Bridge of Canny Abers	95	K3
Bridge of Craigisla Angus	93	J5
Bridge of Dee D & G	70	C4
Bridge of Don C Aber	103	J11
Bridge of Dye Abers	95	K5
Bridge of Earn P & K	92	H11
Bridge of Ericht P & K	91	M5
Bridge of Feugh Abers	95	L3
Bridge of Gairn Abers	94	F3
Bridge of Gaur P & K	91	M5
Bridge of Marnoch Abers	102	D5
Bridge of Muchalls Abers	95	N3
Bridge of Orchy Ag & B	91	J8
Bridge of Tilt P & K	92	D3
Bridge of Tynet Moray	101	M3
Bridge of Walls Shet	111	j4
Bridge of Weir Rens	84	G10
Bridgerule Devon	14	E10
Bridge Sollers Herefs	28	E1
Bridge Street Suffk	34	E6
Bridgetown Somset	16	C9
Bridge Trafford Ches W	49	J1
Bridgham Norfk	44	F11
Bridgnorth Shrops	39	N4
Bridgwater Somset	16	H8
Bridgwater Services Somset	17	J8
Bridlington E R Yk	61	K2
Bridport Dorset	7	L4
Bridstow Herefs	28	G4
Brierfield Lancs	57	Q2
Brierley Barns	59	K11
Brierley Gloucs	28	H6
Brierley Hill Dudley	40	B9
Brierton Hartpl	65	Q6
Briery Cumb	71	K10
Brigg N Linc	52	E3
Briggate Norfk	45	M5
Briggswath N York	67	J6
Brigham Cumb	70	H9
Brigham E R Yk	61	J4
Brighouse Calder	58	F9
Brighstone IoW	9	M10
Brighthampton Oxon	31	K12
Brightley Devon	15	K11
Brightling E Susx	12	D6
Brightlingsea Essex	34	H12
Brighton City Airport W Susx	11	K8
Brighton le Sands Sefton	56	G9
Brightons Falk	85	Q7
Brightwalton W Berk	19	M5
Brightwell Suffk	35	L7
Brightwell Baldwin Oxon	19	Q2
Brightwell-cum-Sotwell Oxon	19	P3
Brightwell Upperton Oxon	19	Q2
Brignall Dur	65	J5
Brig o'Turk Stirlg	85	J2
Brigsley NE Lin	53	J3
Brigsteer Cumb	63	J4
Brigstock Nhants	42	D11
Brill Bucks	31	P10
Brill Cnwll	2	H9
Brilley Herefs	38	F11
Brimfield Herefs	39	K8
Brimfield Cross Herefs	39	K8
Brimington Derbys	51	K6
Brimley Devon	5	Q5
Brimpsfield Gloucs	29	N6
Brimpton W Berk	19	N7
Brimscombe Gloucs	29	M8
Brimstage Wirral	56	F11
Brincliffe Sheff	51	J4
Brind E R Yk	60	C7
Brindister Shet	111	j4
Brindle Lancs	57	L4
Brineton Staffs	49	Q12
Bringhurst Leics	42	B10
Bringsty Common Herefs	39	M10
Brington Cambs	32	F2
Briningham Norfk	44	G4
Brinkhill Lincs	53	L8
Brinkley Cambs	33	Q6
Brinklow Warwks	41	K10
Brinkworth Wilts	18	E4
Brinscall Lancs	57	L5
Brinsley Notts	51	L10
Brinsworth Rothm	51	K3
Brinton Norfk	44	G3
Brinyan Ork	111	h2
Brisley Norfk	44	F6
Brislington Bristl	17	N3
Brissenden Green Kent	12	H3
Bristol Bristl	17	N2
Bristol Airport N Som	17	M3
Bristol Zoo Gardens Bristl	17	N2
Briston Norfk	44	H4
Britford Wilts	8	H2
Brithdir Caerph	27	N8
Brithdir Gwynd	47	M7
British Legion Village Kent	22	E11
Briton Ferry Neath	26	G9
Britwell Salome Oxon	19	R3
Brixham Torbay	6	C10
Brixton Devon	5	L9
Brixton Gt Lon	21	L8
Brixton Deverill Wilts	18	C11
Brixworth Nhants	41	Q12
Brize Norton Oxon	30	H11
Brize Norton Airport Oxon	30	H11
Broad Alley Worcs	30	B1
Broad Blunsdon Swindn	18	G3
Broadbottom Tamesd	50	C3
Broadbridge W Susx	10	D8
Broadbridge Heath W Susx	11	J4
Broad Campden Gloucs	30	F6
Broad Carr Calder	58	E9
Broad Chalke Wilts	8	F3
Broadclyst Devon	6	D4
Broadfield Inver	84	F8
Broadford Highld	96	H5
Broadford Bridge W Susx	10	H6
Broadgairhill Border	79	K6
Broad Green Worcs	39	P10
Broadhaugh Border	81	J4
Broad Haven Pembks	24	F6
Broadheath Traffd	57	N10
Broadhembury Devon	6	E2
Broadhempston Devon	5	Q7
Broad Hinton Wilts	18	G5
Broadland Row E Susx	12	G6
Broadley Moray	101	M3
Broad Marston Worcs	30	F5
Broadmayne Dorset	7	Q5
Broad Meadow Staffs	49	Q6
Broadmoor Pembks	25	J7
Broadoak Dorset	7	L4
Broad Oak E Susx	12	C5
Broad Oak E Susx	12	G6
Broad Oak Herefs	28	F5
Broad Oak St Hel	57	K9
Broadsands Torbay	6	B10
Broad's Green Essex	22	E2
Broadstairs Kent	23	Q9
Broadstone BCP	8	E8
Broadstone Shrops	39	K4
Broad Street E Susx	12	G6
Broad Street Kent	22	G11
Broad Town Wilts	18	G5
Broadwas Worcs	39	N10
Broadwater Herts	33	J11
Broadwater W Susx	11	J8
Broadwaters Worcs	39	Q6
Broadway Pembks	24	F6
Broadway Somset	17	J11
Broadway Worcs	30	E6
Broadwell Gloucs	28	G6
Broadwell Gloucs	30	G8
Broadwell Oxon	30	G12
Broadwell Warwks	31	L2
Broadwindsor Dorset	7	L3
Broadwoodkelly Devon	15	K10
Broadwoodwidger Devon	5	J3
Brochel Highld	104	H12
Brochroy Ag & B	90	D9
Brockamin Worcs	39	P10
Brockbridge Hants	9	Q4
Brockdish Norfk	35	K2
Brockenhurst Hants	9	K7
Brocketsbrae S Lans	78	D2
Brockford Street Suffk	35	J4
Brockhall Nhants	31	N2
Brockham Surrey	21	K12
Brockhampton Gloucs	30	D9
Brockhampton Hants	10	B8
Brockhampton Herefs	28	H4
Brockholes Kirk	58	F11
Brocklesby Lincs	61	K11
Brockley N Som	17	L3
Brockley Suffk	34	D3
Brockley Green Suffk	34	C7
Brockley Green Suffk	34	D6
Brockmoor Dudley	40	B9
Brockton Shrops	38	H3
Brockton Shrops	38	G5
Brockton Shrops	39	L4
Brockweir Gloucs	28	G8
Brockworth Gloucs	29	M5
Brocton Staffs	40	C4
Brodick N Ayrs	75	Q5
Brodie Moray	100	G4
Brodsworth Donc	59	L11
Brogaig Highld	104	F8
Brokenborough Wilts	18	D3
Broken Cross Ches E	50	B6
Brokerswood Wilts	18	C9
Brome Suffk	35	J2
Brome Street Suffk	35	J2
Bromeswell Suffk	35	M6
Bromfield Cumb	71	J6
Bromfield Shrops	39	J6
Bromham Bed	32	E6
Bromham Wilts	18	E7
Bromley Dudley	40	B9
Bromley Gt Lon	21	N9
Bromley Shrops	39	N3
Bromley Cross Bolton	57	N6
Brompton Medway	22	F9
Brompton N York	65	P8
Brompton-by-Sawdon N York	67	K10
Brompton-on-Swale N York	65	L7
Brompton Ralph Somset	16	E9
Brompton Regis Somset	16	C9
Bromsberrow Gloucs	29	K3
Bromsberrow Heath Gloucs	29	K3
Bromsgrove Worcs	40	C12
Bromyard Herefs	39	M10
Bronant Cerdgn	37	K7
Brongest Cerdgn	36	E10
Bronington Wrexhm	49	J7
Bronllys Powys	27	N2
Bronwydd Carmth	25	P4
Bronygarth Shrops	48	F9
Brook Hants	9	J5
Brook IoW	9	L9
Brook Kent	13	K2
Brook Surrey	10	E3
Brooke Norfk	45	L9
Brooke Rutlnd	42	C8
Brookenby Lincs	52	H4
Brookfield Rens	84	G9
Brookhampton Somset	17	P9
Brook Hill Hants	9	J5
Brookhouse Lancs	63	K8
Brookhouse Rothm	51	L3
Brookhouse Green Ches E	49	P4
Brookhouses Derbys	50	D3
Brookland Kent	13	J5
Brooklands Traffd	57	P10
Brookmans Park Herts	21	K3
Brook Street C Beds	32	G8
Brook Street Kent	12	H4
Brookthorpe Gloucs	29	L6
Brookwood Surrey	20	F11
Broom C Beds	32	G8
Broom Rothm	51	K3
Broom Warwks	30	E4
Broome Norfk	45	M10
Broome Shrops	38	H6
Broome Worcs	40	B10
Broomedge Warrtn	57	N10
Broomfield Essex	22	E2
Broomfield Kent	22	G11
Broomfield Kent	23	M9
Broomfield Somset	16	G9
Broomfleet E R Yk	60	E8
Broomhaugh Nthumb	72	H8
Broom Hill Barns	59	K12
Broom Hill Notts	51	M10
Broomhill Nthumb	73	M1
Broompark Dur	73	M11
Brora Highld	107	P2
Broseley Shrops	39	M2
Brotherlee Dur	72	G12
Brotherton N York	59	L8
Brotton R & C	66	F4
Broubster Highld	110	B4
Brough Cumb	64	E5
Brough E R Yk	60	F8
Brough Highld	110	E2
Brough Notts	52	B10
Brough Shet	111	m3
Broughall Shrops	49	K7
Brough Lodge Shet	111	m2
Brough Sowerby Cumb	64	E5
Broughton Border	78	H2
Broughton Cambs	33	J2
Broughton Flints	48	G3
Broughton Hants	9	K2
Broughton Lancs	57	K2
Broughton M Keyn	32	C8
Broughton N Linc	52	D2
Broughton N York	58	C4
Broughton N York	66	H11
Broughton Nhants	32	B2
Broughton Oxon	31	K6
Broughton Salfd	57	P8
Broughton V Glam	27	C3
Broughton Astley Leics	41	M8
Broughton Gifford Wilts	18	C7
Broughton Green Worcs	30	C2
Broughton Hackett Worcs	30	B3
Broughton-in-Furness Cumb	62	E5
Broughton Mains D & G	69	K8
Broughton Mills Cumb	62	E4
Broughton Moor Cumb	70	H8
Broughton Poggs Oxon	30	G12
Broughty Ferry C Dund	93	N9
Brown Candover Hants	19	P11
Brown Edge Staffs	50	B9
Brownhill Abers	102	H7
Brownhills Fife	93	P11
Brownhills Wsall	40	D6
Browninghill Green Hants	19	P8
Brown Lees Staffs	49	Q4
Brownsea Island Dorset	8	F9
Brown's Green Birm	40	D8
Browns Hill Gloucs	29	M8
Brownston Devon	5	N9
Broxa N York	67	K8
Broxbourne Herts	21	M3
Broxburn E Loth	87	N6
Broxburn W Loth	86	C7
Broxted Essex	33	P10
Bruan Highld	110	G7
Bruar P & K	92	C3
Bruchag Ag & B	84	B10
Bruichladdich Ag & B	82	C10
Bruisyard Suffk	35	M4
Bruisyard Street Suffk	35	M4
Brumby N Linc	52	C2
Brund Staffs	50	E8
Brundall Norfk	45	M8
Brundish Suffk	35	L3
Brundish Street Suffk	35	L3
Brunery Highld	89	P2
Brunswick Village N u Ty	73	M6
Brunthwaite C Brad	58	D5
Bruntingthorpe Leics	41	N9
Brunton Fife	93	K10
Brunton Nthumb	81	P9
Brunton Wilts	19	J9
Brushford Devon	15	L9
Brushford Somset	16	C10
Bruton Somset	17	P8
Bryan's Green Worcs	30	B1
Bryanston Dorset	8	C6
Brydekirk D & G	71	K2
Bryher IoS	2	b2
Brympton Somset	17	M11
Bryn Carmth	26	D8
Bryn Neath	26	H9
Bryn Wigan	57	K8

Place	County	Page	Grid
Brynamman	Carmth	26	F6
Brynberian	Pembks	25	J12
Bryncir	Gwynd	46	H3
Bryn-côch	Neath	26	G8
Bryncroes	Gwynd	46	D5
Bryncrug	Gwynd	47	K9
Bryneglwys	Denbgs	48	F3
Brynford	Flints	48	D1
Bryn Gates	Wigan	57	L8
Bryngwran	IoA	54	D6
Bryngwyn	Mons	28	D7
Bryngwyn	Powys	38	E11
Bryn-Henllan	Pembks	24	H2
Brynhoffnant	Cerdgn	36	E9
Brynmawr	Blae G	27	P6
Bryn-mawr	Gwynd	46	D5
Brynmenyn	Brdgnd	27	J10
Brynmill	Swans	26	E9
Brynna	Rhondd	27	L11
Brynrefail	Gwynd	54	H8
Brynsadler	Rhondd	27	L11
Bryn Saith Marchog	Denbgs	48	C5
Brynsiencyn	IoA	54	F7
Brynteg	IoA	54	G5
Bryn-y-Maen	Conwy	55	M6
Bualintur	Highld	96	E5
Bubbenhall	Warwks	41	J11
Bubwith	E R Yk	60	C7
Buccleuch	Border	79	M6
Buchanan Smithy	Stirlg	84	H5
Buchanhaven	Abers	103	M6
Buchanty	P & K	92	D9
Buchany	Stirlg	85	M3
Buchlyvie	Stirlg	85	J4
Buckabank	Cumb	71	M6
Buckden	Cambs	32	H4
Buckden	N York	64	G11
Buckenham	Norfk	45	M8
Buckerell	Devon	6	D4
Buckfast	Devon	5	P6
Buckfastleigh	Devon	5	N7
Buckhaven	Fife	86	G3
Buckholt	Mons	28	F5
Buckhorn Weston	Dorset	17	R10
Buckhurst Hill	Essex	21	N5
Buckie	Moray	101	M3
Buckingham	Bucks	31	P7
Buckland	Bucks	20	E2
Buckland	Devon	5	N10
Buckland	Gloucs	30	C2
Buckland	Herts	33	K9
Buckland	Kent	13	P2
Buckland	Oxon	19	K2
Buckland	Surrey	21	L12
Buckland Brewer	Devon	14	G7
Buckland Common	Bucks	20	E2
Buckland Dinham	Somset	17	R6
Buckland Filleigh	Devon	14	H9
Buckland in the Moor	Devon	5	P5
Buckland Monachorum	Devon	5	K6
Buckland Newton	Dorset	7	P2
Buckland Ripers	Dorset	7	P6
Buckland St Mary	Somset	16	H12
Buckland-Tout-Saints	Devon	5	P10
Bucklebury	W Berk	19	P6
Bucklers Hard	Hants	9	L7
Bucklesham	Suffk	35	L8
Buckley	Flints	48	F3
Bucklow Hill	Ches E	57	N11
Buckminster	Leics	42	C5
Bucknall	C Stke	50	B10
Bucknall	Lincs	52	G9
Bucknell	Oxon	31	M8
Bucknell	Shrops	38	G7
Buckpool	Moray	101	M3
Bucksburn	C Aber	103	J12
Buck's Cross	Devon	14	F7
Bucks Green	W Susx	10	H4
Buckshaw Village	Lancs	57	K4
Bucks Horn Oak	Hants	10	D2
Buck's Mills	Devon	14	F7
Buckton	E R Yk	67	P11
Buckton	Nthumb	81	M6
Buckworth	Cambs	32	G2
Budby	Notts	51	N6
Bude	Cnwll	14	D10
Budge's Shop	Cnwll	4	H8
Budleigh Salterton	Devon	6	E6
Budock Water	Cnwll	2	H9
Buerton	Ches E	49	M6
Bugbrooke	Nhants	31	P3
Bugle	Cnwll	3	M4
Bugley	Dorset	8	B3
Bugthorpe	E R Yk	60	D3
Buildwas	Shrops	39	L2
Builth Wells	Powys	38	B11
Bulbridge	Wilts	8	G2
Bulford	Wilts	18	H11
Bulkeley	Ches E	49	K5
Bulkington	Warwks	41	K9
Bulkington	Wilts	18	D8
Bulkworthy	Devon	14	G8
Bullbrook	Br For	20	E9
Bullington	Hants	19	M11
Bullington	Lincs	52	F7
Bulmer	Essex	34	D8
Bulmer	N York	60	C1
Bulmer Tye	Essex	34	D8
Bulphan	Thurr	22	D6
Bulwark	Abers	103	J6
Bulwell	C Nott	51	M11
Bulwick	Nhants	42	D10
Bumble's Green	Essex	21	N3
Bunacaimb	Highld	97	J11
Bunarkaig	Highld	98	B10
Bunbury	Ches E	49	K4
Bunchrew	Highld	107	K12
Bundalloch	Highld	97	M4
Bunessan	Ag & B	89	J11
Bungay	Suffk	45	M11
Bunny	Notts	41	N2
Buntait	Highld	98	E3
Buntingford	Herts	33	K9
Bunwell	Norfk	45	J10
Burbage	Leics	41	K8
Burbage	Wilts	19	J8
Burchett's Green	W & M	20	D7
Burcombe	Wilts	8	F2
Burcot	Bucks	32	C11
Bures	Essex	34	E9
Burford	Oxon	30	G10
Burford	Shrops	39	L8
Burg	Ag & B	89	J7
Burgess Hill	W Susx	11	L6
Burgh	Suffk	35	K6
Burgh by Sands	Cumb	71	M4
Burgh Castle	Norfk	45	P8
Burghclere	Hants	19	M8
Burghead	Moray	100	H2
Burghfield	W Berk	19	Q7
Burghfield Common	W Berk	19	Q7
Burgh Heath	Surrey	21	K10
Burghill	Herefs	39	J12
Burgh Island	Devon	5	M10
Burgh le Marsh	Lincs	53	N9
Burgh next Aylsham	Norfk	45	K5
Burgh on Bain	Lincs	52	H6
Burgh St Margaret	Norfk	45	P7
Burgh St Peter	Norfk	45	P10
Burghwallis	Donc	59	M10
Burham	Kent	22	E10
Buriton	Hants	10	C6
Burland	Ches E	49	L5
Burlawn	Cnwll	3	M2
Burleigh	Gloucs	29	M8
Burlescombe	Devon	16	E11
Burleston	Dorset	8	B8
Burley	Hants	8	H6
Burley	Rutlnd	42	C7
Burleydam	Ches E	49	L7
Burley Gate	Herefs	39	L11
Burley in Wharfedale	C Brad	58	F5
Burley Street	Hants	8	H6
Burley Wood Head	C Brad	58	F5
Burlton	Shrops	49	J9
Burmarsh	Kent	13	L4
Burmington	Warwks	30	H6
Burn	N York	59	N8
Burnage	Manch	57	Q9
Burnaston	Derbys	40	H2
Burnbrae	N Lans	85	P10
Burnby	E R Yk	60	E5
Burneside	Cumb	63	J3
Burneston	N York	65	N9
Burnett	BaNES	17	P3
Burnfoot	Border	79	N6
Burnfoot	Border	80	C10
Burnfoot	D & G	78	F9
Burnfoot	D & G	79	M10
Burnfoot	D & G	79	N9
Burnfoot	P & K	86	B2
Burnham	Bucks	20	F2
Burnham Deepdale	Norfk	44	D2
Burnham Market	Norfk	44	D2
Burnham Norton	Norfk	44	D2
Burnham-on-Crouch	Essex	23	J4
Burnham-on-Sea	Somset	17	J6
Burnham Overy	Norfk	44	D2
Burnham Overy Staithe	Norfk	44	D2
Burnham Thorpe	Norfk	44	D2
Burnhead	D & G	78	E9
Burnhervie	Abers	102	F10
Burnhill Green	Staffs	39	P3
Burnhope	Dur	73	L10
Burnhouse	N Ayrs	76	G2
Burniston	N York	67	L8
Burnley	Lancs	57	Q3
Burnmouth	Border	81	K3
Burn of Cambus	Stirlg	85	M3
Burnopfield	Dur	73	L9
Burnsall	N York	58	D2
Burnside	Angus	93	M4
Burnside	Angus	93	N5
Burnside	Fife	86	D1
Burnside	Moray	101	J2
Burnside	W Loth	86	C7
Burnside of Duntrune	Angus	93	M8
Burntisland	Fife	86	F6
Burnton	E Ayrs	76	H9
Burntwood	Staffs	40	D5
Burntwood Green	Staffs	40	E6
Burnt Yates	N York	58	G2
Burnworthy	Somset	16	G11
Burpham	Surrey	20	G11
Burpham	W Susx	10	G8
Burradon	Nthumb	73	M7
Burrafirth	Shet	111	m2
Burravoe	Shet	111	k3
Burrells	Cumb	64	C4
Burrelton	P & K	92	H8
Burridge	Devon	15	J7
Burridge	Hants	9	N5
Burrill	N York	65	M9
Burringham	N Linc	52	B2
Burrington	Devon	15	L8
Burrington	Herefs	38	H7
Burrington	N Som	17	L4
Burrough Green	Cambs	33	Q6
Burrough on the Hill	Leics	41	Q5
Burrow	Lancs	63	L7
Burrow	Somset	16	C7
Burrow Bridge	Somset	17	J9
Burrowhill	Surrey	20	F10
Burry Green	Swans	26	B9
Burry Port	Carmth	25	Q8
Burscough	Lancs	56	H6
Burscough Bridge	Lancs	57	J6
Bursea	E R Yk	60	D7
Burseldon	Hants	9	N5
Burstall	Suffk	34	H7
Burstock	Dorset	7	K3
Burston	Norfk	45	J12
Burstow	Surrey	11	L2
Burstwick	E R Yk	61	L8
Burtersett	N York	64	F9
Burtholme	Cumb	71	Q3
Burthorpe Green	Suffk	34	C4
Burtoft	Lincs	43	J3
Burton	BCP	8	H8
Burton	Ches W	48	G1
Burton	Ches W	49	K3
Burton	Pembks	24	H7
Burton	Somset	16	G7
Burton	Wilts	18	B5
Burton Agnes	E R Yk	61	J2
Burton Bradstock	Dorset	7	L5
Burton-by-Lincoln	Lincs	52	D8
Burton Coggles	Lincs	42	E5
Burton End	Essex	33	N11
Burton Fleming	E R Yk	67	M12
Burton Hastings	Warwks	41	K9
Burton-in-Kendal	Cumb	63	K7
Burton in Lonsdale	N York	63	M7
Burton Joyce	Notts	51	N11
Burton Latimer	Nhants	32	C2
Burton Lazars	Leics	41	Q4
Burton Leonard	N York	59	J2
Burton on the Wolds	Leics	41	N4
Burton Overy	Leics	41	P7
Burton Pedwardine	Lincs	42	G2
Burton Pidsea	E R Yk	61	L7
Burton Salmon	N York	59	L8
Burton's Green	Essex	34	D10
Burton upon Stather	N Linc	60	E10
Burton upon Trent	Staffs	40	G3
Burton Waters	Lincs	52	D8
Burtonwood	Warrtn	57	K9
Burwardsley	Ches W	49	K4
Burwarton	Shrops	39	L5
Burwash	E Susx	12	D5
Burwash Common	E Susx	12	D5
Burwash Weald	E Susx	12	D5
Burwell	Cambs	33	P4
Burwell	Lincs	53	K7
Burwen	IoA	54	F3
Burwick	Ork	111	h3
Bury	Bury	57	P6
Bury	Cambs	43	J12
Bury	Somset	16	C10
Bury	W Susx	10	G6
Bury Green	Herts	33	M11
Bury St Edmunds	Suffk	34	E4
Burythorpe	N York	60	D2
Busby	E Rens	85	K10
Buscot	Oxon	19	J2
Bush	Abers	95	M8
Bush Bank	Herefs	39	J10
Bushbury	Wolves	40	B7
Bushey	Herts	21	J4
Bushey Heath	Herts	21	J5
Bush Hill Park	Gt Lon	21	M4
Bushley	Worcs	29	M2
Bushmoor	Shrops	38	H5
Bushton	Wilts	18	F5
Bussage	Gloucs	29	M7
Butcombe	N Som	17	M4
Butleigh	Somset	17	M9
Butleigh Wootton	Somset	17	M9
Butlers Marston	Warwks	30	H4
Butley	Suffk	35	N6
Buttercrambe	N York	60	C3
Butterdean	Border	87	P8
Butterknowle	Dur	65	K3
Butterleigh	Devon	6	C2
Buttermere	Cumb	71	J11
Buttershaw	C Brad	58	F8
Butterstone	P & K	92	F6
Butterton	Staffs	49	P7
Butterton	Staffs	50	E7
Butterwick	Lincs	43	L2
Butterwick	N York	66	G11
Butterwick	N York	67	L12
Buttington	Powys	38	F1
Buttonoak	Shrops	39	N6
Buxhall	Suffk	34	G5
Buxted	E Susx	11	P5
Buxton	Derbys	50	D6
Buxton	Norfk	45	K5
Buxton Heath	Norfk	45	J5
Bwlch	Powys	27	N4
Bwlchgwyn	Wrexhm	48	F4
Bwlchllan	Cerdgn	37	J8
Bwlchtocyn	Gwynd	46	E6
Bwlch-y-cibau	Powys	48	D11
Bwlch-y-ffridd	Powys	38	C3
Bwlch-y-groes	Pembks	25	M2
Bwlch-y-sarnau	Powys	38	B7
Byers Green	Dur	65	L2
Byfield	Nhants	31	M4
Byfleet	Surrey	20	G10
Byford	Herefs	38	H12
Byker	N u Ty	73	M7
Bylchau	Conwy	55	P8
Byley	Ches E	49	N2
Byrness	Nthumb	72	D1
Bystock	Devon	6	D6
Bythorn	Cambs	32	F2
Byton	Herefs	38	G8
Bywell	Nthumb	73	J8
Byworth	W Susx	10	F6

Burton-in-Kendal Services

Place	County	Page	Grid
Cumb		63	K7

C

Place	County	Page	Grid
Cabourne	Lincs	52	G3
Cabrach	Ag & B	82	G9
Cabrach	Moray	101	M9
Cabus	Lancs	63	J11
Cadbury	Devon	6	C2
Cadbury World	Birm	40	D10
Cadder	E Duns	85	K8
Caddington	C Beds	32	F11
Caddonfoot	Border	79	P2
Cadeby	Donc	51	L1
Cadeby	Leics	41	K7
Cadeleigh	Devon	6	C2
Cade Street	E Susx	12	C6
Cadgwith	Cnwll	2	H11
Cadham	Fife	86	F2
Cadishead	Salfd	57	N9
Cadle	Swans	26	E9
Cadley	Lancs	57	K3
Cadley	Wilts	18	H7
Cadley	Wilts	19	J9
Cadmore End	Bucks	20	C5
Cadnam	Hants	9	K5
Cadney	N Linc	52	E3
Cadoxton	V Glam	16	F3
Cadoxton Juxta-Neath	Neath	26	G8
Caeathro	Gwynd	54	G8
Caenby	Lincs	52	E5
Caerau	Brdgnd	27	J9
Caerau	Cardif	16	F2
Caer Farchell	Pembks	24	E4
Caergeiliog	IoA	54	D6
Caergwrle	Flints	48	F4
Caerlanrig	Border	79	N7
Caerleon	Newpt	28	D10
Caernarfon	Gwynd	54	F8
Caernarfon Castle	Gwynd	54	F8
Caerphilly	Caerph	27	N10
Caerwedros	Cerdgn	36	F9
Caerwys	Flints	48	D2
Caerwent	Mons	28	F10
Caio	Carmth	37	L11
Cairinis	W Isls	111	b5
Cairnbaan	Ag & B	83	M5
Cairnbulg	Abers	103	L3
Cairncross	Border	81	J2
Cairncurran	Inver	84	F8
Cairndow	Ag & B	84	C2
Cairneyhill	Fife	86	C5
Cairngarroch	D & G	68	D8
Cairngorms National Park		99	N8
Cairnie	Abers	101	N6
Cairnorrie	Abers	102	H7
Cairnryan	D & G	68	E5
Cairnty	Moray	101	L5
Caister-on-Sea	Norfk	45	Q7
Caistor	Lincs	52	G3
Caistor St Edmund	Norfk	45	K8
Calanais	W Isls	111	c2
Calbourne	IoW	9	M9
Calceed	Flints	48	D1
Calcot	Gloucs	30	E11
Calcot Row	W Berk	19	R6
Calcots	Moray	101	K3
Caldbeck	Cumb	71	M7
Caldecote	Cambs	33	K5
Caldecote	Cambs	42	G11
Caldecote Highfields	Cambs	33	K5
Caldecott	Nhants	32	E3
Caldecott	Oxon	19	N2
Caldecott	Rutlnd	42	C10
Calderbank	N Lans	85	M9
Calder Bridge	Cumb	62	B2
Caldercruix	N Lans	85	N9
Calder Grove	Wakefd	58	H10
Caldermill	S Lans	85	L3
Calder Vale	Lancs	63	K11
Calderwood	S Lans	85	L11
Caldey Island	Pembks	25	K9
Caldicot	Mons	28	F10
Caldmore	Wsall	40	D7
Caldwell	N York	65	L5
Calf of Man	IoM	56	a7
Calfsound	Ork	111	h1
Calgary	Ag & B	89	J6
Califer	Moray	100	G4
California	Falk	85	Q7
California	Norfk	45	Q7
Calke	Derbys	41	J3
Calke Abbey	Derbys	41	J3
Callakille	Highld	105	K10
Callander	Stirlg	85	K2
Callanish	W Isls	111	c2
Callestick	Cnwll	2	H6
Calligarry	Highld	96	H8
Callington	Cnwll	4	H6
Callow	Herefs	28	F2
Callow End	Worcs	39	Q11
Callow Hill	Wilts	18	F4
Calmore	Hants	9	K5
Calmsden	Gloucs	30	D11
Calne	Wilts	18	E6
Calshot	Hants	9	N7
Calstock	Cnwll	5	J6
Calstone Wellington	Wilts	18	F7
Calthorpe	Norfk	45	K4
Calthorpe Street	Norfk	45	N5
Calthwaite	Cumb	71	P7
Calton	Staffs	50	E10
Calveley	Ches E	49	L4
Calver	Derbys	50	G6
Calverhall	Shrops	49	L7
Calverleigh	Devon	16	C12
Calverton	M Keyn	32	B8
Calverton	Notts	51	N10
Calvine	P & K	92	B3
Calzeat	Border	78	H2
Cam	Gloucs	29	K8
Camasachoirce	Highld	89	Q4
Camasine	Highld	89	P4
Camas Luinie	Highld	97	N4
Camastianavaig	Highld	96	F2
Camault Muir	Highld	98	G2
Camber	E Susx	13	J6
Camberley	Surrey	20	E10
Camberwell	Gt Lon	21	L7
Camblesforth	N York	59	N8
Cambo	Nthumb	72	H4
Camborne	Cnwll	2	F7
Camborne & Redruth Mining District	Cnwll	2	F7
Cambourne	Cambs	33	K5
Cambridge	Cambs	33	M5
Cambridge	Gloucs	29	K7
Cambridge Airport	Cambs	33	M5
Cambrose	Cnwll	2	G6
Cambus	Clacks	85	P4
Cambusavie	Highld	107	M3
Cambusbarron	Stirlg	85	N5
Cambuskenneth	Stirlg	85	N4
Cambuslang	S Lans	85	L10
Cambus o' May	Abers	94	G3
Cambuswallace	S Lans	78	G2
Camden Town	Gt Lon	21	L6
Cameley	BaNES	17	N5
Camelford	Cnwll	4	D4
Camelon	Falk	85	P6
Camerory	Highld	100	F8
Camerton	BaNES	17	P5
Camerton	Cumb	70	G8
Camghouran	P & K	91	M5
Camieston	Border	80	D8
Cammachmore	Abers	95	Q3
Cammeringham	Lincs	52	D7
Camore	Highld	107	M4
Campbeltown	Ag & B	75	K8
Campbeltown Airport	Ag & B	75	K7
Cample	D & G	78	E9
Campmuir	P & K	93	J7
Camps	W Loth	86	C8
Campsall	Donc	59	M10
Campsea Ash	Suffk	35	M5
Campton	C Beds	32	G8
Camptown	Border	80	E10
Camrose	Pembks	24	G5
Camserney	P & K	92	C6
Camusnagaul	Highld	90	E2
Camusnagaul	Highld	105	Q5
Camusteel	Highld	97	J2
Camusterrach	Highld	97	J2
Canada	Hants	9	K4
Candacraig	Abers	94	F3
Candlesby	Lincs	53	M9
Candy Mill	Border	78	H1
Cane End	Oxon	20	B7
Canewdon	Essex	22	H5
Canford Cliffs	BCP	8	F8
Canford Heath	BCP	8	F8
Canisbay	Highld	110	G2
Canley	Covtry	40	H11
Cann	Dorset	8	C3
Canna	Highld	96	B8
Cann Common	Dorset	8	C4
Cannich	Highld	98	D3
Cannington	Somset	16	H8
Canning Town	Gt Lon	21	N7
Cannock	Staffs	40	C5
Cannock Chase	Staffs	40	C4
Cannon Bridge	Herefs	28	E1
Canonbie	D & G	71	N1
Canon Frome	Herefs	39	M12
Canon Pyon	Herefs	39	J11
Canons Ashby	Nhants	31	M4
Canonstown	Cnwll	2	D8
Canterbury	Kent	23	M10
Canterbury Cathedral	Kent	23	M10
Cantley	Norfk	45	N8
Canton	Cardif	16	F2
Cantraywood	Highld	107	N11
Cantsfield	Lancs	63	L7
Canvey Island	Essex	22	F6
Canwick	Lincs	52	E9
Canworthy Water	Cnwll	4	F2
Caol	Highld	90	F2
Caolas Scalpaigh	W Isls	111	c3
Caoles	Ag & B	88	D6
Caonich	Highld	97	Q10
Capel	Kent	12	D2
Capel	Surrey	11	J2
Capel Bangor	Cerdgn	37	K5
Capel Coch	IoA	54	F5
Capel Curig	Conwy	55	M9
Capel Dewi	Carmth	26	C5
Capel Dewi	Cerdgn	36	G12
Capel-Dewi	Cerdgn	37	K4
Capel Garmon	Conwy	55	M9
Capel Hendre	Carmth	26	E6
Capel Iwan	Carmth	25	M2
Capel-le-Ferne	Kent	13	N3
Capel Parc	IoA	54	F4
Capel St Andrew	Suffk	35	N7
Capel St Mary	Suffk	34	H8
Capel Seion	Cerdgn	37	K5
Capelulo	Conwy	55	L6
Capenhurst	Ches W	48	G2
Cape Wrath	Highld	108	E1
Capheaton	Nthumb	73	J5
Caplaw	E Rens	84	G10
Cappercleuch	Border	79	K4
Capton	Devon	5	Q9
Caputh	P & K	92	G7
Caradon Mining District	Cnwll	4	G5
Carbeth Inn	Stirlg	85	J7
Carbis Bay	Cnwll	2	D7
Carbost	Highld	96	D4
Carbost	Highld	104	F11
Carbrook	Sheff	51	J3
Carbrooke	Norfk	44	F9
Car Colston	Notts	51	Q11
Carcroft	Donc	59	M11
Cardenden	Fife	86	E4
Cardhu	Moray	101	J6
Cardiff	Cardif	16	G2
Cardiff Airport	V Glam	16	E3
Cardiff Gate Services	Cardif	27	P11
Cardiff West Services	Cardif	27	M11
Cardigan	Cerdgn	36	C10
Cardington	Bed	32	F7
Cardington	Shrops	39	J3
Cardinham	Cnwll	4	D6
Cardrain	D & G	68	F11
Cardrona	Border	79	L2
Cardross	Ag & B	84	F7
Cardryne	D & G	68	F11
Cardurnock	Cumb	71	J4
Careby	Lincs	42	E6
Careston	Angus	95	J9
Carew	Pembks	24	H7
Carew Cheriton	Pembks	24	H7
Carew Newton	Pembks	24	H7
Carey	Herefs	28	G3
Carfin	N Lans	85	N10
Carfraemill	Border	80	C4
Cargate Green	Norfk	45	N7
Cargenbridge	D & G	70	F1
Cargill	P & K	92	H8
Cargo	Cumb	71	M4
Cargreen	Cnwll	5	J7
Carham	Nthumb	80	H6
Carhampton	Somset	16	D7
Carharrack	Cnwll	2	G7
Carie	P & K	91	P5
Carinish	W Isls	111	b5
Carisbrooke	IoW	9	N9
Cark	Cumb	62	G6
Carkeel	Cnwll	5	J7
Càrlabhagh	W Isls	111	c2
Carlbury	Darltn	65	L4
Carlby	Lincs	42	F7
Carleen	Cnwll	2	F8
Carleton Forehoe	Norfk	44	H8
Carleton-in-Craven	N York	58	C4
Carleton Rode	Norfk	44	H10
Carleton St Peter	Norfk	45	M9
Carlincraig	Abers	102	E6
Carlingcott	BaNES	17	Q5
Carlisle	Cumb	71	N4
Carlisle Airport	Cumb	71	P4
Carlops	Border	86	D10
Carloway	W Isls	111	c2
Carlton	Barns	59	J11
Carlton	Bed	32	D6
Carlton	Cambs	33	Q6
Carlton	Leeds	59	J8
Carlton	Leics	41	K6
Carlton	N York	59	N9
Carlton	N York	65	J9

Carlton N York	66	E9
Carlton Notts	51	N11
Carlton S on T	65	P3
Carlton S Lans	35	M4
Carlton Colville Suffk	45	Q11
Carlton Curlieu Leics	41	P7
Carlton Green Cambs	33	Q6
Carlton Husthwaite N York	66	C11
Carlton-in-Cleveland N York	66	F6
Carlton in Lindrick Notts	51	N4
Carlton-le-Moorland Lincs	52	C10
Carlton Miniott N York	65	P10
Carlton-on-Trent Notts	52	B10
Carlton Scroop Lincs	42	D2
Carluke S Lans	77	P2
Carmacoup S Lans	77	N6
Carmarthen Carmth	25	P5
Carmel Carmth	26	D5
Carmel Flints	56	D12
Carmel Gwynd	54	G9
Carmichael S Lans	78	F2
Carmunnock C Glas	85	K10
Carmyle C Glas	85	L9
Carmyllie Angus	93	P7
Carnaby E R Yk	61	K2
Carnbee Fife	87	K2
Carnbo P & K	86	C2
Carn Brea Cnwll	2	
Carnbrogie Abers	102	H9
Candu Highld	97	M4
Carnduff S Lans	77	L3
Carnell E Ayrs	76	H5
Carnforth Lancs	63	J7
Carn-gorm Highld	97	N5
Carnhell Green Cnwll	2	F8
Carnie Abers	95	N2
Carnkie Cnwll	2	G7
Carnkie Cnwll	2	G8
Carno Powys	47	Q11
Carnock Fife	86	C4
Carnon Downs Cnwll	3	J7
Carnousie Abers	102	E5
Carnoustie Angus	93	P8
Carnwath S Lans	86	B11
Carol Green Solhll	40	H11
Carperby N York	64	H9
Carradale Ag & B	75	M5
Carrbridge Highld	99	N4
Carrefour Jersey	7	b1
Carreglefn IoA	54	E4
Carr Gate Wakefd	58	H8
Carrhouse N Linc	60	D11
Carrick Ag & B	83	N5
Carrick Castle Ag & B	84	D4
Carriden Falk	86	B6
Carrington Mdloth	86	G9
Carrington Traffd	57	N9
Carrog Denbgs	48	C6
Carron Falk	85	P6
Carron Moray	101	J4
Carronbridge D & G	78	E8
Carron Bridge Stirlg	85	M6
Carronshore Falk	85	P6
Carr Shield Nthumb	72	E10
Carruth House Inver	84	F9
Carrville Dur	73	N11
Carsaig Ag & B	89	L11
Carseriggan D & G	69	J5
Carsethorn D & G	70	G4
Carshalton Gt Lon	21	L9
Carsington Derbys	50	G9
Carskey Ag & B	75	J10
Carsluith D & G	69	L8
Carsphairn D & G	77	J11
Carstairs S Lans	77	Q3
Carstairs Junction S Lans	77	Q3
Carterton Oxon	30	H11
Carthew Cnwll	3	M5
Carthorpe N York	65	N10
Cartland S Lans	77	P3
Cartmel Cumb	62	H6
Carway Carmth	26	C7
Cashe's Green Gloucs	29	L7
Cassington Oxon	31	L11
Cassop Dur	73	N12
Castel Guern	6	b2
Casterton Cumb	63	L6
Castle Acre Norfk	44	D7
Castle Ashby Nhants	32	C5
Castlebay W Isls	111	a7
Castle Bolton N York	65	J8
Castle Bromwich Solhll	40	F9
Castle Bytham Lincs	42	E6
Castlebythe Pembks	24	H3
Castle Caereinion Powys	38	D2
Castle Camps Cambs	33	P8
Castle Carrock Cumb	71	Q5
Castlecary Falk	85	N7
Castle Cary Somset	17	P8
Castle Combe Wilts	18	C5
Castle Donington Leics	41	K3
Castle Douglas D & G	70	C3
Castle Eaton Swindn	18	G2
Castle Eden Dur	73	Q12
Castleford Wakefd	59	K8
Castle Frome Herefs	39	M11
Castle Gresley Derbys	40	H4
Castle Hedingham Essex	34	D9
Castlehill Border	79	K2
Castlehill Highld	110	E3
Castle Hill Suffk	35	J7
Castlehill W Duns	84	G7
Castle Howard N York	66	G12
Castle Kennedy D & G	68	F7
Castle Lachlan Ag & B	83	Q4
Castlemartin Pembks	24	F8
Castlemilk C Glas	85	K10
Castlemorton Worcs	29	L2
Castlemorton Common Worcs	29	K2
Castle O'er D & G	79	L9
Castle Rising Norfk	43	Q5
Castleside Dur	73	J10
Castle Stuart Highld	107	M10
Castlethorpe M Keyn	32	B7
Castleton Ag & B	83	N4
Castleton Border	79	Q10
Castleton Derbys	50	F4
Castleton N York	66	F6
Castleton Newpt	27	Q11
Castleton Rochdl	58	B11
Castletown Highld	110	E3
Castletown IoM	56	b7
Castletown Sundld	73	P8
Castley N York	58	H5
Caston Norfk	44	F9
Castor C Pete	42	G9
Catacol N Ayrs	75	N3
Catcliffe Rothm	51	K3
Catcomb Wilts	18	E5
Catcott Somset	17	K8
Catcott Burtle Somset	17	K7
Caterham Surrey	21	M11
Catfield Norfk	45	N6
Catford Gt Lon	21	M8
Catforth Lancs	57	J2
Cathcart C Glas	85	K10
Cathedine Powys	27	N4
Catherington Hants	10	B7
Catherston Leweston Dorset	7	K4
Catisfield Hants	9	P6
Catlodge Highld	99	J9
Catmere End Essex	33	M8
Catmore W Berk	19	M5
Caton Lancs	63	K8
Caton Green Lancs	63	K8
Catrine E Ayrs	77	J6
Catsfield E Susx	12	E7
Catsgore Somset	17	M10
Catshill Worcs	40	C11
Cattadale Ag & B	75	K9
Cattal N York	59	K4
Cattawade Suffk	34	H9
Catterall Lancs	57	J1
Catterick N York	65	M7
Catterick Bridge N York	65	M7
Catterlen Cumb	71	P8
Catterline Abers	95	P6
Catterton N York	59	L5
Catteshall Surrey	10	F2
Catthorpe Leics	41	M10
Cattistock Dorset	7	N3
Catton N York	65	P11
Catton Nthumb	72	E8
Catwick E R Yk	61	J5
Catworth Cambs	32	F3
Caudle Green Gloucs	29	N6
Caulcott Oxon	31	L8
Cauldcots Angus	93	Q6
Cauldhame Stirlg	85	L4
Cauldmill Border	80	C10
Cauldon Staffs	50	E10
Cauldwell Derbys	40	G4
Caulkerbush D & G	70	F4
Caulside D & G	79	P11
Caundle Marsh Dorset	17	P12
Caunton Notts	51	Q8
Causeway End D & G	69	K7
Causeway End Essex	34	B11
Causewayend S Lans	78	G2
Causewayhead Stirlg	85	N4
Causeyend Abers	103	K10
Causey Park Bridge Nthumb	73	L2
Cavendish Suffk	34	D7
Cavenham Suffk	34	C3
Caversfield Oxon	31	M8
Caversham Readg	20	B8
Caverswall Staffs	50	C11
Caverton Mill Border	80	G8
Cawdor Highld	100	D5
Cawood N York	59	M6
Cawsand Cnwll	5	J9
Cawston Norfk	45	J5
Cawthorne Barns	58	H11
Caxton Cambs	33	K5
Caynham Shrops	39	K7
Caythorpe Lincs	42	D1
Caythorpe Notts	51	P10
Cayton N York	67	M10
Ceannabeinne Highld	108	H3
Ceann a Bhaigh W Isls	111	a4
Ceannacroc Lodge Highld	98	C6
Cearsiadar W Isls	111	d2
Cefn Newpt	28	C10
Cefn-brîth Conwy	55	N10
Cefn-bryn-brain Carmth	26	G6
Cefn Cribwr Brdgnd	27	J11
Cefneithin Carmth	26	D6
Cefngorwydd Powys	37	P10
Cefn-mawr Wrexhm	48	F7
Cefn-y-pant Carmth	25	L4
Cellardyke Fife	87	L2
Cellarhead Staffs	50	C10
Cemaes IoA	54	E3
Cemmaes Powys	47	N9
Cemmaes Road Powys	47	N9
Cenarth Cerdgn	36	E11
Ceres Fife	93	M12
Cerne Abbas Dorset	7	P3
Cerney Wick Gloucs	18	F2
Cerrigydrudion Conwy	55	P11
Ceunant Gwynd	54	G8
Chaceley Gloucs	29	M3
Chacewater Cnwll	2	H6
Chackmore Bucks	31	P7
Chacombe Nhants	31	L5
Chadbury Worcs	30	D5
Chadderton Oldham	58	B12
Chaddesden C Derb	51	J12
Chaddesley Corbett Worcs	40	B11
Chaddlehanger Devon	5	K5
Chaddleworth W Berk	19	M5
Chadlington Oxon	31	J9
Chadshunt Warwks	31	J4
Chadwell Leics	42	B5
Chadwell Heath Gt Lon	21	P6
Chadwell St Mary Thurr	22	D7
Chadwick Worcs	39	Q8
Chadwick End Solhll	40	G11
Chaffcombe Somset	7	J2
Chafford Hundred Thurr	22	C7
Chagford Devon	5	N3
Chailey E Susx	11	N6
Chainhurst Kent	12	E1
Chaldon Surrey	21	L11
Chaldon Herring Dorset	8	B10
Chale IoW	9	N11
Chale Green IoW	9	N10
Chalfont Common Bucks	20	G5
Chalfont St Giles Bucks	20	F5
Chalfont St Peter Bucks	20	G5
Chalford Gloucs	29	M8
Chalford Wilts	18	C10
Chalgrove Oxon	19	Q2
Chalk Kent	22	D8
Chalkwell Kent	22	H10
Challacombe Devon	15	M4
Challoch D & G	69	K5
Challock Kent	23	J12
Chalton C Beds	32	E10
Chalton Hants	10	B6
Chalvey Slough	20	F7
Chalvington E Susx	11	P8
Chandler's Cross Herts	20	H4
Chandler's Ford Hants	9	M4
Channel Tunnel Terminal Kent	13	M3
Chantry Somset	17	Q6
Chantry Suffk	35	J7
Chapel Fife	86	F4
Chapel Allerton Leeds	58	H6
Chapel Allerton Somset	17	K6
Chapel Amble Cnwll	3	M1
Chapel Brampton Nhants	31	Q2
Chapel Chorlton Staffs	49	P7
Chapelend Way Essex	34	B8
Chapel-en-le-Frith Derbys	50	D5
Chapel Green Warwks	31	L3
Chapel Haddlesey N York	59	M8
Chapelhall N Lans	85	N9
Chapel Hill Abers	103	L8
Chapel Hill Lincs	52	H11
Chapel Hill N York	59	J5
Chapelhope Border	79	K5
Chapelknowe D & G	71	M2
Chapel Lawn Shrops	38	G6
Chapel-le-Dale N York	64	D11
Chapel Leigh Somset	16	F9
Chapel of Garioch Abers	102	F9
Chapel Rossan D & G	68	F9
Chapel Row W Berk	19	P6
Chapel St Leonards Lincs	53	N8
Chapel Stile Cumb	62	G2
Chapelton Abers	95	P4
Chapelton Angus	93	Q6
Chapelton Devon	15	K6
Chapelton S Lans	77	L2
Chapeltown Bl w D	57	N6
Chapeltown Moray	101	K10
Chapeltown Sheff	51	J2
Chapmanslade Wilts	18	C10
Chapmans Well Devon	4	H2
Chapmore End Herts	33	K12
Chappel Essex	34	E10
Chard Somset	7	J2
Chard Junction Somset	7	J2
Chardleigh Green Somset	7	J1
Chardstock Devon	7	J2
Charfield S Glos	29	J9
Charing Kent	23	J12
Charingworth Gloucs	30	G6
Charlbury Oxon	31	J9
Charlcombe BaNES	17	Q3
Charlcutt Wilts	18	E5
Charlecote Warwks	30	H3
Charlemont Sandw	40	D8
Charles Devon	15	M5
Charleston Angus	93	L6
Charlestown C Aber	95	Q2
Charlestown C Brad	58	F6
Charlestown Calder	58	C8
Charlestown Cnwll	3	M5
Charlestown Cnwll	3	M5
Charlestown Fife	86	C5
Charlestown Highld	105	M7
Charlestown Highld	107	K11
Charlestown Salfd	57	P8
Charlestown of Aberlour Moray	101	K6
Charles Tye Suffk	34	G6
Charlesworth Derbys	50	D3
Charlinch Somset	16	H8
Charlottetown Fife	93	K12
Charlton Gt Lon	21	N7
Charlton Nhants	31	M7
Charlton Nthumb	72	E4
Charlton Oxon	19	L3
Charlton Somset	17	H10
Charlton Somset	17	P6
Charlton W Susx	10	E7
Charlton Wilts	8	D3
Charlton Wilts	18	E3
Charlton Worcs	30	D5
Charlton Worcs	49	L12
Charlton Abbots Gloucs	30	D8
Charlton Adam Somset	17	M9
Charlton All Saints Wilts	8	H3
Charlton Down Dorset	7	P4
Charlton Horethorne Somset	17	P10
Charlton Kings Gloucs	29	N5
Charlton Mackrell Somset	17	M9
Charlton Marshall Dorset	8	D6
Charlton Musgrove Somset	17	Q9
Charlton-on-Otmoor Oxon	31	M10
Charlton on the Hill Dorset	8	D6
Charlton St Peter Wilts	18	G9
Charlwood Hants	10	A4
Charlwood Surrey	11	K2
Charminster Dorset	7	P4
Charmouth Dorset	7	J4
Charndon Bucks	31	P8
Charney Bassett Oxon	19	L2
Charnock Richard Lancs	57	K6
Charnock Richard Services Lancs	57	K6
Charsfield Suffk	35	L5
Charter Alley Hants	19	P8
Charterhall Border	80	G5
Charterhouse Somset	17	M5
Chartershall Stirlg	85	N5
Chartham Kent	23	L11
Chartham Hatch Kent	23	L11
Chartridge Bucks	20	E3
Chart Sutton Kent	12	F2
Charvil Wokham	20	C8
Charwelton Nhants	31	M3
Chase Terrace Staffs	40	D5
Chasetown Staffs	40	D6
Chastleton Oxon	30	G8
Chasty Devon	14	F10
Chatburn Lancs	57	P12
Chatcull Staffs	49	P8
Chatham Medway	22	F9
Chatham Green Essex	22	E1
Chathill Nthumb	81	P8
Chatsworth House Derbys	50	H6
Chattenden Medway	22	F8
Chatteris Cambs	43	L11
Chatterton Lancs	57	P5
Chattisham Suffk	34	H8
Chatto Border	80	G10
Chatton Nthumb	81	M8
Chawleigh Devon	15	M9
Chawston Bed	32	G6
Chawton Hants	10	B3
Cheadle Staffs	50	D11
Cheadle Stockp	57	Q10
Cheadle Hulme Stockp	57	Q10
Cheam Gt Lon	21	K10
Chearsley Bucks	31	Q11
Chebsey Staffs	49	Q9
Checkendon Oxon	19	Q4
Checkley Ches E	49	N6
Checkley Staffs	50	D12
Chedburgh Suffk	34	D5
Cheddar Somset	17	L5
Cheddington Bucks	32	D12
Cheddleton Staffs	50	C9
Cheddon Fitzpaine Somset	16	H9
Chedgrave Norfk	45	M9
Chedington Dorset	7	L2
Chediston Suffk	35	M2
Chedworth Gloucs	30	D10
Chedzoy Somset	17	J8
Cheetham Hill Manch	57	Q8
Cheldon Devon	15	M9
Chelford Ches E	49	Q1
Chellaston C Derb	41	J2
Chellington Bed	32	D5
Chelmarsh Shrops	39	N5
Chelmondiston Suffk	35	K8
Chelmorton Derbys	50	E6
Chelmsford Essex	22	E3
Chelmsley Wood Solhll	40	F9
Chelsea Gt Lon	21	L7
Chelsfield Gt Lon	21	P9
Chelsworth Suffk	34	G7
Cheltenham Gloucs	29	N4
Chelveston Nhants	32	E3
Chelvey N Som	17	L3
Chelwood BaNES	17	P4
Chelwood Gate E Susx	11	N4
Cheney Longville Shrops	38	H5
Chenies Bucks	20	G4
Chepstow Mons	28	G9
Cherhill Wilts	18	F6
Cherington Gloucs	29	M8
Cherington Warwks	30	H6
Cheriton Hants	9	P3
Cheriton Kent	13	M3
Cheriton Pembks	24	H8
Cheriton Swans	26	B9
Cheriton Bishop Devon	5	P2
Cheriton Fitzpaine Devon	15	P10
Cherrington Wrekin	49	M10
Cherry Burton E R Yk	60	G6
Cherry Hinton Cambs	33	M5
Cherry Orchard Worcs	39	Q10
Cherry Willingham Lincs	52	E8
Chertsey Surrey	20	G9
Cherwell Valley Services Oxon	31	M8
Cheselbourne Dorset	8	B7
Chesham Bucks	20	F3
Chesham Bury	57	P6
Chesham Bois Bucks	20	F4
Cheshunt Herts	21	M3
Chesil Beach Dorset	7	N6
Cheslyn Hay Staffs	40	C6
Chessetts Wood Warwks	40	F11
Chessington Gt Lon	21	J10
Chessington World of Adventures Gt Lon	21	J10
Chester Ches W	48	H3
Chesterblade Somset	17	P7
Chesterfield Derbys	51	J6
Chesterfield Staffs	40	E6
Chesterhill Mdloth	86	H8
Chester-le-Street Dur	73	M9
Chester Moor Dur	73	M10
Chesters Border	80	E11
Chesters Border	80	E9
Chester Services Ches W	49	J1
Chesterton Cambs	33	M5
Chesterton Cambs	42	G10
Chesterton Gloucs	18	E1
Chesterton Oxon	31	M9
Chesterton Shrops	39	P3
Chesterton Staffs	49	P5
Chesterton Green Warwks	31	J3
Chesterwood Nthumb	72	E7
Chester Zoo Ches W	48	H2
Chestfield Kent	23	L9
Cheston Devon	5	N9
Cheswardine Shrops	49	N9
Cheswick Nthumb	81	N5
Chetnole Dorset	7	N2
Chettiscombe Devon	16	D12
Chettisham Cambs	43	M5
Chettle Dorset	8	D5
Chetton Shrops	39	M4
Chetwynd Wrekin	49	N10
Chetwynd Aston Wrekin	49	N11
Cheveley Cambs	34	B5
Chevening Kent	21	P11
Chevington Suffk	34	D5
Chevithorne Devon	16	D11
Cheviot Hills	80	G11
Chew Magna BaNES	17	N4
Chew Stoke BaNES	17	N4
Chewton Keynsham BaNES	17	P3
Chewton Mendip Somset	17	N5
Chicheley M Keyn	32	C7
Chichester W Susx	10	D8
Chickerell Dorset	7	P6
Chicklade Wilts	8	D2
Chidden Hants	9	Q4
Chiddingfold Surrey	10	F3
Chiddingly E Susx	12	B7
Chiddingstone Kent	11	P2
Chiddingstone Causeway Kent	11	Q1
Chideock Dorset	7	K4
Chidham W Susx	10	C8
Chidswell Kirk	58	H9
Chieveley W Berk	19	M6
Chieveley Services W Berk	19	M6
Chignall St James Essex	22	D2
Chignall Smealy Essex	22	D2
Chigwell Essex	21	N5
Chigwell Row Essex	21	P5
Chilbolton Hants	19	L11
Chilcomb Hants	9	N2
Chilcombe Dorset	7	M5
Chilcompton Somset	17	P6
Chilcote Leics	40	H5
Childer Thornton Ches W	56	G12
Childrey Oxon	19	L3
Child's Ercall Shrops	49	M9
Childswickham Worcs	30	D6
Childwall Lpool	56	H10
Chilfrome Dorset	7	N3
Chilgrove W Susx	10	D7
Chilham Kent	23	K11
Chillaton Devon	5	J4
Chillenden Kent	23	N11
Chillerton IoW	9	N10
Chillesford Suffk	35	N6
Chillington Devon	5	N10
Chillington Somset	7	K1
Chilmark Wilts	8	E2
Chilmington Green Kent	13	J3
Chilson Oxon	30	H9
Chilsworthy Cnwll	5	J6
Chilsworthy Devon	14	F10
Chiltern Hills	20	C4
Chilthorne Domer Somset	17	M11
Chilton Bucks	31	P10
Chilton Dur	65	M2
Chilton Oxon	19	N4
Chilton Candover Hants	19	P11
Chilton Cantelo Somset	17	N10
Chilton Foliat Wilts	19	K6
Chilton Polden Somset	17	K7
Chilton Street Suffk	34	C7
Chilton Trinity Somset	16	H8
Chilwell Notts	41	L1
Chilworth Hants	9	L4
Chilworth Surrey	10	G1
Chimney Oxon	19	L1
Chineham Hants	19	Q9
Chingford Gt Lon	21	M5
Chinley Derbys	50	D4
Chinnor Oxon	20	C3
Chipnall Shrops	49	N8
Chippenham Cambs	33	Q3
Chippenham Wilts	18	D6
Chipperfield Herts	20	G3
Chipping Herts	33	K9
Chipping Lancs	63	L12
Chipping Campden Gloucs	30	F6
Chipping Norton Oxon	30	H8
Chipping Ongar Essex	22	B3
Chipping Sodbury S Glos	29	K11
Chipping Warden Nhants	31	L5
Chipstable Somset	16	E10
Chipstead Kent	21	P11
Chipstead Surrey	21	L11
Chirbury Shrops	38	F3
Chirk Wrexhm	48	F7
Chirnside Border	81	J3
Chirnsidebridge Border	80	H3
Chirton Wilts	18	F8
Chisbury Wilts	19	J7
Chiselborough Somset	17	L12
Chiseldon Swindn	18	H5
Chiselhampton Oxon	19	P2
Chisholme Border	79	N6
Chislehurst Gt Lon	21	N9
Chislet Kent	23	N9
Chisley Calder	58	D8
Chiswell Green Herts	21	J3
Chiswick Gt Lon	21	K7
Chisworth Derbys	50	C3
Chithurst W Susx	10	D5
Chittering Cambs	33	M3
Chitterne Wilts	18	E11
Chittlehamholt Devon	15	L7
Chittlehampton Devon	15	L7
Chittoe Wilts	18	E7
Chivelstone Devon	5	Q11
Chivenor Devon	15	J5
Chlenry D & G	68	F6
Chobham Surrey	20	F10
Cholderton Wilts	19	J11
Cholesbury Bucks	20	E3
Chollerton Nthumb	72	G6
Cholsey Oxon	19	P4
Cholstrey Herefs	39	J9
Chop Gate N York	66	D7
Choppington Nthumb	73	M4
Chopwell Gatesd	73	K8
Chorley Ches E	49	K5
Chorley Lancs	57	L5
Chorley Shrops	39	M5
Chorleywood Herts	20	G4
Chorleywood West Herts	20	G4
Chorlton Ches E	49	N5
Chorlton-cum-Hardy Manch	57	P9
Chorlton Lane Ches W	49	J6
Choulton Shrops	38	H5
Chrishall Essex	33	M8
Chrisswell Inver	84	D7
Christchurch BCP	8	H8
Christchurch Cambs	43	M10
Christchurch Newpt	28	D10
Christian Malford Wilts	18	E5
Christon N Som	17	K5
Christon Bank Nthumb	81	P9
Christow Devon	5	Q4
Chudleigh Devon	6	B6
Chudleigh Knighton Devon	6	B7
Chulmleigh Devon	15	M8
Church Lancs	57	N3
Churcham Gloucs	29	J5
Church Aston Wrekin	49	N11
Church Brampton Nhants	31	Q2
Church Broughton Derbys	40	G2
Church Cove Cnwll	2	G12
Church Crookham Hants	20	D12
Churchdown Gloucs	29	M5
Church Eaton Staffs	49	Q11
Church End C Beds	32	H8
Churchend Essex	23	J5
Church End Essex	34	C10
Church End Gt Lon	21	K5
Church Enstone Oxon	31	J8
Church Fenton N York	59	L6
Churchfield Sandw	40	D8
Church Green Devon	6	G4
Church Hanborough Oxon	31	K10

Church Houses N York 66 F7
Churchill Devon 6 H3
Churchill N Som 17 L4
Churchill Oxon 30 H8
Churchill Worcs 30 B4
Churchill Worcs 39 Q6
Churchinford Somset 6 G1
Church Knowle Dorset 8 D10
Church Langton Leics 41 Q8
Church Lawford Warwks 41 L11
Church Leigh Staffs 40 D1
Church Lench Worcs 30 D4
Church Mayfield Staffs 50 F11
Church Minshull Ches E 49 M4
Church Norton W Susx 10 E10
Churchover Warwks 41 L10
Church Preen Shrops 39 K3
Church Pulverbatch Shrops 38 H2
Churchstanton Somset 16 G12
Churchstow Devon 5 P10
Church Stowe Nhants 31 N3
Church Street Kent 22 E8
Church Stretton Shrops 39 J4
Churchtown Cnwll 4 D5
Churchtown Derbys 50 H8
Churchtown IoM 56 d3
Churchtown Lancs 63 J12
Church Village Rhondd 27 M10
Church Warsop Notts 51 M7
Churston Ferrers Torbay 6 B10
Churt Surrey 10 D3
Churton Ches W 48 H4
Churwell Leeds 58 H8
Chwilog Gwynd 46 G4
Chyandour Cnwll 2 D9
Cilcain Flints 48 D3
Cilcennin Cerdgn 36 H8
Cilfrew Neath 26 G8
Cilfynydd Rhondd 27 M9
Cilgerran Pembks 36 C11
Cilmaengwyn Neath 26 G7
Cilmery Powys 38 B11
Cilsan Carmth 26 E4
Ciltalgarth Gwynd 47 P4
Cilycwm Carmth 37 M11
Cimla Neath 26 G9
Cinderford Gloucs 28 H6
Cinder Hill Wolves 40 B8
Cippenham Slough 20 F7
Cirencester Gloucs 18 F1
City Gt Lon 21 M7
City Airport Gt Lon 21 N7
Clabhach Ag & B 88 F5
Clachaig Ag & B 84 B6
Clachaig Inn Highld 90 F5
Clachan Ag & B 83 L10
Clachan Ag & B 84 B3
Clachan Ag & B 89 Q11
Clachan Ag & B 90 B7
Clachan Highld 96 G3
Clachan-a-Luib W Isls 111 b4
Clachan Mor Ag & B 88 C6
Clachan na Luib W Isls 111 b4
Clachan of Campsie E Duns 85 K7
Clachan-Seil Ag & B 89 Q11
Clachnaharry Highld 107 K11
Clachtoll Highld 108 B9
Clackavoid P & K 94 C8
Clacket Lane Services Surrey 21 N11
Clackmannan Clacks 85 Q5
Clackmannanshire Bridge Fife 85 Q5
Clackmarras Moray 101 K4
Clacton-on-Sea Essex 23 M1
Cladich Ag & B 90 F11
Cladswell Worcs 30 D3
Claggan Highld 89 P6
Claigan Highld 104 C10
Clanfield Hants 10 B6
Clanfield Oxon 19 K1
Clanville Hants 19 K10
Clanville Somset 17 P9
Claonaig Ag & B 83 N10
Clapgate Herts 33 M10
Clapham Bed 32 E6
Clapham Gt Lon 21 L8
Clapham N York 63 N8
Clapham W Susx 10 H8
Clapton Somset 7 K2
Clapton Somset 17 P5
Clapton-in-Gordano N Som 17 L2
Clapton-on-the-Hill Gloucs 30 F9
Claravale Gatesd 73 K7
Clarbeston Pembks 25 J5
Clarbeston Road Pembks 24 H5
Clarborough Notts 51 Q4
Clare Suffk 34 C7
Clarebrand D & G 70 C3
Clarencefield D & G 70 H2
Clarilaw Border 80 C9
Clarkston E Rens 85 J10
Clashmore Highld 107 M5
Clashmore Highld 108 B9
Clashnessie Highld 108 B9
Clashnoir Moray 101 J10
Clathy P & K 92 E10
Clathymore P & K 92 F10
Clatt Abers 102 C9
Clatter Powys 38 B4
Clatworthy Somset 16 E9
Claughton Lancs 57 K1
Claughton Lancs 63 K8
Claughton Wirral 56 F10
Claverdon Warwks 30 G2
Claverham N Som 17 L3
Clavering Essex 33 M9
Claverley Shrops 39 P4
Claverton BaNES 18 B7
Clawdd-coch V Glam 27 M12
Clawdd-newydd Denbgs 48 C5
Clawton Devon 14 F11
Claxby Lincs 52 G5
Claxton N York 59 P3
Claxton Norfk 45 M9
Claybrooke Magna Leics 41 L9
Clay Coton Nhants 41 N11
Clay Cross Derbys 51 K8
Claydon Oxon 31 L4
Claydon Suffk 35 J6
Claygate D & G 79 N11
Claygate Kent 12 E2

Claygate Surrey 21 J10
Clayhall Gt Lon 21 N5
Clayhanger Devon 16 D10
Clayhidon Devon 16 F11
Clayhill E Susx 12 G5
Clayock Highld 110 D4
Claypits Gloucs 29 K7
Claypole Lincs 42 C1
Clayton C Brad 58 E7
Clayton Donc 59 L11
Clayton Swans 11 L7
Clayton-le-Moors Lancs 57 N3
Clayton-le-Woods Lancs 57 K4
Clayton West Kirk 58 H11
Clayworth Notts 51 Q4
Cleadale Highld 96 F11
Cleadon S Tyne 73 P8
Clearbrook Devon 5 L7
Clearwell Gloucs 28 G7
Cleasby N York 65 M5
Cleat Ork 111 h3
Cleatlam Dur 65 K4
Cleator Cumb 70 G11
Cleator Moor Cumb 70 G11
Cleckheaton Kirk 58 F8
Cleehill Shrops 39 L7
Cleekhimin N Lans 85 M10
Clee St Margaret Shrops 39 K5
Cleethorpes NE Lin 53 K2
Cleeton St Mary Shrops 39 L6
Cleeve N Som 17 L3
Cleeve Oxon 19 Q5
Cleeve Hill Gloucs 29 N4
Cleeve Prior Worcs 30 E4
Cleghornie E Loth 87 L5
Clehonger Herefs 28 E2
Cleish P & K 86 C3
Cleland N Lans 85 N10
Clenamacrie Ag & B 90 C9
Clenchwarton Norfk 43 P6
Clenerty Abers 102 G3
Clent Worcs 40 B10
Cleobury Mortimer Shrops 39 M7
Cleobury North Shrops 39 L5
Cleongart Ag & B 83 K5
Clephanton Highld 107 N11
Clerkhill D & G 79 L8
Cleuch-head D & G 78 D8
Clevancy Wilts 18 F6
Clevedon N Som 17 K2
Cleveleys Lancs 62 G12
Cleverton Wilts 18 E4
Clewer Somset 17 L6
Cley next the Sea Norfk 44 H2
Cliburn Cumb 64 B3
Cliddesden Hants 19 Q10
Cliffe Medway 22 E7
Cliffe N York 59 P7
Cliff End E Susx 12 H7
Cliffe Woods Medway 22 E8
Clifford Herefs 38 E11
Clifford Leeds 59 K5
Clifford Chambers Warwks 30 G4
Clifford's Mesne Gloucs 29 J4
Clifton Bristl 17 N2
Clifton C Beds 32 G8
Clifton C Nott 41 M1
Clifton C York 59 N4
Clifton Calder 58 F9
Clifton Cumb 71 Q9
Clifton Derbys 50 F11
Clifton Devon 15 K4
Clifton Donc 51 M2
Clifton Lancs 57 J3
Clifton N York 58 F5
Clifton Oxon 31 L7
Clifton Worcs 39 Q11
Clifton Campville Staffs 40 G5
Clifton Hampden Oxon 19 P2
Clifton Reynes M Keyn 32 C6
Clifton upon Dunsmore Warwks 41 M11
Clifton upon Teme Worcs 39 N9
Cliftonville Kent 23 Q8
Climping W Susx 10 F9
Clink Somset 18 B10
Clint N York 58 H3
Clinterty C Aber 102 H11
Clint Green Norfk 44 G7
Clintmains Border 80 E7
Clippesby Norfk 45 N7
Clipsham Rutlnd 42 D6
Clipston Nhants 41 Q10
Clipston Notts 41 N1
Clipstone C Beds 32 D10
Clipstone Notts 51 N8
Clitheroe Lancs 57 N1
Clive Shrops 49 K9
Cliveden Bucks 20 E6
Clixby Lincs 52 F3
Cloatley Wilts 29 N10
Clocaenog Denbgs 48 C5
Clochan Moray 101 M3
Clodock Herefs 28 C4
Clola Abers 103 K6
Clophill C Beds 32 F8
Clopton Nhants 32 F1
Clopton Suffk 35 K6
Clopton Corner Suffk 35 K6
Clos du Valle Guern 6 c1
Closeburn D & G 78 E9
Closeburnmill D & G 78 E9
Closworth Somset 7 N2
Clothall Herts 33 J9
Clotton Ches W 49 K3
Clough Foot Calder 58 B9
Clough Head Calder 58 E9
Cloughton N York 67 L8
Clousta Shet 111 k4
Clova Angus 94 F7
Clovelly Devon 14 F7
Clovenfords Border 79 P2
Clovullin Highld 90 D4
Clowne Derbys 51 L6
Clows Top Worcs 39 N7
Cluanie Inn Highld 97 Q7
Cluanie Lodge Highld 97 Q7
Clugston D & G 69 J7
Clun Shrops 38 F6
Clunas Highld 100 D6
Clunbury Shrops 38 G6
Clunderwen Carmth 25 K5

Clune Highld 99 L4
Clunes Highld 98 B10
Clungunford Shrops 38 H6
Clunie P & K 92 G6
Clunton Shrops 38 G6
Cluny Fife 86 F3
Clutton BaNES 17 N4
Clutton Ches W 49 J5
Clutton Hill BaNES 17 N4
Clydach Mons 27 P6
Clydach Swans 26 F8
Clydach Vale Rhondd 27 K9
Clydebank W Duns 84 H8
Clyffe Pypard Wilts 18 F5
Clynder Ag & B 84 D6
Clyne Neath 26 H8
Clynnog Fawr Gwynd 54 E10
Clyro Powys 38 E10
Clyst Honiton Devon 6 D4
Clyst Hydon Devon 6 D3
Clyst St George Devon 6 D5
Clyst St Lawrence Devon 6 D3
Clyst St Mary Devon 6 C5
Cnoc W Isls 111 d2
Cnwch Coch Cerdgn 37 L5
Coad's Green Cnwll 4 G7
Coalburn S Lans 78 D2
Coalburns Gatesd 73 K8
Coaley Gloucs 29 K8
Coalhill Essex 22 F4
Coalpit Heath S Glos 29 J11
Coal Pool Wsall 40 D7
Coalport Wrekin 39 M2
Coalsnaughton Clacks 85 Q4
Coaltown of Balgonie Fife 86 G3
Coaltown of Wemyss Fife 86 G3
Coalville Leics 41 K5
Coanwood Nthumb 72 C8
Coat Somset 17 L11
Coatbridge N Lans 85 M9
Coatdyke N Lans 85 M9
Coate Swindn 18 H4
Coate Wilts 18 F8
Coates Cambs 43 K9
Coates Gloucs 29 N8
Coates Lincs 52 C6
Coates W Susx 10 F6
Cobbaton Devon 15 K6
Coberley Gloucs 29 N5
Cobham Kent 22 D9
Cobham Surrey 20 H10
Cobham Services Surrey 20 H11
Cobnash Herefs 39 J9
Cobo Guern 6 b1
Cobridge C Stke 49 Q5
Coburby Abers 103 J3
Cockayne Hatley C Beds 33 J6
Cock Bridge Abers 101 K12
Cockburnspath Border 87 P7
Cock Clarks Essex 22 F3
Cockenzie and Port Seton E Loth 86 H7
Cockerham Lancs 63 J10
Cockermouth Cumb 71 J9
Cockernhoe Herts 32 G11
Cockett Swans 26 E9
Cockfield Dur 65 K3
Cockfield Suffk 34 E6
Cockfosters Gt Lon 21 L4
Cock Green Essex 34 B11
Cocking W Susx 10 E6
Cocking Causeway W Susx 10 E6
Cockington Torbay 6 B9
Cocklake Somset 17 L6
Cockley Cley Norfk 44 B8
Cock Marling E Susx 12 H6
Cockpole Green Wokham 20 C7
Cockshutt Shrops 48 H9
Cockthorpe Norfk 44 G2
Cockwood Devon 6 D6
Cockyard Derbys 50 D5
Coddenham Suffk 35 J6
Coddington Herefs 29 J1
Coddington Notts 52 B11
Codford St Mary Wilts 18 E11
Codford St Peter Wilts 18 E11
Codicote Herts 32 H11
Codmore Hill W Susx 10 G6
Codnor Derbys 51 K10
Codrington S Glos 29 K11
Codsall Staffs 39 Q2
Codsall Wood Staffs 39 Q2
Coedpoeth Wrexhm 48 F5
Coed Talon Flints 48 F4
Coed-y-paen Mons 28 D8
Coffinswell Devon 6 B8
Cofton Devon 6 C6
Cofton Hackett Worcs 40 D11
Cogan V Glam 16 G2
Cogenhoe Nhants 32 B5
Cogges Oxon 31 J11
Coggeshall Essex 34 E11
Coignafearn Highld 99 K5
Coilacriech Abers 94 E3
Coilantogle Stirlg 85 K2
Coillore Highld 96 D3
Coity Brdgnd 27 K11
Col W Isls 111 d2
Colaboll Highld 107 J1
Colan Cnwll 3 K4
Colaton Raleigh Devon 6 E5
Colbost Highld 104 B11
Colburn N York 65 L7
Colby Cumb 64 C4
Colby IoM 56 b6
Colby Norfk 45 L4
Colchester Essex 34 G10
Colchester Zoo Essex 34 F11
Cold Ash W Berk 19 N6
Cold Ashby Nhants 41 P11
Cold Ashton S Glos 17 Q2
Cold Aston Gloucs 30 F9
Coldbackie Highld 109 L4
Cold Brayfield M Keyn 32 D6
Coldean Br & H 11 M8
Coldeast Devon 5 Q5
Colden Calder 58 C8
Colden Common Hants 9 N3
Cold Hanworth Lincs 52 E6
Coldharbour Surrey 11 J2
Cold Higham Nhants 31 P4
Coldingham Border 81 J3
Cold Kirby N York 66 D10

Coldmeece Staffs 49 Q8
Cold Norton Essex 22 G4
Cold Overton Leics 42 B7
Coldred Kent 13 P1
Coldridge Devon 15 M10
Coldstream Border 80 H6
Coldwaltham W Susx 10 G6
Coldwells Abers 103 K7
Cole Somset 17 P9
Colebatch Shrops 38 G5
Colebrook Devon 6 D2
Colebrooke Devon 15 N11
Coleby Lincs 52 D10
Coleby N Linc 60 F9
Coleford Devon 15 N11
Coleford Gloucs 28 G6
Coleford Somset 17 P6
Colegate End Norfk 45 K11
Colehill Dorset 8 F7
Coleman's Hatch E Susx 11 N4
Colemere Shrops 48 H8
Colemore Hants 10 B4
Colenden P & K 92 G9
Colerne Wilts 18 B6
Colesbourne Gloucs 30 D10
Coleshill Bucks 20 F4
Coleshill Oxon 19 J3
Coleshill Warwks 40 G9
Coley BaNES 17 N5
Colgate W Susx 11 K4
Colinsburgh Fife 87 J2
Colinton C Edin 86 E8
Colintraive Ag & B 83 Q7
Colkirk Norfk 44 F5
Coll Ag & B 88 D5
Coll W Isls 111 d2
Collace P & K 93 J8
Collafirth Shet 111 k3
Collaton Devon 5 P11
Collaton St Mary Torbay 6 B9
College of Roseisle Moray 100 H3
College Town Br For 20 D10
Collessie Fife 93 K11
Collier Row Gt Lon 21 P5
Collier's End Herts 33 L11
Collier Street Kent 12 E2
Collieston Abers 103 L9
Collin D & G 70 G1
Collingbourne Ducis Wilts 19 J9
Collingbourne Kingston Wilts 19 J9
Collingham Leeds 59 K5
Collingham Notts 52 B10
Collington Herefs 39 M9
Collingtree Nhants 31 Q3
Collins Green Warrtn 57 K9
Colliston Angus 93 Q6
Colliton Devon 6 E2
Collyweston Nhants 42 E9
Colmonell S Ayrs 68 F2
Colmworth Bed 32 F5
Colnabaichin Abers 101 K12
Colnbrook Slough 20 G7
Colne Cambs 33 L2
Colne Lancs 58 B6
Colne Engaine Essex 34 E10
Colney Norfk 45 K8
Colney Heath Herts 21 K3
Coln Rogers Gloucs 30 E11
Coln St Aldwyns Gloucs 30 F12
Coln St Dennis Gloucs 30 E11
Colonsay Ag & B 82 E4
Colonsay Airport Ag & B 82 E5
Colpy Abers 102 E8
Colquhar Border 79 M1
Colsterworth Lincs 42 D5
Colston Bassett Notts 41 P2
Coltfield Moray 100 H3
Coltishall Norfk 45 L6
Colton Cumb 62 G5
Colton Leeds 59 J7
Colton N York 59 M5
Colton Norfk 44 H7
Colton Staffs 40 D4
Colt's Hill Kent 12 D2
Colvend D & G 70 E5
Colwall Herefs 29 K1
Colwell Nthumb 72 G6
Colwich Staffs 40 D4
Colwinston V Glam 16 C2
Colworth W Susx 10 E9
Colwyn Bay Conwy 55 M6
Colyford Devon 6 H4
Colyton Devon 6 H4
Combe Devon 31 K10
Combe Oxon 31 K10
Combe W Berk 19 L8
Combe Down BaNES 18 B8
Combe Fishacre Devon 6 A9
Combe Florey Somset 16 F9
Combe Hay BaNES 17 Q4
Combeinteignhead Devon 6 B8
Combe Martin Devon 15 K3
Combe Raleigh Devon 6 F3
Comberbach Ches W 57 M12
Comberford Staffs 40 F6
Comberton Cambs 33 L6
Comberton Herefs 39 J8
Combe St Nicholas Somset 7 J1
Combrook Warwks 30 H4
Combs Derbys 50 D5
Combs Suffk 34 H5
Combs Ford Suffk 34 H5
Combwich Somset 16 H7
Comers Abers 95 L1
Comhampton Worcs 39 Q8
Commins Coch Powys 47 N10
Commondale N York 66 F5
Common End Cumb 70 G10
Common Moor Cnwll 4 F6
Compstall Stockp 50 C3
Compstonend D & G 69 P8
Compton Devon 6 B9
Compton Hants 9 M3
Compton Staffs 39 P5
Compton Surrey 10 F1
Compton W Berk 19 N5
Compton W Susx 10 C7
Compton Wilts 18 G9
Compton Abbas Dorset 8 C4
Compton Abdale Gloucs 30 D10
Compton Bassett Wilts 18 F6
Compton Beauchamp Oxon 19 J4

Compton Bishop Somset 17 K5
Compton Chamberlayne Wilts 8 F2
Compton Dando BaNES 17 P4
Compton Dundon Somset 17 L9
Compton Durville Somset 17 K11
Compton Greenfield S Glos 28 G11
Compton Martin BaNES 17 M5
Compton Pauncefoot Somset 17 P10
Compton Valence Dorset 7 N4
Comrie Fife 86 B4
Comrie P & K 92 B10
Conaglen House Highld 90 E3
Conchra Highld 97 M4
Concraigie P & K 92 G6
Conderton Worcs 29 N2
Condicote Gloucs 30 F8
Condorrat N Lans 85 M8
Condover Shrops 39 J2
Coney Hill Gloucs 29 L5
Coneyhurst Common W Susx 10 H5
Coneysthorpe N York 66 G12
Coney Weston Suffk 34 F2
Congerstone Leics 41 J6
Congham Norfk 44 B5
Congleton Ches E 49 Q3
Congresbury N Som 17 L4
Conheath D & G 70 G2
Conicavel Moray 100 F5
Coningsby Lincs 52 H11
Conington Cambs 33 K4
Conington Cambs 42 H11
Conisbrough Donc 51 L2
Conisholme Lincs 53 L4
Coniston Cumb 62 F3
Coniston E R Yk 61 K7
Coniston Cold N York 58 B3
Conistone N York 58 C1
Connah's Quay Flints 48 F2
Connel Ag & B 90 C9
Connel Park E Ayrs 77 K8
Connor Downs Cnwll 2 E7
Conon Bridge Highld 107 J10
Cononley N York 58 C5
Consall Staffs 50 C10
Consett Dur 73 K10
Constable Burton N York 65 L8
Constable Lee Lancs 57 P4
Constantine Cnwll 2 G9
Constantine Bay Cnwll 3 G10
Contin Highld 106 G10
Conwy Conwy 55 L6
Conwy Castle Conwy 55 L6
Conyer's Green Suffk 34 E3
Cooden E Susx 12 E8
Cookbury Devon 14 G10
Cookham W & M 20 E6
Cookham Dean W & M 20 D6
Cookham Rise W & M 20 E6
Cookhill Worcs 30 D3
Cookley Suffk 35 M2
Cookley Worcs 39 Q6
Cookley Green Oxon 20 B5
Cookney Abers 95 P4
Cook's Green Essex 35 K11
Cooks Green Suffk 34 G6
Cooksmill Green Essex 22 D3
Coolham W Susx 10 H5
Cooling Medway 22 F8
Coombe Cnwll 3 L5
Coombe Devon 6 C7
Coombe Devon 6 E4
Coombe Gloucs 29 K9
Coombe Hants 9 Q4
Coombe Bissett Wilts 8 G3
Coombe Cellars Devon 6 B8
Coombe Hill Gloucs 29 M4
Coombe Keynes Dorset 8 C9
Coombe Pafford Torbay 6 C9
Coombes W Susx 11 J8
Coombes-Moor Herefs 38 G9
Coombeswood Dudley 40 C9
Coopersale Common Essex 21 P3
Copdock Suffk 35 J8
Copford Green Essex 34 F11
Copgrove N York 59 J2
Copister Shet 111 k3
Cople Bed 32 F6
Copley Dur 65 J3
Copmanthorpe C York 59 M5
Compere End Staffs 49 P9
Copp Lancs 56 H2
Coppenhall Staffs 40 B4
Copperhouse Cnwll 2 E8
Coppingford Cambs 32 G2
Copplestone Devon 15 N10
Coppull Lancs 57 K6
Copsale W Susx 11 J5
Copster Green Lancs 57 M3
Copston Magna Warwks 41 K9
Cop Street Kent 23 P10
Copt Hewick N York 65 N12
Copthorne W Susx 11 L3
Copt Oak Leics 41 L5
Copythorne Hants 9 K5
Corbets Tey Gt Lon 22 C4
Corbière Jersey 7 a2
Corbridge Nthumb 72 H7
Corby Nhants 42 C11
Corby Glen Lincs 42 E5
Cordon N Ayrs 75 Q6
Coreley Shrops 39 L7
Corfe Somset 16 G11
Corfe Castle Dorset 8 E10
Corfe Mullen Dorset 8 E8
Corfton Shrops 39 J5
Corgarff Abers 94 F1
Corhampton Hants 9 Q4
Corlae D & G 77 L10
Corley Warwks 41 J9
Corley Services Warwks 40 H9
Cormuir Angus 94 E8
Cornard Tye Suffk 34 E8
Cornforth Dur 65 N1
Cornhill Abers 102 D4
Cornhill-on-Tweed Nthumb 81 J6
Cornholme Calder 58 B8
Cornoigmore Ag & B 88 C7
Cornsay Dur 73 K11
Cornsay Colliery Dur 73 L11
Corntown Highld 107 J10
Corntown V Glam 27 J12

Cornwall Airport Newquay
Cnwll 3 K3
Cornwell *Oxon* 30 H8
Cornwood *Devon* 5 M8
Cornworthy *Devon* 5 Q8
Corpach *Highld* 90 F2
Corpusty *Norfk* 45 J4
Corrachree *Abers* 94 H2
Corran *Highld* 90 D4
Corran *Highld* 97 M7
Corrie *D & G* 79 K10
Corrie *N Ayrs* 75 Q4
Corriecravie *N Ayrs* 75 P7
Corriegills *N Ayrs* 75 Q5
Corriegour Lodge Hotel *Highld* 98 C9
Corriemoille *Highld* 106 F9
Corrimony *Highld* 98 E3
Corringham *Lincs* 52 C5
Corringham *Thurr* 22 E6
Corris *Gwynd* 47 M9
Corris Uchaf *Gwynd* 47 M9
Corrow *Ag & B* 84 D3
Corry *Highld* 96 H5
Corscombe *Devon* 15 L11
Corscombe *Dorset* 7 M2
Corse *Gloucs* 29 K3
Corse Lawn *Gloucs* 29 L3
Corsham *Wilts* 18 C6
Corsindae *Abers* 102 F12
Corsley *Wilts* 18 C10
Corsley Heath *Wilts* 18 B10
Corsock *D & G* 78 C12
Corston *BaNES* 17 Q3
Corston *Wilts* 18 D4
Corstorphine *C Edin* 86 E7
Cortachy *Angus* 94 F9
Corton *Suffk* 45 Q10
Corton *Wilts* 18 C11
Corton Denham *Somset* 17 P10
Coruanan *Highld* 90 E3
Corwen *Denbgs* 48 C6
Coryton *Devon* 5 K4
Coryton *Thurr* 22 E6
Cosby *Leics* 41 M8
Coseley *Dudley* 40 C8
Cosgrove *Nhants* 32 B8
Cosham *C Port* 9 Q6
Cosheston *Pembks* 24 H7
Coshieville *P & K* 92 B6
Cossall *Notts* 51 L11
Cossington *Leics* 41 N5
Cossington *Somset* 17 J7
Costessey *Norfk* 45 K7
Costock *Notts* 41 M3
Coston *Leics* 42 B6
Coston *Norfk* 44 H8
Cote *Oxon* 19 L1
Cotebrook *Ches W* 49 L3
Cotehill *Cumb* 71 P5
Cotes *Leics* 41 M4
Cotesbach *Leics* 41 M10
Cotford St Luke *Somset* 16 G9
Cotgrave *Notts* 41 N1
Cothal *Abers* 102 H11
Cotham *Notts* 42 B1
Cotherstone *Dur* 64 H4
Cothill *Oxon* 19 M2
Cotleigh *Devon* 6 G3
Cotmanhay *Derbys* 51 L11
Coton *Cambs* 33 L5
Coton *Nhants* 41 P12
Coton *Staffs* 49 P10
Coton Clanford *Staffs* 49 Q10
Coton Hill *Shrops* 49 J11
Coton in the Elms *Derbys* 40 G4
Cotswolds 30 C11
Cotswold Wildlife Park & Gardens *Oxon* 30 G11
Cott *Devon* 5 Q7
Cottam *Lancs* 57 J3
Cottam *Notts* 52 B7
Cottenham *Cambs* 33 M4
Cottered *Herts* 33 K10
Cotteridge *Birm* 40 D10
Cotterstock *Nhants* 42 F11
Cottesbrooke *Nhants* 41 P11
Cottesmore *Rutlnd* 42 C7
Cottingham *E R Yk* 60 H7
Cottingham *Nhants* 42 B11
Cottingley *C Brad* 58 E6
Cottisford *Oxon* 31 N7
Cotton *Suffk* 34 H4
Cottown *Abers* 101 P9
Cottown *Abers* 102 G11
Cottown of Gight *Abers* 102 H7
Cotts *Devon* 5 J7
Coughton *Warwks* 30 E3
Coulaghailtro *Ag & B* 83 K9
Coulags *Highld* 97 N1
Coull *Abers* 94 H2
Coulport *Ag & B* 84 D5
Coulsdon *Gt Lon* 21 L10
Coulston *Wilts* 18 D9
Coulter *S Lans* 78 G3
Coulton *N York* 66 E11
Coultra *Fife* 93 L10
Cound *Shrops* 39 K2
Coundon *Dur* 65 M2
Countersett *N York* 64 G9
Countess Wear *Devon* 6 C5
Countesthorpe *Leics* 41 N8
Countisbury *Devon* 15 M3
Coupar Angus *P & K* 93 J7
Coupland *Nthumb* 81 K7
Cour *Ag & B* 75 M3
Courteachan *Highld* 97 J9
Courteenhall *Nhants* 31 Q4
Court Henry *Carmth* 26 D4
Courtsend *Essex* 23 K5
Courtway *Somset* 16 G8
Cousland *Mdloth* 86 H8
Cousley Wood *E Susx* 12 D4
Cove *Ag & B* 84 D6
Cove *Border* 87 P7
Cove *Devon* 16 C11
Cove *Hants* 20 D11
Cove *Highld* 105 M4
Cove Bay *C Aber* 95 Q2
Covehithe *Suffk* 35 Q1
Coven *Staffs* 40 B6
Coveney *Cambs* 33 M11

Covenham St Bartholomew *Lincs* 53 K5
Covenham St Mary *Lincs* 53 K5
Coventry *Covtry* 41 J10
Coverack *Cnwll* 2 H11
Coverack Bridges *Cnwll* 2 G9
Coverham *N York* 65 K9
Covington *Cambs* 32 F3
Covington *S Lans* 78 F2
Cowan Bridge *Lancs* 63 L7
Cowbeech *E Susx* 12 C7
Cowbit *Lincs* 43 J6
Cowbridge *V Glam* 16 D2
Cowden *Kent* 11 P3
Cowdenbeath *Fife* 86 D4
Cowers Lane *Derbys* 50 H10
Cowes *IoW* 9 N8
Cowesby *N York* 66 C9
Cowfold *W Susx* 11 K5
Cowhill *S Glos* 28 H10
Cowie *Stirlg* 85 P5
Cowley *Devon* 6 B4
Cowley *Gloucs* 29 N6
Cowley *Gt Lon* 20 G7
Cowley *Oxon* 31 M12
Cowling *Lancs* 57 L5
Cowling *N York* 58 C7
Cowling *N York* 65 M9
Cowlinge *Suffk* 34 B6
Cowpen *Nthumb* 73 N5
Cowplain *Hants* 10 B7
Cowshill *Dur* 72 F11
Cowslip Green *N Som* 17 L4
Cowthorpe *N York* 59 K4
Coxbank *Ches E* 49 M7
Coxbench *Derbys* 51 J11
Coxford *Cnwll* 14 C11
Coxford *Norfk* 44 E4
Coxheath *Kent* 22 E12
Coxhoe *Dur* 65 N1
Coxley *Somset* 17 M7
Coxley Wick *Somset* 17 M7
Coxtie Green *Essex* 22 C4
Coxwold *N York* 66 D11
Coychurch *Brdgnd* 27 K11
Coylton *S Ayrs* 76 G7
Coylumbridge *Highld* 99 N6
Coytrahen *Brdgnd* 27 J10
Crabbs Cross *Worcs* 30 D2
Crabtree *W Susx* 11 K5
Crackenthorpe *Cumb* 64 C3
Crackington Haven *Cnwll* 14 C11
Crackley *Staffs* 49 Q5
Crackleybank *Shrops* 49 N12
Cracoe *N York* 58 C3
Craddock *Devon* 6 E1
Cradley *Dudley* 40 C9
Cradley *Herefs* 39 N11
Cradley Heath *Sandw* 40 C9
Cradoc *Powys* 27 L3
Crafthole *Cnwll* 4 H9
Craggan *Highld* 100 F9
Cragganmore *Moray* 101 J7
Craghead *Dur* 73 L10
Cragside House & Garden *Nthumb* 73 J1
Crai *Powys* 27 J4
Craibstone *Moray* 101 P4
Craichie *Angus* 93 N6
Craig *Angus* 95 L10
Craig *Highld* 105 Q11
Craigbank *E Ayrs* 77 K8
Craigburn *Border* 86 F10
Craigcleuch *D & G* 79 M10
Craigdam *Abers* 102 H8
Craigdhu *Ag & B* 83 M2
Craigearn *Abers* 102 F11
Craigellachie *Moray* 101 K6
Craigend *P & K* 92 G10
Craigend *Rens* 84 H8
Craigendoran *Ag & B* 84 E6
Craigends *Rens* 84 G9
Craighlaw *D & G* 69 J6
Craighouse *Ag & B* 82 G9
Craigie *P & K* 92 G7
Craigie *S Ayrs* 76 G5
Craigieburn *D & G* 79 J3
Craig Llangiwg *Neath* 26 G7
Craiglockhart *C Edin* 86 E7
Craigmillar *C Edin* 86 G7
Craigneston *D & G* 78 C10
Craigneuk *N Lans* 85 N10
Craigneuk *N Lans* 85 N9
Craignure *Ag & B* 89 P8
Craigo *Angus* 95 L8
Craigrothie *Fife* 93 L12
Craigruie *Stirlg* 91 M11
Craigton *Angus* 95 N7
Craigton *C Glas* 85 J9
Craigton *E Rens* 84 H11
Craigton of Airlie *Angus* 93 K5
Crail *Fife* 87 L1
Crailing *Border* 80 F8
Craiselound *N Linc* 51 Q2
Crakehall *N York* 65 M9
Crambe *N York* 60 C2
Cramlington *Nthumb* 73 M5
Cramond *C Edin* 86 E7
Cramond Bridge *C Edin* 86 E7
Cranage *Ches E* 49 N2
Cranberry *Staffs* 49 P8
Cranborne *Dorset* 8 F5
Cranbourne *Br For* 20 E8
Cranbrook *Devon* 6 D4
Cranbrook *Kent* 12 F3
Cranfield *C Beds* 32 D8
Cranford *Gt Lon* 20 H7
Cranford St Andrew *Nhants* 32 D2
Cranford St John *Nhants* 32 D2
Cranham *Gloucs* 29 M6
Crank *St Hel* 57 J8
Cranleigh *Surrey* 10 G3
Cranmore *Somset* 17 P7
Cranoe *Leics* 41 Q8
Cransford *Suffk* 35 M4
Cranshaws *Border* 87 K9
Crantock *Cnwll* 2 H4
Cranwell *Lincs* 52 E12
Cranwich *Norfk* 44 C10
Cranworth *Norfk* 44 G8

Craobh Haven *Ag & B* 83 M2
Crarae *Ag & B* 83 Q4
Crask Inn *Highld* 109 J10
Crask of Aigas *Highld* 98 F1
Craster *Nthumb* 81 Q9
Cratfield *Suffk* 35 M2
Crathes *Abers* 95 M3
Crathie *Abers* 94 E3
Crathie *Highld* 98 H9
Crathorne *N York* 66 B6
Craven Arms *Shrops* 38 H5
Crawcrook *Gatesd* 73 K8
Crawford *S Lans* 78 F5
Crawfordjohn *S Lans* 78 E4
Crawley *Hants* 19 M1
Crawley *Oxon* 31 J10
Crawley *W Susx* 11 L3
Crawley Down *W Susx* 11 M3
Crawton *Abers* 95 P6
Cray *N York* 64 G10
Crayford *Gt Lon* 21 P8
Crayke *N York* 66 D12
Crays Hill *Essex* 22 E5
Creacombe *Devon* 15 P8
Creagan Inn *Ag & B* 90 D7
Creag Ghoraidh *W Isls* 111 b5
Creagorry *W Isls* 111 b5
Creaguaineach Lodge *Highld* 91 J3
Creaton *Nhants* 41 P12
Creca *D & G* 71 K2
Credenhill *Herefs* 39 J12
Crediton *Devon* 15 P11
Creebank *D & G* 69 J4
Creebridge *D & G* 69 K6
Creech Heathfield *Somset* 16 H10
Creech St Michael *Somset* 16 H10
Creed *Cnwll* 3 L6
Creekmouth *Gt Lon* 21 P7
Creeting St Mary *Suffk* 34 H5
Creeton *Lincs* 42 E6
Creetown *D & G* 69 L7
Cregneash *IoM* 56 a7
Creich *Fife* 93 K10
Creigiau *Cardif* 27 M11
Cremyll *Cnwll* 5 K9
Cressage *Shrops* 39 L2
Cressbrook *Derbys* 50 F6
Cresselly *Pembks* 25 J7
Cressex *Bucks* 20 D5
Cressing *Essex* 34 D11
Cresswell *Nthumb* 73 N3
Cresswell *Pembks* 25 J7
Cresswell *Staffs* 50 C11
Creswell *Derbys* 51 M6
Cretingham *Suffk* 35 K5
Cretshengan *Ag & B* 83 K9
Crewe *Ches E* 49 N4
Crewe-by-Farndon *Ches W* 49 N5
Crewe Green *Ches E* 49 N5
Crew Green *Powys* 48 G11
Crewkerne *Somset* 7 L2
Crewton *C Derb* 41 J2
Crianlarich *Stirlg* 91 K10
Cribyn *Cerdgn* 36 H9
Criccieth *Gwynd* 46 H4
Crich *Derbys* 51 J9
Crichton *Mdloth* 86 H9
Crick *Nhants* 41 N11
Crickadarn *Powys* 27 M1
Cricket St Thomas *Somset* 7 K2
Crickhowell *Powys* 27 P5
Cricklade *Wilts* 18 G3
Cricklewood *Gt Lon* 21 K6
Crieff *P & K* 92 C10
Criggion *Powys* 48 F11
Crigglestone *Wakefd* 58 H10
Crimond *Abers* 103 L4
Crimplesham *Norfk* 43 Q8
Crimscote *Warwks* 30 G5
Crinaglack *Highld* 98 F2
Crinan *Ag & B* 83 L4
Crindledyke *N Lans* 85 N10
Cringleford *Norfk* 45 K8
Crinow *Pembks* 25 K6
Croachy *Highld* 99 J4
Crockenhill *Kent* 21 P9
Crocker End *Oxon* 20 B6
Crockernwell *Devon* 5 P2
Crockerton *Wilts* 18 C11
Crocketford *D & G* 70 D2
Crockham Hill *Kent* 21 N12
Croeserw *Neath* 27 J9
Croes-goch *Pembks* 24 E3
Croes-lan *Cerdgn* 36 F10
Croesor *Gwynd* 47 K3
Croesyceiliog *Carmth* 25 P5
Croesyceiliog *Torfn* 28 C9
Croft *Leics* 41 L8
Croft *Lincs* 53 N10
Croft *Warrtn* 57 L9
Croftamie *Stirlg* 84 H6
Crofton *Wakefd* 59 J9
Croft-on-Tees *N York* 65 M5
Croftown *Highld* 106 C5
Crofts *Moray* 101 K5
Crofts Bank *Traffd* 57 N9
Crofts of Dipple *Moray* 101 L4
Crofts of Savoch *Abers* 103 L4
Crofty *Swans* 26 C9
Croggan *Ag & B* 89 P10
Croglin *Cumb* 71 R6
Croick *Highld* 106 H4
Cromarty *Highld* 107 N8
Crombie *Fife* 86 C5
Cromdale *Highld* 100 G9
Cromer *Herts* 33 J10
Cromer *Norfk* 45 K2
Cromford *Derbys* 50 H9
Cromhall *S Glos* 29 J9
Cromor *W Isls* 111 d2
Cromwell *Notts* 52 B10
Cronberry *E Ayrs* 77 K6
Crondall *Hants* 10 C1
Cronton *Knows* 57 J10
Crook *Cumb* 63 J2
Crook *Dur* 65 L1
Crookedholm *E Ayrs* 76 H4
Crookes *Sheff* 51 J4
Crookham *Nthumb* 81 J6
Crookham *W Berk* 19 P7
Crookham Village *Hants* 20 C11
Crook Inn *Border* 78 H4

Crooklands *Cumb* 63 K5
Crook of Devon *P & K* 86 C3
Cropredy *Oxon* 31 L5
Cropston *Leics* 41 M5
Cropthorne *Worcs* 30 D5
Cropton *N York* 66 G9
Cropwell Bishop *Notts* 41 P1
Cropwell Butler *Notts* 51 P12
Cros *W Isls* 111 e1
Crosbost *W Isls* 111 d2
Crosby *Cumb* 70 H7
Crosby *IoM* 56 c5
Crosby *N Linc* 52 F10
Crosby *Sefton* 56 G8
Crosby Garret *Cumb* 63 N1
Crosby Ravensworth *Cumb* 64 B5
Croscombe *Somset* 17 N7
Cross *Somset* 17 K5
Crossaig *Ag & B* 75 M3
Crossapol *Ag & B* 88 C7
Cross Ash *Mons* 28 E5
Cross-at-Hand *Kent* 12 F2
Crossbost *W Isls* 111 d2
Crosscanonby *Cumb* 70 H7
Crossdale Street *Norfk* 45 K3
Cross Flatts *C Brad* 58 E6
Crossford *Fife* 86 C5
Crossford *S Lans* 77 N3
Crossgatehall *E Loth* 86 H8
Crossgates *E Ayrs* 76 F3
Crossgates *Fife* 86 D5
Cross Gates *Leeds* 59 J7
Crossgates *N York* 67 M10
Crossgill *Lancs* 63 K9
Cross Green *Leeds* 59 J7
Cross Green *Suffk* 34 E5
Cross Green *Suffk* 34 G6
Cross Hands *Carmth* 26 D6
Crosshands *E Ayrs* 76 H5
Crosshill *Fife* 86 E3
Crosshill *S Ayrs* 76 F9
Crosshouse *E Ayrs* 76 G4
Cross Houses *Shrops* 39 K1
Cross in Hand *E Susx* 12 C6
Cross Inn *Cerdgn* 36 H8
Cross Keys *Ag & B* 84 F6
Crosskeys *Caerph* 27 P9
Crosskirk *Highld* 110 B2
Cross Lane *IoW* 9 N9
Cross Lane Head *Shrops* 39 N3
Crosslee *Rens* 84 G9
Crossmichael *D & G* 70 C3
Cross of Jackston *Abers* 102 G8
Cross o' th' hands *Derbys* 50 H10
Crossroads *Abers* 95 J1
Crossroads *Abers* 95 M3
Cross Street *Suffk* 35 K2
Crosston *Angus* 93 N5
Cross Town *Ches E* 57 N12
Crossway Green *Worcs* 39 Q8
Crossways *Dorset* 8 B9
Crosswell *Pembks* 25 K2
Crosthwaite *Cumb* 62 H2
Croston *Lancs* 57 J5
Crostwick *Norfk* 45 L7
Crouch End *Gt Lon* 21 L6
Croucheston *Wilts* 8 F3
Crouch Hill *Dorset* 7 Q1
Croughton *Nhants* 31 M7
Crovie *Abers* 102 G3
Crowan *Cnwll* 2 F8
Crowborough *E Susx* 11 P4
Crowborough Warren *E Susx* 11 P4
Crowcombe *Somset* 16 F8
Crowdecote *Derbys* 50 F8
Crowden *Derbys* 50 E2
Crow Edge *Barns* 58 F12
Crowell *Oxon* 20 C4
Crowfield *Suffk* 35 J5
Crowhill *E Loth* 87 N7
Crow Hill *Herefs* 28 H4
Crowhurst *E Susx* 12 F7
Crowhurst *Surrey* 11 M1
Crowland *Lincs* 43 J7
Crowland *Suffk* 34 G3
Crowlas *Cnwll* 2 D8
Crowle *N Linc* 60 D10
Crowle *Worcs* 30 B3
Crowle Green *Worcs* 30 B3
Crowmarsh Gifford *Oxon* 19 Q3
Crown Corner *Suffk* 35 L3
Crownhill *C Plym* 5 K8
Crownpits *Surrey* 10 F2
Crownthorpe *Norfk* 44 H9
Crowntown *Cnwll* 2 F9
Crows-an-Wra *Cnwll* 2 B9
Crowthorne *Wokham* 20 D9
Crowton *Ches W* 49 L1
Croxdale *Dur* 73 M12
Croxden *Staffs* 50 E11
Croxley Green *Herts* 20 H4
Croxteth *Lpool* 56 H9
Croxton *Cambs* 33 J5
Croxton *N Linc* 61 J10
Croxton *Norfk* 44 E11
Croxton *Norfk* 44 G4
Croxton *Staffs* 49 P8
Croxton Kerrial *Leics* 42 B4
Croy *Highld* 107 N11
Croy *N Lans* 85 M7
Croyde *Devon* 14 H4
Croydon *Cambs* 33 K6
Croydon *Gt Lon* 21 L9
Crubenmore *Highld* 99 J6
Cruckmeole *Shrops* 38 H1
Cruckton *Shrops* 48 H11
Cruden Bay *Abers* 103 M7
Crudgington *Wrekin* 49 L11
Crudie *Abers* 102 G4
Crudwell *Wilts* 29 N9
Crumlin *Caerph* 27 P7
Crumplehorn *Cnwll* 4 F9
Crumpsall *Manch* 57 Q8
Crundale *Kent* 13 K1
Crux Easton *Hants* 19 M9
Crwbin *Carmth* 26 C6
Cryers Hill *Bucks* 20 E4
Crymych *Pembks* 25 K3
Crynant *Neath* 26 H7
Crystal Palace *Gt Lon* 21 M8
Cuaig *Highld* 105 K10
Cuan *Ag & B* 89 P12

Cubert *Cnwll* 2 H4
Cublington *Bucks* 32 B11
Cublington *Herefs* 28 E2
Cuckfield *W Susx* 11 L5
Cucklington *Somset* 17 R10
Cuckney *Notts* 51 M6
Cuddesdon *Oxon* 31 N12
Cuddington *Bucks* 31 Q11
Cuddington *Ches W* 49 L2
Cuddington Heath *Ches W* 49 J6
Cudham *Gt Lon* 21 N10
Cudliptown *Devon* 5 L4
Cudnell *BCP* 8 F7
Cudworth *Barns* 59 K11
Cudworth *Somset* 7 K1
Cuffley *Herts* 21 L3
Cuil *Highld* 90 D5
Culbokie *Highld* 107 K9
Culburnie *Highld* 98 G1
Culcabock *Highld* 107 L12
Culcharry *Highld* 100 D5
Culcheth *Warrtn* 57 M9
Culdrain *Abers* 101 P8
Culduie *Highld* 97 K2
Culford *Suffk* 34 D3
Culgaith *Cumb* 64 B2
Culham *Oxon* 19 N2
Culkein *Highld* 108 B8
Culkein Drumbeg *Highld* 108 C8
Culkerton *Gloucs* 29 N9
Cullen *Moray* 101 P2
Cullercoats *N Tyne* 73 P6
Cullerlie *Abers* 95 M2
Cullicudden *Highld* 107 K9
Cullingworth *C Brad* 58 E6
Cuillin Hills *Highld* 96 F5
Cullipool *Ag & B* 83 L1
Cullivoe *Shet* 111 k2
Culloden *Highld* 107 M12
Cullompton *Devon* 6 D2
Cullompton Services *Devon* 6 D2
Culm Davy *Devon* 16 F12
Culmington *Shrops* 39 J6
Culmstock *Devon* 16 E12
Culnacraig *Highld* 106 A2
Culnaightrie *D & G* 70 C5
Culnaknock *Highld* 104 G3
Culrain *Highld* 107 J4
Culross *Fife* 86 B5
Culroy *S Ayrs* 76 F8
Culsalmond *Abers* 102 E8
Culscadden *D & G* 69 L8
Culshabbin *D & G* 69 J8
Culswick *Shet* 111 j4
Cultercullen *Abers* 103 J9
Cults *Aber* 95 P2
Culverstone Green *Kent* 22 D10
Culverthorpe *Lincs* 42 E3
Culworth *Nhants* 31 M5
Culzean Castle & Country Park *S Ayrs* 76 D8
Cumbernauld *N Lans* 85 M7
Cumbernauld Village *N Lans* 85 M7
Cumberworth *Lincs* 53 N8
Cuminestown *Abers* 102 G5
Cumledge *Border* 80 G3
Cummersdale *Cumb* 71 N5
Cummertrees *D & G* 71 J3
Cummingston *Moray* 100 H2
Cumnock *E Ayrs* 77 J7
Cumnor *Oxon* 31 L12
Cumrew *Cumb* 71 Q5
Cumrue *D & G* 78 H10
Cumwhinton *Cumb* 71 P5
Cumwhitton *Cumb* 71 Q5
Cundall *N York* 65 Q11
Cunninghamhead *N Ayrs* 76 F3
Cunningsburgh *Shet* 111 k4
Cupar *Fife* 93 L11
Cupar Muir *Fife* 93 L11
Curbar *Derbys* 50 G6
Curbridge *Hants* 9 N5
Curbridge *Oxon* 31 J11
Curdridge *Hants* 9 N5
Curdworth *Warwks* 40 F8
Curland *Somset* 16 H11
Curridge *W Berk* 19 N6
Currie *C Edin* 86 E8
Curry Mallet *Somset* 17 J10
Curry Rivel *Somset* 17 K10
Curtisden Green *Kent* 12 E3
Curtisknowle *Devon* 5 P9
Cury *Cnwll* 2 G10
Cushnie *Abers* 102 C11
Cusworth *Donc* 59 M12
Cutcloy *D & G* 69 L11
Cutcombe *Somset* 16 C8
Cuthill *Highld* 107 M5
Cutnall Green *Worcs* 39 Q8
Cutsdean *Gloucs* 30 E7
Cutthorpe *Derbys* 51 J6
Cuxham *Oxon* 19 Q2
Cuxton *Medway* 22 E9
Cuxwold *Lincs* 52 G4
Cwm *Denbgs* 56 C12
Cwmafan *Neath* 26 G9
Cwmaman *Rhondd* 27 L8
Cwmbach *Carmth* 25 M4
Cwmbach *Powys* 27 N2
Cwmbach *Rhondd* 27 L8
Cwmbach Llechrhyd *Powys* 38 B10
Cwmbran *Torfn* 28 C9
Cwmcarn *Caerph* 27 P9
Cwmcarvan *Mons* 28 F7
Cwm-cou *Cerdgn* 36 E11
Cwmcrawnon *Powys* 27 N5
Cwmdare *Rhondd* 27 L7
Cwmdu *Carmth* 26 E3
Cwmdu *Powys* 27 P4
Cwmdu *Swans* 26 E9
Cwmduad *Carmth* 25 P3
Cwmfelin *Bridgend* 27 J10
Cwmfelin *Myr Td* 27 M8
Cwmfelin Boeth *Carmth* 25 L5
Cwmfelinfach *Caerph* 27 P9
Cwmffrwd *Carmth* 25 P5
Cwmgiedd *Powys* 26 H6
Cwmgorse *Carmth* 26 F6
Cwmgwili *Carmth* 26 D6
Cwmhiraeth *Carmth* 25 N2
Cwm Llinau *Powys* 47 N9
Cwmllynfell *Neath* 26 G6
Cwmmawr *Carmth* 26 D6

Cwmparc Rhondd......27 K9
Cwmpengraig Carmth......25 N2
Cwmtillery Blae G......27 P7
Cwm-twrch Isaf Powys......26 G6
Cwm-twrch Uchaf Powys......26 G6
Cwm-y-glo Gwynd......54 H8
Cwmystwyth Cerdgn......37 N6
Cwrt-newydd Cerdgn......36 H10
Cyfarthfa Castle Museum
  Myr Td......27 L7
Cyffylliog Denbgs......48 C4
Cylibebyll Neath......26 G7
Cymmer Neath......27 J9
Cymmer Rhondd......27 L10
Cynghordy Carmth......37 N11
Cynonville Neath......26 H9
Cynwyd Denbgs......48 C7
Cynwyl Elfed Carmth......25 P4

D

Daccombe Devon......6 B8
Dacre Cumb......71 P9
Dacre N York......58 F3
Dacre Banks N York......58 G2
Daddry Shield Dur......72 F12
Dadford Bucks......31 P6
Dadlington Leics......41 K7
Dafen Carmth......26 C8
Dagenham Gt Lon......21 P6
Daglingworth Gloucs......30 C12
Dagnall Bucks......32 E12
Dail bho Dheas W Isls......111 d1
Dailly S Ayrs......76 E10
Dairsie Fife......93 M11
Dalabrog W Isls......111 a6
Dalavich Ag & B......83 P1
Dalbeattie D & G......70 D4
Dalby IoM......56 b5
Dalby N York......66 F12
Dalcapon P & K......92 E5
Dalchalm Highld......107 Q2
Dalchreichart Highld......98 D6
Dalchruin P & K......91 Q11
Dalcrue P & K......92 F9
Dalditch Devon......6 E6
Dale Derbys......51 K12
Dale Pembks......24 E7
Dalelia Highld......89 P3
Dalgarven N Ayrs......76 E3
Dalgety Bay Fife......86 E5
Dalgig E Ayrs......77 J8
Dalginross P & K......92 B10
Dalguise P & K......92 E6
Dalhalvaig Highld......109 Q5
Dalham Suffk......34 C4
Daliburgh W Isls......111 a6
Dalkeith Mdloth......86 G8
Dallas Moray......100 H5
Dallinghoo Suffk......35 L6
Dallington E Susx......12 D6
Dallington Nhants......31 Q2
Dalmally Ag & B......90 G10
Dalmary Stirlg......85 J4
Dalmellington E Ayrs......76 H9
Dalmeny C Edin......86 D6
Dalmore Highld......107 L8
Dalmuir W Duns......84 H8
Dalnabreck Highld......89 P3
Dalnacardoch P & K......91 Q3
Dalnahaitnach Highld......99 M6
Dalnaspidal P & K......91 P2
Dalnawillan Lodge Highld......110 B7
Daloist P & K......92 B4
Dalqueich P & K......86 C2
Dalquhairn S Ayrs......76 F11
Dalreavoch Highld......107 M1
Dalry N Ayrs......76 E2
Dalrymple E Ayrs......76 F8
Dalserf S Lans......77 N2
Dalsmeran Ag & B......75 J9
Dalston Gt Lon......21 M5
Dalston Cumb......71 M6
Dalswinton D & G......78 F10
Dalton D & G......70 H2
Dalton N York......65 K6
Dalton N York......66 B11
Dalton N York......73 K6
Dalton Nthumb......73 K5
Dalton-in-Furness Cumb......62 E7
Dalton-le-Dale Dur......73 P10
Dalton-on-Tees N York......65 N6
Dalton Piercy Hartpl......66 C2
Dalveich Stirlg......91 P10
Dalwhinnie Highld......99 J11
Dalwood Devon......6 H3
Damerham Hants......8 G4
Damgate Norfk......45 N8
Damnaglaur D & G......68 F11
Danbury Essex......22 F3
Danby N York......66 G6
Danby Wiske N York......65 N7
Dandaleith Moray......101 K6
Danderhall Mdloth......86 G8
Danebridge Ches E......50 C7
Dane End Herts......33 K11
Danehill E Susx......11 N5
Dane Hills C Leic......41 M6
Dane Street Kent......23 K11
Danshillock Abers......102 F4
Danskine E Loth......87 L8
Darenth Kent......22 C8
Daresbury Halton......57 L11
Darfield Barns......59 K12
Dargate Kent......23 L10
Dargavel Rens......84 G9
Darite Cnwll......4 G6
Darlaston Wsall......40 C7
Darlaston Green Wsall......40 C7
Darley N York......58 G3
Darley Abbey C Derb......51 J12
Darley Bridge Derbys......50 H8
Darley Dale Derbys......50 H7
Darley Green Solhll......40 F11
Darleyhall Herts......32 G11
Darley Head N York......58 G3
Darlingscott Warwks......30 G6
Darlington Darltn......65 M5
Darlton Notts......51 Q6
Darnick Border......80 D7
Darowen Powys......47 N10

Darra Abers......102 F6
Darracott Devon......14 E8
Darracott Devon......14 H4
Darras Hall Nthumb......73 K6
Darrington Wakefd......59 L9
Darsham Suffk......35 N3
Darshill Somset......17 N7
Dartford Kent......22 B8
Dartford Crossing Kent......22 C8
Dartington Devon......5 Q7
Dartmoor National Park
  Devon......5 N4
Dartmouth Devon......6 B11
Darton Barns......58 H11
Darvel E Ayrs......77 J4
Darwen Bl w D......57 M4
Datchet W & M......20 F7
Datchworth Herts......33 J11
Daubhill Bolton......57 M7
Daugh of Kinermony Moray......101 K7
Dauntsey Wilts......18 E4
Dava Moray......100 F7
Davenham Ches W......49 M2
Daventry Nhants......31 M2
Davidson's Mains C Edin......86 E7
Davidstow Cnwll......4 E3
Davington D & G......79 K8
Davington Hill Kent......23 J10
Daviot Abers......102 G9
Daviot Highld......99 K2
Daviot House Highld......99 K2
Davoch of Grange Moray......101 N5
Davyhulme Traffd......57 N9
Daw End Wsall......40 D7
Dawesgreen Surrey......11 K1
Dawley Wrekin......39 M1
Dawlish Devon......6 C7
Dawlish Warren Devon......6 C7
Daybrook Notts......51 M10
Daylesford Gloucs......30 G8
Deal Kent......23 Q11
Dean Cumb......70 H9
Dean Devon......5 M7
Dean Devon......15 M3
Dean Hants......9 P4
Dean Oxon......31 J9
Dean Somset......17 P7
Dean Bottom Kent......22 C9
Deanburnhaugh Border......79 N6
Deancombe Devon......5 P7
Dean Court Oxon......31 L11
Deane Bolton......57 M7
Deane Hants......19 P10
Deanhead Kirk......58 D10
Deanland Dorset......8 E4
Dean Prior Devon......5 Q7
Deanraw Nthumb......72 E8
Deans W Loth......86 B8
Deanscales Cumb......70 H9
Deanshanger Nhants......31 Q6
Deanshaugh Moray......101 L5
Deanston Stirlg......85 M3
Dearham Cumb......70 H8
Debach Suffk......35 L6
Debden Essex......21 N4
Debden Essex......33 N9
Debenham Suffk......35 K4
Deblin's Green Worcs......39 P11
Dechmont W Loth......86 C7
Dechmont Road W Loth......86 B8
Deddington Oxon......31 L7
Dedham Essex......34 H9
Dedworth W & M......20 F8
Deene Nhants......42 D10
Deenethorpe Nhants......42 D10
Deepcar Sheff......50 H2
Deeping Gate C Pete......42 G8
Deeping St James Lincs......42 G8
Deeping St Nicholas Lincs......42 H7
Deerhurst Gloucs......29 M3
Defford Worcs......30 B5
Defynnog Powys......27 K4
Deganwy Conwy......55 L6
Degnish Ag & B......83 L1
Deighton C York......59 N5
Deighton N York......65 P7
Deiniolen Gwynd......54 H8
Delabole Cnwll......4 D4
Delamere Ches W......49 K2
Delfrigs Abers......103 K10
Delliefure Highld......100 G8
Dell Quay W Susx......10 D9
Delnabo Moray......100 H11
Delny Highld......107 M7
Delph Oldham......58 C11
Delves Dur......73 K10
Dembleby Lincs......42 F3
Denaby Donc......51 L2
Denbigh Denbgs......48 C3
Denbrae Fife......93 L11
Denbury Devon......5 Q6
Denby Derbys......51 K10
Denby Dale Kirk......58 G11
Denchworth Oxon......19 L3
Dendron Cumb......62 E7
Denfield P & K......92 E11
Denford Nhants......32 E2
Dengie Essex......23 J3
Denham Bucks......20 G6
Denham Suffk......34 C5
Denham Suffk......35 K2
Denham Green Bucks......20 G6
Denhead Abers......103 K5
Denhead Fife......93 N11
Denhead of Gray C Dund......93 L8
Denholm Border......80 D9
Denholme C Brad......58 E7
Denmead Hants......9 Q5
Denmore C Aber......103 K11
Dennington Suffk......35 L4
Denny Falk......85 N6
Dennyloanhead Falk......85 N7
Den of Lindores Fife......93 J11
Denshaw Oldham......58 C11
Denside Abers......95 N3
Densole Kent......13 N2
Denston Suffk......34 C6
Denstone Staffs......50 E11
Denstroude Kent......23 L10
Dent Cumb......63 N5
Denton Cambs......42 G11
Denton Darltn......65 L4

Denton E Susx......11 P9
Denton Kent......13 N1
Denton Lincs......42 C4
Denton N York......58 F4
Denton Nhants......32 B5
Denton Norfk......45 L11
Denton Tamesd......50 B2
Denver Norfk......43 P9
Denwick Nthumb......81 P10
Deopham Norfk......44 H9
Deopham Green Norfk......44 H9
Depden Suffk......34 C5
Deptford Gt Lon......21 M7
Deptford Wilts......18 E12
Derby C Derb......51 J1
Derby Devon......15 K5
Derbyhaven IoM......56 b7
Derculich P & K......92 D5
Dereham Norfk......44 G7
Deri Caerph......27 N8
Derringstone Kent......23 M12
Derrington Staffs......40 B3
Derry Hill Wilts......18 E6
Derrythorpe N Linc......52 B2
Dersingham Norfk......44 B4
Dervaig Ag & B......89 J6
Derwen Denbgs......48 C5
Derwenlas Powys......47 L10
Derwent Valley Mills Derbys......50 H9
Derwent Water Cumb......71 L10
Desborough Nhants......42 B12
Desford Leics......41 L6
Deskford Moray......101 P3
Detling Kent......22 F10
Devauden Mons......28 F8
Devil's Bridge Cerdgn......37 M5
Devizes Wilts......18 F8
Devonport C Plym......5 K8
Devonside Clacks......85 Q4
Devoran Cnwll......2 H7
Devoran & Perran Cnwll......2 H7
Dewarton Mdloth......86 H9
Dewlish Dorset......7 B7
Dewsbury Kirk......58 G9
Dewsbury Moor Kirk......58 G9
Deytheur Powys......48 E11
Dibden Hants......9 L6
Dibden Purlieu Hants......9 M6
Dickleburgh Norfk......35 J1
Didbrook Gloucs......30 D7
Didcot Oxon......19 N3
Diddington Cambs......32 G4
Diddlebury Shrops......39 K5
Didling W Susx......10 D6
Didmarton Gloucs......18 B4
Didsbury Manch......57 Q9
Digby Lincs......52 F11
Digg Highld......104 F8
Diggle Oldham......58 D11
Digmoor Lancs......57 J7
Dihewyd Cerdgn......36 H9
Dilham Norfk......45 M5
Dilhorne Staffs......50 C11
Dill Hall Lancs......57 N3
Dillington Cambs......32 G4
Dilston Nthumb......72 H8
Dilton Wilts......18 C10
Dilton Marsh Wilts......18 C10
Dilwyn Herefs......38 H10
Dinas Gwynd......46 E4
Dinas Cross Pembks......24 H2
Dinas-Mawddwy Gwynd......47 P8
Dinas Powys V Glam......16 F2
Dinder Somset......17 N7
Dinedor Herefs......28 G2
Dingestow Mons......28 G6
Dingle Lpool......56 G10
Dingley Nhants......41 Q9
Dingwall Highld......107 J9
Dinnet Abers......94 H3
Dinnington N u Ty......73 L6
Dinnington Rothm......51 M4
Dinnington Somset......17 K12
Dinorwic Gwynd......54 H8
Dinton Bucks......31 Q11
Dinton Wilts......8 E2
Dinwoodie D & G......78 H10
Dinworthy Devon......14 F8
Dipford Somset......16 G10
Dippen Ag & B......75 M5
Dippertown Devon......5 M4
Dippin N Ayrs......75 Q7
Dipple Moray......101 M4
Dipple S Ayrs......76 D10
Diptford Devon......5 P8
Dipton Dur......73 K9
Dirleton E Loth......87 K5
Dirt Pot Nthumb......72 F10
Diseworth Leics......41 L3
Dishforth N York......65 P11
Disley Ches E......50 C4
Diss Norfk......35 J1
Distington Cumb......70 G10
Ditchampton Wilts......8 G2
Ditcheat Somset......17 P8
Ditchingham Norfk......45 M11
Ditchling E Susx......11 M7
Ditherington Shrops......49 J11
Ditteridge Wilts......18 B6
Dittisham Devon......6 B10
Ditton Kent......22 E10
Ditton Green Cambs......33 Q5
Ditton Priors Shrops......39 L4
Dixton Mons......28 F6
Dobcross Oldham......58 C11
Dobwalls Cnwll......4 F7
Doccombe Devon......5 M10
Dochgarroch Highld......99 J2
Docking Norfk......44 C3
Docklow Herefs......39 K10
Dockray Cumb......71 N10
Doddinghurst Essex......22 C4
Doddington Cambs......43 L11
Doddington Kent......22 H11
Doddington Lincs......52 C9
Doddington Nthumb......81 L7
Doddington Shrops......39 M6
Doddiscombsleigh Devon......6 B5
Dodd's Green Ches E......49 L6
Dodford Nhants......31 N2
Dodford Worcs......40 C11
Dodington S Glos......29 K11

Dodington Somset......16 G7
Dodleston Ches W......48 G4
Dodside E Rens......84 H11
Dod's Leigh Staffs......40 D1
Dodworth Barns......58 H11
Doe Bank Birm......40 E7
Dogdyke Lincs......52 H11
Dogmersfield Hants......20 C11
Dogsthorpe C Pete......42 H9
Dolanog Powys......48 C11
Dolbenmaen Gwynd......46 H3
Dolfach Powys......47 P10
Dolfor Powys......38 C5
Dolgarrog Conwy......55 L7
Dolgellau Gwynd......47 M7
Doll Highld......107 P2
Dollar Clacks......85 Q4
Dollarfield Clacks......85 Q4
Dolphin Flints......48 E2
Dolphinholme Lancs......63 K10
Dolphinton S Lans......86 D11
Dolton Devon......15 K9
Dolwen Conwy......55 N6
Dolwyddelan Conwy......55 K10
Domgay Powys......48 F10
Doncaster Donc......59 M12
Doncaster North Services
  Donc......59 P11
Doncaster Sheffield Airport
  Donc......51 P2
Donhead St Andrew Wilts......8 D3
Donhead St Mary Wilts......8 D3
Donibristle Fife......86 E5
Doniford Somset......16 E7
Donington Lincs......42 H3
Donington on Bain Lincs......52 H7
Donington Park Services
  Leics......41 L3
Donisthorpe Leics......40 H5
Donnington Gloucs......30 F8
Donnington Shrops......39 L1
Donnington W Berk......19 M7
Donnington W Susx......10 D9
Donnington Wrekin......49 N11
Donnington Wood Wrekin......49 N11
Donyatt Somset......17 J12
Doonfoot S Ayrs......76 F7
Dorback Lodge Highld......100 G11
Dorchester Dorset......7 Q5
Dorchester-on-Thames Oxon......19 P2
Dordon Warwks......40 H7
Dore Sheff......50 H5
Dores Highld......98 H3
Dorking Surrey......21 J12
Dormansland Surrey......11 N2
Dormington Herefs......28 G2
Dormston Worcs......30 C3
Dorney Bucks......20 E7
Dornie Highld......97 M5
Dornoch Highld......107 N4
Dornock D & G......71 K3
Dorrery Highld......110 C5
Dorridge Solhll......40 F11
Dorrington Lincs......52 F11
Dorrington Shrops......39 J2
Dorrington Shrops......49 N7
Dorsington Warwks......30 F4
Dorstone Herefs......28 C1
Dorton Bucks......31 P10
Dosthill Staffs......40 G6
Dotland Nthumb......72 G9
Dottery Dorset......7 M4
Doublebois Cnwll......4 F7
Dougarie N Ayrs......75 N5
Doughton Gloucs......29 M8
Douglas IoM......56 d6
Douglas S Lans......78 D3
Douglas and Angus C Dund......93 M8
Douglas Pier Ag & B......84 D3
Douglastown Angus......93 M6
Douglas Water S Lans......78 E2
Douglas West S Lans......78 D3
Doulting Somset......17 P7
Dounby Ork......111 g2
Doune Highld......106 G3
Doune Stirlg......85 M3
Dounepark S Ayrs......76 D11
Dounie Highld......107 J4
Dousland Devon......5 L6
Dove Dale Derbys......50 F9
Dove Holes Derbys......50 E5
Dovenby Cumb......70 H8
Dover Kent......13 P2
Dover Castle Kent......13 P2
Dovercourt Essex......35 L9
Doverdale Worcs......39 Q8
Doveridge Derbys......40 E1
Doversgreen Surrey......11 K1
Dowally P & K......92 E6
Dowdeswell Gloucs......30 D9
Dowhill S Ayrs......76 D10
Dowlais Myr Td......27 M7
Dowland Devon......15 K9
Dowlish Wake Somset......17 K1
Down Ampney Gloucs......18 G2
Downderry Cnwll......4 G9
Downend Gloucs......29 L8
Downend S Glos......28 H12
Downfield C Dund......93 L8
Downgate Cnwll......4 H5
Downham Essex......22 E4
Downham Gt Lon......21 N8
Downham Lancs......63 P12
Downham Market Norfk......43 P9
Down Hatherley Gloucs......29 M4
Downhead Somset......17 N10
Downhead Somset......17 Q7
Downhill P & K......92 G9
Downholme N York......65 K7
Downies Abers......95 Q3
Downley Bucks......20 D4
Down St Mary Devon......15 M10
Down Thomas Devon......5 K9
Downton Wilts......8 H3
Dowsby Lincs......42 G5
Doynton S Glos......29 J11
Draethen Caerph......27 P10
Draffan S Lans......77 N3
Drakeholes Notts......51 P3
Drakemyre N Ayrs......76 E2
Drakes Broughton Worcs......30 B4
Draughton N York......58 D4
Draughton Nhants......41 Q11
Drax N York......59 P8
Draycote Warwks......41 K12
Draycott Derbys......41 K2
Draycott Gloucs......30 F7

Draycott Somset......17 L6
Draycott in the Clay Staffs......40 F2
Draycott in the Moors Staffs......50 C11
Drayton C Port......9 R6
Drayton Leics......42 B10
Drayton Norfk......45 K7
Drayton Oxon......19 N2
Drayton Oxon......31 K6
Drayton Somset......17 K10
Drayton Worcs......40 B11
Drayton Bassett Staffs......40 F6
Drayton Beauchamp Bucks......20 E2
Drayton Manor Park Staffs......40 G6
Drayton Parslow Bucks......32 B10
Drayton St Leonard Oxon......19 P2
Dreen Hill Pembks......24 G6
Drefach Carmth......25 N2
Drefach Carmth......26 D6
Drefach Cerdgn......36 H10
Dreghorn N Ayrs......76 H3
Drellingore Kent......13 N2
Drem E Loth......87 K6
Dresden C Stke......50 B11
Drewsteignton Devon......5 P3
Driffield E R Yk......60 H3
Driffield Gloucs......18 F2
Drift Cnwll......2 C7
Drigg Cumb......62 C3
Drighlington Leeds......58 G8
Drimnin Highld......89 L5
Drimpton Dorset......7 K2
Drimsallie Highld......90 C1
Dringhouses C York......59 N4
Drinkstone Suffk......34 F5
Drinkstone Green Suffk......34 F5
Drointon Staffs......40 D3
Droitwich Spa Worcs......30 B2
Dron P & K......92 H11
Dronfield Derbys......51 J5
Drongan E Ayrs......76 H7
Dronley Angus......93 L8
Droop Dorset......7 Q2
Droxford Hants......9 Q4
Droylsden Tamesd......50 B2
Druid Denbgs......48 B6
Druidston Pembks......24 F5
Druimarbin Highld......90 E3
Druimavuic Ag & B......90 D7
Druimdrishaig Ag & B......83 L8
Druimindarroch Highld......97 J11
Drum Ag & B......83 P7
Drum P & K......86 C3
Drumalbin S Lans......78 E2
Drumbeg Highld......108 C8
Drumblade Abers......102 E7
Drumbreddon D & G......68 E9
Drumbuie Highld......97 K4
Drumburgh Cumb......71 L4
Drumburn D & G......70 E5
Drumburn D & G......70 F3
Drumchapel C Glas......85 J8
Drumchastle P & K......91 Q5
Drumclog S Lans......77 L4
Drumeldrie Fife......87 J2
Drumelzier Border......79 J3
Drumfearn Highld......97 J6
Drumfrennie Abers......95 M3
Drumguish Highld......99 L8
Drumin Moray......101 J8
Drumjohn D & G......77 J10
Drumlamford S Ayrs......68 H4
Drumlasie Abers......95 K2
Drumleaning Cumb......71 L5
Drumlemble Ag & B......75 K8
Drumlithie Abers......95 N6
Drummoddie D & G......69 K9
Drummore D & G......68 F10
Drummuir Moray......101 M6
Drumnadrochit Highld......98 G3
Drumnagorrach Moray......102 C5
Drumpark D & G......78 E11
Drumrunie Highld......106 C2
Drumshang S Ayrs......76 E8
Drumuie Highld......104 F11
Drumuillie Highld......99 P5
Drumvaich Stirlg......85 L3
Drunzie P & K......86 D1
Drybeck Cumb......64 C5
Drybridge Moray......101 N3
Drybridge N Ayrs......76 F4
Drybrook Gloucs......28 H5
Dryburgh Border......80 D7
Dry Doddington Lincs......42 C2
Dry Drayton Cambs......33 L4
Drymen Stirlg......84 H5
Drymuir Abers......103 J6
Drynoch Highld......96 E4
Dubford Abers......102 G3
Duchally Highld......108 G12
Ducklington Oxon......31 J11
Duddenhoe End Essex......33 M9
Duddingston C Edin......86 F7
Duddington Nhants......42 E9
Duddlestone Somset......16 H11
Duddo Nthumb......81 K6
Duddon Ches W......49 K3
Dudleston Shrops......48 G7
Dudleston Heath Shrops......48 G8
Dudley Dudley......40 C9
Dudley N Tyne......73 M6
Dudley Port Sandw......40 C8
Dudsbury Dorset......8 F7
Duffield Derbys......51 J11
Duffryn Neath......26 H9
Dufftown Moray......101 L7
Duffus Moray......101 J2
Dufton Cumb......64 C3
Duggleby N York......60 F2
Duirinish Highld......97 L4
Duisdalemore Highld......97 J7
Duisky Highld......90 D2
Dukestown Blae G......27 N6
Duke Street Suffk......34 H8
Dukinfield Tamesd......50 C2
Dulcote Somset......17 N7
Dulford Devon......6 E2
Dull P & K......92 B6
Dullatur N Lans......85 M7
Dullingham Cambs......33 Q5
Dulnain Bridge Highld......99 P4
Duloe Bed......32 G5

Place	County	Page	Grid
Duloe	Cnwll	4	F8
Dulsie Bridge	Highld	100	E7
Dulverton	Somset	16	C9
Dulwich	Gt Lon	21	M8
Dumbarton	W Duns	84	G7
Dumbleton	Gloucs	30	D7
Dumfries	D & G	70	F1
Dumgoyne	Stirlg	85	J6
Dummer	Hants	19	P10
Dumpton	Kent	23	Q9
Dun	Angus	95	L9
Dunalastair	P & K	91	Q5
Dunan	Ag & B	84	C8
Dunan	Highld	96	G4
Dunan	P & K	91	L5
Dunaverty	Ag & B	75	K10
Dunball	Somset	17	J7
Dunbar	E Loth	87	M6
Dunbeath	Highld	110	D9
Dunbeg	Ag & B	90	B9
Dunblane	Stirlg	85	N3
Dunbog	Fife	93	K11
Duncanston	Highld	107	J10
Duncanstone	Abers	102	D9
Dunchideock	Devon	6	B5
Dunchurch	Warwks	41	L12
Duncow	D & G	78	F11
Duncrievie	P & K	86	D1
Duncton	W Susx	10	F6
Dundee	C Dund	93	M9
Dundee Airport	*C Dund*	*93*	*L9*
Dundon	Somset	17	L9
Dundonald	S Ayrs	76	F5
Dundonnell	Highld	106	B5
Dundraw	Cumb	71	K5
Dundreggan	Highld	98	D6
Dundrennan	D & G	70	C6
Dundry	N Som	17	N3
Dunecht	Abers	102	G12
Dunfermline	Fife	86	C5
Dunfield	Gloucs	18	G2
Dungavel	S Lans	77	L4
Dungeness	Kent	13	L6
Dunham Massey	*Traffd*	*57*	*N10*
Dunham-on-the-Hill	Ches W	49	J2
Dunham-on-Trent	Notts	52	B8
Dunhampton	Worcs	39	Q8
Dunham Town	Traffd	57	N10
Dunham Woodhouses	Traffd	57	N10
Dunholme	Lincs	52	E7
Dunino	Fife	93	P12
Dunipace	Falk	85	N6
Dunkeld	P & K	92	F7
Dunkerton	BaNES	17	Q4
Dunkeswell	Devon	6	F2
Dunkeswick	N York	58	H5
Dunkirk	Kent	23	L10
Dunkirk	S Glos	18	B4
Dunk's Green	Kent	22	C11
Dunlappie	Angus	95	K8
Dunley	Worcs	39	P8
Dunlop	E Ayrs	76	G2
Dunmaglass	Highld	98	H5
Dunmore	Falk	85	P5
Dunnet	Highld	110	E2
Dunnichen	Angus	93	N6
Dunning	P & K	92	F11
Dunnington	C York	59	P4
Dunnington	E R Yk	61	K4
Dunnington	Warwks	30	E4
Dunoon	Ag & B	84	C7
Dunphail	Moray	100	F5
Dunragit	D & G	68	F7
Duns	Border	80	G4
Dunsby	Lincs	42	F5
Dunscore	D & G	78	E11
Dunscroft	Donc	59	P11
Dunsdale	R & Cl	66	E4
Dunsden Green	Oxon	20	B7
Dunsdon	Devon	14	F9
Dunsfold	Surrey	10	G3
Dunsford	Devon	5	Q3
Dunshalt	Fife	86	F1
Dunshillock	Abers	103	K5
Dunsill	Notts	51	L8
Dunsley	N York	67	J5
Dunsley	Staffs	39	Q5
Dunsmore	Bucks	20	D3
Dunsop Bridge	Lancs	63	M11
Dunstable	C Beds	32	E11
Dunstall	Staffs	40	F4
Dunstan	Nthumb	81	Q9
Dunster	Somset	16	D7
Duns Tew	Oxon	31	L8
Dunston	Gatesd	73	M8
Dunston	Lincs	52	F10
Dunston	Norfk	45	K9
Dunston	Staffs	40	B4
Dunstone	Devon	5	M9
Dunstone	Devon	5	P5
Dunsville	Donc	59	N11
Dunswell	E R Yk	61	J7
Dunsyre	S Lans	86	C11
Dunterton	Devon	5	H4
Duntisbourne Abbots	Gloucs	29	N7
Duntisbourne Rouse	Gloucs	29	N7
Duntish	Dorset	7	Q2
Duntocher	W Duns	84	H8
Dunton	Bucks	32	B11
Dunton	C Beds	33	J7
Dunton	Norfk	44	E4
Dunton Bassett	Leics	41	M8
Dunton Green	Kent	21	P11
Duntulm	Highld	104	F7
Dunure	S Ayrs	76	E8
Dunvant	Swans	26	D9
Dunvegan	Highld	104	C11
Dunwich	Suffk	35	P3
Durgan	Cnwll	2	H9
Durham	Dur	73	M11
Durham Cathedral	*Dur*	*73*	*M11*
Durham Services	*Dur*	*73*	*N12*
Durham Tees Valley Airport	*S on T*	*65*	*P5*
Durisdeer	D & G	78	E8
Durisdeermill	D & G	78	E8
Durleigh	Somset	16	H8
Durley	Hants	9	N4
Durley	Wilts	18	H7
Durley Street	Hants	9	N4
Durlock	Kent	23	P10
Durlock	Kent	23	P9
Durness	Highld	108	G3
Durno	Abers	102	F9
Duror	Highld	90	D5
Durran	Ag & B	83	P2
Durrington	W Susx	10	H8
Durrington	Wilts	18	H10
Durris	Abers	95	M3
Dursley	Gloucs	29	K8
Dursley Cross	Gloucs	29	J5
Durston	Somset	16	H9
Durweston	Dorset	8	C6
Duston	Nhants	31	Q2
Duthil	Highld	99	P4
Dutton	Ches W	57	L11
Duxford	Cambs	33	M7
Duxford	Oxon	19	L2
Duxford IWM	*Cambs*	*33*	*M7*
Dwygyfylchi	Conwy	55	K6
Dwyran	IoA	54	F8
Dyce	C Aber	103	J11
Dyffryn Ardudwy	Gwynd	47	J6
Dyffryn Cellwen	Neath	27	J4
Dyke	Lincs	42	F5
Dyke	Moray	100	F4
Dykehead	Angus	93	J5
Dykehead	Angus	94	F9
Dykehead	N Lans	85	P10
Dykehead	Stirlg	85	K4
Dykelands	Abers	95	L8
Dykends	Angus	93	J4
Dykeside	Abers	102	F6
Dymchurch	Kent	13	L4
Dymock	Gloucs	29	J3
Dyrham	S Glos	17	Q2
Dysart	Fife	86	G4
Dyserth	Denbgs	56	C11

E

Place	County	Page	Grid
Eagland Hill	Lancs	62	H12
Eagle	Lincs	52	C9
Eaglesfield	Cumb	70	H9
Eaglesfield	D & G	71	K1
Eaglesham	E Rens	85	J11
Eagley	Bolton	57	N6
Eakring	Notts	51	P8
Ealand	N Linc	60	D10
Ealing	Gt Lon	21	J7
Eals	Nthumb	72	C9
Eamont Bridge	Cumb	71	Q9
Earby	Lancs	58	B5
Earcroft	Bl w D	57	N4
Eardington	Shrops	39	N4
Eardisland	Herefs	38	H9
Eardisley	Herefs	38	F11
Eardiston	Shrops	48	G9
Eardiston	Worcs	39	M8
Earith	Cambs	33	L2
Earlestown	St Hel	57	L9
Earley	Wokham	20	C8
Earlham	Norfk	45	K8
Earlish	Highld	104	E9
Earls Barton	Nhants	32	C4
Earls Colne	Essex	34	E10
Earls Common	Worcs	30	C3
Earl's Croome	Worcs	29	M1
Earlsdon	Covtry	40	H10
Earlsferry	Fife	87	J3
Earlsfield	Gt Lon	21	K8
Earlsford	Abers	102	H8
Earlsheaton	Kirk	58	H9
Earl Shilton	Leics	41	L7
Earl Soham	Suffk	35	K4
Earl Sterndale	Derbys	50	E7
Earlston	Border	80	D6
Earlston	E Ayrs	76	G4
Earlswood	Surrey	21	L12
Earlswood	Warwks	40	E11
Earnley	W Susx	10	D10
Earsdon	N Tyne	73	N6
Earsham	Norfk	45	M11
Eartham	W Susx	10	F8
Easby	N York	66	E6
Easdale	Ag & B	89	P11
Easebourne	W Susx	10	E5
Easenhall	Warwks	41	L10
Eashing	Surrey	10	F2
Easington	Bucks	31	P11
Easington	Dur	73	P11
Easington	E R Yk	61	P9
Easington	R & Cl	66	G4
Easington Colliery	Dur	73	Q11
Easington Lane	Sundld	73	P10
Easingwold	N York	59	M1
Eassie and Nevay	Angus	93	L6
East Aberthaw	V Glam	16	D3
East Allington	Devon	5	P9
East Anstey	Devon	15	P9
East Ashey	IoW	9	P9
East Ashling	W Susx	10	D8
East Ayton	N York	67	L9
East Barkwith	Lincs	52	H7
East Barming	Kent	22	E11
East Barnby	N York	66	H5
East Barnet	Gt Lon	21	L4
East Barns	E Loth	87	P4
East Barsham	Norfk	44	F4
East Beckham	Norfk	45	J3
East Bedfont	Gt Lon	20	H8
East Bergholt	Suffk	34	H9
East Bilney	Norfk	44	F6
East Blatchington	E Susx	11	P9
East Boldon	S Tyne	73	P8
East Boldre	Hants	9	L7
Eastbourne	Darltn	65	N6
Eastbourne	E Susx	12	C9
East Bradenham	Norfk	44	F8
East Brent	Somset	17	J6
Eastbridge	Suffk	35	P4
East Bridgford	Notts	51	P11
East Buckland	Devon	15	L6
East Budleigh	Devon	6	E6
Eastburn	C Brad	58	D5
Eastbury	W Berk	19	M4
East Butterwick	N Linc	52	B3
Eastby	N York	58	D4
East Calder	W Loth	86	C8
East Carleton	Norfk	45	K9
East Carlton	Leeds	58	G5
East Carlton	Nhants	42	B11
East Chaldon	Dorset	8	B10
East Challow	Oxon	19	L3
East Charleton	Devon	5	P10
East Chelborough	Dorset	7	M2
East Chiltington	E Susx	11	M7
East Chinnock	Somset	17	L12
East Chisenbury	Wilts	18	G9
Eastchurch	Kent	23	J8
East Clandon	Surrey	20	G11
East Claydon	Bucks	31	Q8
East Coker	Somset	7	M1
Eastcombe	Gloucs	29	M7
East Compton	Somset	17	N7
Eastcote	Gt Lon	20	H6
Eastcote	Nhants	31	P4
Eastcote	Solhll	40	G10
Eastcott	Wilts	18	F9
East Cottingwith	E R Yk	60	C6
Eastcourt	Wilts	19	J8
East Cowes	IoW	9	N8
East Cowick	E R Yk	59	P9
East Cowton	N York	65	N6
East Cranmore	Somset	17	P7
East Dean	E Susx	12	C9
East Dean	Gloucs	28	H5
East Dean	Hants	9	J3
East Dean	W Susx	10	E7
East Drayton	Notts	51	Q6
East Dulwich	Gt Lon	21	M8
East Dundry	N Som	17	N3
East Ella	C KuH	60	H8
Eastend	Essex	22	H5
East End	Hants	9	L7
East End	Hants	19	M8
East End	Kent	12	G3
East End	Oxon	31	K10
East End	Somset	17	P6
Easter Balmoral	Abers	94	E3
Easter Compton	S Glos	28	G11
Easter Dalziel	Highld	107	M11
Eastergate	W Susx	10	F8
Easterhouse	C Glas	85	L9
Easter Howgate	Mdloth	86	F9
Easter Kinkell	Highld	107	J10
Easter Moniack	Highld	98	H1
Eastern Green	Covtry	40	H10
Easter Ord	Abers	95	N2
Easter Pitkierie	Fife	87	L2
Easter Skeld	Shet	111	k4
Easter Softlaw	Border	80	G7
Easterton	Wilts	18	F9
East Everleigh	Wilts	18	H9
East Farleigh	Kent	22	E11
East Farndon	Nhants	41	Q9
East Ferry	Lincs	52	B4
Eastfield	N Lans	85	P9
Eastfield	N York	67	M10
East Fortune	E Loth	87	K6
East Garston	W Berk	19	L5
Eastgate	Dur	72	G12
Eastgate	Lincs	42	F6
Eastgate	Norfk	45	J5
East Goscote	Leics	41	N5
East Grafton	Wilts	19	J8
East Grimstead	Wilts	9	J2
East Grinstead	W Susx	11	N3
East Guldeford	E Susx	12	H6
East Haddon	Nhants	31	P1
East Hagbourne	Oxon	19	N3
East Halton	N Linc	61	K9
East Ham	Gt Lon	21	N6
Easthampton	Herefs	38	H9
East Hanney	Oxon	19	M3
East Hanningfield	Essex	22	F3
East Hardwick	Wakefd	59	K9
East Harling	Norfk	44	G11
East Harlsey	N York	65	P7
East Harnham	Wilts	8	G2
East Harptree	BaNES	17	N5
East Harting	W Susx	10	C6
East Hatch	Wilts	8	D2
East Hatley	Cambs	33	J6
East Hauxwell	N York	65	L8
East Haven	Angus	93	P7
East Heckington	Lincs	42	H2
East Hedleyhope	Dur	73	K11
East Helmsdale	Highld	110	B11
East Hendred	Oxon	19	M3
East Heslerton	N York	67	K11
East Hoathly	E Susx	11	P7
East Holme	Dorset	8	D9
Easthope	Shrops	39	K3
Easthorpe	Essex	34	F11
East Horrington	Somset	17	N6
East Horsley	Surrey	20	H11
East Howe	BCP	8	F8
East Huntington	C York	59	N3
East Huntspill	Somset	17	J7
East Ilsley	W Berk	19	N5
Eastington	Devon	15	M9
Eastington	Gloucs	29	K7
Eastington	Gloucs	30	F10
East Keal	Lincs	53	L10
East Kennett	Wilts	18	G7
East Keswick	Leeds	59	J5
East Kilbride	S Lans	85	K11
East Kirkby	Lincs	53	K10
East Knighton	Dorset	8	B9
East Knoyle	Wilts	8	C2
East Lambrook	Somset	17	L11
Eastlands	D & G	70	D2
East Langdon	Kent	13	P2
East Langton	Leics	41	Q8
East Lavant	W Susx	10	D8
East Lavington	W Susx	10	F6
East Layton	N York	65	L5
Eastleach Martin	Gloucs	30	G12
Eastleach Turville	Gloucs	30	G12
East Leake	Notts	41	M3
Eastleigh	Devon	14	H6
Eastleigh	Hants	9	M4
East Lexham	Norfk	44	E6
East Linton	E Loth	87	L6
East Lockinge	Oxon	19	M4
East Lound	N Linc	52	B4
East Lulworth	Dorset	8	C10
East Lutton	N York	60	G1
East Lydford	Somset	17	N9
East Malling	Kent	22	E11
East Marden	W Susx	10	D7
East Markham	Notts	51	Q6
East Martin	Hants	8	F4
East Marton	N York	58	B4
East Meon	Hants	10	B5
East Mersea	Essex	23	K1
East Midlands Airport	*Leics*	*41*	*K3*
East Molesey	Surrey	21	J9
East Morden	Dorset	8	D8
East Morton	C Brad	58	E6
East Morton	D & G	78	E8
East Ness	N York	66	F10
Eastney	C Port	9	Q7
Eastnor	Herefs	29	K2
East Norton	Leics	42	B9
Eastoft	N Linc	60	D10
East Ogwell	Devon	5	P3
Easton	Cambs	32	G3
Easton	Devon	5	P3
Easton	Dorset	7	Q8
Easton	Hants	9	N2
Easton	Lincs	42	D5
Easton	Norfk	45	J7
Easton	Somset	17	M6
Easton	Suffk	35	L5
Easton	Wilts	18	D6
Easton Grey	Wilts	18	C4
Easton-in-Gordano	N Som	17	M2
Easton Maudit	Nhants	32	C5
Easton-on-the-Hill	Nhants	42	E8
Easton Royal	Wilts	18	H8
East Orchard	Dorset	8	C4
East Peckham	Kent	12	D1
East Pennard	Somset	17	N8
East Perry	Cambs	32	G4
East Portlemouth	Devon	5	P11
East Prawle	Devon	5	Q11
East Preston	W Susx	10	H9
East Putford	Devon	14	G8
East Quantoxhead	Somset	16	F7
East Rainton	Sundld	73	N10
East Ravendale	NE Lin	52	H4
East Raynham	Norfk	44	E5
Eastrea	Cambs	43	J10
Eastriggs	D & G	71	L3
East Rigton	Leeds	59	J5
Eastrington	E R Yk	60	D8
Eastrop	Swindn	18	H3
East Rounton	N York	65	P6
East Rudham	Norfk	44	D5
East Runton	Norfk	45	K2
East Ruston	Norfk	45	M5
Eastry	Kent	23	P11
East Saltoun	E Loth	87	J8
East Sheen	Gt Lon	21	K8
East Shefford	W Berk	19	L6
East Stockwith	Lincs	52	B5
East Stoke	Dorset	8	C9
East Stoke	Notts	51	Q10
East Stour	Dorset	8	B3
East Stourmouth	Kent	23	N10
East Stowford	Devon	15	L6
East Stratton	Hants	19	P11
East Studdal	Kent	23	P12
East Taphouse	Cnwll	4	E7
East-the-Water	Devon	14	H6
East Thirston	Nthumb	73	L2
East Tilbury	Thurr	22	D7
East Tisted	Hants	10	B4
East Torrington	Lincs	52	G6
East Tuddenham	Norfk	44	H7
East Tytherley	Hants	9	K2
East Tytherton	Wilts	18	E6
East Village	Devon	15	P10
Eastville	Bristl	17	N2
Eastville	Lincs	53	L11
East Walton	Norfk	44	C6
East Week	Devon	5	N2
Eastwell	Leics	41	Q2
East Wellow	Hants	9	K4
East Wemyss	Fife	86	G3
East Whitburn	W Loth	85	N9
Eastwick	Herts	21	N1
East Wickham	Gt Lon	21	P7
East Williamston	Pembks	25	J7
East Winch	Norfk	44	B6
East Winterslow	Wilts	9	J1
East Wittering	W Susx	10	C9
East Witton	N York	65	K9
Eastwood	Notts	51	L10
Eastwood	Sthend	22	G6
East Woodburn	Nthumb	72	G4
East Woodhay	Hants	19	L8
East Worldham	Hants	10	C3
East Wretham	Norfk	44	F11
Eathorpe	Warwks	31	K1
Eaton	Ches E	49	Q3
Eaton	Ches W	49	L3
Eaton	Leics	42	B4
Eaton	Norfk	45	K8
Eaton	Notts	51	P5
Eaton	Oxon	31	K12
Eaton	Shrops	39	J4
Eaton Bray	C Beds	32	D11
Eaton Constantine	Shrops	39	L2
Eaton Green	C Beds	32	D11
Eaton Hastings	Oxon	19	J2
Eaton Mascott	Shrops	39	K2
Eaton Socon	Cambs	32	G5
Eaton upon Tern	Shrops	49	M10
Ebberston	N York	67	K10
Ebbesborne Wake	Wilts	8	E3
Ebbw Vale	Blae G	27	N6
Ebchester	Dur	73	K9
Ebford	Devon	6	D5
Ebley	Gloucs	29	L7
Ebnal	Ches W	49	J6
Ecchinswell	Hants	19	N8
Ecclaw	Border	87	P8
Ecclefechan	D & G	71	K1
Eccles	Border	80	G6
Eccles	Kent	22	E10
Eccles	Salfd	57	P8
Ecclesall	Sheff	50	H4
Ecclesfield	Sheff	51	J3
Eccleshall	Staffs	49	P9
Eccleshill	C Brad	58	F7
Ecclesmachan	W Loth	86	C7
Eccles Road	Norfk	44	G11
Eccleston	Ches W	48	H3
Eccleston	Lancs	57	K5
Eccleston	St Hel	57	J9
Echt	Abers	95	M2
Eckford	Border	80	F8
Eckington	Derbys	51	K5
Eckington	Worcs	29	N1
Ecton	Nhants	32	B4
Edale	Derbys	50	E4
Eday	Ork	111	h1
Eday Airport	*Ork*	*111*	*h1*
Edburton	W Susx	11	K7
Edderton	Highld	107	L5
Eddleston	Border	86	F10
Eddlewood	S Lans	85	M11
Edenbridge	Kent	11	N2
Edenfield	Lancs	57	P5
Edenhall	Cumb	71	Q8
Edenham	Lincs	42	F6
Eden Park	Gt Lon	21	M9
Eden Project	*Cnwll*	*3*	*M5*
Edensor	Derbys	50	G6
Edentaggart	Ag & B	84	F7
Edenthorpe	Donc	59	N11
Edern	Gwynd	46	E4
Edgbaston	Birm	40	D9
Edgcott	Bucks	31	P9
Edgcott	Somset	15	P4
Edge	Gloucs	29	L6
Edgefield	Norfk	44	H4
Edgefield Green	Norfk	44	H4
Edgerton	Kirk	58	F10
Edgeworth	Gloucs	29	N7
Edgmond	Wrekin	49	N10
Edgton	Shrops	38	H5
Edgware	Gt Lon	21	J5
Edgworth	Bl w D	57	N5
Edinbane	Highld	104	D11
Edinburgh	C Edin	86	F7
Edinburgh Airport	*C Edin*	*86*	*D7*
Edinburgh Castle	C Edin	86	F7
Edinburgh Old & New Town	C Edin	86	F7
Edinburgh Royal Botanic Gardens	C Edin	86	F7
Edinburgh Zoo RZSS	C Edin	86	E7
Edingale	Staffs	40	G5
Edingham	D & G	70	D3
Edingley	Notts	51	P9
Edingthorpe	Norfk	45	M4
Edingthorpe Green	Norfk	45	M4
Edington	Border	81	J3
Edington	Nthumb	73	K4
Edington	Somset	17	K8
Edington	Wilts	18	D9
Edington Burtle	Somset	17	K7
Edingworth	Somset	17	J5
Edithmead	Somset	17	J6
Edith Weston	Rutlnd	42	D8
Edlesborough	Bucks	32	D11
Edlingham	Nthumb	81	M11
Edlington	Lincs	52	H8
Edmondsham	Dorset	8	F5
Edmondsley	Dur	73	M10
Edmondthorpe	Leics	42	C6
Edmonton	Gt Lon	21	M5
Edmundbyers	Dur	72	H10
Ednam	Border	80	G6
Ednaston	Derbys	50	G10
Edradynate	P & K	92	D5
Edrom	Border	80	H3
Edstaston	Shrops	49	K8
Edstone	Warwks	30	F2
Edwalton	Notts	41	N1
Edwinstowe	Notts	51	N7
Edworth	C Beds	32	H8
Edwyn Ralph	Herefs	39	M9
Edzell	Angus	95	K8
Edzell Woods	Abers	95	K7
Efail-fach	Neath	26	G9
Efail Isaf	Rhondd	27	M11
Efailnewydd	Gwynd	46	F4
Efailwen	Carmth	25	K4
Efenechtyd	Denbgs	48	C4
Effgill	D & G	79	L9
Effingham	Surrey	20	H11
Egerton	Bolton	57	N6
Egerton	Kent	12	H1
Eggborough	N York	59	M9
Eggbuckland	C Plym	5	K8
Eggesford	Devon	15	M9
Eggington	C Beds	32	D10
Egginton	Derbys	40	H2
Eggleston	Dur	64	H3
Egham	Surrey	20	G8
Egleton	Rutlnd	42	C8
Egloshayle	Cnwll	3	M2
Egloskerry	Cnwll	4	G3
Eglwysbach	Conwy	55	L7
Eglwys Cross	Wrexhm	49	J7
Eglwyswrw	Pembks	25	K2
Egmanton	Notts	51	Q7
Egremont	Cumb	70	G12
Egremont	Wirral	56	G9
Egton	N York	66	H6
Egton Bridge	N York	66	H6
Egypt	Bucks	20	F6
Eigg	Highld	96	F11
Eight Ash Green	Essex	34	F10
Eilanreach	Highld	97	L6
Eilean Donan Castle	*Highld*	*97*	*M5*
Eisgein	W Isls	111	d3
Eishken	W Isls	111	d3
Elan Valley	Powys	37	P7
Elan Village	Powys	37	P7
Elberton	S Glos	28	H10
Elburton	C Plym	5	K8
Elcombe	Swindn	18	G5
Eldersfield	Worcs	29	L3
Elderslie	Rens	84	H9
Eldon	Dur	65	M2
Elerch	Cerdgn	37	L4
Elfhill	Abers	95	N5
Elford	Staffs	40	F5
Elgin	Moray	101	J3
Elgol	Highld	96	G6
Elham	Kent	13	M2
Elie	Fife	87	K3
Elim	IoA	54	E5
Eling	Hants	9	L5
Elkesley	Notts	51	P6
Elkstone	Gloucs	29	N6
Ella	Abers	102	E7
Ellacombe	Torbay	6	C9
Elland	Calder	58	E9

Ellary Ag & B 83 L7
Ellastone Staffs 50 E11
Ellel Lancs 63 J10
Ellemford Border 87 N9
Ellenabeich Ag & B 89 P11
Ellenhall Staffs 49 Q9
Ellen's Green Surrey 10 H3
Ellerbeck N York 66 B8
Ellerby N York 66 H5
Ellerdine Heath Wrekin 49 L10
Elleric Ag & B 90 E6
Ellerker E R Yk 60 F8
Ellerton E R Yk 60 C6
Ellerton Shrops 65 M7
Ellesborough Bucks 20 D3
Ellesmere Shrops 48 H8
Ellesmere Port Ches W 56 H12
Ellingham Norfk 45 N10
Ellingham Nthumb 81 N8
Ellingstring N York 65 L10
Ellington Cambs 32 G3
Ellington Nthumb 73 M9
Elliots Green Somset 18 B10
Ellisfield Hants 19 Q10
Ellishader Highld 104 G8
Ellistown Leics 41 K5
Ellon Abers 103 K8
Ellonby Cumb 71 N8
Elloughton E R Yk 60 G8
Ellwood Gloucs 28 G7
Elm Cambs 43 M8
Elmbridge Worcs 30 B1
Elmdon Essex 33 M8
Elmdon Solhll 40 F10
Elmer W Susx 10 F9
Elmers End Gt Lon 21 M9
Elmer's Green Lancs 57 J7
Elmesthorpe Leics 41 L8
Elmhurst Staffs 40 E5
Elmley Castle Worcs 29 N1
Elmley Lovett Worcs 39 Q8
Elmore Gloucs 29 K6
Elmore Back Gloucs 29 K5
Elm Park Gt Lon 21 Q6
Elmsett Suffk 34 H7
Elmstead Market Essex 34 H10
Elmsted Kent 13 L2
Elmstone Kent 23 N10
Elmstone Hardwicke Gloucs 29 M4
Elmswell E R Yk 60 H3
Elmswell Suffk 34 G4
Elmton Derbys 51 L6
Elphin Highld 108 E12
Elphinstone E Loth 86 H8
Elrick Abers 95 N1
Elrig D & G 69 J9
Elrington Nthumb 72 F8
Elsdon Nthumb 72 G3
Elsenham Essex 33 N10
Elsfield Oxon 31 M11
Elsham N Linc 60 H10
Elsing Norfk 44 H6
Elslack N York 58 B4
Elson Hants 9 P7
Elsrickle S Lans 86 C12
Elstead Surrey 10 E2
Elsted W Susx 10 D6
Elsthorpe Lincs 42 F5
Elston Notts 51 Q10
Elstow Bed 32 F7
Elstree Herts 21 J4
Elstronwick E R Yk 61 L7
Elswick Lancs 56 H2
Elswick N u Ty 73 M7
Elsworth Cambs 33 K4
Elterwater Cumb 62 G2
Eltham Gt Lon 21 N8
Eltisley Cambs 33 J5
Elton Cambs 42 F10
Elton Ches W 49 J1
Elton Derbys 51 G8
Elton Herefs 39 J7
Elton S on T 65 P4
Elton-on-the-Hill Notts 51 Q11
Eltringham Nthumb 73 J8
Elvanfoot S Lans 78 F6
Elvaston Derbys 41 K2
Elveden Suffk 34 D2
Elvetham Heath Hants 20 C11
Elvingston E Loth 87 J7
Elvington C York 60 C5
Elvington Kent 23 P12
Elwick Hartpl 66 C2
Elworth Ches E 49 N3
Elworthy Somset 16 E8
Ely Cambs 33 N1
Ely Cardif 16 F2
Emberton M Keyn 32 C6
Embleton Cumb 71 J9
Embleton Nthumb 81 P9
Embo Highld 107 N4
Emborough Somset 17 N6
Embo Street Highld 107 N4
Embsay N York 58 D3
Emery Down Hants 9 K6
Emley Kirk 58 G10
Emmington Oxon 20 C3
Emneth Norfk 43 M8
Emneth Hungate Norfk 43 N8
Empingham Rutlnd 42 D8
Empshott Hants 10 C4
Emsworth Hants 10 C8
Enborne W Berk 19 M7
Enborne Row W Berk 19 M7
Enderby Leics 41 M7
Endmoor Cumb 63 K5
Endon Staffs 50 B9
Endon Bank Staffs 50 B9
Enfield Gt Lon 21 M4
Enfield Lock Gt Lon 21 M4
Enfield Wash Gt Lon 21 M4
Enford Wilts 18 G9
Engine Common S Glos 29 J11
Englefield W Berk 19 Q6
Englefield Green Surrey 20 G8
English Bicknor Gloucs 28 G5
Englishcombe BaNES 17 Q4
English Frankton Shrops 49 J9
Enham Alamein Hants 19 L10
Enmore Somset 16 H8
Enmore Green Dorset 8 C3
Ennerdale Bridge Cumb 70 H11

Enochdhu P & K 92 F3
Ensay Ag & B 88 H6
Ensbury BCP 8 F8
Ensdon Shrops 48 H11
Enstone Oxon 31 J8
Enterkinfoot D & G 78 E7
Enville Staffs 39 P5
Eòlaigearraidh W Isls 111 a6
Eoligarry W Isls 111 a6
Epney Gloucs 29 K6
Epperstone Notts 51 P10
Epping Essex 21 P3
Epping Green Essex 21 N3
Epping Upland Essex 21 N3
Eppleby N York 65 L5
Epsom Surrey 21 K10
Epwell Oxon 31 J6
Epworth N Linc 52 A3
Erbistock Wrexhm 48 G7
Erdington Birm 40 E8
Eridge Green E Susx 12 B3
Erines Ag & B 83 M3
Eriska Ag & B 90 C7
Eriskay W Isls 111 b6
Eriswell Suffk 34 C3
Erith Gt Lon 21 P7
Erlestoke Wilts 18 E8
Ermington Devon 5 M9
Erpingham Norfk 45 K4
Errogie Highld 98 H5
Errol P & K 93 J10
Erskine Rens 84 H8
Erskine Bridge Rens 84 H8
Ervie D & G 68 D5
Erwarton Suffk 35 K9
Erwood Powys 38 C12
Eryholme N York 65 N6
Eryrys Denbgs 48 F3
Escomb Dur 65 L2
Escrick N York 59 N5
Esgairgeiliog Powys 47 M9
Esh Dur 73 L11
Esher Surrey 21 J9
Eshott Nthumb 73 L2
Esh Winning Dur 73 L11
Eskadale Highld 98 F2
Eskbank Mdloth 86 G8
Eskdale Green Cumb 62 D3
Eskdalemuir D & G 79 L8
Esprick Lancs 56 H2
Essendine Rutlnd 42 E7
Essendon Herts 21 L2
Essich Highld 99 J2
Essington Staffs 40 C6
Esslemont Abers 103 J8
Eston R & Cl 66 D4
Etal Nthumb 81 K6
Etchilhampton Wilts 18 F8
Etchingham E Susx 12 E5
Etchinghill Kent 13 M3
Etchinghill Staffs 40 D4
Eton W & M 20 G7
Eton Wick W & M 20 F7
Etruria C Stke 49 Q5
Etteridge Highld 99 K9
Ettersgill Dur 64 F3
Ettiley Heath Ches E 49 N4
Ettingshall Wolves 40 B8
Ettington Warwks 30 H4
Etton C Pete 42 G8
Etton E R Yk 60 G5
Ettrick Border 79 L6
Ettrickbridge Border 79 M4
Ettrickhill Border 79 L6
Etwall Derbys 40 H2
Euston Suffk 34 E2
Euxton Lancs 57 K5
Evanton Highld 107 K8
Evedon Lincs 42 F2
Evelix Highld 107 M4
Evenjobb Powys 38 F9
Evenley Nhants 31 N7
Evenlode Gloucs 30 G9
Evenwood Dur 65 K3
Evercreech Somset 17 P8
Everingham E R Yk 60 D6
Everleigh Wilts 18 H9
Eversholt C Beds 32 E9
Evershot Dorset 7 N2
Eversley Hants 20 C10
Eversley Cross Hants 20 C10
Everthorpe E R Yk 60 F7
Everton C Beds 32 H6
Everton Hants 9 K8
Everton Lpool 56 G9
Everton Notts 51 P3
Evertown D & G 71 M1
Evesbatch Herefs 39 M11
Evesham Worcs 30 D5
Evington C Leic 41 N6
Ewden Village Sheff 50 H4
Ewell Surrey 21 K10
Ewell Minnis Kent 13 N2
Ewelme Oxon 19 Q3
Ewen Gloucs 18 E2
Ewenny V Glam 27 J12
Ewerby Lincs 42 G11
Ewhurst Surrey 10 H2
Ewhurst Green E Susx 12 F5
Ewhurst Green Surrey 10 H2
Ewloe Flints 48 F3
Ewood Bl w D 57 M4
Eworthy Devon 5 J2
Ewshot Hants 20 D12
Ewyas Harold Herefs 28 D3
Exbourne Devon 15 K10
Exbury Hants 9 M7
Exebridge Somset 16 C10
Exelby N York 65 N9
Exeter Devon 6 C4
Exeter Airport Devon 6 C4
Exeter Services Devon 6 C4
Exford Somset 15 P5
Exfordsgreen Shrops 39 J2
Exhall Warwks 30 E3
Exhall Warwks 41 J9
Exlade Street Oxon 19 Q4
Exminster Devon 6 C5
Exmoor National Park 15 P4
Exmouth Devon 6 D6
Exning Suffk 33 Q4
Exton Devon 6 D5

Exton Hants 9 Q4
Exton Rutlnd 42 D7
Exton Somset 16 C9
Exwick Devon 6 B4
Eyam Derbys 50 G5
Eydon Nhants 31 M4
Eye C Pete 42 H9
Eye Herefs 39 J8
Eye Suffk 35 J3
Eyemouth Border 81 K2
Eyeworth C Beds 33 J7
Eyhorne Street Kent 22 G11
Eyke Suffk 35 M6
Eynesbury Cambs 32 H5
Eynsford Kent 22 B9
Eynsham Oxon 31 K11
Eype Dorset 7 L5
Eyre Highld 104 F11
Eythorne Kent 23 P12
Eyton Herefs 39 J9
Eyton Shrops 48 H10
Eyton on Severn Shrops 39 L2
Eyton upon the Weald Moors Wrekin 49 M11

F

Faccombe Hants 19 L8
Faceby N York 66 C7
Fachwen Powys 48 B11
Faddiley Ches E 49 L5
Fadmoor N York 66 F9
Faerdre Swans 26 F8
Faifley W Duns 84 H8
Failand N Som 17 M2
Failford S Ayrs 76 H6
Failsworth Oldham 50 B1
Fairbourne Gwynd 47 K8
Fairburn N York 59 L8
Fairfield Derbys 50 E6
Fairfield Worcs 40 C11
Fairford Gloucs 18 H1
Fairgirth D & G 70 E4
Fair Green Norfk 43 Q6
Fairhaven Lancs 56 G4
Fair Isle Shet 111 m5
Fair Isle Airport Shet 111 m5
Fairlands Surrey 20 F11
Fairlie N Ayrs 84 D11
Fairlight E Susx 12 G7
Fairmile Devon 6 E4
Fairmile Surrey 20 H10
Fairmilee Border 79 P3
Fairoak Staffs 49 N8
Fair Oak Hants 9 N4
Fair Oak Green Hants 19 Q8
Fairseat Kent 22 D10
Fairstead Essex 34 C12
Fairstead Norfk 43 Q6
Fairwarp E Susx 11 P5
Fairwater Cardif 27 N12
Fairy Cross Devon 14 G7
Fakenham Norfk 44 F4
Fakenham Magna Suffk 34 E2
Fala Mdloth 87 J9
Fala Dam Mdloth 87 J9
Faldingworth Lincs 52 F6
Faldouët Jersey 7 c2
Falfield S Glos 29 J9
Falkenham Suffk 35 L8
Falkirk Falk 85 P7
Falkirk Wheel Falk 85 P7
Falkland Fife 86 F2
Fallburn S Lans 86 B11
Fallin Stirlg 85 N5
Fallodon Nthumb 81 P9
Fallowfield Manch 57 Q9
Fallowfield Nthumb 72 H7
Falmer E Susx 11 M8
Falmouth Cnwll 3 J8
Falnash Border 79 N7
Falsgrave N York 67 M9
Falstone Nthumb 72 D4
Fanagmore Highld 108 D6
Fancott C Beds 32 E10
Fanellan Highld 98 G1
Fangdale Beck N York 66 D8
Fangfoss E R Yk 60 D4
Fanmore Ag & B 89 J7
Fannich Lodge Highld 106 D8
Fans Border 80 E6
Far Bletchley M Keyn 32 C9
Farcet Cambs 42 H10
Far Cotton Nhants 31 Q3
Fareham Hants 9 P6
Farewell Staffs 40 E5
Faringdon Oxon 19 K2
Farington Lancs 57 K4
Farlam Cumb 71 Q4
Farleigh N Som 17 M3
Farleigh Surrey 21 M10
Farleigh Hungerford Somset 18 B8
Farleigh Wallop Hants 19 Q10
Farlesthorpe Lincs 53 M8
Farleton Cumb 63 K6
Farleton Lancs 63 K6
Farley Staffs 50 E11
Farley Wilts 9 J2
Farley Green Surrey 10 G2
Farley Hill Wokham 20 C9
Farleys End Gloucs 29 K6
Farlington C Port 10 B8
Farlington N York 59 N1
Farlow Shrops 39 L6
Farmborough BaNES 17 P4
Farmcote Gloucs 30 D9
Farmoor Oxon 31 L11
Far Moor Wigan 57 K7
Farmtown Moray 101 P5
Farnborough Gt Lon 21 N9
Farnborough Hants 20 E11
Farnborough W Berk 19 M4
Farnborough Warwks 31 K4
Farnborough Park Hants 20 E11
Farncombe Surrey 10 F2
Farndish Bed 32 D4
Farndon Ches W 48 H5
Farndon Notts 51 Q9
Farne Islands Nthumb 81 P6

Farnell Angus 93 Q5
Farnham Dorset 8 E4
Farnham Essex 33 M10
Farnham N York 59 J3
Farnham Suffk 35 M5
Farnham Surrey 10 D1
Farnham Common Bucks 20 F6
Farnham Royal Bucks 20 F6
Farningham Kent 22 B9
Farnley Leeds 58 G7
Farnley N York 58 G5
Farnley Tyas Kirk 58 F10
Farnsfield Notts 51 P9
Farnworth Bolton 57 N7
Farnworth Halton 57 K10
Far Oakridge Gloucs 29 N7
Farr Highld 99 K3
Farr Highld 99 M8
Farr Highld 109 M3
Farraline Highld 98 H5
Farringdon Devon 6 D5
Farrington Gurney BaNES 17 P5
Far Sawrey Cumb 62 H3
Farthinghoe Nhants 31 M6
Farthingstone Nhants 31 N3
Fartown Kirk 58 F9
Fasnacloich Ag & B 90 D6
Fasnakyle Highld 98 D4
Fassfern Highld 90 D1
Fatfield Sundld 73 N9
Fauldhouse W Loth 85 Q10
Faulkbourne Essex 34 D12
Faulkland Somset 17 Q5
Fauls Shrops 49 L8
Faversham Kent 23 K10
Fawdington N York 66 B11
Fawdon N u Ty 73 M7
Fawkham Green Kent 22 C9
Fawler Oxon 31 J10
Fawley Bucks 20 C6
Fawley Hants 9 M6
Fawley W Berk 19 L5
Faxfleet E R Yk 60 E8
Faygate W Susx 11 K3
Fazakerley Lpool 56 G9
Fazeley Staffs 40 G7
Fearby N York 65 L10
Fearn Highld 107 N7
Fearnan P & K 91 Q7
Fearnbeg Highld 105 L9
Fearnmore Highld 105 K9
Fearnoch Ag & B 83 P7
Featherstone Staffs 40 C6
Featherstone Wakefd 59 K9
Feckenham Worcs 30 D2
Feering Essex 34 E11
Feetham N York 64 H7
Felbridge Surrey 11 M3
Felbrigg Norfk 45 K3
Felcourt Surrey 11 M2
Felindre Carmth 25 N2
Felindre Carmth 26 D5
Felindre Powys 38 D6
Felindre Swans 26 E8
Felindre Farchog Pembks 36 B11
Felinfoel Carmth 26 C8
Felingwm Isaf Carmth 26 C4
Felingwm Uchaf Carmth 26 C4
Felixkirk N York 66 C10
Felixstowe Suffk 35 L9
Felling Gatesd 73 M8
Felmersham Bed 32 E5
Felmingham Norfk 45 L4
Felpham W Susx 10 F9
Felsham Suffk 34 F5
Felsted Essex 34 B11
Feltham Gt Lon 20 H8
Felthamhill Surrey 20 H8
Felthorpe Norfk 45 J6
Felton Herefs 39 L11
Felton N Som 17 M3
Felton Nthumb 73 L2
Felton Butler Shrops 48 H11
Feltwell Norfk 44 B11
Fence Lancs 57 P2
Fence Rothm 51 K4
Fencott Oxon 31 M10
Fendike Corner Lincs 53 M10
Fen Ditton Cambs 33 M5
Fen Drayton Cambs 33 K3
Feniton Devon 6 F3
Fenn Green Shrops 39 P5
Fenn Street Medway 22 F8
Fenny Bentley Derbys 50 F10
Fenny Bridges Devon 6 F3
Fenny Compton Warwks 31 K4
Fenny Drayton Leics 41 J7
Fenstanton Cambs 33 K3
Fen Street Norfk 44 G10
Fenton Cambs 33 K2
Fenton Cumb 71 Q4
Fenton Lincs 52 C12
Fenton Lincs 52 B6
Fenton Nthumb 81 K7
Fenton Barns E Loth 87 K6
Fenwick Donc 59 N10
Fenwick E Ayrs 76 H3
Fenwick Nthumb 73 J6
Fenwick Nthumb 81 M6
Feock Cnwll 3 J7
Feolin Ferry Ag & B 82 F8
Fergushill N Ayrs 76 F2
Feriniquarrie Highld 104 B11
Fern Angus 93 J9
Ferndale Rhondd 27 L3
Ferndown Dorset 8 F7
Ferness Highld 100 E6
Fernham Oxon 19 K3
Fernhill Heath Worcs 39 Q9
Fernhurst W Susx 10 D5
Fernie Fife 93 K11
Ferniegair S Lans 85 M11
Fernilea Highld 96 D3
Fernilee Derbys 50 D5
Fernwood Notts 52 B12
Ferrensby N York 59 J3
Ferrindonald Highld 97 J7
Ferring W Susx 10 H9
Ferrybridge Services Wakefd 59 L9

Ferryden Angus 95 M9
Ferryhill Dur 65 M2
Ferryhill Station Dur 65 N2
Ferry Point Highld 107 M5
Ferryside Carmth 25 N6
Ferrytown Highld 107 M5
Fersfield Norfk 44 H12
Fersit Highld 91 K2
Feshiebridge Highld 99 M8
Fetcham Surrey 21 J11
Fetlar Shet 111 m2
Fetterangus Abers 103 K5
Fettercairn Abers 95 K7
Fewston N York 58 G4
Ffairfach Carmth 26 E5
Ffair Rhos Cerdgn 37 M7
Ffarmers Carmth 37 K10
Ffestiniog Gwynd 47 L3
Ffestiniog Railway Gwynd 47 K3
Fforest Carmth 26 D7
Ffostrasol Cerdgn 36 F10
Ffrith Flints 48 F4
Ffynnongroyw Flints 56 D11
Fickleshole Surrey 21 M10
Fiddington Somset 16 G7
Fiddleford Dorset 8 B5
Fiddlers Green Cnwll 3 J5
Field Staffs 40 D2
Field Dalling Norfk 44 G3
Field Head Leics 41 L5
Fifehead Magdalen Dorset 8 B3
Fifehead Neville Dorset 8 B5
Fifehead St Quintin Dorset 8 B5
Fife Keith Moray 101 M5
Fifield Oxon 30 G10
Fifield W & M 20 E7
Figheldean Wilts 18 H10
Filby Norfk 45 P7
Filey N York 67 N10
Filgrave M Keyn 32 C7
Filkins Oxon 30 G12
Filleigh Devon 15 L6
Fillingham Lincs 52 D6
Fillongley Warwks 40 H9
Filton S Glos 28 H11
Fimber E R Yk 60 F3
Finavon Angus 93 N4
Fincham Norfk 44 B8
Finchampstead Wokham 20 C10
Finchdean Hants 10 B7
Finchingfield Essex 34 B9
Finchley Gt Lon 21 L5
Findern Derbys 40 H2
Findhorn Moray 100 G3
Findhorn Bridge Highld 99 M2
Findochty Moray 101 N2
Findo Gask P & K 92 G10
Findon Abers 95 Q3
Findon W Susx 10 H8
Findon Mains Highld 107 K8
Findrack House Abers 95 K2
Finedon Nhants 32 D3
Fingask P & K 92 H10
Fingest Bucks 20 C5
Finghall N York 65 L9
Fingland D & G 77 L9
Finglesham Kent 23 P11
Fingringhoe Essex 34 G11
Finlarig Stirlg 91 N9
Finmere Oxon 31 N7
Finnart P & K 91 M5
Finningham Suffk 34 H4
Finningley Donc 51 P2
Finsbay W Isls 111 c4
Finstall Worcs 40 C12
Finsthwaite Cumb 62 G5
Finstock Oxon 31 J10
Finstown Ork 111 h2
Fintry Abers 102 G4
Fintry Stirlg 85 K5
Finzean Abers 95 K4
Fionnphort Ag & B 88 G10
Fionnsbhagh W Isls 111 c4
Firbank Cumb 63 L4
Firbeck Rothm 51 M3
Firby N York 60 C2
Firby N York 65 M9
Firle E Susx 11 P8
Firsby Lincs 53 M10
Fir Tree Dur 65 K1
Fishbourne IoW 9 P8
Fishbourne W Susx 10 D8
Fishbourne Roman Palace W Susx 10 D8
Fishburn Dur 65 P2
Fishcross Clacks 85 P4
Fisherford Abers 102 E8
Fisherrow E Loth 86 G7
Fisher's Pond Hants 9 N4
Fisherton Highld 107 M11
Fisherton S Ayrs 76 E7
Fisherton de la Mere Wilts 18 E11
Fishery Estate W & M 20 E7
Fishguard Pembks 24 G2
Fishlake Donc 59 P10
Fishnish Pier Ag & B 89 N7
Fishponds Bristl 17 P2
Fishtoft Lincs 43 K2
Fishtoft Drove Lincs 43 K1
Fishwick Lancs 57 K3
Fiskavaig Highld 96 D3
Fiskerton Lincs 52 F8
Fiskerton Notts 51 Q9
Fittleton Wilts 18 G10
Fittleworth W Susx 10 G6
Fitz Shrops 49 J11
Fitzhead Somset 16 F9
Fitzwilliam Wakefd 59 K10
Five Ash Down E Susx 11 P5
Five Ashes E Susx 12 B5
Fivehead Somset 17 J10
Fivelanes Cnwll 4 F4
Five Oak Green Kent 12 D2
Five Oaks Jersey 7 c2
Five Oaks W Susx 10 H4
Five Roads Carmth 26 C7
Flackwell Heath Bucks 20 E5
Fladbury Worcs 30 C5
Fladdabister Shet 111 k4
Flagg Derbys 50 F7
Flamborough E R Yk 67 Q12

Place	County	Page	Grid
Flamborough Head	E R Yk	67	Q12
Flamingo Land Theme Park	N York	66	H10
Flamstead	Herts	20	H1
Flamstead End	Herts	21	M3
Flansham	W Susx	10	F9
Flanshaw	Wakefd	58	H9
Flasby	N York	58	C3
Flash	Staffs	50	D7
Flashader	Highld	104	D10
Flaunden	Herts	20	G4
Flawborough	Notts	42	B2
Flawith	N York	59	L2
Flax Bourton	N Som	17	M3
Flaxby	N York	59	K3
Flaxley	Gloucs	29	J6
Flaxpool	Somset	16	F8
Flaxton	N York	59	P2
Fleckney	Leics	41	P8
Flecknoe	Warwks	31	L2
Fledborough	Notts	52	B8
Fleet	Dorset	7	P6
Fleet	Hants	20	D11
Fleet	Lincs	43	L5
Fleet Hargate	Lincs	43	L5
Fleet Services	Hants	20	C11
Fleetwood	Lancs	62	G11
Fleggburgh	Norfk	45	P7
Flemingston	V Glam	16	D3
Flemington	S Lans	85	L10
Flempton	Suffk	34	D3
Fletchertown	Cumb	71	K7
Fletching	E Susx	11	N5
Flexbury	Cnwll	14	D10
Flexford	Surrey	20	E12
Flimby	Cumb	70	G8
Flimwell	E Susx	12	E4
Flint	Flints	48	E2
Flintham	Notts	51	Q10
Flinton	E R Yk	61	L7
Flitcham	Norfk	44	C5
Flitton	C Beds	32	F9
Flitwick	C Beds	32	E9
Flixborough	N Linc	60	E10
Flixborough Stather	N Linc	60	E10
Flixton	N York	67	M10
Flixton	Suffk	45	M11
Flixton	Traffd	57	N9
Flockton	Kirk	58	G10
Flockton Green	Kirk	58	G10
Flodigarry	Highld	104	F7
Flookburgh	Cumb	62	G7
Flordon	Norfk	45	K10
Flore	Nhants	31	N3
Flowton	Suffk	34	H7
Flushing	Cnwll	3	J8
Fluxton	Devon	6	E4
Flyford Flavell	Worcs	30	C3
Fobbing	Thurr	22	E6
Fochabers	Moray	101	L4
Fochriw	Caerph	27	M7
Fockerby	N Linc	60	E9
Foddington	Somset	17	N9
Foel	Powys	48	B12
Foggathorpe	E R Yk	60	D6
Fogo	Border	80	G4
Fogwatt	Moray	101	K4
Foindle	Highld	108	D6
Folda	Angus	94	C8
Fole	Staffs	50	D12
Foleshill	Covtry	41	J10
Folke	Dorset	17	P12
Folkestone	Kent	13	N3
Folkingham	Lincs	42	F4
Folkington	E Susx	12	C8
Folksworth	Cambs	42	G11
Folkton	N York	67	M10
Folla Rule	Abers	102	F8
Follifoot	N York	59	J4
Folly Gate	Devon	15	K11
Fonthill Bishop	Wilts	8	D2
Fonthill Gifford	Wilts	8	D2
Fontmell Magna	Dorset	8	C4
Fontmell Parva	Dorset	8	C5
Fontwell	W Susx	10	F8
Foolow	Derbys	50	F5
Forbestown	Abers	101	M11
Forcett	N York	65	L5
Ford	Ag & B	83	N3
Ford	Bucks	31	Q11
Ford	Derbys	51	K5
Ford	Devon	14	G7
Ford	Gloucs	30	E8
Ford	Nthumb	81	K6
Ford	Somset	16	E9
Ford	Staffs	50	E9
Ford	W Susx	10	F8
Ford	Wilts	18	C6
Fordcombe	Kent	11	Q3
Fordell	Fife	86	D5
Forden	Powys	38	E2
Ford End	Essex	34	B12
Forder Green	Devon	5	Q6
Fordham	Cambs	33	Q3
Fordham	Essex	34	F10
Fordham	Norfk	43	P9
Fordingbridge	Hants	8	G5
Fordon	E R Yk	67	M11
Fordoun	Abers	95	M6
Fordstreet	Essex	34	F10
Ford Street	Somset	16	F11
Fordwich	Kent	23	M10
Fordyce	Abers	102	D3
Forebridge	Staffs	40	B3
Forest	Guern	6	b2
Forest Chapel	Ches E	50	C6
Forest Gate	Gt Lon	21	N6
Forest Green	Surrey	10	H2
Forest Hall	N Tyne	73	M6
Forest Hill	Gt Lon	21	M8
Forest Hill	Oxon	31	N11
Forest Lane Head	N York	59	J3
Forest Mill	Clacks	85	Q4
Forest of Bowland	Lancs	63	L10
Forest of Dean	Gloucs	28	H6
Forest Row	E Susx	11	N3
Forestside	W Susx	10	C7
Forfar	Angus	93	M5
Forgandenny	P & K	92	G11
Forge	Guern	6	b2
Forge Hammer	Torfn	28	C9
Forgie	Moray	101	M4
Forgieside	Moray	101	M5
Forgue	Abers	102	D6
Formby	Sefton	56	F7
Forncett End	Norfk	45	J10
Forncett St Mary	Norfk	45	J10
Forncett St Peter	Norfk	45	L6
Fornham All Saints	Suffk	34	D4
Fornham St Martin	Suffk	34	E4
Fornighty	Highld	100	E5
Forres	Moray	100	F4
Forsbrook	Staffs	50	C11
Forse	Highld	110	E8
Forsinard	Highld	109	Q7
Forss	Highld	110	B3
Fort Augustus	Highld	98	E7
Forteviot	P & K	92	F11
Forth	S Lans	85	Q11
Forthampton	Gloucs	29	M3
Forth Rail Bridge	C Edin	86	D6
Forth Road Bridge	Fife	86	D6
Fortingall	P & K	91	Q6
Forton	Hants	19	M11
Forton	Lancs	63	J11
Forton	Shrops	48	H11
Forton	Somset	7	J2
Forton	Staffs	49	N10
Fortrie	Abers	102	E6
Fortrose	Highld	107	M10
Fortuneswell	Dorset	7	P7
Fort William	Highld	90	F2
Forty Hill	Gt Lon	21	M4
Fosbury	Wilts	19	K8
Foscot	Oxon	30	G9
Fosdyke	Lincs	43	K4
Foss	P & K	92	B4
Fossebridge	Gloucs	30	E11
Foster Street	Essex	21	P2
Foston	Derbys	40	F2
Foston	Leics	41	N8
Foston	Lincs	42	C2
Foston	N York	59	P2
Foston on the Wolds	E R Yk	61	J3
Fotherby	Lincs	53	K5
Fotheringhay	Nhants	42	F10
Foula	Shet	111	j5
Foula Airport	Shet	111	j5
Foulden	Border	81	K3
Foulden	Norfk	44	C9
Foul End	Warwks	40	G8
Foulness Island	Essex	23	J5
Foulridge	Lancs	58	B6
Foulsham	Norfk	44	G5
Fountainhall	Border	87	J11
Four Ashes	Suffk	34	G3
Four Crosses	Powys	48	F10
Four Elms	Kent	11	P1
Four Forks	Somset	16	G8
Four Gotes	Cambs	43	M6
Four Lanes	Cnwll	2	H7
Four Marks	Hants	9	R1
Four Mile Bridge	IoA	54	C6
Four Oaks	Birm	40	E7
Four Oaks	Solhll	40	G10
Fourpenny	Highld	107	N4
Four Roads	Carmth	25	Q7
Fourstones	Nthumb	72	F7
Four Throws	Kent	12	F4
Fovant	Wilts	8	E2
Foveran	Abers	103	K9
Fowey	Cnwll	4	D9
Fowlhall	Kent	12	E2
Fowlis	Angus	93	M8
Fowlis Wester	P & K	92	D10
Fowlmere	Cambs	33	L7
Fownhope	Herefs	28	G3
Foxbar	Rens	84	H10
Foxcote	Somset	17	Q5
Foxdale	IoM	56	b5
Foxearth	Essex	34	D7
Foxfield	Cumb	62	E5
Foxhole	Cnwll	3	M5
Foxholes	N York	67	L11
Foxley	Norfk	44	H6
Foxt	Staffs	50	D10
Foxton	Cambs	33	L7
Foxton	Leics	41	P9
Foxton	N York	65	Q8
Foxwood	Shrops	39	L6
Foy	Herefs	28	H3
Foyers	Highld	98	G5
Foynesfield	Highld	100	D5
Fraddon	Cnwll	3	K4
Fradley	Staffs	40	F5
Fradswell	Staffs	40	C2
Fraisthorpe	E R Yk	61	K2
Framfield	E Susx	11	P6
Framingham Earl	Norfk	45	L9
Framingham Pigot	Norfk	45	L9
Framlingham	Suffk	35	L4
Frampton	Dorset	7	P4
Frampton	Lincs	43	K3
Frampton Cotterell	S Glos	29	J11
Frampton Mansell	Gloucs	29	N8
Frampton-on-Severn	Gloucs	29	K7
Framsden	Suffk	35	K5
Framwellgate Moor	Dur	73	M11
Franche	Worcs	39	P6
Frankby	Wirral	56	E10
Frankley	Worcs	40	C10
Frankley Services	Worcs	40	C10
Frankton	Warwks	41	K12
Frant	E Susx	12	C3
Fraserburgh	Abers	103	K2
Frating	Essex	34	H11
Frating Green	Essex	34	H11
Fratton	C Port	9	Q7
Freathy	Cnwll	5	J9
Freckenham	Suffk	33	Q3
Freckleton	Lancs	56	H3
Freeby	Leics	42	B6
Freefolk	Hants	19	N10
Freeland	Oxon	31	K10
Freethorpe	Norfk	45	N8
Freethorpe Common	Norfk	45	N8
Freiston	Lincs	43	L2
Fremington	Devon	15	J6
Fremington	N York	65	J7
Frenchay	S Glos	28	H12
Frenich	P & K	92	C4
Frensham	Surrey	10	D2
Freshfield	Sefton	56	F7
Freshford	Wilts	18	B8
Freshwater	IoW	9	K9
Fressingfield	Suffk	35	L2
Freston	Suffk	35	J8
Freswick	Highld	110	G3
Fretherne	Gloucs	29	K6
Frettenham	Norfk	45	L6
Freuchie	Fife	86	F2
Freystrop	Pembks	24	G6
Friar Park	Sandw	40	D8
Friday Bridge	Cambs	43	M8
Friday Street	Suffk	35	N5
Fridaythorpe	E R Yk	60	E3
Friern Barnet	Gt Lon	21	L5
Friesthorpe	Lincs	52	F6
Frieston	Lincs	42	D1
Frieth	Bucks	20	C5
Friford	Oxon	19	M2
Frilsham	W Berk	19	P6
Frimley	Surrey	20	E10
Frindsbury	Medway	22	E9
Fring	Norfk	44	C3
Fringford	Oxon	31	N8
Frinsted	Kent	22	H11
Frinton-on-Sea	Essex	35	K11
Friockheim	Angus	93	Q6
Frisby on the Wreake	Leics	41	P4
Friskney	Lincs	53	M11
Friston	E Susx	12	B9
Friston	Suffk	35	N5
Fritchley	Derbys	51	J9
Fritham	Hants	9	J5
Frithelstock	Devon	14	H8
Frithelstock Stone	Devon	14	H8
Frithville	Lincs	53	K12
Frittenden	Kent	12	F2
Frittiscombe	Devon	5	Q10
Fritton	Norfk	45	K10
Fritton	Norfk	45	M4
Fritwell	Oxon	31	M8
Frizinghall	C Brad	58	F7
Frizington	Cumb	70	G11
Frocester	Gloucs	29	K8
Frodesley	Shrops	39	K2
Frodsham	Ches W	57	K12
Frogden	Border	80	G8
Frog End	Cambs	33	L7
Froggatt	Derbys	50	G5
Froghall	Staffs	50	D10
Frogmore	Devon	5	P10
Frognall	Lincs	42	G7
Frog Pool	Worcs	39	P8
Frogwell	Cnwll	4	H6
Frolesworth	Leics	41	L8
Frome	Somset	18	B10
Frome St Quintin	Dorset	7	N3
Fromes Hill	Herefs	39	M11
Froncysyllte	Wrexhm	48	F7
Fron-goch	Gwynd	47	P4
Fron Isaf	Wrexhm	48	F7
Frosterley	Dur	72	H12
Froxfield	Wilts	19	K7
Froxfield Green	Hants	10	B5
Fryern Hill	Hants	9	M4
Fryerning	Essex	22	D4
Fuinary	Highld	89	M7
Fulbeck	Lincs	52	D12
Fulbourn	Cambs	33	N5
Fulbrook	Oxon	30	H10
Fulflood	Hants	9	M2
Fulford	C York	59	N4
Fulford	Somset	16	G9
Fulford	Staffs	50	C12
Fulham	Gt Lon	21	K8
Fulking	W Susx	11	K7
Fullarton	N Ayrs	76	F4
Fuller Street	Essex	34	C12
Fullerton	Hants	19	L11
Fulletby	Lincs	53	J8
Fullready	Warwks	30	H5
Full Sutton	E R Yk	60	D3
Fullwood	E Ayrs	76	G2
Fulmer	Bucks	20	F6
Fulmodeston	Norfk	44	G4
Fulnetby	Lincs	52	F7
Fulney	Lincs	43	J5
Fulstow	Lincs	53	K4
Fulwell	Sundld	73	P8
Fulwood	Lancs	57	K3
Fulwood	Sheff	50	H4
Fundenhall	Norfk	45	J10
Funtington	W Susx	10	C8
Funtullch	P & K	92	B9
Furley	Devon	6	H2
Furnace	Ag & B	83	Q3
Furnace	Carmth	26	C8
Furness Vale	Derbys	50	D4
Furneux Pelham	Herts	33	L10
Furzley	Hants	9	K4
Fyfield	Essex	22	C3
Fyfield	Hants	19	K10
Fyfield	Oxon	19	M2
Fyfield	Wilts	18	G7
Fyfield	Wilts	18	H8
Fylingthorpe	N York	67	K6
Fyning	W Susx	10	D5
Fyvie	Abers	102	G7

G

Place	County	Page	Grid
Gabroc Hill	E Ayrs	76	H2
Gaddesby	Leics	41	P5
Gaddesden Row	Herts	20	G2
Gadgirth	S Ayrs	76	G6
Gaerllwyd	Mons	28	E9
Gaerwen	IoA	54	F7
Gailes	N Ayrs	76	F4
Gailey	Staffs	40	B5
Gainford	Dur	65	L5
Gainsborough	Lincs	52	B5
Gainsford End	Essex	34	C9
Gairloch	Highld	105	M7
Gairlochy	Highld	98	B10
Gairneybridge	P & K	86	D3
Gaitsgill	Cumb	71	N6
Galashiels	Border	80	C7
Galgate	Lancs	63	J11
Galhampton	Somset	17	P9
Gallanachbeg	Ag & B	90	B10
Gallanachmore	Ag & B	89	R10
Gallatown	Fife	86	G4
Galley Common	Warwks	41	J7
Galleywood	Essex	22	E3
Gallovie	Highld	98	H10
Galloway Forest Park	D & G	69	L5
Gallowfauld	Angus	93	M7
Gallowhill	P & K	92	H9
Galltair	Highld	97	L5
Galmisdale	Highld	96	F11
Galmpton	Devon	5	N11
Galmpton	Torbay	6	B10
Galphay	N York	65	M11
Galston	E Ayrs	76	H4
Gamblesby	Cumb	72	B11
Gamlingay	Cambs	33	J6
Gamlingay Great Heath	Cambs	32	H6
Gamrie	Abers	102	G3
Gamston	Notts	51	N12
Gamston	Notts	51	P5
Ganavan Bay	Ag & B	90	B9
Ganllwyd	Gwynd	47	N6
Gannachy	Angus	95	K7
Ganstead	E R Yk	61	K7
Ganthorpe	N York	66	F12
Ganton	N York	67	L11
Garbity	Moray	101	L3
Garboldisham	Norfk	34	G1
Garbole	Highld	99	L4
Garchory	Abers	101	L12
Gardeners Green	Wokham	20	D9
Gardenstown	Abers	102	G3
Garden Village	Sheff	50	H2
Garderhouse	Shet	111	k4
Gare Hill	Somset	18	B11
Garelochhead	Ag & B	84	D5
Garford	Oxon	19	M2
Garforth	Leeds	59	K7
Gargrave	N York	58	B4
Gargunnock	Stirlg	85	M4
Garlic Street	Norfk	45	K12
Garlieston	D & G	69	L9
Garlinge	Kent	23	P9
Garlinge Green	Kent	23	L11
Garlogie	Abers	95	M2
Garmond	Abers	102	G5
Garmouth	Moray	101	L3
Garmston	Shrops	39	L2
Garndolbenmaen	Gwynd	46	H3
Garrabost	W Isls	111	d2
Garrallan	E Ayrs	77	J7
Garras	Cnwll	2	G10
Garreg	Gwynd	47	K3
Garrigill	Cumb	72	D11
Garroch	D & G	69	L3
Garrochtrie	D & G	68	F10
Garrochty	Ag & B	84	B11
Garros	Highld	104	G9
Garsdale Head	Cumb	64	C8
Garsdon	Wilts	18	E4
Garshall Green	Staffs	40	C1
Garsington	Oxon	31	M12
Garstang	Lancs	63	J12
Garston	Herts	20	H4
Garston	Lpool	56	H11
Gartachossan	Ag & B	82	E10
Gartcosh	N Lans	85	L9
Garth	Powys	37	Q10
Garth	Wrexhm	48	F7
Garthamlock	C Glas	85	L9
Garthmyl	Powys	38	E3
Garthorpe	Leics	42	B6
Garthorpe	N Linc	60	E9
Garth Row	Cumb	63	K3
Gartly	Abers	102	C8
Gartmore	Stirlg	85	J4
Gartness	N Lans	85	N9
Gartness	Stirlg	84	H5
Gartocharn	W Duns	84	H5
Garton-on-the-Wolds	E R Yk	60	H3
Gartymore	Highld	110	B11
Garva Bridge	Highld	98	G9
Garvald	Abers	86	C11
Garvald	E Loth	87	L7
Garvan	Highld	90	D2
Garvard	Ag & B	82	E5
Garve	Highld	106	G9
Garvellachs	Ag & B	83	K2
Garvestone	Norfk	44	G8
Garvock	Inver	84	E8
Garway	Herefs	28	E4
Garynahine	W Isls	111	c2
Garyvard	W Isls	111	d2
Gasper	Wilts	8	B2
Gastard	Wilts	18	C7
Gasthorpe	Norfk	34	F1
Gaston Green	Essex	33	N12
Gatcombe	IoW	9	N9
Gate Burton	Lincs	52	B7
Gateforth	N York	59	M8
Gatehead	E Ayrs	76	G4
Gate Helmsley	N York	59	P3
Gatehouse	Nthumb	72	F9
Gatehouse of Fleet	D & G	69	N7
Gateley	Norfk	44	G6
Gatenby	N York	65	N9
Gateshaw	Border	80	G9
Gateshead	Gatesd	73	M8
Gateside	Angus	93	M6
Gateside	E Rens	84	H10
Gateside	Fife	86	E1
Gateside	N Ayrs	84	F11
Gateslack	D & G	78	E8
Gatley	Stockp	57	Q10
Gattonside	Border	80	D7
Gatwick Airport	W Susx	11	L2
Gaulby	Leics	41	P7
Gauldry	Fife	93	L10
Gauldswell	P & K	93	J5
Gautby	Lincs	52	H8
Gavinton	Border	80	G4
Gawcott	Bucks	31	P7
Gawsworth	Ches E	50	B6
Gawthrop	Cumb	63	M5
Gawthwaite	Cumb	62	F5
Gaydon	Warwks	31	J4
Gayhurst	M Keyn	32	C7
Gayle	N York	64	F9
Gayles	N York	65	K6
Gayton	Nhants	31	P4
Gayton	Norfk	44	C7
Gayton	Staffs	40	C2
Gayton le Marsh	Lincs	53	L6
Gayton Thorpe	Norfk	44	C7
Gaywood	Norfk	43	Q6
Gazeley	Suffk	34	C4
Gearraidh Bhaird	W Isls	111	d2
Gearraidh na h-Aibhne	W Isls	111	c2
Geary	Highld	104	C9
Gedding	Suffk	34	F5
Geddington	Nhants	42	C12
Gedling	Notts	51	N11
Gedney	Lincs	43	L5
Gedney Broadgate	Lincs	43	L5
Gedney Drove End	Lincs	43	M4
Gedney Dyke	Lincs	43	L5
Gedney Hill	Lincs	43	K7
Geeston	Rutlnd	42	E8
Geldeston	Norfk	45	N10
Gellifor	Denbgs	48	D3
Gelligaer	Caerph	27	N9
Gellilydan	Gwynd	47	L4
Gellinudd	Neath	26	G7
Gellyburn	P & K	92	G7
Gellywen	Carmth	25	M4
Gelston	D & G	70	C4
Gelston	Lincs	42	C2
Gembling	E R Yk	61	J3
Gentleshaw	Staffs	40	D5
Georgefield	D & G	79	L9
Georgeham	Devon	14	H4
Georgemas Junction Station	Highld	110	D4
George Nympton	Devon	15	M7
Georth	Ork	111	h2
Germansweek	Devon	5	J2
Gerrans	Cnwll	3	K8
Gerrards Cross	Bucks	20	G6
Gerrick	R & C	66	G5
Gestingthorpe	Essex	34	D8
Geuffordd	Powys	48	E11
Gidea Park	Gt Lon	21	Q5
Giffnock	E Rens	85	J10
Gifford	E Loth	87	K8
Giffordtown	Fife	93	K12
Giggleswick	N York	63	P9
Gigha	Ag & B	75	J3
Gilberdyke	E R Yk	60	E8
Gilchriston	E Loth	87	J8
Gilcrux	Cumb	70	H7
Gildersome	Leeds	58	G8
Gildingwells	Rothm	51	M4
Gilesgate Moor	Dur	73	N11
Gileston	V Glam	16	D3
Gilfach	Caerph	27	N8
Gilfach Goch	Brdgnd	27	K10
Gilfachrheda	Cerdgn	36	G8
Gilgarran	Cumb	70	G10
Gillamoor	N York	66	F9
Gillen	Highld	104	C9
Gillesbie	D & G	79	J9
Gilling East	N York	66	E11
Gillingham	Dorset	8	B3
Gillingham	Medway	22	F9
Gillingham	Norfk	45	N10
Gilling West	N York	65	L6
Gillock	Highld	110	E4
Gills	Highld	110	G2
Gilmanscleuch	Border	79	M5
Gilmerton	C Edin	86	F8
Gilmerton	P & K	92	D10
Gilmonby	Dur	64	H5
Gilmorton	Leics	41	M9
Gilsland	Nthumb	72	B7
Gilston	Border	87	J10
Gilston	Herts	21	N2
Giltbrook	Notts	51	L11
Gilwern	Mons	27	Q6
Gimingham	Norfk	45	L3
Gipping	Suffk	34	H4
Gipsey Bridge	Lincs	53	J12
Girdle Toll	N Ayrs	76	F3
Girlsta	Shet	111	k4
Girsby	N York	65	N6
Girthon	D & G	69	N8
Girton	Cambs	33	L4
Girton	Notts	52	B9
Girvan	S Ayrs	76	D10
Gisburn	Lancs	63	P11
Gisleham	Suffk	45	Q11
Gislingham	Suffk	34	H3
Gissing	Norfk	45	J11
Gittisham	Devon	6	F3
Gladestry	Powys	38	E10
Gladsmuir	E Loth	87	J7
Glais	Swans	26	F8
Glaisdale	N York	66	H6
Glamis	Angus	93	L6
Glanaman	Carmth	26	G7
Glandford	Norfk	44	H2
Glandwr	Pembks	25	L3
Glandyfi	Cerdgn	47	L11
Glanllynfi	Brdgnd	27	J10
Glan-rhyd	Powys	26	G7
Glanton	Nthumb	81	M10
Glanvilles Wootton	Dorset	7	P2
Glan-y-don	Flints	56	D11
Glapthorn	Nhants	42	E11
Glapwell	Derbys	51	L7
Glasbury	Powys	27	P2
Glascoed	Mons	28	D8
Glascote	Staffs	40	G6
Glascwm	Powys	38	D10
Glasfryn	Conwy	55	N10
Glasgow	C Glas	85	K9
Glasgow Airport	Rens	84	H9
Glasgow Prestwick Airport	S Ayrs	76	F6
Glasgow Science Centre	C Glas	85	J9
Glasinfryn	Gwynd	54	H7
Glasnacardoch Bay	Highld	97	J9
Glasnakille	Highld	96	G12
Glasphein	Highld	104	B11
Glassford	S Lans	77	M2
Glasshouse	Gloucs	29	J5
Glasshouses	N York	58	F2
Glasslaw	Abers	102	H4
Glasson	Cumb	71	L4
Glasson	Lancs	63	J11
Glassonby	Cumb	72	B12
Glasterlaw	Angus	93	Q5
Glaston	Rutlnd	42	C9
Glastonbury	Somset	17	M8
Glatton	Cambs	42	G11
Glazebrook	Warrtn	57	M9
Glazebury	Warrtn	57	M9

Glazeley Shrops....39 N5
Gleaston Cumb....62 F7
Glebe Highld....98 G5
Gledhow Leeds....58 H4
Gledpark D & G....69 P8
Gledrid Shrops....48 F7
Glemsford Suffk....34 D7
Glenallachie Moray....101 K7
Glenancross Highld....97 J10
Glenaros House Ag & B....89 L7
Glen Auldyn IoM....56 d3
Glenbarr Ag & B....75 K5
Glenbarry Abers....102 D4
Glenbeg Highld....89 M4
Glenbervie Abers....95 M6
Glenboig N Lans....85 M8
Glenborrodale Highld....89 M4
Glenbranter Ag & B....84 B4
Glenbreck Border....78 H5
Glenbrittle Highld....96 E5
Glenbuck E Ayrs....77 M5
Glencally Angus....94 F8
Glencaple D & G....70 G2
Glencarse P & K....92 H10
Glencoe Highld....90 F5
Glencothe Border....78 H3
Glencraig Fife....86 E4
Glencrosh D & G....78 C10
Glendale Highld....104 B11
Glendaruel Ag & B....83 Q6
Glendevon P & K....86 B2
Glendoe Lodge Highld....98 E7
Glendoick P & K....93 J10
Glenduckie Fife....93 K11
Glenegedale Ag & B....74 D3
Glenelg Highld....97 L6
Glenernie Moray....100 F9
Glenfarg P & K....92 G12
Glenfield Leics....41 M6
Glenfinnan Highld....90 C1
Glenfintaig Lodge Highld....98 C10
Glenfoot P & K....92 H11
Glenfyne Lodge Ag & B....90 G12
Glengarnock N Ayrs....84 F11
Glengolly Highld....110 D3
Glengorm Castle Ag & B....89 K5
Glengrasco Highld....96 E1
Glenholm Border....78 H3
Glenhoul D & G....69 N2
Glenisla Angus....94 D9
Glenkin Ag & B....84 C7
Glenkindie Abers....101 N11
Glenlivet Moray....101 J9
Glenlochar D & G....70 C3
Glenlomond P & K....86 E2
Glenluce D & G....68 G2
Glenmassan Ag & B....84 B5
Glenmavis N Lans....85 M9
Glen Maye IoM....56 b5
Glenmore Highld....96 E2
Glenmore Lodge Highld....99 P7
Glen Nevis House Highld....90 F12
Glenochil Clacks....85 P4
Glen Parva Leics....41 M7
Glenquiech Angus....94 G9
Glenralloch Ag & B....83 M8
Glenridding Cumb....71 N11
Glenrothes Fife....86 F3
Glenshero Lodge Highld....98 H9
Glenstriven Ag & B....84 B7
Glentham Lincs....52 E5
Glentrool D & G....69 J4
Glen Trool Lodge D & G....69 K3
Glentruim Highld....99 K9
Glentworth Lincs....52 D6
Glenuig Highld....89 N2
Glenvarragill Highld....96 F2
Glen Vine IoM....56 c5
Glenwhilly D & G....68 G5
Glespin S Lans....78 D4
Glewstone Herefs....28 G4
Glinton C Pete....42 G8
Glooston Leics....41 Q8
Glossop Derbys....50 D3

Gloster Hill Nthumb....81 Q12
Gloucester Gloucs....29 L5
Gloucester Services Gloucs....29 L6
Gloucestershire Airport Gloucs....29 M5
Glusburn N York....58 D5
Glutt Lodge Highld....110 B8
Glympton Oxon....31 K9
Glynarthen Cerdgn....36 E10
Glyn Ceiriog Wrexhm....48 E7
Glyncoch Rhondd....27 M9
Glyncorrwg Neath....27 J8
Glynde E Susx....11 P8
Glyndyfrdwy Denbgs....48 D7
Glynneath Neath....27 J7
Glyntawe Powys....26 H5
Glynteg Carmth....25 N2
Gnosall Staffs....49 P10
Gnosall Heath Staffs....49 P10
Goadby Leics....41 Q7
Goadby Marwood Leics....41 R3
Goatacre Wilts....18 F5
Goathill Dorset....17 P11
Goathland N York....67 J7
Goathurst Somset....16 H8
Goat Lees Kent....13 K2
Gobowen Shrops....48 F8
Godalming Surrey....10 F2
Goddard's Green Kent....12 G3
Godmanchester Cambs....33 J3
Godmanstone Dorset....7 P4
Godmersham Kent....23 K12
Godney Somset....17 L7
Godolphin Cross Cnwll....2 F9
Godre'r-graig Neath....26 H3
Godshill IoW....9 N10
Godstone Surrey....21 M11
Goetre Mons....28 C7
Goff's Oak Herts....21 M3
Gogar C Edin....86 E7
Goginan Cerdgn....37 L4
Golan Gwynd....46 H3
Golant Cnwll....4 C5
Golberdon Cnwll....4 H6
Golborne Wigan....57 L8
Golcar Kirk....58 E10
Goldcliff Newpt....28 D11
Golden Green Kent....12 D1

Goldenhill C Stke....49 Q5
Golden Pot Hants....10 B2
Golders Green Gt Lon....21 K6
Goldhanger Essex....22 H2
Goldington Bed....32 F6
Goldsborough N York....59 J3
Goldsborough N York....67 J3
Golds Green Sandw....40 C8
Goldsithney Cnwll....2 E9
Goldthorpe Barns....59 L12
Goldworthy Devon....14 G7
Gollanfield Highld....107 N10
Golspie Highld....107 N3
Gomeldon Wilts....8 H1
Gomshall Surrey....10 H1
Gonalston Notts....51 P10
Gonerby Hill Foot Lincs....42 C3
Gonfirth Shet....111 k3
Good Easter Essex....22 D2
Gooderstone Norfk....44 C9
Goodleigh Devon....15 K5
Goodmanham E R Yk....60 F5
Goodmayes Gt Lon....21 P6
Goodnestone Kent....23 K10
Goodnestone Kent....23 N11
Goodrich Herefs....28 G5
Goodrington Torbay....6 B10
Goodshaw Lancs....57 P4
Goodwick Pembks....24 G2
Goodworth Clatford Hants....19 L11
Goole E R Yk....60 C9
Goom's Hill Worcs....30 D3
Goonbell Cnwll....2 G6
Goonhavern Cnwll....2 H5
Goonvrea Cnwll....2 K2
Goosecruives Abers....95 M5
Gooseford Devon....5 N7
Goose Green Essex....35 J10
Goose Green S Glos....17 P2
Gooseham Cnwll....14 E8
Goosey Oxon....19 L3
Goosnargh Lancs....57 K2
Goostrey Ches E....49 P2
Gordano Services N Som....17 M2
Gordon Border....80 E5
Gordon Arms Hotel Border....79 L4
Gordonstown Abers....102 D4
Gordonstown Abers....102 F7
Gorebridge Mdloth....86 G9
Gorefield Cambs....43 L7
Gores Wilts....18 G8
Gorey Jersey....7 c2
Goring Oxon....19 P5
Goring-by-Sea W Susx....10 H9
Gorleston on Sea Norfk....45 Q8
Gorrachie Abers....102 F4
Gorran Churchtown Cnwll....3 M7
Gorran Haven Cnwll....3 M7
Gorsedd Flints....56 D12
Gorse Hill Swindn....18 H4
Gorseinon Swans....26 D8
Gorsgoch Cerdgn....36 H9
Gorslas Carmth....26 D6
Gorsley Gloucs....29 J4
Gorsley Common Herefs....29 J4
Gorstan Highld....106 F9
Gorsten Ag & B....89 P9
Gorsty Hill Staffs....40 E2
Gorthleck Highld....98 G5
Gorton Manch....50 B2
Gosbeck Suffk....35 J5
Gosberton Lincs....43 J4
Gosfield Essex....34 D10
Gosforth Cumb....62 C2
Gosforth N u Ty....73 M7
Gosport Hants....9 Q7
Gossington Gloucs....29 K8
Gotham Notts....41 M2
Gotherington Gloucs....29 N3
Gotton Somset....16 H9
Goudhurst Kent....12 E3
Goulceby Lincs....53 J7
Gourdas Abers....102 G7
Gourdie C Dund....93 L8
Gourdon Abers....95 N7
Gourock Inver....84 D7
Govan C Glas....85 J9
Goveton Devon....5 P10
Govilon Mons....28 B6
Gowdall E R Yk....59 N9
Gower Highld....106 H10
Gower Swans....26 C10
Gowerton Swans....26 D9
Gowkhall Fife....86 C5
Goxhill E R Yk....61 K5
Goxhill N Linc....61 J9
Grabhair W Isls....111 d3
Graffham W Susx....10 E6
Grafham Cambs....32 G3
Grafham Surrey....10 G2
Grafton N York....59 K2
Grafton Oxon....19 J1
Grafton Shrops....48 H10
Grafton Worcs....29 N2
Grafton Flyford Worcs....30 C3
Grafton Regis Nhants....31 Q5
Grafton Underwood Nhants....32 D2
Grafty Green Kent....12 G1
Graig Conwy....55 L7
Graigfechan Denbgs....48 D5
Grain Medway....22 H7
Grainsby Lincs....53 J4
Grainthorpe Lincs....53 L4
Grampound Cnwll....3 L6
Grampound Road Cnwll....3 K5
Gramsdal W Isls....111 b5
Gramsdale W Isls....111 b5
Granborough Bucks....31 Q8
Granby Notts....41 Q1
Grandborough Warwks....31 L2
Grand Chemins Jersey....7 c2
Grandes Rocques Guern....6 b1
Grandtully P & K....92 D5
Grange Cumb....71 L11
Grange Medway....22 F9
Grange P & K....93 K10
Grange Crossroads Moray....101 N4
Grange Hall Moray....100 G3
Grangehall S Lans....78 F1
Grange Hill Essex....21 N5
Grangemill Derbys....50 G8
Grange Moor Kirk....58 G10

Grangemouth Falk....85 Q6
Grange of Lindores Fife....93 J11
Grange-over-Sands Cumb....62 H6
Grangepans Falk....86 B6
Grange Park Nhants....31 Q3
Grangetown R & Cl....66 D4
Grangetown Sundld....73 P9
Grange Villa Dur....73 M9
Gransmoor E R Yk....61 J3
Granston Pembks....24 F2
Grantchester Cambs....33 M6
Grantham Lincs....42 D3
Granton C Edin....86 F6
Grantown-on-Spey Highld....100 F9
Grantshouse Border....87 P8
Grasby Lincs....52 F3
Grasmere Cumb....62 G1
Grasscroft Oldham....58 C12
Grassendale Lpool....56 H10
Grassington N York....58 D2
Grassmoor Derbys....51 K7
Grassthorpe Notts....52 B9
Grateley Hants....19 J11
Graveley Cambs....33 J4
Graveley Herts....32 H10
Gravelly Hill Birm....40 E8
Graveney Kent....23 K10
Gravesend Kent....22 D8
Gravir W Isls....111 d3
Grayingham Lincs....52 D4
Grayrigg Cumb....63 L3
Grays Thurr....22 C7
Grayshott Hants....10 E3
Grayswood Surrey....10 E3
Greasbrough Rothm....51 K2
Greasby Wirral....56 F10
Great Abington Cambs....33 N7
Great Addington Nhants....32 D2
Great Alne Warwks....30 E3
Great Altcar Lancs....56 G6
Great Amwell Herts....21 M2
Great Asby Cumb....64 C5
Great Ashfield Suffk....34 G4
Great Ayton N York....66 E5
Great Baddow Essex....22 E3
Great Badminton S Glos....18 B4
Great Bardfield Essex....34 B10
Great Barford Bed....32 G6
Great Barr Sandw....40 D8
Great Barrington Gloucs....30 G10
Great Barrow Ches W....49 J2
Great Barton Suffk....34 E4
Great Barugh N York....66 G10
Great Bavington Nthumb....72 H5
Great Bealings Suffk....35 K7
Great Bedwyn Wilts....19 J7
Great Bentley Essex....35 J11
Great Billing Nhants....32 B4
Great Bircham Norfk....44 C4
Great Blakenham Suffk....35 J6
Great Blencow Cumb....71 P8
Great Bolas Wrekin....49 M10
Great Bookham Surrey....21 J11
Great Bourton Oxon....31 L5
Great Bowden Leics....41 Q9
Great Bradley Suffk....34 B6
Great Braxted Essex....22 G1
Great Bricett Suffk....34 G6
Great Brickhill Bucks....32 C10
Great Bridgeford Staffs....40 B3
Great Brington Nhants....31 P2
Great Bromley Essex....34 H10
Great Broughton Cumb....70 H8
Great Broughton N York....66 D6
Great Budworth Ches W....57 M12
Great Burdon Darltn....65 N4
Great Burstead Essex....22 D5
Great Busby N York....66 D6
Great Carlton Lincs....53 L6
Great Casterton Rutlnd....42 E8
Great Chalfield Wilts....18 C7
Great Chart Kent....13 J2
Great Chatwell Staffs....49 P11
Great Chell C Stke....49 Q5
Great Chesterford Essex....33 N8
Great Cheverell Wilts....18 E9
Great Chishill Cambs....33 L8
Great Clacton Essex....35 K12
Great Clifton Cumb....70 G9
Great Coates NE Lin....61 L11
Great Comberton Worcs....29 N1
Great Corby Cumb....71 P5
Great Cornard Suffk....34 E8
Great Cowden E R Yk....61 L6
Great Coxwell Oxon....19 J3
Great Cransley Nhants....32 B2
Great Cressingham Norfk....44 E9
Great Crosthwaite Cumb....71 L10
Great Cubley Derbys....50 F12
Great Cumbrae Island N Ayrs....84 C10
Great Dalby Leics....41 Q5
Great Denham Bed....32 E7
Great Doddington Nhants....32 C4
Great Dunham Norfk....44 E7
Great Dunmow Essex....33 Q11
Great Durnford Wilts....18 G12
Great Easton Essex....33 P10
Great Easton Leics....42 C10
Great Eccleston Lancs....56 H2
Great Ellingham Norfk....44 G10
Great Elm Somset....17 Q6
Great Everdon Nhants....31 N4
Great Eversden Cambs....33 K6
Great Fencote N York....65 M8
Great Finborough Suffk....34 G5
Greatford Lincs....42 F7
Great Fransham Norfk....44 E7
Great Gaddesden Herts....20 G2
Great Gidding Cambs....42 G12
Great Givendale E R Yk....60 E4
Great Glemham Suffk....35 M4
Great Glen Leics....41 P7
Great Gonerby Lincs....42 C3
Great Gransden Cambs....33 J6
Great Green Cambs....33 J7
Great Green Suffk....34 F5
Great Habton N York....66 G11
Great Hale Lincs....42 G2
Great Hallingbury Essex....33 N11
Greatham Hants....10 C4
Greatham Hartpl....66 C3

Greatham W Susx....10 G6
Great Hampden Bucks....20 D3
Great Harrowden Nhants....32 C3
Great Harwood Lancs....57 N3
Great Haseley Oxon....19 Q1
Great Hatfield E R Yk....61 K5
Great Haywood Staffs....40 D3
Great Heck N York....59 N9
Great Henny Essex....34 E8
Great Hinton Wilts....18 D8
Great Hockham Norfk....44 F10
Great Holland Essex....35 K11
Great Hollands Br For....20 D9
Great Horkesley Essex....34 F9
Great Hormead Herts....33 L10
Great Horton C Brad....58 F7
Great Horwood Bucks....31 Q7
Great Houghton Barns....59 K11
Great Houghton Nhants....32 B5
Great Hucklow Derbys....50 F5
Great Kelk E R Yk....61 J3
Great Kimble Bucks....20 D3
Great Kingshill Bucks....20 E4
Great Langdale Cumb....62 F2
Great Langton N York....65 N8
Great Leighs Essex....34 C12
Great Limber Lincs....52 G2
Great Linford M Keyn....32 C8
Great Livermere Suffk....34 E3
Great Longstone Derbys....50 G6
Great Lumley Dur....73 N10
Great Malvern Worcs....39 P11
Great Maplestead Essex....34 D9
Great Marton Bpool....56 G2
Great Massingham Norfk....44 D5
Great Milton Oxon....19 Q1
Great Missenden Bucks....20 E3
Great Mitton Lancs....57 N2
Great Mongeham Kent....23 Q12
Great Moulton Norfk....45 J11
Great Musgrave Cumb....64 C4
Great Ness Shrops....48 H10
Great Notley Essex....34 C11
Great Oak Mons....28 D6
Great Oakley Essex....35 K10
Great Oakley Nhants....42 C11
Great Offley Herts....32 G10
Great Ormside Cumb....64 C4
Great Orton Cumb....71 M5
Great Ouseburn N York....59 K2
Great Oxendon Nhants....41 Q10
Great Park N u Ty....73 L6
Great Parndon Essex....21 N2
Great Paxton Cambs....32 H4
Great Plumpton Lancs....56 H3
Great Plumstead Norfk....45 L7
Great Ponton Lincs....42 D4
Great Preston Leeds....59 K8
Great Raveley Cambs....33 J1
Great Rissington Gloucs....30 G10
Great Rollright Oxon....31 J7
Great Ryburgh Norfk....44 F5
Great Ryton Shrops....39 J2
Great Saling Essex....34 B10
Great Salkeld Cumb....71 Q8
Great Sampford Essex....33 Q9
Great Saughall Ches W....48 G2
Great Shefford W Berk....19 L6
Great Shelford Cambs....33 M6
Great Smeaton N York....65 N6
Great Snoring Norfk....44 F4
Great Somerford Wilts....18 E4
Great Soudley Shrops....49 N9
Great Stainton Darltn....65 N3
Great Stambridge Essex....22 H5
Great Staughton Cambs....32 G4
Great Steeping Lincs....53 M9
Great Stoke S Glos....28 H11
Greatstone-on-Sea Kent....13 L5
Great Strickland Cumb....71 Q10
Great Stukeley Cambs....32 H2
Great Sturton Lincs....52 H7
Great Swinburne Nthumb....72 G6
Great Tew Oxon....31 K8
Great Tey Essex....34 E10
Great Thurlow Suffk....34 B6
Great Torrington Devon....15 J8
Great Tosson Nthumb....72 H2
Great Totham Essex....22 G2
Great Totham Essex....22 G2
Great Urswick Cumb....62 F7
Great Wakering Essex....22 H6
Great Waldingfield Suffk....34 E8
Great Walsingham Norfk....44 F3
Great Waltham Essex....22 E2
Great Warley Essex....22 C5
Great Washbourne Gloucs....29 N2
Great Weeke Devon....5 P4
Great Wenham Suffk....34 H8
Great Whittington Nthumb....72 H6
Great Wigborough Essex....23 J1
Great Wilbraham Cambs....33 N5
Great Wishford Wilts....8 F1
Great Witcombe Gloucs....29 M8
Great Witley Worcs....39 N8
Great Wolford Warwks....30 H5
Greatworth Nhants....31 M6
Great Wratting Suffk....34 B7
Great Wymondley Herts....32 H10
Great Wyrley Staffs....40 C6
Great Yarmouth Norfk....45 Q8
Great Yeldham Essex....34 C8
Greenburn W Loth....85 Q10
Green End Herts....33 K9
Greenfield Ag & B....90 D5
Greenfield C Beds....32 F9
Greenfield Flints....56 E12
Greenfield Oldham....58 C12
Greenford Gt Lon....21 J6
Greengairs N Lans....85 N8
Greengates C Brad....58 G6
Greenham Somset....16 E11
Green Hammerton N York....59 K3
Greenhaugh Nthumb....72 E4
Greenhead Nthumb....72 C7
Green Heath Staffs....40 C5
Greenhill D & G....78 H11
Greenhill Falk....85 N7
Greenhill Kent....23 M9
Greenhill S Lans....78 F3

Greenhills S Lans....85 K11
Greenhithe Kent....22 C8
Greenholm E Ayrs....77 J4
Greenhouse Border....80 D9
Greenhow Hill N York....58 E2
Greenland Highld....110 E3
Greenland Sheff....51 K3
Greenlaw Border....80 F5
Greenlea D & G....70 G1
Greenloaning P & K....85 N2
Greenmount Bury....57 N5
Greenock Inver....84 E7
Greenodd Cumb....62 G5
Green Ore Somset....17 N6
Green Quarter Cumb....63 J2
Greenshields S Lans....86 B12
Greenside Gatesd....73 K8
Greenside Kirk....58 F10
Greens Norton Nhants....31 P4
Greenstead Green Essex....34 D10
Green Street Herts....21 J4
Green Street Herts....33 M11
Green Tye Herts....33 M11
Greenway Somset....17 J11
Greenwich Gt Lon....21 M7
Greenwich Maritime Gt Lon....21 M7
Greet Gloucs....30 D7
Greete Shrops....39 L7
Greetham Lincs....53 K8
Greetham Rutlnd....42 D7
Greetland Calder....58 E9
Greinton Somset....17 K8
Grenaby IoM....56 b6
Grendon Nhants....32 C5
Grendon Warwks....40 H7
Grendon Underwood Bucks....31 P9
Grenoside Sheff....51 J3
Greosabhagh W Isls....111 c3
Gresford Wrexhm....48 G5
Gresham Norfk....45 J3
Greshornish Highld....104 D10
Gressenhall Norfk....44 F7
Gressenhall Green Norfk....44 F6
Gressingham Lancs....63 K8
Greta Bridge Dur....65 J5
Gretna D & G....71 M3
Gretna Green D & G....71 M2
Gretna Services D & G....71 L2
Gretton Gloucs....30 D7
Gretton Nhants....42 C10
Gretton Shrops....39 K3
Grewelthorpe N York....65 M11
Greygarth D & G....78 H10
Greys Green Oxon....20 B6
Greysouthen Cumb....70 H9
Greystoke Cumb....71 P8
Greystone Angus....93 P7
Greywell Hants....20 B12
Griff Warwks....41 J9
Griffithstown Torfn....28 C8
Grimeford Village Lancs....57 L6
Grimesthorpe Sheff....51 J3
Grimethorpe Barns....59 K11
Grimley Worcs....39 Q9
Grimmet S Ayrs....76 F8
Grimoldby Lincs....53 L6
Grimpo Shrops....48 G9
Grimsargh Lancs....57 L3
Grimsby NE Lin....61 M11
Grimscote Nhants....31 P4
Grimscott Cnwll....14 E10
Grimshader W Isls....111 d2
Grimsthorpe Lincs....42 F5
Grimston Leics....41 P3
Grimston Norfk....44 C5
Grimstone Dorset....7 P4
Grimstone End Suffk....34 F3
Grindale E R Yk....67 N12
Grindleford Derbys....50 G5
Grindleton Lancs....63 N11
Grindley Brook Shrops....49 K7
Grindlow Derbys....50 F5
Grindon Staffs....50 E9
Gringley on the Hill Notts....51 Q3
Grinsdale Cumb....71 M4
Grinshill Shrops....49 K10
Grinton N York....65 J7
Griomaisiader W Isls....111 d2
Grishipoll Ag & B....88 F5
Gristhorpe N York....67 M10
Griston Norfk....44 F9
Gritley Ork....111 h2
Grittenham Wilts....18 F4
Grittleton Wilts....18 C5
Grizebeck Cumb....62 E5
Grizedale Cumb....62 G4
Groby Leics....41 M6
Groes Conwy....55 Q8
Groes-faen Rhondd....27 M11
Groeslon Gwynd....54 F9
Groes-Wen Caerph....27 N10
Grogarry W Isls....111 a5
Grogport Ag & B....75 M4
Groigearraidh W Isls....111 a5
Gronant Flints....56 C11
Groombridge E Susx....11 Q3
Grosebay W Isls....111 c3
Grosmont Mons....28 E4
Grosmont N York....67 J6
Groton Suffk....34 F8
Grouville Jersey....7 c2
Grove Notts....51 Q5
Grove Oxon....19 L3
Grove Green Kent....22 F11
Grove Park Gt Lon....21 N8
Grovesend Swans....26 D8
Gruinard Highld....105 P4
Gruinart Ag & B....82 D9
Grula Highld....96 D4
Gruline Ag & B....89 L8
Grundisburgh Suffk....35 K6
Gruting Shet....111 j4
Grutness Shet....111 k5
Gualachulain Highld....90 F7
Guardbridge Fife....93 M11
Guarlford Worcs....39 P11
Guay P & K....92 E6
Guernsey Guern....6 b2
Guernsey Airport Guern....6 b2
Guestling Green E Susx....12 G6
Guestling Thorn E Susx....12 G6
Guestwick Norfk....44 H5

Guide Bridge Tamesd......50 B2
Guilden Morden Cambs......33 J7
Guilden Sutton Ches W......49 J2
Guildford Surrey......20 F12
Guildtown P & K......92 G8
Guilsborough Nhants......41 P11
Guilsfield Powys......48 E12
Guiltreehill S Ayrs......76 F8
Guineaford Devon......15 J5
Guisborough R & Cl......66 E4
Guiseley Leeds......58 G6
Guist Norfk......44 G5
Guiting Power Gloucs......30 E8
Gullane E Loth......87 J5
Gulval Cnwll......2 D9
Gulworthy Devon......5 K5
Gumfreston Pembks......25 J8
Gumley Leics......41 P9
Gunby Lincs......42 D6
Gunby Lincs......53 M9
Gundleton Hants......9 Q2
Gun Hill E Susx......12 C7
Gunn Devon......15 L5
Gunnerside N York......64 G7
Gunnerton Nthumb......72 G6
Gunness N Linc......60 E11
Gunnislake Cnwll......5 J6
Gunnista Shet......111 k4
Gunthorpe C Pete......42 H9
Gunthorpe N Linc......52 B4
Gunthorpe Norfk......44 G3
Gunthorpe Notts......51 P11
Gunwalloe Cnwll......2 F10
Gurnard IoW......9 N8
Gurney Slade Somset......17 N6
Gurnos Powys......26 G7
Gussage All Saints Dorset......8 E5
Gussage St Andrew Dorset......8 E5
Gussage St Michael Dorset......8 E5
Guston Kent......13 P2
Gutcher Shet......111 k2
Guthrie Angus......93 P5
Guyhirn Cambs......43 L8
Guyzance Nthumb......81 P12
Gwaenysgor Flints......56 C11
Gwalchmai IoA......54 E6
Gwaun-Cae-Gurwen Carmth......26 F6
Gweek Cnwll......2 G9
Gwenddwr Powys......38 C12
Gwennap Cnwll......2 H7
Gwennap Mining District Cnwll......2 H7
Gwernaffield Flints......48 E3
Gwernesney Mons......28 E8
Gwernogle Carmth......26 D3
Gwernymynydd Flints......48 E3
Gwespyr Flints......56 C11
Gwinear Cnwll......2 E8
Gwithian Cnwll......2 E7
Gwyddelwern Denbgs......48 C6
Gwyddgrug Carmth......26 C2
Gwytherin Conwy......55 N8

H

Habberley Shrops......38 H2
Habberley Worcs......39 P6
Habergham Lancs......57 P3
Habertoft Lincs......53 N9
Habrough NE Lin......61 K10
Hacconby Lincs......42 F5
Haceby Lincs......42 E3
Hacheston Suffk......35 M5
Hackbridge Gt Lon......21 L9
Hackenthorpe Sheff......51 K4
Hackford Norfk......44 H9
Hackforth N York......65 M8
Hackland Ork......111 h2
Hackleton Nhants......32 B6
Hacklinge Kent......23 Q11
Hackness N York......67 L9
Hackney Gt Lon......21 M6
Hackthorn Lincs......52 E7
Hackthorpe Cumb......71 Q10
Hadden Border......80 G7
Haddenham Bucks......20 B2
Haddenham Cambs......33 M2
Haddington E Loth......87 K7
Haddington Lincs......52 D10
Haddiscoe Norfk......45 P10
Haddo Abers......102 H7
Haddon Cambs......42 G10
Hadfield Derbys......50 D2
Hadham Ford Herts......33 M11
Hadleigh Essex......22 F6
Hadleigh Suffk......34 G8
Hadley Worcs......39 Q8
Hadley Wrekin......49 M12
Hadley End Staffs......40 F4
Hadley Wood Gt Lon......21 L4
Hadlow Kent......22 D12
Hadlow Down E Susx......11 Q5
Hadnall Shrops......49 K10
Hadrian's Wall......72 G6
Hadstock Essex......33 N7
Hadzor Worcs......30 B2
Haggersta Shet......111 k4
Haggerston Nthumb......81 L5
Haggs Falk......85 N7
Hagley Herefs......28 G1
Hagley Worcs......40 B10
Hagworthingham Lincs......53 K9
Haile Cumb......62 B1
Hailey Oxon......31 J10
Hailsham E Susx......12 C8
Hail Weston Cambs......32 G4
Hainault Gt Lon......21 P5
Hainford Norfk......45 K6
Hainton Lincs......52 H6
Haisthorpe E R Yk......61 J2
Hakin Pembks......24 F7
Halam Notts......51 P9
Halbeath Fife......86 D5
Halberton Devon......6 D1
Halcro Highld......110 E4
Hale Cumb......63 J6
Hale Halton......57 J11
Hale Hants......8 H4
Hale Surrey......10 D1
Hale Traffd......57 P10

Hale Barns Traffd......57 P10
Hales Norfk......45 N10
Hales Staffs......49 N8
Halesowen Dudley......40 C10
Hales Place Kent......23 M10
Hale Street Kent......22 D12
Halesworth Suffk......35 N2
Halewood Knows......57 J10
Halford Devon......5 Q5
Halford Warwks......30 H5
Halfpenny Green Staffs......39 P4
Halfway House Shrops......48 G12
Halfway Houses Kent......22 H8
Halifax Calder......58 E8
Halket E Ayrs......84 G11
Halkirk Highld......110 D4
Halkyn Flints......48 E2
Hall E Rens......84 G11
Hallam Leics......42 B10
Hallatrow BaNES......17 P5
Hallbankgate Cumb......72 B8
Hall Dunnerdale Cumb......62 E3
Hallen S Glos......28 G11
Hallgarth Dur......73 N11
Hallglen Falk......85 P7
Hallin Highld......104 C9
Halling Medway......22 E10
Hallington Lincs......53 K6
Hallington Nthumb......72 H6
Halliwell Bolton......57 M6
Halloughton Notts......51 P9
Hallow Worcs......39 P9
Hall's Green Herts......33 J10
Hallyne Border......79 K2
Halmore Gloucs......29 J8
Halnaker W Susx......10 E8
Halsall Lancs......56 G6
Halse Nhants......31 M6
Halse Somset......16 F9
Halsetown Cnwll......2 D7
Halsham E R Yk......61 M8
Halstead Essex......34 D10
Halstead Kent......21 P10
Halstead Leics......41 Q6
Halstock Dorset......7 M2
Haltham Lincs......53 J10
Halton Bucks......20 E2
Halton Halton......57 K11
Halton Lancs......63 J8
Halton Leeds......59 J7
Halton Nthumb......72 H7
Halton Wrexhm......48 F7
Halton East N York......58 D4
Halton Gill N York......64 F11
Halton Holegate Lincs......53 L9
Halton Lea Gate Nthumb......72 C8
Halton Shields Nthumb......72 H7
Halton West N York......63 Q10
Haltwhistle Nthumb......72 D7
Halvergate Norfk......45 N8
Halwell Devon......5 Q9
Halwill Devon......14 H11
Halwill Junction Devon......14 H11
Ham Devon......6 H3
Ham Gloucs......29 J8
Ham Gt Lon......21 J8
Ham Kent......23 P11
Ham Somset......16 H10
Ham Wilts......19 K8
Hambleden Bucks......20 C6
Hambledon Hants......9 Q4
Hambledon Surrey......10 F3
Hamble-le-Rice Hants......9 N6
Hambleton Lancs......56 G1
Hambleton N York......59 M7
Hambridge Somset......17 K10
Hambrook W Susx......10 C8
Hameringham Lincs......53 K9
Hamerton Cambs......32 G2
Ham Green Worcs......30 D2
Hamilton S Lans......85 M11
Hamilton Services S Lans......85 M10
Hamlet Dorset......7 N2
Hammersmith Gt Lon......21 K7
Hammerwich Staffs......40 E6
Hammoon Dorset......8 B5
Hamnavoe Shet......111 k4
Hampden Park E Susx......12 C9
Hampnett Gloucs......30 E10
Hampole Donc......59 L11
Hampreston Dorset......8 F7
Hampstead Gt Lon......21 L6
Hampstead Norreys W Berk......19 N5
Hampsthwaite N York......58 H3
Hampton C Pete......42 G10
Hampton Gt Lon......21 J9
Hampton Kent......23 M9
Hampton Shrops......39 N5
Hampton Swindn......18 H3
Hampton Worcs......30 D5
Hampton Bishop Herefs......28 G2
Hampton Court Palace Gt Lon......21 J9
Hampton Heath Ches W......49 J5
Hampton-in-Arden Solhll......40 G10
Hampton Lovett Worcs......30 B2
Hampton Lucy Warwks......30 G3
Hampton Magna Warwks......30 H2
Hampton Poyle Oxon......31 L10
Hampton Wick Gt Lon......21 J9
Hamptworth Wilts......9 J4
Hamsey E Susx......11 N7
Hamstall Ridware Staffs......40 E4
Hamstead Birm......40 D8
Hamstead Marshall W Berk......19 M7
Hamsterley Dur......65 K2
Hamsterley Dur......73 K9
Hamstreet Kent......13 J4
Ham Street Somset......17 M8
Hamworthy BCP......8 E8
Hanbury Staffs......40 F2
Hanbury Worcs......30 C2
Hanchurch Staffs......49 Q7
Handa Island Highld......108 D7
Hand and Pen Devon......6 E4
Handbridge Ches W......48 H3
Handcross W Susx......11 L4
Handforth Ches E......57 Q11
Handley Ches W......49 J4
Handley Derbys......51 J8
Handsworth Birm......40 D8
Handsworth Sheff......51 K4

Handsworth Sheff......51 K4
Hanford C Stke......49 Q7
Hanging Heaton Kirk......58 G9
Hanging Houghton Nhants......41 Q11
Hanging Langford Wilts......18 F12
Hangleton Br & H......11 L8
Hanham S Glos......17 Q2
Hankelow Ches E......49 M6
Hankerton Wilts......29 M9
Hanley C Stke......50 B10
Hanley Castle Worcs......39 Q12
Hanley Child Worcs......39 M8
Hanley Swan Worcs......39 P12
Hanley William Worcs......39 M8
Hanlith N York......58 B2
Hanmer Wrexhm......49 J7
Hannaford Devon......15 L6
Hannington Hants......19 N9
Hannington Nhants......32 B3
Hannington Swindn......18 H3
Hannington Wick Swindn......18 H2
Hanslope M Keyn......32 B7
Hanthorpe Lincs......42 F5
Hanwell Gt Lon......21 J7
Hanwell Oxon......31 K5
Hanwood Shrops......49 J12
Hanworth Gt Lon......21 H8
Hanworth Norfk......45 K3
Happendon S Lans......78 E3
Happendon Services S Lans......78 D3
Happisburgh Norfk......45 N4
Happisburgh Common Norfk......45 N4
Hapsford Ches W......49 J1
Hapton Lancs......57 P3
Hapton Norfk......45 K10
Harberton Devon......5 Q8
Harbertonford Devon......5 Q8
Harbledown Kent......23 L10
Harborne Birm......40 D9
Harborough Magna Warwks......41 L10
Harbottle Nthumb......81 K12
Harbourneford Devon......5 P7
Harbury Warwks......31 J3
Harby Leics......41 Q2
Harby Notts......52 C8
Harcombe Devon......6 B6
Harcombe Devon......6 F5
Harcombe Bottom Devon......7 J4
Harden C Brad......58 E6
Harden Wsall......40 D7
Hardenhuish Wilts......18 D6
Hardgate Abers......95 M2
Hardgate D & G......70 D3
Hardgate W Duns......84 H8
Hardham W Susx......10 G6
Hardingham Norfk......44 H9
Hardingstone Nhants......31 Q3
Hardington Somset......17 Q5
Hardington Mandeville Somset......7 M2
Hardington Marsh Somset......7 M2
Hardington Moor Somset......7 M1
Hardisworthy Devon......14 E7
Hardley Hants......9 M6
Hardley Street Norfk......45 N9
Hardraw N York......64 F8
Hardstoft Derbys......51 K8
Hardway Hants......9 Q7
Hardway Somset......17 Q8
Hardwick Bucks......32 B11
Hardwick Cambs......33 L5
Hardwick Nhants......32 C3
Hardwick Norfk......45 K11
Hardwick Oxon......31 J11
Hardwick Oxon......31 M7
Hardwick Wsall......40 E7
Hardwicke Gloucs......29 L6
Hardwicke Gloucs......29 M4
Hardwick Hall Derbys......51 L7
Hardy's Green Essex......34 F11
Hare Croft C Brad......58 E7
Harefield Gt Lon......20 H5
Hare Green Essex......34 H10
Hare Hatch Wokham......20 C7
Harehill Derbys......40 F1
Harehills Leeds......59 J7
Harelaw Border......80 C9
Harelaw D & G......79 N12
Harescombe Gloucs......29 L6
Haresfield Gloucs......29 L6
Harestock Hants......9 M2
Hare Street Essex......21 N2
Hare Street Herts......33 L10
Harewood Leeds......58 H5
Harewood End Herefs......28 F4
Harford Devon......5 M8
Hargrave Ches W......49 J3
Hargrave Nhants......32 E3
Hargrave Suffk......34 C5
Harkstead Suffk......35 K9
Harlaston Staffs......40 G5
Harlaxton Lincs......42 C4
Harlech Gwynd......47 J5
Harlech Castle Gwynd......47 J5
Harlescott Shrops......49 J11
Harlesden Gt Lon......21 K6
Harlesthorpe Derbys......51 L5
Harleston Devon......5 Q10
Harleston Norfk......45 L12
Harleston Suffk......34 G5
Harlestone Nhants......31 P2
Harle Syke Lancs......57 Q2
Harley Rothm......51 J2
Harley Shrops......39 L2
Harlington C Beds......32 E10
Harlington Donc......51 L1
Harlington Gt Lon......21 H7
Harlosh Highld......96 C2
Harlow Essex......21 N2
Harlow Carr RHS N York......58 H4
Harlow Hill Nthumb......73 J7
Harlthorpe E R Yk......60 C6
Harlton Cambs......33 L6
Harlyn Cnwll......3 K1
Harman's Cross Dorset......8 E10
Harmby N York......65 K9
Harmer Green Herts......33 J12
Harmer Hill Shrops......49 J10
Harmston Lincs......52 D10
Harnage Shrops......39 K2
Harnhill Gloucs......18 F1
Harold Hill Gt Lon......21 Q5

Haroldston West Pembks......24 F6
Haroldswick Shet......111 m2
Harold Wood Gt Lon......22 B5
Harome N York......66 F10
Harpenden Herts......21 J1
Harpford Devon......6 E5
Harpham E R Yk......61 J2
Harpley Norfk......44 D5
Harpley Worcs......39 M9
Harpole Nhants......31 P2
Harpsdale Highld......110 D5
Harpswell Lincs......52 D5
Harpurhey Manch......57 Q8
Harraby Cumb......71 N5
Harracott Devon......15 K6
Harrapool Highld......97 J5
Harrietfield P & K......92 E9
Harrietsham Kent......22 G11
Harringay Gt Lon......21 L6
Harrington Cumb......70 G9
Harrington Lincs......53 L8
Harrington Nhants......41 Q10
Harringworth Nhants......42 D10
Harris W Isls......111 c3
Harrogate N York......58 H3
Harrold Bed......32 D5
Harrow Gt Lon......21 J6
Harrowbarrow Cnwll......5 J6
Harrowgate Village Darltn......65 N4
Harrow Green Suffk......34 E6
Harrow on the Hill Gt Lon......21 J6
Harrow Weald Gt Lon......21 J5
Harston Cambs......33 L6
Harston Leics......42 B4
Harswell E R Yk......60 E6
Hart Hartpl......66 C1
Hartburn Nthumb......73 J4
Hartburn S on T......65 Q4
Hartest Suffk......34 D6
Hartfield E Susx......11 P3
Hartford Cambs......33 J3
Hartford Ches W......49 L2
Hartfordbridge Hants......20 C10
Hartford End Essex......34 B12
Hartforth N York......65 L6
Hartgrove Dorset......8 C4
Harthill Ches W......49 J4
Harthill N Lans......85 L9
Harthill Rothm......51 L5
Harthope D & G......78 G6
Hartington Derbys......50 F8
Hartland Devon......14 E7
Hartland Quay Devon......14 D7
Hartlebury Worcs......39 Q7
Hartlepool Hartpl......66 C2
Hartley Cumb......64 E6
Hartley Kent......12 F3
Hartley Kent......22 C9
Hartley Wespall Hants......20 B10
Hartley Wintney Hants......20 C11
Hartlip Kent......22 G9
Harton N York......60 C2
Harton S Tyne......73 P7
Hartpury Gloucs......29 L4
Hartshead Kirk......58 F9
Hartshead Moor Services Calder......58 F8
Hartshill C Stke......49 Q6
Hartshill Warwks......41 J8
Hartshorne Derbys......41 J4
Hartwell Nhants......32 B6
Hartwith N York......58 G2
Hartwood N Lans......85 N10
Hartwoodmyres Border......79 N4
Harvel Kent......22 D9
Harvington Worcs......30 D4
Harvington Worcs......39 Q7
Harwell Notts......51 P3
Harwell Oxon......19 N3
Harwich Essex......35 L9
Harwood Nthumb......72 H3
Harwood Dale N York......67 L8
Harworth Notts......51 N3
Hasbury Dudley......40 C10
Hascombe Surrey......10 G3
Haselbech Nhants......41 P11
Haselbury Plucknett Somset......7 L1
Haseley Warwks......30 H2
Haselor Warwks......30 E3
Hasfield Gloucs......29 L4
Haskayne Lancs......56 G7
Hasketon Suffk......35 L6
Haslemere Surrey......10 E4
Haslingden Lancs......57 P4
Haslingfield Cambs......33 L6
Haslington Ches E......49 N4
Hassingham Norfk......45 N8
Hassocks W Susx......11 L7
Hassop Derbys......50 G6
Haster Highld......110 G5
Hastingleigh Kent......13 L2
Hastings E Susx......12 G7
Hastingwood Essex......21 P2
Hastoe Herts......20 E2
Haswell Dur......73 P11
Haswell Plough Dur......73 P11
Hatch Beauchamp Somset......17 J11
Hatch End Gt Lon......21 J5
Hatchmere Ches W......49 K2
Hatcliffe NE Lin......52 H4
Hatfield Donc......59 P11
Hatfield Herefs......39 L9
Hatfield Herts......21 K2
Hatfield Broad Oak Essex......33 N12
Hatfield Heath Essex......21 Q1
Hatfield Peverel Essex......22 F2
Hatfield Woodhouse Donc......59 P11
Hatford Oxon......19 K2
Hatherden Hants......19 L9
Hatherleigh Devon......15 J10
Hathern Leics......41 L3
Hatherop Gloucs......30 F11
Hathersage Derbys......50 G5
Hathersage Booths Derbys......50 G5
Hatherton Ches E......49 M5
Hatherton Staffs......40 C5
Hatley St George Cambs......33 J6
Hatt Cnwll......5 J7
Hattersley Tamesd......50 D2
Hatton Abers......103 L7
Hatton Angus......93 N7
Hatton Derbys......40 G2

Hatton Gt Lon......20 H8
Hatton Lincs......52 H7
Hatton Shrops......39 J4
Hatton Warrtn......57 L11
Hatton Warwks......30 H2
Hatton of Fintray Abers......102 H11
Haugh E Ayrs......76 H6
Haugham Lincs......53 K7
Haughhead E Duns......85 K7
Haughley Suffk......34 G4
Haughley Green Suffk......34 G4
Haugh of Glass Moray......101 M7
Haugh of Urr D & G......70 D3
Haughs of Kinnaird Angus......93 Q4
Haughton Ches E......49 L4
Haughton Shrops......48 H9
Haughton Staffs......49 Q10
Haughton le Skerne Darltn......65 N4
Haultwick Herts......33 K11
Haunton Staffs......40 G5
Hauxton Cambs......33 M6
Havant Hants......10 B8
Havenstreet IoW......9 P8
Havercroft Wakefd......59 K10
Haverfordwest Pembks......24 G6
Haverhill Suffk......33 Q7
Haverigg Cumb......62 D6
Havering-atte-Bower Gt Lon......21 P5
Haversham M Keyn......32 B8
Haverthwaite Cumb......62 G5
Havyatt N Som......17 L4
Hawarden Flints......48 G3
Hawbush Green Essex......34 D11
Hawen Cerdgn......36 F10
Hawes N York......64 F9
Hawe's Green Norfk......45 L9
Hawford Worcs......39 Q9
Hawick Border......80 C10
Hawkchurch Devon......7 J3
Hawkedon Suffk......34 D6
Hawkeridge Wilts......18 C9
Hawkesbury S Glos......18 B4
Hawkesbury Upton S Glos......18 B4
Hawkhurst Kent......12 F4
Hawkinge Kent......13 N3
Hawkley Hants......10 C4
Hawkridge Somset......15 P6
Hawkshead Cumb......62 G3
Hawkshead Hill Cumb......62 G3
Hawksland S Lans......78 D2
Hawkstone Shrops......49 L9
Hawkswick N York......64 G12
Hawksworth Leeds......58 F6
Hawksworth Notts......51 Q11
Hawkwell Essex......22 G5
Hawley Hants......20 D10
Hawling Gloucs......30 E9
Hawnby N York......66 D9
Haworth C Brad......58 D6
Hawstead Suffk......34 E5
Hawthorn Dur......73 P10
Hawthorn Hill Lincs......52 H11
Hawton Notts......52 B12
Haxby C York......59 N3
Haxey N Linc......51 Q2
Haydock St Hel......57 K9
Haydon Bridge Nthumb......72 F7
Haydon Wick Swindn......18 G4
Hayes Gt Lon......20 H7
Hayes Gt Lon......21 N9
Hayes End Gt Lon......20 H7
Hayfield Ag & B......90 E10
Hayfield Derbys......50 D4
Hayhillock Angus......93 N7
Hayle Cnwll......2 E8
Hayle Port Cnwll......2 E8
Hayley Green Dudley......40 C10
Hayling Island Hants......10 B9
Hayne Devon......5 P3
Haynes C Beds......32 F8
Haynes Church End C Beds......32 F8
Haynes West End C Beds......32 F8
Hay-on-Wye Powys......27 P1
Hayscastle Pembks......24 F4
Hayscastle Cross Pembks......24 G4
Hay Street Herts......33 L10
Hayton Cumb......70 H7
Hayton Cumb......71 Q4
Hayton E R Yk......60 E5
Hayton Notts......51 Q4
Haytor Vale Devon......5 P5
Haytown Devon......14 G8
Haywards Heath W Susx......11 M5
Haywood Donc......59 N10
Hazelbank S Lans......77 P3
Hazeleigh Essex......22 G3
Hazel Grove Stockp......50 B4
Hazelton Walls Fife......93 L10
Hazelwood Derbys......51 J10
Hazlemere Bucks......20 E4
Hazlerigg N u Ty......73 M6
Hazleton Gloucs......30 E9
Heacham Norfk......44 B3
Headbourne Worthy Hants......9 N2
Headcorn Kent......12 G2
Headingley Leeds......58 H7
Headington Oxon......31 M11
Headlam Dur......65 L4
Headlesscross N Lans......85 Q10
Headless Cross Worcs......30 D2
Headley Hants......10 D3
Headley Hants......19 N8
Headley Surrey......21 K11
Headley Down Hants......10 D3
Headon Notts......51 Q5
Heads Nook Cumb......71 P5
Heage Derbys......51 J10
Healaugh N York......64 G8
Heald Green Stockp......57 Q10
Heale Somset......16 H11
Heale Somset......17 K10
Healey N York......65 L9
Healeyfield Dur......73 J10
Healing NE Lin......61 L11
Heamoor Cnwll......2 C9
Heanor Derbys......51 K10
Heanton Punchardon Devon......15 J5
Heapham Lincs......52 C6
Heart of Scotland Services N Lans......85 Q9

Heasley Mill Devon 15 M6
Heaste Highld. 96 H6
Heath Derbys 51 K7
Heath Wakefd. 59 J9
Heath and Reach C Beds 32 D10
Heathcote Derbys 50 F8
Heather Leics 41 K5
Heathfield E Susx 12 C6
Heathfield Somset 16 F10
Heath Green Worcs 40 E12
Heath Hall D & G 78 G11
Heath Hayes & Wimblebury Staffs 40 D5
Heath Hill Shrops 49 N11
Heathrow Airport Gt Lon 20 H8
Heathton Shrops 39 P4
Heath Town Wolves 40 B7
Heatley Warrtn 57 N10
Heaton C Brad 58 F7
Heaton N u Ty. 73 M7
Heaton Staffs 50 C8
Heaton Chapel Stockp 57 Q9
Heaton Mersey Stockp 57 Q10
Heaton Norris Stockp 50 B3
Heaton's Bridge Lancs 56 H6
Heaverham Kent 22 C10
Heavitree Devon 6 C4
Hebburn S Tyne 73 N7
Hebden N York 58 D2
Hebden Bridge Calder 58 C8
Hebing End Herts 33 K11
Hebron Carmth 25 L4
Hebron Nthumb 73 L3
Heckfield Hants 20 B10
Heckfield Green Suffk 35 K2
Heckfordbridge Essex 34 F11
Heckington Lincs 42 G2
Heckmondwike Kirk 58 G9
Heddington Wilts 18 E7
Heddon-on-the-Wall Nthumb 73 K7
Hedenham Norfk 45 M10
Hedge End Hants 9 N5
Hedgerley Bucks 20 F6
Hedging Somset 17 J9
Hedley on the Hill Nthumb 73 J8
Hednesford Staffs 40 C5
Hedon E R Yk 61 K8
Hedsor Bucks 20 E6
Heeley Sheff 51 J4
Heglibister Shet 111 k4
Heighington Darltn 65 M3
Heighington Lincs 52 E9
Heightington Worcs 39 N7
Heiton Border 80 F7
Hele Devon 6 D3
Hele Devon 15 J3
Helensburgh Ag & B 84 E6
Helenton S Ayrs 76 G5
Helford Cnwll 2 H9
Helford Passage Cnwll 2 H9
Helhoughton Norfk 44 E5
Helions Bumpstead Essex 33 Q8
Helland Cnwll 3 N2
Hellescott Cnwll 4 G3
Hellesdon Norfk 45 K7
Hellidon Nhants 31 M3
Hellifield N York 63 Q10
Hellingly E Susx 12 C7
Helmdon Nhants 31 N5
Helme Kirk 58 E10
Helmingham Suffk 35 K5
Helmsdale Highld 110 B11
Helmshore Lancs 57 P5
Helmsley N York 66 E10
Helperby N York 59 K1
Helperthorpe N York 67 K12
Helpringham Lincs 42 G3
Helpston C Pete 42 G8
Helsby Ches W 49 J1
Helston Cnwll 2 F9
Helstone Cnwll 4 D4
Helton Cumb 71 Q10
Hemel Hempstead Herts 20 G2
Hemerdon Devon 5 L8
Hemingbrough N York 59 P7
Hemingby Lincs 53 J8
Hemingford Abbots Cambs 33 J3
Hemingford Grey Cambs 33 J3
Hemingstone Suffk 35 J6
Hemington Leics 41 L2
Hemington Nhants 42 F12
Hemington Somset 17 Q5
Hemley Suffk 35 L8
Hemlington Middsb 66 C5
Hempnall Norfk 45 L10
Hempnall Green Norfk 45 L10
Hempriggs Moray 100 H3
Hempstead Essex 33 Q8
Hempstead Medway 22 F9
Hempstead Norfk 44 H3
Hempstead Norfk 45 N5
Hempton Norfk 44 E4
Hempton Oxon 31 K7
Hemsby Norfk 45 P6
Hemswell Lincs 52 D5
Hemswell Cliff Lincs 52 D5
Hemsworth Wakefd 59 K10
Hemyock Devon 16 F12
Henbury Bristl 28 G11
Hendon Gt Lon 21 K5
Hendon Sundld 73 P9
Hendy Carmth 26 D7
Henfield W Susx 11 K6
Hengoed Caerph 27 N9
Hengoed Powys 38 E10
Hengrave Suffk 34 D3
Henham Essex 33 N10
Heniarth Powys 38 D1
Henlade Somset 16 H10
Henley Dorset 7 Q2
Henley Somset 17 L9
Henley Suffk 35 J6
Henley W Susx 10 E5
Henley Green Covtry 41 J10
Henley-in-Arden Warwks 30 F2
Henley-on-Thames Oxon 20 C6
Henley's Down E Susx 12 E7
Henllan Cerdgn 36 F11
Henllan Denbgs 55 Q7
Henllys Torfn 28 B9
Henlow C Beds 32 H8
Hennock Devon 5 Q4

Henny Street Essex 34 E8
Henryd Conwy 55 L6
Henry's Moat (Castell Hendre) Pembks 24 H4
Hensall N York 59 N9
Henshaw Nthumb 72 D7
Hensingham Cumb 70 G11
Henstead Suffk 45 P11
Hensting Hants 9 N3
Henstridge Somset 17 Q11
Henstridge Ash Somset 17 Q11
Henton Oxon 20 C3
Henton Somset 17 L7
Henwick Worcs 39 Q10
Henwood Cnwll 4 G5
Heol-y-Cyw Brdgnd 27 K11
Hepple Nthumb 72 H1
Hepscott Nthumb 73 L4
Heptonstall Calder 58 C8
Hepworth Kirk 58 F11
Hepworth Suffk 34 G2
Herbrandston Pembks 24 F7
Hereford Herefs 28 F2
Hereson Kent 23 Q9
Heribusta Highld 104 E8
Heriot Border 86 H10
Hermiston C Edin 86 E8
Hermitage Border 79 P9
Hermitage Dorset 7 P2
Hermitage W Berk 19 N6
Hermon Carmth 25 N3
Hermon Pembks 25 L3
Herne Kent 23 M9
Herne Bay Kent 23 M9
Herne Hill Gt Lon 21 L8
Herne Pound Kent 22 D11
Hernhill Kent 23 K10
Herodsfoot Cnwll 4 F7
Heronsford S Ayrs 68 F3
Herriard Hants 19 Q10
Herringfleet Suffk 45 P9
Herringswell Suffk 34 C3
Herringthorpe Rothm 51 K3
Herrington Sundld 73 P9
Hersden Kent 23 M10
Hersham Surrey 20 H9
Herstmonceux E Susx 12 D7
Herston Ork 111 h3
Hertford Herts 21 M2
Hertford Heath Herts 21 M2
Hertingfordbury Herts 21 L2
Hesketh Bank Lancs 57 J4
Hesketh Lane Lancs 57 L1
Hesket Newmarket Cumb 71 M7
Hesleden Dur 73 Q12
Heslington C York 59 N4
Hessay C York 59 M4
Hessenford Cnwll 4 G8
Hessett Suffk 34 F4
Hessle E R Yk 60 H8
Hessle Wakefd 59 K10
Hest Bank Lancs 63 J8
Heston Gt Lon 20 H7
Heston Services Gt Lon 20 H7
Hestwall Ork 111 g2
Heswall Wirral 56 F11
Hethe Oxon 31 N8
Hethersett Norfk 45 J8
Hethersgill Cumb 71 P3
Hett Dur 73 M12
Hetton N York 58 C3
Hetton-le-Hole Sundld 73 N10
Heugh Nthumb 73 J6
Heughhead Abers 101 M11
Heugh Head Border 87 Q9
Heveningham Suffk 35 M3
Hever Kent 11 P2
Heversham Cumb 63 J5
Hevingham Norfk 45 K6
Hewas Water Cnwll 3 L6
Hewelsfield Gloucs 28 G8
Hewish Somset 7 K2
Hewood Dorset 7 J3
Hexham Nthumb 72 G7
Hextable Kent 21 P8
Hexthorpe Donc 51 M1
Hexton Herts 32 F10
Hexworthy Cnwll 4 H4
Hexworthy Devon 5 N6
Heybridge Essex 22 D4
Heybridge Essex 22 G2
Heybrook Bay Devon 5 K9
Heydon Cambs 33 M8
Heydon Norfk 45 J5
Heydour Lincs 42 E3
Heylipoll Ag & B 88 B7
Heylor Shet 111 j3
Heysham Lancs 62 H9
Heyshott W Susx 10 E6
Heytesbury Wilts 18 D11
Heythrop Oxon 31 J8
Heywood Rochdl 57 Q6
Heywood Wilts 18 C9
Hibaldstow N Linc 52 D3
Hickleton Donc 59 L12
Hickling Norfk 45 N5
Hickling Notts 41 P2
Hickling Green Norfk 45 N5
Hickstead W Susx 11 L6
Hidcote Bartrim Gloucs 30 F5
Hidcote Boyce Gloucs 30 F6
High Ackworth Wakefd 59 K9
Higham Barns 58 H11
Higham Derbys 51 K8
Higham Kent 12 C1
Higham Kent 22 E8
Higham Lancs 57 P2
Higham Suffk 34 C4
Higham Suffk 34 G3
Higham Ferrers Nhants 32 D3
Higham Gobion C Beds 32 F9
Higham Hill Gt Lon 21 M5
Higham on the Hill Leics 41 J8
Highampton Devon 14 H10
Highams Park Gt Lon 21 M5
High Ardwell D & G 68 E9
High Auldgirth D & G 78 E10
High Bankhill Cumb 71 Q7
High Beach Essex 21 N4
High Bentham N York 63 M8
High Bickington Devon 15 K7
High Biggins Cumb 63 L6

High Blantyre S Lans 85 L10
High Bonnybridge Falk 85 N10
High Bray Devon 15 M5
Highbridge Somset 17 J6
Highbrook W Susx 11 M4
High Brooms Kent 12 C2
Highburton Kirk 58 F10
Highbury Gt Lon 21 L6
Highbury Somset 17 Q6
High Catton E R Yk 60 C4
Highclere Hants 19 M8
Highcliffe BCP 8 H8
High Coniscliffe Darltn 65 M5
High Crosby Cumb 71 P4
High Cross E Ayrs 76 G3
High Cross Hants 10 B5
High Cross Herts 33 L11
High Cross Warwks 30 G1
High Drummore D & G 68 F11
High Easter Essex 22 C1
High Ellington N York 65 L10
Higher Ansty Dorset 8 B3
Higher Bartle Lancs 57 J3
Higher Bockhampton Dorset 7 Q4
Higher Brixham Torbay 6 C10
Higher Chillington Somset 7 K2
Higher Folds Wigan 57 M8
Higher Gabwell Devon 6 C8
Higher Heysham Lancs 62 H9
Higher Irlam Salfd 57 N9
Higher Kinnerton Flints 48 G3
Higher Muddiford Devon 15 K5
Higher Penwortham Lancs 57 K3
Higher Prestacott Devon 14 G2
Higher Town Cnwll 3 J6
Higher Town Cnwll 3 M4
Higher Town IoS 2 c1
Higher Walton Lancs 57 L4
Higher Walton Warrtn 57 L10
Higher Wambrook Somset 6 H2
Higher Waterston Dorset 7 Q4
Higher Wheelton Lancs 57 L4
Higher Whitley Ches W 57 L11
Higher Wincham Ches W 57 M12
Higher Wraxall Dorset 7 N3
Higher Wych Ches W 49 J6
High Etherley Dur 65 L2
Highfield Gatesd 73 K8
Highfield N Ayrs 76 F2
High Garrett Essex 34 C10
Highgate Gt Lon 21 L6
Highgate Kent 12 F4
High Grantley N York 65 M12
High Green Norfk 45 J11
High Green Norfk 45 J8
High Green Sheff 51 J2
High Halden Kent 12 H3
High Halstow Medway 22 F8
High Ham Somset 17 K9
High Harrington Cumb 70 G9
High Harrogate N York 58 H3
High Hatton Shrops 49 L9
High Hauxley Nthumb 73 M1
High Hawsker N York 67 K6
High Hesket Cumb 71 P6
High Hoyland Barns 58 H11
High Hurstwood E Susx 11 P5
High Hutton N York 60 D1
High Ireby Cumb 71 K7
High Kilburn N York 66 D10
High Lands Dur 65 K3
Highlane Derbys 51 K4
High Lane Stockp 50 C4
High Lanes Cnwll 2 F7
Highleadon Gloucs 29 K4
High Legh Ches E 57 M11
Highleigh W Susx 10 D9
High Leven S on T 66 C5
Highley Shrops 39 N5
High Littleton BaNES 17 P5
High Lorton Cumb 71 J9
High Marnham Notts 52 B9
High Melton Donc 51 L11
High Mickley Nthumb 73 J8
Highmoor Oxon 20 B6
Highmoor Cross Oxon 20 B6
Highnam Gloucs 29 K5
High Newport Sundld 73 P9
High Newton Cumb 62 H5
High Nibthwaite Cumb 62 F4
High Offley Staffs 49 P9
High Ongar Essex 22 C3
High Onn Staffs 49 P11
High Park Corner Essex 34 G11
High Pennyvenie E Ayrs 76 H9
High Roding Essex 33 P12
High Salvington W Susx 10 H8
High Spen Gatesd 73 K8
Highsted Kent 22 H10
High Street Cnwll 3 L5
Highstreet Kent 23 L10
Highstreet Green Surrey 10 F3
Hightae D & G 78 H11
Highter's Heath Birm 40 E10
Hightown Sefton 56 F7
Hightown Green Suffk 34 F5
High Toynton Lincs 53 J9
High Valleyfield Fife 86 B5
Highweek Devon 6 B8
Highwood Essex 22 D3
Highwood Hill Gt Lon 21 K5
High Wray Cumb 62 G3
High Wych Herts 21 P1
High Wycombe Bucks 20 D5
Hilborough Norfk 44 D9
Hilcott Wilts 18 G8
Hildenborough Kent 21 P12
Hilden Park Kent 12 C1
Hildersham Cambs 33 N6
Hilderstone Staffs 40 C1
Hilderthorpe E R Yk 61 J2
Hilgay Norfk 43 P9
Hill S Glos 28 H9
Hill Warwks 31 L2
Hillam N York 59 L8
Hill Brow Hants 10 C5
Hillbutts Dorset 8 E7
Hill Chorlton Staffs 49 P7
Hillclifflane Derbys 50 H10
Hill Common Somset 16 F10

Hilldyke Lincs 43 K1
Hill End Fife 86 C3
Hillend Fife 86 D5
Hill End Gloucs 29 M2
Hillend Mdloth 86 F8
Hillend N Herts 85 N9
Hillesden Bucks 31 P8
Hillesley Gloucs 29 K10
Hillfarrance Somset 16 F10
Hill Green Kent 22 G10
Hillhead Abers 102 D8
Hill Head Hants 9 P6
Hillhead S Lans 78 F2
Hillhead of Cocklaw Abers 103 M6
Hilliclay Highld 110 D3
Hillingdon Gt Lon 20 H6
Hillington C Glas 85 J9
Hillington Norfk 44 C5
Hillmorton Warwks 41 M11
Hill of Beath Fife 86 D4
Hill of Fearn Highld 107 N6
Hillowton D & G 70 C3
Hill Ridware Staffs 40 E4
Hillside Abers 95 Q3
Hillside Angus 95 L9
Hill Side Kirk 58 F10
Hills Town Derbys 51 L6
Hillstreet Hants 9 K4
Hillswick Shet 111 j3
Hill Top Sandw 40 C8
Hill Top Wakefd 59 J10
Hillwell Shet 111 k5
Hilmarton Wilts 18 E6
Hilperton Wilts 18 C8
Hilsea C Port 9 Q6
Hilston E R Yk 61 M7
Hilton Border 81 J4
Hilton Cambs 33 J4
Hilton Cumb 64 D4
Hilton Derbys 40 G2
Hilton Dorset 8 B4
Hilton Dur 65 L3
Hilton Highld 107 P7
Hilton S on T 66 C5
Himbleton Worcs 30 C3
Himley Staffs 39 Q4
Hincaster Cumb 63 K5
Hinchley Wood Surrey 21 J9
Hinckley Leics 41 K8
Hinderclay Suffk 34 G2
Hinderwell N York 66 H4
Hindhead Surrey 10 E3
Hindhead Tunnel Surrey 10 E3
Hindley Wigan 57 L7
Hindlip Worcs 39 Q9
Hindolveston Norfk 44 G4
Hindon Wilts 8 D2
Hindringham Norfk 44 G3
Hingham Norfk 44 G9
Hinstock Shrops 49 M9
Hintlesham Suffk 34 H7
Hinton Herefs 28 D2
Hinton S Glos 17 Q2
Hinton Shrops 38 H1
Hinton Ampner Hants 9 P2
Hinton Blewett BaNES 17 N5
Hinton Charterhouse BaNES 18 B8
Hinton-in-the-Hedges Nhants 31 M6
Hinton Martell Dorset 8 E6
Hinton on the Green Worcs 30 D5
Hinton Parva Swindn 19 J4
Hinton St George Somset 7 K2
Hinton St Mary Dorset 8 B4
Hinton Waldrist Oxon 19 L2
Hints Staffs 40 F6
Hinwick Bed 32 D5
Hinxhill Kent 13 K2
Hinxton Cambs 33 M7
Hinxworth Herts 32 H8
Hipperholme Calder 58 E8
Hipswell N York 65 L7
Hirn Abers 95 M2
Hirnant Powys 48 B10
Hirst Nthumb 73 M4
Hirst Courtney N York 59 N8
Hirwaun Rhondd 27 K7
Hiscott Devon 15 J7
Histon Cambs 33 M4
Hitcham Suffk 34 G6
Hitcham Causeway Suffk 34 G6
Hitcham Street Suffk 34 G6
Hitchin Herts 32 H10
Hither Green Gt Lon 21 M8
Hittisleigh Devon 5 P2
Hive E R Yk 60 E7
Hixon Staffs 40 D3
Hoaden Kent 23 N10
Hoar Cross Staffs 40 F3
Hoarwithy Herefs 28 G3
Hoath Kent 23 N9
Hobarris Shrops 38 F6
Hobkirk Border 80 D11
Hobson Dur 73 L9
Hoby Leics 41 P4
Hockering Norfk 44 H7
Hockerton Notts 51 Q9
Hockley Essex 22 H5
Hockley Heath Solhll 40 F11
Hocklifffe C Beds 32 D10
Hockwold cum Wilton Norfk 44 C11
Hockworthy Devon 16 E11
Hoddesdon Herts 21 M2
Hoddlesden Bl w D 57 N4
Hoddom Cross D & G 71 J2
Hoddom Mains D & G 71 J2
Hodgeston Pembks 24 H8
Hodnet Shrops 49 L9
Hodsock Notts 51 N4
Hodsoll Street Kent 22 D10
Hodson Swindn 18 H5
Hodthorpe Derbys 51 M5
Hoe Norfk 44 G6
Hogben's Hill Kent 23 K11
Hoggeston Bucks 32 B9
Hoggrill's End Warwks 40 G8
Hoghton Lancs 57 L4
Hognaston Derbys 50 G10
Hogsthorpe Lincs 53 N8
Holbeach Lincs 43 K5

Holbeach Bank Lincs 43 K5
Holbeach Clough Lincs 43 K5
Holbeach Drove Lincs 43 K7
Holbeach Hurn Lincs 43 L5
Holbeach St Johns Lincs 43 K6
Holbeach St Mark's Lincs 43 L4
Holbeach St Matthew Lincs 43 L4
Holbeck Notts 51 M6
Holberrow Green Worcs 30 D3
Holbeton Devon 5 M9
Holborn Gt Lon 21 L7
Holbrook Derbys 51 J11
Holbrook Suffk 35 J9
Holbrooks Covtry 41 J10
Holbury Hants 9 M6
Holcombe Devon 6 C7
Holcombe Somset 17 P6
Holcombe Rogus Devon 16 E11
Holcot Nhants 32 B3
Holden Lancs 63 P11
Holdenby Nhants 31 P1
Holder's Green Essex 33 Q10
Holdgate Shrops 39 K4
Holdingham Lincs 42 F1
Holditch Dorset 7 J3
Holemoor Devon 14 H10
Holford Somset 16 F7
Holgate C York 59 N4
Holker Cumb 62 G6
Holkham Norfk 44 E2
Hollacombe Devon 14 G10
Holland Fen Lincs 52 H12
Holland-on-Sea Essex 35 K12
Hollandstoun Ork 111 i1
Hollee D & G 71 L2
Hollesley Suffk 35 M7
Hollicombe Torbay 6 B9
Hollingbourne Kent 22 G11
Hollington Br & H 11 L8
Hollingdon Bucks 32 C10
Hollington Derbys 50 G11
Hollington Staffs 50 D11
Hollingworth Tamesd 50 D2
Hollinsclough Staffs 50 E7
Hollins End Derbys 51 J4
Hollins Green Warrtn 57 M10
Hollinswood Wrekin 39 N1
Hollocombe Devon 15 J9
Holloway Derbys 51 J9
Holloway Gt Lon 21 L6
Hollowell Nhants 41 P11
Hollowmoor Heath Ches W 49 J2
Hollows D & G 79 N12
Hollybush Caerph 27 N7
Hollybush E Ayrs 76 G8
Hollybush Herefs 29 K2
Hollym E R Yk 61 N8
Holmbridge Kirk 58 F11
Holmbury St Mary Surrey 10 H2
Holmbush Cnwll 3 M5
Holmcroft Staffs 40 B3
Holme Cambs 42 H11
Holme Cumb 63 K6
Holme Kirk 58 E11
Holme N York 65 P10
Holme Notts 52 B10
Holme Chapel Lancs 57 Q3
Holme Hale Norfk 44 E8
Holme Lacy Herefs 28 G2
Holme Marsh Herefs 38 G10
Holme next the Sea Norfk 44 B2
Holme on the Wolds E R Yk 60 G5
Holme Pierrepont Notts 51 N11
Holmer Herefs 28 F1
Holmer Green Bucks 20 E4
Holme St Cuthbert Cumb 70 H6
Holmes Chapel Ches E 49 N3
Holmesfield Derbys 50 H5
Holmeswood Lancs 56 H5
Holmethorpe Surrey 21 L12
Holme upon Spalding Moor E R Yk 60 D6
Holmewood Derbys 51 K7
Holmfirth Kirk 58 F11
Holmhead E Ayrs 77 J5
Holmpton E R Yk 61 N9
Holmrook Cumb 62 D2
Holmside Dur 73 L10
Holne Devon 5 P7
Holnicote Somset 16 C7
Holsworthy Devon 14 F10
Holsworthy Beacon Devon 14 G9
Holt Dorset 8 F6
Holt Norfk 44 H3
Holt Wilts 18 C8
Holt Worcs 39 P9
Holt Wrexhm 48 H5
Holtby C York 59 P4
Holt End Worcs 40 E12
Holt Heath Worcs 39 P9
Holton Oxon 31 N11
Holton Somset 17 P10
Holton Suffk 35 N2
Holton cum Beckering Lincs 52 G6
Holton le Clay Lincs 53 J3
Holton le Moor Lincs 52 H4
Holton St Mary Suffk 34 H8
Holwell Dorset 7 Q1
Holwell Herts 32 G9
Holwell Leics 41 Q3
Holwell Oxon 30 G11
Holwick Dur 64 G3
Holybourne Hants 10 B2
Holyhead IoA 54 C5
Holy Island IoA 54 C5
Holy Island Nthumb 81 N5
Holymoorside Derbys 51 J7
Holyport W & M 20 E7
Holystone Nthumb 72 G1
Holytown N Lans 85 M10
Holywell C Beds 32 E12
Holywell Cambs 33 K3
Holywell Cnwll 2 H4
Holywell Dorset 7 N2
Holywell Flints 48 E1
Holywell Green Calder 58 E9
Holywell Lake Somset 16 F11
Holywell Row Suffk 34 B2
Holywood D & G 78 F11
Holywood Village D & G 78 F11
Homer Shrops 39 L1

Place	Page	Ref
Homersfield Suffk	45	L11
Homington Wilts	8	G3
Honeybourne Worcs	30	E5
Honeychurch Devon	15	L10
Honeystreet Wilts	18	G8
Honey Tye Suffk	34	F9
Honiley Warwks	40	G11
Honing Norfk	45	M5
Honingham Norfk	44	H7
Honington Lincs	42	D2
Honington Suffk	34	E2
Honington Warwks	30	H5
Honiton Devon	6	F3
Honley Kirk	58	F10
Hooe C Plym	5	K9
Hooe E Susx	12	E7
Hoo Green Ches E	57	N11
Hoohill Bpool	56	G2
Hook E R Yk	60	D8
Hook Gt Lon	21	J9
Hook Hants	20	B11
Hook Pembks	24	G6
Hook Wilts	18	F4
Hooke Dorset	7	M3
Hook Green Kent	12	D3
Hook Norton Oxon	31	J7
Hookway Devon	15	P11
Hooley Surrey	21	L11
Hoo St Werburgh Medway	22	F8
Hooton Levitt Rothm	51	M3
Hooton Pagnell Donc	59	L11
Hooton Roberts Rothm	51	L2
Hope Derbys	50	F4
Hope Devon	5	N11
Hope Flints	48	F4
Hope Staffs	50	E9
Hope Bagot Shrops	39	L7
Hope Bowdler Shrops	39	J4
Hopehouse Border	79	L5
Hopeman Moray	100	H2
Hope Mansell Herefs	28	H5
Hopesay Shrops	38	H5
Hope under Dinmore Herefs	39	K10
Hopgrove C York	59	N3
Hopperton N York	59	K3
Hopstone Shrops	39	P4
Hopton Derbys	50	H9
Hopton Staffs	40	C3
Hopton Suffk	34	G2
Hopton Cangeford Shrops	39	K6
Hopton Castle Shrops	38	G6
Hoptonheath Shrops	38	H6
Hopton on Sea Norfk	45	Q9
Hopton Wafers Shrops	39	M6
Hopwas Staffs	40	F6
Hopwood Worcs	40	D11
Hopwood Park Services Worcs	40	D11
Horam E Susx	12	C6
Horbling Lincs	42	G3
Horbury Wakefd	58	H9
Horden Dur	73	Q11
Hordle Hants	9	J8
Hordley Shrops	48	H8
Horfield Bristl	17	N2
Horham Suffk	35	K3
Horkesley Heath Essex	34	G10
Horkstow N Linc	60	G9
Horley Oxon	31	K5
Horley Surrey	11	L2
Hornblotton Green Somset	17	N9
Hornby Lancs	63	L8
Hornby N York	65	L8
Hornby N York	65	P6
Horncastle Lincs	53	J9
Hornchurch Gt Lon	21	Q6
Horncliffe Nthumb	81	K4
Horndean Border	81	J4
Horndean Hants	10	B7
Horndon Devon	5	L4
Horndon on the Hill Thurr	22	D6
Horne Surrey	11	M2
Horner Somset	16	B7
Horning Norfk	45	M6
Horninghold Leics	42	B10
Horninglow Staffs	40	G3
Horningsea Cambs	33	M4
Horningsham Wilts	18	B11
Horningtoft Norfk	44	F5
Horns Cross Devon	14	G7
Hornsea E R Yk	61	K5
Hornsey Gt Lon	21	L5
Hornton Oxon	31	K5
Horra Shet	111	k2
Horrabridge Devon	5	K6
Horringer Suffk	34	D4
Horrocksford Lancs	63	N12
Horsebridge Devon	5	J5
Horsebridge E Susx	12	C7
Horsebridge Hants	9	L2
Horsehay Wrekin	39	M1
Horseheath Cambs	33	P7
Horsehouse N York	65	J10
Horsell Surrey	20	F10
Horseman's Green Wrexhm	49	J7
Horsey Norfk	45	P5
Horsey Somset	17	J8
Horsford Norfk	45	K7
Horsforth Leeds	58	G6
Horsham W Susx	11	J4
Horsham Worcs	39	N9
Horsham St Faith Norfk	45	K7
Horsington Lincs	52	H9
Horsington Somset	17	Q10
Horsley Derbys	51	J11
Horsley Gloucs	29	L8
Horsley Nthumb	72	F2
Horsley Nthumb	73	J7
Horsleycross Street Essex	35	J10
Horsleyhill Border	80	C9
Horsley Woodhouse Derbys	51	K11
Horsmonden Kent	12	E2
Horspath Oxon	31	M12
Horstead Norfk	45	L6
Horsted Keynes W Susx	11	M5
Horton Dorset	8	F6
Horton Lancs	63	Q11
Horton Nhants	32	B6
Horton S Glos	18	A4
Horton Somset	17	J12
Horton Staffs	50	C8
Horton Swans	26	C10
Horton W & M	20	G8
Horton Wilts	18	F7
Horton Wrekin	49	M11
Horton-cum-Studley Oxon	31	N10
Horton Green Ches W	49	J5
Horton-in-Ribblesdale N York	64	E12
Horton Kirby Kent	22	C9
Horwich Bolton	57	M6
Horwood Devon	15	J6
Hoscote Border	79	N6
Hose Leics	41	Q2
Hosh P & K	92	C10
Hoswick Shet	111	k5
Hotham E R Yk	60	F7
Hothfield Kent	13	J2
Hoton Leics	41	M3
Hough Ches E	49	N5
Hougham Lincs	42	C2
Hough Green Halton	57	J12
Hough-on-the-Hill Lincs	42	D2
Houghton Cambs	33	J3
Houghton Hants	9	K2
Houghton Pembks	24	H7
Houghton W Susx	10	G7
Houghton Conquest C Beds	32	F8
Houghton Green E Susx	12	H5
Houghton-le-Spring Sundld	73	N10
Houghton on the Hill Leics	41	P6
Houghton Regis C Beds	32	E11
Houghton St Giles Norfk	44	F3
Hound Green Hants	20	B10
Houndslow Border	80	E5
Houndwood Border	87	Q9
Hounslow Gt Lon	21	J8
Househill Highld	100	D4
Houses Hill Kirk	58	G10
Housieside Abers	103	J9
Houston Rens	84	G9
Houstry Highld	110	D8
Houton Ork	111	g2
Hove Br & H	11	L8
Hoveringham Notts	51	P10
Hoveton Norfk	45	M6
Hovingham N York	66	F11
How Caple Herefs	28	H3
Howden E R Yk	60	D8
Howden-le-Wear Dur	65	L2
Howe Highld	110	F4
Howe N York	65	P10
Howe Norfk	45	L9
Howe Green Essex	22	E3
Howegreen Essex	22	G3
Howell Lincs	42	G2
Howe of Teuchar Abers	102	G6
Howes D & G	71	K3
Howe Street Essex	22	E1
Howe Street Essex	34	B9
Howey Powys	38	C9
Howgate Cumb	70	G10
Howgate Mdloth	86	F10
Howick Nthumb	81	Q10
Howlett End Essex	33	P9
Howley Somset	6	H2
How Mill Cumb	71	Q4
Howmore W Isls	111	a5
Hownam Border	80	G9
Howsham N Linc	52	E3
Howsham N York	60	C2
Howtel Nthumb	81	J7
How Wood Herts	21	J3
Howwood Rens	84	G10
Hoxa Ork	111	h3
Hoxne Suffk	35	K2
Hoy Ork	111	g3
Hoylake Wirral	56	E10
Hoyland Barns	51	J1
Hoylandswaine Barns	58	H12
Hubberston Pembks	24	F7
Huby N York	58	H4
Huby N York	59	M2
Hucclecote Gloucs	29	M5
Hucking Kent	22	G10
Hucknall Notts	51	M10
Huddersfield Kirk	58	F10
Huddington Worcs	30	C3
Hudswell N York	65	K7
Huggate E R Yk	60	F4
Hughenden Valley Bucks	20	D4
Hughley Shrops	39	K3
Hugh Town IoS	2	c2
Huish Devon	15	J9
Huish Wilts	18	G7
Huish Champflower Somset	16	E9
Huish Episcopi Somset	17	L10
Hùisinis W Isls	111	b3
Huisinish W Isls	111	b3
Hulcott Bucks	32	C12
Hulham Devon	6	D6
Hulland Derbys	50	G10
Hulland Ward Derbys	50	G10
Hullavington Wilts	18	D4
Hullbridge Essex	22	F4
Hull, Kingston upon C KuH	61	J8
Hulme Manch	57	Q9
Hulme Leics	50	C10
Hulme Warrtn	57	L9
Hulme End Staffs	50	E8
Hulme Walfield Ches E	49	Q3
Hulverstone IoW	9	L9
Hulver Street Suffk	45	P11
Humber Bridge N Linc	60	H8
Humberside Airport N Linc	61	J11
Humberston NE Lin	53	K3
Humberstone C Leic	41	N6
Humbie E Loth	87	J9
Humbleton E R Yk	61	L7
Humby Lincs	42	E4
Hume Border	80	F6
Humshaugh Nthumb	72	G6
Huna Highld	110	G2
Huncote Leics	41	M7
Hundalee Border	80	E9
Hunderthwaite Dur	64	H4
Hundleby Lincs	53	L9
Hundleton Pembks	24	G8
Hundon Suffk	34	C7
Hundred House Powys	38	C10
Hungarton Leics	41	P6
Hungerford Somset	16	E7
Hungerford W Berk	19	K7
Hungerford Newtown W Berk	19	L6
Hungerstone Herefs	28	E2
Hunmanby N York	67	N11
Hunningham Warwks	31	J1
Hunsbury Hill Nhants	31	Q3
Hunsdon Herts	21	N1
Hunsingore N York	59	K4
Hunslet Leeds	58	H7
Hunsonby Cumb	64	B1
Hunstanton Norfk	43	Q3
Hunston Suffk	34	F3
Hunston W Susx	10	D9
Hunstrete BaNES	17	P4
Hunsworth Kirk	58	F8
Hunter's Quay Ag & B	84	C7
Huntham Somset	17	J10
Hunthill Lodge Angus	94	H7
Huntingdon Cambs	33	J3
Huntingfield Suffk	35	M2
Huntington C York	59	N3
Huntington Ches W	48	H3
Huntington E Loth	87	J7
Huntington Herefs	38	F10
Huntington Staffs	40	C5
Huntingtowerfield P & K	92	G9
Huntley Gloucs	29	J5
Huntly Abers	102	C7
Hunton Kent	22	E12
Hunton N York	65	L8
Hunton Somset	16	C7
Huntscott Somset	16	C7
Huntsham Devon	16	D11
Huntshaw Devon	15	J7
Huntspill Somset	17	J7
Huntstile Somset	16	H9
Huntworth Somset	17	J8
Hunwick Dur	65	L2
Hunworth Norfk	44	H3
Hurcott Somset	17	K11
Hurdcott Wilts	8	H1
Hurdsfield Ches E	50	B6
Hurley W & M	20	D6
Hurley Warwks	40	G8
Hurley Common Warwks	40	G8
Hurlford E Ayrs	76	H4
Hurn BCP	8	G7
Hursley Hants	9	M3
Hurst Wokham	20	C8
Hurstbourne Priors Hants	19	M10
Hurstbourne Tarrant Hants	19	L9
Hurst Green E Susx	12	E5
Hurst Green Essex	34	H12
Hurst Green Lancs	57	M2
Hurst Green Surrey	21	N12
Hurst Hill Dudley	40	B8
Hurstpierpoint W Susx	11	L6
Hurstwood Lancs	57	Q3
Hurtiso Ork	111	h2
Hurworth-on-Tees Darltn	65	N5
Hurworth Place Darltn	65	N5
Husbands Bosworth Leics	41	N10
Husborne Crawley C Beds	32	D9
Husthwaite N York	66	D11
Huthwaite Notts	51	L8
Huttoft Lincs	53	N8
Hutton Border	81	J4
Hutton E R Yk	60	H4
Hutton Essex	22	D4
Hutton Lancs	57	J4
Hutton N Som	17	J4
Hutton Buscel N York	67	L10
Hutton Conyers N York	65	N11
Hutton Cranswick E R Yk	60	H4
Hutton End Cumb	71	P7
Hutton Henry Dur	65	Q1
Hutton-le-Hole N York	66	G9
Hutton Lowcross R & Cl	66	E5
Hutton Magna Dur	65	K5
Hutton Roof Cumb	63	K6
Hutton Roof Cumb	71	M8
Hutton Rudby N York	66	C6
Hutton Sessay N York	66	C11
Hutton Wandesley N York	59	L4
Huxham Devon	6	C4
Huxley Ches W	49	K3
Huyton Knows	57	J10
Hycemoor Cumb	62	C4
Hyde Tamesd	50	C2
Hyde Heath Bucks	20	E4
Hyde Lea Staffs	40	B4
Hylands House & Park Essex	22	D3
Hyndford Bridge S Lans	78	E1
Hynish Ag & B	88	C8
Hyssington Powys	38	F4
Hythe Essex	34	G10
Hythe Hants	9	M6
Hythe Kent	13	M3
Hythe End W & M	20	G8

I

Place	Page	Ref
Ibberton Dorset	8	B6
Ible Derbys	50	G9
Ibsley Hants	8	H5
Ibstock Leics	41	K5
Ibstone Bucks	20	C5
Ibthorpe Hants	19	L9
Iburndale N York	67	J6
Ibworth Hants	19	P9
Ichrachan Ag & B	90	D9
Ickburgh Norfk	44	D10
Ickenham Gt Lon	20	H6
Ickford Bucks	31	N10
Ickham Kent	23	N10
Ickleford Herts	32	H9
Icklesham E Susx	12	G6
Ickleton Cambs	33	M7
Icklingham Suffk	34	C3
Ickornshaw N York	58	C5
Ickwell Green C Beds	32	G7
Icomb Gloucs	30	G9
Idbury Oxon	30	G9
Iddesleigh Devon	15	K9
Ide Devon	6	B5
Ideford Devon	6	B7
Ide Hill Kent	21	P11
Iden E Susx	12	H5
Iden Green Kent	12	F4
Iden Green Kent	12	F4
Idle C Brad	58	F6
Idless Cnwll	3	J6
Idlicote Warwks	30	H5
Idmiston Wilts	18	H12
Idole Carmth	25	P6
Idridgehay Derbys	50	H10
Idrigill Highld	104	E9
Idstone Oxon	19	J4
Iffley Oxon	31	M12
Ifield W Susx	11	K3
Ifold W Susx	10	G4
Iford BCP	8	G8
Iford E Susx	11	N8
Ifton Mons	28	F10
Ightfield Shrops	49	L7
Ightham Kent	22	C11
Ilam Staffs	50	F10
Ilchester Somset	17	M10
Ilderton Nthumb	81	N9
Ilford Gt Lon	21	N6
Ilford Somset	17	K11
Ilfracombe Devon	15	J3
Ilkeston Derbys	51	L11
Ilketshall St Andrew Suffk	45	M11
Ilketshall St Margaret Suffk	45	M11
Ilkley C Brad	58	E5
Illand Cnwll	4	G5
Illey Dudley	40	C10
Illogan Cnwll	2	G7
Illston on the Hill Leics	41	P7
Ilmer Bucks	20	C3
Ilmington Warwks	30	G5
Ilminster Somset	17	J12
Ilsington Devon	5	Q4
Ilston Swans	26	D10
Ilton N York	65	L11
Ilton Somset	17	J11
Imachar N Ayrs	75	N4
Immingham NE Lin	61	K10
Immingham Dock NE Lin	61	K10
Impington Cambs	33	M4
Ince Ches W	57	J12
Ince Blundell Sefton	56	G8
Ince-in-Makerfield Wigan	57	L7
Inchbae Lodge Hotel Highld	106	F3
Inchbare Angus	95	K8
Inchberry Moray	101	L4
Incheril Highld	105	Q3
Inchinnan Rens	84	H8
Inchlaggan Highld	98	B8
Inchmichael P & K	93	J9
Inchmore Highld	107	J12
Inchnacardoch Highld	98	E10
Inchnadamph Highld	108	E10
Inchture P & K	93	K9
Inchvuilt Highld	98	C2
Inchyra P & K	92	H10
Indian Queens Cnwll	3	K4
Ingatestone Essex	22	D4
Ingbirchworth Barns	58	G11
Ingerthorpe N York	58	E2
Ingestre Staffs	40	C3
Ingham Lincs	52	D6
Ingham Norfk	45	N5
Ingham Suffk	34	E3
Ingham Corner Norfk	45	N5
Ingleby Derbys	41	J3
Ingleby Arncliffe N York	66	C7
Ingleby Barwick S on T	66	C5
Ingleby Greenhow N York	66	E6
Ingleigh Green Devon	15	K10
Inglesbatch BaNES	17	Q4
Inglesham Swindn	18	H2
Ingleston D & G	70	D5
Ingleton Dur	65	L4
Ingleton N York	63	M7
Inglewhite Lancs	57	K2
Ingoe Nthumb	73	J6
Ingol Lancs	57	K3
Ingoldisthorpe Norfk	44	B4
Ingoldmells Lincs	53	N9
Ingoldsby Lincs	42	E4
Ingram Nthumb	81	L10
Ingrave Essex	22	D5
Ingrow C Brad	58	D6
Ings Cumb	63	J3
Ingst S Glos	28	G10
Ingthorpe RutInd	42	E8
Ingworth Norfk	45	K4
Inkberrow Worcs	30	D3
Inkhorn Abers	103	J7
Inkpen W Berk	19	L7
Inkstack Highld	110	F2
Innellan Ag & B	84	C8
Innerleithen Border	79	M2
Innerleven Fife	86	H3
Innermessan D & G	68	E6
Innerwick E Loth	87	N7
Innesmill Moray	101	K3
Insch Abers	102	E9
Insh Highld	99	M8
Inskip Lancs	57	J2
Instow Devon	14	H6
Intake Sheff	51	K4
Inver Abers	94	D4
Inver Highld	107	P6
Inver P & K	92	F7
Inverailort Highld	97	K12
Inverallochy Abers	103	L3
Inveran Highld	107	J3
Inveraray Ag & B	84	B2
Inverarish Highld	96	G3
Inverarity Angus	93	M6
Inverarnan Stirlg	91	J11
Inverasdale Highld	105	M5
Inverbeg Ag & B	84	F4
Inverbervie Abers	95	N7
Inverboyndie Abers	102	E3
Invercreran House Hotel Ag & B	90	D7
Inverdruie Highld	99	N6
Inveresk E Loth	86	G7
Inveresragan Ag & B	90	D8
Inverey Abers	94	B4
Inverfarigaig Highld	98	G4
Inverfolla Ag & B	90	C7
Invergarry Highld	98	D8
Invergeldie P & K	91	N9
Invergloy Highld	98	C10
Invergordon Highld	107	L8
Invergowrie P & K	93	L9
Inverguseran Highld	97	K8
Inverhadden P & K	91	P5
Inverie Highld	97	K9
Inverinan Ag & B	90	D11
Inverinate Highld	97	N5
Inverkeilor Angus	93	R6
Inverkeithing Fife	86	D5
Inverkeithny Abers	102	E6
Inverkip Inver	84	D8
Inverkirkaig Highld	108	B10
Inverlael Highld	106	C3
Inverlair Highld	98	D11
Inverliever Lodge Ag & B	83	N2
Inverlochy Angus	90	G10
Invermark Angus	94	G6
Invermoriston Highld	98	F5
Invernaver Highld	109	M4
Inverneill Ag & B	83	M6
Inverness Highld	107	L12
Inverness Airport Highld	107	M11
Invernettie Abers	103	M6
Invernoaden Ag & B	84	C4
Inveroran Hotel Ag & B	90	H7
Inverquharity Angus	93	M4
Inverquhomery Abers	103	L6
Inverroy Highld	98	C11
Inversanda Highld	90	C4
Invershiel Highld	97	N6
Invershin Highld	107	J3
Invershore Highld	110	F8
Inversnaid Hotel Stirlg	84	F2
Inverugie Abers	103	M6
Inveruglas Ag & B	84	F2
Inveruglass Highld	99	M8
Inverurie Abers	102	G10
Inwardleigh Devon	15	K11
Inworth Essex	34	E12
Iochdar W Isls	111	a5
Iona Ag & B	88	G10
Iping W Susx	10	D5
iPort Logistics Park Donc	51	N2
Ipplepen Devon	5	Q7
Ipsden Oxon	19	Q4
Ipstones Staffs	50	D10
Ipswich Suffk	35	J7
Irby Wirral	56	F11
Irby in the Marsh Lincs	53	M10
Irby upon Humber NE Lin	52	H3
Irchester Nhants	32	D4
Ireby Cumb	71	K7
Ireby Lancs	63	M7
Ireland Cumb	62	E6
Ireleth Cumb	62	E5
Ireshopeburn Dur	72	F12
Irlam Salfd	57	N9
Irnham Lincs	42	E5
Iron Acton S Glos	29	J11
Ironbridge Wrekin	39	M2
Ironbridge Gorge Wrekin	39	M2
Ironmacannie D & G	69	P4
Ironville Derbys	51	K9
Irstead Norfk	45	M6
Irthington Cumb	71	P4
Irthlingborough Nhants	32	D3
Irton N York	67	L10
Irvine N Ayrs	76	F4
Isauld Highld	110	A3
Isbister Shet	111	k2
Isbister Shet	111	m3
Isfield E Susx	11	N6
Isham Nhants	32	C3
Isington Hants	10	C2
Islay Ag & B	82	E7
Islay Airport Ag & B	74	D3
Isle Abbotts Somset	17	J11
Isle Brewers Somset	17	K11
Isleham Cambs	33	Q2
Isle of Dogs Gt Lon	21	M7
Isle of Grain Medway	22	G7
Isle of Lewis W Isls	111	d2
Isle of Man IoM	56	c4
Isle of Man Ronaldsway Airport IoM	56	b7
Isle of Mull Ag & B	89	M8
Isle of Purbeck Dorset	8	E10
Isle of Sheppey Kent	23	J9
Isle of Skye Highld	96	E3
Isle of Thanet Kent	23	P9
Isle of Walney Cumb	62	E8
Isle of Whithorn D & G	69	L10
Isle of Wight IoW	9	N9
Isleornsay Highld	97	J7
Isles of Scilly IoS	2	c2
Isles of Scilly St Mary's Airport IoS	2	c2
Islesteps D & G	70	F2
Isleworth Gt Lon	21	J8
Isley Walton Leics	41	K3
Islibhig W Isls	111	b2
Islington Gt Lon	21	L6
Islip Nhants	32	E2
Islip Oxon	31	M10
Islivig W Isls	111	b2
Isombridge Wrekin	49	L11
Istead Rise Kent	22	D9
Itchen Abbas Hants	9	N2
Itchen Stoke Hants	9	P2
Itchingfield W Susx	11	J4
Itteringham Norfk	45	J4
Itton Mons	28	F9
Itton Common Mons	28	F9
Ivegill Cumb	71	N6
Iver Bucks	20	G7
Iver Heath Bucks	20	G6
Iveston Dur	73	K10
Ivinghoe Bucks	32	D12
Ivinghoe Aston Bucks	32	D12
Ivington Herefs	39	J10
Ivybridge Devon	5	M8
Ivychurch Kent	13	K5
Ivy Hatch Kent	22	C11
Iwade Kent	22	H9
Iwerne Courtney Dorset	8	C5
Iwerne Minster Dorset	8	C5
Ixworth Suffk	34	F3
Ixworth Thorpe Suffk	34	F3

J

Place	Page	Ref
Jack-in-the-Green Devon	6	D4
Jackton S Lans	85	K11
Jacobstow Cnwll	4	F2
Jacobstowe Devon	15	K10
Jameston Pembks	25	J8
Jamestown Highld	106	H10

Jamestown W Duns 84 G6
Janetstown Highld 110 E8
Janetstown Highld 110 G5
Jardine Hall D & G 78 H10
Jarrow S Tyne 73 N7
Jasper's Green Essex 34 C10
Jawcraig Falk 85 P7
Jaywick Essex 23 M1
Jedburgh Border 80 E9
Jeffreyston Pembks 25 J7
Jemimaville Highld 107 M8
Jerbourg Guern 6 c2
Jersey Jersey 7 b1
Jersey Airport Jersey 7 a2
Jesmond N u Ty 73 M7
Jevington E Susx 12 C9
Jockey End Herts 20 G1
Johnby Cumb 71 N8
John Lennon Airport Lpool 56 H11
John o' Groats Highld 110 H2
Johnshaven Abers 95 N8
Johnston Pembks 24 G6
Johnstone D & G 79 L8
Johnstone Rens 84 G9
Johnstonebridge D & G. 78 H9
Johnstown Carmth 25 P5
Johnstown Wrexhm 48 F6
Joppa C Edin 86 G7
Joppa Cerdgn 37 J7
Joppa S Ayrs 76 G7
Jordanston Pembks 24 G3
Joyden's Wood Kent 21 P8
Juniper Nthumb 72 G8
Juniper Green C Edin 86 E8
Jura Ag & B 82 G6
Jurassic Coast Devon 7 J5
Jurby IoM 56 c2

K

Kaber Cumb 64 E5
Kaimend S Lans 86 B11
Kames Ag & B 83 P8
Kames E Ayrs 77 L6
Kea Cnwll 3 J7
Keadby N Linc 60 E10
Keal Cotes Lincs 53 K10
Kearsley Bolton 57 N7
Kearsney Kent 13 P2
Kearstwick Cumb 63 L6
Kedington Suffk 34 B7
Kedleston Derbys 50 H11
Keelby Lincs 61 K11
Keele Staffs 49 P6
Keele Services Staffs 49 P6
Keelham C Brad 58 E7
Keeston Pembks 24 F5
Keevil Wilts 18 D8
Kegworth Leics 41 L3
Kehelland Cnwll 2 F7
Keig Abers 102 D10
Keighley C Brad 58 D6
Keilarsbrae Clacks 85 P4
Keillour P & K 92 E9
Keiloch Abers 94 C4
Keils Ag & B 82 G8
Keinton Mandeville Somset 17 M9
Keir Mill D & G 78 E9
Keisley Cumb 64 D3
Keiss Highld 110 G4
Keith Moray 101 N5
Keithick P & K 93 J7
Keithock Angus 95 K8
Keithtown Highld 106 H10
Kelbrook Lancs 58 B5
Kelby Lincs 42 E2
Keld N York 64 F7
Kelfield N York 59 N6
Kelham Notts 51 Q9
Kelhead D & G 71 J2
Kellamergh Lancs 56 H3
Kellas Angus 93 M8
Kellas Moray 101 J5
Kellaton Devon 5 Q11
Kelling Norfk 44 H2
Kellington N York 59 M8
Kelloe Dur 73 N12
Kelloholm D & G 77 N8
Kells Cumb 70 F11
Kelly Devon 5 J4
Kelmarsh Nhants 41 Q10
Kelmscott Oxon 19 J2
Kelsale Suffk 35 N4
Kelsall Ches W 49 K2
Kelshall Herts 33 K9
Kelsick Cumb 71 K5
Kelso Border 80 G7
Kelstedge Derbys 51 J7
Kelstern Lincs 53 J5
Kelston BaNES 17 Q3
Keltneyburn P & K 92 B6
Kelton D & G 70 G2
Kelty Fife 86 D4
Kelvedon Essex 34 E11
Kelvedon Hatch Essex 22 C4
Kelynack Cnwll 2 B9
Kemback Fife 93 M11
Kemberton Shrops 39 N2
Kemble Gloucs 29 P8
Kemerton Worcs 29 N2
Kemeys Commander Mons 28 D7
Kemnay Abers 102 F11
Kempley Gloucs 29 J3
Kempley Green Gloucs 29 J3
Kempsey Worcs 39 Q11
Kempsford Gloucs 18 H2
Kempshott Hants 19 P10
Kempston Bed 32 E7
Kempton Shrops 38 G5
Kemp Town Br & H 11 M8
Kemsing Kent 22 B10
Kenardington Kent 13 J4
Kenchester Herefs 38 H12
Kencot Oxon 30 G12
Kendal Cumb 63 K4
Kenfig Brdgnd 26 H11
Kenilworth Warwks 40 H12
Kenley Gt Lon 21 L10
Kenley Shrops 39 K3
Kenmore Highld 105 L10

Kenmore P & K 92 B6
Kenn Devon 6 C6
Kenn N Som 17 K3
Kennacraig Ag & B 83 M9
Kennall Vale Cnwll 2 H8
Kennerleigh Devon 15 P10
Kennet Clacks 85 Q5
Kennethmont Abers 102 C9
Kennett Cambs 34 B3
Kennford Devon 6 C5
Kenninghall Norfk 44 G11
Kennington Kent 13 K2
Kennington Oxon 19 N1
Kennoway Fife 86 G2
Kenny Somset 17 J11
Kenny Hill Suffk 33 Q2
Kennythorpe N York 60 D2
Kenovay Ag & B 88 C7
Kensaleyre Highld 104 F11
Kensington Gt Lon 21 L7
Kensington Palace Gt Lon 21 K7
Kensworth Common C Beds 32 E12
Kentallen Highld 90 D5
Kentchurch Herefs 28 E4
Kentford Suffk 34 B4
Kentisbeare Devon 6 E2
Kentisbury Devon 15 L4
Kentish Town Gt Lon 21 L6
Kentmere Cumb 63 J2
Kenton Devon 6 C6
Kenton Gt Lon 21 J6
Kenton N u Ty 73 L7
Kenton Suffk 35 K4
Kenton Bankfoot N u Ty 73 L7
Kentra Highld 89 N3
Kent's Green Gloucs 29 K4
Kent's Oak Hants 9 K3
Kenwyn Cnwll 3 J6
Keoldale Highld 108 G3
Keppoch Highld 97 M5
Kepwick N York 66 C8
Keresley Covtry 40 H10
Kerrera Ag & B 89 Q10
Kerry Powys 38 D4
Kerrycroy Ag & B 84 B10
Kersall Notts 51 Q8
Kersbrook Devon 6 E6
Kersey Suffk 34 G7
Kershader W Isls 111 d2
Kerswell Devon 6 E2
Kerswell Green Worcs 39 Q11
Kesgrave Suffk 35 K7
Kessingland Suffk 45 Q11
Kestle Cnwll 3 L4
Kestle Mill Cnwll 3 J4
Keston Gt Lon 21 N9
Keswick Cumb 71 L10
Keswick Norfk 45 K8
Kettering Nhants 32 C12
Ketteringham Norfk 45 J9
Kettins P & K 93 J7
Kettlebaston Suffk 34 F6
Kettlebridge Fife 86 G2
Kettlebrook Staffs 40 G6
Kettleburgh Suffk 35 L5
Kettleholm D & G 79 J12
Kettleshulme Ches E 50 C5
Kettlesing N York 58 G3
Kettlesing Bottom N York 58 G3
Kettlestone Norfk 44 F4
Kettlethorpe Lincs 52 C8
Kettletoft Ork 111 i1
Kettlewell N York 64 H11
Ketton Rutlnd 42 E8
Kew Gt Lon 21 J7
Kew Royal Botanic Gardens Gt Lon 21 J7
Kewstoke N Som 17 J4
Kexby C York 60 C4
Kexby Lincs 52 C6
Key Green Ches E 50 B7
Keyham Leics 41 P6
Keyhaven Hants 9 K8
Keyingham E R Yk 61 L8
Keymer W Susx 11 L7
Keynsham BaNES 17 P3
Keysoe Bed 32 F4
Keysoe Row Bed 32 F5
Keyston Cambs 32 F2
Keyworth Notts 41 N2
Kibblesworth Gatesd 73 M9
Kibworth Beauchamp Leics 41 P8
Kibworth Harcourt Leics 41 P8
Kidbrooke Gt Lon 21 N7
Kidderminster Worcs 39 Q6
Kidlington Oxon 31 L10
Kidmore End Oxon 20 B7
Kidsdale D & G 69 L10
Kidsgrove Staffs 49 Q5
Kidwelly Carmth 25 P7
Kiel Crofts Ag & B 90 C8
Kielder Nthumb 72 B3
Kielder Forest 72 B4
Kiells Ag & B 82 F8
Kilbarchan Rens 84 G9
Kilbeg Highld 97 J8
Kilberry Ag & B 83 K9
Kilbirnie N Ayrs 84 E11
Kilbride Ag & B 83 L7
Kilbride Ag & B 83 Q9
Kilbuiack Moray 100 G4
Kilburn Derbys 51 J10
Kilburn Gt Lon 21 K6
Kilburn N York 66 D10
Kilby Leics 41 N8
Kilchamaig Ag & B 83 M10
Kilchattan Ag & B 82 E4
Kilchattan Ag & B 84 B11
Kilcheran Ag & B 89 Q8
Kilchoan Highld 89 K4
Kilchoman Ag & B 82 C9
Kilchrenan Ag & B 90 E10
Kilconquhar Fife 87 J2
Kilcot Gloucs 29 J4
Kilcoy Highld 107 J11
Kilcreggan Ag & B 84 D6
Kildale N York 66 E5
Kildalloig Ag & B 75 L8
Kildary Highld 107 M7
Kildavanan Ag & B 83 Q9
Kildonan Ag & B 83 Q9
Kildonan Highld 109 Q10

Kildonan N Ayrs 75 Q8
Kildonan Lodge Highld 109 Q10
Kildonnan Highld 96 F11
Kildrochet House D & G 68 E7
Kildrummy Abers 101 N10
Kildwick N York 58 D5
Kilfinan Ag & B 83 P7
Kilfinnan Highld 98 C9
Kilgetty Pembks 25 K7
Kilgrammie S Ayrs 76 E10
Kilham E R Yk 60 H2
Kilham Nthumb 81 J7
Kilkenneth Ag & B 88 B7
Kilkenzie Ag & B 75 K7
Kilkerran Ag & B 75 L8
Kilkhampton Cnwll 14 E9
Killamarsh Derbys 51 L5
Killay Swans 26 E9
Killean Stirlg 85 J6
Killen Highld 107 L10
Killerby Darltn 65 L4
Killerton Devon 6 D3
Killichonan P & K 91 M5
Killiechonate Highld 98 C11
Killiechronan Ag & B 89 L7
Killiecrankie P & K 92 D3
Killilan Highld 97 N4
Killimster Highld 110 G4
Killin Stirlg 91 M9
Killinghall N York 58 H3
Killington Cumb 63 L6
Killington Lake Services Cumb 63 L4
Killingworth N Tyne 73 M6
Killochyett Border 87 J12
Kilmacolm Inver 84 F8
Kilmahog Stirlg 85 K2
Kilmahumaig Ag & B 83 L4
Kilmaluag Highld 104 F7
Kilmany Fife 93 L10
Kilmarnock E Ayrs 76 G4
Kilmartin Ag & B 83 M3
Kilmaurs E Ayrs 76 G3
Kilmelford Ag & B 83 L1
Kilmersdon Somset 17 Q6
Kilmeston Hants 9 P3
Kilmichael Ag & B 75 K7
Kilmichael Glassary Ag & B 83 N4
Kilmichael of Inverlussa Ag & B 83 L3
Kilmington Devon 6 H4
Kilmington Wilts 18 B12
Kilmington Common Wilts 8 B1
Kilmington Street Wilts 8 B1
Kilmorack Highld 106 H12
Kilmore Ag & B 90 B10
Kilmore Highld 97 J8
Kilmory Ag & B 83 K7
Kilmory Highld 89 L3
Kilmory N Ayrs 75 P8
Kilmuir Highld 104 C11
Kilmuir Highld 104 E8
Kilmuir Highld 107 L11
Kilmuir Highld 107 M7
Kilmun Ag & B 84 C6
Kilnave Ag & B 82 D8
Kilncadzow S Lans 77 P2
Kildown Kent 12 E3
Kilninver Ag & B 89 Q11
Kilnsea E R Yk 61 P10
Kilnsey N York 58 C1
Kilnwick E R Yk 60 G4
Kiloran Ag & B 82 E4
Kilpatrick N Ayrs 75 N7
Kilpeck Herefs 28 E3
Kilpin E R Yk 60 D8
Kilrenny Fife 87 L2
Kilsby Nhants 41 M12
Kilspindie P & K 93 J9
Kilstay D & G 68 F10
Kilsyth N Lans 85 M7
Kiltarlity Highld 98 G12
Kilton R & Cl 66 F4
Kilton Thorpe R & Cl 66 F4
Kilvaxter Highld 104 E8
Kilve Somset 16 F7
Kilvington Notts 42 B2
Kilwinning N Ayrs 76 E3
Kimberley Norfk 44 H8
Kimberley Notts 51 L11
Kimberworth Rothm 51 K3
Kimblesworth Dur 73 M10
Kimbolton Cambs 32 F4
Kimbolton Herefs 39 K9
Kimcote Leics 41 N9
Kimmeridge Dorset 8 D10
Kimpton Hants 19 J10
Kimpton Herts 32 H11
Kinbrace Highld 109 Q8
Kinbuck Stirlg 85 N3
Kincaple Fife 93 N11
Kincardine Fife 85 Q5
Kincardine Highld 107 K5
Kincardine Bridge Fife 85 P5
Kincardine O'Neil Abers 95 K3
Kinclaven P & K 92 H7
Kincorth C Aber 95 Q2
Kincorth House Moray 100 F4
Kincraig Highld 99 M7
Kincraigie P & K 92 E6
Kindallachan P & K 92 E6
Kineton Gloucs 30 E8
Kineton Warwks 31 J4
Kinfauns P & K 92 H10
Kingarth Ag & B 84 B10
Kingcausie Abers 95 P3
Kingcoed Mons 28 E7
Kingerby Lincs 52 F5
Kingford Devon 14 H10
Kingham Oxon 30 H8
Kingholm Quay D & G 70 F2
Kinghorn Fife 86 F5
Kinglassie Fife 86 E3
Kingoodie P & K 93 L9
Kingsand Cnwll 5 J9
Kingsbarns Fife 93 N12
Kingsbridge Devon 5 P10
Kingsbridge Somset 16 D8
King's Bromley Staffs 40 E4
Kingsburgh Highld 104 E10
Kingsbury Gt Lon 21 J5
Kingsbury Warwks 40 G8

Kingsbury Episcopi Somset 17 L11
King's Caple Herefs 28 G3
Kingsclere Hants 19 N8
King's Cliffe Nhants 42 E10
Kings Clipstone Notts 51 N7
Kingscote Gloucs 29 L9
Kingscott Devon 15 J8
King's Coughton Warwks 30 E3
Kingscross N Ayrs 75 Q6
Kingsdon Somset 17 M10
Kingsdown Kent 13 Q1
Kingsdown Swindn 18 H4
Kingsdown Wilts 18 B7
Kingseat Abers 103 J10
Kingseat Fife 86 D4
Kingsey Bucks 20 C3
Kingsfold W Susx 11 J3
Kingsford E Ayrs 76 G4
Kingsford Worcs 39 Q5
Kingsgate Kent 23 Q8
Kingshall Street Suffk 34 F4
King's Heath Birm 40 E9
Kings Hill Kent 22 D11
King's Hill Wsall 40 C8
Kings House Hotel Highld 90 H5
Kingshurst Solhll 40 F9
Kingskerswell Devon 6 B8
Kingskettle Fife 86 G1
Kingsland Herefs 39 J9
Kingsland IoA 54 C5
Kings Langley Herts 20 H3
Kingsley Ches W 49 L2
Kingsley Hants 10 C3
Kingsley Staffs 50 D10
Kingsley Green W Susx 10 E4
Kingsley Park Nhants 31 Q2
King's Lynn Norfk 43 P6
Kings Meaburn Cumb 64 B4
King's Mills Guern 6 b2
Kingsmuir Angus 93 N6
Kings Muir Border 79 L2
Kingsmuir Fife 87 K1
Kingsnorth Kent 13 J3
King's Norton Birm 40 D10
King's Norton Leics 41 P7
King's Nympton Devon 15 M8
King's Pyon Herefs 38 H11
Kings Ripton Cambs 33 J2
King's Somborne Hants 9 L2
King's Stag Dorset 7 Q1
King's Stanley Gloucs 29 L7
King's Sutton Nhants 31 L6
Kingstanding Birm 40 E8
Kingsteignton Devon 6 B8
Kingsthorne Herefs 28 F3
Kingsthorpe Nhants 31 Q2
Kingston Cambs 33 K6
Kingston Cnwll 4 H5
Kingston Devon 5 M10
Kingston Dorset 7 Q2
Kingston Dorset 8 D10
Kingston E Loth 87 K6
Kingston IoW 9 N10
Kingston Kent 23 M12
Kingston Bagpuize Oxon 19 L2
Kingston Blount Oxon 20 B4
Kingston Deverill Wilts 18 C12
Kingstone Herefs 28 E2
Kingstone Somset 17 K12
Kingstone Staffs 40 D2
Kingston Lacy House & Gardens Dorset 8 E7
Kingston Lisle Oxon 19 K4
Kingston near Lewes E Susx 11 N8
Kingston on Soar Notts 41 L2
Kingston on Spey Moray 101 L3
Kingston Russell Dorset 7 N5
Kingston St Mary Somset 16 H10
Kingston Seymour N Som 17 K3
Kingston upon Hull C KuH 61 J8
Kingston upon Thames Gt Lon 21 J9
King's Walden Herts 32 G11
Kingswear Devon 6 B11
Kingswells C Aber 95 P1
Kings Weston Bristl 28 G12
Kingswinford Dudley 40 B9
Kingswood Bucks 31 P9
Kingswood Gloucs 29 K9
Kingswood S Glos 17 P2
Kingswood Somset 16 F8
Kingswood Surrey 21 K11
Kingswood Warwks 40 F12
Kingswood Common Staffs 39 Q2
Kings Worthy Hants 9 N2
Kingthorpe Lincs 52 G8
Kington Herefs 38 F10
Kington S Glos 28 H10
Kington Worcs 30 C3
Kington Langley Wilts 18 D5
Kington Magna Dorset 8 B12
Kington St Michael Wilts 18 D5
Kingussie Highld 99 L8
Kingweston Somset 17 M9
Kinharrachie Abers 103 J8
Kinharvie D & G 70 F3
Kinkell Bridge P & K 92 D11
Kinknockie Abers 103 L7
Kinleith C Edin 86 E8
Kinlet Shrops 39 N6
Kinloch Highld 96 E9
Kinloch Highld 108 G6
Kinloch Highld 109 K5
Kinloch P & K 92 H6
Kinlochard Stirlg 84 H3
Kinlochbervie Highld 108 E4
Kinlocheil Highld 90 D1
Kinlochewe Highld 105 Q9
Kinloch Hourn Highld 97 N8
Kinlochlaggan Highld 98 G4
Kinlochleven Highld 90 G4
Kinlochmoidart Highld 89 P2
Kinlochnanuagh Highld 97 K11
Kinloch Rannoch P & K 91 P5
Kinloss Moray 100 G4
Kinmel Bay Conwy 55 P5
Kinmuck Abers 102 H10
Kinmundy Abers 103 J10
Kinnabus Ag & B 82 B11
Kinnadie Abers 103 K6
Kinnaird P & K 92 H7
Kinneff Abers 95 N6
Kinnelhead D & G 78 G8

Kinnell Angus 93 Q5
Kinnerley Shrops 48 G10
Kinnersley Herefs 38 G11
Kinnersley Worcs 39 Q12
Kinnerton Powys 38 E9
Kinnesswood P & K 86 E2
Kinnordy Angus 93 L5
Kinoulton Notts 41 P2
Kinross P & K 86 D2
Kinrossie P & K 92 H8
Kinross Services P & K 86 D2
Kinsham Herefs 38 G8
Kinsham Worcs 29 N2
Kinsley Wakefd 59 K10
Kinson BCP 8 F7
Kintail Highld 97 P6
Kintbury W Berk 19 L7
Kintessack Moray 100 F4
Kintillo P & K 92 G11
Kinton Herefs 38 H7
Kinton Shrops 48 G10
Kintore Abers 102 G11
Kintour Ag & B 74 F3
Kintra Ag & B 74 D3
Kintra Ag & B 88 H10
Kintraw Ag & B 83 M3
Kintyre Ag & B 75 L5
Kinveachy Highld 99 N5
Kinver Staffs 39 Q5
Kippax Leeds 59 K7
Kippen Stirlg 85 L4
Kippford D & G 70 D5
Kipping's Cross Kent 12 D3
Kirbister Ork 111 h2
Kirby Bedon Norfk 45 L8
Kirby Bellars Leics 41 Q4
Kirby Cane Norfk 45 N10
Kirby Cross Essex 35 K11
Kirby Grindalythe N York 60 F1
Kirby Hill N York 59 K1
Kirby Hill N York 65 K6
Kirby Knowle N York 66 C9
Kirby-le-Soken Essex 35 K11
Kirby Misperton N York 66 H10
Kirby Muxloe Leics 41 M6
Kirby Underdale E R Yk 60 D3
Kirby Wiske N York 65 P9
Kirdford W Susx 10 G5
Kirk Highld 110 F4
Kirkabister Shet 111 k4
Kirkandrews D & G 69 N9
Kirkandrews upon Eden Cumb 71 M4
Kirkbampton Cumb 71 L4
Kirkbean D & G 70 F4
Kirk Bramwith Donc 59 N10
Kirkbride Cumb 71 K4
Kirkbuddo Angus 93 N7
Kirkburn Border 79 L2
Kirkburn E R Yk 60 G3
Kirkburton Kirk 58 G10
Kirkby Knows 56 H8
Kirkby Lincs 52 F5
Kirkby N York 66 D6
Kirkby Fleetham N York 65 M8
Kirkby Green Lincs 52 F11
Kirkby-in-Ashfield Notts 51 L9
Kirkby-in-Furness Cumb 62 E6
Kirkby la Thorpe Lincs 42 F2
Kirkby Lonsdale Cumb 63 L6
Kirkby Malham N York 58 B3
Kirkby Mallory Leics 41 L7
Kirkby Malzeard N York 65 M11
Kirkbymoorside N York 66 F9
Kirkby on Bain Lincs 53 J10
Kirkby Overblow N York 59 J4
Kirkby Stephen Cumb 64 E6
Kirkby Thore Cumb 64 B3
Kirkby Underwood Lincs 42 F5
Kirkby Wharf N York 59 L6
Kirkcaldy Fife 86 F4
Kirkcambeck Cumb 71 Q2
Kirkchrist D & G 69 P8
Kirkcolm D & G 68 D5
Kirkconnel D & G 77 M8
Kirkconnell D & G 70 F2
Kirkcowan D & G 69 J7
Kirkcudbright D & G 69 P8
Kirkdale Lpool 56 G9
Kirk Deighton N York 59 K4
Kirk Ella E R Yk 60 H8
Kirkfieldbank S Lans 77 P3
Kirkgunzeon D & G 70 E3
Kirk Hallam Derbys 51 L11
Kirkham Lancs 56 H3
Kirkham N York 60 C2
Kirkhamgate Wakefd 58 H9
Kirk Hammerton N York 59 L3
Kirkhaugh Nthumb 72 C10
Kirkheaton Kirk 58 F9
Kirkheaton Nthumb 72 H5
Kirkhill Highld 107 J12
Kirkhope S Lans 78 F7
Kirkibost Highld 96 G6
Kirkinch P & K 93 K6
Kirkinner D & G 69 K8
Kirkintilloch E Duns 85 L8
Kirk Ireton Derbys 50 H10
Kirkland Cumb 70 H11
Kirkland D & G 77 M8
Kirkland D & G 78 D10
Kirkland D & G 78 D10
Kirk Langley Derbys 50 H11
Kirkleatham R & Cl 66 E3
Kirklevington S on T 66 B5
Kirkley Suffk 45 Q10
Kirklington N York 65 N10
Kirklington Notts 51 N9
Kirklinton Cumb 71 N3
Kirkliston C Edin 86 D7
Kirkmabreck D & G 69 L7
Kirkmaiden D & G 68 F10
Kirk Merrington Dur 65 M2
Kirk Michael IoM 56 c4
Kirkmichael P & K 94 B9
Kirkmichael S Ayrs 76 F9
Kirkmuirhill S Lans 77 N3
Kirknewton Nthumb 81 J8
Kirknewton W Loth 86 D8
Kirkney Abers 101 P8
Kirk of Shotts N Lans 85 N9
Kirkoswald Cumb 71 P6
Kirkoswald S Ayrs 76 D9

Kirkpatrick D & G 78 E10
Kirkpatrick Durham D & G 70 C2
Kirkpatrick-Fleming D & G 71 L2
Kirk Sandall Donc 59 N11
Kirksanton Cumb 62 D6
Kirk Smeaton N York 59 M10
Kirkstall Leeds 58 H7
Kirkstead Lincs 52 H10
Kirkstile Abers 102 C8
Kirkstile D & G 79 M10
Kirkstyle Highld 110 G2
Kirkthorpe Wakefd 59 J9
Kirkton Abers 102 E9
Kirkton D & G 78 F11
Kirkton Fife 93 L10
Kirkton Highld 97 L4
Kirkton Highld 97 N2
Kirkton P & K 92 E11
Kirkton Manor Border 79 K2
Kirkton of Airlie Angus 93 K5
Kirkton of Auchterhouse Angus 93 L7
Kirkton of Barevan Highld 107 N11
Kirkton of Collace P & K 92 H8
Kirkton of Glenbuchat Abers 101 M11
Kirkton of Kingoldrum Angus 93 L5
Kirkton of Lethendy P & K 92 G7
Kirkton of Logie Buchan Abers 103 K8
Kirkton of Maryculter Abers 95 P3
Kirkton of Menmuir Angus 95 J8
Kirkton of Monikie Angus 93 N7
Kirkton of Rayne Abers 102 F8
Kirkton of Skene Abers 95 N1
Kirkton of Tealing Angus 93 M7
Kirkton of Tough Abers 102 D11
Kirktown Abers 103 K3
Kirktown Abers 103 M5
Kirktown of Alvah Abers 102 E4
Kirktown of Bourtie Abers 102 G9
Kirktown of Fetteresso Abers 95 P5
Kirktown of Mortlach Moray 101 L7
Kirktown of Slains Abers 103 L9
Kirkurd Border 86 D12
Kirkwall Ork 111 h2
Kirkwall Airport Ork 111 h2
Kirkwhelpington Nthumb 72 H4
Kirk Yetholm Border 80 H8
Kirmington N Linc 61 J11
Kirmond le Mire Lincs 52 H5
Kirn Ag & B 84 C7
Kirriemuir Angus 93 L5
Kirstead Green Norfk 45 L10
Kirtlebridge D & G 71 K2
Kirtling Cambs 34 B5
Kirtling Green Cambs 34 B5
Kirtlington Oxon 31 L9
Kirtomy Highld 109 N3
Kirton Lincs 43 K3
Kirton Notts 51 P7
Kirton Suffk 35 L8
Kirtonhill W Duns 84 G7
Kirton in Lindsey N Linc 52 D4
Kirwaugh D & G 69 K8
Kishorn Highld 97 L2
Kislingbury Nhants 31 P3
Kittisford Somset 16 E10
Kitt's Green Birm 40 F9
Kittybrewster C Aber 95 Q1
Kivernoll Herefs 28 F3
Kiveton Park Rothm 51 L4
Knaith Lincs 52 B6
Knap Corner Dorset 8 B3
Knaphill Surrey 20 F10
Knapp Somset 17 J10
Knapton C York 59 M4
Knapton N York 67 J11
Knapton Norfk 45 M4
Knapwell Cambs 33 K4
Knaresborough N York 59 J3
Knarsdale Nthumb 72 C9
Knaven Abers 103 J6
Knayton N York 66 B9
Knebworth Herts 33 J11
Knedlington E R Yk 60 C8
Kneesall Notts 51 P7
Kneeton Notts 51 P10
Knelston Swans 26 C10
Knenhall Staffs 50 B12
Knightcote Warwks 31 K4
Knightley Staffs 49 P9
Knighton C Leic 41 N7
Knighton Dorset 7 N1
Knighton Powys 38 F7
Knighton Somset 16 G7
Knighton Staffs 49 N7
Knighton Staffs 49 N9
Knighton on Teme Worcs 39 L7
Knightwick Worcs 39 N10
Knill Herefs 38 F9
Knipoch Ag & B 90 B10
Knipton Leics 42 B4
Kniveton Derbys 50 G10
Knock Cumb 64 C3
Knock Highld 97 J7
Knock Moray 102 C5
Knock W Isls 111 d2
Knockally Highld 110 D9
Knockan Highld 106 D1
Knockando Moray 101 J7
Knockbain Highld 98 H1
Knockbain Highld 107 K10
Knock Castle N Ayrs 84 D9
Knockdee Highld 110 D4
Knockdow Ag & B 84 B8
Knockdown Wilts 18 C3
Knockeen S Ayrs 76 E11
Knockenkelly N Ayrs 75 Q7
Knockentiber E Ayrs 76 G4
Knockholt Kent 21 P10
Knockholt Pound Kent 21 P10
Knockin Shrops 48 G10
Knockinlaw E Ayrs 76 G4
Knocknain D & G 68 C6
Knockrome Ag & B 82 H8
Knocksharry IoM 56 b4
Knocksheen D & G 69 N3
Knockvennie Smithy D & G 70 C2
Knodishall Suffk 35 N4
Knodishall Common Suffk 35 P5
Knole Somset 17 L10
Knolls Green Ches E 57 P11

Knolton Wrexhm 48 H7
Knook Wilts 18 D11
Knossington Leics 42 B8
Knott End-on-Sea Lancs 62 G11
Knotting Bed 32 E4
Knotting Green Bed 32 E4
Knottingley Wakefd 59 L9
Knotty Ash Lpool 56 H9
Knowbury Shrops 39 L7
Knowe D & G 69 J5
Knowehead D & G 69 N2
Knoweside S Ayrs 76 E8
Knowle Bristl 17 N3
Knowle Devon 6 D2
Knowle Devon 6 E6
Knowle Devon 15 J5
Knowle Devon 15 N10
Knowle Shrops 39 L7
Knowle Solhll 40 F11
Knowle Somset 16 C7
Knowlefield Cumb 71 N4
Knowle Green Lancs 57 L2
Knowle St Giles Somset 7 J1
Knowl Hill W & M 20 D7
Knowsley Knows 56 H9
Knowsley Safari Park Knows 57 J9
Knowstone Devon 15 P7
Knox Bridge Kent 12 F2
Knoydart Highld 97 L8
Knucklas Powys 38 F7
Knuston Nhants 32 D4
Knutsford Ches E 57 N12
Knutsford Services Ches E 57 N12
Krumlin Calder 58 D9
Kuggar Cnwll 2 G11
Kyleakin Highld 97 K4
Kyle of Lochalsh Highld 97 K4
Kylerhea Highld 97 L5
Kylesku Highld 108 E8
Kylesmorar Highld 97 L10
Kyles Scalpay W Isls 111 c3
Kylestrome Highld 108 E8
Kynnersley Wrekin 49 M11
Kyrewood Worcs 39 L8

L

Lacasaigh W Isls 111 d2
Lacasdal W Isls 111 d2
Laceby NE Lin 52 H3
Lacey Green Bucks 20 D4
Lach Dennis Ches W 49 N2
Lackford Suffk 34 D3
Lackford Green Suffk 34 D3
Lacock Wilts 18 D7
Ladbroke Warwks 31 K3
Laddingford Kent 12 E1
Ladock Cnwll 3 K5
Lady Ork 111 i1
Ladybank Fife 93 K12
Ladygill S Lans 78 F4
Lady Hall Cumb 62 E5
Ladykirk Border 81 J5
Ladywood Birm 40 D9
Ladywood Worcs 39 Q9
La Fontenelle Guern 6 c1
Lag D & G 78 E10
Laga Highld 89 N4
Lagavulin Ag & B 74 F4
Lagg N Ayrs 75 P7
Laggan Highld 98 D9
Laggan Highld 99 J9
Lagganlia Highld 99 M8
La Grève de Lecq Jersey 7 a1
Laid Highld 108 H4
Laide Highld 105 N4
Laig Highld 96 F11
Laigh Clunch E Ayrs 76 H2
Laigh Fenwick E Ayrs 76 H3
Laigh Glenmuir E Ayrs 77 K7
Laighstonehall S Lans 85 M11
Laindon Essex 22 D5
Lairg Highld 107 J2
Laisterdyke C Brad 58 F7
Lake IoW 9 P10
Lake Wilts 18 G11
Lake District Cumb 71 K12
Lake District National Park Cumb 71 K12
Lakenheath Suffk 44 B12
Lakes End Norfk 43 N10
Laleston Brdgnd 27 J11
Lamarsh Essex 34 E9
Lamas Norfk 45 L5
Lambden Border 80 G5
Lamberhurst Kent 12 D3
Lamberhurst Down Kent 12 D3
Lamberton Border 81 K3
Lambeth Gt Lon 21 L7
Lambfair Green Suffk 34 B6
Lambley Notts 51 N10
Lambley Nthumb 72 C8
Lambourn W Berk 19 K5
Lambourne End Essex 21 P5
Lambs Green W Susx 11 K3
Lamerton Devon 5 K5
Lamesley Gatesd 73 M8
Lamington S Lans 78 F3
Lamlash N Ayrs 75 Q6
Lamonby Cumb 71 N8
Lamorna Cnwll 2 C10
Lamorran Cnwll 3 K7
Lampeter Cerdgn 37 J10
Lampeter Velfrey Pembks 25 K6
Lamphey Pembks 24 H8
Lamplugh Cumb 70 H10
Lamport Nhants 41 Q11
Lamyatt Somset 17 P8
Lanark S Lans 78 F3
Lancaster Lancs 63 J10
Lancaster Services Lancs 63 J10
Lanchester Dur 73 L10
Lancing W Susx 11 J8
L'Ancresse Guern 6 c1
Landbeach Cambs 33 M4
Landcross Devon 14 H7
Landerberry Abers 95 M2
Landford Wilts 9 J4
Land-hallow Highld 110 E8
Landimore Swans 26 C9

Landkey Devon 15 K6
Landore Swans 26 F9
Landrake Cnwll 4 H7
Land's End Airport Cnwll 2 B9
Landulph Cnwll 5 J7
Lane Cnwll 3 J4
Laneast Cnwll 4 F4
Lane End Bucks 20 D5
Lane End Wilts 18 B10
Lane Ends Derbys 40 G1
Laneham Notts 52 B8
Lane Head Dur 65 K5
Lanehead Dur 72 F11
Lane Head Wsall 40 C7
Lane Side Lancs 57 P4
Langal Highld 89 P3
Langaller Somset 16 H10
Langar Notts 41 Q1
Langbank Rens 84 G8
Langbar N York 58 E4
Langcliffe N York 63 P8
Langdale End N York 67 K8
Langdon Cnwll 4 G3
Langdon Beck Dur 72 F11
Langdown Hants 9 M6
Langdyke Fife 86 G2
Langenhoe Essex 34 G11
Langford C Beds 32 H8
Langford Devon 6 D3
Langford Essex 22 G2
Langford Notts 52 B10
Langford Oxon 30 G12
Langford Budville Somset 16 F10
Langham Essex 34 G9
Langham Norfk 44 G2
Langham Rutlnd 42 B7
Langham Suffk 34 F3
Langho Lancs 57 N3
Langholm D & G 79 M11
Langland Swans 26 E10
Langlee Border 80 C7
Langley Hants 9 M6
Langley Herts 32 H11
Langley Kent 22 F11
Langley Nthumb 72 E8
Langley Slough 20 G7
Langley Somset 16 E9
Langley W Susx 10 D4
Langley Warwks 30 F2
Langley Burrell Wilts 18 D6
Langley Green Essex 34 E11
Langley Marsh Somset 16 E9
Langley Mill Derbys 51 K10
Langley Park Dur 73 L11
Langley Street Norfk 45 N9
Langley Upper Green Essex 33 M9
Langney E Susx 12 D9
Langold Notts 51 N4
Langore Cnwll 4 G3
Langport Somset 17 K10
Langrick Lincs 43 J1
Langridge BaNES 17 Q3
Langrigg Cumb 71 J6
Langrish Hants 10 B5
Langsett Barns 50 G2
Langside P & K 92 B11
Langstone Hants 10 B8
Langthorne N York 65 M6
Langthorpe N York 59 K1
Langthwaite N York 64 H7
Langtoft E R Yk 60 H2
Langtoft Lincs 42 G7
Langton Dur 65 L4
Langton Lincs 52 H9
Langton Lincs 53 L9
Langton N York 60 D2
Langton by Wragby Lincs 52 G7
Langton Green Kent 12 B3
Langton Herring Dorset 7 N6
Langton Matravers Dorset 8 E10
Langtree Devon 14 H8
Langwathby Cumb 71 R8
Langwell House Highld 110 D8
Langwith Derbys 51 M6
Langwith Junction Derbys 51 L7
Langworth Lincs 52 F8
Lanhydrock House & Gardens Cnwll 3 N3
Lanivet Cnwll 3 M3
Lanlivery Cnwll 3 N4
Lanner Cnwll 2 G7
Lanreath Cnwll 4 E8
Lansallos Cnwll 4 E9
Lanteglos Cnwll 4 D4
Lanteglos Highway Cnwll 4 E9
Lanton Border 80 E7
Lanton Nthumb 81 K7
Lapford Devon 15 M9
Laphroaig Ag & B 74 E4
Lapley Staffs 49 Q11
Lapworth Warwks 40 F12
Larachbeg Highld 89 N6
Larbert Falk 85 P6
Largie Abers 102 D8
Largiemore Ag & B 83 P6
Largoward Fife 87 J1
Largs N Ayrs 84 D10
Largybeg N Ayrs 75 Q7
Largymore N Ayrs 75 Q7
Larkfield Inver 84 D7
Larkfield Kent 22 E11
Larkhall S Lans 77 M2
Larkhill Wilts 18 G11
Larling Norfk 44 G11
La Rocque Jersey 7 c2
Lartington Dur 65 J4
Lasham Hants 19 Q11
Lashenden Kent 12 G2
Lastingham N York 66 G9
Latchford Warrtn 57 L10
Latchingdon Essex 22 G3
Latchley Cnwll 5 J5
Lathbury M Keyn 32 C7
Latheron Highld 110 E8
Latheronwheel Highld 110 E8
Lathones Fife 87 J1
Latimer Bucks 20 G4
Latteridge S Glos 29 J10
Lattiford Somset 17 P10
Latton Wilts 18 G2
Lauder Border 80 C5
Laugharne Carmth 25 M6
Laughterton Lincs 52 B8
Laughton E Susx 11 P7

Laughton Leics 41 P9
Laughton Lincs 42 F4
Laughton Lincs 52 B4
Laughton-en-le-Morthen Rothm 51 M4
Launceston Cnwll 4 H4
Launton Oxon 31 N9
Laurencekirk Abers 95 L7
Laurieston D & G 69 P6
Laurieston Falk 85 Q7
Lavendon M Keyn 32 D6
Lavenham Suffk 34 F7
Lavernock V Glam 16 G3
Laversdale Cumb 71 P3
Laverstock Wilts 8 H2
Laverstoke Hants 19 N10
Laverton Gloucs 30 E7
Laverton N York 65 M11
Laverton Somset 18 B9
La Villette Guern 6 b2
Lavister Wrexhm 48 G4
Law S Lans 85 N11
Lawers P & K 91 Q8
Lawford Essex 34 H9
Lawford Somset 16 F8
Law Hill S Lans 85 N11
Lawhitton Cnwll 4 H4
Lawkland N York 63 P8
Lawrence Weston Bristl 28 G11
Lawrenny Pembks 24 H7
Lawshall Suffk 34 E6
Laxay W Isls 111 d2
Laxdale W Isls 111 d2
Laxey IoM 56 d4
Laxfield Suffk 35 L3
Laxford Bridge Highld 108 E6
Laxo Shet 111 k3
Laxton E R Yk 60 D8
Laxton Nhants 42 D10
Laxton Notts 51 Q7
Laycock C Brad 58 D6
Layer Breton Essex 34 F12
Layer-de-la-Haye Essex 34 F11
Layer Marney Essex 34 F12
Layham Suffk 34 G8
Laymore Dorset 7 K2
Laytham E R Yk 60 D6
Lazonby Cumb 71 Q7
Lea Derbys 51 J8
Lea Herefs 28 H4
Lea Lincs 52 B6
Lea Shrops 38 G4
Lea Wilts 18 E4
Leachkin Highld 107 K12
Leadburn Border 86 F10
Leadenham Lincs 52 D11
Leaden Roding Essex 22 C1
Leadgate Dur 73 K9
Leadhills S Lans 78 E6
Leafield Oxon 30 H10
Leagrave Luton 32 F11
Leake Common Side Lincs 53 L11
Lealholm N York 66 G6
Lealt Ag & B 104 G9
Lea Marston Warwks 40 G8
Leamington Hastings Warwks 31 K1
Leamington Spa Warwks 30 H2
Leap Cross E Susx 12 C7
Leasgill Cumb 63 J5
Leasingham Lincs 42 F1
Leasingthorne Dur 65 M2
Leatherhead Surrey 21 J11
Leathley N York 58 G5
Leaton Shrops 49 J10
Leaveland Kent 23 J11
Leavenheath Suffk 34 F8
Leavening N York 60 D2
Leaves Green Gt Lon 21 N10
Lebberston N York 67 M10
Le Bourg Guern 6 b2
Lechlade on Thames Gloucs 18 H2
Lecht Gruinart Ag & B 82 D8
Leck Lancs 63 M6
Leckbuie P & K 91 Q8
Leckford Hants 19 L12
Leckhampstead Bucks 31 Q6
Leckhampstead W Berk 19 M5
Leckhampstead Thicket W Berk 19 M5
Leckhampton Gloucs 29 N5
Leckmelm Highld 106 C4
Leconfield E R Yk 60 H5
Ledaig Ag & B 90 C8
Ledburn Bucks 32 C11
Ledbury Herefs 29 J2
Ledgemoor Herefs 38 H11
Ledmore Highld 108 E12
Ledsham Leeds 59 L8
Ledston Leeds 59 L8
Ledwell Oxon 31 K8
Lee Devon 14 H3
Lee Gt Lon 21 M8
Leebotwood Shrops 39 J3
Lee Brockhurst Shrops 49 K9
Leece Cumb 62 E8
Lee Chapel Essex 22 E6
Lee Clump Bucks 20 E3
Leeds Kent 22 G11
Leeds Leeds 58 H7
Leeds Bradford Airport Leeds 58 G6
Leeds Castle Kent 22 G11
Leedstown Cnwll 2 E8
Leek Staffs 50 C9
Leek Wootton Warwks 30 H1
Lee Mill Devon 5 M8
Leeming N York 65 M9
Leeming Bar N York 65 M9
Lee-on-the-Solent Hants 9 N7
Lees Derbys 50 H12
Lees Oldham 58 C12
Lees Green Derbys 50 H12
Leeswood Flints 48 F4
Leetown P & K 93 J9
Leftwich Ches W 49 M2
Legbourne Lincs 53 L6
Legerwood Border 80 D5
Legoland W & M 20 F8
Legsby Lincs 52 G6
Leicester C Leic 41 N6
Leicester Forest East Services Leics 41 M7

Leigh Dorset 7 N2
Leigh Gloucs 29 M4
Leigh Kent 12 B2
Leigh Surrey 11 K1
Leigh Wigan 57 M8
Leigh Wilts 18 F3
Leigh Worcs 39 P10
Leigh Beck Essex 22 F6
Leigh Delamere Wilts 18 C5
Leigh Delamere Services Wilts 18 D5
Leigh Green Kent 12 H4
Leigh Knoweglass S Lans 77 K2
Leigh-on-Sea Shend 22 G6
Leigh Park Dorset 8 F7
Leigh Park Hants 10 B8
Leigh Sinton Worcs 39 P11
Leighswood Wsall 40 D7
Leighterton Gloucs 29 L9
Leighton Powys 38 E2
Leighton Shrops 39 L2
Leighton Bromswold Cambs 32 G2
Leighton Buzzard C Beds 32 D10
Leigh upon Mendip Somset 17 Q6
Leigh Woods N Som 17 N2
Leinthall Earls Herefs 39 H8
Leinthall Starkes Herefs 38 H8
Leintwardine Herefs 38 H7
Leire Leics 41 M9
Leiston Suffk 35 P4
Leith C Edin 86 F7
Leitholm Border 80 G5
Lelant Cnwll 2 E8
Lelley E R Yk 61 L7
Lempitlaw Border 80 G7
Lemreway W Isls 111 d3
Lemsford Herts 21 K2
Lenchwick Worcs 30 D5
Lendalfoot S Ayrs 68 F2
Lendrick Stirlg 85 J2
Lendrum Terrace Abers 103 M7
Lenham Kent 22 H11
Lenham Heath Kent 22 H12
Lenie Highld 98 G4
Lennel Border 80 H6
Lennox Plunton D & G 69 N8
Lennoxtown E Duns 85 K7
Lenton C Nott 51 M11
Lenton Lincs 42 E4
Lenwade Norfk 44 H6
Lenzie E Duns 85 L8
Leochel-Cushnie Abers 102 C12
Leominster Herefs 39 J9
Leonard Stanley Gloucs 29 L7
Lephin Highld 104 B11
Leppington N York 60 D2
Lepton Kirk 58 G10
Lerags Ag & B 90 B10
L'Erée Guern 6 a2
Lerryn Cnwll 4 E8
Lerwick Shet 111 k4
Lesbury Nthumb 81 P10
Leslie Abers 102 D9
Leslie Fife 86 F2
Lesmahagow S Lans 78 D2
Lesnewth Cnwll 4 E3
Les Quartiers Guern 6 c1
Les Quennevais Jersey 7 a2
Lessingham Norfk 45 N5
Lessonhall Cumb 71 K5
Leswalt D & G 68 D6
L'Etacq Jersey 7 a1
Letchmore Heath Herts 21 J4
Letchworth Garden City Herts 32 H9
Letcombe Bassett Oxon 19 L4
Letcombe Regis Oxon 19 L4
Letham Angus 93 P6
Letham Border 80 F11
Letham Falk 85 P6
Letham Fife 93 K11
Letham Grange Angus 93 Q6
Lethenty Abers 102 D10
Lethenty Abers 102 H7
Letheringham Suffk 35 L5
Letheringsett Norfk 44 H3
Letterewe Highld 105 P7
Letterfearn Highld 97 M5
Letterfinlay Lodge Hotel Highld 98 C10
Lettermorar Highld 97 K10
Letters Highld 106 C5
Lettershaw S Lans 78 E5
Letterston Pembks 24 G3
Lettoch Highld 99 Q5
Lettoch Highld 100 H6
Letton Herefs 38 G11
Letty Green Herts 21 L2
Letwell Rothm 51 M4
Leuchars Fife 93 M10
Leumrabhagh W Isls 111 d3
Leurbost W Isls 111 d2
Levedale Staffs 40 B4
Leven E R Yk 61 J5
Leven Fife 86 H3
Levens Cumb 63 J5
Levens Green Herts 33 K11
Levenshulme Manch 57 Q9
Levenwick Shet 111 k5
Leverburgh W Isls 111 c4
Leverington Cambs 43 M7
Leverstock Green Herts 20 H3
Leverton Lincs 43 L3
Le Villocq Guern 6 b1
Levington Suffk 35 K8
Levisham N York 67 J9
Lew Oxon 31 J11
Lewannick Cnwll 4 K3
Lewdown Devon 5 K3
Lewes E Susx 11 N7
Leweston Pembks 24 G4
Lewisham Gt Lon 21 M8
Lewiston Highld 98 G4
Lewknor Oxon 20 B4
Lewson Street Kent 23 J10
Lewtrenchard Devon 5 K3
Lexden Essex 34 F10
Lexworthy Somset 16 H8
Leybourne Kent 22 D10
Leyburn N York 65 K9
Leygreen Herts 32 G10

Ley Hill Bucks 20 F3
Leyland Lancs 57 K4
Leylodge Abers 102 G11
Leys Abers 103 K5
Leys P & K 93 J7
Leysdown-on-Sea Kent 23 K8
Leysmill Angus 93 Q6
Leys of Cossans Angus 93 L6
Leysters Herefs 39 K8
Leyton Gt Lon 21 M6
Leytonstone Gt Lon 21 N6
Lezant Cnwll 4 H4
Lhanbryde Moray 101 K3
Libanus Powys 27 L4
Libberton S Lans 78 G1
Liberton C Edin 86 F8
Lichfield Staffs 40 E5
Lickey Worcs 40 C11
Lickey End Worcs 40 C11
Lickfold W Susx 10 E5
Liddesdale Highld 89 Q4
Liddington Swindn 18 H5
Lidgate Suffk 34 C5
Lidlington C Beds 32 E8
Liff Angus 93 L8
Lifford Birm 40 D10
Lifton Devon 5 J3
Liftondown Devon 4 H3
Lighthorne Warwks 31 J3
Lighthorne Heath Warwks 31 J3
Lightwater Surrey 20 E10
Lightwater Valley Theme
   Park N York 65 M11
Lightwood C Stke 50 B11
Lilbourne Nhants 41 M11
Lilleshall Wrekin 49 N11
Lilley Herts 32 G10
Lilliesleaf Border 80 C8
Lillingstone Dayrell Bucks 31 P6
Lillingstone Lovell Bucks 31 P6
Lillington Dorset 7 P1
Lilliput BCP 8 F9
Lilstock Somset 16 F7
Limbury Luton 32 F11
Limekilnburn S Lans 77 M2
Limekilns Fife 86 C5
Limerigg Falk 85 P8
Limerstone IoW 9 M10
Lime Street Worcs 29 L3
Limington Somset 17 M10
Limmerhaugh E Ayrs 77 K6
Limpenhoe Norfk 45 N8
Limpley Stoke Wilts 18 B8
Limpsfield Surrey 21 N11
Limpsfield Chart Surrey 21 N11
Linby Notts 51 M9
Linchmere W Susx 10 D4
Lincluden D & G 78 F12
Lincoln Lincs 52 D8
Lincomb Worcs 39 P8
Lindale Cumb 62 H6
Lindal in Furness Cumb 62 F7
Lindfield W Susx 11 M5
Lindford Hants 10 D3
Lindley Kirk 58 E9
Lindores Fife 93 K11
Lindridge Worcs 39 M8
Lindsell Essex 33 Q10
Lindsey Suffk 34 G7
Lindsey Tye Suffk 34 G7
Lingdale R & Cl 66 F4
Lingen Herefs 38 G8
Lingfield Surrey 11 M2
Lingwood Norfk 45 M8
Liniclate W Isls 111 b5
Linicro Highld 104 E8
Linkend Worcs 29 L3
Linkenholt Hants 19 L8
Linkinhorne Cnwll 4 G5
Linktown Fife 86 F4
Linkwood Moray 101 K3
Linley Shrops 38 G4
Linley Green Herefs 39 M10
Linlithgow W Loth 86 B6
Linsidemore Highld 107 J3
Linslade C Beds 32 C10
Linstead Parva Suffk 35 M2
Linstock Cumb 71 N4
Linthurst Worcs 40 D11
Linthwaite Kirk 58 E10
Lintlaw Border 87 Q9
Lintmill Moray 101 P3
Linton Border 80 G8
Linton Cambs 33 P7
Linton Derbys 40 H4
Linton Herefs 28 H4
Linton Kent 22 F12
Linton Leeds 59 K5
Linton N York 58 C2
Linton Hill Herefs 29 J4
Linton-on-Ouse N York 59 L3
Linwood Lincs 52 G6
Linwood Rens 84 G9
Lionacleit W Isls 111 b5
Lional W Isls 111 e1
Liphook Hants 10 D4
Liscard Wirral 56 F9
Liscombe Somset 15 P5
Liskeard Cnwll 4 F7
Lismore Ag & B 90 B7
Liss Hants 10 C5
Lissett E R Yk 61 K3
Lissington Lincs 52 G6
Lisvane Cardif 27 P11
Liswerry Newpt 28 D10
Litcham Norfk 44 E6
Litchborough Nhants 31 N4
Litchfield Hants 19 M9
Litherland Sefton 56 G8
Litlington Cambs 33 K8
Litlington E Susx 11 Q9
Little Abington Cambs 33 N7
Little Addington Nhants 32 D3
Little Airies D & G 69 K9
Little Alne Warwks 30 F2
Little Altcar Sefton 56 F7
Little Amwell Herts 21 M2
Little Aston Staffs 40 E7
Little Ayton N York 66 D5
Little Baddow Essex 22 H4
Little Badminton S Glos 18 B4
Little Bampton Cumb 71 L5

Little Bardfield Essex 33 Q9
Little Barford Bed 32 H5
Little Barningham Norfk 45 J4
Little Barrington Gloucs 30 G10
Little Barrow Ches W 49 J2
Little Bavington Nthumb 72 H5
Little Bedwyn Wilts 19 K7
Little Bentley Essex 35 J10
Little Berkhamsted Herts 21 L2
Little Billing Nhants 32 B4
Little Billington C Beds 32 D11
Little Birch Herefs 28 F3
Little Blakenham Suffk 34 H7
Little Blencow Cumb 71 P8
Little Bognor W Susx 10 G6
Little Bollington Ches E 57 N10
Little Bookham Surrey 20 H11
Littleborough Notts 52 B7
Littleborough Rochdl 58 C10
Littlebourne Kent 23 N11
Little Bourton Oxon 31 L5
Little Braxted Essex 22 G1
Little Brechin Angus 95 J9
Littlebredy Dorset 7 N5
Little Brickhill M Keyn 32 C9
Little Brington Nhants 31 P2
Little Bromley Essex 34 H10
Little Budworth Ches W 49 L3
Littleburn Highld 107 K10
Little Burstead Essex 22 D5
Littlebury Essex 33 N8
Littlebury Green Essex 33 M8
Little Bytham Lincs 42 E6
Little Carlton Lincs 53 L6
Little Casterton Rutlnd 42 E8
Little Cawthorpe Lincs 53 K6
Little Chalfont Bucks 20 F4
Little Chart Kent 12 H2
Little Chesterford Essex 33 N8
Little Cheverell Wilts 18 E9
Little Chishill Cambs 33 L8
Little Clacton Essex 35 J11
Little Clifton Cumb 70 H9
Little Coates NE Lin 53 J2
Little Comberton Worcs 30 C5
Little Common E Susx 12 E8
Little Compton Warwks 30 H7
Little Cornard Suffk 34 E8
Little Cowarne Herefs 39 L11
Little Coxwell Oxon 19 K3
Little Crakehall N York 65 M9
Little Cressingham Norfk 44 E9
Little Crosby Sefton 56 G8
Little Cubley Derbys 50 F12
Little Dalby Leics 41 Q5
Littledean Gloucs 29 J6
Little Dewchurch Herefs 28 F3
Little Ditton Cambs 33 Q5
Little Downham Cambs 43 N12
Little Driffield E R Yk 60 H3
Little Dunham Norfk 44 E7
Little Dunkeld P & K 92 F7
Little Dunmow Essex 33 Q11
Little Durnford Wilts 8 G1
Little Easton Essex 33 P11
Little Eaton Derbys 51 J11
Little Ellingham Norfk 44 G9
Little Everdon Nhants 31 N3
Little Eversden Cambs 33 L6
Little Faringdon Oxon 19 J1
Little Fencote N York 65 M8
Little Fenton N York 59 M7
Littleferry Highld 107 N4
Little Fransham Norfk 44 F7
Little Gaddesden Herts 20 F2
Little Glemham Suffk 35 M5
Little Gorsley Herefs 29 J4
Little Gransden Cambs 33 J6
Little Green Somset 17 Q6
Little Hadham Herts 33 M11
Little Hale Lincs 42 G2
Little Hallam Derbys 51 L11
Little Hallingbury Essex 33 N11
Littleham Devon 6 D6
Littleham Devon 14 H7
Littlehampton W Susx 10 G9
Little Harrowden Nhants 32 C3
Little Haseley Oxon 19 Q1
Little Haven Pembks 24 F6
Littlehaven W Susx 10 J4
Little Hay Staffs 40 E7
Little Haywood Staffs 40 D3
Littlehempston Devon 5 Q7
Little Hereford Herefs 39 L8
Little Horkesley Essex 34 F9
Little Hormead Herts 33 L10
Little Horsted E Susx 11 P6
Little Horton C Brad 58 F7
Little Horwood Bucks 32 B10
Little Houghton Barns 59 K11
Little Houghton Nhants 32 B5
Little Hucklow Derbys 50 F5
Little Hutton N York 66 C11
Little Irchester Nhants 32 C4
Little Keyford Somset 18 B10
Little Kimble Bucks 20 D3
Little Kineton Warwks 31 J4
Little Kingshill Bucks 20 E4
Little Knox D & G 70 D4
Little Langdale Cumb 62 G2
Little Langford Wilts 18 F12
Little Leigh Ches W 49 L1
Little Leighs Essex 34 C12
Little Lever Bolton 57 N7
Little Linford M Keyn 32 B7
Little Load Somset 17 L10
Little London Cambs 43 L10
Little London E Susx 12 C6
Little London Hants 19 L10
Little London Hants 19 Q8
Little Longstone Derbys 50 F6
Little Maplestead Essex 34 D9
Little Marcle Herefs 29 J2
Little Marlow Bucks 20 E6
Little Massingham Norfk 44 D5
Little Melton Norfk 45 J8
Littlemill Abers 94 E3
Littlemill Highld 100 E5
Little Mill Mons 28 C8
Little Milton Oxon 19 Q1
Little Missenden Bucks 20 E4
Littlemore Oxon 19 M1

Little Musgrave Cumb 64 D5
Little Ness Shrops 48 H10
Little Newcastle Pembks 24 G3
Little Newsham Dur 65 K4
Little Norton Somset 17 L11
Little Oakley Essex 35 K10
Little Oakley Nhants 42 C11
Little Orton Cumb 71 M5
Littleover C Derb 41 J1
Little Packington Warwks 40 G9
Little Paxton Cambs 32 H4
Little Petherick Cnwll 3 K2
Little Plumstead Norfk 45 M7
Little Ponton Lincs 42 D4
Littleport Cambs 43 P11
Little Preston Nhants 31 N4
Little Raveley Cambs 33 J2
Little Reedness E R Yk 60 D9
Little Ribston N York 59 J4
Little Rissington Gloucs 30 F9
Little Rollright Oxon 30 H7
Little Ryburgh Norfk 44 F5
Little Ryle Nthumb 81 L9
Little Salkeld Cumb 71 Q8
Little Sampford Essex 33 Q9
Little Saughall Ches W 48 G2
Little Saxham Suffk 34 D4
Little Scatwell Highld 106 F10
Little Shelford Cambs 33 M6
Little Singleton Lancs 56 G2
Little Skipwith N York 59 P6
Little Smeaton N York 59 M10
Little Snoring Norfk 44 F4
Little Sodbury S Glos 18 A4
Little Somborne Hants 9 L2
Little Somerford Wilts 18 E4
Little Soudley Shrops 49 N9
Little Stainton Darltn 65 N4
Little Stanney Ches W 48 H1
Little Staughton Bed 32 G4
Little Steeping Lincs 53 M10
Little Stoke Staffs 40 B2
Littlestone-on-Sea Kent 13 L5
Little Stonham Suffk 35 J5
Little Stretton Leics 41 P7
Little Stretton Shrops 39 J4
Little Strickland Cumb 71 Q10
Little Stukeley Cambs 32 H2
Little Sugnall Staffs 49 P8
Little Swinburne Nthumb 72 G5
Little Sypland D & G 70 B5
Little Tew Oxon 31 J8
Little Tey Essex 34 E11
Little Thetford Cambs 33 N2
Little Thorpe Dur 73 Q11
Littlethorpe Leics 41 M7
Littlethorpe N York 59 J1
Little Thurlow Suffk 34 B6
Little Thurrock Thurr 22 D7
Littleton Angus 93 L5
Littleton Ches W 48 H3
Littleton D & G 69 P7
Littleton Hants 9 M2
Littleton Somset 17 L9
Littleton Surrey 20 H9
Littleton Drew Wilts 18 C5
Littleton-on-Severn S Glos 28 H10
Littleton Pannell Wilts 18 E9
Little Torrington Devon 15 J8
Littletown Dur 73 N11
Little Town Lancs 57 M2
Little Urswick Cumb 62 F7
Little Wakering Essex 22 H6
Little Walden Essex 33 N8
Little Waldingfield Suffk 34 F7
Little Walsingham Norfk 44 F4
Little Waltham Essex 22 E2
Little Weighton E R Yk 60 G7
Little Wenlock Wrekin 39 M2
Little Weston Somset 17 N10
Little Whitefield IoW 9 P9
Littlewick Green W & M 20 D7
Little Wilbraham Cambs 33 N5
Little Witcombe Gloucs 29 M6
Little Witley Worcs 39 P8
Little Wittenham Oxon 19 P3
Little Wolford Warwks 30 H7
Littleworth Gt Lon 21 L10
Littleworth Staffs 40 C3
Littleworth W Susx 10 J4
Littleworth Worcs 30 B4
Little Wymington Bed 32 D4
Little Wymondley Herts 32 H10
Little Wyrley Staffs 40 D6
Little Yeldham Essex 34 C8
Littley Green Essex 34 B12
Litton Derbys 50 F6
Litton N York 64 G11
Litton Somset 17 M5
Litton Cheney Dorset 7 M5
Liurbost W Isls 111 d2
Liverpool Lpool 56 G10
Liverpool Maritime
   Mercantile City Lpool 56 G10
Liversedge Kirk 58 G9
Liverton Devon 5 Q4
Liverton R & Cl 66 G4
Livingston W Loth 86 C8
Livingston Village W Loth 86 C8
Lixwm Flints 48 D2
Lizard Cnwll 2 G12
Llanaelhaearn Gwynd 46 E4
Llanafan Cerdgn 37 L6
Llanafan-Fawr Powys 37 Q9
Llanallgo IoA 54 G5
Llanarmon Dyffryn Ceiriog
   Wrexhm 48 D8
Llanarmon-yn-Ial Denbgs 48 E4
Llanarth Cerdgn 36 G9
Llanarth Mons 28 D6
Llanarthne Carmth 26 D5
Llanasa Flints 56 C11
Llanbadarn Fawr Cerdgn 37 K4
Llanbadarn Fynydd Powys 38 C6
Llanbadoc Mons 28 D8
Llanbeder Newpt 28 D10
Llanbedr Gwynd 47 J6
Llanbedr Powys 27 P5
Llanbedr-Dyffryn-Clwyd
   Denbgs 48 D4
Llanbedrgoch IoA 54 G5
Llanbedrog Gwynd 46 E5
Llanbedr-y-Cennin Conwy 55 L7

Llanberis Gwynd 54 H9
Llanbethêry V Glam 16 D3
Llanbister Powys 38 C7
Llanblethian V Glam 16 D2
Llanboidy Carmth 25 L4
Llanbradach Caerph 27 N10
Llanbrynmair Powys 47 P10
Llancadle V Glam 16 D3
Llancarfan V Glam 16 E3
Llancloudy Herefs 28 F5
Llandaff Cardif 27 N12
Llandanwg Gwynd 47 J5
Llanddaniel Fab IoA 54 G7
Llanddarog Carmth 26 C5
Llanddeiniol Cerdgn 37 J6
Llanddeiniolen Gwynd 54 G8
Llandderfel Gwynd 47 R4
Llanddeusant Carmth 26 G5
Llanddew Powys 27 M3
Llanddewi Swans 26 B10
Llanddewi Brefi Cerdgn 37 L9
Llanddewi Rhydderch Mons 28 D6
Llanddewi Velfrey Pembks 25 K5
Llanddewi Ystradenni Powys 38 C8
Llanddoged Conwy 55 L8
Llanddona IoA 54 H5
Llanddowror Carmth 25 M6
Llanddulas Conwy 55 N6
Llanddwywe Gwynd 47 J6
Llanddyfnan IoA 54 G6
Llandefaelog-Tre'r-Graig
   Powys 27 N3
Llandefalle Powys 27 M2
Llandegfan IoA 54 H6
Llandegla Denbgs 48 E5
Llandegley Powys 38 D9
Llandegveth Mons 28 D9
Llandeilo Carmth 26 E4
Llandeilo Graban Powys 38 C12
Llandeloy Pembks 24 F4
Llandenny Mons 28 E7
Llandevaud Newpt 28 E10
Llandevenny Mons 28 E10
Llandinam Powys 38 B5
Llandissilio Pembks 25 K5
Llandogo Mons 28 F7
Llandough V Glam 16 D2
Llandough V Glam 16 F2
Llandovery Carmth 26 G2
Llandow V Glam 16 C2
Llandre Carmth 37 L11
Llandre Cerdgn 37 K4
Llandre Isaf Pembks 25 K3
Llandrillo Denbgs 48 B7
Llandrillo-yn-Rhos Conwy 55 M5
Llandrindod Wells Powys 38 C9
Llandrinio Powys 48 F11
Llandudno Conwy 55 L5
Llandudno Junction Conwy 55 L6
Llandulas Powys 37 F9
Llandwrog Gwynd 54 F9
Llandybie Carmth 26 E6
Llandyfaelog Carmth 25 P6
Llandyfriog Cerdgn 36 F11
Llandygai Gwynd 54 H7
Llandygwydd Cerdgn 36 D11
Llandyrnog Denbgs 48 C3
Llandyssil Powys 38 E3
Llandysul Cerdgn 36 G11
Llanedeyrn Cardif 27 P11
Llaneglwys Powys 27 M2
Llanegryn Gwynd 47 K9
Llanegwad Carmth 26 C5
Llaneilian IoA 54 F3
Llanelian-yn-Rhôs Conwy 55 M6
Llanelidan Denbgs 48 C5
Llanelieu Powys 27 P3
Llanellen Mons 28 C6
Llanelli Carmth 26 C6
Llanelltyd Gwynd 47 L7
Llanelwedd Powys 38 B10
Llanenddwyn Gwynd 47 J6
Llanengan Gwynd 46 C6
Llanerchymedd IoA 54 F5
Llanerfyl Powys 38 B1
Llanfachraeth IoA 54 D5
Llanfachreth Gwynd 47 M6
Llanfaelog IoA 54 D7
Llanfaelrhys Gwynd 46 D6
Llanfaethlu IoA 54 D4
Llanfair Gwynd 47 J5
Llanfair Caereinion Powys 38 C2
Llanfair Clydogau Cerdgn 37 K9
Llanfair Dyffryn Clwyd
   Denbgs 48 D4
Llanfairfechan Conwy 55 K6
Llanfairpwllgwyngyll IoA 54 G7
Llanfair Talhaiarn Conwy 55 N7
Llanfair Waterdine Shrops 38 E6
Llanfairynghornwy IoA 54 D4
Llanfair-yn-Neubwll IoA 54 D6
Llanfallteg Carmth 25 K5
Llanfallteg West Carmth 25 K5
Llanfarian Cerdgn 37 J5
Llanfechain Powys 48 E10
Llanfechell IoA 54 E4
Llanferres Denbgs 48 E4
Llanfihangel-ar-arth Carmth 36 G11
Llanfihangel Glyn Myfyr
   Conwy 55 P10
Llanfihangel Nant Bran
   Powys 27 K2
Llanfihangel Rhydithon
   Powys 38 D8
Llanfihangel Rogiet Mons 28 E10
Llanfihangel-y-Creuddyn
   Cerdgn 37 L5
Llanfihangel-yng-Ngwynfa
   Powys 48 C11
Llanfihangel yn Nhowyn IoA 54 D6
Llanfihangel-y-traethau
   Gwynd 47 J4
Llanfilo Powys 27 N3
Llanfoist Mons 28 D5
Llanfor Gwynd 47 Q4
Llanfrechfa Torfn 28 C9
Llanfrynach Powys 27 M3
Llanfwrog Denbgs 48 D4
Llanfwrog IoA 54 D5
Llanfyllin Powys 48 D10
Llanfynydd Carmth 26 D4
Llanfynydd Flints 48 F4

Llanfyrnach Pembks 25 L3
Llangadfan Powys 48 B12
Llangadog Carmth 26 F3
Llangadwaladr IoA 54 F7
Llangaffo IoA 54 F7
Llangammarch Wells Powys 37 Q10
Llangan V Glam 27 K12
Llangarron Herefs 28 F5
Llangathen Carmth 26 D4
Llangattock Powys 27 P5
Llangattock Lingoed Mons 28 D5
Llangedwyn Powys 48 E10
Llangefni IoA 54 F6
Llangeinor Brdgnd 27 J10
Llangeitho Cerdgn 37 K8
Llangeler Carmth 36 F11
Llangelynin Gwynd 47 J9
Llangendeirne Carmth 26 B6
Llangennech Carmth 26 D8
Llangennith Swans 25 P9
Llangenny Powys 27 N7
Llangernyw Conwy 55 N7
Llangian Gwynd 46 E5
Llangloffan Pembks 24 F3
Llanglydwen Carmth 25 L4
Llangoed IoA 54 H6
Llangollen Denbgs 48 E7
Llangolman Pembks 25 K4
Llangors Powys 27 N4
Llangower Gwynd 47 P5
Llangrannog Cerdgn 36 F9
Llangristiolus IoA 54 F6
Llangrove Herefs 28 F5
Llangunllo Powys 38 E7
Llangunnor Carmth 25 P5
Llangurig Powys 37 P5
Llangwm Conwy 47 Q3
Llangwm Mons 28 E8
Llangwm Pembks 24 H6
Llangwnnadl Gwynd 46 D5
Llangwyryfon Cerdgn 37 K6
Llangybi Cerdgn 37 K8
Llangybi Gwynd 46 G3
Llangybi Mons 28 D9
Llangynhafal Denbgs 48 D3
Llangynidr Powys 27 N5
Llangynin Carmth 25 M5
Llangynog Carmth 25 N6
Llangynog Powys 48 B9
Llangynwyd Brdgnd 27 J10
Llanhamlach Powys 27 M4
Llanharan Rhondd 27 L11
Llanharry Rhondd 27 L11
Llanhennock Mons 28 D9
Llanhilleth Blae G 27 P8
Llanidloes Powys 37 Q4
Llaniestyn Gwynd 46 E5
Llanigon Powys 27 P2
Llanilar Cerdgn 37 K5
Llanilid Rhondd 27 K11
Llanina Cerdgn 36 G8
Llanishen Cardif 27 N11
Llanishen Mons 28 F7
Llanllechid Gwynd 55 J7
Llanllowell Mons 28 D8
Llanllugan Powys 38 C2
Llanllwch Carmth 25 P5
Llanllwchaiarn Powys 38 D4
Llanllwni Carmth 36 H11
Llanllyfni Gwynd 54 F10
Llanmadoc Swans 25 Q9
Llanmaes V Glam 16 D3
Llanmartin Newpt 28 D10
Llanmiloe Carmth 25 M7
Llannefydd Conwy 55 P7
Llannon Carmth 26 D7
Llannor Gwynd 46 F4
Llanon Cerdgn 36 H7
Llanover Mons 28 C7
Llanpumsaint Carmth 25 P3
Llanrhaeadr-ym-Mochnant
   Powys 48 D9
Llanrhian Pembks 24 E3
Llanrhidian Swans 25 C9
Llanrhychwyn Conwy 55 L8
Llanrhyddlad IoA 54 D4
Llanrhystud Cerdgn 37 J6
Llanrug Gwynd 54 G8
Llanrumney Cardif 27 P11
Llanrwst Conwy 55 L8
Llansadurnen Carmth 25 M6
Llansadwrn Carmth 26 F3
Llansadwrn IoA 54 H6
Llansaint Carmth 25 P7
Llansamlet Swans 26 F8
Llansanffraid Glan Conwy
   Conwy 55 L5
Llansannan Conwy 55 N8
Llansantffraed Powys 27 N4
Llansantffraed-
   Cwmdeuddwr Powys 37 Q7
Llansantffraed-in-Elvel
   Powys 38 C10
Llansantffraid Cerdgn 36 H7
Llansantffraid-ym-Mechain
   Powys 48 E10
Llansawel Carmth 26 E2
Llansilin Powys 48 E9
Llansoy Mons 28 E8
Llanspyddid Powys 27 L3
Llanstadwell Pembks 24 G7
Llansteffan Carmth 25 N6
Llantarnam Torfn 28 C9
Llanteg Pembks 25 L6
Llanthewy Skirrid Mons 28 D5
Llanthony Mons 28 C4
Llantilio-Crossenny Mons 28 D5
Llantilio Pertholey Mons 28 D5
Llantrisant Mons 28 D9
Llantrisant Rhondd 27 L11
Llantrithyd V Glam 16 E2
Llantwit Fardre Rhondd 27 M10
Llantwit Major V Glam 16 C3
Llanuwchllyn Gwynd 47 N5
Llanvaches Newpt 28 E9
Llanvair Discoed Mons 28 E9
Llanvapley Mons 28 D6
Llanvetherine Mons 28 D5
Llanvihangel Crucorney Mons 28 C5
Llanwddyn Powys 48 B10
Llanwenog Cerdgn 36 H10
Llanwern Newpt 28 D10
Llanwinio Carmth 25 M4

Llanwnda – Maiden Newton 179

Llanwnda Gwynd 54 F9
Llanwnda Pembks 24 G2
Llanwnnen Cerdgn 37 J10
Llanwnog Powys 38 B4
Llanwrda Carmth 26 F3
Llanwrin Powys 47 M9
Llanwrthwl Powys 37 Q7
Llanwrtyd Wells Powys 37 P10
Llanwyddelan Powys 38 C2
Llanyblodwel Shrops 48 E10
Llanybri Carmth 25 N6
Llanybydder Carmth 36 H10
Llanycefn Pembks 25 J4
Llanychaer Pembks 24 H2
Llanymawddwy Gwynd 47 P7
Llanymynech Powys 48 F10
Llanynghenedl IoA 54 D5
Llanynys Denbgs 58 C3
Llanyre Powys 38 B9
Llanystumdwy Gwynd 46 H4
Llanywern Powys 27 M3
Llawhaden Pembks 25 J5
Llawryglyn Powys 37 Q3
Llay Wrexhm 48 G4
Llechrhyd Caerph 27 M7
Llechryd Cerdgn 36 D11
Lledrod Cerdgn 37 K6
Lleyn Peninsula Gwynd 46 E4
Llithfaen Gwynd 46 F3
Lloc Flints 56 D12
Llowes Powys 27 P1
Llwydcoed Rhondd 27 L7
Llwydiarth Powys 48 B11
Llwyncelyn Cerdgn 36 G8
Llwyndafydd Cerdgn 36 F9
Llwyngwril Gwynd 47 J9
Llwynmawr Wrexhm 48 E7
Llwynypia Rhondd 27 L9
Llynclys Shrops 48 F10
Llynfaes IoA 54 E6
Llysfaen Conwy 55 N6
Llyswen Powys 27 N2
Llysworney V Glam 16 C2
Llys-y-frân Pembks 24 H4
Llywel Powys 27 J3
Loan Falk 85 Q7
Loanhead Mdloth 86 F8
Loaningfoot D & G 70 F4
Loans S Ayrs 76 F5
Lobhillcross Devon 5 K3
Lochailort Highld 97 K12
Lochaline Highld 89 N7
Lochans D & G 68 E7
Locharbriggs D & G 78 G11
Lochavich Ag & B 90 C12
Lochawe Ag & B 90 F10
Loch Baghasdail W Isls 111 b6
Lochboisdale W Isls 111 b6
Lochbuie Ag & B 89 M10
Lochcarron Highld 97 M2
Lochdon Ag & B 89 P9
Lochdonhead Ag & B 89 P9
Lochead Ag & B 83 L7
Lochearnhead Stirlg 91 N10
Lochee C Dund 93 L8
Locheilside Station Highld 90 D1
Lochend Highld 98 H2
Locheport W Isls 111 b4
Loch Euphoirt W Isls 111 b4
Lochfoot D & G 70 E2
Lochgair Ag & B 83 P5
Lochgelly Fife 86 E4
Lochgilphead Ag & B 83 N5
Lochgoilhead Ag & B 84 D3
Lochieheads Fife 93 J11
Lochill Moray 101 K3
Lochindorb Lodge Highld 100 E8
Lochinver Highld 108 C10
Loch Lomond and The Trossachs National Park 84 H1
Loch Loyal Lodge Highld 109 L6
Lochluichart Highld 106 F9
Lochmaben D & G 78 H11
Lochmaddy W Isls 111 b4
Loch nam Madadh W Isls 111 b4
Loch Ness Highld 98 G4
Lochore Fife 86 E3
Lochranza N Ayrs 75 P3
Loch Sgioport W Isls 111 b5
Lochside Abers 95 M8
Lochside D & G 78 F12
Lochside Highld 107 N11
Lochskipport W Isls 111 b5
Lochslin Highld 107 N6
Lochton S Ayrs 68 H3
Lochty Angus 95 J9
Lochty Fife 87 K1
Lochuisge Highld 89 Q5
Lochwinnoch Rens 84 F10
Lochwood D & G 78 H9
Lockengate Cnwll 3 M4
Lockerbie D & G 79 J11
Lockeridge Wilts 18 G7
Lockerley Hants 9 K3
Locking N Som 17 J4
Locking Stumps Warrtn 57 M9
Lockington E R Yk 60 G5
Lockleywood Shrops 49 M9
Locksbottom Gt Lon 21 N9
Locks Heath Hants 9 N6
Lockton N York 67 J9
Loddington Leics 42 B9
Loddington Nhants 32 B2
Loddiswell Devon 5 P9
Loddon Norfk 45 M9
Lode Cambs 33 N4
Lode Heath Solhll 40 F10
Loders Dorset 7 L4
Lodsworth W Susx 10 E5
Lofthouse Leeds 59 J8
Lofthouse N York 65 K11
Lofthouse Gate Wakefd 59 J8
Loftus R & Cl 66 G4
Logan E Ayrs 77 K7
Loganlea W Loth 86 B9
Loggerheads Staffs 49 N8
Logie Angus 95 L8
Logie Fife 93 M10
Logie Moray 100 F5
Logie Coldstone Abers 94 G2
Logie Newton Abers 102 E7
Logie Pert Angus 95 L8
Logierait P & K 92 E5
Logierieve Abers 103 J9
Login Carmth 25 K4
Lolworth Cambs 33 L4
Lonbain Highld 105 K10
Londesborough E R Yk 60 E5
London Gt Lon 21 M7
London Apprentice Cnwll 3 M6
London Colney Herts 21 J3
Londonderry N York 65 N9
London Gateway Services Gt Lon 21 K5
London Gatwick Airport W Susx 11 L2
London Heathrow Airport Gt Lon 20 H8
London Luton Airport Luton 32 G11
London Oxford Airport Oxon 31 L10
London Southend Airport Essex 22 G5
London Stansted Airport Essex 33 N11
Londonthorpe Lincs 42 D3
London Zoo ZSL Gt Lon 21 L6
Londubh Highld 105 M6
Lonemore Highld 105 L6
Long Ashton N Som 17 M3
Long Bank Worcs 39 N7
Long Bennington Lincs 42 B2
Longbenton N Tyne 73 M7
Longborough Gloucs 30 F8
Long Bredy Dorset 7 N5
Longbridge Birm 40 D11
Longbridge Deverill Wilts 18 C11
Long Buckby Nhants 31 N1
Longburton Dorset 7 P1
Long Clawson Leics 41 Q3
Longcliffe Derbys 50 G9
Longcombe Devon 5 Q8
Long Compton Staffs 49 Q10
Long Compton Warwks 30 H7
Longcot Oxon 19 J3
Long Crendon Bucks 20 B2
Long Crichel Dorset 8 E5
Longden Shrops 38 H2
Long Ditton Surrey 21 J9
Longdon Staffs 40 E5
Longdon Worcs 29 L2
Longdon Green Staffs 40 E5
Longdon upon Tern Wrekin 49 L11
Longdown Devon 6 B5
Longdowns Cnwll 2 H8
Long Duckmanton Derbys 51 K6
Long Eaton Derbys 41 L2
Longfield Kent 22 C9
Longford Covtry 41 J10
Longford Derbys 50 G12
Longford Gloucs 29 L5
Longford Shrops 49 M8
Longford Wrekin 49 N10
Longforgan P & K 93 K9
Longformacus Border 87 N10
Longframlington Nthumb 73 K1
Long Green Ches W 49 J2
Longham Dorset 8 F7
Longham Norfk 44 F7
Long Hanborough Oxon 31 K10
Longhaven Abers 103 M7
Longhirst Nthumb 73 L3
Longhope Gloucs 29 J5
Longhope Ork 111 g3
Longhorsley Nthumb 73 K2
Longhoughton Nthumb 81 P10
Long Itchington Warwks 31 K2
Longlane Derbys 50 G12
Long Lawford Warwks 41 L11
Longleat Safari & Adventure Park Wilts 18 B11
Longlevens Gloucs 29 L5
Longleys P & K 93 K7
Long Load Somset 17 L10
Longmanhill Abers 102 F3
Long Marston Herts 20 E1
Long Marston N York 59 L4
Long Marston Warwks 30 F4
Long Marton Cumb 64 C3
Long Melford Suffk 34 E7
Longmoor Camp Hants 10 C4
Longmorn Moray 101 K4
Longmoss Ches E 50 B6
Long Newnton Gloucs 29 M9
Longnewton Border 80 D8
Long Newton E Loth 87 K8
Longnewton S on T 65 P4
Longney Gloucs 29 K6
Longniddry E Loth 87 J7
Longnor Shrops 39 J3
Longnor Staffs 50 E7
Longparish Hants 19 M10
Long Preston N York 63 Q9
Longridge Lancs 57 L2
Longridge W Loth 85 Q9
Longriggend N Lans 85 N8
Long Riston E R Yk 61 J6
Longrock Cnwll 2 D9
Longsdon Staffs 50 C9
Longside Abers 103 L6
Longstanton Cambs 33 L4
Longstock Hants 19 L12
Longstowe Cambs 33 K6
Long Stratton Norfk 45 K10
Long Street M Keyn 32 B7
Longstreet Wilts 18 G9
Long Sutton Hants 10 B1
Long Sutton Lincs 43 L5
Long Sutton Somset 17 L10
Longthorpe C Pete 42 G9
Long Thurlow Suffk 34 G3
Longthwaite Cumb 71 N10
Longton Lancs 57 J4
Longtown Cumb 71 N2
Longtown Herefs 28 C3
Longueville Jersey 7 c2
Longville in the Dale Shrops 39 K4
Long Waste Wrekin 49 L11
Long Whatton Leics 41 L3
Longwick Bucks 20 C3
Long Wittenham Oxon 19 P3
Longwitton Nthumb 73 J3
Longwood D & G 70 B4
Longworth Oxon 19 L2
Longyester E Loth 87 K8
Lonmay Abers 103 L4
Lonmore Highld 104 C12
Looe Cnwll 4 F9
Loose Kent 22 F11
Loosley Row Bucks 20 D4
Lootcherbrae Abers 102 D5
Lopen Somset 17 K12
Loppington Shrops 49 J9
Lordshill C Sotn 9 L4
Lords Wood Medway 22 F10
Lornty P & K 92 H6
Loscoe Derbys 51 K10
Losgaintir W Isls 111 c3
Lossiemouth Moray 101 K2
Lostock Gralam Ches W 49 M1
Lostock Green Ches W 49 M2
Lostwithiel Cnwll 4 D8
Lothbeg Highld 107 Q1
Lothersdale N York 58 C5
Lothmore Highld 110 A12
Loudwater Bucks 20 E5
Loughborough Leics 41 M4
Loughor Swans 26 D8
Loughton Essex 21 N4
Loughton M Keyn 32 B8
Lound Lincs 42 F6
Lound Notts 51 P4
Lound Suffk 45 Q9
Lount Leics 41 K4
Louth Lincs 53 K6
Lover Wilts 8 H4
Loversall Donc 51 M2
Loveston Pembks 25 J7
Lovington Somset 17 N9
Low Ackworth Wakefd 59 K10
Low Barbeth D & G 68 D6
Low Bentham N York 63 M8
Low Biggins Cumb 63 L6
Low Borrowbridge Cumb 63 L3
Low Bradfield Sheff 50 H3
Low Bradley N York 58 D5
Low Burnham N Linc 52 A3
Lowca Cumb 70 F10
Low Catton E R Yk 60 C4
Low Crosby Cumb 71 P4
Lowdham Notts 51 P10
Low Dinsdale Darltn 65 N5
Lower Aisholt Somset 16 G8
Lower Ansty Dorset 8 B6
Lower Apperley Gloucs 29 M4
Lower Arboll Highld 107 P6
Lower Ashton Devon 6 A6
Lower Assendon Oxon 20 C6
Lower Badcall Highld 108 D7
Lower Bartle Lancs 57 J3
Lower Basildon W Berk 19 Q5
Lower Beeding W Susx 11 K5
Lower Benefield Nhants 42 E11
Lower Bentley Worcs 30 C2
Lower Boddington Nhants 31 L4
Lower Bourne Surrey 10 D2
Lower Brailes Warwks 30 H6
Lower Breakish Highld 97 J5
Lower Broadheath Worcs 39 P10
Lower Broxwood Herefs 38 G10
Lower Bullingham Herefs 28 F2
Lower Burgate Hants 8 H4
Lower Caldecote C Beds 32 H7
Lower Chapel Powys 27 L2
Lower Chicksgrove Wilts 8 E2
Lower Chute Wilts 19 K9
Lower Clapton Gt Lon 21 M6
Lower Clent Worcs 40 B10
Lower Cumberworth Kirk 58 G11
Lower Darwen Bl w D 57 M4
Lower Dean Bed 32 F3
Lower Diabaig Highld 105 L9
Lower Dicker E Susx 12 B7
Lower Down Shrops 38 G5
Lower Dunsforth N York 59 K2
Lower Egleton Herefs 39 L11
Lower End M Keyn 32 D8
Lower Eythorne Kent 23 P12
Lower Failand N Som 17 M2
Lower Farringdon Hants 10 B3
Lower Feltham Gt Lon 20 H8
Lower Froyle Hants 10 C2
Lower Gabwell Devon 6 C8
Lower Gledfield Highld 107 K4
Lower Godney Somset 17 L7
Lower Gornal Dudley 40 B8
Lower Gravenhurst C Beds 32 G9
Lower Green Kent 12 C3
Lower Green Kent 12 D2
Lower Halstow Kent 22 G9
Lower Hamworthy BCP 8 E8
Lower Hardres Kent 23 M11
Lower Hartwell Bucks 20 C2
Lower Hergest Herefs 38 F10
Lower Heyford Oxon 31 L8
Lower Heysham Lancs 62 H9
Lower Houses Kirk 58 F10
Lower Irlam Salfd 57 N9
Lower Killeyan Ag & B 74 D4
Lower Langford N Som 17 L4
Lower Largo Fife 86 H2
Lower Leigh Staffs 40 D1
Lower Loxhore Devon 15 K5
Lower Lydbrook Gloucs 28 G5
Lower Lye Herefs 38 H8
Lower Machen Newpt 27 P10
Lower Merridge Somset 16 G8
Lower Middleton Cheney Nhants 31 L6
Lower Moor Worcs 30 C5
Lower Morton S Glos 28 H9
Lower Nazeing Essex 21 N3
Lower Penarth V Glam 16 G3
Lower Penn Staffs 39 Q3
Lower Peover Ches E 49 N1
Lower Place Rochdl 58 B10
Lower Quinton Warwks 30 F5
Lower Raydon Suffk 34 G8
Lower Roadwater Somset 16 D8
Lower Seagry Wilts 18 E5
Lower Shelton C Beds 32 E8
Lower Shiplake Oxon 20 C7
Lower Shuckburgh Warwks 31 L2
Lower Slaughter Gloucs 30 F9
Lower Standen Kent 13 N3
Lower Stanton St Quintin Wilts 18 D5
Lower Stoke Medway 22 G8
Lower Stondon C Beds 32 G9
Lower Stone Gloucs 29 J9
Lower Stow Bedon Norfk 44 F10
Lower Street Norfk 45 L3
Lower Street Suffk 35 J6
Lower Swanwick Hants 9 N5
Lower Swell Gloucs 30 F8
Lower Tasburgh Norfk 45 K10
Lower Tean Staffs 50 D12
Lower Town Devon 5 P5
Lower Town Pembks 24 G2
Lower Upham Hants 9 N4
Lower Weare Somset 17 K5
Lower Welson Herefs 38 F11
Lower Westmancote Worcs 29 N2
Lower Whatley Somset 17 Q6
Lower Whitley Ches W 57 L11
Lower Wield Hants 19 Q11
Lower Willingdon E Susx 12 C9
Lower Withington Ches E 49 P2
Lower Woodford Wilts 8 G1
Lower Wraxhall Dorset 7 N3
Lowesby Leics 41 Q6
Lowestoft Suffk 45 Q10
Loweswater Cumb 71 J10
Low Fell Gatesd 73 M8
Lowfield Heath W Susx 11 L3
Low Gartachorrans Stirlg 84 H6
Low Grantley N York 65 M12
Low Ham Somset 17 L9
Low Harrogate N York 58 H3
Low Hesket Cumb 71 P6
Low Hutton N York 60 D1
Lowick Nhants 32 E1
Lowick Nthumb 81 L6
Lowick Green Cumb 62 F5
Low Lorton Cumb 71 J9
Low Marnham Notts 52 B9
Low Mill N York 66 F8
Low Moorsley Sundld 73 N10
Low Moresby Cumb 70 G10
Low Newton Cumb 62 H6
Low Row Cumb 72 B8
Low Row N York 64 H7
Low Salchrie D & G 68 D6
Low Santon N Linc 60 G10
Lowsonford Warwks 30 F1
Low Tharston Norfk 45 K10
Lowther Cumb 71 Q10
Lowthorpe E R Yk 61 J3
Lowton Somset 16 G11
Low Torry Fife 86 B5
Low Worsall N York 65 P5
Low Wray Cumb 62 G2
Loxbeare Devon 16 C11
Loxhill Surrey 10 G3
Loxhore Devon 15 K4
Loxley Warwks 30 H4
Loxton N Som 17 K5
Loxwood W Susx 10 G4
Lubenham Leics 41 P9
Luccombe Somset 16 C7
Luccombe Village IoW 9 P10
Lucker Nthumb 81 N8
Luckett Cnwll 5 J5
Lucking Street Essex 34 D9
Luckington Wilts 18 C4
Lucklawhill Fife 93 M10
Luckwell Bridge Somset 16 B8
Lucton Herefs 38 H8
Ludag W Isls 111 b6
Ludborough Lincs 53 J4
Ludbrook Devon 5 N8
Ludchurch Pembks 25 K6
Luddenden Calder 58 D8
Luddenden Foot Calder 58 D8
Luddesdown Kent 22 D9
Luddington N Linc 60 E10
Luddington Warwks 30 F4
Luddington in the Brook Nhants 42 F12
Ludford Lincs 52 H5
Ludford Shrops 39 K7
Ludgershall Bucks 31 P10
Ludgershall Wilts 19 J9
Ludgvan Cnwll 2 D8
Ludham Norfk 45 N6
Ludlow Shrops 39 K7
Ludney Somset 7 K1
Ludwell Wilts 8 D3
Ludworth Dur 73 P11
Luffness E Loth 87 J6
Lugar E Ayrs 77 K7
Luggate Burn E Loth 87 L7
Luggiebank N Lans 85 M8
Lugton E Ayrs 84 G11
Lugwardine Herefs 28 G1
Luib Highld 96 G4
Luing Ag & B 83 L2
Lulham Herefs 28 E1
Lullington Derbys 40 G5
Lullington Somset 18 B9
Lulsgate Bottom N Som 17 M3
Lulsley Worcs 39 N10
Lumb Calder 58 D9
Lumby N York 59 L7
Lumphanan Abers 95 J2
Lumphinnans Fife 86 E4
Lumsden Abers 101 N10
Lunan Angus 95 L10
Lunanhead Angus 93 N5
Luncarty P & K 92 G9
Lund E R Yk 60 G5
Lund N York 59 P7
Lundie Angus 93 K8
Lundin Links Fife 86 H2
Lundin Mill Fife 86 H2
Lundy Devon 14 C3
Lunga Ag & B 83 K2
Lunna Shet 111 k3
Lunsford Kent 22 E10
Lunsford's Cross E Susx 12 E7
Lunt Sefton 56 G8
Luppitt Devon 6 F2
Lupset Wakefd 58 H9
Lupton Cumb 63 K6
Lurgashall W Susx 10 F5
Lurley Devon 16 C12
Luscombe Devon 5 Q8
Luss Ag & B 84 F4
Lussagiven Ag & B 83 J6
Lusta Highld 104 C10
Lustleigh Devon 5 Q4
Luston Herefs 39 J9
Luthermuir Abers 95 L8
Luthrie Fife 93 K10
Luton Devon 6 B7
Luton Devon 6 E3
Luton Luton 32 F11
Luton Medway 22 F9
Luton Airport Luton 32 G11
Lutterworth Leics 41 M9
Lutton Devon 5 M8
Lutton Devon 5 N7
Lutton Lincs 43 M5
Lutton Nhants 42 G11
Luxborough Somset 16 D8
Luxulyan Cnwll 3 M4
Luxulyan Valley Cnwll 3 N4
Lybster Highld 110 F8
Lydbury North Shrops 38 G5
Lydd Kent 13 K6
Lydd Airport Kent 13 K6
Lydden Kent 13 N2
Lydden Kent 23 Q9
Lyddington Rutlnd 42 C10
Lydeard St Lawrence Somset 16 F9
Lydford Devon 5 K3
Lydford on Fosse Somset 17 N9
Lydgate Calder 58 B8
Lydham Shrops 38 G4
Lydiard Millicent Wilts 18 G4
Lydiard Tregoze Swindn 18 G4
Lydiate Sefton 56 G7
Lydiate Ash Worcs 40 C11
Lydlinch Dorset 17 Q12
Lydney Gloucs 28 H7
Lydstep Pembks 25 J8
Lye Dudley 40 B10
Lye Green E Susx 11 P4
Lye Green Warwks 30 G2
Lye's Green Wilts 18 B10
Lyford Oxon 19 L2
Lymbridge Green Kent 13 L2
Lyme Regis Dorset 7 J4
Lyminge Kent 13 M2
Lymington Hants 9 K8
Lyminster W Susx 10 G8
Lymm Warrtn 57 M10
Lymm Services Warrtn 57 M11
Lympne Kent 13 L3
Lympsham Somset 17 J5
Lympstone Devon 6 D6
Lynchat Highld 99 L8
Lynch Green Norfk 45 J8
Lyndhurst Hants 9 K6
Lyndon Rutlnd 42 C8
Lyndon Green Birm 40 F9
Lyne Border 79 K1
Lyne Surrey 20 G9
Lyneal Shrops 49 J8
Lyneham Oxon 30 H9
Lyneham Wilts 18 F5
Lynemouth Nthumb 73 N3
Lyne of Skene Abers 102 G12
Lyness Ork 111 g3
Lyng Norfk 44 H6
Lyng Somset 17 J9
Lynmouth Devon 15 M3
Lynsted Kent 22 H10
Lynton Devon 15 M3
Lyon's Gate Dorset 7 P2
Lyonshall Herefs 38 G10
Lytchett Matravers Dorset 8 D8
Lytchett Minster Dorset 8 E8
Lyth Highld 110 F3
Lytham Lancs 56 G4
Lytham St Annes Lancs 56 G4
Lythe N York 67 J5
Lythmore Highld 110 C3

M

Mabe Burnthouse Cnwll 2 H8
Mablethorpe Lincs 53 N6
Macclesfield Ches E 50 B6
Macduff Abers 102 F3
Macharioch Ag & B 75 L9
Machen Caerph 27 P10
Machrie N Ayrs 75 N5
Machrihanish Ag & B 75 J8
Machrins Ag & B 82 E4
Machynlleth Powys 47 M10
Machynys Carmth 26 C8
Mackworth Derbys 50 H12
Macmerry E Loth 87 J7
Madderty P & K 92 E10
Maddiston Falk 85 Q7
Madeley Staffs 49 P6
Madeley Wrekin 39 M2
Madingley Cambs 33 L5
Madley Herefs 28 E2
Madresfield Worcs 39 P11
Madron Cnwll 2 C9
Maenclochog Pembks 25 J4
Maendy V Glam 16 D2
Maentwrog Gwynd 47 L3
Maen-y-groes Cerdgn 36 F8
Maer Staffs 49 P7
Maerdy Conwy 48 B6
Maerdy Rhondd 27 K8
Maesbrook Shrops 48 F10
Maesbury Shrops 48 F9
Maesbury Marsh Shrops 48 G9
Maesllyn Cerdgn 36 F10
Maesteg Brdgnd 27 J10
Maesybont Carmth 26 D5
Maesycwmmer Caerph 27 N9
Maggieknockater Moray 101 L6
Magham Down E Susx 12 C7
Maghull Sefton 56 G8
Magna Park Leics 41 L9
Magor Mons 28 E10
Magor Services Mons 28 E10
Maidenbower W Susx 11 L3
Maiden Bradley Wilts 18 B11
Maidencombe Torbay 6 C8
Maidenhayne Devon 6 H4
Maiden Head N Som 17 N3
Maidenhead W & M 20 E7
Maiden Newton Dorset 7 N4

Maidens S Ayrs 76 D9
Maiden's Green Br For 20 E8
Maiden Wells Pembks 24 G8
Maidford Nhants 31 N4
Maids Moreton Bucks 31 P7
Maidstone Kent 22 F11
Maidstone Services Kent 22 G11
Maidwell Nhants 41 Q11
Mail Shet 111 k4
Maindee Newpt 28 C10
Mainland Ork 111 h2
Mainland Shet 111 k4
Mainsforth Dur 65 N2
Mains of Balhall Angus 94 H8
Mains of Balnakettle Abers 95 K7
Mains of Dalvey Highld 100 H8
Mains of Haulkerton Abers 95 L11
Mains of Lesmoir Abers 101 N9
Mains of Melgunds Angus 93 P5
Mainsriddle D & G 70 F4
Mainstone Shrops 38 F5
Maisemore Gloucs 29 L5
Major's Green Worcs 40 E11
Malborough Devon 5 P11
Maldon Essex 22 G3
Malham N York 58 B2
Maligar Highld 104 G9
Mallaig Highld 97 J9
Mallaigvaig Highld 97 J9
Malleny Mills C Edin 86 E8
Malltraeth IoA 54 E7
Mallwyd Gwynd 47 P4
Malmesbury Wilts 18 D4
Malmsmead Devon 15 N3
Malpas Ches W 49 J6
Malpas Cnwll 3 J7
Malpas Newpt 28 C10
Maltby Rothm 51 M3
Maltby S on T 66 C5
Maltby le Marsh Lincs 53 M7
Maltman's Hill Kent 12 H2
Malton N York 66 H12
Malvern Worcs 39 P11
Malvern Hills 39 P12
Malvern Link Worcs 39 P11
Malvern Wells Worcs 29 K1
Mamble Worcs 39 M7
Mamhilad Mons 28 C7
Manaccan Cnwll 2 H10
Manafon Powys 38 C2
Manais W Isls 111 c3
Manaton Devon 5 P4
Manby Lincs 53 L6
Mancetter Warwks 40 H7
Manchester Manch 57 Q8
Manchester Airport Manch 57 P11
Mancot Flints 48 G3
Mandally Highld 98 C6
Manea Cambs 43 M11
Maney Birm 40 E8
Manfield N York 65 L5
Mangersta W Isls 111 b2
Mangotsfield S Glos 17 P2
Mangurstadh W Isls 111 b2
Manish W Isls 111 c3
Manley Ches W 49 J2
Manmoel Caerph 27 P7
Mannal Ag & B 88 C8
Manningford Bohune Wilts 18 G8
Manningford Bruce Wilts 18 G8
Manningham C Brad 58 F7
Mannings Heath W Susx 11 K4
Mannington Dorset 8 F6
Manningtree Essex 34 H9
Mannofield C Aber 95 Q2
Manorbier Pembks 25 J8
Manorbier Newton Pembks 24 H8
Manorhill Border 80 F7
Manorowen Pembks 24 G2
Manor Park Gt Lon 21 N6
Mansell Gamage Herefs 38 H12
Mansell Lacy Herefs 38 H11
Mansfield E Ayrs 77 K8
Mansfield Notts 51 M8
Mansfield Woodhouse Notts 51 M7
Manston Dorset 8 B4
Manston Kent 23 Q9
Manston Leeds 59 J7
Manswood Dorset 8 E6
Manthorpe Lincs 42 F7
Manton N Linc 52 D3
Manton Rutlnd 42 C8
Manton Wilts 18 H7
Manuden Essex 33 M10
Maperton Somset 17 P10
Maplebeck Notts 51 P8
Mapledurham Oxon 19 R5
Mapledurwell Hants 20 B12
Maplehurst W Susx 11 J5
Maplescombe Kent 22 C9
Mapleton Derbys 50 F10
Mapperley Derbys 51 K11
Mapperley Park C Nott 51 M11
Mapperton Dorset 7 M3
Mappleborough Green Warwks 30 E2
Mappleton E R Yk 61 L5
Mapplewell Barns 59 J11
Mappowder Dorset 7 Q2
Marazion Cnwll 2 D9
Marbhig W Isls 111 d2
Marbury Ches E 49 K6
March Cambs 43 L10
March S Lans 78 G6
Marcham Oxon 19 M2
Marchamley Shrops 49 L9
Marchington Staffs 40 F2
Marchros Gwynd 46 E6
Marchwiel Wrexhm 48 G6
Marchwood Hants 9 L5
Marcross V Glam 16 C3
Marden Herefs 39 K11
Marden Kent 12 E2
Marden Wilts 18 G8
Marden Thorn Kent 12 F2
Mardy Mons 28 C5
Mareham le Fen Lincs 53 J10
Mareham on the Hill Lincs 53 J9
Marehill W Susx 10 G6
Maresfield E Susx 11 P5
Marfleet C KuH 61 K8
Marford Wrexhm 48 G4

Margam Neath 26 G10
Margaret Marsh Dorset 8 B4
Margaretting Essex 22 D3
Margaretting Tye Essex 22 D4
Margate Kent 23 Q8
Margnaheglish N Ayrs 75 Q6
Margrie D & G 69 N8
Margrove Park R & Cl 66 F4
Marham Norfk 44 B7
Marhamchurch Cnwll 14 D10
Marholm C Pete 42 G9
Mariansleigh Devon 15 M7
Marine Town Kent 22 H8
Marionburgh Abers 95 L1
Marishader Highld 104 G9
Maristow Devon 5 K7
Marjoriebanks D & G 78 H11
Mark Somset 17 K6
Markbeech Kent 11 P2
Markby Lincs 53 M7
Mark Cross E Susx 12 C4
Market Bosworth Leics 41 K6
Market Deeping Lincs 42 G7
Market Drayton Shrops 49 M8
Market Harborough Leics 41 Q9
Market Lavington Wilts 18 E9
Market Overton Rutlnd 42 C6
Market Rasen Lincs 52 G5
Market Stainton Lincs 52 H7
Market Warsop Notts 51 M7
Market Weighton E R Yk 60 F6
Market Weston Suffk 34 G2
Markfield Leics 41 L5
Markham Caerph 27 N8
Markham Moor Notts 51 Q6
Markinch Fife 86 G2
Markington N York 58 H2
Markle E Loth 87 L6
Marksbury BaNES 17 P4
Marks Tey Essex 34 E11
Markyate Herts 32 F12
Marlborough Wilts 18 H7
Marlcliff Warwks 30 E4
Marldon Devon 6 B9
Marlesford Suffk 35 M5
Marlingford Norfk 45 J8
Marloes Pembks 24 E7
Marlow Bucks 20 D6
Marlow Bottom Bucks 20 D6
Marlpit Hill Kent 11 N1
Marnhull Dorset 8 B4
Marple Stockp 50 C3
Marr Donc 59 L12
Marrick N York 65 J7
Marsden Kirk 58 D10
Marsden S Tyne 73 P7
Marshalswick Herts 21 J2
Marsham Norfk 45 K5
Marsh Baldon Oxon 19 P2
Marshborough Kent 23 P11
Marshbrook Shrops 38 H4
Marshchapel Lincs 53 K4
Marsh Farm Luton 32 F10
Marshfield Newpt 28 B11
Marshfield S Glos 18 B6
Marshgate Cnwll 4 E2
Marsh Gibbon Bucks 31 N9
Marsh Green Devon 6 E4
Marsh Green Kent 11 N2
Marshland St James Norfk 43 N8
Marsh Lane Derbys 51 K5
Marsh Street Somset 16 D7
Marshwood Dorset 7 K3
Marske N York 65 K7
Marske-by-the-Sea R & Cl 66 E3
Marston Herefs 38 G10
Marston Lincs 42 C2
Marston Oxon 31 M11
Marston Staffs 40 B3
Marston Wilts 18 E9
Marston Green Solhll 40 F9
Marston Magna Somset 17 N10
Marston Meysey Wilts 18 G2
Marston Montgomery Derbys 50 F12
Marston Moretaine C Beds 32 E8
Marston on Dove Derbys 40 G2
Marston St Lawrence Nhants 31 M6
Marston Trussell Nhants 41 P9
Marstow Herefs 28 G5
Marsworth Bucks 20 E1
Marten Wilts 19 K8
Martham Norfk 45 P6
Martin Hants 8 F4
Martin Kent 13 Q1
Martin Lincs 52 G10
Martinhoe Devon 15 L3
Martin Hussingtree Worcs 39 Q9
Martinstown Dorset 7 P5
Martlesham Suffk 35 L7
Martlesham Heath Suffk 35 L7
Martletwy Pembks 24 H6
Martley Worcs 39 N9
Martock Somset 17 L11
Marton Ches E 49 Q2
Marton E R Yk 61 K6
Marton Lincs 52 B7
Marton Middsb 66 D4
Marton N York 59 K2
Marton N York 66 G10
Marton Shrops 38 F2
Marton Warwks 31 K1
Marton-le-Moor N York 65 P12
Martyr Worthy Hants 9 N2
Marvig W Isls 111 d2
Marwell Wildlife Hants 9 N3
Marwick Ork 111 g2
Marwood Devon 15 J5
Marybank Highld 106 H10
Maryburgh Highld 107 J10
Marygold Border 87 P9
Maryhill C Glas 85 J8
Marykirk Abers 95 L8
Marylebone Gt Lon 21 L7
Marylebone Wigan 57 L7
Marypark Moray 101 J7
Maryport Cumb 70 G8
Maryport D & G 68 F11
Marystow Devon 5 J4
Mary Tavy Devon 5 K4
Maryton Angus 95 L10
Marywell Abers 95 J3
Marywell Abers 95 Q3

Marywell Angus 93 Q6
Masham N York 65 L10
Masongill N York 63 M7
Mastin Moor Derbys 51 L5
Matching Green Essex 21 Q2
Matching Tye Essex 21 P2
Matfen Nthumb 73 J6
Matfield Kent 12 D2
Mathern Mons 28 F9
Mathry Pembks 24 F3
Matlask Norfk 45 J3
Matlock Derbys 50 H8
Matlock Bath Derbys 50 H8
Matson Gloucs 29 L5
Mattersey Notts 51 P3
Mattingley Hants 20 B10
Mattishall Norfk 44 H7
Mattishall Burgh Norfk 44 H7
Mauchline E Ayrs 76 H6
Maud Abers 103 J6
Maufant Jersey 7 c1
Maugersbury Gloucs 30 G8
Maughold IoM 56 e3
Mauld Highld 98 E2
Maulden C Beds 32 F8
Maulds Meaburn Cumb 64 B4
Maunby N York 65 N9
Maund Bryan Herefs 39 L10
Maundown Somset 16 E9
Mautby Norfk 45 P7
Mavesyn Ridware Staffs 40 E4
Mavis Enderby Lincs 53 K9
Mawbray Cumb 70 H6
Mawdesley Lancs 57 J6
Mawdlam Brdgnd 26 H11
Mawgan Cnwll 2 G10
Mawgan Porth Cnwll 3 J3
Mawla Cnwll 2 G6
Mawnan Cnwll 2 H9
Mawnan Smith Cnwll 2 H9
Mawsley Nhants 32 B2
Maxey C Pete 42 G8
Maxstoke Warwks 40 G9
Maxton Border 80 E7
Maxton Kent 13 P2
Maxwellheugh Border 80 F7
Maxwelltown D & G 70 F1
Maxworthy Cnwll 4 G2
May Bank Staffs 49 Q6
Maybole S Ayrs 76 E8
Maybury Surrey 20 G10
Mayfield E Susx 12 C5
Mayfield Mdloth 86 G8
Mayfield Staffs 50 F10
Mayford Surrey 20 F11
May Hill Gloucs 29 J5
Mayland Essex 22 H3
Maylandsea Essex 22 H3
Maynard's Green E Susx 12 C6
Maypole Birm 40 E10
Maypole Green Norfk 45 N10
Maypole Green Suffk 34 F5
Meadgate BaNES 17 P5
Meadle Bucks 20 C3
Meadowfield Dur 73 M11
Meadwell Devon 5 J4
Mealabost W Isls 111 d2
Meanwood Leeds 58 H6
Meare Somset 17 L7
Meare Green Somset 16 H10
Meare Green Somset 17 J10
Mearns E Rens 85 J11
Mears Ashby Nhants 32 B4
Measham Leics 41 J5
Meath Green Surrey 11 L2
Meathop Cumb 62 H6
Meavaig W Isls 111 c2
Meavy Devon 5 L6
Medbourne Leics 42 B10
Meddon Devon 14 E8
Meden Vale Notts 51 M6
Medmenham Bucks 20 D6
Medomsley Dur 73 K9
Medstead Hants 19 Q12
Medway Services Medway 22 G10
Meerbrook Staffs 50 C8
Meesden Herts 33 L9
Meeth Devon 15 J9
Meeting House Hill Norfk 45 M5
Meidrim Carmth 25 M5
Meifod Powys 48 D11
Meigle P & K 93 K6
Meikle Carco D & G 77 N8
Meikle Earnock S Lans 85 M11
Meikle Kilmory Ag & B 83 R5
Meikle Obney P & K 92 F8
Meikleour P & K 92 H7
Meikle Wartle Abers 102 F8
Meinciau Carmth 26 B6
Meir C Stke 50 C11
Melbost W Isls 111 d2
Melbourn Cambs 33 L7
Melbourne Derbys 41 J3
Melbourne E R Yk 60 D5
Melbury Abbas Dorset 8 C4
Melbury Bubb Dorset 7 N2
Melbury Osmond Dorset 7 N2
Melchbourne Bed 32 E4
Melcombe Bingham Dorset 8 B6
Meldon Devon 5 L2
Meldon Nthumb 73 K4
Meldreth Cambs 33 L7
Meldrum Stirlg 85 M3
Melfort Ag & B 90 B12
Meliden Denbgs 56 C11
Melin-y-wig Denbgs 48 B6
Melkinthorpe Cumb 71 Q9
Melkridge Nthumb 72 D7
Melksham Wilts 18 D7
Melling Lancs 63 L7
Melling Sefton 56 H8
Mellis Suffk 34 H2
Mellon Charles Highld 105 M4
Mellon Udrigle Highld 105 N3
Mellor Lancs 57 M3
Mellor Stockp 50 C3
Mellor Brook Lancs 57 M3
Mells Somset 17 Q6
Melmerby Cumb 72 B12
Melmerby N York 65 J9
Melmerby N York 65 N11
Melness Highld 109 K4
Melplash Dorset 7 L3

Melrose Border 80 D7
Melsetter Ork 111 g3
Melsonby N York 65 L6
Meltham Kirk 58 E11
Melton E R Yk 60 G8
Melton Suffk 35 L6
Melton Constable Norfk 44 H4
Melton Mowbray Leics 41 Q4
Melton Ross N Linc 60 H11
Melvaig Highld 105 L5
Melverley Shrops 48 G11
Melvich Highld 109 Q3
Membury Devon 6 H3
Membury Services W Berk 19 K5
Memsie Abers 103 K3
Memus Angus 93 M4
Menai Bridge IoA 54 H7
Mendham Suffk 45 L12
Mendip Hills 17 M5
Mendlesham Suffk 34 H4
Mendlesham Green Suffk 34 H4
Menheniot Cnwll 4 G7
Mennock D & G 77 N9
Menston C Brad 58 F5
Menstrie Clacks 85 P4
Mentmore Bucks 32 C11
Meoble Highld 97 L11
Meole Brace Shrops 49 J12
Meonstoke Hants 9 Q4
Meopham Kent 22 D9
Mepal Cambs 33 M1
Meppershall C Beds 32 G9
Mere Ches E 57 N11
Mere Wilts 8 B2
Mere Brow Lancs 56 H5
Mereclough Lancs 57 Q3
Mere Green Birm 40 E7
Mereworth Kent 22 D10
Meriden Solhll 40 G10
Merkadale Highld 96 D4
Merley BCP 8 F7
Merrion Pembks 24 G8
Merriott Somset 7 L1
Merrow Surrey 20 G12
Merry Hill Herts 21 J5
Merryhill Wolves 40 B7
Merrymeet Cnwll 4 G2
Mersea Island Essex 23 K1
Mersey Crossing Halton 57 K11
Mersham Kent 13 K3
Merstham Surrey 21 L11
Merston W Susx 10 E9
Merstone IoW 9 N9
Merther Cnwll 3 L6
Merthyr Cynog Powys 27 L2
Merthyr Mawr Brdgnd 27 J12
Merthyr Tydfil Myr Td 27 M7
Merthyr Vale Myr Td 27 M8
Merton Devon 15 J9
Merton Gt Lon 21 K9
Merton Norfk 44 F9
Merton Oxon 31 M9
Meshaw Devon 15 M8
Messing Essex 34 E11
Messingham N Linc 52 C3
Metfield Suffk 35 L1
Metherell Cnwll 5 J6
Metheringham Lincs 52 F10
Methil Fife 86 H3
Methilhill Fife 86 G3
Methlick Abers 102 H7
Methven P & K 92 F9
Methwold Norfk 44 C10
Methwold Hythe Norfk 44 B10
Mettingham Suffk 45 M11
Metton Norfk 45 K3
Mevagissey Cnwll 3 M6
Mexborough Donc 51 L2
Mey Highld 110 F2
Meysey Hampton Gloucs 18 G1
Miabhaig W Isls 111 c2
Michaelchurch Herefs 28 F4
Michaelchurch Escley Herefs 28 C3
Michaelstone-y-Fedw Newpt 27 P11
Michaelston-le-Pit V Glam 16 F2
Michaelstow Cnwll 4 D4
Michaelwood Services Gloucs 29 J9
Micheldever Hants 19 N11
Micheldever Station Hants 19 N11
Michelmersh Hants 9 L3
Mickfield Suffk 35 J4
Micklebring Donc 51 L2
Micklebly N York 66 H4
Micklefield Leeds 59 K7
Mickleham Surrey 21 J11
Mickleover C Derb 40 H1
Mickleton Dur 64 H3
Mickleton Gloucs 30 F5
Mickletown Leeds 59 K8
Mickle Trafford Ches W 49 J2
Mickley N York 65 M11
Mickley Square Nthumb 73 J8
Mid Ardlaw Abers 103 K3
Midbea Ork 111 h1
Mid Beltie Abers 95 K2
Mid Calder W Loth 86 C8
Mid Clyth Highld 110 F8
Mid Culbuckie Abers 102 E3
Middle Aston Oxon 31 L8
Middle Barton Oxon 31 K8
Middlebie D & G 71 K2
Middlebridge P & K 92 D3
Middle Chinnock Somset 7 L1
Middle Claydon Bucks 31 Q8
Middleham N York 65 K9
Middle Handley Derbys 51 K5
Middlehill Wilts 18 B7
Middlehope Shrops 39 J4
Middle Kames Ag & B 83 N5
Middle Littleton Worcs 30 E5
Middlemarsh Dorset 7 P2
Middle Mayfield Staffs 50 F10
Middle Rasen Lincs 52 F5
Middle Rocombe Devon 6 B8
Middlesbrough Middsb 66 C4
Middleshaw Cumb 63 K4
Middlesmoor N York 65 J11
Middle Stoke Medway 22 G8
Middlestone Dur 65 M2
Middlestown Wakefd 58 H10
Middlethird Border 80 F5
Middleton Ag & B 88 B7
Middleton Derbys 50 G8

Middleton Derbys 50 H9
Middleton Essex 34 E8
Middleton Hants 19 M11
Middleton Herefs 39 K8
Middleton Leeds 58 H8
Middleton N York 58 E4
Middleton N York 66 H9
Middleton Nhants 42 B11
Middleton Norfk 43 Q6
Middleton Nthumb 73 J4
Middleton P & K 86 D2
Middleton Rochdl 57 Q6
Middleton Shrops 39 K6
Middleton Suffk 35 N3
Middleton Swans 25 P10
Middleton Warwks 40 F7
Middleton Cheney Nhants 31 L6
Middleton-in-Teesdale Dur 64 G3
Middleton Moor Suffk 35 N4
Middleton One Row Darltn 65 N5
Middleton-on-Sea W Susx 10 F9
Middleton on the Hill Herefs 39 K8
Middleton on the Wolds E R Yk 60 G4
Middleton Park C Aber 103 J11
Middleton Quernhow N York 65 N10
Middleton St George Darltn 65 N5
Middleton Scriven Shrops 39 M5
Middleton Stoney Oxon 31 M9
Middleton Tyas N York 65 M6
Middle Town IoS 2 b3
Middletown Powys 48 F11
Middle Tysoe Warwks 31 J5
Middle Wallop Hants 19 K12
Middlewich Ches E 49 N3
Middle Winterslow Wilts 9 J2
Middlewood Cnwll 4 G5
Middle Woodford Wilts 18 G12
Middlewood Green Suffk 34 H5
Middlezoy Somset 17 K9
Midford BaNES 18 B8
Midgham W Berk 19 P7
Midgley Calder 58 D8
Midgley Wakefd 58 H10
Midhopestones Sheff 50 G2
Midhurst W Susx 10 E6
Mid Lavant W Susx 10 D8
Midlem Border 80 C8
Mid Mains Highld 98 F12
Midpark Ag & B 83 Q10
Midsomer Norton BaNES 17 P5
Midtown Highld 109 K4
Mid Yell Shet 111 k2
Migdale Highld 107 K4
Migvie Abers 94 G1
Milborne Port Somset 17 P11
Milborne St Andrew Dorset 8 B8
Milborne Wick Somset 17 P11
Milbourne Nthumb 73 K6
Milbourne Wilts 18 D4
Milburn Cumb 64 B2
Milbury Heath S Glos 29 J10
Milby N York 59 K1
Milcombe Oxon 31 K7
Milden Suffk 34 F7
Mildenhall Suffk 34 B2
Mildenhall Wilts 18 H6
Mileham Norfk 44 F6
Mile Oak Br & H 11 K8
Milesmark Fife 86 C5
Miles Platting Manch 57 Q8
Mile Town Kent 22 H8
Milfield Nthumb 81 K7
Milford Derbys 51 J10
Milford Devon 14 E7
Milford Staffs 40 C4
Milford Surrey 10 F2
Milford Haven Pembks 24 F7
Milford on Sea Hants 9 K8
Milkwall Gloucs 28 G7
Milland W Susx 10 D4
Mill Bank Calder 58 D9
Millbreck Abers 103 K6
Millbridge Surrey 10 D2
Millbrook C Beds 32 E8
Millbrook C Sotn 9 L5
Millbrook Cnwll 5 J9
Millbrook Jersey 7 b2
Mill Brow Stockp 50 C3
Millbuie Abers 102 G12
Millbuie Highld 107 J11
Millcorner E Susx 12 G5
Millcraig Highld 107 L7
Milldale Staffs 50 F9
Mill End Bucks 20 C6
Mill End Herts 33 K9
Millerhill Mdloth 86 G8
Miller's Dale Derbys 50 F6
Millerston C Glas 85 L9
Mill Green Cambs 33 P7
Mill Green Essex 22 D3
Mill Green Lincs 43 J5
Mill Green Suffk 34 H8
Mill Green Suffk 34 G5
Mill Green Suffk 35 J5
Millhalf Herefs 38 F11
Millheugh S Lans 77 M2
Mill Hill Gt Lon 21 L5
Millhouse Ag & B 83 P8
Millhousebridge D & G 78 H10
Millhouse Green Barns 58 G12
Millhouses Sheff 51 J4
Milliken Park Rens 84 G9
Millington E R Yk 60 E4
Millmeece Staffs 49 Q8
Mill of Drummond P & K 92 C11
Mill of Haldane W Duns 84 G6
Millom Cumb 62 D6
Millport N Ayrs 84 C11
Mill Street Suffk 34 H3
Millthrop Cumb 63 M4
Milltimber C Aber 95 P2
Milltown Abers 101 K12
Milltown Abers 101 N11
Milltown D & G 71 M1
Milltown Devon 15 K4
Milltown Highld 97 J2
Milltown of Auchindoun Moray 101 L2
Milltown of Campfield Abers 95 L2
Milltown of Edinvillie Moray 101 K7
Milltown of Learney Abers 95 K2

Milltown of Rothiemay Moray ...102 D5
Milnathort P & K ...86 D2
Milngavie E Duns ...85 J7
Milnrow Rochdl ...58 B10
Milnthorpe Cumb ...63 J6
Milovaig Highld ...104 B11
Milson Shrops ...39 M7
Milstead Kent ...22 H10
Milston Wilts ...18 H10
Milthorpe Nhants ...31 N5
Milton C Stke ...50 B10
Milton Cambs ...33 M4
Milton Cumb ...71 Q4
Milton D & G ...68 G8
Milton D & G ...70 D2
Milton Derbys ...40 H3
Milton Highld ...98 G3
Milton Highld ...107 J11
Milton Highld ...107 M7
Milton Highld ...110 G5
Milton Inver ...84 F8
Milton Kent ...22 D8
Milton Moray ...101 J10
Milton Moray ...101 P3
Milton N Som ...17 J4
Milton Notts ...51 P6
Milton Oxon ...19 N3
Milton Oxon ...31 L7
Milton P & K ...94 B9
Milton Pembks ...24 H8
Milton Somset ...17 L10
Milton Stirlg ...84 H3
Milton W Duns ...84 G7
Milton Abbas Dorset ...8 B4
Milton Abbot Devon ...5 J4
Milton Bridge Mdloth ...86 F9
Milton Bryan C Beds ...32 D10
Milton Clevedon Somset ...17 P8
Milton Combe Devon ...5 K7
Milton Damerel Devon ...14 G9
Milton Ernest Bed ...32 E5
Milton Green Ches W ...49 J4
Milton Hill Oxon ...19 M3
Milton Keynes M Keyn ...32 C8
Milton Lilbourne Wilts ...18 H8
Milton Malsor Nhants ...31 Q3
Milton Morenish P & K ...91 P8
Milton of Auchinhove Abers ...95 J2
Milton of Balgonie Fife ...86 G3
Milton of Buchanan Stirlg ...84 G5
Milton of Campsie E Duns ...85 L7
Milton of Finavon Angus ...93 N4
Milton of Leys Highld ...99 K1
Milton of Murtle C Aber ...95 P2
Milton on Stour Dorset ...8 B4
Milton Regis Kent ...22 H9
Milton-under-Wychwood Oxon ...30 H9
Milverton Somset ...16 F10
Milverton Warwks ...30 H2
Milwich Staffs ...40 C2
Minard Ag & B ...83 P4
Minchinhampton Gloucs ...29 M8
Minehead Somset ...16 C6
Minera Wrexhm ...48 F5
Minety Wilts ...18 F3
Minffordd Gwynd ...47 J4
Mingarrypark Highld ...89 N3
Miningsby Lincs ...53 K10
Minions Cnwll ...4 G6
Minishant S Ayrs ...76 F8
Minllyn Gwynd ...47 P8
Minnigaff D & G ...69 K6
Minnonie Abers ...102 G4
Minskip N York ...59 K2
Minstead Hants ...9 K5
Minsted W Susx ...10 D6
Minster Kent ...23 P9
Minsterley Shrops ...38 G2
Minster Lovell Oxon ...30 H10
Minster-on-Sea Kent ...23 J8
Minsterworth Gloucs ...29 K5
Minterne Magna Dorset ...7 P2
Minting Lincs ...52 H8
Mintlaw Abers ...103 K6
Minto Border ...80 D9
Minton Shrops ...38 H4
Mirehouse Cumb ...70 F11
Mireland Highld ...110 G4
Mirfield Kirk ...58 G9
Miserden Gloucs ...29 N7
Miskin Rhondd ...27 L11
Misson Notts ...51 P2
Misterton Notts ...51 Q2
Misterton Somset ...7 L2
Mistley Essex ...35 J9
Mitcham Gt Lon ...21 L9
Mitcheldean Gloucs ...29 J5
Mitchell Cnwll ...3 J5
Mitchellslacks D & G ...78 F9
Mitchel Troy Mons ...28 F6
Mitford Nthumb ...73 L4
Mithian Cnwll ...2 H5
Mixbury Oxon ...31 N7
Mobberley Ches E ...57 P11
Mobberley Staffs ...50 D11
Mochdre Powys ...38 C4
Mochrum D & G ...69 J9
Mockbeggar Kent ...12 E1
Mockerkin Cumb ...70 H10
Modbury Devon ...5 N9
Moddershall Staffs ...50 B12
Moelfre IoA ...54 G4
Moelfre Powys ...48 E9
Moffat D & G ...78 H7
Moggerhanger C Beds ...32 G6
Moira Leics ...40 H4
Molash Kent ...23 K11
Mol-chlach Highld ...96 E7
Mold Flints ...48 E3
Moldgreen Kirk ...58 F10
Molehill Green Essex ...33 P10
Molescroft E R Yk ...60 H6
Molesworth Cambs ...32 F2
Moll Highld ...96 G4
Molland Devon ...15 N6
Mollington Ches W ...48 H2
Mollington Oxon ...31 K5
Mollinsburn N Lans ...85 M8
Mondynes Abers ...95 M6
Monewden Suffk ...35 L5
Moneydie P & K ...92 F9

Moniaive D & G ...78 C10
Monifieth Angus ...93 N8
Monikie Angus ...93 N7
Monimail Fife ...93 K11
Monken Hadley Gt Lon ...21 K4
Monk Fryston N York ...59 L8
Monkhide Herefs ...39 L12
Monkhill Cumb ...71 M4
Monkhopton Shrops ...39 L4
Monkland Herefs ...39 J10
Monkleigh Devon ...14 H7
Monknash V Glam ...16 C3
Monkokehampton Devon ...15 K10
Monkseaton N Tyne ...73 N6
Monks Eleigh Suffk ...34 F7
Monk's Gate W Susx ...11 K5
Monks Heath Ches E ...49 Q1
Monk Sherborne Hants ...19 Q9
Monksilver Somset ...16 E8
Monks Kirby Warwks ...41 L10
Monk Soham Suffk ...35 K4
Monks Risborough Bucks ...20 D3
Monksthorpe Lincs ...53 M9
Monk Street Essex ...33 P10
Monkswood Mons ...28 D8
Monkton Devon ...6 G3
Monkton Kent ...23 P9
Monkton S Ayrs ...76 F6
Monkton S Tyne ...73 N8
Monkton Combe BaNES ...18 B8
Monkton Deverill Wilts ...18 C12
Monkton Farleigh Wilts ...18 B7
Monkton Heathfield Somset ...16 H10
Monkton Wyld Dorset ...7 J4
Monkwood Hants ...9 Q2
Monmore Green Wolves ...40 B7
Monmouth Mons ...28 F6
Monnington on Wye Herefs ...38 G12
Monreith D & G ...69 J10
Montacute Somset ...17 M11
Montford Shrops ...48 H11
Montford Bridge Shrops ...48 H11
Montgarrie Abers ...102 D10
Montgomery Powys ...38 E3
Montrose Angus ...95 L9
Mont Saint Guern ...b2
Monxton Hants ...19 K11
Monyash Derbys ...50 F7
Monymusk Abers ...102 F11
Monzie P & K ...92 C9
Moodiesburn N Lans ...85 L8
Moonzie Fife ...93 L11
Moor Allerton Leeds ...58 H6
Moorby Lincs ...53 J10
Moor Crichel Dorset ...8 E6
Moordown BCP ...8 G8
Moore Halton ...57 L11
Moor End Calder ...58 D8
Moorends Donc ...59 P10
Moorhead C Brad ...58 F6
Moorhouse Cumb ...71 M4
Moorhouse Notts ...51 Q7
Moorhouse Bank Surrey ...21 N11
Moorlinch Somset ...17 K8
Moor Monkton N York ...59 L3
Moorsholm R & Cl ...66 F5
Moorside Dorset ...8 B4
Moor Street Birm ...40 C10
Moorswater Cnwll ...4 F7
Moorthorpe Wakefd ...59 L11
Moortown Leeds ...58 H6
Moortown Lincs ...52 F4
Morangie Highld ...107 M6
Morar Highld ...97 J10
Morborne Cambs ...42 G10
Morchard Bishop Devon ...15 N10
Morcombelake Dorset ...7 K4
Morcott Rutlnd ...42 D9
Morda Shrops ...48 F9
Morden Dorset ...8 D8
Morden Gt Lon ...21 K9
Mordiford Herefs ...28 G2
Mordon Dur ...65 N3
More Shrops ...38 G4
Morebath Devon ...16 C10
Morebattle Border ...80 G8
Morecambe Lancs ...62 H8
Moredon Swindn ...18 G4
Morefield Highld ...106 B4
Morehall Kent ...13 N3
Moreleigh Devon ...5 P9
Morenish P & K ...91 N8
Morestead Hants ...9 N3
Moreton Dorset ...8 B9
Moreton Essex ...21 Q3
Moreton Herefs ...39 J8
Moreton Oxon ...20 B3
Moreton Wirral ...56 F10
Moreton Corbet Shrops ...49 K10
Moretonhampstead Devon ...5 P3
Moreton-in-Marsh Gloucs ...30 G7
Moreton Jeffries Herefs ...39 L11
Moreton Morrell Warwks ...30 H3
Moreton on Lugg Herefs ...39 J11
Moreton Pinkney Nhants ...31 M4
Moreton Say Shrops ...49 L8
Moreton Valence Gloucs ...29 K6
Morfa Nefyn Gwynd ...46 E4
Morham E Loth ...87 K7
Morland Cumb ...64 B3
Morley Derbys ...51 K11
Morley Leeds ...58 H8
Morley Green Ches E ...57 P11
Morley St Botolph Norfk ...44 H9
Morningside C Edin ...86 F7
Morningside N Lans ...85 N11
Morningthorpe Norfk ...45 K10
Morpeth Nthumb ...73 L3
Morphie Abers ...95 L8
Morrey Staffs ...40 E4
Morriston Swans ...26 F8
Morston Norfk ...44 G2
Mortehoe Devon ...14 H3
Morthen Rothm ...51 L3
Mortimer W Berk ...19 Q7
Mortimer West End Hants ...19 Q7
Mortlake Gt Lon ...21 K8
Morton Cumb ...71 N5
Morton Derbys ...51 K8
Morton Lincs ...42 F5

Morton Lincs ...52 B5
Morton Notts ...51 Q9
Morton Shrops ...48 F9
Morton-on-Swale N York ...65 N8
Morvah Cnwll ...2 C8
Morville Shrops ...39 M4
Morwenstow Cnwll ...14 D8
Mosborough Sheff ...51 K5
Moscow E Ayrs ...76 H4
Moseley Birm ...40 E10
Moseley Wolves ...40 C7
Moseley Worcs ...39 P9
Moss Ag & B ...88 B7
Moss Donc ...59 N10
Mossat Abers ...101 N10
Mossbank Shet ...111 k3
Moss Bank St Hel ...57 K8
Mossbay Cumb ...70 G9
Mossblown S Ayrs ...76 G6
Mossburnford Border ...80 F10
Mossdale D & G ...69 P5
Mossdale E Ayrs ...76 H9
Moss Edge Lancs ...62 H12
Mossend N Lans ...85 M10
Mossley Tamesd ...50 C1
Mosspaul Hotel Border ...79 N8
Moss-side Highld ...100 D4
Mosstodloch Moray ...101 L4
Mossyard D & G ...69 M8
Mossy Lea Lancs ...57 K6
Mosterton Dorset ...7 L2
Moston Manch ...57 Q8
Mostyn Flints ...56 D11
Motcombe Dorset ...8 C3
Mothecombe Devon ...5 M10
Motherby Cumb ...71 N9
Motherwell N Lans ...85 M10
Motspur Park Gt Lon ...21 K9
Mottingham Gt Lon ...21 N8
Mottisfont Hants ...9 K3
Mottistone IoW ...9 L10
Mottram in Longdendale Tamesd ...50 C2
Mottram St Andrew Ches E ...57 Q12
Mouldsworth Ches W ...49 J2
Moulin P & K ...92 E4
Moulsecoomb Br & H ...11 M8
Moulsford Oxon ...19 P4
Moulsoe M Keyn ...32 C8
Moultavie Highld ...107 K9
Moulton Ches W ...49 M2
Moulton Lincs ...43 K5
Moulton N York ...65 M6
Moulton Nhants ...32 B4
Moulton Suffk ...34 B4
Moulton V Glam ...16 E3
Moulton Chapel Lincs ...43 J6
Moulton St Mary Norfk ...45 N8
Moulton Seas End Lincs ...43 K5
Mount Cnwll ...4 E6
Mountain C Brad ...58 E7
Mountain Ash Rhondd ...27 L8
Mountain Cross Border ...86 D11
Mount Ambrose Cnwll ...2 G7
Mount Bures Essex ...34 E9
Mountfield E Susx ...12 E6
Mountgerald Highld ...107 J9
Mount Hawke Cnwll ...2 G7
Mountjoy Cnwll ...3 K4
Mount Lothian Mdloth ...86 F10
Mountnessing Essex ...22 D4
Mounton Mons ...28 F9
Mount Pleasant Derbys ...51 J10
Mount Pleasant Suffk ...34 C7
Mountsorrel Leics ...41 M5
Mount Tabor Calder ...58 D8
Mousehole Cnwll ...2 C9
Mouswald D & G ...70 H2
Mow Cop Ches E ...49 Q4
Mowhaugh Border ...80 H9
Mowmacre Hill C Leic ...41 N6
Mowsley Leics ...41 N9
Moy Highld ...98 H11
Moy Highld ...99 L3
Moyle Highld ...97 M6
Moylegrove Pembks ...36 B10
Muasdale Ag & B ...75 K4
Muchalls Abers ...95 P4
Much Birch Herefs ...28 F3
Much Cowarne Herefs ...39 L11
Much Dewchurch Herefs ...28 F3
Muchelney Somset ...17 K10
Muchelney Ham Somset ...17 L10
Much Hadham Herts ...33 L11
Much Hoole Lancs ...57 J4
Muchlarnick Cnwll ...4 F8
Much Marcle Herefs ...28 H3
Much Wenlock Shrops ...39 L3
Muck Highld ...89 J1
Muckleburgh Collection Norfk ...44 H2
Mucklestone Staffs ...49 N7
Muckton Lincs ...53 L7
Muddiford Devon ...15 K5
Muddles Green E Susx ...12 B7
Mudeford BCP ...8 H8
Mudford Somset ...17 N11
Mudford Sock Somset ...17 M11
Mugdock Stirlg ...85 J7
Mugeary Highld ...96 E2
Mugginton Derbys ...50 H11
Muirden Abers ...102 F5
Muirdrum Angus ...93 P8
Muiresk Abers ...102 F5
Muirhead Angus ...93 M8
Muirhead Fife ...86 F2
Muirhead N Lans ...85 L8
Muirhouses Falk ...86 B6
Muirkirk E Ayrs ...77 L6
Muirmill Stirlg ...85 M6
Muir of Fowlis Abers ...102 D11
Muir of Miltonduff Moray ...101 J4
Muir of Ord Highld ...107 J11
Muirshearlich Highld ...98 A11
Muirtack Abers ...103 K7
Muirton P & K ...85 Q2
Muirton Mains Highld ...106 H10
Muirton of Ardblair P & K ...92 H7
Muker N York ...64 G7

Mulbarton Norfk ...45 K9
Mulben Moray ...101 L5
Mull Ag & B ...89 M8
Mullion Cnwll ...2 G11
Mullion Cove Cnwll ...2 F11
Mumby Lincs ...53 N8
Munderfield Row Herefs ...39 M10
Munderfield Stocks Herefs ...39 M11
Mundesley Norfk ...45 M3
Mundford Norfk ...44 D10
Mundham Norfk ...45 M9
Mundon Hill Essex ...22 G3
Mungrisdale Cumb ...71 M9
Munlochy Highld ...107 K10
Munnoch N Ayrs ...76 E2
Munsley Herefs ...29 J1
Munslow Shrops ...39 K5
Murchington Devon ...5 N3
Murcott Oxon ...31 N10
Murkle Highld ...110 D3
Murlaggan Highld ...97 P10
Murroes Angus ...93 N8
Murrow Cambs ...43 L8
Mursley Bucks ...32 B10
Murthill Angus ...93 N4
Murthly P & K ...92 G7
Murton C York ...59 P4
Murton Cumb ...64 D3
Murton Dur ...73 P10
Murton Nthumb ...81 K5
Musbury Devon ...6 H4
Musselburgh E Loth ...86 G7
Muston Leics ...42 B3
Muston N York ...67 N10
Muswell Hill Gt Lon ...21 L5
Mutehill D & G ...69 P8
Mutford Suffk ...45 P11
Muthill P & K ...92 C11
Mybster Highld ...110 D5
Myddfai Carmth ...26 G3
Myddle Shrops ...49 J10
Mydroilyn Cerdgn ...36 G9
Mylor Cnwll ...3 J8
Mylor Bridge Cnwll ...3 J8
Mynachlog ddu Pembks ...25 K3
Mynydd-bach Mons ...28 F9
Mynydd-Bach Swans ...26 E8
Mynyddgarreg Carmth ...25 P7
Mynydd Isa Flints ...48 F3
Myrebird Abers ...95 M3
Myredykes Border ...72 B2
Mytchett Surrey ...20 E11
Mytholm Calder ...58 C8
Mytholmroyd Calder ...58 D8
Myton-on-Swale N York ...59 K2

N

Naast Highld ...105 M6
Na Buirgh W Isls ...111 c3
Naburn C York ...59 N5
Nackington Kent ...23 M11
Nacton Suffk ...35 K8
Nafferton E R Yk ...60 H3
Nailbourne Somset ...16 G9
Nailsea N Som ...17 L3
Nailstone Leics ...41 K6
Nailsworth Gloucs ...29 L8
Nairn Highld ...100 D4
Nannerch Flints ...48 D2
Nanpantan Leics ...41 L4
Nanpean Cnwll ...3 L5
Nanstallon Cnwll ...3 M3
Nanternis Cerdgn ...36 F8
Nantgaredig Carmth ...26 C5
Nantglyn Denbgs ...55 Q8
Nantmel Powys ...38 B8
Nantmor Gwynd ...47 K3
Nant Peris Gwynd ...54 H9
Nantwich Ches E ...49 M5
Nantyglo Blae G ...27 P6
Nant-y-moel Brdgnd ...27 K9
Naphill Bucks ...20 D4
Napton on the Hill Warwks ...31 L2
Narberth Pembks ...25 J6
Narborough Leics ...41 M7
Narborough Norfk ...44 C7
Nasareth Gwynd ...54 F10
Naseby Nhants ...41 P10
Nash Bucks ...32 B9
Nash Newpt ...28 D11
Nash Shrops ...39 L7
Nassington Nhants ...42 F10
Nateby Cumb ...64 E6
Nateby Lancs ...63 J12
National Memorial Arboretum Staffs ...40 F5
National Motor Museum (Beaulieu) Hants ...9 L6
National Space Centre C Leic ...41 N6
Natland Cumb ...63 K4
Naughton Suffk ...34 G7
Naunton Gloucs ...30 E9
Naunton Worcs ...29 M2
Naunton Beauchamp Worcs ...30 C4
Navenby Lincs ...52 E10
Navestock Essex ...21 Q4
Navestock Side Essex ...22 C4
Navidale Highld ...110 B11
Navity Highld ...107 N8
Nawton N York ...66 F9
Nayland Suffk ...34 F9
Nazeing Essex ...21 N3
Neap Shet ...111 k4
Near Cotton Staffs ...50 D10
Near Sawrey Cumb ...62 G3
Neasden Gt Lon ...21 K6
Neasham Darltn ...65 N6
Neath Neath ...26 G8
Neatham Hants ...10 C3
Neatishead Norfk ...45 M6
Nebo Cerdgn ...37 J7
Nebo Conwy ...55 M10
Nebo Gwynd ...54 F10
Nebo IoA ...54 F4
Necton Norfk ...44 E8
Nedd Highld ...108 C8
Nedging Suffk ...34 G7
Nedging Tye Suffk ...34 G6
Needham Norfk ...45 K1

Needham Market Suffk ...34 H6
Needingworth Cambs ...33 K3
Neen Savage Shrops ...39 M6
Neen Sollars Shrops ...39 M7
Neenton Shrops ...39 M5
Nefyn Gwynd ...46 E4
Neilston E Rens ...84 H10
Nelson Caerph ...27 M9
Nelson Lancs ...57 Q2
Nemphlar S Lans ...77 P3
Nempnett Thrubwell BaNES ...17 N4
Nenthead Cumb ...72 E11
Nenthorn Border ...80 F6
Nerabus Ag & B ...82 C11
Nercwys Flints ...48 E4
Nerston S Lans ...85 L10
Nesbit Nthumb ...81 K7
Nesfield N York ...58 E4
Nesscliffe Shrops ...48 H10
Neston Ches W ...56 F12
Neston Wilts ...18 C7
Netchwood Shrops ...39 L4
Nether Abington S Lans ...78 F4
Nether Alderley Ches E ...49 Q1
Netheravon Wilts ...18 G10
Nether Blainslie Border ...80 D5
Netherbrae Abers ...102 G4
Nether Broughton Leics ...41 P3
Netherburn S Lans ...77 N2
Netherbury Dorset ...7 L3
Netherby N York ...59 J5
Nether Cerne Dorset ...7 P3
Nether Compton Dorset ...17 N11
Nethercleuch D & G ...79 J10
Nether Crimond Abers ...102 H10
Nether Dallachy Moray ...101 M3
Netherend Gloucs ...28 G8
Netherfield E Susx ...12 E6
Netherfield Notts ...51 N11
Nether Fingland S Lans ...78 F6
Netherhampton Wilts ...8 G2
Nether Handwick Angus ...93 L7
Nether Haugh Rothm ...51 K2
Netherhay Dorset ...7 K2
Nether Headon Notts ...51 Q5
Nether Heage Derbys ...51 J10
Nether Heyford Nhants ...31 P3
Nether Kellet Lancs ...63 J8
Nether Kinmundy Abers ...103 L6
Nether Langwith Notts ...51 M6
Netherlaw D & G ...70 C6
Netherley Abers ...95 P4
Nethermill D & G ...78 G10
Nethermuir Abers ...103 J6
Nether Padley Derbys ...50 G5
Nether Poppleton C York ...59 M4
Netherseal Derbys ...40 H5
Nether Silton N York ...66 C8
Nether Stowey Somset ...16 G8
Netherthong Kirk ...58 F11
Netherthorpe Angus ...93 P4
Netherton Devon ...6 B8
Netherton Dudley ...40 C9
Netherton Kirk ...58 F10
Netherton N Lans ...81 N11
Netherton Nthumb ...81 K11
Netherton P & K ...92 H5
Netherton Sefton ...56 G8
Netherton Stirlg ...85 J7
Netherton Wakefd ...58 H10
Nethertown Cumb ...62 B1
Nethertown Highld ...110 G1
Nethertown Staffs ...40 E4
Netherurd Border ...86 D12
Nether Wallop Hants ...19 K12
Nether Wasdale Cumb ...62 D2
Nether Westcote Gloucs ...30 G9
Nether Whitacre Warwks ...40 G8
Nether Whitecleuch S Lans ...78 D5
Nether Winchendon Bucks ...31 Q10
Netherwitton Nthumb ...73 K3
Nethy Bridge Highld ...99 Q5
Netley Hants ...9 M6
Netley Marsh Hants ...9 K5
Nettlebed Oxon ...20 B6
Nettlebridge Somset ...17 P6
Nettlecombe Dorset ...7 M4
Nettleden Herts ...32 G2
Nettleham Lincs ...52 E8
Nettlestead Kent ...22 D11
Nettlestead Green Kent ...22 D12
Nettlestone IoW ...9 Q8
Nettlesworth Dur ...73 M10
Nettleton Lincs ...52 G4
Nettleton Wilts ...18 B5
Netton Wilts ...18 G12
Nevern Pembks ...36 B11
Nevill Holt Leics ...42 B10
New Abbey D & G ...70 F3
New Aberdour Abers ...103 J3
New Addington Gt Lon ...21 M10
Newall Leeds ...58 G5
New Alresford Hants ...9 P2
New Alyth P & K ...93 J6
Newark C Pete ...42 H9
Newark Ork ...111 i1
Newark-on-Trent Notts ...52 B11
Newarthill N Lans ...85 N10
New Ash Green Kent ...22 C9
New Balderton Notts ...52 B11
New Barn Kent ...22 C9
New Barnet Gt Lon ...21 L4
Newbattle Mdloth ...86 G8
New Bewick Nthumb ...81 M9
Newbie D & G ...71 K3
Newbiggin Cumb ...71 B2
Newbiggin Cumb ...71 P9
Newbiggin Cumb ...71 Q6
Newbiggin Dur ...64 G3
Newbiggin N York ...64 H9
Newbiggin-by-the-Sea Nthumb ...73 N4
Newbigging Angus ...93 K7
Newbigging Angus ...93 M8
Newbigging Angus ...93 N8
Newbigging S Lans ...86 B11
Newbiggin-on-Lune Cumb ...63 N2
New Bilton Warwks ...41 L11
Newbold Derbys ...51 J6
Newbold on Avon Warwks ...41 L11

182 Newbold on Stour – Nymans

Newbold on Stour Warwks 30 G5
Newbold Pacey Warwks 30 H3
Newbold Verdon Leics 41 K6
New Bolingbroke Lincs 53 K11
Newborough C Pete 42 H8
Newborough IoA 54 F8
Newborough Staffs 40 F3
New Boultham Lincs 52 D8
Newbourne Suffk 35 L8
New Bradwell M Keyn 32 B8
New Brampton Derbys 51 J6
New Brancepeth Dur 73 M11
Newbridge C Edin 86 D7
Newbridge Caerph 27 P8
Newbridge Cnwll 2 C9
Newbridge D & G 78 F11
Newbridge Hants 9 K4
Newbridge IoW 9 M9
Newbridge Green Worcs 29 L2
Newbridge-on-Wye Powys 38 B9
New Brighton Wirral 56 F9
Newbrough Nthumb 72 F7
New Buckenham Norfk 44 H11
Newbuildings Devon 15 N10
Newburgh Abers 103 K4
Newburgh Abers 103 K9
Newburgh Fife 93 J11
Newburgh Lancs 57 J6
Newburn N u Ty 73 L7
Newbury Somset 17 Q6
Newbury W Berk 19 M7
Newbury Park Gt Lon 21 N6
Newby Cumb 64 B4
Newby Lancs 63 P11
Newby N York 63 N8
Newby N York 66 C5
Newby Bridge Cumb 62 G5
Newby East Cumb 71 P4
New Byth Abers 102 H5
Newby West Cumb 71 M5
Newcastle Mons 28 E5
Newcastle Shrops 38 F5
Newcastle Airport Nthumb 73 L6
Newcastle Emlyn Carmth 36 E11
Newcastleton Border 79 P10
Newcastle-under-Lyme Staffs 49 Q6
Newcastle upon Tyne N u Ty 73 M7
Newchapel Pembks 36 D11
Newchapel Surrey 11 M2
Newchurch IoW 9 P9
Newchurch Kent 13 K4
Newchurch Mons 28 E8
Newchurch Powys 38 E11
Newchurch Staffs 40 F3
New Costessey Norfk 45 K7
Newcraighall C Edin 86 G7
New Crofton Wakefd 59 K10
New Cross Gt Lon 21 M7
New Cross Somset 17 K11
New Cumnock E Ayrs 77 K8
New Deer Abers 103 J6
New Denham Bucks 20 G6
Newdigate Surrey 11 K2
New Duston Nhants 31 Q2
New Earswick C York 59 N3
New Edlington Donc 51 M2
New Elgin Moray 101 J3
New Ellerby E R Yk 61 K6
Newell Green Br For 20 E8
New Eltham Gt Lon 21 N8
New End Worcs 30 D3
Newenden Kent 12 G5
New England C Pete 42 H9
Newent Gloucs 29 J4
New Ferry Wirral 56 G10
Newfield Dur 65 L2
Newfield Highld 107 N7
New Fletton C Pete 42 H9
New Forest National Park 9 K6
Newgale Pembks 24 E4
New Galloway D & G 69 P4
Newgate Street Herts 21 L3
New Gilston Fife 87 J1
New Grimsby IoS 2 b1
Newhall Ches E 49 L6
New Hartley Nthumb 73 N5
Newhaven C Edin 86 F7
Newhaven E Susx 11 N9
New Haw Surrey 20 G10
New Hedges Pembks 25 K8
New Holland N Linc 61 J9
Newholm N York 67 J5
New Houghton Derbys 51 L7
New Houghton Norfk 44 D5
Newhouse N Lans 85 N10
New Hutton Cumb 63 K4
Newick E Susx 11 N6
Newington Kent 13 M3
Newington Kent 22 G9
Newington Oxon 19 Q2
New Inn Carmth 26 C2
New Inn Torfn 28 C8
New Invention Shrops 38 F6
New Lakenham Norfk 45 K8
New Lanark S Lans 78 E1
New Lanark Village S Lans 78 E1
Newland C KuH 61 J7
Newland Gloucs 28 G6
Newland N York 59 P8
Newland Somset 15 P5
Newland Worcs 39 P11
Newlandrig Mdloth 86 H9
Newlands Border 79 Q9
Newlands Nthumb 73 J9
Newlands of Dundurcas Moray 101 L5
New Langholm D & G 79 M11
New Leake Lincs 53 L11
New Leeds Abers 103 K4
New Lodge Barns 59 J11
New Longton Lancs 57 K4
New Luce D & G 68 G6
Newlyn Cnwll 2 C9
Newmachar Abers 103 J10
Newmains N Lans 85 N10
New Malden Gt Lon 21 K9
Newman's Green Suffk 34 E7
Newmarket Suffk 33 Q4
Newmarket W Isls 111 d2
New Marske R & Cl 66 E4
New Marston Oxon 31 M11
New Mill Abers 95 N5
Newmill Border 79 P6
New Mill Cnwll 2 C8
New Mill Kirk 58 F11
Newmill Moray 101 N5
Newmillerdam Wakefd 59 J10
Newmill of Inshewan Angus 94 G9
Newmills C Edin 86 E8
New Mills Derbys 50 D4
Newmills Fife 86 B5
Newmills Mons 28 F7
New Mills Powys 38 C2
Newmiln P & K 92 G9
Newmilns E Ayrs 77 J4
New Milton Hants 9 J8
New Mistley Essex 35 J9
New Moat Pembks 25 J4
Newney Green Essex 22 D3
Newnham Hants 20 B11
Newnham Herts 33 J8
Newnham Kent 23 J11
Newnham Nhants 31 M3
Newnham Bridge Worcs 39 M8
Newnham on Severn Gloucs 29 J6
New Ollerton Notts 51 P7
New Oscott Birm 40 E8
New Pitsligo Abers 103 J4
Newport Cnwll 4 H3
Newport E R Yk 60 E7
Newport Essex 33 N9
Newport Gloucs 29 J8
Newport Highld 110 D10
Newport IoW 9 N9
Newport Newpt 28 C10
Newport Pembks 25 J2
Newport Wrekin 49 N10
Newport-on-Tay Fife 93 M9
Newport Pagnell M Keyn 32 C7
Newport Pagnell Services M Keyn 32 C7
New Prestwick S Ayrs 76 F6
New Quay Cerdgn 36 F8
Newquay Cnwll 3 J4
Newquay Zoo Cnwll 3 J4
New Rackheath Norfk 45 L7
New Radnor Powys 38 E9
New Ridley Nthumb 73 J8
New Romney Kent 13 K5
New Rossington Donc 51 N2
New Sauchie Clacks 85 P4
Newseat Abers 102 F8
Newsham Lancs 57 K2
Newsham N York 65 K5
Newsham N York 65 P9
Newsham Nthumb 73 N5
New Sharlston Wakefd 59 J9
Newsholme E R Yk 60 C8
New Silksworth Sundld 73 P9
Newsome Kirk 58 F10
New Somerby Lincs 42 D3
Newstead Border 80 D7
Newstead Notts 51 L9
Newstead Nthumb 81 N8
New Stevenston N Lans 85 M10
Newthorpe Notts 51 L10
New Thundersley Essex 22 F5
Newton Ag & B 83 Q4
Newton Border 80 E9
Newton Brdgnd 26 H12
Newton C Beds 32 H7
Newton Cambs 33 M6
Newton Cambs 43 M7
Newton Ches W 48 H2
Newton Ches W 49 J4
Newton Cumb 62 E7
Newton Derbys 51 K8
Newton Herefs 28 D3
Newton Herefs 39 K10
Newton Highld 107 J11
Newton Highld 107 M11
Newton Highld 107 M8
Newton Highld 110 G6
Newton Lincs 42 F3
Newton Mdloth 86 G8
Newton Moray 100 H3
Newton Moray 101 L3
Newton Nhants 42 C12
Newton Norfk 44 D7
Newton Notts 51 P11
Newton Nthumb 73 J7
Newton S Lans 78 F3
Newton S Lans 85 L10
Newton Sandw 40 D8
Newton Staffs 40 D3
Newton Suffk 34 F8
Newton W Loth 86 C6
Newton Warwks 41 M10
Newton Abbot Devon 6 B8
Newton Arlosh Cumb 71 K5
Newton Aycliffe Dur 65 M3
Newton Bewley Hartpl 66 C3
Newton Blossomville M Keyn 32 D6
Newton Bromswold Nhants 32 E4
Newton Burgoland Leics 41 J6
Newton-by-the-Sea Nthumb 81 P8
Newton by Toft Lincs 52 F6
Newton Ferrers Devon 5 L9
Newton Ferry W Isls 111 b4
Newton Flotman Norfk 45 K9
Newtongrange Mdloth 86 G8
Newton Green Mons 28 F9
Newton Harcourt Leics 41 N7
Newton Heath Manch 57 Q8
Newtonhill Abers 95 P4
Newton-in-Bowland Lancs 63 M11
Newton Kyme N York 59 L5
Newton-le-Willows N York 65 L9
Newton-le-Willows St Hel 57 L9
Newtonloan Mdloth 86 G9
Newton Longville Bucks 32 C9
Newton Mearns E Rens 85 J11
Newtonmill Angus 95 K8
Newtonmore Highld 99 K8
Newton Morrell N York 65 M5
Newton of Balcanquhal P & K 92 H12
Newton of Balcormo Fife 87 K2
Newton-on-Ouse N York 59 L3
Newton-on-Rawcliffe N York 66 H9
Newton-on-the-Moor Nthumb 81 N12
Newton on Trent Lincs 52 B8
Newton Poppleford Devon 6 E5
Newton Purcell Oxon 31 N7
Newton Regis Warwks 40 H6
Newton Reigny Cumb 71 P8
Newton St Cyres Devon 15 Q11
Newton St Faith Norfk 45 K6
Newton St Loe BaNES 17 Q3
Newton St Petrock Devon 14 G9
Newton Solney Derbys 40 H3
Newton Stacey Hants 19 M11
Newton Stewart D & G 69 K6
Newton Tony Wilts 19 J11
Newton Tracey Devon 15 J6
Newton under Roseberry R & Cl 66 D5
Newton upon Derwent E R Yk 60 C4
Newton Valence Hants 10 B4
Newton Wamphray D & G 78 H9
Newton with Scales Lancs 57 J3
Newtown BCP 8 F8
Newtown Cumb 70 H6
Newtown Cumb 71 P3
Newtown D & G 77 N8
Newtown Devon 6 E3
Newtown Devon 15 N7
New Town E Susx 11 P6
Newtown Gloucs 29 J8
Newtown Hants 9 Q5
Newtown Herefs 39 L12
Newtown Highld 98 E7
Newtown IoW 9 M8
Newtown Nthumb 81 L8
Newtown Powys 38 C4
Newtown Shrops 49 J8
Newtown Somset 6 H1
Newtown Staffs 50 B8
Newtown Wigan 57 K7
Newtown Worcs 39 Q10
Newtown Linford Leics 41 M5
Newtown of Beltrees Rens 84 F10
Newtown St Boswells Border 80 D7
New Tredegar Caerph 27 N8
New Trows S Lans 77 N4
Newtyle Angus 93 K7
New Walsoken Cambs 43 M8
New Waltham NE Lin 53 J3
New Winton E Loth 87 J7
Newyork Ag & B 83 P2
New York Lincs 53 J11
New York N Tyne 73 N6
Neyland Pembks 24 G7
Nicholashayne Devon 16 E11
Nicholaston Swans 26 C10
Nidd N York 58 H3
Nigg C Aber 95 Q2
Nigg Highld 107 N7
Nigg Ferry Highld 107 N8
Ninebanks Nthumb 72 E9
Nine Elms Swindn 18 G4
Ninfield E Susx 12 E7
Ningwood IoW 9 L9
Nisbet Border 80 F8
Nisbet Hill Border 80 H4
Niton IoW 9 N11
Nitshill C Glas 85 J10
Nocton Lincs 52 F10
Noke Oxon 31 M10
Nolton Pembks 24 F5
Nolton Haven Pembks 24 F5
No Man's Heath Ches W 49 K6
No Man's Heath Warwks 40 H6
Nomansland Devon 15 P9
Nomansland Wilts 9 J4
Noneley Shrops 49 J9
Nonington Kent 23 N11
Nook Cumb 63 K6
Norbiton Gt Lon 21 K9
Norbury Ches E 49 K6
Norbury Derbys 50 F11
Norbury Gt Lon 21 L9
Norbury Shrops 38 G4
Norbury Staffs 49 P10
Norchard Worcs 39 Q8
Nordelph Norfk 43 N9
Nordley Shrops 39 M3
Norfolk Broads Norfk 45 P8
Norham Nthumb 81 J5
Norley Ches W 49 K2
Norleywood Hants 9 L7
Normanby Lincs 52 E6
Normanby N Linc 60 F10
Normanby N York 66 G10
Normanby R & Cl 66 D4
Normanby le Wold Lincs 52 G5
Normandy Surrey 20 E11
Norman's Green Devon 6 E3
Normanton C Derb 41 J2
Normanton Leics 42 B2
Normanton Notts 51 P9
Normanton Wakefd 59 J9
Normanton le Heath Leics 41 J5
Normanton on Cliffe Lincs 42 D2
Normanton on Soar Notts 41 L3
Normanton on the Wolds Notts 41 N2
Normanton on Trent Notts 52 B9
Norris Green Lpool 56 H9
Norris Hill Leics 41 J4
Norristhorpe Kirk 58 G9
Northall Bucks 32 D11
Northallerton N York 65 P8
Northam C Sotn 9 M5
Northam Devon 14 H6
Northampton Nhants 31 Q2
Northampton Worcs 39 Q8
Northampton Services Nhants 31 Q3
North Anston Rothm 51 M4
North Ascot Br For 20 E9
North Aston Oxon 31 L8
Northaw Herts 21 L3
Northay Somset 6 H1
North Baddesley Hants 9 L4
North Ballachulish Highld 90 E4
North Barrow Somset 17 N9
North Barsham Norfk 44 F3
Northbay W Isls 111 a7
North Benfleet Essex 22 F5
North Berwick E Loth 87 K5
North Boarhunt Hants 9 P5
Northborough C Pete 42 G8
Northbourne Kent 23 P11
North Bovey Devon 5 P4
North Bradley Wilts 18 C9
North Brentor Devon 5 K4
North Brewham Somset 17 Q8
Northbrook Hants 19 N11
North Buckland Devon 14 H4
North Burlingham Norfk 45 N7
North Cadbury Somset 17 P10
North Carlton Lincs 52 D7
North Carlton Notts 51 N4
North Cave E R Yk 60 F7
North Cerney Gloucs 30 D11
North Chailey E Susx 11 N6
Northchapel W Susx 10 F4
North Charford Hants 8 H4
North Charlton Nthumb 81 N9
North Cheam Gt Lon 21 K9
North Cheriton Somset 17 Q10
North Chideock Dorset 7 K4
Northchurch Herts 20 F2
North Cliffe E R Yk 60 E6
North Clifton Notts 52 B8
North Cockerington Lincs 53 L5
North Connel Ag & B 90 C9
North Cornelly Brdgnd 26 H11
North Cotes Lincs 53 K4
Northcott Devon 4 H2
Northcourt Oxon 19 N2
North Cove Suffk 45 P11
North Cowton N York 65 M6
North Crawley M Keyn 32 D7
North Creake Norfk 44 E3
North Curry Somset 17 J10
North Dalton E R Yk 60 F4
North Deighton N York 59 K4
Northdown Kent 23 Q8
North Downs 22 H11
North Duffield N York 59 P6
North Elmham Norfk 44 G6
North Elmsall Wakefd 59 L10
North End C Port 9 Q7
North End Essex 33 Q11
North End Hants 8 G4
North End Nhants 32 D3
North End W Susx 10 F8
Northend Warwks 31 K4
Northenden Manch 57 P10
North Erradale Highld 105 L6
North Evington C Leic 41 N6
North Fambridge Essex 22 G4
North Ferriby E R Yk 60 G8
Northfield Birm 40 D10
Northfield C Aber 95 P1
Northfield E R Yk 60 H8
Northfields Lincs 42 E8
Northfleet Kent 22 D8
North Frodingham E R Yk 61 J4
North Gorley Hants 8 H5
North Green Suffk 35 M4
North Greetwell Lincs 52 E8
North Grimston N York 60 E1
North Haven Shet 111 m5
North Hayling Hants 10 B9
North Hill Cnwll 4 G5
North Hillingdon Gt Lon 20 H6
North Hinksey Village Oxon 31 L11
North Holmwood Surrey 11 J1
North Huish Devon 5 P8
North Hykeham Lincs 52 D9
Northiam E Susx 12 G5
Northill C Beds 32 G7
Northington Hants 19 P12
North Kelsey Lincs 52 F3
North Kessock Highld 107 L11
North Killingholme N Linc 61 K10
North Kilvington N York 65 Q9
North Kilworth Leics 41 N10
North Kyme Lincs 52 G11
North Landing E R Yk 67 Q12
Northlands Lincs 53 K11
Northleach Gloucs 30 E10
North Lee Bucks 20 D2
Northleigh Devon 6 G4
North Leigh Oxon 31 K10
North Leverton with Habblesthorpe Notts 52 B7
Northlew Devon 15 J11
North Littleton Worcs 30 E5
North Lopham Norfk 44 G12
North Luffenham RutInd 42 D9
North Marden W Susx 10 D6
North Marston Bucks 31 Q9
North Middleton Mdloth 86 G9
North Millbrex Abers 102 H6
North Milmain D & G 68 E8
North Molton Devon 15 M6
Northmoor Oxon 19 M1
North Moreton Oxon 19 P3
Northmuir Angus 93 L5
North Mundham W Susx 10 E9
North Muskham Notts 52 B10
North Newbald E R Yk 60 F6
North Newington Oxon 31 K6
North Newnton Wilts 18 G8
North Newton Somset 17 J9
Northney Hants 10 B8
North Nibley Gloucs 29 K9
Northolt Gt Lon 21 J6
Northolt Airport Gt Lon 20 H6
Northop Flints 48 E2
Northop Hall Flints 48 F2
North Ormesby Middsb 66 D4
North Ormsby Lincs 53 J5
Northorpe Kirk 58 G9
Northorpe Lincs 42 H3
Northorpe Lincs 52 C4
North Otterington N York 65 P9
North Owersby Lincs 52 F5
Northowram Calder 58 E8
North Perrott Somset 7 L2
North Petherton Somset 16 H9
North Petherwin Cnwll 4 G3
North Pickenham Norfk 44 E8
North Piddle Worcs 30 C3
North Poorton Dorset 7 M3
Northport Dorset 8 D9
North Queensferry Fife 86 D6
North Rauceby Lincs 42 E2
Northrepps Norfk 45 L3
North Reston Lincs 53 L6
North Rigton N York 58 H4
North Rode Ches E 50 B7
North Ronaldsay Ork 111 i1
North Ronaldsay Airport Ork 111 i1
North Runcton Norfk 43 Q6
North Scarle Lincs 52 C9
North Shian Ag & B 90 C7
North Shields N Tyne 73 N7
North Shoebury Sthend 22 H6
North Shore Bpool 56 F2
North Side C Pete 43 J9
North Somercotes Lincs 53 L4
North Stainley N York 65 M11
North Stifford Thurr 22 C7
North Stoke BaNES 17 Q3
North Stoke Oxon 19 Q4
North Stoke W Susx 10 G7
North Street Kent 23 K10
North Street W Berk 19 Q6
North Sunderland Nthumb 81 P7
North Tamerton Cnwll 14 F11
North Tawton Devon 15 L10
North Third Stirlg 85 M5
North Thoresby Lincs 53 J4
North Tolsta W Isls 111 e1
Northton W Isls 111 b3
North Town Devon 15 J9
North Town Somset 17 N7
North Town W & M 20 E7
North Tuddenham Norfk 44 G7
North Uist W Isls 111 a4
Northumberland National Park Nthumb 72 E5
North Walsham Norfk 45 L4
North Waltham Hants 19 P10
North Warnborough Hants 20 B12
North Weald Bassett Essex 21 P3
North Wheatley Notts 51 Q4
Northwich Ches W 49 M2
Northwick Worcs 39 Q9
North Widcombe BaNES 17 N5
North Willingham Lincs 52 G6
North Wingfield Derbys 51 K7
North Witham Lincs 42 D6
Northwold Norfk 44 C10
Northwood C Stke 50 B10
Northwood Gt Lon 20 H5
Northwood IoW 9 N8
Northwood Shrops 49 J8
Northwood Green Gloucs 29 J5
North Wootton Dorset 17 P12
North Wootton Norfk 43 Q5
North Wootton Somset 17 N7
North Wraxall Wilts 18 B6
North York Moors National Park 66 G7
Norton Donc 59 M10
Norton E Susx 11 P9
Norton Gloucs 29 M4
Norton Halton 57 K11
Norton Nhants 31 N2
Norton Notts 51 M6
Norton Powys 38 F8
Norton S on T 66 C3
Norton Sheff 51 J5
Norton Shrops 39 N3
Norton Suffk 34 F4
Norton Swans 26 E10
Norton W Susx 10 E8
Norton Wilts 18 C4
Norton Worcs 30 D5
Norton Worcs 39 Q11
Norton Bavant Wilts 18 D11
Norton Canes Staffs 40 D6
Norton Canes Services Staffs 40 D6
Norton Canon Herefs 38 H11
Norton Disney Lincs 52 C10
Norton Fitzwarren Somset 16 G10
Norton Green IoW 9 K9
Norton Hawkfield BaNES 17 N4
Norton Heath Essex 22 C3
Norton in Hales Shrops 49 N7
Norton-Juxta-Twycross Leics 41 J6
Norton-le-Clay N York 65 P12
Norton-le-Moors C Stke 50 B9
Norton Lindsey Warwks 30 G2
Norton Little Green Suffk 34 F4
Norton Malreward BaNES 17 N3
Norton-on-Derwent N York 66 H12
Norton St Philip Somset 18 B9
Norton Subcourse Norfk 45 N9
Norton sub Hamdon Somset 17 L11
Norwell Notts 51 Q8
Norwell Woodhouse Notts 51 Q8
Norwich Norfk 45 K8
Norwich Airport Norfk 45 K7
Norwick Shet 111 m2
Norwood Clacks 85 P4
Norwood Green Gt Lon 21 J7
Norwood Hill Surrey 11 K2
Norwoodside Cambs 43 L9
Noss Mayo Devon 5 L10
Nosterfield N York 65 M10
Nostie Highld 97 M4
Notgrove Gloucs 30 E9
Nottage Brdgnd 26 H12
Nottingham C Nott 51 M11
Notton Wakefd 59 J10
Notton Wilts 18 D6
Noutard's Green Worcs 39 P8
Nuffield Oxon 19 Q4
Nunburnholme E R Yk 60 E5
Nuneaton Warwks 41 J8
Nunhead Gt Lon 21 M8
Nun Monkton N York 59 L3
Nunney Somset 17 Q7
Nunnington N York 66 F10
Nunsthorpe NE Lin 53 J2
Nunthorpe C York 59 N4
Nunthorpe Middsb 66 D5
Nunthorpe Village Middsb 66 D5
Nunton Wilts 8 H3
Nunwick N York 65 N11
Nursling Hants 9 L4
Nutbourne W Susx 10 C8
Nutbourne W Susx 10 H6
Nutfield Surrey 21 L12
Nuthall Notts 51 M11
Nuthampstead Herts 33 L9
Nuthurst W Susx 11 J5
Nutley E Susx 11 N5
Nuttall Bury 57 P5
Nybster Highld 110 G3
Nyetimber W Susx 10 E9
Nyewood W Susx 10 C6
Nymans W Susx 11 L4

Nymet Rowland Devon 15 M9
Nymet Tracey Devon 15 M11
Nympsfield Gloucs 29 L8
Nynehead Somset 16 F10
Nyton W Susx 10 E8

O

Oadby Leics 41 N7
Oad Street Kent 22 G10
Oakamoor Staffs 50 D11
Oakbank W Loth 86 C8
Oak Cross Devon 15 J11
Oakdale Caerph 27 P8
Oake Somset 16 F10
Oaken Staffs 39 Q2
Oakenclough Lancs 63 K11
Oakengates Wrekin 49 M12
Oakenshaw Dur 73 L12
Oakenshaw Kirk 58 F8
Oakford Cerdgn 36 G8
Oakford Devon 16 C11
Oakham Rutlnd 42 C8
Oakhanger Hants 10 C3
Oakhill Somset 17 P6
Oakington Cambs 33 L4
Oakle Street Gloucs 29 K5
Oakley Bed 32 E6
Oakley Bucks 31 N10
Oakley Fife 86 B4
Oakley Hants 19 P9
Oakley Suffk 35 J2
Oakridge Lynch Gloucs 29 M7
Oaksey Wilts 29 P9
Oakthorpe Leics 40 H5
Oakwood C Derb 51 J12
Oakworth C Brad 58 D6
Oare Kent 23 J10
Oare Somset 15 N3
Oare Wilts 18 H7
Oasby Lincs 42 E3
Oath Somset 17 K10
Oathlaw Angus 93 N4
Oatlands Park Surrey 20 H9
Oban Ag & B 90 B9
Oban Airport Ag & B 90 C8
Obley Shrops 38 G6
Obney P & K 92 F8
Oborne Dorset 17 P11
Occold Suffk 35 J3
Occumster Highld 110 F8
Ochiltree E Ayrs 76 H7
Ockbrook Derbys 41 K1
Ocker Hill Sandw 40 C8
Ockham Surrey 20 H11
Ockle Highld 89 L3
Ockley Surrey 11 J3
Ocle Pychard Herefs 39 L11
Odcombe Somset 17 M11
Odd Down BaNES 17 Q4
Oddingley Worcs 30 B3
Oddington Gloucs 30 G8
Oddington Oxon 31 M10
Odell Bed 32 D5
Odiham Hants 20 C12
Odsal C Brad 58 F8
Odsey Cambs 33 J8
Odstock Wilts 8 G3
Odstone Leics 41 K6
Offchurch Warwks 31 J2
Offenham Worcs 30 D5
Offerton Stockp 50 B3
Offham E Susx 11 N7
Offham Kent 22 D11
Offham W Susx 10 G8
Offord Cluny Cambs 32 H4
Offord D'Arcy Cambs 32 H4
Offton Suffk 34 H6
Offwell Devon 6 G3
Ogbourne Maizey Wilts 18 H6
Ogbourne St Andrew Wilts 18 H6
Ogbourne St George Wilts 18 H6
Ogle Nthumb 73 K5
Oglet Lpool 56 H11
Ogmore V Glam 16 B2
Ogmore-by-Sea V Glam 16 B2
Ogmore Vale Brdgnd 27 K10
Okeford Fitzpaine Dorset 8 B5
Okehampton Devon 5 M2
Oker Side Derbys 50 H8
Okewood Hill Surrey 11 J3
Old Nhants 32 B3
Old Aberdeen C Aber 95 Q1
Old Alresford Hants 9 P1
Oldany Highld 108 C8
Old Auchenbrack D & G 77 M11
Old Basford C Nott 51 M11
Old Basing Hants 19 Q9
Old Beetley Norfk 44 F6
Oldberrow Warwks 30 E2
Old Bewick Nthumb 81 M9
Old Bolingbroke Lincs 53 K9
Old Bramhope Leeds 58 G5
Old Brampton Derbys 51 J6
Old Bridge of Urr D & G 70 C3
Old Buckenham Norfk 44 H10
Old Burghclere Hants 19 M8
Oldbury Sandw 40 C9
Oldbury Shrops 39 N4
Oldbury Warwks 40 H8
Oldbury-on-Severn S Glos 28 H9
Oldbury on the Hill Gloucs 18 B3
Old Byland N York 66 D9
Old Cantley Donc 51 N1
Oldcastle Mons 28 C4
Old Catton Norfk 45 K7
Old Clee NE Lin 53 J2
Old Cleeve Somset 16 E7
Old Colwyn Conwy 55 N6
Oldcotes Notts 51 N3
Old Coulsdon Gt Lon 21 L11
Old Dailly S Ayrs 76 D10
Old Dalby Leics 41 P3
Old Deer Abers 103 K6
Old Edlington Donc 51 M2
Old Felixstowe Suffk 35 M9
Oldfield Worcs 39 Q8
Old Fletton C Pete 42 H10
Oldford Somset 18 B10

Old Forge Herefs 28 G5
Old Grimsby IoS 2 b1
Old Hall Green Herts 33 L11
Oldham Oldham 58 B12
Oldhamstocks E Loth 87 N7
Old Harlow Essex 21 P2
Old Hunstanton Norfk 44 B2
Old Hurst Cambs 33 J2
Old Hutton Cumb 63 K5
Old Inns Services N Lans 85 N7
Old Kilpatrick W Duns 84 H8
Old Knebworth Herts 32 H11
Old Lakenham Norfk 45 K8
Oldland S Glos 17 P2
Old Langho Lancs 57 M2
Old Leake Lincs 53 L12
Old Malton N York 66 H11
Oldmeldrum Abers 102 H9
Oldmill Cnwll 4 H5
Old Milverton Warwks 30 H1
Oldmixon N Som 17 J5
Old Newton Suffk 34 H4
Old Portlethen Abers 95 Q3
Old Radford C Nott 51 M11
Old Radnor Powys 38 F9
Old Rayne Abers 102 E9
Old Romney Kent 13 K5
Old Shoreham W Susx 11 K8
Oldshoremore Highld 108 D4
Old Sodbury S Glos 29 K11
Old Somerby Lincs 42 D4
Oldstead N York 66 D10
Old Stratford Nhants 31 Q6
Old Struan P & K 92 C3
Old Swinford Dudley 40 B10
Old Thirsk N York 66 B10
Old Town Cumb 63 L5
Old Town E Susx 12 C9
Old Town IoS 2 c2
Old Trafford Traffd 57 P9
Oldwall Cumb 71 P4
Oldwalls Swans 26 C9
Old Warden C Beds 32 G7
Old Weston Cambs 32 F2
Old Wick Highld 110 G6
Old Windsor W & M 20 F8
Old Wives Lees Kent 23 K11
Old Woking Surrey 20 G11
Olgrinmore Highld 110 C5
Olive Green Staffs 40 E4
Oliver's Battery Hants 9 M2
Ollaberry Shet 111 k3
Ollach Highld 96 F3
Ollerton Ches E 57 P12
Ollerton Notts 51 P7
Ollerton Shrops 49 M9
Olney M Keyn 32 C6
Olrig House Highld 110 E3
Olton Solhll 40 F10
Olveston S Glos 28 H10
Ombersley Worcs 39 Q8
Ompton Notts 51 P7
Onchan IoM 56 d5
Onecote Staffs 50 D9
Onibury Shrops 39 J6
Onich Highld 90 E4
Onllwyn Neath 26 H6
Onneley Staffs 49 N6
Onslow Green Essex 33 Q12
Onslow Village Surrey 20 F12
Onston Ches W 49 L1
Opinan Highld 105 L7
Orbliston Moray 101 L4
Orbost Highld 96 B2
Orby Lincs 53 M9
Orchard Portman Somset 16 H10
Orcheston Wilts 18 F10
Orcop Herefs 28 F4
Orcop Hill Herefs 28 F4
Ord Abers 102 E4
Ordhead Abers 102 E12
Ordie Abers 94 G2
Ordiequish Moray 101 L4
Ordsall Notts 51 P5
Ore E Susx 12 G7
Orford Suffk 35 N6
Orford Warrtn 57 L10
Organford Dorset 8 D8
Orkney Islands Ork 111 h2
Orkney Neolithic Ork 111 g2
Orlestone Kent 13 J3
Orleton Herefs 39 J8
Orleton Worcs 39 M8
Orlingbury Nhants 32 C3
Ormesby R & Cl 66 D4
Ormesby St Margaret Norfk 45 P7
Ormesby St Michael Norfk 45 P7
Ormiscaig Highld 105 M4
Ormiston E Loth 86 H8
Ormsaigmore Highld 89 K4
Ormsary Ag & B 83 L8
Ormskirk Lancs 56 H7
Oronsay Ag & B 82 E5
Orphir Ork 111 h2
Orpington Gt Lon 21 P9
Orrell Sefton 56 G9
Orrell Wigan 57 K7
Orroland D & G 70 C6
Orsett Thurr 22 D7
Orslow Staffs 49 P11
Orston Notts 51 Q11
Orton Cumb 63 L1
Orton Nhants 32 B2
Orton Staffs 39 Q3
Orton Longueville C Pete 42 G10
Orton-on-the-Hill Leics 40 H6
Orton Waterville C Pete 42 G10
Orwell Cambs 33 K6
Osbaldeston Lancs 57 M3
Osbaldwick C York 59 N4
Osbaston Leics 41 K6
Osbaston Shrops 48 G10
Osborne House IoW 9 N8
Osbournby Lincs 42 F3
Oscroft Ches W 49 J3
Ose Highld 96 C2
Osgathorpe Leics 41 K4
Osgodby Lincs 52 F5
Osgodby N York 59 N7
Osgodby N York 67 M9
Oskaig Highld 96 G3
Oskamull Ag & B 89 K8

Osmaston Derbys 50 G11
Osmington Dorset 7 Q6
Osmington Mills Dorset 7 Q6
Osmondthorpe Leeds 59 J7
Osmotherley N York 66 C7
Osney Oxon 31 L11
Ospringe Kent 23 J10
Ossett Wakefd 58 H9
Ossington Notts 51 Q7
Osterley Gt Lon 21 J7
Oswaldkirk N York 66 E10
Oswaldtwistle Lancs 57 N4
Oswestry Shrops 48 F9
Otford Kent 21 Q10
Otham Kent 22 F11
Othery Somset 17 K9
Otterbourne Hants 9 M3
Otterburn N York 63 Q9
Otterburn Nthumb 72 F3
Otter Ferry Ag & B 83 P6
Otterham Cnwll 4 E3
Otterhampton Somset 16 H7
Otternish W Isls 111 b4
Ottershaw Surrey 20 G9
Otterswick Shet 111 k3
Otterton Devon 6 E6
Ottery St Mary Devon 6 E4
Ottinge Kent 13 M2
Ottringham E R Yk 61 M8
Oughterside Cumb 71 J7
Oughtibridge Sheff 50 H3
Oughtrington Warrtn 57 M10
Oulston N York 66 D11
Oulton Cumb 71 K5
Oulton Norfk 45 J4
Oulton Staffs 40 B1
Oulton Staffs 45 Q10
Oulton Broad Suffk 45 Q10
Oulton Street Norfk 45 J5
Oundle Nhants 42 E11
Ousdale Highld 110 E8
Ousden Suffk 34 C5
Ousefleet E R Yk 60 E9
Ouston Dur 73 M9
Outgate Cumb 62 G3
Outhgill Cumb 64 B1
Outhill Warwks 30 E2
Outlane Kirk 58 E9
Out Rawcliffe Lancs 56 H1
Out Skerries Shet 111 m3
Outwell Norfk 43 N8
Outwood Surrey 11 L2
Outwoods Staffs 49 P10
Ouzlewell Green Leeds 59 J8
Over Cambs 33 L3
Overbury Worcs 29 N2
Overcombe Dorset 7 Q6
Over Compton Dorset 17 N11
Over Haddon Derbys 50 G7
Over Kellet Lancs 63 K8
Over Kiddington Oxon 31 K9
Overleigh Somset 17 L8
Over Norton Oxon 30 H8
Over Peover Ches E 49 P1
Overpool Ches W 48 H12
Overscaig Highld 108 H10
Overseal Derbys 40 H4
Over Silton N York 66 C8
Oversland Kent 23 K11
Overstone Nhants 32 B4
Over Stowey Somset 16 G8
Overstrand Norfk 45 L3
Over Stratton Somset 17 L11
Overthorpe Nhants 31 L6
Overton C Aber 102 H11
Overton Hants 19 N10
Overton Lancs 62 H9
Overton N York 59 M3
Overton Shrops 39 J7
Overton Swans 26 B10
Overton Wakefd 58 H10
Overton Wrexhm 48 H7
Overtown N Lans 85 N11
Over Wallop Hants 19 K11
Over Whitacre Warwks 40 G8
Over Worton Oxon 31 K8
Oving Bucks 32 A11
Oving W Susx 10 E8
Ovingdean Br & H 11 M8
Ovingham Nthumb 73 J7
Ovington Dur 65 K5
Ovington Essex 34 C8
Ovington Hants 9 P2
Ovington Norfk 44 F9
Ovington Nthumb 73 J7
Ower Hants 9 K4
Owermoigne Dorset 8 B9
Owlerton Sheff 51 J3
Owlsmoor Br For 20 D10
Owlswick Bucks 20 C3
Owmby Lincs 52 E6
Owmby Lincs 52 F2
Owslebury Hants 9 N3
Owston Donc 59 M11
Owston Leics 41 Q6
Owston Ferry N Linc 52 B4
Owstwick E R Yk 61 M7
Owthorne E R Yk 61 N8
Owthorpe Notts 41 P2
Owton Manor Hartpl 66 C2
Oxborough Norfk 44 C9
Oxcombe Lincs 53 K7
Oxenholme Cumb 63 K3
Oxenhope C Brad 58 D7
Oxen Park Cumb 62 G4
Oxenpill Somset 17 L7
Oxenton Gloucs 29 M6
Oxenwood Wilts 19 K8
Oxford Oxon 31 L11
Oxford Airport Oxon 31 L10
Oxford Services Oxon 31 N12
Oxhey Herts 20 H4
Oxhill Dur 73 L9
Oxhill Warwks 30 H5
Oxley Wolves 40 B7
Oxley Green Essex 22 H1
Oxlode Cambs 43 M11
Oxnam Border 80 F9

Oxnead Norfk 45 K5
Oxshott Surrey 21 J10
Oxspring Barns 50 H1
Oxted Surrey 21 N11
Oxton Border 80 C4
Oxton N York 59 L5
Oxton Notts 51 N9
Oxton Wirral 56 F10
Oxwich Swans 26 C10
Oxwich Green Swans 26 C10
Oykel Bridge Highld 106 C11
Oyne Abers 102 E9
Oystermouth Swans 26 E10

P

Pabail W Isls 111 e2
Packington Leics 41 J5
Packmoor C Stke 49 Q5
Padanaram Angus 93 M5
Padbury Bucks 31 Q7
Paddington Gt Lon 21 L7
Paddlesworth Kent 13 M3
Paddlesworth Kent 22 D10
Paddock Wood Kent 12 D2
Padiham Lancs 57 P3
Padside N York 58 F3
Padstow Cnwll 3 K1
Padworth W Berk 19 Q7
Pagham W Susx 10 E9
Paglesham Essex 22 H5
Paignton Torbay 6 B10
Pailton Warwks 41 L10
Painscastle Powys 38 D11
Painshawfield Nthumb 73 J8
Painsthorpe E R Yk 60 E3
Painswick Gloucs 29 M6
Painter's Forstal Kent 23 J10
Paisley Rens 84 H9
Pakefield Suffk 45 Q11
Pakenham Suffk 34 F4
Paley Street W & M 20 E7
Palfrey Wsall 40 D7
Palgrave Suffk 35 J2
Pallington Dorset 8 B8
Palmerston E Ayrs 76 H7
Palnackie D & G 70 D4
Palnure D & G 69 L6
Palterton Derbys 51 L7
Pamber End Hants 19 Q8
Pamber Green Hants 19 Q8
Pamber Heath Hants 19 Q8
Pamington Gloucs 29 N3
Pamphill Dorset 8 E7
Pampisford Cambs 33 N7
Panbride Angus 93 P8
Pancrasweek Devon 14 F10
Pandy Mons 28 D4
Pandy Tudur Conwy 55 N8
Panfield Essex 34 C10
Pangbourne W Berk 19 Q5
Pangdean W Susx 11 L7
Pannal N York 58 H4
Pannal Ash N York 58 H4
Pant Shrops 48 F10
Pantasaph Flints 48 D1
Pant-ffrwyth Brdgnd 27 K11
Pant Glas Gwynd 46 H2
Pantglas Powys 47 M10
Panton Lincs 52 H7
Pant-y-dwr Powys 37 R6
Pant-y-mwyn Flints 48 E3
Panxworth Norfk 45 M7
Papa Stour Shet 111 j3
Papa Stour Airport Shet 111 j4
Papa Westray Ork 111 h1
Papa Westray Airport Ork 111 h1
Papcastle Cumb 70 H8
Papigoe Highld 110 H5
Papple E Loth 87 L7
Papplewick Notts 51 M9
Papworth Everard Cambs 33 J4
Papworth St Agnes Cambs 33 J4
Par Cnwll 3 N5
Parbold Lancs 57 J7
Parbrook Somset 17 N8
Parc Gwynd 47 P5
Parc Seymour Newpt 28 E9
Pardshaw Cumb 70 H9
Parham Suffk 35 M5
Park Nthumb 72 C8
Park D & G 78 E10
Park Corner Oxon 20 B6
Parkend Gloucs 28 H7
Parker's Green Kent 12 C1
Park Farm Kent 13 J3
Parkgate Ches W 56 F12
Parkgate D & G 78 G10
Park Gate Hants 9 N6
Park Gate Leeds 58 F6
Parkgate Surrey 11 K2
Parkhall W Duns 84 H8
Parkham Devon 14 G7
Parkmill Swans 26 D10
Park Royal Gt Lon 21 K7
Parkside N Lans 85 N10
Parkside Dur 73 Q10
Parkstone BCP 8 F8
Park Street Herts 21 J3
Parracombe Devon 15 L3
Parson Drove Cambs 43 L8
Parson's Heath Essex 34 G10
Partick C Glas 85 J9
Partington Traffd 57 N9
Partney Lincs 53 L9
Parton Cumb 70 F10
Partridge Green W Susx 11 J6
Parwich Derbys 50 F9
Passenham Nhants 32 A8
Paston C Pete 42 H9
Paston Norfk 45 M4
Patcham Br & H 11 L8
Patching W Susx 10 H8
Patchway S Glos 28 H11
Pateley Bridge N York 58 F2
Pathhead Fife 86 H3
Pathhead Mdloth 86 H9
Path of Condie P & K 92 G12
Patna E Ayrs 76 H7
Patney Wilts 18 F8

Patrick IoM 56 b5
Patrick Brompton N York 65 L8
Patricroft Salfd 57 N8
Patrington E R Yk 61 M9
Patrington Haven E R Yk 61 M9
Patrixbourne Kent 23 M11
Patterdale Cumb 71 N11
Pattingham Staffs 39 P3
Pattishall Nhants 31 P4
Pattiswick Green Essex 34 D11
Paul Cnwll 2 C9
Paulerspury Nhants 31 Q5
Paull E R Yk 61 K8
Paulton BaNES 17 P5
Paultons Park Hants 9 K4
Pauperhaugh Nthumb 73 K2
Pavenham Bed 32 E5
Pawlett Somset 16 H7
Paxford Gloucs 30 F6
Paxton Border 81 K4
Payhembury Devon 6 E3
Paythorne Lancs 63 P10
Peacehaven E Susx 11 N9
Peak District National Park 50 F3
Peak Forest Derbys 50 E5
Peakirk C Pete 42 G8
Peasedown St John BaNES 17 Q5
Peasemore W Berk 19 M5
Peasenhall Suffk 35 M3
Pease Pottage W Susx 11 L4
Pease Pottage Services W Susx 11 L4
Peaslake Surrey 10 H2
Peasley Cross St Hel 57 K9
Peasmarsh E Susx 12 H5
Peathill Abers 103 J3
Peat Inn Fife 87 J1
Peatling Magna Leics 41 N8
Peatling Parva Leics 41 N9
Pebmarsh Essex 34 E9
Pebsham E Susx 12 F8
Pebworth Worcs 30 F5
Pecket Well Calder 58 C8
Peckforton Ches E 49 K4
Peckham Gt Lon 21 M8
Peckleton Leics 41 L7
Pedlinge Kent 13 L3
Pedmore Dudley 40 B10
Pedwell Somset 17 K8
Peebles Border 79 L2
Peel IoM 56 b4
Peene Kent 13 M3
Pegsdon C Beds 32 G9
Pegswood Nthumb 73 M4
Pegwell Kent 23 Q9
Peinchorran Highld 96 G3
Peinlich Highld 104 F10
Peldon Essex 34 G12
Pelsall Wsall 40 D6
Pelton Dur 73 M9
Pelynt Cnwll 4 F8
Pemberton Carmth 26 D8
Pemberton Wigan 57 K7
Pembrey Carmth 25 P8
Pembridge Herefs 38 H9
Pembroke Pembks 24 H8
Pembroke Dock Pembks 24 G7
Pembrokeshire Coast National Park Pembks 24 E5
Pembury Kent 12 D2
Pen-allt Herefs 28 G3
Penallt Mons 28 F6
Penally Pembks 25 K8
Penarth V Glam 16 G2
Pen-bont Rhydybeddau Cerdgn 37 L4
Penbryn Cerdgn 36 E9
Pencader Carmth 25 Q2
Pencaitland E Loth 87 J8
Pencarnisiog IoA 54 D6
Pencarreg Carmth 37 J10
Pencelli Powys 27 M4
Penclawdd Swans 26 D9
Pencoed Brdgnd 27 K11
Pencombe Herefs 39 L10
Pencraig Herefs 28 G5
Pencraig Powys 48 B9
Pendeen Cnwll 2 B8
Penderyn Rhondd 27 K7
Pendine Carmth 25 L7
Pendlebury Salfd 57 P8
Pendleton Lancs 57 N2
Pendock Worcs 29 K3
Pendoggett Cnwll 4 C4
Pendomer Somset 7 M1
Pendoylan V Glam 16 E2
Penegoes Powys 47 M10
Pen-ffordd Pembks 25 J4
Pengam Caerph 27 N8
Pengam Cardif 27 P12
Penge Gt Lon 21 M8
Pengelly Cnwll 4 D4
Penhallow Cnwll 2 H5
Penhalvean Cnwll 2 G8
Penhill Swindn 18 H3
Penhow Newpt 28 E10
Penicuik Mdloth 86 F9
Penifiler Highld 96 F2
Peninver Ag & B 75 L7
Penistone Barns 50 G1
Penkill S Ayrs 76 D10
Penkridge Staffs 40 B5
Penley Wrexhm 48 H7
Penllyn V Glam 16 C2
Penmachno Conwy 55 L10
Penmaen Caerph 27 P8
Penmaen Swans 26 D10
Penmaenmawr Conwy 55 K6
Penmaenpool Gwynd 47 L9
Penmark V Glam 16 E3
Penmorfa Gwynd 47 J4
Penmynydd IoA 54 G6
Pennal Gwynd 47 L10
Pennan Abers 102 H3
Pennant Powys 47 P10
Pennerley Shrops 38 G3
Pennines 57 C7
Pennington Cumb 62 F6
Pennorth Powys 27 M4
Penn Street Bucks 20 E4
Penny Bridge Cumb 62 F5
Pennycross Ag & B 89 L10

Place	Region	Page	Grid
Pennyghael	Ag & B	89	L10
Pennyglen	S Ayrs	76	E8
Pennymoor	Devon	15	P9
Pennywell	Sundld	73	P9
Penparc	Cerdgn	36	D10
Penperlleni	Mons	28	C7
Penpoll	Cnwll	4	E8
Penponds	Cnwll	2	F7
Penpont	D & G	78	D9
Pen-rhiw	Pembks	36	D11
Penrhiwceiber	Rhondd	27	M8
Pen Rhiwfawr	Neath	26	G6
Penrhiwllan	Cerdgn	36	F11
Penrhiw-pal	Cerdgn	36	F10
Penrhos	Gwynd	46	F6
Penrhos	Mons	28	E6
Penrhyn Bay	Conwy	55	M5
Penrhyn-coch	Cerdgn	37	K4
Penrhyndeudraeth	Gwynd	47	K4
Penrice	Swans	26	C10
Penrioch	N Ayrs	75	N4
Penrith	Cumb	71	Q9
Penrose	Cnwll	3	K2
Penruddock	Cumb	71	N9
Penryn	Cnwll	2	H8
Pensarn	Carmth	55	P6
Pensax	Worcs	39	N8
Penselwood	Somset	17	R9
Pensford	BaNES	17	N4
Pensham	Worcs	30	C5
Penshaw	Sundld	73	N9
Penshurst	Kent	11	Q2
Pensilva	Cnwll	4	G6
Pensnett	Dudley	40	B9
Pentewan	Cnwll	3	M6
Pentir	Gwynd	54	H8
Pentire	Cnwll	3	H4
Pentlow	Essex	34	D7
Pentney	Norfk	44	C7
Pentonbridge	Cumb	79	P12
Penton Mewsey	Hants	19	K10
Pentraeth	IoA	54	G6
Pentre	Mons	28	E8
Pentre	Rhondd	27	K9
Pentre	Shrops	48	G11
Pentrebach	Myr Td	27	M7
Pentre-bach	Powys	27	J3
Pentre Berw	IoA	54	F7
Pentrecelyn	Denbgs	48	D5
Pentre-celyn	Powys	47	P9
Pentre-chwyth	Swans	26	F9
Pentre-cwrt	Carmth	25	P2
Pentredwr	Denbgs	48	E6
Pentrefelin	Gwynd	47	J4
Pentrefoelas	Conwy	55	M10
Pentregat	Cerdgn	36	F9
Pentre-Gwenlais	Carmth	26	E5
Pentre Hodrey	Shrops	38	G6
Pentre Llanrhaeadr	Denbgs	48	C3
Pentre Meyrick	V Glam	16	C2
Pentre-tafarn-y-fedw	Conwy	55	M8
Pentrich	Derbys	51	J9
Pentridge	Dorset	8	F4
Pen-twyn	Mons	28	F7
Pentwynmaur	Caerph	27	P9
Pentyrch	Cardif	27	M11
Penwithick	Cnwll	3	M5
Penybanc	Carmth	26	E4
Penybont	Powys	38	C8
Pen-y-bont	Powys	48	E10
Penybontfawr	Powys	48	C9
Pen-y-bryn	Pembks	36	C11
Penycae	Wrexhm	48	F6
Pen-y-clawdd	Mons	28	E7
Pen-y-coedcae	Rhondd	27	M10
Penycwn	Pembks	24	E4
Pen-y-felin	Flints	48	D2
Penyffordd	Flints	48	F4
Pen-y-Garnedd	Powys	48	C10
Pen-y-graig	Gwynd	46	C5
Penygraig	Rhondd	27	L10
Penygroes	Carmth	26	D6
Penygroes	Gwynd	54	F10
Pen-y-Mynydd	Carmth	26	C7
Penymynydd	Flints	48	F3
Penysarn	IoA	54	F4
Pen-y-stryt	Denbgs	48	E5
Penywaun	Rhondd	27	K7
Penzance	Cnwll	2	D9
Peopleton	Worcs	30	C4
Peplow	Shrops	49	L9
Perceton	N Ayrs	76	F4
Percyhorner	Abers	103	K3
Perham Down	Wilts	19	J10
Periton	Somset	16	C7
Perivale	Gt Lon	21	J6
Perkins Village	Devon	6	D5
Perlethorpe	Notts	51	N6
Perranarworthal	Cnwll	2	H7
Perranporth	Cnwll	2	H5
Perranuthnoe	Cnwll	2	D9
Perranwell	Cnwll	2	H7
Perranzabuloe	Cnwll	2	H5
Perry	Birm	40	E8
Perry Barr	Birm	40	E8
Perry Green	Wilts	18	E3
Pershall	Staffs	49	P9
Pershore	Worcs	30	C5
Pertenhall	Bed	32	F4
Perth	P & K	92	G10
Perthy	Shrops	48	G8
Perton	Herefs	28	H2
Perton	Staffs	39	Q3
Peterborough	C Pete	42	H9
Peterborough Services	Cambs	42	G10
Peterchurch	Herefs	28	D2
Peterculter	C Aber	95	N2
Peterhead	Abers	103	M6
Peterlee	Dur	73	Q11
Petersfield	Hants	10	C5
Petersham	Gt Lon	21	J8
Peters Marland	Devon	14	H9
Peterstone Wentlooge	Newpt	28	B11
Peterston-super-Ely	V Glam	16	E2
Peterstow	Herefs	28	G4
Peter Tavy	Devon	5	K5
Petham	Kent	23	L12
Petherwin Gate	Cnwll	4	G3
Petrockstow	Devon	14	H9
Pett	E Susx	12	G7
Pettaugh	Suffk	35	J5
Petterden	Angus	93	M7
Pettinain	S Lans	77	Q3
Pettistree	Suffk	35	L6
Petton	Devon	16	D10
Petts Wood	Gt Lon	21	N9
Pettycur	Fife	86	F5
Pettymuk	Abers	103	J9
Petworth	W Susx	10	F6
Pevensey	E Susx	12	D8
Pevensey Bay	E Susx	12	D8
Pewsey	Wilts	18	H8
Pewsham	Wilts	18	D6
Phepson	Worcs	30	B3
Philham	Devon	14	E7
Philiphaugh	Border	79	N4
Phillack	Cnwll	2	E7
Philleigh	Cnwll	3	K7
Philpstown	W Loth	86	C6
Phoenix Green	Hants	20	C11
Pibsbury	Somset	17	L10
Pickburn	Donc	59	L11
Pickering	N York	66	H10
Pickford	Covtry	40	H10
Pickhill	N York	65	N10
Picklescott	Shrops	38	H3
Pickmere	Ches E	57	M12
Pickney	Somset	16	G9
Pickwell	Leics	42	B7
Pickworth	Lincs	42	F4
Pickworth	Rutlnd	42	E7
Picton	Ches W	48	H2
Picton	N York	65	P6
Piddinghoe	E Susx	11	N9
Piddington	Nhants	32	B6
Piddington	Oxon	31	N10
Piddlehinton	Dorset	7	Q4
Piddletrenthide	Dorset	7	Q3
Pidley	Cambs	33	K2
Piercebridge	Darltn	65	L4
Pierowall	Ork	111	h1
Pilgrims Hatch	Essex	22	C4
Pilham	Lincs	52	C5
Pillaton	Cnwll	4	H7
Pillerton Hersey	Warwks	30	H4
Pillerton Priors	Warwks	30	H5
Pilley	Barns	51	J1
Pilley	Hants	9	K7
Pillgwenlly	Newpt	28	C10
Pilling	Lancs	62	H11
Pilning	S Glos	28	G10
Pilsbury	Derbys	50	F7
Pilsdon	Dorset	7	K3
Pilsley	Derbys	50	G8
Pilsley	Derbys	51	K8
Pilson Green	Norfk	45	N7
Piltdown	E Susx	11	N5
Pilton	Devon	15	K5
Pilton	Nhants	42	E12
Pilton	Rutlnd	42	D9
Pilton	Somset	17	N7
Pimlico	Herts	20	H3
Pimperne	Dorset	8	D5
Pinchbeck	Lincs	43	J5
Pin Green	Herts	33	J3
Pinhoe	Devon	6	C4
Pinley Green	Warwks	30	G2
Pinminnoch	S Ayrs	76	D11
Pinmore	S Ayrs	76	D11
Pinn	Devon	6	E5
Pinner	Gt Lon	20	H5
Pinner Green	Gt Lon	20	H5
Pinvin	Worcs	30	C4
Pinwherry	S Ayrs	68	G2
Pinxton	Derbys	51	L9
Pipe and Lyde	Herefs	39	J12
Pipe Aston	Herefs	39	J7
Pipe Gate	Shrops	49	N7
Piperdam	Angus	93	K8
Piperhill	Highld	100	D5
Pipewell	Nhants	42	B11
Pirbright	Surrey	20	F11
Pirnie	Border	80	E8
Pirnmill	N Ayrs	75	N4
Pirton	Herts	32	G9
Pishill	Oxon	20	B5
Pistyll	Gwynd	46	E3
Pitblae	Abers	103	K3
Pitcairngreen	P & K	92	F9
Pitcalnie	Highld	107	N7
Pitcaple	Abers	102	F9
Pitcairity	Angus	94	F8
Pitchcombe	Gloucs	29	L7
Pitchcott	Bucks	31	Q9
Pitchford	Shrops	39	K2
Pitch Green	Bucks	20	C3
Pitchroy	Moray	101	J7
Pitcombe	Somset	17	P9
Pitcox	E Loth	87	M7
Pitfichie	Abers	102	E11
Pitglassie	Abers	102	F6
Pitgrudy	Highld	107	N4
Pitlessie	Fife	86	G1
Pitlochry	P & K	92	D4
Pitmachie	Abers	102	E8
Pitmain	Highld	99	L8
Pitmedden	Abers	103	J9
Pitmedden Garden	Abers	103	J9
Pitminster	Somset	16	G11
Pitmuies	Angus	93	P6
Pitmunie	Abers	102	E11
Pitney	Somset	17	L9
Pitroddie	P & K	93	J10
Pitscottie	Fife	93	M11
Pitsea	Essex	22	E6
Pitsford	Nhants	31	Q1
Pitstone	Bucks	20	F1
Pittarrow	Abers	95	M7
Pittenweem	Fife	87	K1
Pittington	Dur	73	N11
Pittodrie House Hotel	Abers	102	F9
Pitton	Wilts	8	H2
Pittulie	Abers	103	K2
Pity Me	Dur	73	M10
Pixham	Surrey	21	J12
Plains	N Lans	85	N9
Plaish	Shrops	39	K3
Plaistow	Gt Lon	21	N6
Plaistow	W Susx	10	G4
Plaitford	Hants	9	J4
Plawsworth	Dur	73	M10
Plaxtol	Kent	22	C11
Playden	E Susx	12	H6
Playford	Suffk	35	K7
Play Hatch	Oxon	20	B7
Playing Place	Cnwll	3	J7
Playley Green	Gloucs	29	K3
Plealey	Shrops	38	H2
Plean	Stirlg	85	P5
Pleasance	Fife	93	J12
Pleasington	Bl w D	57	M4
Pleasley	Derbys	51	L7
Pleasurewood Hills	Suffk	45	Q10
Plemstall	Ches W	49	J2
Pleshey	Essex	22	D1
Plockton	Highld	97	L3
Plowden	Shrops	38	H5
Pluckley	Kent	12	H2
Pluckley Thorne	Kent	12	H2
Plumbland	Cumb	71	J7
Plumley	Ches E	49	N1
Plumpton	Cumb	71	P7
Plumpton	E Susx	11	M7
Plumpton	Nhants	31	N5
Plumpton Green	E Susx	11	M6
Plumstead	Gt Lon	21	N7
Plumstead	Norfk	45	J3
Plumtree	Notts	41	N2
Plungar	Leics	42	Q1
Plurenden	Kent	12	H3
Plush	Dorset	7	Q3
Plwmp	Cerdgn	36	F9
Plymouth	C Plym	5	K8
Plympton	C Plym	5	L8
Plymstock	C Plym	5	L9
Plymtree	Devon	6	E3
Pockley	N York	66	F9
Pocklington	E R Yk	60	D4
Podimore	Somset	17	M10
Podington	Bed	32	D4
Podmore	Staffs	49	P8
Pointon	Lincs	42	G4
Pokesdown	BCP	8	G8
Polbain	Highld	105	Q1
Polbathic	Cnwll	4	H8
Polbeth	W Loth	86	B9
Poldark Mine	Cnwll	2	G9
Polebrook	Nhants	42	F11
Polegate	E Susx	12	C8
Polesden Lacey	Surrey	21	J11
Polesworth	Warwks	40	H7
Polglass	Highld	105	Q2
Polgooth	Cnwll	3	M5
Polgown	D & G	77	M9
Poling	W Susx	10	G8
Poling Corner	W Susx	10	G8
Polkerris	Cnwll	4	D9
Pollington	E R Yk	59	N9
Polloch	Highld	89	Q3
Pollokshaws	C Glas	85	J10
Pollokshields	C Glas	85	J9
Polmassick	Cnwll	3	L6
Polmont	Falk	85	Q7
Polnish	Highld	97	K12
Polperro	Cnwll	4	F9
Polruan	Cnwll	4	E9
Polstead	Suffk	34	G8
Poltalloch	Ag & B	83	M4
Poltimore	Devon	6	C4
Polton	Mdloth	86	F8
Polwarth	Border	80	G4
Polyphant	Cnwll	4	G4
Polzeath	Cnwll	4	C4
Pomathorn	Mdloth	86	F9
Pondersbridge	Cambs	43	J10
Ponders End	Gt Lon	21	M4
Ponsanooth	Cnwll	2	H8
Ponsworthy	Devon	5	N5
Pont Abraham Services	Carmth	26	D7
Pontantwn	Carmth	25	Q4
Pontardawe	Neath	26	F7
Pontarddulais	Swans	26	D7
Pont-ar-gothi	Carmth	26	C5
Pontarsais	Carmth	25	Q3
Pontblyddyn	Flints	48	F4
Pontcysyllte Aqueduct	Wrexhm	48	F7
Pontefract	Wakefd	59	L9
Ponteland	Nthumb	73	L6
Ponterwyd	Cerdgn	37	M4
Pontesbury	Shrops	38	H2
Pontesford	Shrops	38	H2
Pontfadog	Wrexhm	48	E7
Pontfaen	Pembks	24	H3
Pont-faen	Powys	27	L3
Pontgarreg	Cerdgn	36	F9
Ponthenri	Carmth	26	C7
Ponthir	Torfn	28	C9
Ponthirwaun	Cerdgn	36	D10
Pontllanfraith	Caerph	27	P9
Pontlliw	Swans	26	E8
Pontllyfni	Gwynd	54	F10
Pontlottyn	Caerph	27	N7
Pontnêddfechan	Neath	27	J6
Pontnewydd	Torfn	28	C9
Pontrhydfendigaid	Cerdgn	37	M7
Pont-rhyd-y-fen	Neath	26	H9
Pontrhydygroes	Cerdgn	37	M6
Pontrilas	Herefs	28	D4
Pont Robert	Powys	48	C11
Pontshaen	Cerdgn	36	G10
Pontsticill	Myr Td	27	M6
Pontwelly	Carmth	36	G11
Pontyates	Carmth	26	C7
Pontybodkin	Flints	48	F4
Pontyberem	Carmth	26	C6
Pontyclun	Rhondd	27	L11
Pontycymer	Brdgnd	27	J9
Pontymister	Caerph	27	P10
Pont-y-pant	Conwy	55	L10
Pontypool	Torfn	28	C8
Pontypridd	Rhondd	27	M10
Pontywaun	Caerph	27	P9
Pool	Cnwll	2	G7
Poole	BCP	8	E9
Poole Keynes	Gloucs	18	E2
Poolewe	Highld	105	M6
Pooley Bridge	Cumb	71	P10
Poolfold	Staffs	50	B8
Poolhill	Gloucs	29	J3
Pool in Wharfedale	Leeds	58	G5
Pool of Muckhart	Clacks	86	B3
Pool Street	Essex	34	C8
Poplar	Gt Lon	21	M7
Porchfield	IoW	9	M8
Poringland	Norfk	45	L9
Porkellis	Cnwll	2	G8
Porlock	Somset	15	Q3
Porlock Weir	Somset	15	P3
Portachoillan	Ag & B	83	L10
Port Appin	Ag & B	90	C7
Port Askaig	Ag & B	82	E8
Portavadie	Ag & B	83	P8
Port Bannatyne	Ag & B	84	B9
Portbury	N Som	17	M2
Port Carlisle	Cumb	71	L3
Port Charlotte	Ag & B	82	C10
Portchester	Hants	9	Q6
Port Driseach	Ag & B	83	Q8
Port Ellen	Ag & B	74	E4
Port Elphinstone	Abers	102	G10
Portencalzie	D & G	68	D5
Portencross	N Ayrs	76	C2
Port Erin	IoM	56	a6
Portesham	Dorset	7	N5
Portessie	Moray	101	N3
Port Eynon	Swans	26	C10
Portfield Gate	Pembks	24	G6
Portgate	Devon	5	J3
Port Gaverne	Cnwll	4	C4
Port Glasgow	Inver	84	F7
Portgordon	Moray	101	M3
Portgower	Highld	110	B11
Porth	Cnwll	3	J4
Porth	Rhondd	27	L9
Porthallow	Cnwll	2	H10
Porthallow	Cnwll	4	F9
Porthcawl	Brdgnd	26	H12
Porthcothan	Cnwll	3	K2
Porthcurno	Cnwll	2	B10
Port Henderson	Highld	105	L7
Porthgain	Pembks	24	E3
Porthgwarra	Cnwll	2	B10
Porthill	Staffs	49	Q6
Porthkerry	V Glam	16	E3
Porthleven	Cnwll	2	F9
Porthmadog	Gwynd	47	J4
Porth Navas	Cnwll	2	H9
Porthoustock	Cnwll	3	J10
Porthpean	Cnwll	3	M5
Porthtowan	Cnwll	2	G6
Porthyrhyd	Carmth	26	C5
Portincaple	Ag & B	84	D4
Portington	E R Yk	60	D7
Portinnisherrich	Ag & B	83	P2
Portinscale	Cumb	71	L10
Port Isaac	Cnwll	4	C4
Portishead	N Som	17	L2
Portknockie	Moray	101	N2
Portland	Dorset	7	P8
Portlethen	Abers	95	Q3
Portling	D & G	70	E5
Portloe	Cnwll	3	L7
Port Logan	D & G	68	E10
Portmahomack	Highld	107	Q5
Portmeirion	Gwynd	47	J4
Portmellon	Cnwll	3	M7
Port Mòr	Highld	89	J1
Portnacroish	Ag & B	90	C6
Portnaguran	W Isls	111	e2
Portnahaven	Ag & B	74	B2
Portnalong	Highld	96	D3
Port nan Giuran	W Isls	111	e2
Port nan Long	W Isls	111	b4
Port Nis	W Isls	111	e1
Portobello	C Edin	86	G7
Portobello	Wolves	40	C7
Port of Menteith	Stirlg	85	J3
Port of Ness	W Isls	111	e1
Porton	Wilts	18	H12
Portpatrick	D & G	68	D8
Port Quin	Cnwll	4	B4
Port Ramsay	Ag & B	90	B7
Portreath	Cnwll	2	F6
Portreath Harbour	Cnwll	2	F6
Portree	Highld	96	F2
Port Righ	Ag & B	75	M5
Port St Mary	IoM	56	b7
Portscatho	Cnwll	3	K8
Portsea	C Port	9	Q7
Portskerra	Highld	109	Q3
Portskewett	Mons	28	F10
Portslade	Br & H	11	K8
Portslade-by-Sea	Br & H	11	L8
Portslogan	D & G	68	D7
Portsmouth	C Port	9	Q7
Portsmouth	Calder	58	B8
Portsmouth Dockyard	C Port	9	Q7
Port Soderick	IoM	56	c6
Portsonachan Hotel	Ag & B	90	E11
Portsoy	Abers	102	D3
Port Sunlight	Wirral	56	G11
Portswood	C Sotn	9	M5
Port Talbot	Neath	26	G10
Port Tennant	Swans	26	F9
Portuairk	Highld	89	J4
Portway	Sandw	40	C9
Portway	Worcs	40	E11
Port Wemyss	Ag & B	74	B3
Port William	D & G	69	J9
Portwrinkle	Cnwll	4	H9
Portyerrock	D & G	69	L10
Poslingford	Suffk	34	C7
Posso	Border	79	K3
Postbridge	Devon	5	N4
Postcombe	Oxon	20	B4
Postling	Kent	13	M3
Postwick	Norfk	45	L8
Potarch	Abers	95	K3
Potten End	Herts	20	G2
Potter Brompton	N York	67	L11
Potterhanworth	Lincs	52	E9
Potterhanworth Booths	Lincs	52	F9
Potter Heigham	Norfk	45	N6
Potterne	Wilts	18	E8
Potterne Wick	Wilts	18	F8
Potters Bar	Herts	21	K3
Potters Crouch	Herts	20	H3
Potters Green	Covtry	41	J10
Potters Marston	Leics	41	L8
Potterspury	Nhants	31	Q5
Potter Street	Essex	21	P2
Potterton	Abers	103	K11
Potto	N York	66	C6
Potton	C Beds	32	H6
Pott Shrigley	Ches E	50	C5
Poughill	Cnwll	14	D10
Poughill	Devon	15	P9
Poulner	Hants	8	H6
Poulshot	Wilts	18	E8
Poulton	Gloucs	18	G1
Poulton	Wirral	56	F10
Poulton-le-Fylde	Lancs	56	G2
Poundbury	Dorset	7	P5
Pound Green	E Susx	11	P5
Pound Green	Suffk	34	C6
Pound Hill	W Susx	11	L3
Poundon	Bucks	31	N8
Poundsgate	Devon	5	N6
Poundstock	Cnwll	14	D11
Pouton	D & G	69	L9
Povey Cross	Surrey	11	L2
Powburn	Nthumb	81	M10
Powderham	Devon	6	C6
Powerstock	Dorset	7	M4
Powfoot	D & G	71	J3
Powick	Worcs	39	Q10
Powmill	P & K	86	B3
Poxwell	Dorset	7	Q6
Poyle	Slough	20	G7
Poynings	W Susx	11	L7
Poyntington	Dorset	17	P11
Poynton	Ches E	50	B4
Poynton Green	Wrekin	49	K10
Praa Sands	Cnwll	2	E9
Praze-an-Beeble	Cnwll	2	F8
Prees	Shrops	49	K8
Preesall	Lancs	62	G11
Prees Green	Shrops	49	K8
Prees Heath	Shrops	49	K7
Prees Higher Heath	Shrops	49	K8
Pren-gwyn	Cerdgn	36	G10
Prenteg	Gwynd	47	J3
Prescot	Knows	57	J9
Prescott	Devon	16	E12
Presnerb	Angus	94	C8
Prestatyn	Denbgs	56	C11
Prestbury	Ches E	50	B4
Prestbury	Gloucs	29	N4
Presteigne	Powys	38	G8
Prestleigh	Somset	17	P7
Preston	Border	87	P10
Preston	Br & H	11	L8
Preston	Devon	6	B7
Preston	Dorset	7	Q6
Preston	E R Yk	61	K7
Preston	Gloucs	18	F1
Preston	Herts	32	H10
Preston	Kent	23	K10
Preston	Kent	23	N10
Preston	Lancs	57	K4
Preston	Nthumb	81	P8
Preston	Rutlnd	42	C9
Preston	Somset	16	E8
Preston	Torbay	6	B9
Preston	Wilts	18	F5
Preston Bagot	Warwks	30	F2
Preston Bissett	Bucks	31	P8
Preston Bowyer	Somset	16	F10
Preston Brockhurst	Shrops	49	K9
Preston Brook	Halton	57	K11
Preston Candover	Hants	19	Q11
Preston Capes	Nhants	31	M3
Preston Green	Warwks	30	F2
Preston Gubbals	Shrops	49	J10
Preston on Stour	Warwks	30	G4
Preston on the Hill	Halton	57	K11
Preston on Wye	Herefs	28	D1
Prestonpans	E Loth	86	H7
Preston Patrick	Cumb	63	K5
Preston Plucknett	Somset	17	M11
Preston St Mary	Suffk	34	F6
Preston-under-Scar	N York	65	J8
Preston upon the Weald Moors	Wrekin	49	M11
Preston Wynne	Herefs	39	K11
Prestwich	Bury	57	P7
Prestwick	S Ayrs	76	F6
Prestwick Airport	S Ayrs	76	F6
Prestwood	Bucks	20	E4
Prickwillow	Cambs	33	P1
Priddy	Somset	17	M6
Priest Hutton	Lancs	63	K7
Priestland	E Ayrs	77	J4
Priest Weston	Shrops	38	F3
Primrosehill	Border	87	P10
Primrose Hill	Dudley	40	C9
Primsidemill	Border	80	H8
Prince of Wales Bridge	Mons	28	F10
Princes Risborough	Bucks	20	D3
Princethorpe	Warwks	41	K12
Princetown	Devon	5	M5
Priors Hardwick	Warwks	31	L3
Priorslee	Wrekin	49	N12
Priors Marston	Warwks	31	L3
Priors Norton	Gloucs	29	M4
Priston	BaNES	17	Q4
Prittlewell	Sthend	22	G6
Privett	Hants	10	B5
Prixford	Devon	15	J5
Probus	Cnwll	3	K6
Prora	E Loth	87	K6
Prospect	Cumb	71	J7
Prospidnick	Cnwll	2	F9
Prostonhill	Abers	102	H3
Prudhoe	Nthumb	73	K8
Pubil	P & K	91	L7
Publow	BaNES	17	P4
Puckeridge	Herts	33	L11
Puckington	Somset	17	K11
Pucklechurch	S Glos	17	Q2
Puddington	Ches W	48	G2
Puddington	Devon	15	P9
Puddletown	Dorset	7	Q4
Pudsey	Leeds	58	G7
Pulborough	W Susx	10	G6
Pulford	Ches W	48	G4
Pulham	Dorset	7	Q2
Pulham Market	Norfk	45	K11
Pulham St Mary	Norfk	45	L11
Pulloxhill	C Beds	32	F8
Pulverbatch	Shrops	38	H2
Pumpherston	W Loth	86	C8
Pumsaint	Carmth	37	K11

Puncheston – Roster 185

Puncheston Pembks 24 H3
Puncknowle Dorset 7 M5
Punnett's Town E Susx 12 C6
Purbrook Hants 10 A8
Purfleet Thurr 22 B7
Puriton Somset 17 J7
Purleigh Essex 22 G3
Purley Gt Lon 21 L10
Purley on Thames W Berk 19 Q5
Purse Caundle Dorset 17 Q11
Purtington Somset 7 K2
Purton Gloucs 29 J7
Purton Gloucs 29 J7
Purton Wilts 18 G4
Purton Stoke Wilts 18 G3
Pury End Nhants 31 P5
Pusey Oxon 19 L2
Putley Herefs 28 H2
Putley Green Herefs 28 H2
Putney Gt Lon 21 K8
Puttenham Surrey 10 E1
Puxley Nhants 31 Q6
Puxton N Som 17 K4
Pwll Carmth 26 C8
Pwll-glâs Denbgs 48 C5
Pwllgloyw Powys 27 L3
Pwllheli Gwynd 46 F4
Pwllmeyric Mons 28 F9
Pwll-trap Carmth 25 M5
Pwll-y-glaw Neath 26 H9
Pye Bridge Derbys 51 K9
Pyecombe W Susx 11 L7
Pyle Brdgnd 26 H11
Pyleigh Somset 16 F9
Pylle Somset 17 N8
Pymoor Cambs 43 M11
Pymore Dorset 7 L4
Pyrford Surrey 20 G10
Pyrton Oxon 20 B4
Pytchley Nhants 32 C2
Pyworthy Devon 14 F10

Q

Quadring Lincs 42 H4
Quadring Eaudike Lincs 43 J4
Quainton Bucks 31 Q9
Quantock Hills Somset 16 G8
Quarff Shet 111 k4
Quarley Hants 19 J11
Quarndon Derbys 51 J11
Quarrier's Village Inver 84 F9
Quarrington Lincs 42 F2
Quarrington Hill Dur 73 N12
Quarry Bank Dudley 40 B9
Quarrywood Moray 101 J3
Quarter N Ayrs 84 D10
Quarter S Lans 85 M11
Quatford Shrops 39 N4
Quatt Shrops 39 N5
Quebec Dur 73 L11
Quedgeley Gloucs 29 L6
Queen Adelaide Cambs 33 P1
Queenborough Kent 22 H8
Queen Camel Somset 17 N10
Queen Charlton BaNES 17 P3
Queen Elizabeth Forest Park Stirlg 84 H3
Queenhill Worcs 29 M2
Queen Oak Dorset 8 B2
Queen's Bower IoW 9 P9
Queensbury C Brad 58 E7
Queensferry Flints 48 G2
Queensferry Crossing Fife 86 D6
Queenslie C Glas 85 L9
Queen's Park Bed 32 E6
Queen's Park Nhants 31 Q2
Queenzieburn N Lans 85 L7
Quendon Essex 33 N10
Queniborough Leics 41 N5
Quenington Gloucs 30 F12
Queslett Birm 40 E8
Quethiock Cnwll 4 G7
Quidenham Norfk 44 G11
Quidhampton Wilts 8 G2
Quinton Nhants 31 R4
Quintrell Downs Cnwll 3 J4
Quixwood Border 87 P9
Quoig P & K 92 C10
Quorn Leics 41 M4
Quothquan S Lans 78 G2
Quoyburray Ork 111 h2
Quoyloo Ork 111 g2

R

Raasay Highld 96 G2
Rachan Mill Border 79 J3
Rachub Gwynd 55 J7
Rackenford Devon 15 P8
Rackham W Susx 10 G7
Rackheath Norfk 45 L7
Racks D & G 70 G1
Rackwick Ork 111 g3
Radbourne Derbys 40 H1
Radcliffe Bury 57 P7
Radcliffe on Trent Notts 51 N11
Radclive Bucks 31 P7
Raddery Highld 107 L9
Radernie Fife 87 J1
Radford Covtry 41 J10
Radford Semele Warwks 31 J2
Radlett Herts 21 J4
Radley Oxon 19 N2
Radley Green Essex 22 D3
Radnage Bucks 20 C4
Radstock BaNES 17 P5
Radstone Nhants 31 N6
Radway Warwks 31 J5
Radwell Bed 32 E5
Radwell Herts 32 H9
Radwinter Essex 33 P8
Radyr Cardif 27 N11
Rafford Moray 100 G4
RAF Museum Cosford Shrops 39 P2
RAF Museum Hendon Gt Lon 21 K5
Ragdale Leics 41 P4
Raglan Mons 28 E7
Ragnall Notts 52 B8
Raigbeg Highld 99 M4
Rainbow Hill Worcs 39 Q10
Rainford St Hel 57 J8
Rainham Gt Lon 21 Q7
Rainham Medway 22 F9
Rainhill St Hel 57 J9
Rainhill Stoops St Hel 57 J10
Rainow Ches E 50 C6
Rainton N York 65 P11
Rainworth Notts 51 N8
Rait P & K 93 J9
Raithby Lincs 53 K6
Raithby Lincs 53 L9
Rake Hants 10 C5
Ralia Highld 99 K9
Ramasaig Highld 96 A2
Rame Cnwll 2 G8
Rame Cnwll 5 J9
Rampisham Dorset 7 N3
Rampside Cumb 62 E8
Rampton Cambs 33 L3
Rampton Notts 52 B7
Ramsbottom Bury 57 P5
Ramsbury Wilts 19 J6
Ramscraigs Highld 110 D9
Ramsdean Hants 10 B5
Ramsdell Hants 19 P8
Ramsden Oxon 31 J10
Ramsden Bellhouse Essex 22 E5
Ramsey Cambs 43 J11
Ramsey Essex 35 K10
Ramsey IoM 56 e3
Ramsey Forty Foot Cambs 43 K11
Ramsey Heights Cambs 43 J12
Ramsey Island Essex 23 J3
Ramsey Island Pembks 24 C4
Ramsey Mereside Cambs 43 J11
Ramsey St Mary's Cambs 43 J11
Ramsgate Kent 23 Q9
Ramsgill N York 65 K12
Ramshope Nthumb 80 G12
Ramshorn Staffs 50 E10
Ramsnest Common Surrey 10 F4
Ranby Lincs 52 H7
Ranby Notts 51 P5
Rand Lincs 52 F7
Randwick Gloucs 29 L7
Ranfurly Rens 84 G9
Rangemore Staffs 40 F3
Rangeworthy S Glos 29 J10
Rankinston E Ayrs 76 H8
Rannoch Station P & K 91 L5
Ranscombe Somset 16 C7
Ranskill Notts 51 P4
Ranton Staffs 49 Q10
Ranton Green Staffs 49 Q10
Ranworth Norfk 45 M7
Raploch Stirlg 85 N4
Rapness Ork 111 h1
Rascarrel D & G 70 D6
Rashfield Ag & B 84 C6
Rashwood Worcs 30 B2
Raskelf N York 66 C12
Rastrick Calder 58 F9
Ratagan Highld 97 N6
Ratby Leics 41 L6
Ratcliffe Culey Leics 41 J7
Ratcliffe on Soar Notts 41 L2
Ratcliffe on the Wreake Leics 41 N5
Rathen Abers 103 K3
Rathillet Fife 93 L10
Rathmell N York 63 P9
Ratho C Edin 86 D7
Ratho Station C Edin 86 D7
Rathven Moray 101 N3
Ratley Warwks 31 J5
Ratling Kent 23 N11
Ratlinghope Shrops 38 H3
Rattar Highld 110 F2
Rattery Devon 5 P7
Rattlesden Suffk 34 F5
Ratton Village E Susx 12 C9
Rattray P & K 92 H6
Raunds Nhants 32 E3
Ravenfield Rothm 51 L2
Ravenglass Cumb 62 C3
Raveningham Norfk 45 N10
Ravenscar N York 67 L7
Ravenscraig N Lans 85 N10
Ravensden Bed 32 F6
Ravenshead Notts 51 M9
Ravensthorpe Kirk 58 G9
Ravensthorpe Nhants 41 P12
Ravenstone Leics 41 K5
Ravenstone M Keyn 32 C6
Ravenstonedale Cumb 63 N2
Ravenstruther S Lans 77 Q3
Ravensworth N York 65 K6
Rawcliffe C York 59 M4
Rawcliffe E R Yk 59 P9
Rawdon Leeds 58 G6
Rawling Street Kent 22 H10
Rawmarsh Rothm 51 K2
Rawreth Essex 22 F5
Rawridge Devon 6 G2
Rawtenstall Lancs 57 P4
Raydon Suffk 34 H8
Rayleigh Essex 22 F5
Rayne Essex 34 C11
Raynes Park Gt Lon 21 K9
Reach Cambs 33 P4
Read Lancs 57 P2
Reading Readg 20 B8
Reading Services W Berk 20 A9
Reading Street Kent 12 H4
Reading Street Kent 23 Q9
Reagill Cumb 64 B4
Realwa Cnwll 2 F8
Rearquhar Highld 107 M4
Rearsby Leics 41 P5
Reay Highld 110 A3
Reculver Kent 23 N9
Red Ball Devon 16 E11
Redberth Pembks 25 J7
Redbourn Herts 20 H2
Redbourne N Linc 52 D4
Redbrook Gloucs 28 G6
Redbrook Wrexhm 49 K7
Redbrook Street Kent 12 H3
Redburn Highld 100 E6
Redcar R & Cl 66 E3
Redcastle D & G 70 D3
Redcastle Highld 107 J11
Redding Falk 85 Q7
Reddingmuirhead Falk 85 Q7
Reddish Stockp 50 B3
Redditch Worcs 30 D1
Rede Suffk 34 D5
Redenhall Norfk 45 L12
Redesmouth Nthumb 72 F5
Redford Abers 95 M7
Redford Angus 93 P6
Redford W Susx 10 D5
Redfordgreen Border 79 M6
Redgate Rhondd 27 L10
Redgorton P & K 92 G9
Redgrave Suffk 34 H2
Redhill Abers 95 M2
Red Hill BCP 8 G8
Redhill Herts 33 J9
Redhill N Som 17 M4
Redhill Surrey 21 L12
Redisham Suffk 45 N12
Redland Bristl 17 N2
Redland Ork 111 h2
Redlingfield Suffk 35 K3
Redlingfield Green Suffk 35 K3
Red Lodge Suffk 34 B3
Redlynch Somset 17 Q9
Redlynch Wilts 8 H3
Redmarley Worcs 39 N8
Redmarley D'Abitot Gloucs 29 K3
Redmarshall S on T 65 P4
Redmile Leics 42 B3
Redmire N York 65 J8
Redmyre Abers 95 M6
Rednal Shrops 48 G9
Redpath Border 80 D7
Redpoint Highld 105 K8
Red Roses Carmth 25 L6
Red Row Nthumb 73 M2
Redruth Cnwll 2 G7
Redstone P & K 92 H8
Red Street Staffs 49 P5
Red Wharf Bay IoA 54 G5
Redwick Newpt 28 E11
Redwick S Glos 28 G10
Redworth Darltn 65 M3
Reed Herts 33 K9
Reedham Norfk 45 N9
Reedness E R Yk 60 D9
Reeds Holme Lancs 57 P4
Reepham Lincs 52 E8
Reepham Norfk 44 H5
Reeth N York 65 J7
Reeves Green Solhll 40 H11
Regil N Som 17 M4
Reiff Highld 108 A11
Reigate Surrey 21 K12
Reighton N York 67 N11
Reinigeadal W Isls 111 c3
Reisque Abers 103 J10
Reiss Highld 110 G5
Relubbus Cnwll 2 E8
Relugas Moray 100 F5
Remenham Wokham 20 C6
Remenham Hill Wokham 20 C6
Rempstone Notts 41 M3
Rendcomb Gloucs 30 D11
Rendham Suffk 35 M4
Rendlesham Suffk 35 M6
Renfrew Rens 84 H9
Renhold Bed 32 F6
Renishaw Derbys 51 K5
Rennington Nthumb 81 P9
Renton W Duns 84 G7
Renwick Cumb 72 B11
Repps Norfk 45 N6
Repton Derbys 40 H3
Reraig Highld 97 L4
Resaurie Highld 107 L12
Resipole Burn Highld 89 P4
Reskadinnick Cnwll 2 F7
Resolis Highld 107 L8
Resolven Neath 26 H8
Rest and be thankful Ag & B 84 D2
Reston Border 87 R9
Reswallie Angus 93 N5
Retford Notts 51 P5
Rettendon Essex 22 F4
Revesby Lincs 53 J10
Rewe Devon 6 C3
Rew Street IoW 9 M8
Reymerston Norfk 44 G8
Reynalton Pembks 25 J7
Reynoldston Swans 26 C10
Rezare Cnwll 4 H5
Rhandirmwyn Carmth 37 M11
Rhayader Powys 37 Q7
Rheindown Highld 106 H11
Rhenigidale W Isls 111 c3
Rhes-y-cae Flints 48 E2
Rhewl Denbgs 48 C4
Rhewl Denbgs 48 D6
Rhicarn Highld 108 C10
Rhiconich Highld 108 E5
Rhicullen Highld 107 L7
Rhigos Rhondd 27 K7
Rhives Highld 107 N3
Rhiwbina Cardif 27 N11
Rhiwderyn Newpt 28 B10
Rhiwlas Gwynd 54 H8
Rhoden Green Kent 12 D2
Rhodes Minnis Kent 13 M2
Rhodiad-y-brenin Pembks 24 D4
Rhonehouse D & G 70 C4
Rhoose V Glam 16 E3
Rhos Carmth 25 P2
Rhos Neath 26 G8
Rhoscolyn IoA 54 C6
Rhoscrowther Pembks 24 F8
Rhosesmor Flints 48 E2
Rhosgoch Powys 38 E11
Rhoshill Pembks 36 C11
Rhoshirwaun Gwynd 46 C5
Rhoslefain Gwynd 47 J9
Rhosllanerchrugog Wrexhm 48 F6
Rhosmeirch IoA 54 F6
Rhosneigr IoA 54 D7
Rhosnesni Wrexhm 48 G5
Rhôs-on-Sea Conwy 55 M5
Rhossili Swans 25 P10
Rhostryfan Gwynd 54 G9
Rhostyllen Wrexhm 48 F6
Rhosybol IoA 54 F4
Rhos-y-gwaliau Gwynd 47 Q4
Rhosymedre Wrexhm 48 F7
Rhu Ag & B 84 E6
Rhuallt Denbgs 48 C1
Rhubodach Ag & B 83 Q8
Rhuddlan Denbgs 55 Q6
Rhunahaorine Ag & B 75 K3
Rhyd Gwynd 47 K3
Rhydargaeau Carmth 25 Q4
Rhydcymerau Carmth 26 D2
Rhyd-Ddu Gwynd 54 H10
Rhydlewis Cerdgn 36 F10
Rhydowen Cerdgn 36 G10
Rhyd-uchaf Gwynd 47 P4
Rhyd-y-clafdy Gwynd 46 E4
Rhyd-y-foel Conwy 55 N6
Rhydyfro Neath 26 F7
Rhyd-y-groes Gwynd 54 H8
Rhyd-y-pennau Cerdgn 37 K4
Rhyl Denbgs 55 Q5
Rhymney Caerph 27 N7
Rhynd P & K 92 H10
Rhynie Abers 101 P9
Rhynie Highld 107 P6
Ribbesford Worcs 39 P7
Ribbleton Lancs 57 K3
Ribchester Lancs 57 M2
Riby Lincs 52 H3
Riccall N York 59 N6
Riccarton Border 79 Q9
Riccarton E Ayrs 76 G4
Richards Castle Herefs 39 J8
Richmond Gt Lon 21 J8
Richmond N York 65 L7
Richmond Sheff 51 K4
Rickerscote Staffs 40 B4
Rickford N Som 17 L4
Rickham Devon 5 P11
Rickinghall Suffk 34 H2
Rickling Green Essex 33 N10
Rickmansworth Herts 20 G5
Riddell Border 80 C8
Riddlecombe Devon 15 K8
Riddlesden C Brad 58 E5
Ridge Dorset 8 D9
Ridge Herts 21 K4
Ridge Wilts 8 D2
Ridge Lane Warwks 40 H8
Ridgeway Derbys 51 K5
Ridgewell Essex 34 C8
Ridgewood E Susx 11 P6
Ridgmont C Beds 32 D9
Riding Mill Nthumb 72 H8
Ridlington Norfk 45 M4
Ridlington Rutlnd 42 C9
Ridsdale Nthumb 72 G4
Rievaulx N York 66 E9
Rigg D & G 71 L3
Riggend N Lans 85 M8
Righoul Highld 100 D5
Rigsby Lincs 53 L8
Rigside S Lans 78 E2
Riley Green Lancs 57 L4
Rilla Mill Cnwll 4 G5
Rillington N York 67 J11
Rimington Lancs 63 P11
Rimpton Somset 17 N10
Rimswell E R Yk 61 M8
Rinaston Pembks 24 H4
Rindleford Shrops 39 N3
Ringford D & G 69 Q7
Ringland Norfk 45 J7
Ringmer E Susx 11 N7
Ringmore Devon 5 N10
Ringmore Devon 6 C8
Ringorm Moray 101 K6
Ringsfield Suffk 45 N11
Ringsfield Corner Suffk 45 N11
Ringshall Herts 20 F1
Ringshall Suffk 34 G6
Ringshall Stocks Suffk 34 H6
Ringstead Nhants 32 E2
Ringstead Norfk 44 B3
Ringwood Hants 8 H6
Ringwould Kent 13 Q1
Rinmore Abers 101 M11
Ripe E Susx 11 P7
Ripley Derbys 51 K10
Ripley Hants 8 H7
Ripley N York 58 H3
Ripley Surrey 20 G11
Riplington Hants 9 Q3
Ripon N York 65 N12
Rippingale Lincs 42 F5
Ripple Kent 23 Q12
Ripple Worcs 29 M2
Ripponden Calder 58 D9
Risabus Ag & B 74 D4
Risbury Herefs 39 K10
Risby Suffk 34 D4
Risca Caerph 27 P9
Rise E R Yk 61 K6
Risegate Lincs 42 H4
Riseley Bed 32 F4
Riseley Wokham 20 B10
Rishangles Suffk 35 J3
Rishton Lancs 57 N3
Rishworth Calder 58 D9
Risley Derbys 41 L1
Risley Warrtn 57 M9
Risplith N York 58 G1
River Kent 13 P2
River W Susx 10 F5
Riverford Highld 107 J10
Riverhead Kent 21 P11
Rivington Lancs 57 L6
Rivington Services Lancs 57 L6
Roade Nhants 31 Q4
Roadmeetings S Lans 77 P2
Roadside E Ayrs 77 K7
Roadside Highld 110 D4
Roadwater Somset 16 D8
Roag Highld 96 C2
Roan of Craigoch S Ayrs 76 E9
Roath Cardif 27 P12
Roberton Border 79 N6
Roberton S Lans 78 F3
Robertsbridge E Susx 12 E5
Roberttown Kirk 58 G9
Robeston Wathen Pembks 25 J5
Robgill Tower D & G 71 L2
Robin Hood's Bay N York 67 K6
Roborough Devon 5 K7
Roborough Devon 15 K8
Robroyston C Glas 85 K8
Roby Knows 56 H10
Rocester Staffs 50 E11
Roch Pembks 24 F5
Rochdale Rochdl 58 B10
Roche Cnwll 3 L4
Rochester Medway 22 E9
Rochester Nthumb 72 E2
Rochford Essex 22 G5
Rochford Worcs 39 L8
Rock Cnwll 3 L1
Rock Nthumb 81 P9
Rock Worcs 39 N7
Rockbeare Devon 6 D4
Rockbourne Hants 8 G4
Rockcliffe Cumb 71 M4
Rockcliffe D & G 70 D5
Rockend Torbay 6 C9
Rock Ferry Wirral 56 G10
Rockfield Highld 107 Q6
Rockfield Mons 28 F6
Rockford Devon 15 N3
Rockhampton S Glos 28 H9
Rockhill Shrops 38 F6
Rockingham Nhants 42 C10
Rockland All Saints Norfk 44 G10
Rockland St Mary Norfk 45 M8
Rockland St Peter Norfk 44 G9
Rockley Notts 51 Q6
Rockville Ag & B 84 D5
Rockwell End Bucks 20 C6
Rodborough Gloucs 29 L7
Rodbourne Swindn 18 G4
Rodbourne Wilts 18 D4
Rodden Dorset 7 N6
Rode Somset 18 B9
Rode Heath Ches E 49 P4
Rodel W Isls 111 c4
Roden Wrekin 49 L11
Rodhuish Somset 16 D8
Rodington Wrekin 49 L11
Rodington Heath Wrekin 49 L11
Rodley Gloucs 29 K6
Rodmarton Gloucs 29 N8
Rodmell E Susx 11 N8
Rodmersham Kent 22 H10
Rodmersham Green Kent 22 H10
Rodney Stoke Somset 17 L6
Rodsley Derbys 50 G11
Roecliffe N York 59 J2
Roe Green Herts 21 K2
Roe Green Herts 33 K9
Roehampton Gt Lon 21 K8
Roffey W Susx 11 K4
Rogart Highld 107 M2
Rogate W Susx 10 D5
Rogerstone Newpt 28 C10
Roghadal W Isls 111 c4
Rogiet Mons 28 E10
Roke Oxon 19 Q3
Roker Sundld 73 P8
Rollesby Norfk 45 P7
Rolleston Leics 41 Q7
Rolleston Notts 51 Q9
Rolleston on Dove Staffs 40 G3
Rolston E R Yk 61 L5
Rolvenden Kent 12 G4
Rolvenden Layne Kent 12 G4
Romaldkirk Dur 64 H3
Romanby N York 65 P8
Romanno Bridge Border 86 D11
Romansleigh Devon 15 M7
Romesdal Highld 104 E10
Romford Dorset 8 F5
Romford Gt Lon 21 P5
Romiley Stockp 50 C3
Romsey Cambs 33 M5
Romsey Hants 9 L3
Romsley Shrops 39 P5
Romsley Worcs 40 C10
Rona Highld 105 J10
Ronachan Ag & B 83 L11
Rookhope Dur 72 G11
Rookley IoW 9 N9
Rooks Bridge Somset 17 K5
Rooks Nest Somset 16 E9
Rookwith N York 65 L9
Roos E R Yk 61 M7
Roothams Green Bed 32 F5
Ropley Hants 9 Q2
Ropley Dean Hants 9 Q2
Ropsley Lincs 42 E4
Rora Abers 103 L5
Rorrington Shrops 38 F3
Rosarie Moray 101 M5
Rose Cnwll 2 H5
Rose Ash Devon 15 N7
Rosebank S Lans 77 N2
Rosebush Pembks 25 J3
Rosedale Abbey N York 66 G8
Rose Green Essex 34 E10
Rose Green Suffk 34 F7
Rose Green Suffk 34 F8
Rose Green W Susx 10 E9
Rosehall Highld 106 H2
Rosehearty Abers 103 J2
Rose Hill Lancs 57 P3
Roseisle Moray 100 H2
Roselands E Susx 12 C9
Rosemarket Pembks 24 G7
Rosemarkie Highld 107 M10
Rosemary Lane Devon 16 F12
Rosemount P & K 92 H7
Rosenannon Cnwll 3 L3
Rosewell Mdloth 86 F9
Roseworth S on T 65 Q3
Rosgill Cumb 71 Q11
Roskhill Highld 96 C1
Rosley Cumb 71 M6
Roslin Mdloth 86 F9
Rosliston Derbys 40 G4
Rosneath Ag & B 84 E6
Ross D & G 69 P9
Rossett Wrexhm 48 G4
Rossett Green N York 58 H4
Rossington Donc 51 N2
Ross-on-Wye Herefs 28 H4
Roster Highld 110 F7

186 Rostherne – Scampston

Rostherne Ches E 57 N11
Rosthwaite Cumb 71 L11
Roston Derbys 50 F11
Rosyth Fife 86 D5
Rothbury Nthumb 73 J1
Rotherby Leics 41 P4
Rotherfield E Susx 12 B4
Rotherfield Greys Oxon 20 B7
Rotherfield Peppard Oxon 20 B7
Rotherham Rothm 51 K3
Rothersthorpe Nhants 31 Q3
Rotherwick Hants 20 B11
Rothes Moray 101 K5
Rothesay Ag & B 84 B9
Rothiebrisbane Abers 102 G7
Rothiemurchus Lodge Highld 99 P7
Rothienorman Abers 102 F7
Rothley Leics 41 N5
Rothmaise Abers 102 F8
Rothwell Leeds 59 J8
Rothwell Lincs 52 G4
Rothwell Nhants 32 B1
Rottal Lodge Angus 94 F7
Rottingdean Br & H 11 M9
Rottington Cumb 70 F11
Roucan D & G 78 G12
Rougham Norfk 44 D6
Rougham Suffk 34 E4
Rough Common Kent 23 L10
Roughpark Abers 101 L11
Roughton Lincs 53 J9
Roughton Norfk 45 K3
Roughton Shrops 39 N4
Roundbush Green Essex 22 C1
Round Green Luton 32 F11
Roundham Somset 7 K2
Roundhay Leeds 59 J6
Rounds Green Sandw 40 C9
Roundswell Devon 15 J6
Roundway Wilts 18 E7
Roundyhill Angus 93 L5
Rousay Ork 111 h1
Rousdon Devon 6 H5
Rousham Oxon 31 L8
Rous Lench Worcs 30 D4
Routenburn N Ayrs 84 D10
Routh E R Yk 61 J6
Row Cumb 63 J4
Rowanburn D & G 79 N12
Rowardennan Stirlg 84 F4
Rowarth Derbys 50 D3
Rowberrow Somset 17 L5
Rowde Wilts 18 E8
Rowen Conwy 55 L7
Rowfoot Nthumb 72 C8
Rowhedge Essex 34 G11
Rowington Warwks 30 G1
Rowland Derbys 50 G6
Rowland's Castle Hants 10 B7
Rowlands Gill Gatesd 73 L8
Rowledge Surrey 10 D2
Rowley Dur 73 J10
Rowley Regis Sandw 40 C9
Rowlstone Herefs 28 D4
Rowly Surrey 10 G2
Rowner Hants 9 P7
Rowney Green Worcs 40 D12
Rownhams Hants 9 L4
Rownhams Services Hants 9 L4
Rowrah Cumb 70 H10
Rowsham Bucks 32 C12
Rowsley Derbys 50 G7
Rowston Lincs 52 F11
Rowton Ches W 49 J3
Rowton Wrekin 49 L10
Roxburgh Border 80 F7
Roxby N Linc 60 F10
Roxton Bed 32 G6
Roxwell Essex 22 D2
Royal Leamington Spa Warwks 30 H2
Royal Sutton Coldfield Birm 40 E8
Royal Tunbridge Wells Kent 12 C3
Royal Wootton Bassett Wilts 18 F4
Royal Yacht Britannia C Edin 86 F6
Roy Bridge Highld 98 C11
Roydon Essex 21 N2
Roydon Norfk 34 H1
Roydon Norfk 44 B5
Roydon Hamlet Essex 21 N2
Royston Barns 59 J11
Royston Herts 33 K8
Royton Oldham 58 B11
Rozel Jersey 7 c1
Ruabon Wrexhm 48 F6
Ruaig Ag & B 88 D6
Ruan Lanihorne Cnwll 3 K7
Ruan Major Cnwll 2 G11
Ruan Minor Cnwll 2 G11
Ruardean Gloucs 28 H5
Ruardean Hill Gloucs 28 H5
Ruardean Woodside Gloucs 28 H5
Rubery Birm 40 C11
Rubha Ban W Isls 111 b6
Ruckhall Herefs 28 E2
Ruckinge Kent 13 K4
Ruckley Shrops 39 K3
Rudby N York 66 C6
Rudchester Nthumb 73 K7
Ruddington Notts 41 M2
Rudge Somset 18 C9
Rudgeway S Glos 28 H10
Rudgwick W Susx 10 H4
Rudheath Ches W 49 M2
Rudley Green Essex 22 G3
Rudloe Wilts 18 C6
Rudry Caerph 27 P10
Rudston E R Yk 61 J1
Rudyard Staffs 50 C8
Ruecastle Border 80 E9
Rufford Lancs 57 J6
Rufford Abbey Notts 51 N7
Rufforth C York 59 M4
Rugby Warwks 41 L11
Rugeley Staffs 40 D4
Ruigh'riabhach Highld 105 Q4
Ruisgarry W Isls 111 b4
Ruishton Somset 16 H10
Ruisigearraidh W Isls 111 b4
Ruislip Gt Lon 20 H6
Rùm Highld 96 D9
Rumbach Moray 101 M5
Rumbling Bridge P & K 86 B3
Rumburgh Suffk 35 M1
Rumford Cnwll 3 K2
Rumford Falk 85 Q7
Rumney Cardif 27 P11
Runcorn Halton 57 K11
Runcton W Susx 10 E9
Runcton Holme Norfk 43 P8
Runfold Surrey 10 D1
Runhall Norfk 44 H8
Runham Norfk 45 P7
Runnington Somset 16 F10
Runswick N York 66 H4
Runtaleave Angus 94 E8
Runwell Essex 22 F5
Ruscombe Wokham 20 C8
Rushall Herefs 28 H2
Rushall Norfk 45 K12
Rushall Wilts 18 G9
Rushall Wsall 40 D7
Rushbrooke Suffk 34 E5
Rushbury Shrops 39 K4
Rushden Herts 33 K9
Rushden Nhants 32 D4
Rushenden Kent 22 H8
Rushford Norfk 34 F1
Rush Green Essex 23 M1
Rush Green Gt Lon 21 P6
Rush Green Warrtn 57 M10
Rushlake Green E Susx 12 D6
Rushmere Suffk 45 P11
Rushmoor Surrey 10 E3
Rushock Worcs 40 B12
Rusholme Manch 57 Q9
Rushton Nhants 42 B12
Rushton Spencer Staffs 50 C8
Rushwick Worcs 39 P10
Rushyford Dur 65 M2
Ruskie Stirlg 85 K3
Ruskington Lincs 52 F12
Rusland Cross Cumb 62 G5
Rusper W Susx 11 K3
Ruspidge Gloucs 29 J6
Russell's Water Oxon 20 B5
Russ Hill Surrey 11 K3
Rusthall Kent 12 C3
Rustington W Susx 10 G9
Ruston N York 67 K10
Ruston Parva E R Yk 60 H2
Ruswarp N York 67 J5
Rutherford Border 80 E7
Rutherglen S Lans 85 K10
Ruthernbridge Cnwll 3 M3
Ruthin Denbgs 48 D4
Ruthrieston C Aber 95 Q2
Ruthven Abers 101 P6
Ruthven Angus 93 K6
Ruthven Highld 99 L8
Ruthven Highld 99 M3
Ruthvoes Cnwll 3 K4
Ruthwell D & G 70 H3
Ruyton-XI-Towns Shrops 48 H10
Ryal Nthumb 72 H6
Ryall Dorset 7 K4
Ryall Worcs 29 M1
Ryarsh Kent 22 D10
Rydal Cumb 62 G2
Ryde IoW 9 P8
Rye E Susx 12 H6
Rye Foreign E Susx 12 H5
Rye Street Worcs 29 K2
Ryhall Rutlnd 42 E7
Ryhill Wakefd 59 J10
Ryhope Sundld 73 P9
Ryland Lincs 52 E7
Rylands Notts 41 M1
Rylstone N York 58 C3
Ryme Intrinseca Dorset 7 N1
Ryther N York 59 M6
Ryton Gatesd 73 K7
Ryton Shrops 39 N2
Ryton-on-Dunsmore Warwks 41 J11
RZSS Edinburgh Zoo C Edin 86 E7

S

Sabden Lancs 57 P2
Sacombe Herts 33 K11
Sacriston Dur 73 M10
Sadberge Darltn 65 N4
Saddell Ag & B 75 L6
Saddington Leics 41 P8
Saddlebow Norfk 43 P7
Saddlescombe W Susx 11 L7
Saffron Walden Essex 33 N8
Sageston Pembks 25 J7
Saham Hills Norfk 44 E9
Saham Toney Norfk 44 E9
Saighton Ches W 49 J3
St Abbs Border 81 J1
St Agnes Border 87 M9
St Agnes Cnwll 2 G5
St Agnes IoS 2 b3
St Agnes Mining District Cnwll 2 G6
St Albans Herts 21 J2
St Allen Cnwll 3 J5
St Andrew Guern 6 b2
St Andrews Fife 93 N11
St Andrews Botanic Garden Fife 93 N11
St Andrews Major V Glam 16 F2
St Andrews Well Dorset 7 L4
St Anne's Lancs 56 G3
St Ann's D & G 78 H9
St Ann's Chapel Cnwll 5 J6
St Ann's Chapel Devon 5 N10
St Anthony-in-Meneage Cnwll 2 H10
St Anthony's Hill E Susx 12 D9
St Arvans Mons 28 F9
St Asaph Denbgs 48 B1
St Athan V Glam 16 D3
St Aubin Jersey 7 b2
St Austell Cnwll 3 M5
St Bees Cumb 70 F12
St Blazey Cnwll 3 N5
St Boswells Border 80 D7
St Brelade Jersey 7 a2
St Brelade's Bay Jersey 7 a2
St Breock Cnwll 3 L2
St Breward Cnwll 4 D5
St Briavels Gloucs 28 G7
St Bride's Major V Glam 16 B2
St Brides-super-Ely V Glam 27 M12
St Brides Wentlooge Newpt 28 C11
St Budeaux C Plym 5 K8
Saintbury Gloucs 30 E6
St Buryan Cnwll 2 C9
St Catherines Ag & B 84 C2
St Chloe Gloucs 29 L8
St Clears Carmth 25 M5
St Cleer Cnwll 4 F6
St Clement Cnwll 3 J7
St Clement Jersey 7 c2
St Clether Cnwll 4 F4
St Colmac Ag & B 83 Q9
St Columb Major Cnwll 3 K3
St Columb Minor Cnwll 3 J4
St Columb Road Cnwll 3 K4
St Combs Abers 103 L3
St Cross South Elmham Suffk 45 L12
St Cyrus Abers 95 M8
St David's P & K 92 E10
St Davids Pembks 24 D4
St Davids Cathedral Pembks 24 D4
St Day Cnwll 2 G7
St Dennis Cnwll 3 L4
St Dogmaels Pembks 36 C10
St Dominick Cnwll 5 J6
St Donats V Glam 16 C3
St Endellion Cnwll 4 C5
St Enoder Cnwll 3 K4
St Erme Cnwll 3 J6
St Erney Cnwll 4 H8
St Erth Cnwll 2 E8
St Erth Praze Cnwll 2 E8
St Ervan Cnwll 3 K2
St Eval Cnwll 3 K3
St Ewe Cnwll 3 L6
St Fagans Cardif 27 N12
St Fagans: National History Museum Cardif 27 N12
St Fergus Abers 103 M5
St Fillans P & K 91 Q10
St Florence Pembks 25 J8
St Gennys Cnwll 14 C11
St George Conwy 55 P6
St Georges N Som 17 K4
St George's V Glam 16 E2
St Germans Cnwll 4 H8
St Giles in the Wood Devon 15 J8
St Giles-on-the-Heath Devon 4 H3
St Harmon Powys 38 B7
St Helen Auckland Dur 65 L3
St Helen's E Susx 12 G7
St Helens IoW 9 Q9
St Helens St Hel 57 K9
St Helier Gt Lon 21 L9
St Helier Jersey 7 b2
St Hilary Cnwll 2 E9
St Hilary V Glam 16 D2
St Ippolyts Herts 32 H10
St Ishmael's Pembks 24 E7
St Issey Cnwll 3 L2
St Ive Cnwll 4 G6
St Ives Cambs 33 K3
St Ives Cnwll 2 D7
St James's End Nhants 31 Q3
St James South Elmham Suffk 35 M1
St Jidgey Cnwll 3 L2
St John Cnwll 5 J9
St John Jersey 7 b1
St John's E Susx 11 P4
St John's IoM 56 b5
St John's Kent 21 Q11
St Johns Surrey 20 F10
St Johns Worcs 39 Q10
St John's Chapel Devon 15 J6
St John's Chapel Dur 72 F12
St John's Fen End Norfk 43 N7
St John's Kirk S Lans 78 F2
St John's Town of Dalry D & G 69 N3
St John's Wood Gt Lon 21 L6
St Judes IoM 56 d3
St Just Cnwll 2 B9
St Just-in-Roseland Cnwll 3 J8
St Just Mining District Cnwll 2 B8
St Katherines Abers 102 G8
St Keverne Cnwll 2 H10
St Kew Cnwll 3 M1
St Kew Highway Cnwll 3 M1
St Keyne Cnwll 4 F7
St Lawrence Essex 23 J3
St Lawrence IoW 9 N11
St Lawrence Jersey 7 b1
St Lawrence Kent 23 Q9
St Leonards Bucks 20 E3
St Leonards Dorset 8 G6
St Leonards E Susx 12 F8
St Levan Cnwll 2 B10
St Lythans V Glam 16 F2
St Mabyn Cnwll 3 M2
St Madoes P & K 92 H10
St Margarets Herefs 28 D3
St Margarets Herts 21 M2
St Margaret's at Cliffe Kent 13 Q2
St Margaret's Hope Ork 111 h3
St Margaret South Elmham Suffk 45 M12
St Marks IoM 56 c6
St Martin Cnwll 2 H10
St Martin Cnwll 4 G8
St Martin Guern 6 b2
St Martin Jersey 7 c1
St Martin's IoS 2 c1
St Martin's P & K 92 H9
St Martin's Shrops 48 G8
St Mary Jersey 7 a1
St Mary Bourne Hants 19 M10
St Marychurch Torbay 6 C9
St Mary Church V Glam 16 D2
St Mary Cray Gt Lon 21 P9
St Mary in the Marsh Kent 13 K5
St Mary's IoS 2 c2
St Mary's Ork 111 h2
St Mary's Bay Kent 13 L5
St Mary's Hoo Medway 22 F7
St Mary's Platt Kent 22 D11
St Maughans Green Mons 28 F5
St Mawes Cnwll 3 J8
St Mawgan Cnwll 3 K3
St Mellion Cnwll 5 J7
St Mellons Cardif 27 P11
St Merryn Cnwll 3 K2
St Michael Caerhays Cnwll 3 L7
St Michael Church Somset 17 J9
St Michael Penkevil Cnwll 3 J7
St Michaels Kent 12 H3
St Michaels Worcs 39 L8
St Michael's Mount Cnwll 2 D9
St Michael's on Wyre Lancs 57 J1
St Minver Cnwll 3 L1
St Monans Fife 87 K2
St Neot Cnwll 4 E6
St Neots Cambs 32 H5
St Newlyn East Cnwll 3 J5
St Nicholas Pembks 24 F2
St Nicholas V Glam 16 E2
St Nicholas-at-Wade Kent 23 N9
St Ninians Stirlg 85 N5
St Olaves Norfk 45 P9
St Osyth Essex 23 L1
St Ouen Jersey 7 a1
St Owen's Cross Herefs 28 G4
St Paul's Cray Gt Lon 21 P9
St Paul's Walden Herts 32 H11
St Peter Jersey 7 a1
St Peter Port Guern 6 c2
St Peter's Guern 6 b2
St Peter's Kent 23 Q9
St Peter's Hill Cambs 33 J3
St Pinnock Cnwll 4 F7
St Quivox S Ayrs 76 F6
St Sampson Guern 6 c1
St Saviour Guern 6 b2
St Saviour Jersey 7 b2
St Stephen Cnwll 3 L5
St Stephens Cnwll 4 H3
St Stephens Cnwll 5 J8
St Teath Cnwll 4 D4
St Thomas Devon 6 B5
St Tudy Cnwll 3 N1
St Twynnells Pembks 24 G8
St Veep Cnwll 4 E8
St Vigeans Angus 93 Q7
St Wenn Cnwll 3 L3
St Weonards Herefs 28 F4
Salcombe Devon 5 P11
Salcombe Regis Devon 6 F5
Salcott-cum-Virley Essex 23 J1
Sale Traffd 57 P9
Saleby Lincs 53 M7
Sale Green Worcs 30 B3
Salehurst E Susx 12 E5
Salem Cerdgn 37 L4
Salen Ag & B 89 M7
Salen Highld 89 N4
Salford C Beds 32 D8
Salford Oxon 30 H8
Salford Salfd 57 P8
Salford Priors Warwks 30 E4
Salfords Surrey 11 L2
Salhouse Norfk 45 M7
Saline Fife 86 B4
Salisbury Wilts 8 G2
Salisbury Plain Wilts 18 F10
Salkeld Dykes Cumb 71 Q7
Salle Norfk 45 J5
Salmonby Lincs 53 K8
Salperton Gloucs 30 E9
Salsburgh N Lans 85 N9
Salt Staffs 40 C2
Saltaire C Brad 58 F6
Saltaire C Brad 58 F6
Saltash Cnwll 5 J8
Saltburn Highld 107 M8
Saltburn-by-the-Sea R & Cl 66 F4
Saltby Leics 42 C5
Saltcoats N Ayrs 76 D3
Saltdean Br & H 11 M9
Salterbeck Cumb 70 G9
Salterforth Lancs 58 B5
Salterton Wilts 18 G12
Saltfleet Lincs 53 M5
Saltfleetby All Saints Lincs 53 M5
Saltfleetby St Clement Lincs 53 M5
Saltfleetby St Peter Lincs 53 M5
Saltford BaNES 17 P3
Salthouse Norfk 44 H2
Saltley Birm 40 E9
Saltmarshe E R Yk 60 D8
Saltney Flints 48 H3
Salton N York 66 G10
Saltrens Devon 14 H7
Saltwood Kent 13 M3
Salvington W Susx 10 H8
Salwarpe Worcs 39 Q9
Salway Ash Dorset 7 L4
Sambourne Warwks 30 D2
Sambrook Wrekin 49 N9
Sampford Arundel Somset 16 F11
Sampford Brett Somset 16 E7
Sampford Courtenay Devon 15 L11
Sampford Moor Somset 16 F11
Sampford Peverell Devon 16 D12
Sampford Spiney Devon 5 L6
Samsonlane Ork 111 i2
Samuelston E Loth 87 J7
Sanaigmore Ag & B 82 C8
Sancreed Cnwll 2 C9
Sancton E R Yk 60 F6
Sandaig Highld 97 K8
Sandal Magna Wakefd 59 J9
Sanday Ork 111 i1
Sanday Airport Ork 111 i1
Sandbach Ches E 49 N4
Sandbach Services Ches E 49 P4
Sandbank Ag & B 84 C6
Sandbanks BCP 8 F9
Sandend Abers 102 D3
Sanderstead Gt Lon 21 M10
Sandford Cumb 64 D4
Sandford Devon 15 P10
Sandford Dorset 8 D9
Sandford Hants 8 H7
Sandford IoW 9 N10
Sandford N Som 17 K4
Sandford S Lans 77 M3
Sandford-on-Thames Oxon 19 N1
Sandford Orcas Dorset 17 P11
Sandford St Martin Oxon 31 K8
Sandgate Kent 13 M3
Sandhaven Abers 103 K2
Sandhead D & G 68 E8
Sand Hills Leeds 59 J6
Sandhills Oxon 31 M11
Sandhills Surrey 10 F3
Sandhoe Nthumb 72 H7
Sandhole Ag & B 83 Q4
Sand Hole E R Yk 60 D6
Sandholme E R Yk 60 E7
Sandhurst Br For 20 D10
Sandhurst Gloucs 29 L4
Sandhurst Kent 12 F4
Sand Hutton N York 59 P3
Sandhutton N York 65 P10
Sandiacre Derbys 51 L12
Sandilands Lincs 53 N7
Sandleheath Hants 8 G4
Sandleigh Oxon 19 M1
Sandley Dorset 8 B3
Sandness Shet 111 j4
Sandon Essex 22 E3
Sandon Herts 33 K9
Sandon Staffs 40 C2
Sandon Bank Staffs 40 C2
Sandown IoW 9 P9
Sandplace Cnwll 4 F8
Sandridge Herts 21 J2
Sandringham Norfk 44 B4
Sandsend N York 67 J5
Sandtoft N Linc 60 D11
Sandway Kent 22 H12
Sandwich Kent 23 P10
Sandwick Shet 111 k5
Sandwick W Isls 111 d2
Sandwith Cumb 70 F11
Sandy C Beds 32 G7
Sandyford D & G 79 K9
Sandygate Devon 6 B7
Sandygate IoM 56 d3
Sandyhills D & G 70 E5
Sandylands Lancs 62 H9
Sandy Lane Wilts 18 E7
Sandy Park Devon 5 P3
Sangobeg Highld 108 H3
Sangomore Highld 108 H3
Sankyn's Green Worcs 39 P8
Sanna Highld 89 K3
Sanndabhaig W Isls 111 d2
Sannox N Ayrs 75 Q4
Sanquhar D & G 77 N8
Santon Bridge Cumb 62 C2
Santon Downham Suffk 44 D11
Sapcote Leics 41 L8
Sapey Common Herefs 39 M8
Sapiston Suffk 34 F2
Sapley Cambs 33 J2
Sapperton Gloucs 29 N7
Sapperton Lincs 42 E4
Saracen's Head Lincs 43 K5
Sarclet Highld 110 G7
Sarisbury Hants 9 N5
Sarn Powys 38 E4
Sarnau Cerdgn 36 E9
Sarnau Powys 48 E11
Sarn Mellteyrn Gwynd 46 D5
Sarn Park Services Brdgnd 27 J11
Saron Carmth 26 E6
Saron Gwynd 54 G8
Sarratt Herts 20 G4
Sarre Kent 23 N9
Sarsden Oxon 30 H9
Satley Dur 73 K11
Satterleigh Devon 15 L7
Satterthwaite Cumb 62 G4
Sauchen Abers 102 F11
Saucher P & K 92 H8
Sauchieburn Abers 95 L7
Saul Gloucs 29 K7
Saundby Notts 52 B6
Saundersfoot Pembks 25 K7
Saunderton Bucks 20 C3
Saunton Devon 14 H5
Sausthorpe Lincs 53 L9
Savile Town Kirk 58 G9
Sawbridge Warwks 31 L2
Sawbridgeworth Herts 21 P1
Sawdon N York 67 K9
Sawley Lancs 63 P11
Sawley N York 58 G1
Sawston Cambs 33 M7
Sawtry Cambs 42 G12
Saxby Leics 42 B6
Saxby Lincs 52 E6
Saxby All Saints N Linc 60 G10
Saxelbye Leics 41 P4
Saxham Street Suffk 34 H5
Saxilby Lincs 52 C8
Saxlingham Norfk 44 G3
Saxlingham Green Norfk 45 L10
Saxlingham Nethergate Norfk 45 K10
Saxlingham Thorpe Norfk 45 K9
Saxmundham Suffk 35 N4
Saxondale Notts 51 P11
Saxon Street Cambs 34 B5
Saxtead Suffk 35 L4
Saxtead Green Suffk 35 L4
Saxtead Little Green Suffk 35 L4
Saxthorpe Norfk 45 J4
Saxton N York 59 L6
Sayers Common W Susx 11 L6
Scackleton N York 66 F11
Scadabay W Isls 111 c3
Scadabhagh W Isls 111 c3
Scafell Pike Cumb 62 E2
Scaftworth Notts 51 P3
Scagglethorpe N York 67 J11
Scalasaig Ag & B 82 E4
Scalby E R Yk 60 E8
Scalby N York 67 L9
Scaldwell Nhants 41 Q11
Scaleby Cumb 71 P3
Scalebyhill Cumb 71 P3
Scales Cumb 62 F7
Scales Cumb 71 M9
Scalford Leics 41 Q3
Scaling N York 66 G5
Scalloway Shet 111 k4
Scalpay Highld 96 H4
Scalpay W Isls 111 c3
Scamblesby Lincs 53 J7
Scamodale Highld 90 B2
Scampston N York 67 J11

Scampton Lincs 52 D7
Scaniport Highld 99 J2
Scapegoat Hill Kirk 58 E10
Scarba Ag & B 83 K3
Scarborough N York 67 M9
Scarcewater Cnwll 3 K5
Scarcliffe Derbys 51 L7
Scarcroft Leeds 59 J6
Scarfskerry Highld 110 H2
Scarinish Ag & B 88 C7
Scarisbrick Lancs 56 H6
Scarning Norfk 44 F7
Scarrington Notts 51 Q11
Scartho NE Lin 53 J3
Scatsta Airport Shet 111 k3
Scaur D & G 70 D5
Scawby N Linc 52 D3
Scawsby Donc 59 M12
Scawthorpe Donc 59 M11
Scawton N York 66 D10
Scayne's Hill W Susx 11 M5
Scethrog Powys 27 M4
Scholar Green Ches E 49 Q4
Scholes Kirk 58 F11
Scholes Leeds 59 J6
Scholes Rothm 51 K2
Scholes Wigan 57 L7
Scissett Kirk 58 G11
Scleddau Pembks 24 G2
Scofton Notts 51 N5
Scole Norfk 35 J2
Scone P & K 92 H9
Sconser Highld 96 F4
Scoonie Fife 86 H2
Scopwick Lincs 52 F11
Scoraig Highld 105 Q3
Scorborough E R Yk 60 H5
Scorrier Cnwll 2 G7
Scorton Lancs 63 J11
Scorton N York 65 M7
Scotby Cumb 71 P5
Scotch Corner N York 65 L6
Scotch Corner Rest Area
  N York 65 L6
Scotforth Lancs 63 J9
Scothern Lincs 52 E7
Scotlandwell P & K 86 F2
Scotscalder Station Highld 110 C5
Scot's Gap Nthumb 73 J4
Scotsmill Abers 102 D10
Scotstoun C Glas 85 J9
Scotswood N u Ty 73 L7
Scotter Lincs 52 C4
Scotterthorpe Lincs 52 C3
Scottish Seabird Centre
  E Loth 87 K5
Scottish Wool Centre Stirlg 85 J3
Scotton Lincs 52 C4
Scotton N York 59 J3
Scotton N York 65 L8
Scoulton Norfk 44 G9
Scourie Highld 108 D6
Scourie More Highld 108 D7
Scousburgh Shet 111 k5
Scrabster Highld 110 C2
Scraesburgh Border 80 F9
Scrane End Lincs 43 L2
Scraptoft Leics 41 P6
Scratby Norfk 45 Q7
Scrayingham N York 60 C3
Scredington Lincs 42 F3
Scremby Lincs 53 M9
Scremerston Nthumb 81 L4
Screveton Notts 51 Q11
Scriven N York 59 J3
Scrooby Notts 51 P3
Scropton Derbys 40 G2
Scrub Hill Lincs 52 H11
Scruton N York 65 N8
Scullomie Highld 109 L4
Sculthorpe Norfk 44 E4
Scunthorpe N Linc 60 F11
Seaborough Dorset 7 K2
Seabridge Staffs 49 Q6
Seabrook Kent 13 M3
Seaburn Sundld 73 P8
Seacombe Wirral 56 G10
Seacroft Leeds 59 J7
Seafield W Loth 86 B8
Seaford E Susx 11 P9
Seaforth Sefton 56 G9
Seagrave Leics 41 N4
Seaham Dur 73 P10
Seahouses Nthumb 81 P7
Seal Kent 22 B11
Sealand Flints 48 G2
Seale Surrey 10 E1
Seamer N York 66 C5
Seamer N York 67 L10
Seamill N Ayrs 76 D2
Sea Palling Norfk 45 N5
Searby Lincs 52 F3
Seasalter Kent 23 L9
Seascale Cumb 62 B3
Seathwaite Cumb 62 E3
Seatoller Cumb 71 L11
Seaton Cnwll 4 G8
Seaton Cumb 70 G8
Seaton Devon 6 H5
Seaton E R Yk 61 K5
Seaton Kent 23 N10
Seaton Nthumb 73 N5
Seaton Rutlnd 42 C9
Seaton Carew Hartpl 66 D2
Seaton Delaval Nthumb 73 N6
Seaton Ross E R Yk 60 D6
Seaton Sluice Nthumb 73 N5
Seatown Dorset 7 K4
Seave Green N York 66 D7
Seaview IoW 9 Q8
Seaville Cumb 71 J5
Seavington St Mary Somset 17 K12
Seavington St Michael
  Somset 17 K12
Sebergham Cumb 71 M7
Seckington Warwks 40 H6
Second Severn Crossing
  Mons 28 F10
Sedbergh Cumb 63 M4
Sedbury Gloucs 28 G9
Sedbusk N York 64 F8
Sedgeberrow Worcs 30 D6

Sedgebrook Lincs 42 C3
Sedgefield Dur 65 P2
Sedgeford Norfk 44 B3
Sedgehill Wilts 8 C2
Sedgemoor Services Somset 17 J5
Sedgley Dudley 40 B8
Sedgley Park Bury 57 P8
Sedgwick Cumb 63 K5
Sedlescombe E Susx 12 F6
Sedrup Bucks 20 C2
Seend Wilts 18 D8
Seend Cleeve Wilts 18 D8
Seer Green Bucks 20 F5
Seething Norfk 45 M9
Sefton Sefton 56 G8
Seighford Staffs 49 Q9
Seion Gwynd 54 H8
Seisdon Staffs 39 Q3
Selattyn Shrops 48 F8
Selborne Hants 10 C4
Selby N York 59 N7
Selham W Susx 10 E6
Selhurst Gt Lon 21 M9
Selkirk Border 79 P3
Sellack Herefs 28 G4
Sellafield Station Cumb 62 B2
Sellindge Kent 13 L3
Selling Kent 23 K11
Sells Green Wilts 18 D8
Selly Oak Birm 40 D10
Selmeston E Susx 11 P8
Selsdon Gt Lon 21 M10
Selsey W Susx 10 D10
Selside N York 64 E11
Selsley Gloucs 29 L7
Selsted Kent 13 N2
Selston Notts 51 L9
Selworthy Somset 16 C6
Semer Suffk 34 G7
Semington Wilts 18 D8
Semley Wilts 8 D3
Send Surrey 20 G11
Senghenydd Caerph 27 N10
Sennen Cnwll 2 B10
Sennen Cove Cnwll 2 B9
Sennybridge Powys 27 K3
Sessay N York 66 C11
Setchey Norfk 43 Q7
Seton Mains E Loth 87 J7
Settle N York 63 P9
Settrington N York 67 J12
Sevenhampton Gloucs 30 D9
Sevenhampton Swindn 18 H3
Seven Kings Gt Lon 21 P6
Sevenoaks Kent 21 Q11
Sevenoaks Weald Kent 21 Q12
Seven Sisters Neath 26 H7
Seven Star Green Essex 34 F10
Severn Beach S Glos 28 G10
Severn Bridge S Glos 28 G10
Severn Stoke Worcs 39 Q12
Severn View Services S Glos 28 G10
Sevington Kent 13 K2
Sewards End Essex 33 P8
Sewell C Beds 32 E11
Sewerby E R Yk 61 L1
Seworgan Cnwll 2 G9
Sewstern Leics 42 C6
Sgalpaigh W Isls 111 c3
Sgiogarstaigh W Isls 111 e1
Shabbington Bucks 31 P11
Shackerstone Leics 41 J6
Shackleford Surrey 10 E2
Shader W Isls 111 d1
Shadforth Dur 73 N11
Shadingfield Suffk 45 P12
Shadoxhurst Kent 13 J3
Shadwell Leeds 59 J6
Shadwell Norfk 44 F12
Shaftenhoe End Herts 33 L8
Shaftesbury Dorset 8 C3
Shafton Barns 59 K11
Shakerley Wigan 57 M8
Shalbourne Wilts 19 K7
Shalden Hants 10 B2
Shaldon Devon 6 C8
Shalfleet IoW 9 M9
Shalford Essex 34 C10
Shalford Surrey 10 G1
Shalford Green Essex 34 C10
Shalmsford Street Kent 23 L11
Shalstone Bucks 31 N6
Shamley Green Surrey 10 G2
Shandford Angus 94 H9
Shandon Ag & B 84 E6
Shandwick Highld 107 P7
Shangton Leics 41 Q8
Shanklin IoW 9 M10
Shantron Ag & B 84 F5
Shap Cumb 71 Q11
Shapinsay Ork 111 h2
Shapwick Dorset 8 D7
Shapwick Somset 17 K8
Shard End Birm 40 F9
Shardlow Derbys 41 K2
Shareshill Staffs 40 C6
Sharlston Wakefd 59 K9
Sharman's Cross Solhll 40 F10
Sharnbrook Bed 32 E5
Sharnford Leics 41 L8
Sharoe Green Lancs 57 N12
Sharow N York 65 N12
Sharpenhoe C Beds 32 F10
Sharperton Nthumb 81 K12
Sharpness Gloucs 29 J8
Sharrington Norfk 44 G3
Shatterford Worcs 39 P6
Shaugh Prior Devon 5 L7
Shavington Ches E 49 M5
Shaw Oldham 58 C11
Shaw Swindn 18 G4
Shaw W Berk 19 N7
Shaw Wilts 18 D7
Shawbirch Wrekin 39 M11
Shawbost W Isls 111 d1
Shawbury Shrops 49 M10
Shawell Leics 41 M10
Shawford Hants 9 M3
Shawhead D & G 70 E2
Shaw Mills N York 58 H3
Shawsburn S Lans 77 N2

Shearington D & G 70 G3
Shearsby Leics 41 N11
Shearston Somset 16 H9
Shebbear Devon 14 H9
Shebdon Staffs 49 N9
Shebster Highld 110 B3
Shedfield Hants 9 P5
Sheen Staffs 50 E8
Sheepscar Leeds 58 H7
Sheepscombe Gloucs 29 M6
Sheepstor Devon 5 L6
Sheepwash Devon 14 H10
Sheepy Magna Leics 41 J7
Sheepy Parva Leics 41 J7
Sheering Essex 21 P1
Sheerness Kent 22 H8
Sheerwater Surrey 20 G10
Sheet Hants 10 C5
Sheffield Sheff 51 J4
Sheffield Park E Susx 11 N5
Shefford C Beds 32 G8
Sheigra Highld 108 D4
Sheinton Shrops 39 L2
Shelderton Shrops 38 H6
Sheldon Birm 40 F9
Sheldon Derbys 50 F7
Sheldon Devon 6 G2
Sheldwich Kent 23 K11
Shelfanger Norfk 45 J12
Shelford Notts 51 P11
Shelley Kirk 58 G11
Shelley Suffk 34 G8
Shellingford Oxon 19 K3
Shellow Bowells Essex 22 C2
Shelsley Beauchamp Worcs 39 N9
Shelsley Walsh Worcs 39 N9
Shelton Bed 32 E3
Shelton Norfk 45 K11
Shelton Notts 42 B2
Shelton Lock C Derb 41 J2
Shelton Under Harley Staffs 49 P7
Shelve Shrops 38 G3
Shelwick Herefs 28 F1
Shenfield Essex 22 C4
Shenington Oxon 31 J5
Shenley Herts 21 J4
Shenley Brook End M Keyn 32 B9
Shenley Church End M Keyn 32 B9
Shenmore Herefs 28 D2
Shennanton D & G 69 J6
Shenstone Staffs 40 E6
Shenstone Worcs 39 Q7
Shenton Leics 41 J7
Shenval Moray 101 J8
Shephall Herts 33 J11
Shepherd's Bush Gt Lon 21 K7
Shepherdswell Kent 13 N1
Shepley Kirk 58 G11
Shepperton Surrey 20 H9
Shepreth Cambs 33 L7
Shepshed Leics 41 L4
Shepton Beauchamp Somset 17 K11
Shepton Mallet Somset 17 N7
Shepton Montague Somset 17 P9
Shepway Kent 22 F11
Sheraton Dur 66 C1
Sherborne Dorset 17 P11
Sherborne Gloucs 30 F10
Sherborne Somset 17 N5
Sherborne St John Hants 19 Q9
Sherbourne Warwks 30 H2
Sherburn Dur 73 N11
Sherburn N York 67 K11
Sherburn Hill Dur 73 N11
Sherburn in Elmet N York 59 L7
Shere Surrey 10 H1
Shereford Norfk 44 E4
Sherfield English Hants 9 K3
Sherfield on Loddon Hants 20 B10
Sherford Devon 5 Q10
Sheriffhales Shrops 49 N11
Sheriff Hutton N York 59 P2
Sheringham Norfk 45 J2
Sherington M Keyn 32 C7
Shernborne Norfk 44 B4
Sherrington Wilts 18 E11
Sherston Wilts 18 C4
Sherwood C Nott 51 M11
Sherwood Forest Notts 51 N10
Shettleston C Glas 85 L9
Shevington Wigan 57 K7
Sheviock Cnwll 4 H8
Shibden Head C Brad 58 E8
Shide IoW 9 N9
Shidlaw Nthumb 80 H6
Shiel Bridge Highld 97 N6
Shieldaig Highld 105 M3
Shieldhill D & G 78 G11
Shieldhill Falk 85 P7
Shieldhill House Hotel S Lans 78 G2
Shields N Lans 85 N11
Shielfoot Highld 89 N3
Shielhill Angus 93 M4
Shielhill Inver 84 D8
Shifnal Shrops 39 N1
Shilbottle Nthumb 81 P11
Shildon Dur 65 M3
Shillford E Rens 84 H10
Shillingford Devon 16 D10
Shillingford Oxon 19 P3
Shillingford Abbot Devon 6 B5
Shillingford St George Devon 6 B5
Shillingstone Dorset 8 C5
Shillington C Beds 32 G9
Shilton Oxon 30 H11
Shilton Warwks 41 K9
Shimpling Norfk 45 J12
Shimpling Suffk 34 E6
Shimpling Street Suffk 34 E6
Shincliffe Dur 73 N11
Shiney Row Sundld 73 N9
Shinfield Wokham 20 B9
Shinness Highld 109 M11
Shipbourne Kent 22 C11
Shipdham Norfk 44 F9
Shipham Somset 17 L5
Shiphay Torbay 6 C7
Shiplake Oxon 20 C7
Shipley C Brad 58 F6
Shipley W Susx 11 J6

Shipley Bridge Surrey 11 L3
Shipmeadow Suffk 45 N11
Shippon Oxon 19 N2
Shipston-on-Stour Warwks 30 G5
Shipton Gloucs 30 D9
Shipton N York 59 M3
Shipton Shrops 39 K4
Shipton Bellinger Hants 19 J10
Shipton Gorge Dorset 7 M5
Shipton Green W Susx 10 C9
Shipton Moyne Gloucs 29 M10
Shipton-on-Cherwell Oxon 31 L10
Shiptonthorpe E R Yk 60 E5
Shipton-under-Wychwood
  Oxon 30 H9
Shirburn Oxon 19 B4
Shirdley Hill Lancs 56 G6
Shirebrook Derbys 51 M7
Shiregreen Sheff 51 J3
Shirehampton Bristl 28 G12
Shiremoor N Tyne 73 N6
Shirenewton Mons 28 F9
Shireoaks Notts 51 M5
Shirland Derbys 51 K8
Shirley C Sotn 9 L5
Shirley Derbys 50 G11
Shirley Gt Lon 21 M9
Shirley Solhll 40 E10
Shirrell Heath Hants 9 P5
Shirwell Devon 15 K5
Shiskine N Ayrs 75 N6
Shobdon Herefs 38 H9
Shobrooke Devon 15 P11
Shoby Leics 41 P4
Shocklach Ches W 48 H5
Shoeburyness Sthend 22 H6
Sholden Kent 23 Q11
Sholing C Sotn 9 M5
Shop Cnwll 14 D8
Shoreditch Gt Lon 21 M6
Shoreditch Somset 16 H10
Shoreham Kent 21 P10
Shoreham-by-Sea W Susx 11 K8
Shorley Hants 9 P3
Shorne Kent 22 E8
Shortgate E Susx 11 P7
Short Heath Birm 40 E8
Short Heath Wsall 40 C7
Shortlanesend Cnwll 3 J6
Shortlees E Ayrs 76 G4
Shorwell IoW 9 M10
Shoscombe BaNES 17 Q5
Shotesham Norfk 45 L9
Shotgate Essex 22 F5
Shotley Suffk 35 K9
Shotley Bridge Dur 73 J9
Shotley Gate Suffk 35 L9
Shotley Street Suffk 35 K9
Shottenden Kent 23 K11
Shottery Warwks 30 F3
Shotteswell Warwks 31 K5
Shottisham Suffk 35 M7
Shottlegate Derbys 50 H10
Shotton Dur 73 P11
Shotton Flints 48 F2
Shotton Colliery Dur 73 P11
Shotts N Lans 85 P10
Shotwick Ches W 48 G2
Shougle Moray 101 J4
Shouldham Norfk 44 B8
Shouldham Thorpe Norfk 43 Q8
Shoulton Worcs 39 P9
Shrawardine Shrops 48 H11
Shrawley Worcs 39 P8
Shrewley Warwks 30 G1
Shrewsbury Shrops 49 J11
Shrewton Wilts 18 F11
Shripney W Susx 10 F9
Shrivenham Oxon 19 J3
Shropham Norfk 44 G10
Shroton Dorset 8 C5
Shucknall Herefs 28 G1
Shudy Camps Cambs 33 P7
Shuna Ag & B 83 L2
Shurdington Gloucs 29 N5
Shurlock Row W & M 20 D9
Shurrery Highld 110 B4
Shurrery Lodge Highld 110 B4
Shurton Somset 16 G7
Shustoke Warwks 40 G9
Shute Devon 6 H4
Shute Devon 15 Q11
Shutford Oxon 31 J4
Shut Heath Staffs 49 Q10
Shuthonger Gloucs 29 M2
Shutlanger Nhants 31 Q4
Shuttington Warwks 40 G6
Shuttlewood Derbys 51 L6
Shuttleworth Bury 57 P5
Siabost W Isls 111 d1
Siadar W Isls 111 d1
Sibbertoft Nhants 41 P10
Sibford Ferris Oxon 31 J6
Sibford Gower Oxon 31 J6
Sible Hedingham Essex 34 C9
Sibley's Green Essex 33 P10
Sibsey Lincs 53 K12
Sibson Cambs 42 F10
Sibson Leics 41 J7
Sibster Highld 110 G5
Sibthorpe Notts 51 Q10
Sibthorpe Notts 51 P11
Sibton Suffk 35 M2
Sicklesmere Suffk 34 E5
Sicklinghall N York 59 J5
Sidbury Devon 6 F4
Sidbury Shrops 39 M5
Sidcot N Som 17 K5
Sidcup Gt Lon 21 P8
Siddington Ches E 49 Q2
Siddington Gloucs 29 P2
Sidestrand Norfk 45 L3
Sidford Devon 6 F4
Sidlesham W Susx 10 D9
Sidley E Susx 12 E8
Sidmouth Devon 6 F5
Sigglesthorne E R Yk 61 K5
Sigingstone V Glam 16 C3
Silchester Hants 19 Q8
Sileby Leics 41 N5
Silecroft Cumb 62 D6
Silfield Norfk 45 J9

Silkstone Barns 58 H11
Silkstone Common Barns 58 H12
Silloth Cumb 70 H5
Silpho N York 67 L8
Silsden C Brad 58 D5
Silsoe C Beds 32 F9
Silton Dorset 8 B2
Silverburn Mdloth 86 E9
Silverdale Lancs 63 J7
Silverdale Staffs 49 P6
Silver End Essex 34 D11
Silverford Abers 102 H3
Silverstone Nhants 31 P5
Silverton Devon 6 C3
Silvington Shrops 39 L6
Simonburn Nthumb 72 F6
Simonsbath Somset 15 N4
Simonstone Lancs 57 P3
Simprim Border 80 H5
Simpson M Keyn 32 C9
Simpson Cross Pembks 24 F5
Sinclair's Hill Border 80 H4
Sinclairston E Ayrs 76 H7
Sinderby N York 65 N10
Sinderland Green Traffd 57 N10
Sindlesham Wokham 20 C9
Sinfin C Derb 41 J2
Singleton Kent 13 J2
Singleton Lancs 56 H2
Singleton W Susx 10 E7
Singlewell Kent 22 D8
Sinnarhard Abers 101 N11
Sinnington N York 66 G9
Sinton Worcs 39 P9
Sinton Worcs 39 Q9
Sinton Green Worcs 39 P9
Sissinghurst Kent 12 F3
Siston S Glos 17 P2
Sithney Cnwll 2 F9
Sittingbourne Kent 22 H10
Six Ashes Shrops 39 P4
Sixhills Lincs 52 G6
Six Mile Bottom Cambs 33 P5
Sixpenny Handley Dorset 8 E4
Skaill Ork 111 h2
Skara Brae Ork 111 g2
Skares E Ayrs 77 J7
Skateraw Abers 95 P4
Skateraw E Loth 87 N7
Skeabost Highld 104 F11
Skeeby N York 65 L7
Skeffington Leics 41 Q7
Skeffling E R Yk 61 N9
Skegby Notts 51 L8
Skegby Notts 52 B9
Skegness Lincs 53 P10
Skelbo Highld 107 N4
Skelbo Street Highld 107 N4
Skelbrooke Donc 59 L10
Skeldyke Lincs 43 K3
Skellingthorpe Lincs 52 D8
Skellow Donc 59 M11
Skelmanthorpe Kirk 58 G11
Skelmersdale Lancs 57 J7
Skelmorlie N Ayrs 84 D9
Skelpick Highld 109 M5
Skelston D & G 78 D10
Skelton C York 59 M3
Skelton Cumb 71 N8
Skelton E R Yk 60 D8
Skelton R & Cl 66 F4
Skelton on Ure N York 59 J1
Skelwith Bridge Cumb 62 G2
Skendleby Lincs 53 M9
Skene House Abers 102 G12
Skenfrith Mons 28 E5
Skerne E R Yk 60 H3
Skerray Highld 109 L3
Skerricha Highld 108 E5
Skerton Lancs 63 J9
Sketchley Leics 41 K8
Sketty Swans 26 E9
Skewsby N York 66 E12
Skiall Highld 110 B3
Skidby E R Yk 60 H7
Skigersta W Isls 111 e1
Skilgate Somset 16 D10
Skillington Lincs 42 C5
Skinburness Cumb 71 J4
Skinflats Falk 85 Q6
Skinidin Highld 104 C11
Skipness Ag & B 83 N10
Skipper's Bridge D & G 79 M11
Skipsea E R Yk 61 K3
Skipton N York 58 C4
Skipton-on-Swale N York 65 P10
Skipwith N York 59 P6
Skirlaugh E R Yk 61 K6
Skirling Border 78 H2
Skirmett Bucks 20 C5
Skirpenbeck E R Yk 60 D3
Skirwith Cumb 64 B2
Skirza Highld 110 H3
Skokholm Island Pembks 24 D7
Skomer Island Pembks 24 D7
Skulamus Highld 97 J5
Skye Green Essex 34 E11
Skye of Curr Highld 99 P4
Slack D & G 78 C8
Slacks of Cairnbanno Abers 102 H6
Slad Gloucs 29 M7
Slade Devon 15 J3
Slade Green Gt Lon 21 Q7
Slade Hooton Rothm 51 M3
Slaggyford Nthumb 72 C9
Slaidburn Lancs 63 N10
Slaithwaite Kirk 58 E10
Slaley Nthumb 72 H8
Slamannan Falk 85 Q9
Slapton Bucks 32 D11
Slapton Devon 5 Q10
Slapton Nhants 31 N5
Slaugham W Susx 11 K5
Slaughterford Wilts 18 C6
Slawston Leics 41 R8
Sleaford Hants 10 C3
Sleaford Lincs 42 F2
Sleagill Cumb 64 B4
Sleapford Wrekin 49 L11
Sleasdairidh Highld 107 K3
Sledmere E R Yk 60 H2

188 Sleetbeck – Sternfield

- **Sleetbeck** Cumb 79 P12
- **Sleights** N York 67 J6
- **Slickly** Highld 110 F3
- **Sliddery** N Ayrs 75 P7
- **Sligachan** Highld 96 F4
- **Sligrachan** Ag & B 84 C5
- **Slimbridge** Gloucs 29 K7
- **Slindon** Staffs 49 P8
- **Slindon** W Susx 10 F8
- **Slinfold** W Susx 10 H4
- **Slingsby** N York 66 F11
- **Slip End** C Beds 32 F11
- **Slip End** Herts 33 J8
- **Slipton** Nhants 32 D2
- **Slitting Mill** Staffs 40 D4
- **Slockavullin** Ag & B 83 M4
- **Sloncombe** Devon 5 P3
- **Sloothby** Lincs 53 M8
- **Slough** Slough 20 F7
- **Slough Green** Somset 16 H11
- **Slumbay** Highld 97 M2
- **Slyne** Lancs 63 J8
- **Smailholm** Border 80 E7
- **Smallburgh** Norfk 45 M5
- **Smallburn** E Ayrs 77 L6
- **Small Dole** W Susx 11 K7
- **Smalley** Derbys 51 K11
- **Smallfield** Surrey 11 L2
- **Small Heath** Birm 40 E9
- **Small Hythe** Kent 12 H4
- **Smallridge** Devon 7 J3
- **Smallthorne** C Stke 50 B10
- **Smallworth** Norfk 34 G1
- **Smannell** Hants 19 L10
- **Smarden** Kent 12 G2
- **Smarden Bell** Kent 12 G2
- **Smart's Hill** Kent 11 Q2
- **Smeatharpe** Devon 6 G1
- **Smeeth** Kent 13 K3
- **Smeeton Westerby** Leics 41 P8
- **Smerral** Highld 110 D8
- **Smestow** Staffs 39 Q4
- **Smethwick** Sandw 40 D9
- **Smirisary** Highld 89 N2
- **Smisby** Derbys 41 J4
- **Smithfield** Cumb 71 P3
- **Smith's Green** Essex 33 Q8
- **Smithstown** Highld 105 L6
- **Smithton** Highld 107 L12
- **Smoo** Highld 108 H3
- **Smythe's Green** Essex 34 F11
- **Snade** D & G 78 D10
- **Snailbeach** Shrops 38 G2
- **Snailwell** Cambs 33 Q4
- **Snainton** N York 67 K10
- **Snaith** E R Yk 59 N9
- **Snape** N York 65 M10
- **Snape** Suffk 35 N5
- **Snape Street** Suffk 35 N5
- **Snaresbrook** Gt Lon 21 N5
- **Snarestone** Leics 41 J5
- **Snarford** Lincs 52 F7
- **Snargate** Kent 13 J4
- **Snave** Kent 13 K4
- **Sneaton** N York 67 J6
- **Snelland** Lincs 52 F7
- **Snelston** Derbys 50 F11
- **Snetterton** Norfk 44 G11
- **Snettisham** Norfk 44 B4
- **Snitter** Nthumb 81 L12
- **Snitterby** Lincs 52 E5
- **Snitterfield** Warwks 30 G3
- **Snitton** Shrops 39 K7
- **Snodland** Kent 22 E10
- **Snowdon** Gwynd 54 H10
- *Snowdonia National Park* 47 N5
- **Snow End** Herts 33 L9
- **Snowshill** Gloucs 30 E7
- **Soake** Hants 9 Q5
- **Soay** Highld 96 E7
- **Soberton** Hants 9 Q4
- **Soberton Heath** Hants 9 P5
- **Sockburn** Darltn 65 N6
- **Soham** Cambs 33 P3
- **Solas** W Isls 111 b4
- **Soldridge** Hants 9 Q1
- **Sole Street** Kent 22 D9
- **Sole Street** Kent 23 L12
- **Solihull** Solhll 40 F10
- **Sollers Dilwyn** Herefs 38 H10
- **Sollers Hope** Herefs 28 H3
- **Solva** Pembks 24 E4
- **Solwaybank** D & G 79 L12
- **Somerby** Leics 41 R5
- **Somerby** Lincs 52 F3
- **Somercotes** Derbys 51 K9
- **Somerford** BCP 8 H8
- **Somerford Keynes** Gloucs 18 E2
- **Somerley** W Susx 10 D9
- **Somerleyton** Suffk 45 P10
- **Somersal Herbert** Derbys 40 F1
- **Somersby** Lincs 53 K8
- **Somersham** Cambs 33 K2
- **Somersham** Suffk 34 H7
- **Somerton** Oxon 31 L8
- **Somerton** Somset 17 L9
- **Somerton** Suffk 34 D6
- **Sompting** W Susx 11 J8
- **Sonning** Wokham 20 C8
- **Sonning Common** Oxon 20 B7
- **Sopley** Hants 8 H7
- **Sopwell** Herts 21 J3
- **Sopworth** Wilts 18 C4
- **Sorbie** D & G 69 L9
- **Sordale** Highld 110 D4
- **Sorisdale** Ag & B 88 G4
- **Sorn** E Ayrs 77 J6
- **Sornhill** E Ayrs 77 J4
- **Sortat** Highld 110 F3
- **Sotby** Lincs 52 H7
- **Sotterley** Suffk 45 P12
- **Soughton** Flints 48 E3
- **Soulbury** Bucks 32 C10
- **Soulby** Cumb 64 D5
- **Souldern** Oxon 31 M7
- **Souldrop** Bed 32 E4
- **Sound** Ches E 49 L6
- **Sound Muir** Moray 101 M5
- **Soundwell** S Glos 17 P2
- **Sourton** Devon 5 L3
- **Soutergate** Cumb 62 E6
- **South Acre** Norfk 44 D7
- **South Alkham** Kent 13 N2
- **Southall** Gt Lon 20 H7
- **South Allington** Devon 5 Q11
- **South Alloa** Falk 85 P5
- **Southam** Gloucs 29 N4
- **Southam** Warwks 31 K2
- **South Ambersham** W Susx 10 E6
- **Southampton** C Sotn 9 M5
- *Southampton Airport* Hants 9 M4
- **South Anston** Rothm 51 L4
- **South Ashford** Kent 13 J2
- **South Baddesley** Hants 9 L7
- **South Ballachulish** Highld 90 E5
- **South Bank** C York 59 N4
- **South Barrow** Somset 17 N9
- **South Beddington** Gt Lon 21 L10
- **South Benfleet** Essex 22 F6
- **Southborough** Gt Lon 21 N9
- **Southborough** Kent 12 C2
- **Southbourne** BCP 8 G8
- **Southbourne** W Susx 10 C8
- **South Bramwith** Donc 59 N11
- **South Brent** Devon 5 N8
- **South Brewham** Somset 17 Q8
- **South Broomhill** Nthumb 73 M2
- **Southburgh** Norfk 44 G8
- **South Burlingham** Norfk 45 N8
- **Southburn** E R Yk 60 G4
- **South Cadbury** Somset 17 P10
- **South Carlton** Lincs 52 D8
- **South Carlton** Notts 51 N4
- **South Cave** E R Yk 60 F7
- **South Cerney** Gloucs 18 F2
- **South Chailey** E Susx 11 N6
- **South Charlton** Nthumb 81 N9
- **South Cheriton** Somset 17 Q10
- **South Church** Dur 65 L2
- **Southchurch** Sthend 22 H6
- **South Cliffe** E R Yk 60 E7
- **South Clifton** Notts 52 B9
- **South Cockerington** Lincs 53 L6
- **South Cornelly** Brdgnd 26 H11
- **Southcott** Cnwll 4 F2
- **Southcott** Devon 5 P4
- **Southcourt** Bucks 20 D2
- **South Cove** Suffk 35 P1
- **South Creake** Norfk 44 E3
- **South Croxton** Leics 41 P5
- **South Dalton** E R Yk 60 G5
- **South Darenth** Kent 22 C9
- **South Dell** W Isls 111 d1
- *South Downs National Park* 11 M8
- **South Duffield** N York 59 P7
- **South Earlswood** Surrey 11 L1
- **Southease** E Susx 11 N8
- **South Elkington** Lincs 53 J6
- **South Elmsall** Wakefd 59 L11
- **Southend** Ag & B 75 K10
- *Southend Airport* Essex 22 G5
- **Southend-on-Sea** Sthend 22 H6
- **Southerndown** V Glam 16 B2
- **Southerness** D & G 70 F5
- **South Erradale** Highld 105 L7
- **Southerton** Devon 6 E5
- **Southery** Norfk 43 P10
- **South Fambridge** Essex 22 G5
- **South Ferriby** N Linc 60 G9
- **South Field** E R Yk 60 H8
- **Southfield** Falk 85 P8
- **Southfleet** Kent 22 C8
- **Southgate** Gt Lon 21 L5
- **Southgate** Swans 26 D10
- **South Gorley** Hants 8 H5
- **South Gosforth** N u Ty 73 M7
- **South Green** Essex 22 D5
- **South Green** Kent 22 G10
- **South Green** Norfk 44 H7
- **South Gyle** C Edin 86 E7
- **South Hanningfield** Essex 22 E4
- **South Harting** W Susx 10 C6
- **South Hayling** Hants 10 B9
- **South Heath** Bucks 20 E3
- **South Heighton** E Susx 11 N9
- **South Hetton** Dur 73 P10
- **South Hiendley** Wakefd 59 K10
- **South Hill** Cnwll 4 H5
- **South Hinksey** Oxon 31 L12
- **South Holmwood** Surrey 11 J2
- **South Hornchurch** Gt Lon 21 P6
- **South Huish** Devon 5 N11
- **South Hykeham** Lincs 52 D9
- **South Hylton** Sundld 73 P9
- **Southill** C Beds 32 G8
- **Southington** Hants 19 N10
- **South Kelsey** Lincs 52 E4
- **South Kessock** Highld 107 L11
- **South Killingholme** N Linc 61 K10
- **South Kilvington** N York 65 Q10
- **South Kilworth** Leics 41 N10
- **South Kirkby** Wakefd 59 K11
- **South Kyme** Lincs 52 G12
- **Southleigh** Devon 6 G4
- **South Leigh** Oxon 31 K11
- **South Leverton** Notts 52 A7
- **South Littleton** Worcs 30 E5
- **South Lopham** Norfk 34 G1
- **South Luffenham** Rutlnd 42 D9
- **South Lynn** Norfk 43 P6
- **South Malling** E Susx 11 N7
- **South Marston** Swindn 18 H3
- **South Merstham** Surrey 21 L11
- **South Milford** N York 59 L7
- **South Milton** Devon 5 N10
- **South Mimms** Herts 21 K3
- *South Mimms Services* Herts 21 K4
- **Southminster** Essex 23 J4
- **South Molton** Devon 15 M7
- **South Moor** Dur 73 L9
- **Southmoor** Oxon 19 L2
- **South Moreton** Oxon 19 P3
- **Southmuir** Angus 93 L5
- **South Mundham** W Susx 10 E9
- **South Newbald** E R Yk 60 F7
- **South Newington** Oxon 31 K7
- **South Newton** Wilts 8 G1
- **South Normanton** Derbys 51 K9
- **South Norwood** Gt Lon 21 M9
- **South Ockendon** Thurr 22 C6
- **Southoe** Cambs 32 H4
- **Southolt** Suffk 35 K3
- **South Ormsby** Lincs 53 L8
- **Southorpe** C Pete 42 F9
- **South Otterington** N York 65 P9
- **Southover** Dorset 7 N4
- **South Owersby** Lincs 52 F5
- **Southowram** Calder 58 E9
- **South Park** Surrey 11 K1
- **South Perrott** Dorset 7 L2
- **South Petherton** Somset 17 L11
- **South Petherwin** Cnwll 4 G4
- **South Pickenham** Norfk 44 E8
- **South Pill** Cnwll 5 J8
- **South Pool** Devon 5 Q11
- **South Poorton** Dorset 7 M4
- **Southport** Sefton 56 G5
- **South Queensferry** C Edin 86 D6
- **South Rauceby** Lincs 42 E2
- **South Raynham** Norfk 44 E5
- **South Reddish** Stockp 50 B3
- **Southrepps** Norfk 45 L3
- **South Reston** Lincs 53 L6
- **Southrey** Lincs 52 G9
- **South Ronaldsay** Ork 111 h3
- **Southrop** Gloucs 30 G12
- **Southrope** Hants 19 Q10
- **South Runcton** Norfk 43 Q8
- **South Scarle** Notts 52 B10
- **Southsea** C Port 9 Q7
- **South Shian** Ag & B 90 C7
- **South Shields** S Tyne 73 P7
- **South Shore** Bpool 56 F3
- **Southside** Dur 65 K3
- **South Stainley** N York 58 H2
- **South Stifford** Thurr 22 C7
- **South Stoke** BaNES 17 Q4
- **South Stoke** Oxon 19 P4
- **South Stoke** W Susx 10 G7
- **South Street** Kent 23 K10
- **South Street** Kent 23 L9
- **South Tarbrax** S Lans 86 B10
- **South Tawton** Devon 5 N2
- **South Tehidy** Cnwll 2 F7
- **South Thoresby** Lincs 53 L7
- **Southtown** Norfk 45 Q8
- **South Uist** W Isls 111 b6
- **Southwaite** Cumb 71 P6
- *Southwaite Services* Cumb 71 P6
- **South Walsham** Norfk 45 M7
- **Southwark** Gt Lon 21 L7
- **South Warnborough** Hants 10 B1
- **Southwater** W Susx 11 J5
- **Southway** C Plym 5 K7
- **South Weald** Essex 22 C5
- **Southwell** Notts 51 P9
- **South Weston** Oxon 20 B4
- **South Wheatley** Notts 51 Q4
- **Southwick** Hants 9 Q6
- **Southwick** Nhants 42 E10
- **Southwick** Sundld 73 P8
- **Southwick** W Susx 11 K8
- **Southwick** Wilts 18 C9
- **South Widcombe** BaNES 17 N5
- **South Wigston** Leics 41 N7
- **South Willesborough** Kent 13 K2
- **South Willingham** Lincs 52 H6
- **South Wingfield** Derbys 51 J9
- **South Witham** Lincs 42 D6
- **Southwold** Suffk 35 Q2
- **South Woodham Ferrers** Essex 22 F4
- **South Wootton** Norfk 43 Q5
- **South Wraxall** Wilts 18 C7
- **South Zeal** Devon 5 N2
- **Sovereign Harbour** E Susx 12 D9
- **Sowerby** Calder 58 D9
- **Sowerby** N York 66 B10
- **Sowerby Bridge** Calder 58 D9
- **Sowood** Calder 58 E9
- **Sowton** Devon 5 K7
- **Sowton** Devon 6 D4
- **Soyland Town** Calder 58 D9
- **Spain's End** Essex 33 Q8
- **Spalding** Lincs 43 J5
- **Spaldington** E R Yk 60 D7
- **Spaldwick** Cambs 32 G3
- **Spalford** Notts 52 B9
- **Spanby** Lincs 42 F3
- **Sparham** Norfk 44 H6
- **Spark Bridge** Cumb 62 F5
- **Sparkford** Somset 17 N10
- **Sparkhill** Birm 40 E10
- **Sparkwell** Devon 5 M8
- **Sparrowpit** Derbys 50 E5
- **Sparrows Green** E Susx 12 D4
- **Sparsholt** Hants 9 M2
- **Sparsholt** Oxon 19 L4
- **Spaunton** N York 66 G9
- **Spaxton** Somset 16 G8
- **Spean Bridge** Highld 98 C11
- **Spearywell** Hants 9 K2
- **Speen** Bucks 20 D4
- **Speen** W Berk 19 M7
- **Speeton** N York 67 N11
- **Speke** Lpool 56 H11
- **Speldhurst** Kent 12 B2
- **Spellbrook** Herts 33 M12
- **Spencers Wood** Wokham 20 B9
- **Spen Green** Ches E 49 P4
- **Spennithorne** N York 65 K9
- **Spennymoor** Dur 65 M2
- **Spetchley** Worcs 30 B4
- **Spetisbury** Dorset 8 D7
- **Spexhall** Suffk 35 N2
- **Spey Bay** Moray 101 L3
- **Speybridge** Highld 100 G9
- **Speyview** Moray 101 K6
- **Spilsby** Lincs 53 L9
- **Spinkhill** Derbys 51 L5
- **Spinningdale** Highld 107 L4
- **Spital** Wirral 56 G11
- **Spital Hill** Donc 51 N3
- **Spittal** E Loth 87 J6
- **Spittal** Highld 110 D5
- **Spittal** Nthumb 81 L4
- **Spittal** Pembks 24 G4
- **Spittalfield** P & K 92 G7
- **Spittal of Glenmuick** Abers 94 E5
- **Spittal of Glenshee** P & K 94 B7
- **Spittal-on-Rule** Border 80 D9
- **Spixworth** Norfk 45 L7
- **Splatt** Devon 15 K10
- **Splayne's Green** E Susx 11 N5
- **Splott** Cardif 16 G2
- **Spofforth** N York 59 J4
- **Spondon** C Derb 41 K1
- **Spooner Row** Norfk 44 H10
- **Sporle** Norfk 44 E7
- **Spott** E Loth 87 M7
- **Spottiswoode** Border 80 E4
- **Spratton** Nhants 41 Q12
- **Spreakley** Surrey 10 D2
- **Spreyton** Devon 15 M11
- **Spriddlestone** Devon 5 L9
- **Spridlington** Lincs 52 E6
- **Springburn** C Glas 85 K8
- **Springfield** D & G 71 M2
- **Springfield** Essex 22 E2
- **Springfield** Fife 93 L12
- **Springholm** D & G 70 D2
- **Springside** N Ayrs 76 F4
- **Springthorpe** Lincs 52 C5
- **Springwell** Sundld 73 M8
- **Sproatley** E R Yk 61 K7
- **Sproston Green** Ches W 49 N3
- **Sprotbrough** Donc 51 M1
- **Sproughton** Suffk 35 J7
- **Sprouston** Border 80 G7
- **Sprowston** Norfk 45 L7
- **Sproxton** Leics 42 C5
- **Sproxton** N York 66 E10
- **Spurstow** Ches E 49 K4
- **Spyway** Dorset 7 M4
- **Stableford** Shrops 39 N3
- **Stacey Bank** Sheff 50 H3
- **Stackhouse** N York 63 P8
- **Stackpole** Pembks 24 H9
- **Stackpole Elidor** Pembks 24 H8
- **Staddiscombe** C Plym 5 K9
- **Stadhampton** Oxon 19 Q2
- **Stadhlaigearraidh** W Isls 111 a5
- **Staffield** Cumb 71 Q7
- **Staffin** Highld 104 G8
- **Stafford** Staffs 40 B3
- *Stafford Services (northbound)* Staffs 40 B2
- *Stafford Services (southbound)* Staffs 40 B2
- **Stagsden** Bed 32 E7
- **Stainburn** Cumb 70 G9
- **Stainby** Lincs 42 C5
- **Staincross** Barns 59 J11
- **Staindrop** Dur 65 K4
- **Staines-upon-Thames** Surrey 20 G8
- **Stainforth** Donc 59 N10
- **Stainforth** N York 63 P8
- **Staining** Lancs 56 G2
- **Stainland** Calder 58 E9
- **Stainsacre** N York 67 K6
- **Stainton** Cumb 63 K5
- **Stainton** Cumb 71 P9
- **Stainton** Donc 51 M3
- **Stainton** Dur 65 J4
- **Stainton** Middsb 66 C5
- **Stainton by Langworth** Lincs 52 F7
- **Staintondale** N York 67 L7
- **Stainton le Vale** Lincs 52 H5
- **Stainton with Adgarley** Cumb 62 F7
- **Stair** E Ayrs 76 G6
- **Stairhaven** D & G 68 G8
- **Staithes** N York 66 H4
- **Stakes** Hants 10 B8
- **Stalbridge** Dorset 17 Q11
- **Stalbridge Weston** Dorset 17 Q11
- **Stalham** Norfk 45 N5
- **Stalisfield Green** Kent 23 J11
- **Stallen** Dorset 17 N11
- **Stallingborough** NE Lin 61 K11
- **Stalmine** Lancs 62 G12
- **Stalybridge** Tamesd 50 C2
- **Stambourne** Essex 34 C8
- **Stambourne Green** Essex 34 B8
- **Stamford** Lincs 42 E8
- **Stamford** Nthumb 81 P9
- **Stamford Bridge** Ches W 49 J3
- **Stamford Bridge** E R Yk 60 C3
- **Stamfordham** Nthumb 73 J6
- **Stamford Hill** Gt Lon 21 M6
- **Stanbridge** C Beds 32 D11
- **Stanbury** C Brad 58 D6
- **Stand** N Lans 85 M8
- **Standburn** Falk 85 Q7
- **Standeford** Staffs 40 B6
- **Standen** Kent 12 G3
- **Standerwick** Somset 18 B10
- **Standford** Hants 10 D3
- **Standingstone** Cumb 70 H8
- **Standish** Wigan 57 K6
- **Standlake** Oxon 31 K12
- **Standon** Hants 9 M3
- **Standon** Herts 33 L11
- **Standon** Staffs 49 P8
- **Stane** N Lans 85 P10
- **Stanfield** Norfk 44 F6
- **Stanford** C Beds 32 G8
- **Stanford** Kent 13 L3
- **Stanford Bishop** Herefs 39 M10
- **Stanford Bridge** Worcs 39 N8
- **Stanford Dingley** W Berk 19 P6
- **Stanford in the Vale** Oxon 19 K3
- **Stanford le Hope** Thurr 22 D7
- **Stanford on Avon** Nhants 41 N10
- **Stanford on Soar** Notts 41 M3
- **Stanford on Teme** Worcs 39 N8
- **Stanfree** Derbys 51 L6
- **Stanghow** R & Cl 66 F4
- **Stanground** C Pete 42 H10
- **Stanhoe** Norfk 44 D3
- **Stanhope** Border 79 J3
- **Stanhope** Dur 72 H11
- **Stanhope** Kent 13 J2
- **Stanion** Nhants 42 D11
- **Stanley** Derbys 51 K11
- **Stanley** Dur 73 L9
- **Stanley** P & K 92 G8
- **Stanley** Staffs 50 B9
- **Stanley Crook** Dur 73 L12
- **Stanley Pontlarge** Gloucs 30 D7
- **Stanmer** Br & H 11 M7
- **Stanmore** Gt Lon 21 J5
- **Stanmore** Hants 9 M2
- **Stannersburn** Nthumb 72 D4
- **Stanningfield** Suffk 34 E5
- **Stannington** Nthumb 73 L5
- **Stannington** Sheff 50 H4
- **Stannington Station** Nthumb 73 L5
- **Stansbatch** Herefs 38 G9
- **Stansfield** Suffk 34 D6
- **Stanstead** Suffk 34 D7
- **Stanstead Abbotts** Herts 21 M2
- **Stansted** Kent 22 C10
- *Stansted Airport* Essex 33 N11
- **Stansted Mountfitchet** Essex 33 N10
- **Stanton** Gloucs 30 E7
- **Stanton** Nthumb 73 K3
- **Stanton** Staffs 50 E10
- **Stanton** Suffk 34 F3
- **Stanton by Bridge** Derbys 41 J3
- **Stanton by Dale** Derbys 51 L12
- **Stanton Drew** BaNES 17 N4
- **Stanton Fitzwarren** Swindn 18 H3
- **Stanton Harcourt** Oxon 31 K11
- **Stanton in Peak** Derbys 50 G7
- **Stanton Lacy** Shrops 39 J6
- **Stanton Lees** Derbys 50 G8
- **Stanton Long** Shrops 39 L4
- **Stanton-on-the-Wolds** Notts 41 N2
- **Stanton Prior** BaNES 17 P4
- **Stanton St Bernard** Wilts 18 G8
- **Stanton St John** Oxon 31 M11
- **Stanton St Quintin** Wilts 18 D5
- **Stanton Street** Suffk 34 F4
- **Stanton under Bardon** Leics 41 L5
- **Stanton upon Hine Heath** Shrops 49 K10
- **Stanton Wick** BaNES 17 N4
- **Stanway** Essex 34 F11
- **Stanway** Gloucs 30 D7
- **Stanwell** Surrey 20 G8
- **Stanwick** Nhants 32 E3
- **Stanwix** Cumb 71 N4
- **Staoinebrig** W Isls 111 a5
- **Stape** N York 66 H8
- **Stapeley** Ches E 49 M5
- **Stapenhill** Staffs 40 G3
- **Staple** Kent 23 P11
- **Staple Cross** Devon 16 D11
- **Staplecross** E Susx 12 F5
- **Staplefield** W Susx 11 L5
- **Staple Fitzpaine** Somset 16 H11
- **Stapleford** Cambs 33 M6
- **Stapleford** Herts 33 K12
- **Stapleford** Leics 42 B6
- **Stapleford** Lincs 52 C11
- **Stapleford** Notts 51 L12
- **Stapleford** Wilts 18 F12
- **Stapleford Abbotts** Essex 21 P5
- **Staplegrove** Somset 16 G10
- **Staplehay** Somset 16 G10
- **Staplehurst** Kent 12 F2
- **Staplers** IoW 9 N9
- **Staplestreet** Kent 23 K10
- **Stapleton** Herefs 38 G8
- **Stapleton** Leics 41 K7
- **Stapleton** N York 65 M5
- **Stapleton** Shrops 39 J2
- **Stapleton** Somset 17 L11
- **Stapley** Somset 16 G12
- **Staploe** Bed 32 G5
- **Staplow** Herefs 29 J1
- **Star** Fife 86 G2
- **Star** Pembks 25 M2
- **Star** Somset 17 L5
- **Starbeck** N York 59 J3
- **Starbotton** N York 64 G11
- **Starcross** Devon 6 C6
- **Stareton** Warwks 41 J12
- **Starlings Green** Essex 33 M9
- **Starston** Norfk 45 K12
- **Startforth** Dur 65 J4
- **Startley** Wilts 18 D4
- **Statenborough** Kent 23 P11
- **Statham** Warrtn 57 M10
- **Stathe** Somset 17 K9
- **Stathern** Leics 41 Q2
- **Staughton Green** Cambs 32 G4
- **Staunton** Gloucs 28 G6
- **Staunton** Gloucs 29 K3
- **Staunton on Arrow** Herefs 38 G9
- **Staunton on Wye** Herefs 38 G12
- **Staveley** Cumb 63 J3
- **Staveley** Derbys 51 K6
- **Staveley** N York 59 J2
- **Staveley-in-Cartmel** Cumb 62 H5
- **Staverton** Devon 5 Q7
- **Staverton** Gloucs 29 M4
- **Staverton** Nhants 31 M2
- **Staverton** Wilts 18 C8
- **Stawell** Somset 17 K8
- **Stawley** Somset 16 E10
- **Staxigoe** Highld 110 H5
- **Staxton** N York 67 L10
- **Staynall** Lancs 62 G12
- **Stean** N York 65 J11
- **Stearsby** N York 66 E12
- **Steart** Somset 16 H7
- **Stebbing** Essex 33 Q11
- **Stechford** Birm 40 F9
- **Stedham** W Susx 10 D5
- **Steelend** Fife 86 B4
- **Steele Road** Border 79 Q9
- **Steen's Bridge** Herefs 39 K10
- **Steep** Hants 10 C5
- **Steep Lane** Calder 58 D9
- **Steeple** Essex 22 H3
- **Steeple Ashton** Wilts 18 D9
- **Steeple Aston** Oxon 31 L8
- **Steeple Bumpstead** Essex 34 B8
- **Steeple Claydon** Bucks 31 P8
- **Steeple Gidding** Cambs 32 G1
- **Steeple Langford** Wilts 18 F12
- **Steeple Morden** Cambs 33 J8
- **Steeton** C Brad 58 D5
- **Stein** Highld 104 C10
- **Stelling Minnis** Kent 13 M1
- **Stembridge** Somset 17 K11
- **Stenalees** Cnwll 3 M4
- **Stenhouse** D & G 77 N11
- **Stenhousemuir** Falk 85 P6
- **Stenscholl** Highld 104 F8
- **Stenson Fields** Derbys 41 J2
- **Stenton** E Loth 87 M7
- **Steornabhagh** W Isls 111 d2
- **Stepaside** Pembks 25 K7
- **Stepford** D & G 78 E11
- **Stepney** Gt Lon 21 M7
- **Steppingley** C Beds 32 E9
- **Stepps** N Lans 85 L8
- **Sternfield** Suffk 35 N5

Stert Wilts 18 F8
Stetchworth Cambs 33 Q5
Stevenage Herts 32 H10
Stevenston N Ayrs 76 E3
Steventon Hants 19 P10
Steventon Oxon 19 M3
Steventon End Essex 33 P8
Stevington Bed 32 E6
Stewartby Bed 32 E8
Stewartfield S Lans 85 K11
Stewarton Ag & B 75 K8
Stewarton E Ayrs 76 G3
Stewkley Bucks 32 C10
Stewley Somset 17 J11
Steyning W Susx 11 J7
Steynton Pembks 24 G7
Stibb Cnwll 14 D9
Stibbard Norfk 44 G4
Stibb Cross Devon 14 H8
Stibb Green Wilts 19 J8
Stibbington Cambs 42 F9
Stichill Border 80 F6
Sticker Cnwll 3 L6
Stickford Lincs 53 K10
Sticklepath Devon 5 M2
Stickney Lincs 53 K11
Stiffkey Norfk 44 F2
Stifford Clays Thurr 22 C7
Stilligarry W Isls 111 a5
Stillingfleet N York 59 N6
Stillington N York 59 N1
Stillington S on T 65 P3
Stilton Cambs 42 G11
Stinchcombe Gloucs 29 K8
Stinsford Dorset 7 Q5
Stiperstones Shrops 38 G3
Stirchley Wrekin 39 M1
Stirling Abers 103 M6
Stirling Stirlg 85 N4
Stirling Castle Stirlg 85 N4
Stirling Services Stirlg 85 N5
Stirtloe Cambs 32 H4
Stirton N York 58 C4
Stisted Essex 34 D10
Stithians Cnwll 2 G8
Stivichall Covtry 41 J11
Stixwould Lincs 52 H9
St Michaels Fife 93 M10
Stoak Ches W 48 H2
Stobo Border 79 K2
Stoborough Dorset 8 D9
Stobs Castle Border 80 C11
Stobswood Nthumb 73 L2
Stock Essex 22 E4
Stock N Som 17 L4
Stockbridge Hants 9 L1
Stockbriggs S Lans 77 N4
Stockbury Kent 22 G10
Stockcross W Berk 19 M7
Stockerston Leics 42 B9
Stock Green Worcs 30 C3
Stocking Herefs 28 H3
Stockingford Warwks 41 J8
Stocking Pelham Herts 33 M10
Stockland Devon 6 H2
Stockland Bristol Somset 16 H7
Stockleigh English Devon 15 P10
Stockleigh Pomeroy Devon 15 P10
Stockley Wilts 18 E7
Stocklinch Somset 17 K11
Stockport Stockp 50 B3
Stocksbridge Sheff 50 H2
Stocksfield Nthumb 73 J8
Stockton Herefs 39 K9
Stockton Norfk 45 N10
Stockton Shrops 39 N3
Stockton Warwks 31 K2
Stockton Wilts 18 E12
Stockton Wrekin 49 P11
Stockton Brook Staffs 50 B9
Stockton Heath Warrtn 57 L10
Stockton-on-Tees S on T 66 C4
Stockton on Teme Worcs 39 N8
Stockton on the Forest C York 59 P3
Stockwell End Wolves 40 B7
Stockwood Bristl 17 P3
Stockwood Dorset 7 N2
Stock Wood Worcs 30 D3
Stodmarsh Kent 23 N10
Stody Norfk 44 H3
Stoer Highld 108 B9
Stoford Somset 17 N12
Stoford Wilts 8 F1
Stogumber Somset 16 E8
Stogursey Somset 16 G7
Stoke Covtry 41 J10
Stoke Devon 14 E7
Stoke Hants 10 B9
Stoke Hants 19 L9
Stoke Medway 22 G8
Stoke Abbott Dorset 7 L3
Stoke Albany Nhants 42 B11
Stoke Ash Suffk 35 J3
Stoke Bardolph Notts 51 N11
Stoke Bliss Worcs 39 M9
Stoke Bruerne Nhants 31 Q4
Stoke-by-Clare Suffk 34 C7
Stoke-by-Nayland Suffk 34 G7
Stoke Canon Devon 6 C3
Stoke Charity Hants 19 N11
Stoke Climsland Cnwll 4 H5
Stoke Cross Herefs 39 L11
Stoke D'Abernon Surrey 20 H10
Stoke Doyle Nhants 42 E11
Stoke Dry Rutlnd 42 C10
Stoke Edith Herefs 28 H1
Stoke Farthing Wilts 8 F3
Stoke Ferry Norfk 44 B9
Stoke Fleming Devon 6 B11
Stokeford Dorset 8 C9
Stoke Gabriel Devon 6 B10
Stoke Gifford S Glos 28 H11
Stoke Golding Leics 41 K7
Stoke Goldington M Keyn 32 B7
Stokeham Notts 52 A7
Stoke Hammond Bucks 32 C10
Stoke Holy Cross Norfk 45 K9
Stokeinteignhead Devon 6 C8
Stoke Lacy Herefs 39 L11
Stoke Lyne Oxon 31 M8
Stoke Mandeville Bucks 20 D2
Stokenchurch Bucks 20 C4

Stoke Newington Gt Lon 21 M6
Stokenham Devon 5 C10
Stoke-on-Trent C Stke 50 B10
Stoke Orchard Gloucs 29 M3
Stoke Poges Bucks 20 F6
Stoke Prior Herefs 39 K10
Stoke Prior Worcs 30 C1
Stoke Rivers Devon 15 L5
Stoke Rochford Lincs 42 D5
Stoke Row Oxon 20 B6
Stoke St Gregory Somset 17 J10
Stoke St Mary Somset 16 H10
Stoke St Michael Somset 17 P6
Stoke St Milborough Shrops 39 K5
Stokesby Norfk 45 N7
Stokesley N York 66 D6
Stoke sub Hamdon Somset 17 L11
Stoke Talmage Oxon 19 B4
Stoke Trister Somset 17 Q9
Stoke upon Tern Shrops 49 M9
Stolford Somset 16 G7
Stondon Massey Essex 22 C4
Stone Bucks 20 C2
Stone Gloucs 29 J9
Stone Rothm 51 M3
Stone Staffs 40 B1
Stone Worcs 30 B1
Stone Allerton Somset 17 K6
Ston Easton Somset 17 N5
Stonebridge N Som 17 K4
Stonebridge Warwks 40 G10
Stonebroom Derbys 51 K8
Stone Cross Kent 23 P11
Stonecrouch Kent 12 E4
Stoneferry C KuH 61 J7
Stonefield Castle Hotel Ag & B 83 N8
Stonegate E Susx 12 D4
Stonegrave N York 66 F11
Stonehaven Abers 95 P5
Stonehenge Wilts 18 G11
Stonehouse C Plym 5 K9
Stonehouse Gloucs 29 L7
Stonehouse S Lans 77 M3
Stone in Oxney Kent 12 H5
Stoneleigh Warwks 41 J11
Stonesby Leics 42 B5
Stonesfield Oxon 31 K10
Stones Green Essex 35 J10
Stone Street Kent 22 C11
Stone Street Suffk 35 N1
Stonewells Moray 101 K3
Stoneybridge W Isls 111 a5
Stoneyburn W Loth 86 B9
Stoneygate C Leic 41 N7
Stoneykirk D & G 68 E8
Stoney Middleton Derbys 50 G6
Stoney Stanton Leics 41 L8
Stoney Stoke Somset 17 Q9
Stoney Stretton Shrops 17 P8
Stoneywood C Aber 103 J11
Stoneywood Falk 85 N6
Stonham Aspal Suffk 35 J5
Stonnall Staffs 40 E6
Stonor Oxon 20 B6
Stonton Wyville Leics 41 Q8
Stony Houghton Derbys 51 L7
Stony Stratford M Keyn 32 B8
Stoodleigh Devon 15 L6
Stoodleigh Devon 16 C11
Stop 24 Services Kent 13 L3
Stopham W Susx 10 G6
Stopsley Luton 32 F11
Stornoway W Isls 111 d2
Stornoway Airport W Isls 111 d2
Storridge Herefs 39 N11
Storrington W Susx 10 H7
Storth Cumb 63 J6
Storwood E R Yk 60 C5
Stotfield Moray 101 J2
Stotfold C Beds 32 H9
Stottesdon Shrops 39 M5
Stoughton Leics 41 N7
Stoughton Surrey 20 F12
Stoughton W Susx 10 C7
Stoulton Worcs 30 B4
Stourbridge Dudley 40 B10
Stourhead Wilts 8 B1
Stourpaine Dorset 8 C5
Stourport-on-Severn Worcs 39 P7
Stour Provost Dorset 8 B3
Stour Row Dorset 8 C3
Stourton Staffs 39 Q5
Stourton Warwks 30 H6
Stourton Wilts 8 B1
Stourton Caundle Dorset 17 Q12
Stove Shet 111 k5
Stoven Suffk 35 P1
Stow Border 87 J12
Stow Lincs 52 C7
Stow Bardolph Norfk 43 P8
Stow Bedon Norfk 44 F10
Stowbridge Norfk 43 P8
Stow-cum-Quy Cambs 33 N5
Stowe Shrops 38 F7
Stowe by Chartley Staffs 40 D3
Stowell Somset 17 P10
Stowey BaNES 17 N4
Stowford Devon 5 J3
Stowlangtoft Suffk 34 G3
Stow Longa Cambs 32 G3
Stow Maries Essex 22 G4
Stowmarket Suffk 34 H5
Stow-on-the-Wold Gloucs 30 F8
Stowting Kent 13 L2
Stowupland Suffk 34 H5
Straanruie Highld 99 P6
Strachan Abers 95 L4
Strachur Ag & B 84 B3
Stradbroke Suffk 35 K3
Stradishall Suffk 34 C6
Stradsett Norfk 43 Q8
Stragglethorpe Lincs 52 C11
Straiton Mdloth 86 F8
Straiton S Ayrs 76 G9
Straloch Abers 102 H10
Straloch P & K 92 F3
Stramshall Staffs 40 E1
Strang IoM 56 c5
Strangeways Salfd 57 P8
Strangford Herefs 28 G4
Stranraer D & G 68 E7
Stratfield Mortimer W Berk 19 Q7
Stratfield Saye Hants 20 B10

Stratfield Turgis Hants 20 B10
Stratford Gt Lon 21 M6
Stratford St Andrew Suffk 35 M5
Stratford St Mary Suffk 34 H7
Stratford sub Castle Wilts 8 G2
Stratford Tony Wilts 8 G3
Stratford-upon-Avon Warwks 30 G3
Strath Highld 105 L6
Strathan Highld 108 C3
Strathan Highld 109 K3
Strathaven S Lans 77 L3
Strathblane Stirlg 85 J7
Strathcanaird Highld 106 C3
Strathcarron Highld 97 N2
Strathcoil Ag & B 89 N9
Strathdon Abers 101 L11
Strathkinness Fife 93 M11
Strathloanhead W Loth 85 Q8
Strathmashie House Highld 98 H10
Strathmiglo Fife 86 E1
Strathpeffer Highld 106 H10
Strathtay P & K 92 D3
Strathwhillan N Ayrs 75 Q5
Strathy Highld 109 P3
Strathy Inn Highld 109 P3
Strathyre Stirlg 91 N11
Stratton Cnwll 14 E10
Stratton Dorset 7 P4
Stratton Gloucs 30 D12
Stratton Audley Oxon 31 N8
Stratton-on-the-Fosse Somset 17 N6
Stratton St Margaret Swindn 18 H4
Stratton St Michael Norfk 45 K10
Stratton Strawless Norfk 45 K6
Streat E Susx 11 M7
Streatham Gt Lon 21 L8
Streatley C Beds 32 F10
Streatley W Berk 19 P5
Street Devon 6 G5
Street Somset 17 L8
Street Ashton Warwks 41 L10
Street Dinas Shrops 48 G7
Street End Kent 23 M11
Street End W Susx 10 D9
Streethay Staffs 40 F5
Streetlam N York 65 N7
Streetly End Cambs 33 P7
Street on the Fosse Somset 17 N8
Strelitz P & K 92 H11
Strelley Notts 51 L11
Strensall C York 59 N3
Strensham Services (northbound) Worcs 29 M1
Strensham Services (southbound) Worcs 29 M2
Stretcholt Somset 16 H7
Strete Devon 5 R10
Stretford Traffd 57 P9
Strethall Essex 33 M8
Stretham Cambs 33 N2
Strettington W Susx 10 E8
Stretton Derbys 51 K8
Stretton Rutlnd 42 D7
Stretton Staffs 40 B5
Stretton Staffs 40 G3
Stretton Warrtn 57 L11
Stretton Grandison Herefs 39 L12
Stretton-on-Dunsmore Warwks 41 K11
Stretton on Fosse Warwks 30 G6
Stretton Sugwas Herefs 28 E1
Stretton under Fosse Warwks 41 L10
Stretton Westwood Shrops 39 L3
Strichen Abers 103 K4
Stringston Somset 16 G7
Strixton Nhants 32 C4
Stroat Gloucs 28 G8
Strollamus Highld 96 H4
Stroma Highld 110 G1
Stromeferry Highld 97 M3
Stromness Ork 111 g2
Stronaba Highld 98 B11
Stronachlachar Stirlg 84 G2
Stronafian Ag & B 83 Q6
Stronchrubie Highld 108 E11
Strone Ag & B 84 D6
Strone Highld 98 A11
Strone Highld 98 G4
Stronmilchan Ag & B 90 F10
Stronsay Ork 111 i2
Stronsay Airport Ork 111 i2
Strontian Highld 89 Q4
Strood Medway 22 E9
Strood Gloucs 29 L7
Stroud Hants 10 B5
Stroud Green Gloucs 29 L7
Stroxton Lincs 42 C4
Struan Highld 96 D3
Struan P & K 92 B3
Strumpshaw Norfk 45 M8
Strutherhill S Lans 77 M2
Struthers Fife 86 H1
Struy Highld 98 E2
Stuartfield Abers 103 K6
Stubbington Hants 9 N5
Stubbins Lancs 57 P5
Stubton Lincs 42 C11
Stuckton Hants 8 H5
Studham C Beds 32 E12
Studland Dorset 8 F10
Studley Warwks 30 E2
Studley Wilts 18 E6
Studley Roger N York 65 M12
Studley Royal N York 65 M12
Studley Royal Park & Fountains Abbey N York 58 H1
Stuntney Cambs 33 N2
Sturmer Essex 34 B7
Sturminster Common Dorset 8 B5
Sturminster Marshall Dorset 8 D7
Sturminster Newton Dorset 8 B5
Sturry Kent 23 N10
Sturton N Linc 52 D3
Sturton by Stow Lincs 52 C7
Sturton le Steeple Notts 52 B6
Stuston Suffk 35 J2
Stutton N York 59 L6
Stutton Suffk 35 J8
Styal Ches E 57 Q11
Stynie Moray 101 L3
Styrrup Notts 51 N3

Succoth Ag & B 84 E2
Suckley Worcs 39 N10
Sudborough Nhants 32 D1
Sudbourne Suffk 35 N6
Sudbrook Lincs 42 D2
Sudbrook Mons 28 F10
Sudbrooke Lincs 52 E8
Sudbury Derbys 40 F2
Sudbury Gt Lon 21 J6
Sudbury Suffk 34 E8
Suffield N York 67 L8
Suffield Norfk 45 K4
Sugnall Staffs 49 P8
Sugwas Pool Herefs 28 E1
Suisnish Highld 96 H6
Sulby IoM 56 d3
Sulgrave Nhants 31 M5
Sulham W Berk 19 Q6
Sulhamstead W Berk 19 Q7
Sullom Shet 111 k3
Sullom Voe Shet 111 k3
Sully V Glam 16 F3
Sumburgh Airport Shet 111 k5
Summerbridge N York 58 G2
Summercourt Cnwll 3 K5
Summerfield Norfk 44 C3
Summerhill Pembks 25 K7
Summerhouse Darltn 65 L4
Summersdale W Susx 10 D8
Summerseat Bury 57 P6
Summertown Oxon 31 L11
Sunbury-on-Thames Surrey 20 H9
Sundaywell D & G 78 D11
Sunderland Ag & B 82 C9
Sunderland Cumb 71 J8
Sunderland Lancs 62 H10
Sunderland Sundld 73 P9
Sunderland Bridge Dur 73 M12
Sundhope Border 79 M4
Sundon Park Luton 32 F10
Sundridge Kent 21 P11
Sunningdale W & M 20 F9
Sunninghill W & M 20 F9
Sunningwell Oxon 19 N1
Sunniside Dur 73 K12
Sunniside Gatesd 73 L8
Sunnyhill C Derb 41 J2
Sunnyhurst Bl w D 57 M4
Sunnylaw Stirlg 85 N4
Sunnymead Oxon 31 L11
Surbiton Gt Lon 21 J9
Surfleet Lincs 43 J5
Surlingham Norfk 45 M8
Surrex Essex 34 E11
Sustead Norfk 45 K3
Susworth Lincs 52 B3
Sutcombe Devon 14 F9
Sutcombemill Devon 14 F9
Sutterby Lincs 53 L8
Sutterton Lincs 43 J3
Sutton C Beds 32 H7
Sutton C Pete 42 F9
Sutton Cambs 33 M2
Sutton Devon 5 N10
Sutton E Susx 11 P9
Sutton Gt Lon 21 K9
Sutton Kent 23 P12
Sutton N York 59 L8
Sutton Norfk 45 N5
Sutton Notts 51 Q12
Sutton Oxon 31 K11
Sutton Shrops 39 N5
Sutton Shrops 49 J12
Sutton Staffs 49 N10
Sutton Suffk 35 M7
Sutton W Susx 10 F7
Sutton-at-Hone Kent 22 B9
Sutton Bassett Nhants 41 Q9
Sutton Benger Wilts 18 D5
Sutton Bonington Notts 41 L3
Sutton Bridge Lincs 43 M6
Sutton Cheney Leics 41 K7
Sutton Coldfield Birm 40 E8
Sutton Courtenay Oxon 19 N2
Sutton cum Lound Notts 51 P4
Sutton Green Surrey 20 G11
Sutton Howgrave N York 65 N10
Sutton-in-Ashfield Notts 51 L8
Sutton-in-Craven N York 58 D5
Sutton Maddock Shrops 39 N2
Sutton Mallet Somset 17 K8
Sutton Mandeville Wilts 8 E2
Sutton Montis Somset 17 P10
Sutton-on-Hull C KuH 61 J7
Sutton on Sea Lincs 53 N7
Sutton-on-the-Forest N York 59 M2
Sutton on the Hill Derbys 40 G2
Sutton on Trent Notts 52 B9
Sutton St Edmund Lincs 43 L7
Sutton St James Lincs 43 L6
Sutton St Nicholas Herefs 39 K11
Sutton Scotney Hants 19 M11
Sutton-under-Brailes Warwks 30 H6
Sutton-under-Whitestonecliffe N York 66 C10
Sutton upon Derwent E R Yk 60 C5
Sutton Valence Kent 12 F1
Sutton Veny Wilts 18 D11
Sutton Waldron Dorset 8 C4
Sutton Weaver Ches W 57 K11
Sutton Wick BaNES 17 N4
Sutton Wick Oxon 19 N2
Swaby Lincs 53 L7
Swadlincote Derbys 40 H4
Swaffham Norfk 44 D8
Swaffham Bulbeck Cambs 33 N4
Swaffham Prior Cambs 33 N4
Swafield Norfk 45 L4
Swainby N York 66 C7
Swainshill Herefs 28 E1
Swainsthorpe Norfk 45 K9
Swainswick BaNES 18 B7
Swalcliffe Oxon 31 J6
Swalecliffe Kent 23 L9
Swallow Lincs 52 H3
Swallow Beck Lincs 52 D9
Swallowcliffe Wilts 8 E3
Swallowfield Wokham 20 B9
Swallownest Rothm 51 K4
Swanage Dorset 8 F11
Swanbourne Bucks 32 B10
Swan Green Ches W 49 N2
Swanland E R Yk 60 G8
Swanley Kent 21 P9
Swanley Village Kent 21 Q9
Swanmore Hants 9 P4
Swannington Leics 41 K4
Swannington Norfk 45 J6
Swanpool Lincs 52 D9
Swanscombe Kent 22 C8
Swansea Swans 26 E9
Swansea Airport Swans 26 D9
Swansea West Services Swans 26 E8
Swanton Abbot Norfk 45 L5
Swanton Morley Norfk 44 G6
Swanton Novers Norfk 44 G4
Swan Village Sandw 40 C8
Swanwick Derbys 51 K9
Swanwick Hants 9 N5
Swarby Lincs 42 F3
Swardeston Norfk 45 K9
Swarkestone Derbys 41 J2
Swarland Nthumb 81 N12
Swarraton Hants 19 P12
Swarthmoor Cumb 62 F6
Swaton Lincs 42 G3
Swavesey Cambs 33 K3
Sway Hants 9 J7
Swayfield Lincs 42 E5
Swaythling C Sotn 9 M4
Sweetham Devon 15 Q11
Sweethaws E Susx 11 P4
Sweets Cnwll 4 E2
Sweetshouse Cnwll 3 N4
Swefling Suffk 35 M4
Swepstone Leics 41 J5
Swerford Oxon 31 J7
Swettenham Ches E 49 P3
Swilland Suffk 35 K6
Swillington Leeds 59 J7
Swimbridge Devon 15 L6
Swimbridge Newland Devon 15 K6
Swinbrook Oxon 30 H10
Swincliffe N York 58 G3
Swinderby Lincs 52 C10
Swindon Gloucs 29 N4
Swindon Staffs 39 Q4
Swindon Swindn 18 H4
Swine E R Yk 61 K7
Swinefleet E R Yk 60 D9
Swineshead Bed 32 F4
Swineshead Lincs 43 J3
Swiney Highld 110 E8
Swinford Leics 41 M10
Swingfield Minnis Kent 13 N2
Swingfield Street Kent 13 N2
Swingleton Green Suffk 34 F7
Swinhoe Nthumb 81 P8
Swinithwaite N York 65 J9
Swinside Cumb 71 K10
Swinstead Lincs 42 E5
Swinton Border 80 H5
Swinton N York 65 L10
Swinton N York 66 G11
Swinton Rothm 51 K2
Swinton Salfd 57 P8
Swithland Leics 41 M5
Swordale Highld 107 J8
Swordland Highld 97 L10
Swordly Highld 109 N3
Swynnerton Staffs 49 Q8
Swyre Dorset 7 M5
Sychtyn Powys 38 B1
Syde Gloucs 29 N6
Sydenham Gt Lon 21 M8
Sydenham Oxon 20 B3
Sydenham Damerel Devon 5 J5
Syderstone Norfk 44 D4
Sydling St Nicholas Dorset 7 P3
Sydmonton Hants 19 N8
Syerston Notts 51 Q10
Sykehouse Donc 59 N10
Symbister Shet 111 k3
Symington S Ayrs 76 G5
Symington S Lans 78 G2
Symondsbury Dorset 7 L4
Symonds Yat (West) Herefs 28 G5
Syre Highld 109 M7
Syreford Gloucs 30 D9
Syresham Nhants 31 N6
Syston Leics 41 N5
Syston Lincs 42 D2
Sytchampton Worcs 39 Q8
Sywell Nhants 32 B4

T

Tackley Oxon 31 L9
Tacolneston Norfk 45 J10
Tadcaster N York 59 L5
Taddington Derbys 50 F6
Tadley Hants 19 P8
Tadlow Cambs 33 J7
Tadmarton Oxon 31 K6
Tadworth Surrey 21 K11
Taff's Well Rhondd 27 N11
Taibach Neath 26 G10
Tain Highld 107 M6
Tain Highld 110 E3
Tairbeart W Isls 111 c3
Takeley Essex 33 P11
Takeley Street Essex 33 N11
Talaton Devon 6 E3
Talbenny Pembks 24 E6
Talbot Village BCP 8 F8
Taleford Devon 6 E4
Talerddig Powys 37 Q2
Talgarreg Cerdgn 36 G9
Talgarth Powys 27 N3
Talisker Highld 96 D3
Talke Staffs 49 P5
Talke Pits Staffs 49 P5
Talkin Cumb 71 Q4
Talladale Highld 105 N8
Talla Linnfoots Border 79 J5
Tallaminnock S Ayrs 76 G10
Tallarn Green Wrexhm 49 J6
Tallentire Cumb 70 H8
Talley Carmth 26 E3
Tallington Lincs 42 F8
Talmine Highld 109 K3
Talog Carmth 25 N4
Talsarn Cerdgn 37 J9

Place	County	Page	Grid
Talsarnau	Gwynd	47	K4
Talskiddy	Cnwll	3	K3
Talwrn	IoA	54	G6
Tal-y-Bont	Cerdgn	37	K3
Tal-y-Bont	Conwy	55	L7
Tal-y-bont	Gwynd	47	J2
Tal-y-bont	Gwynd	54	H7
Talybont-on-Usk	Powys	27	N4
Tal-y-Cafn	Conwy	55	L7
Tal-y-coed	Mons	28	E6
Talysarn	Gwynd	54	G10
Tamar Valley Mining District	Devon	5	J7
Tamerton Foliot	C Plym	5	K7
Tamworth	Staffs	40	G6
Tamworth Services	Warwks	40	G7
Tandridge	Surrey	21	M12
Tanfield	Dur	73	K10
Tanfield Lea	Dur	73	L10
Tangasdale	W Isls	111	a7
Tangley	Hants	19	K9
Tangmere	W Susx	10	E8
Tankerness	Ork	111	h2
Tankersley	Barns	51	K2
Tankerton	Kent	23	L9
Tannach	Highld	110	G6
Tannachie	Abers	95	N5
Tannadice	Angus	93	N4
Tanner's Green	Worcs	40	E11
Tannington	Suffk	35	L4
Tannochside	N Lans	85	L10
Tansley	Derbys	51	J8
Tansor	Nhants	42	F11
Tantobie	Dur	73	L9
Tanworth in Arden	Warwks	40	E12
Tan-y-groes	Cerdgn	36	E10
Taobh Tuath	W Isls	111	b3
Taplow	Bucks	20	E7
Tarbert	Ag & B	75	J3
Tarbert	Ag & B	83	N8
Tarbert	W Isls	111	c3
Tarbet	Ag & B	84	F3
Tarbet	Highld	97	L10
Tarbet	Highld	108	D6
Tarbolton	S Ayrs	76	G6
Tarbrax	S Lans	86	B10
Tardebigge	Worcs	30	D3
Tarfside	Angus	94	H1
Tarland	Abers	94	H2
Tarleton	Lancs	57	J5
Tarlton	Gloucs	29	N8
Tarnock	Somset	17	K5
Tarporley	Ches W	49	K3
Tarrant Crawford	Dorset	8	D5
Tarrant Gunville	Dorset	8	D5
Tarrant Hinton	Dorset	8	D5
Tarrant Keyneston	Dorset	8	D6
Tarrant Launceston	Dorset	8	D6
Tarrant Monkton	Dorset	8	D6
Tarrant Rawston	Dorset	8	D6
Tarrant Rushton	Dorset	8	D6
Tarring Neville	E Susx	11	N8
Tarrington	Herefs	28	H1
Tarskavaig	Highld	96	H7
Tarves	Abers	102	H8
Tarvin	Ches W	49	J3
Tasburgh	Norfk	45	K10
Tatenhill	Staffs	40	G3
Tathwell	Lincs	53	K6
Tatsfield	Surrey	21	N11
Tattenhall	Ches W	49	J4
Tatterford	Norfk	44	E5
Tattersett	Norfk	44	E4
Tattershall	Lincs	52	H11
Tattershall Thorpe	Lincs	52	H10
Tattingstone	Suffk	35	J8
Tattingstone White Horse	Suffk	35	J8
Tatton Park	Ches E	57	N10
Tatworth	Somset	7	J2
Tauchers	Moray	101	M5
Taunton	Somset	16	G10
Taunton Deane Services	Somset	16	G11
Taverham	Norfk	45	J7
Tavernspite	Pembks	25	L6
Tavistock	Devon	5	K5
Tavistock	Devon	5	K5
Taw Green	Devon	15	L11
Tawstock	Devon	15	K6
Taxal	Derbys	50	D5
Tay Bridge	C Dund	93	M9
Taychreggan Hotel	Ag & B	90	E11
Tay Forest Park	P & K	92	B4
Tayinloan	Ag & B	75	K4
Taynton	Gloucs	29	J4
Taynton	Oxon	30	G10
Taynuilt	Ag & B	90	D9
Tayport	Fife	93	M9
Tayvallich	Ag & B	83	L5
Tealby	Lincs	52	G5
Tealing	Angus	93	M7
Team Valley	Gatesd	73	M8
Teangue	Highld	97	J7
Teanord	Highld	107	K9
Tebay	Cumb	63	J2
Tebay Services	Cumb	63	L2
Tebworth	C Beds	32	E10
Tedburn St Mary	Devon	5	Q2
Teddington	Gloucs	29	N3
Teddington	Gt Lon	21	J8
Tedstone Delamere	Herefs	39	M9
Tedstone Wafer	Herefs	39	M9
Teeton	Nhants	41	P12
Teffont Evias	Wilts	8	E2
Teffont Magna	Wilts	8	E2
Tegryn	Pembks	25	L3
Teigh	Rutlnd	42	C7
Teigngrace	Devon	6	B7
Teignmouth	Devon	6	B8
Teindside	Border	79	P7
Telford	Wrekin	39	M1
Telford Services	Shrops	39	N1
Tellisford	Somset	18	B9
Telscombe	E Susx	11	N8
Tempar	P & K	91	Q5
Templand	D & G	78	G10
Temple	Cnwll	4	E5
Temple	Mdloth	86	G9
Temple Bar	Cerdgn	37	J9
Temple Cloud	BaNES	17	P5
Templecombe	Somset	17	Q10
Temple Grafton	Warwks	30	E3
Temple Guiting	Gloucs	30	E8
Temple Hirst	N York	59	N8
Temple Normanton	Derbys	51	K7
Temple of Fiddes	Abers	95	N5
Temple Sowerby	Cumb	64	B3
Templeton	Devon	15	Q9
Templeton	Pembks	25	K6
Templetown	Dur	73	K10
Tempsford	C Beds	32	G6
Tenbury Wells	Worcs	39	L8
Tenby	Pembks	25	K8
Tendring	Essex	35	J11
Tendring Green	Essex	35	J10
Tendring Heath	Essex	35	J10
Ten Mile Bank	Norfk	43	P10
Tenterden	Kent	12	H4
Terling	Essex	22	F1
Ternhill	Shrops	49	L8
Terregles	D & G	78	F12
Terrington	N York	66	F12
Terrington St Clement	Norfk	43	N6
Terrington St John	Norfk	43	N7
Teston	Kent	22	E11
Testwood	Hants	9	L5
Tetbury	Gloucs	29	M9
Tetchill	Shrops	48	H8
Tetcott	Devon	14	F11
Tetford	Lincs	53	K8
Tetney	Lincs	53	K4
Tetsworth	Oxon	20	B3
Tettenhall	Wolves	40	B7
Tettenhall Wood	Wolves	39	Q3
Teversal	Notts	51	L8
Teversham	Cambs	33	M5
Teviothead	Border	79	N7
Tewin	Herts	21	L1
Tewkesbury	Gloucs	29	M3
Teynham	Kent	23	J10
Thackley	C Brad	58	F6
Thainstone	Abers	102	G10
Thakeham	W Susx	10	H6
Thame	Oxon	20	B3
Thames Ditton	Surrey	21	J9
Thamesmead	Gt Lon	21	P7
Thamesport	Medway	22	G8
Thanington	Kent	23	L11
Thankerton	S Lans	78	F2
Tharston	Norfk	45	K10
Thatcham	W Berk	19	N7
Thaxted	Essex	33	P9
Theakston	N York	65	N9
Thealby	N Linc	60	F9
Theale	Somset	17	L7
Theale	W Berk	19	Q6
Thearne	E R Yk	61	J6
The Beeches	Gloucs	18	F1
Theberton	Suffk	35	P4
The Braes	Highld	96	G3
The Broads		45	P8
The Brunt	E Loth	87	M7
The Bungalow	IoM	56	d4
The Burf	Worcs	39	P8
The City	Bucks	20	C4
The Common	Wilts	9	J2
Theddingworth	Leics	41	P9
Theddlethorpe All Saints	Lincs	53	M6
Theddlethorpe St Helen	Lincs	53	M6
The Deep	C KuH	61	J8
The Den	N Ayrs	76	F2
The Forstal	Kent	13	K3
The Green	Cumb	62	D5
The Green	Essex	34	C11
The Green	N York	66	H6
The Green	Wilts	8	C2
The Headland	Hartpl	66	D1
The Hill	Cumb	62	D5
The Lee	Bucks	20	E3
The Lhen	IoM	56	d2
Thelnetham	Suffk	34	G2
The Lochs	Moray	101	L3
Thelveton	Norfk	35	J1
Thelwall	Warrtn	57	M10
Themelthorpe	Norfk	44	H5
The Middles	Dur	73	L9
The Moor	Kent	12	F4
The Mumbles	Swans	26	E10
The Murray	S Lans	85	K11
The Neuk	Abers	95	M3
Thenford	Nhants	31	M6
The Reddings	Gloucs	29	M5
Therfield	Herts	33	K8
The Ross	P & K	92	B10
The Spring	Warwks	40	H11
The Stocks	Kent	12	H5
The Strand	Wilts	18	D8
Thetford	Norfk	44	E12
Thetford Forest Park		44	D11
Theydon Bois	Essex	21	N4
Thickwood	Wilts	18	C6
Thimbleby	Lincs	53	J9
Thimbleby	N York	66	C8
Thingwall	Wirral	56	F11
Thirkleby	N York	66	C10
Thirlby	N York	66	C10
Thirlestane	Border	80	D5
Thirn	N York	65	M9
Thirsk	N York	65	Q10
Thistleton	Lancs	56	H2
Thistleton	Rutlnd	42	D6
Thistley Green	Suffk	33	Q2
Thixendale	N York	60	E3
Thockrington	Nthumb	72	G5
Tholomas Drove	Cambs	43	L8
Tholthorpe	N York	59	L2
Thomastown	Abers	102	D7
Thompson	Norfk	44	F10
Thongsbridge	Kirk	58	F11
Thoralby	N York	64	H9
Thoresway	Lincs	52	G4
Thorganby	Lincs	52	H4
Thorganby	N York	59	P6
Thorgill	N York	66	G7
Thorington	Suffk	35	N2
Thorington Street	Suffk	34	G9
Thorlby	N York	58	C4
Thorley	Herts	33	M11
Thorley Street	IoW	9	L9
Thormanby	N York	66	C11
Thornaby-on-Tees	S on T	66	C4
Thornage	Norfk	44	H3
Thornborough	Bucks	31	Q7
Thornborough	N York	65	N10
Thornbury	C Brad	58	G7
Thornbury	Devon	14	G9
Thornbury	Herefs	39	L9
Thornbury	S Glos	28	H10
Thornby	Nhants	41	P11
Thorncliff	Staffs	50	D8
Thorncombe	Dorset	7	K3
Thorndon	Suffk	35	J3
Thorndon Cross	Devon	5	L2
Thorne	Donc	59	P10
Thorner	Leeds	59	J6
Thorne St Margaret	Somset	16	E11
Thorney	C Pete	43	J8
Thorney	Notts	52	C8
Thorney	Somset	17	K10
Thorney Hill	Hants	8	H7
Thorney Island	W Susx	10	C9
Thornfalcon	Somset	16	H10
Thornford	Dorset	17	N12
Thorngrafton	Nthumb	72	E7
Thorngumbald	E R Yk	61	L8
Thornham	Norfk	44	C2
Thornham Magna	Suffk	34	H3
Thornham Parva	Suffk	35	J3
Thornhaugh	C Pete	42	F9
Thornhill	C Sotn	9	M5
Thornhill	Cumb	62	B1
Thornhill	D & G	78	E9
Thornhill	Derbys	50	G4
Thornhill	Kirk	58	G9
Thornhill	Stirlg	85	L3
Thornholme	E R Yk	61	J2
Thornicombe	Dorset	8	C6
Thornington	Nthumb	81	J7
Thornley	Dur	73	K12
Thornley	Dur	73	P11
Thornliebank	E Rens	85	J10
Thorns	Suffk	34	C6
Thornsett	Derbys	50	D4
Thornthwaite	Cumb	71	K9
Thornthwaite	N York	58	F3
Thornton	Angus	93	M6
Thornton	Bucks	31	Q7
Thornton	C Brad	58	E7
Thornton	E R Yk	60	D5
Thornton	Fife	86	F3
Thornton	Lancs	56	G1
Thornton	Leics	41	L6
Thornton	Middsb	66	C5
Thornton	Nthumb	81	K5
Thornton Curtis	N Linc	61	J9
Thorntonhall	S Lans	85	K11
Thornton Heath	Gt Lon	21	L9
Thornton Hough	Wirral	56	F11
Thornton-in-Craven	N York	58	B5
Thornton in Lonsdale	N York	63	M7
Thornton-le-Beans	N York	65	P9
Thornton-le-Clay	N York	59	P2
Thornton-le-Dale	N York	67	J10
Thornton le Moor	Lincs	52	F4
Thornton-le-Moor	N York	65	P9
Thornton-le-Moors	Ches W	48	H1
Thornton-le-Street	N York	65	P9
Thorntonloch	E Loth	87	N7
Thornton Rust	N York	64	G9
Thornton Steward	N York	65	L9
Thornton Watlass	N York	65	M9
Thornydykes	Border	80	E5
Thornythwaite	Cumb	71	N10
Thoroton	Notts	51	Q11
Thorp Arch	Leeds	59	K5
Thorpe	Derbys	50	F10
Thorpe	E R Yk	60	G5
Thorpe	N York	58	D2
Thorpe	Notts	51	Q10
Thorpe	Surrey	20	G9
Thorpe Abbotts	Norfk	35	K2
Thorpe Arnold	Leics	41	Q4
Thorpe Audlin	Wakefd	59	L10
Thorpe Bassett	N York	67	J11
Thorpe Bay	Sthend	22	H6
Thorpe by Water	Rutlnd	42	C10
Thorpe Constantine	Staffs	40	H6
Thorpe End	Norfk	45	L7
Thorpe Green	Essex	35	J11
Thorpe Green	Suffk	34	F6
Thorpe Hesley	Rothm	51	J2
Thorpe in Balne	Donc	59	N11
Thorpe Langton	Leics	41	Q8
Thorpe Lea	Surrey	20	G8
Thorpe-le-Soken	Essex	35	K11
Thorpe le Street	E R Yk	60	E5
Thorpe Malsor	Nhants	32	B2
Thorpe Mandeville	Nhants	31	M5
Thorpe Market	Norfk	45	L3
Thorpe Marriot	Norfk	45	K7
Thorpe Morieux	Suffk	34	F6
Thorpeness	Suffk	35	P5
Thorpe on the Hill	Lincs	52	C9
Thorpe Park	Surrey	20	G9
Thorpe St Andrew	Norfk	45	L8
Thorpe St Peter	Lincs	53	M10
Thorpe Salvin	Rothm	51	M5
Thorpe Satchville	Leics	41	Q5
Thorpe Thewles	S on T	65	P3
Thorpe Tilney	Lincs	52	G11
Thorpe Underwood	N York	59	L3
Thorpe Waterville	Nhants	32	E1
Thorpe Willoughby	N York	59	M7
Thorrington	Essex	34	H11
Thorverton	Devon	6	C3
Thrandeston	Suffk	35	J2
Thrapston	Nhants	32	E2
Threapwood	Ches W	48	H6
Threapwood	Staffs	50	D11
Threave	S Ayrs	76	F9
Three Bridges	W Susx	11	L3
Three Chimneys	Kent	12	G3
Three Cocks	Powys	27	N2
Three Crosses	Swans	26	D9
Three Cups Corner	E Susx	12	D6
Threekingham	Lincs	42	F3
Three Leg Cross	E Susx	12	D4
Three Legged Cross	Dorset	8	F6
Three Mile Cross	Wokham	20	B9
Threemilestone	Cnwll	3	L5
Threemiletown	W Loth	86	C7
Three Oaks	E Susx	12	G7
Threlkeld	Cumb	71	M9
Threshers Bush	Essex	21	P2
Threshfield	N York	58	C2
Thrigby	Norfk	45	P7
Thrintoft	N York	65	N8
Thriplow	Cambs	33	M7
Throcking	Herts	33	K10
Throckley	N u Ty	73	K7
Throckmorton	Worcs	30	C4
Throop	BCP	8	G8
Throphill	Nthumb	72	H1
Thropton	Nthumb	81	J1
Throsk	Stirlg	85	P5
Throughgate	D & G	78	E11
Throwleigh	Devon	5	N3
Throwley Forstal	Kent	23	J11
Thrumpton	Notts	41	L2
Thrumster	Highld	110	G6
Thrunscoe	NE Lin	53	K2
Thrupp	Gloucs	29	M7
Thrussington	Leics	41	P4
Thruxton	Hants	19	K10
Thruxton	Herefs	28	E2
Thrybergh	Rothm	51	L2
Thulston	Derbys	41	K2
Thundersley	Essex	22	F6
Thurcaston	Leics	41	M5
Thurcroft	Rothm	51	L3
Thurgarton	Norfk	45	J3
Thurgarton	Notts	51	P10
Thurgoland	Barns	50	H1
Thurlaston	Leics	41	L7
Thurlaston	Warwks	41	L12
Thurlbear	Somset	16	H11
Thurlby	Lincs	42	F6
Thurlby	Lincs	52	C10
Thurlby	Lincs	53	M8
Thurleigh	Bed	32	F5
Thurlestone	Devon	5	N10
Thurloxton	Somset	16	H9
Thurlstone	Barns	58	G12
Thurlton	Norfk	45	N9
Thurmaston	Leics	41	N5
Thurnby	Leics	41	N6
Thurne	Norfk	45	N7
Thurnham	Kent	22	F11
Thurning	Nhants	42	F12
Thurning	Norfk	44	H4
Thurnscoe	Barns	51	L11
Thursby	Cumb	71	M5
Thursford	Norfk	44	F4
Thursley	Surrey	10	E3
Thurso	Highld	110	D3
Thurstaston	Wirral	56	F11
Thurston	Suffk	34	F4
Thurstonfield	Cumb	71	M4
Thurstonland	Kirk	58	F11
Thurton	Norfk	45	M9
Thurvaston	Derbys	50	G12
Thuxton	Norfk	44	G8
Thwaite	N York	64	F7
Thwaite	Suffk	35	J4
Thwaite Head	Cumb	62	G4
Thwaite St Mary	Norfk	45	N10
Thwing	E R Yk	67	M12
Tibbermore	P & K	92	F10
Tibbers	D & G	78	E9
Tibberton	Gloucs	29	K4
Tibberton	Worcs	30	B3
Tibberton	Wrekin	49	M10
Tibenham	Norfk	45	J11
Tibshelf	Derbys	51	K8
Tibthorpe	E R Yk	60	G3
Ticehurst	E Susx	12	E4
Tichborne	Hants	9	P2
Tickencote	Rutlnd	42	E8
Tickenham	N Som	17	L2
Tickhill	Donc	51	N3
Ticklerton	Shrops	39	J4
Ticknall	Derbys	41	J3
Tickton	E R Yk	60	H6
Tidcombe	Wilts	19	K8
Tiddington	Oxon	31	P12
Tiddington	Warwks	30	G3
Tidebrook	E Susx	12	C4
Tideford	Cnwll	4	H8
Tidenham	Gloucs	28	G9
Tideswell	Derbys	50	F6
Tidmarsh	W Berk	19	Q6
Tidmington	Warwks	30	H6
Tidworth	Wilts	19	J10
Tiers Cross	Pembks	24	F6
Tiffield	Nhants	31	P4
Tigerton	Angus	93	J8
Tigh a' Ghearraidh	W Isls	111	a4
Tigharry	W Isls	111	a4
Tighnabruaich	Ag & B	83	P8
Tilbrook	Cambs	32	F3
Tilbury	Thurr	22	D8
Tile Cross	Birm	40	F9
Tile Hill	Covtry	40	H11
Tilehurst	Readg	19	Q6
Tilford	Surrey	10	E2
Tilgate	W Susx	11	L3
Tilham Street	Somset	17	M8
Tillicoultry	Clacks	85	Q4
Tillietudlem	S Lans	77	N3
Tillingham	Essex	23	J3
Tillington	Herefs	39	J12
Tillington	W Susx	10	F6
Tillington Common	Herefs	39	J11
Tillybirloch	Abers	95	L1
Tillyfourie	Abers	102	E11
Tillygreig	Abers	103	J10
Tillyrie	P & K	86	D2
Tilmanstone	Kent	23	P12
Tilney All Saints	Norfk	43	P6
Tilney High End	Norfk	43	N6
Tilney St Lawrence	Norfk	43	N7
Tilshead	Wilts	18	F11
Tilstock	Shrops	49	K7
Tilston	Ches W	49	J5
Tilstone Fearnall	Ches W	49	K4
Tilsworth	C Beds	32	E11
Tilton on the Hill	Leics	41	Q6
Tiltups End	Gloucs	29	L8
Timberland	Lincs	52	G10
Timbersbrook	Ches E	50	B8
Timberscombe	Somset	16	C7
Timble	N York	58	F4
Timpanheck	D & G	71	M1
Timperley	Traffd	57	P10
Timsbury	BaNES	17	P4
Timsbury	Hants	9	L3
Timsgarry	W Isls	111	c2
Timsgearraidh	W Isls	111	c2
Timworth	Suffk	34	E3
Timworth Green	Suffk	34	E3
Tincleton	Dorset	8	B8
Tindale	Cumb	72	B8
Tingewick	Bucks	31	P7
Tingrith	C Beds	32	E9
Tingwall Airport	Shet	111	k4
Tingwall	Ork	111	h2
Tinhay	Devon	5	J3
Tinsley	Sheff	51	K3
Tinsley Green	W Susx	11	L3
Tintagel	Cnwll	4	C3
Tintern	Mons	28	F8
Tintinhull	Somset	17	M11
Tintwistle	Derbys	50	D2
Tinwald	D & G	78	G11
Tinwell	Rutlnd	42	E8
Tipton	Sandw	40	C8
Tipton Green	Sandw	40	C8
Tipton St John	Devon	6	E5
Tiptree	Essex	34	E12
Tiptree Heath	Essex	22	G1
Tirabad	Powys	37	P11
Tiree	Ag & B	88	C7
Tiree Airport	Ag & B	88	C7
Tiretigan	Ag & B	83	K9
Tirley	Gloucs	29	L3
Tiroran	Ag & B	89	K10
Tirphil	Caerph	27	N7
Tirril	Cumb	71	P9
Tisbury	Wilts	8	D2
Tissington	Derbys	50	F9
Titchberry	Devon	14	E6
Titchfield	Hants	9	P6
Titchmarsh	Nhants	32	E2
Titchwell	Norfk	44	C2
Tithby	Notts	51	P12
Titley	Herefs	38	G9
Titsey	Surrey	21	N11
Titson	Cnwll	14	E10
Tittensor	Staffs	49	Q7
Tittleshall	Norfk	44	E6
Titton	Worcs	39	P7
Tiverton	Ches W	49	K4
Tiverton	Devon	6	C1
Tivetshall St Margaret	Norfk	45	K11
Tivetshall St Mary	Norfk	45	J11
Tixall	Staffs	40	C3
Tixover	Rutlnd	42	D9
Toab	Shet	111	k5
Tobermory	Ag & B	89	L5
Toberonochy	Ag & B	83	L2
Tobha Mòr	W Isls	111	a5
Tocher	Abers	102	F8
Tochieneal	Moray	101	P3
Tockenham	Wilts	18	F5
Tockholes	Bl w D	57	M4
Tockington	S Glos	28	H10
Tockwith	N York	59	L4
Todber	Dorset	8	B4
Toddington	C Beds	32	E10
Toddington	Gloucs	30	D7
Toddington Services	C Beds	32	E10
Todenham	Gloucs	30	G7
Todhills	Angus	93	M7
Todhills Rest Area	Cumb	71	N3
Todmorden	Calder	58	C8
Todwick	Rothm	51	L4
Toft	Cambs	33	K5
Toft	Lincs	42	F7
Toft	Shet	111	k3
Toft Hill	Dur	65	K2
Toft Monks	Norfk	45	N10
Toft next Newton	Lincs	52	E6
Toftrees	Norfk	44	E5
Togston	Nthumb	73	M1
Tokavaig	Highld	96	H7
Tokers Green	Oxon	20	B7
Tolastadh bho Thuath	W Isls	111	e1
Tolland	Somset	16	E9
Tollard Royal	Wilts	8	D4
Toll Bar	Donc	59	M11
Toller Fratrum	Dorset	7	N4
Toller Porcorum	Dorset	7	N3
Tollerton	N York	59	L2
Tollerton	Notts	41	N1
Tollesbury	Essex	23	J2
Tolleshunt D'Arcy	Essex	22	H2
Tolleshunt Knights	Essex	22	H2
Tolleshunt Major	Essex	22	H2
Toll of Birness	Abers	103	K8
Tolpuddle	Dorset	8	B8
Tolworth	Gt Lon	21	J9
Tomatin	Highld	99	M4
Tomchrasky	Highld	98	C6
Tomdoun	Highld	98	B8
Tomich	Highld	98	D4
Tomich	Highld	107	J11
Tomich	Highld	107	K2
Tomich	Highld	107	L8
Tomintoul	Moray	101	J9
Tomnacross	Highld	98	G2
Tomnavoulin	Moray	101	J9
Tonbridge	Kent	12	C2
Tondu	Brdgnd	27	J11
Tonedale	Somset	16	F11
Tong	C Brad	58	G7
Tong	Kent	23	J11
Tong	Shrops	39	P1
Tong	W Isls	111	d2
Tonge	Leics	41	K3
Tongham	Surrey	10	E1
Tongland	D & G	69	Q8
Tong Norton	Shrops	39	P1
Tongue	Highld	109	K4
Tongwynlais	Cardif	27	N11
Tonmawr	Neath	26	H9
Tonna	Neath	26	G8
Tonwell	Herts	33	K12
Tonypandy	Rhondd	27	L9
Tonyrefail	Rhondd	27	L10
Toot Baldon	Oxon	19	P1
Toot Hill	Essex	21	P3
Toothill	Swindn	18	G4
Tooting	Gt Lon	21	L8
Tooting Bec	Gt Lon	21	L8
Topcliffe	N York	65	P11
Topcroft	Norfk	45	L10

Topcroft Street – Upton 191

Topcroft Street Norfk 45 L10
Toppesfield Essex 34 C8
Toprow Norfk 45 J9
Topsham Devon 6 C5
Torbeg N Ayrs 75 N6
Torboll Highld 107 M3
Torbreck Highld 99 J2
Torbryan Devon 5 Q6
Torcastle Highld 90 F1
Torcross Devon 5 Q10
Tore Highld 107 K10
Torinturk Ag & B 83 M9
Torksey Lincs 52 B7
Torlundy Highld 90 F2
Tormarton S Glos 18 B5
Tormore N Ayrs 75 N6
Tornagrain Highld 107 M11
Tornaveen Abers 95 K2
Torness Highld 98 H4
Toronto Dur 65 L2
Torpenhow Cumb 71 K7
Torphichen W Loth 86 A7
Torphins Abers 95 K2
Torpoint Cnwll 5 J8
Torquay Torbay 6 C9
Torquhan Border 87 J11
Torran Highld 104 H11
Torrance E Duns 85 K8
Torranyard N Ayrs 76 F3
Torridon Highld 105 N10
Torridon House Highld 105 M10
Torrin Highld 96 G5
Torrisdale Ag & B 75 M5
Torrisdale Highld 109 M4
Torrish Highld 110 A11
Torrisholme Lancs 63 J9
Torrobull Highld 107 K2
Torry C Aber 95 Q2
Torryburn Fife 86 B5
Torteval Guern 6 a2
Torthorwald D & G 78 G12
Tortington W Susx 10 G8
Torton Worcs 39 Q7
Tortworth S Glos 29 J9
Torvaig Highld 96 F2
Torver Cumb 62 F4
Torwood Falk 85 P6
Torwoodlee Border 79 P2
Torworth Notts 51 P4
Toscaig Highld 97 J3
Toseland Cambs 33 J4
Tosside Lancs 63 P10
Tostock Suffk 34 F4
Totaig Highld 104 B11
Tote Highld 104 F11
Tote Highld 104 G9
Totland IoW 9 K9
Totley Sheff 50 H5
Totley Brook Sheff 50 H5
Totnes Devon 5 Q7
Toton Notts 41 L1
Totronald Ag & B 88 E5
Totscore Highld 104 E8
Tottenham Gt Lon 21 M5
Tottenhill Norfk 43 Q7
Totteridge Gt Lon 21 K5
Totternhoe C Beds 32 E11
Tottington Bury 57 P6
Totton Hants 9 L5
Toulton Somset 16 G9
Toulvaddie Highld 107 P6
Tovil Kent 22 F11
Toward Ag & B 84 C8
Toward Quay Ag & B 84 B9
Towcester Nhants 31 P4
Towednack Cnwll 2 D7
Tower of London Gt Lon 21 M7
Towersey Oxon 20 B3
Towie Abers 101 N11
Tow Law Dur 73 K11
Town End Cambs 43 L10
Townend W Duns 84 G7
Townhead Barns 50 F1
Townhead D & G 78 G10
Townhead of Greenlaw D & G 70 C3
Townhill Fife 86 D4
Town Littleworth E Susx 11 N6
Townshend Cnwll 2 E8
Town Street Suffk 44 C11
Town Yetholm Border 80 H8
Towthorpe C York 59 N3
Towton N York 59 L6
Towyn Conwy 55 P6
Toxteth Lpool 56 G10
Toynton All Saints Lincs 53 L10
Toy's Hill Kent 21 P12
Trabboch E Ayrs 76 G7
Trabbochburn E Ayrs 76 H7
Tradespark Highld 100 D4
Trafford Park Traffd 57 P9
Trallong Powys 27 K3
Tranent E Loth 86 H7
Tranmere Wirral 56 G10
Trantelbeg Highld 109 Q5
Trantlemore Highld 109 Q5
Trap Carmth 26 E5
Traprain E Loth 87 L7
Traquair Border 79 M3
Trawden Lancs 58 B6
Trawsfynydd Gwynd 47 L4
Trealaw Rhondd 27 L9
Treales Lancs 56 H3
Trearddur Bay IoA 54 C6
Trebetherick Cnwll 4 B5
Treborough Somset 16 D8
Trebullett Cnwll 4 H5
Treburley Cnwll 4 H5
Trecastle Powys 27 J3
Trecwn Pembks 24 G3
Trecynon Rhondd 27 L7
Tredegar Blae G 27 N7
Tredington Gloucs 29 M3
Tredington Warwks 30 H5
Tredunnock Mons 28 D9
Treen Cnwll 2 B10
Treeton Rothm 51 K4
Trefasser Pembks 24 F2
Trefecca Powys 27 N3
Trefeglwys Powys 37 Q3
Treffgarne Pembks 24 G4
Treffgarne Owen Pembks 24 F4
Trefilan Cerdgn 37 J8
Trefin Pembks 24 E3
Trefnant Denbgs 48 B2
Trefonen Shrops 48 F9
Trefor Gwynd 46 F3
Treforest Rhondd 27 M10
Trefriw Conwy 55 L8
Tregadillett Cnwll 4 G4
Tregare Mons 28 E6
Tregaron Cerdgn 37 L8
Tregarth Gwynd 54 H7
Tregeare Cnwll 4 F3
Tregeiriog Wrexhm 48 D8
Tregele IoA 54 E3
Treglemais Pembks 24 E3
Tregonetha Cnwll 3 L3
Tregonning & Gwinear Mining District Cnwll 2 E9
Tregony Cnwll 3 K6
Tregorrick Cnwll 3 M5
Tregoyd Powys 27 P2
Tre-groes Cerdgn 36 G10
Tregynon Powys 38 C3
Tre-gynwr Carmth 25 P5
Trehafod Rhondd 27 L10
Trehan Cnwll 5 J8
Treharris Myr Td 27 M9
Treherbert Rhondd 27 K8
Trekenner Cnwll 4 H5
Treknow Cnwll 4 C3
Trelawnyd Flints 56 C11
Trelech Carmth 25 M3
Treleddyd-fawr Pembks 24 D3
Trelewis Myr Td 27 M9
Trelights Cnwll 4 B4
Trelill Cnwll 4 C5
Trellech Mons 28 F7
Trelogan Flints 56 D11
Tremadog Gwynd 47 J4
Tremail Cnwll 4 E3
Tremain Cerdgn 36 D10
Tremaine Cnwll 4 F3
Tremar Cnwll 4 G6
Trematon Cnwll 5 J8
Tremeirchion Denbgs 48 C2
Trenance Cnwll 3 J3
Trenance Cnwll 3 L2
Trench Wrekin 49 M11
Trenear Cnwll 2 G9
Treneglos Cnwll 4 F3
Trent Dorset 17 N11
Trentham C Stke 49 Q7
Trentishoe Devon 15 L3
Trent Vale C Stke 49 Q6
Treoes V Glam 27 K12
Treorchy Rhondd 27 K8
Trequite Cnwll 3 M1
Trerhyngyll V Glam 27 L12
Trerulefoot Cnwll 4 H8
Tresaith Cerdgn 36 E9
Tresco IoS 2 b2
Trescowe Cnwll 2 E9
Tresean Cnwll 2 H4
Tresham Gloucs 29 L9
Treshnish Isles Ag & B 88 G7
Tresillian Cnwll 3 K6
Treskinnick Cross Cnwll 14 D11
Tresmeer Cnwll 4 F4
Tresparrett Cnwll 4 E2
Tressait P & K 92 C4
Tresta Shet 111 k4
Tresta Shet 111 m2
Treswell Notts 52 A7
Tre Taliesin Cerdgn 37 L3
Trethevey Cnwll 4 D3
Trethewey Cnwll 2 B10
Trethurgy Cnwll 3 M5
Tretire Herefs 28 F4
Tretower Powys 27 P5
Treuddyn Flints 48 F4
Trevalga Cnwll 4 D3
Trevalyn Wrexhm 48 H4
Trevarrian Cnwll 3 J3
Treveal Cnwll 2 H4
Treveighan Cnwll 4 D4
Trevellas Downs Cnwll 2 H5
Trevelmond Cnwll 4 F7
Treverva Cnwll 2 H9
Trevescan Cnwll 2 B10
Treviscoe Cnwll 3 L5
Trevone Cnwll 3 K1
Trevor Wrexhm 48 F7
Trewalder Cnwll 4 D4
Trewarmett Cnwll 4 D3
Trewavas Mining District Cnwll 2 E9
Trewen Cnwll 4 F4
Trewint Cnwll 4 F4
Trewithian Cnwll 3 K8
Trewoon Cnwll 3 L5
Treyford W Susx 10 D6
Trimdon Dur 65 P1
Trimdon Colliery Dur 65 P1
Trimdon Grange Dur 65 P1
Trimingham Norfk 45 L3
Trimley St Martin Suffk 35 L8
Trimley St Mary Suffk 35 L9
Trimsaran Carmth 26 B7
Trimstone Devon 15 J4
Trinafour P & K 91 Q4
Tring Herts 20 E2
Trinity Angus 95 K9
Trinity Jersey 7 b1
Trinity Gask P & K 92 E11
Triscombe Somset 16 F8
Trislaig Highld 90 E2
Trispen Cnwll 3 J6
Tritlington Nthumb 73 L3
Trochry P & K 92 E7
Troedyraur Cerdgn 36 E10
Troedyrhiw Myr Td 27 M8
Troon Cnwll 2 F8
Troon S Ayrs 76 F5
Tropical World Roundhay Park Leeds 59 J6
Trossachs Stirlg 84 H2
Trossachs Pier Stirlg 84 H2
Troston Suffk 34 E3
Trotshill Worcs 30 B3
Trottiscliffe Kent 22 D10
Trotton W Susx 10 D5
Troutbeck Cumb 62 H2
Troutbeck Bridge Cumb 62 H3
Troway Derbys 51 K5
Trowbridge Wilts 18 C8
Trowell Notts 51 L11
Trowell Services Notts 51 L11
Trowse Newton Norfk 45 L8
Trudoxhill Somset 17 Q7
Trull Somset 16 G10
Trumpan Highld 104 C9
Trumpet Herefs 28 H2
Trumpington Cambs 33 M6
Trunch Norfk 45 L3
Truro Cnwll 3 J6
Trusham Devon 6 B6
Trusley Derbys 40 G1
Trusthorpe Lincs 53 N6
Trysull Staffs 39 Q4
Tubney Oxon 19 M2
Tuckenhay Devon 5 Q8
Tuckhill Shrops 39 P5
Tuckingmill Cnwll 2 F7
Tuckingmill Wilts 8 D2
Tuckton BCP 8 G8
Tuddenham Suffk 34 C3
Tuddenham Suffk 35 K7
Tudeley Kent 12 C2
Tudhoe Dur 65 M1
Tudweiliog Gwynd 46 D4
Tuffley Gloucs 29 L6
Tufton Hants 19 M10
Tufton Pembks 24 H3
Tugby Leics 41 Q7
Tugford Shrops 39 K5
Tughall Nthumb 81 P8
Tullibody Clacks 85 P4
Tullich Abers 94 F3
Tullich Highld 99 J4
Tullich Highld 107 P7
Tulliemet P & K 92 E5
Tulloch Abers 102 G8
Tullochgorm Ag & B 83 P4
Tulloch Station Highld 98 E11
Tullymurdoch P & K 92 H5
Tullynessle Abers 102 D10
Tulse Hill Gt Lon 21 L8
Tumble Carmth 26 D6
Tumby Lincs 53 J10
Tumby Woodside Lincs 53 J11
Tummel Bridge P & K 92 B4
Tunbridge Wells Kent 12 C3
Tundergarth D & G 79 J11
Tunga W Isls 111 d2
Tunley BaNES 17 Q4
Tunstall E R Yk 61 M7
Tunstall Kent 22 H10
Tunstall Lancs 63 L7
Tunstall N York 65 L8
Tunstall Norfk 45 N8
Tunstall Staffs 49 P9
Tunstall Suffk 35 M6
Tunstall Sundld 73 P9
Tunstead Derbys 50 E6
Tunstead Norfk 45 L6
Tunstead Milton Derbys 50 D5
Tupsley Herefs 28 G2
Turgis Green Hants 20 B10
Turkdean Gloucs 30 E9
Tur Langton Leics 41 Q8
Turleigh Wilts 18 B8
Turnastone Herefs 28 D2
Turnberry S Ayrs 76 D9
Turnditch Derbys 50 H10
Turners Hill W Susx 11 M3
Turnhouse C Edin 86 D7
Turnworth Dorset 8 B6
Turriff Abers 102 F5
Turton Bottoms Bl w D 57 N6
Turves Cambs 43 K10
Turvey Bed 32 D6
Turville Bucks 20 C5
Turweston Bucks 31 N6
Tushielaw Inn Border 79 L5
Tutbury Staffs 40 G2
Tutshill Gloucs 28 G9
Tuttington Norfk 45 K5
Tuxford Notts 51 Q6
Twatt Ork 111 g2
Twatt Shet 111 k4
Twechar E Duns 85 L7
Tweedbank Border 80 C7
Tweedmouth Nthumb 81 L4
Tweedsmuir Border 78 H4
Twelveheads Cnwll 2 H7
Twemlow Green Ches E 49 P2
Twenty Lincs 42 G6
Twerton BaNES 17 Q4
Twickenham Gt Lon 21 J8
Twigworth Gloucs 29 L4
Twineham W Susx 11 K6
Twinstead Essex 34 E9
Twitchen Devon 15 N6
Two Dales Derbys 50 H8
Two Gates Staffs 40 G7
Two Waters Herts 20 G3
Twycross Leics 41 J6
Twycross Zoo Leics 40 H6
Twyford Bucks 31 P8
Twyford Hants 9 N3
Twyford Leics 41 Q5
Twyford Norfk 44 G5
Twyford Wokham 20 C8
Twynholm D & G 69 P8
Twyning Green Gloucs 29 M2
Twynllanan Carmth 26 G4
Twywell Nhants 32 D2
Tyberton Herefs 28 D2
Tyburn Birm 40 F8
Tycroes Carmth 26 E6
Tycrwyn Powys 48 C10
Tydd Gote Lincs 43 M6
Tydd St Giles Cambs 43 L6
Tydd St Mary Lincs 43 M6
Tye Green Essex 33 P9
Tyldesley Wigan 57 M8
Tyler Hill Kent 23 L10
Tylorstown Rhondd 27 L9
Ty-nant Conwy 48 B6
Tyndrum Stirlg 91 J9
Ty'n-dwr Denbgs 48 E7
Tynemouth N Tyne 73 P7
Tyne Tunnel S Tyne 73 N7
Tyninghame E Loth 87 L6
Tynron D & G 77 N11
Tynygraig Cerdgn 37 L6
Ty'n-y-Groes Conwy 55 L7
Tyrie Abers 103 J3
Tyringham M Keyn 32 C7
Tyseley Birm 40 E9
Tythegston Brdgnd 27 J11
Tytherington Ches E 50 B6
Tytherington S Glos 29 J10
Tytherington Wilts 18 D11
Tytherleigh Devon 7 J3
Tytherton Lucas Wilts 18 D6
Tywardreath Cnwll 3 N5
Tywyn Gwynd 47 J10

U

Ubbeston Green Suffk 35 M3
Ubley BaNES 17 M5
Uckfield E Susx 11 P6
Uckinghall Worcs 29 M2
Uckington Gloucs 29 M4
Uddingston S Lans 85 L10
Uddington S Lans 78 E3
Udimore E Susx 12 G6
Udny Green Abers 103 J9
Udny Station Abers 103 J9
Uffculme Devon 16 E12
Uffington Lincs 42 F8
Uffington Oxon 19 K3
Uffington Shrops 49 K11
Ufford C Pete 42 F8
Ufford Suffk 35 L6
Ufton Warwks 31 J2
Ufton Nervet W Berk 19 Q7
Ugadale Ag & B 75 L6
Ugborough Devon 5 N8
Uggeshall Suffk 35 P2
Ugglebarnby N York 67 J6
Ughill Sheff 50 G3
Ugley Essex 33 N10
Ugley Green Essex 33 N10
Ugthorpe N York 66 H5
Uibhist A Deas W Isls 111 b6
Uibhist A Tuath W Isls 111 a4
Uig Ag & B 88 E5
Uig Highld 104 B10
Uig Highld 104 E9
Uig W Isls 111 c2
Uigshader Highld 104 F12
Uisken Ag & B 89 J11
Ulbster Highld 110 G7
Ulceby Lincs 53 L8
Ulceby N Linc 61 J10
Ulceby Skitter N Linc 61 J10
Ulcombe Kent 12 G1
Uldale Cumb 71 L7
Uley Gloucs 29 K8
Ulgham Nthumb 73 M3
Ullapool Highld 106 B4
Ullenhall Warwks 30 E1
Ulleskelf N York 59 M6
Ullesthorpe Leics 41 L9
Ulley Rothm 51 L4
Ullingswick Herefs 39 L11
Ullinish Lodge Hotel Highld 96 C3
Ullock Cumb 70 H10
Ullswater Cumb 71 N10
Ullswater Steamers Cumb 71 N11
Ulpha Cumb 62 E4
Ulrome E R Yk 61 K3
Ulsta Shet 111 k3
Ulva Ag & B 89 J8
Ulverley Green Solhll 40 F10
Ulverston Cumb 62 F6
Ulwell Dorset 8 F10
Ulzieside D & G 77 N9
Umberleigh Devon 15 K7
Unapool Highld 108 E8
Underbarrow Cumb 63 J4
Under Burnmouth Border 79 P11
Undercliffe C Brad 58 F7
Underdale Shrops 49 J11
Underriver Kent 22 B11
Underwood Notts 51 L10
Undy Mons 28 E10
Union Mills IoM 56 c5
Unst Shet 111 m2
Unstone Derbys 51 J5
Upavon Wilts 18 G9
Upchurch Kent 22 G9
Upcott Devon 15 N6
Up Exe Devon 6 C3
Upgate Norfk 45 J6
Uphall Dorset 7 M3
Uphall W Loth 86 C7
Upham Devon 15 Q9
Upham Hants 9 N4
Uphampton Herefs 38 H9
Uphampton Worcs 39 Q8
Uphill N Som 17 J5
Up Holland Lancs 57 K7
Uplawmoor E Rens 84 G11
Upleadon Gloucs 29 K4
Upleatham R & Cl 66 E4
Uploders Dorset 7 M4
Uplowman Devon 16 D11
Uplyme Devon 7 J4
Up Marden W Susx 10 C7
Upminster Gt Lon 22 C6
Up Mudford Somset 17 N11
Up Nately Hants 20 B11
Upottery Devon 6 G2
Upper Affcot Shrops 39 J5
Upper Arley Worcs 39 N6
Upper Badcall Highld 108 D7
Upper Basildon W Berk 19 P5
Upper Beeding W Susx 11 K7
Upper Benefield Nhants 42 E11
Upper Bentley Worcs 30 C2
Upper Bighouse Highld 109 Q4
Upper Boddington Nhants 31 L4
Upper Brailes Warwks 30 H6
Upper Broadheath Worcs 39 P10
Upper Broughton Notts 41 P3
Upper Bucklebury W Berk 19 P7
Upper Burgate Hants 8 H4
Upperby Cumb 71 N5
Upper Caldecote C Beds 32 G7
Upper Chapel Powys 27 L1
Upper Chicksgrove Wilts 8 E2
Upper Chute Wilts 19 K9
Upper Clapton Gt Lon 21 M6
Upper Clatford Hants 19 L11
Upper Cound Shrops 39 K2
Upper Cumberworth Kirk 58 G11
Upper Dallachy Moray 101 M3
Upper Deal Kent 23 Q11
Upper Dean Bed 32 F4
Upper Denby Kirk 58 G11
Upper Dicker E Susx 12 B7
Upper Dounreay Highld 110 B3
Upper Dovercourt Essex 35 K9
Upper Drumbane Stirlg 85 L2
Upper Dunsforth N York 59 K2
Upper Eashing Surrey 10 F2
Upper Eathie Highld 107 M9
Upper Egleton Herefs 39 M12
Upper Elkstone Staffs 50 D8
Upper Ellastone Staffs 50 E11
Upper Farringdon Hants 10 B3
Upper Framilode Gloucs 29 K6
Upper Froyle Hants 10 C2
Upperglen Highld 104 D11
Upper Godney Somset 17 L7
Upper Gravenhurst C Beds 32 G9
Upper Green W Berk 19 L7
Upper Grove Common Herefs 28 G4
Upper Hale Surrey 10 D1
Upper Halliford Surrey 20 H9
Upper Hambleton Rutlnd 42 C8
Upper Harbledown Kent 23 L10
Upper Hartfield E Susx 11 P3
Upper Hatherley Gloucs 29 M5
Upper Heaton Kirk 58 F9
Upper Helmsley N York 59 P3
Upper Hergest Herefs 38 F10
Upper Heyford Nhants 31 P3
Upper Heyford Oxon 31 L8
Upper Hill Herefs 39 J10
Upper Hopton Kirk 58 G9
Upper Hulme Staffs 50 D8
Upper Inglesham Swindn 18 H2
Upper Killay Swans 26 D9
Upper Kinchrackine Ag & B 90 G10
Upper Knockando Moray 101 J6
Upper Lambourn W Berk 19 K5
Upper Landywood Staffs 40 C6
Upper Langford N Som 17 L4
Upper Langwith Derbys 51 L6
Upper Largo Fife 87 J2
Upper Leigh Staffs 50 D12
Upper Lochton Abers 95 L3
Upper Longdon Staffs 40 D5
Upper Lybster Highld 110 F8
Upper Lydbrook Gloucs 28 H6
Upper Lye Herefs 38 H8
Uppermill Oldham 58 C11
Upper Milton Worcs 39 P7
Upper Minety Wilts 18 E3
Upper Mulben Moray 101 L5
Upper Netchwood Shrops 39 L4
Upper Nobut Staffs 40 D1
Upper Norwood W Susx 10 F6
Upper Poppleton C York 59 M4
Upper Ratley Hants 9 K3
Upper Rissington Gloucs 30 G9
Upper Rochford Worcs 39 L8
Upper Ruscoe D & G 69 N6
Upper Sapey Herefs 39 M8
Upper Seagry Wilts 18 D5
Upper Shelton C Beds 32 E7
Upper Sheringham Norfk 45 J2
Upper Skelmorlie N Ayrs 84 D9
Upper Slaughter Gloucs 30 F9
Upper Soudley Gloucs 28 H6
Upper Standen Kent 13 N3
Upper Stoke Norfk 45 L9
Upper Stondon C Beds 32 G9
Upper Stowe Nhants 31 N3
Upper Street Hants 8 H4
Upper Street Norfk 45 M6
Upper Street Norfk 45 M6
Upper Street Suffk 34 C6
Upper Street Suffk 34 H6
Upper Sundon C Beds 32 F10
Upper Swell Gloucs 30 F8
Upper Tean Staffs 50 D11
Upperthong Kirk 58 F11
Upperton W Susx 10 F5
Upper Town Herefs 39 L11
Uppertown Highld 110 G1
Upper Town N Som 17 M3
Upper Town Suffk 34 F4
Upper Tumble Carmth 26 D6
Upper Tysoe Warwks 31 J5
Upper Victoria Angus 93 P8
Upper Wardington Oxon 31 L5
Upper Welland Worcs 29 K1
Upper Wellingham E Susx 11 N7
Upper Weybread Suffk 35 K2
Upper Wield Hants 19 Q11
Upper Winchendon Bucks 31 Q10
Upper Woodford Wilts 18 G12
Upper Wraxall Wilts 18 B6
Uppingham Rutlnd 42 C9
Uppington Shrops 39 L1
Upsall N York 66 C9
Upsettlington Border 81 J5
Upshire Essex 21 N4
Up Somborne Hants 9 L2
Upstreet Kent 23 N10
Upton Bucks 31 Q10
Upton C Pete 42 G9
Upton Cambs 32 H2
Upton Ches W 48 H2
Upton Cnwll 4 G6
Upton Devon 5 N10
Upton Devon 6 E3
Upton Dorset 7 Q6
Upton Dorset 8 E8
Upton Halton 57 J10
Upton Hants 9 L4
Upton Hants 19 L9
Upton Leics 41 J7
Upton Lincs 52 C6
Upton Norfk 45 N7
Upton Notts 51 Q5
Upton Notts 51 Q9
Upton Oxon 19 N4
Upton Slough 20 F7
Upton Somset 16 D9
Upton Somset 17 L10

Upton Wakefd 59 L10
Upton Wirral 56 F10
Upton Bishop Herefs 28 H4
Upton Cheyney S Glos 17 Q3
Upton Cressett Shrops 39 M4
Upton Grey Hants 10 B1
Upton Hellions Devon 15 P10
Upton Lovell Wilts 18 D11
Upton Magna Shrops 49 K11
Upton Noble Somset 17 Q8
Upton Pyne Devon 6 C3
Upton St Leonards Gloucs 29 M6
Upton Scudamore Wilts 18 C10
Upton Snodsbury Worcs 30 C4
Upton-upon-Severn Worcs 29 L1
Upton Warren Worcs 30 B1
Upwaltham W Susx 10 F7
Upwell Norfk 43 N9
Upwood Cambs 43 J12
Urchfont Wilts 18 F8
Urmston Traffd 57 P9
Urquhart Moray 101 K3
Urquhart Castle Highld 98 E7
Urra N York 66 D7
Urray Highld 106 H10
Usan Angus 95 M10
Ushaw Moor Dur 73 M11
Usk Mons 28 D8
Usselby Lincs 52 F5
Usworth Sundld 73 N8
Utkinton Ches W 49 K3
Utley C Brad 58 C3
Uton Devon 15 P11
Utterby Lincs 53 K5
Uttoxeter Staffs 40 E6
Uxbridge Gt Lon 20 G6
Uyeasound Shet 111 m2
Uzmaston Pembks 24 G6

V

Vale Guern 6 c1
Valley IoA 54 D6
Valtos Highld 104 G9
Valtos W Isls 111 c2
Vange Essex 22 E6
Vatsetter Shet 111 k2
Vatten Highld 96 C2
Vaynor Myr Td 27 L6
Veensgarth Shet 111 k4
Velindre Powys 27 P2
Venngreen Devon 14 G9
Venn Ottery Devon 6 E5
Ventnor IoW 9 P11
Venton Devon 5 M8
Vernham Dean Hants 19 K9
Vernham Street Hants 19 L8
Verwood Dorset 8 G5
Veryan Cnwll 3 K7
Vickerstown Cumb 62 E8
Victoria Cnwll 3 L4
Vidlin Shet 111 k3
Viewfield Moray 101 K3
Viewpark N Lans 85 M10
Vigo Kent 22 D10
Village de Putron Guern 6 c2
Vines Cross E Susx 12 C6
Virginia Water Surrey 20 G8
Virginstow Devon 4 H2
Vobster Somset 17 Q6
Voe Shet 111 k3
Vowchurch Herefs 28 D2

W

Waberthwaite Cumb 62 C4
Wackerfield Dur 65 K3
Wacton Norfk 45 K10
Wadborough Worcs 30 B5
Waddesdon Bucks 31 Q10
Waddesdon Manor Bucks 31 Q10
Waddeton Devon 6 B10
Waddingham Lincs 52 E4
Waddington Lancs 63 N12
Waddington Lincs 52 D9
Waddon Gt Lon 21 L9
Wadebridge Cnwll 3 L2
Wadeford Somset 7 J1
Wadenhoe Nhants 42 E12
Wadesmill Herts 33 K12
Wadhurst E Susx 12 D4
Wadshelf Derbys 50 H6
Wadworth Donc 51 M2
Wainfleet All Saints Lincs 53 N10
Wainfleet St Mary Lincs 53 N10
Wainhouse Corner Cnwll 4 E2
Wainscott Medway 22 E8
Wainstalls Calder 58 D8
Waitby Cumb 64 D6
Waithe Lincs 53 J4
Wakefield Wakefd 59 J9
Wake Green Birm 40 E10
Wakehurst Place W Susx 11 M4
Wakerley Nhants 42 D9
Wakes Colne Essex 34 E10
Walberswick Suffk 35 P2
Walberton W Susx 10 F8
Walbutt D & G 70 C2
Walcombe Somset 17 M6
Walcot Lincs 42 F3
Walcot Shrops 49 L11
Walcot Swindn 18 H4
Walcote Leics 41 M10
Walcot Green Norfk 35 J2
Walcott Lincs 52 G11
Walcott Norfk 45 M4
Walden Stubbs N York 59 M10
Walderslade Medway 22 F10
Walderton W Susx 10 C7
Walditch Dorset 7 L4
Waldridge Dur 73 M10
Waldringfield Suffk 35 L7
Waldron E Susx 12 B6
Wales Rothm 51 L4
Wales Somset 17 N10
Walesby Lincs 52 F5
Walesby Notts 51 P6
Walford Herefs 28 G5

Walford Herefs 38 H7
Walford Heath Shrops 49 J10
Walgherton Ches E 49 M6
Walgrave Nhants 32 B3
Walkden Salfd 57 N8
Walker N u Ty 73 M7
Walkerburn Border 79 M2
Walkeringham Notts 51 Q3
Walkerith Lincs 52 B5
Walkern Herts 33 J10
Walker's Heath Birm 40 D10
Walkerton Fife 86 F3
Walkford BCP 8 H8
Walkhampton Devon 5 L6
Walkington E R Yk 60 G6
Walkley Sheff 51 J3
Walk Mill Lancs 57 Q3
Walkwood Worcs 30 D2
Wall Nthumb 72 G7
Wall Staffs 40 E6
Wallacetown S Ayrs 76 E10
Wallacetown S Ayrs 76 F6
Wallands Park E Susx 11 N7
Wallasey Wirral 56 F9
Wallasey (Kingsway) Tunnel Wirral 56 G9
Wall Heath Dudley 40 B9
Wallingford Oxon 19 P3
Wallington Gt Lon 21 L9
Wallington Hants 9 P6
Wallington Herts 33 J9
Wallisdown BCP 8 F8
Walliswood Surrey 10 H3
Walls Shet 111 j4
Wallsend N Tyne 73 N7
Wallyford E Loth 86 H7
Walmer Kent 23 Q12
Walmer Bridge Lancs 57 J4
Walmley Birm 40 F8
Walmley Ash Birm 40 F8
Walpole Suffk 35 M2
Walpole Cross Keys Norfk 43 N6
Walpole Highway Norfk 43 N7
Walpole St Andrew Norfk 43 N6
Walpole St Peter Norfk 43 N6
Walsall Wsall 40 D7
Walsden Calder 58 C9
Walsgrave on Sowe Covtry 41 J10
Walsham le Willows Suffk 34 G3
Walshford N York 59 K4
Walsoken Norfk 43 M7
Walston S Lans 86 C12
Walsworth Herts 32 H10
Walter's Ash Bucks 20 D4
Waltham Kent 13 L1
Waltham NE Lin 53 J3
Waltham Abbey Essex 21 M4
Waltham Chase Hants 9 P4
Waltham Cross Herts 21 M4
Waltham on the Wolds Leics 41 N4
Waltham St Lawrence W & M 20 D7
Walthamstow Gt Lon 21 M5
Walton C Pete 42 H9
Walton Cumb 71 Q3
Walton Derbys 51 J7
Walton Leeds 59 K5
Walton Leics 41 N9
Walton M Keyn 32 C9
Walton Powys 38 F9
Walton Somset 17 L8
Walton Suffk 35 L9
Walton Suffk 10 D8
Walton Wakefd 59 J10
Walton Wrekin 49 L10
Walton Cardiff Gloucs 29 M3
Walton East Pembks 24 H4
Walton Highway Norfk 43 M7
Walton-in-Gordano N Som 17 K2
Walton-le-Dale Lancs 57 K4
Walton-on-Thames Surrey 20 H9
Walton-on-the-Hill Staffs 40 C4
Walton-on-the-Hill Surrey 21 K11
Walton-on-the-Naze Essex 35 L11
Walton on the Wolds Leics 41 N4
Walton-on-Trent Derbys 40 G4
Walton Park N Som 17 K2
Walton West Pembks 24 F6
Walworth Darltn 65 M4
Walworth Gt Lon 21 M7
Walwyn's Castle Pembks 24 F6
Wambrook Somset 6 H2
Wanborough Surrey 10 E1
Wanborough Swindn 18 H4
Wandsworth Gt Lon 21 K8
Wangford Suffk 35 P2
Wanlip Leics 41 N5
Wanlockhead D & G 78 E6
Wannock E Susx 12 C8
Wansford C Pete 42 F9
Wansford E R Yk 60 H3
Wanshurst Green Kent 12 F2
Wanstead Gt Lon 21 N6
Wanstrow Somset 17 Q7
Wanswell Gloucs 29 J8
Wantage Oxon 19 L3
Wappenbury Warwks 41 J12
Wappenham Nhants 31 N5
Warbleton E Susx 12 C6
Warborough Oxon 19 P3
Warboys Cambs 33 K2
Warbreck Bpool 56 G2
Warbstow Cnwll 4 F3
Warburton Traffd 57 M10
Warcop Cumb 64 D5
Warden Nthumb 72 G7
Ward End Birm 40 E9
Wardington Oxon 31 L5
Wardle Ches E 49 M4
Wardle Rochdl 58 B10
Wardley Gatesd 73 N8
Wardley Rutlnd 42 B9
Wardlow Derbys 50 F6
Wardy Hill Cambs 33 M1
Ware Herts 21 M1
Wareham Dorset 8 D9
Warehorne Kent 13 J4
Warenford Nthumb 81 N8
Wareside Herts 21 N1
Waresley Cambs 33 J6
Warfield Br For 20 E8
Warfleet Devon 6 B11
Wargrave Wokham 20 C7

Warham Norfk 44 F2
Wark Nthumb 72 F5
Wark Nthumb 80 H6
Warkleigh Devon 15 L7
Warkton Nhants 32 C2
Warkworth Nhants 31 L6
Warkworth Nthumb 81 P11
Warlaby N York 65 N9
Warleggan Cnwll 4 E6
Warley Town Calder 58 D8
Warlingham Surrey 21 M10
Warmfield Wakefd 59 J9
Warmingham Ches E 49 N4
Warmington Nhants 42 F11
Warmington Warwks 31 K5
Warminster Wilts 18 C10
Warmley S Glos 17 P2
Warmsworth Donc 51 M1
Warmwell Dorset 7 Q5
Warner Bros. Studio Tour Herts 20 H3
Warnford Hants 9 Q3
Warnham W Susx 11 J4
Warningcamp W Susx 10 G8
Warninglid W Susx 11 L5
Warren Ches E 50 B6
Warren Pembks 24 G8
Warrenhill S Lans 78 F2
Warren Row W & M 20 D7
Warren Street Kent 22 H11
Warrington M Keyn 32 C6
Warrington Warrtn 57 L10
Warriston C Edin 86 F7
Warsash Hants 9 N6
Warslow Staffs 50 E8
Warter E R Yk 60 E4
Warthermaske N York 65 L10
Warthill N York 59 P3
Wartling E Susx 12 D8
Wartnaby Leics 41 P3
Warton Lancs 56 H3
Warton Lancs 63 J7
Warton Warwks 40 H6
Warwick Warwks 30 H2
Warwick Bridge Cumb 71 P4
Warwick Castle Warwks 30 H2
Warwick Services Warwks 31 J3
Wasbister Ork 111 h1
Wasdale Head Cumb 62 E1
Washaway Cnwll 3 M2
Washbourne Devon 5 Q8
Washbrook Suffk 35 J8
Washfield Devon 16 C11
Washford Somset 16 E7
Washford Pyne Devon 15 N9
Washingborough Lincs 52 E8
Washington Sundld 73 N9
Washington W Susx 10 H7
Washington Services Gatesd 73 M9
Washwood Heath Birm 40 E9
Wasperton Warwks 30 H3
Wass N York 66 D10
Wast Water Cumb 62 D2
Watchet Somset 16 E7
Watchfield Oxon 19 J3
Watchgate Cumb 63 K3
Water Devon 5 P4
Waterbeach Cambs 33 M4
Waterbeach W Susx 10 E8
Waterbeck D & G 79 L12
Water End E R Yk 60 D6
Waterfall Staffs 50 E9
Waterfoot Ag & B 75 M5
Waterfoot E Rens 85 J11
Waterford Herts 21 L1
Waterheads Border 86 F11
Waterhouses Staffs 50 E10
Wateringbury Kent 22 E11
Waterloo Highld 97 J5
Waterloo N Lans 85 N11
Waterloo P & K 92 F8
Waterloo Pembks 24 G7
Waterloo Sefton 56 G8
Waterlooville Hants 10 B7
Watermead Bucks 20 D1
Watermillock Cumb 71 P10
Water Newton Cambs 42 G10
Water Orton Warwks 40 F8
Waterperry Oxon 31 N11
Waterrow Somset 16 E10
Watersfield W Susx 10 G6
Waterside Bl w D 57 N4
Waterside E Ayrs 76 G9
Waterside E Ayrs 76 H3
Waterside E Duns 85 L8
Waterstein Highld 104 A11
Waterstock Oxon 31 N11
Waterston Pembks 24 G7
Water Stratford Bucks 31 P7
Waters Upton Wrekin 49 L10
Watford Herts 21 H4
Watford Nhants 31 N1
Watford Gap Services Nhants 31 L6
Wath N York 58 F1
Wath N York 65 N11
Wath upon Dearne Rothm 51 K1
Watlington Norfk 43 P7
Watlington Oxon 20 B5
Watten Highld 110 E4
Wattisfield Suffk 34 G2
Wattisham Suffk 34 G6
Watton Dorset 7 L4
Watton E R Yk 60 H4
Watton Norfk 44 F9
Watton-at-Stone Herts 33 K11
Wattston N Lans 85 N8
Wattsville Caerph 27 P9
Waulkmill Abers 95 K4
Waunarlwydd Swans 26 E9
Waunfawr Cerdgn 37 K4
Waunfawr Gwynd 54 G9
Wavendon M Keyn 32 C8
Waverbridge Cumb 71 K6
Waverton Ches W 49 J3
Waverton Cumb 71 K6
Wawne E R Yk 61 J6
Waxham Norfk 45 P5
Wayford Somset 7 K2
Way Village Devon 15 Q9
Weacombe Somset 16 F7
Weald Oxon 19 K1

Wealdstone Gt Lon 21 J5
Weardley Leeds 58 H5
Weare Somset 17 K5
Weare Giffard Devon 14 H7
Wearhead Dur 72 F11
Wearne Somset 17 L5
Weasenham All Saints Norfk 44 E6
Weasenham St Peter Norfk 44 E5
Weaste Salfd 57 P8
Weaverham Ches W 49 L1
Weaverthorpe N York 67 L12
Webheath Worcs 30 D2
Wedderlairs Abers 102 H8
Weddington Warwks 41 J8
Wedhampton Wilts 18 F8
Wedmore Somset 17 L6
Wednesbury Sandw 40 C8
Wednesfield Wolves 40 C7
Weedon Bucks 32 B12
Weedon Bec Nhants 31 N3
Weedon Lois Nhants 31 N5
Weeford Staffs 40 F6
Weeke Hants 9 N1
Weekley Nhants 32 C1
Week St Mary Cnwll 14 E11
Weel E R Yk 60 H6
Weeley Essex 35 J11
Weeley Heath Essex 35 J11
Weem P & K 92 C6
Weethley Warwks 30 D3
Weeting Norfk 44 C11
Weeton E R Yk 61 N9
Weeton Lancs 56 H2
Weeton N York 58 H5
Weetwood Leeds 58 H6
Weir Lancs 57 Q4
Weir Quay Devon 5 J7
Weisdale Shet 111 k4
Welborne Norfk 44 H7
Welbourn Lincs 52 D11
Welburn N York 66 G12
Welbury N York 65 P7
Welby Lincs 42 D3
Welcombe Devon 14 E8
Weldon Nhants 42 D11
Welford Nhants 41 N10
Welford W Berk 19 L6
Welford-on-Avon Warwks 30 F4
Welham Leics 41 Q8
Welham Notts 51 Q5
Welham Green Herts 21 K3
Well Hants 10 C2
Well Lincs 53 M8
Well N York 65 M10
Welland Worcs 29 L2
Wellbank Angus 93 N8
Wellesbourne Warwks 30 H3
Well Head Herts 32 H10
Welling Gt Lon 21 P8
Wellingborough Nhants 32 C3
Wellingham Norfk 44 E6
Wellingore Lincs 52 E11
Wellington Cumb 62 C2
Wellington Herefs 39 J11
Wellington Somset 16 F11
Wellington Wrekin 49 M12
Wellington Heath Herefs 29 J1
Wellow BaNES 17 Q5
Wellow IoW 9 L9
Wellow Notts 51 P7
Wells Somset 17 M7
Wells-next-the-Sea Norfk 44 F2
Wellstye Green Essex 33 Q11
Welltree P & K 92 E10
Wellwood Fife 86 C5
Welney Norfk 43 N10
Welshampton Shrops 48 H8
Welsh Frankton Shrops 48 G8
Welsh Newton Herefs 28 F5
Welshpool Powys 38 E1
Welsh St Donats V Glam 16 D2
Welton Cumb 71 M6
Welton E R Yk 60 G8
Welton Lincs 52 E7
Welton Nhants 31 N2
Welton le Marsh Lincs 53 M9
Welton le Wold Lincs 53 J6
Welwick E R Yk 61 N9
Welwyn Herts 32 H12
Welwyn Garden City Herts 21 K2
Wem Shrops 49 K9
Wembdon Somset 16 H8
Wembley Gt Lon 21 J6
Wembury Devon 5 L9
Wembworthy Devon 15 L9
Wemyss Bay Inver 84 D8
Wendens Ambo Essex 33 N9
Wendlebury Oxon 31 M9
Wendling Norfk 44 F7
Wendover Bucks 20 D2
Wendron Cnwll 2 G9
Wendron Mining District Cnwll 2 G8
Wendy Cambs 33 K7
Wenhaston Suffk 35 N2
Wennington Cambs 33 J2
Wennington Gt Lon 22 B7
Wennington Lancs 63 L8
Wensley Derbys 50 H8
Wensley N York 65 J9
Wentbridge Wakefd 59 L10
Wentnor Shrops 38 H4
Wentworth Cambs 33 M2
Wentworth Rothm 51 J2
Wenvoe V Glam 16 F2
Weobley Herefs 38 H10
Wepham W Susx 10 G8
Wereham Norfk 44 B9
Werrington C Pete 42 G9
Werrington Cnwll 4 H4
Wervin Ches W 48 H2
Wesham Lancs 56 H3
Wessington Derbys 50 H8
West Acre Norfk 44 C7
West Alvington Devon 5 P10
West Anstey Devon 15 P6
West Ashby Lincs 53 J8
West Ashling W Susx 10 D8
West Ashton Wilts 18 C9
West Auckland Dur 65 L3
West Ayton N York 67 L9
West Bagborough Somset 16 G9

West Bank Halton 57 K11
West Barkwith Lincs 52 G7
West Barnby N York 66 H5
West Barns E Loth 87 M6
West Barsham Norfk 44 E4
West Bay Dorset 7 L5
West Beckham Norfk 45 J3
West Bedfont Surrey 20 H8
Westbere Kent 23 M10
West Bergholt Essex 34 F10
West Bexington Dorset 7 M5
West Bilney Norfk 44 B7
West Blatchington Br & H 11 L8
West Boldon S Tyne 73 P8
Westborough Lincs 42 C2
Westbourne BCP 8 F8
Westbourne W Susx 10 C8
West Bowling C Brad 58 F7
West Bradenham Norfk 44 F8
West Bradford Lancs 63 N12
West Bradley Somset 17 M8
West Bretton Wakefd 58 H10
West Bridgford Notts 51 N11
West Bromwich Sandw 40 D8
Westbrook Kent 23 Q8
Westbrook W Berk 19 M6
West Buckland Devon 15 L6
West Buckland Somset 16 G11
West Burrafirth Shet 111 j4
West Burton N York 64 H9
Westbury Bucks 31 N7
Westbury Shrops 38 G1
Westbury Wilts 18 C9
Westbury Leigh Wilts 18 C10
Westbury-on-Severn Gloucs 29 J6
Westbury-on-Trym Bristl 28 G12
Westbury-sub-Mendip Somset 17 M6
West Butterwick N Linc 52 B3
Westby Lancs 56 H3
West Byfleet Surrey 20 G10
West Cairngaan D & G 68 F12
West Caister Norfk 45 Q7
West Calder W Loth 86 B9
West Camel Somset 17 N10
West Chaldon Dorset 8 B10
West Challow Oxon 19 L3
West Charleton Devon 5 P10
West Chiltington W Susx 10 H6
West Chinnock Somset 17 L12
West Clandon Surrey 20 G11
West Cliffe Kent 13 Q2
Westcliff-on-Sea Sthend 22 G6
West Coker Somset 17 M12
Westcombe Somset 17 P8
West Compton Somset 17 N7
West Compton Abbas Dorset 7 N4
Westcote Gloucs 30 G9
Westcote Barton Oxon 31 K8
Westcott Bucks 31 Q10
Westcott Devon 6 C3
Westcott Surrey 11 J1
West Cottingwith N York 59 P6
Westcourt Wilts 19 J8
West Cowick E R Yk 59 P9
West Cross Swans 26 E10
West Curthwaite Cumb 71 M6
Westdean E Susx 11 Q9
West Dean W Susx 10 D7
West Dean Wilts 9 J3
West Deeping Lincs 42 G8
West Derby Lpool 56 H9
West Dereham Norfk 43 Q9
West Down Devon 15 J4
Westdowns Cnwll 4
West Drayton Gt Lon 20 G7
West Drayton Notts 51 P6
West Dunnet Highld 110 D2
West Ella E R Yk 60 H8
West End Bed 32 E6
West End Hants 9 M5
West End N Som 17 L3
West End Norfk 45 Q7
West End Surrey 20 F10
West End Surrey 20 H10
West End Wilts 8 E3
West End Green Hants 19 Q8
Wester Aberchalder Highld 98 H5
Westerdale Highld 110 D5
Westerdale N York 66 F6
Westerfield Suffk 35 K7
Westergate W Susx 10 F8
Westerham Kent 21 N11
Westerhope N u Ty 73 L7
Westerland Devon 6 B9
Westerleigh S Glos 29 J11
Western Isles W Isls 111 c3
Wester Ochiltree W Loth 86 B7
Wester Pitkierie Fife 87 K2
Wester Ross Highld 105 P9
Westerton of Rossie Angus 93 R5
Westerwick Shet 111 j4
West Farleigh Kent 22 E11
West Farndon Nhants 31 M4
West Felton Shrops 48 G9
Westfield BaNES 17 P5
Westfield E Susx 12 F7
Westfield Highld 110 C3
Westfield N Lans 85 M8
Westfield Norfk 44 G8
Westfield W Loth 85 Q8
Westfields Herefs 28 F1
Westfields of Rattray P & K 92 H6
Westgate Dur 72 G12
Westgate N Linc 52 B3
Westgate-on-Sea Kent 23 P8
West Grafton Wilts 19 J8
West Green Hants 20 C11
West Grimstead Wilts 8 H3
West Grinstead W Susx 11 J5
West Haddlesey N York 59 M8
West Haddon Nhants 41 N12
West Hagbourne Oxon 19 N3
West Hagley Worcs 40 B10
Westhall Suffk 35 N1
West Hallam Derbys 51 K11
West Halton N Linc 60 F8
Westham Dorset 7 P7
West Ham Gt Lon 21 N6
Westham E Susx 12 D8
Westham Somset 17 L7
Westhampnett W Susx 10 E8

West Handley Derbys 51 K5
West Hanney Oxon 19 L3
West Hanningfield Essex 22 E4
West Harnham Wilts 8 G2
West Harptree BaNES 17 M5
West Harting W Susx 10 C6
West Hatch Somset 16 H11
West Hatch Wilts 8 D2
West Haven Angus 93 P8
Westhay Somset 17 L7
West Heath Birm 40 D11
West Helmsdale Highld 110 B11
West Hendred Oxon 19 M3
West Heslerton N York 67 K11
West Hewish N Som 17 K4
Westhide Herefs 39 L12
Westhill Abers 95 N1
West Hill Devon 6 E4
Westhill Highld 107 L12
West Hoathly W Susx 11 M4
West Holme Dorset 8 C9
Westhope Herefs 39 J11
Westhope Shrops 39 J5
West Horndon Essex 22 D6
Westhorpe Lincs 42 H4
Westhorpe Suffk 34 H3
West Horrington Somset 17 N6
West Horsley Surrey 20 H11
West Hougham Kent 13 N3
Westhoughton Bolton 57 M7
Westhouse N York 63 M7
Westhouses Derbys 51 K8
West Howe BCP 8 F8
Westhumble Surrey 21 J11
West Huntingtower P & K 92 G10
West Huntspill Somset 17 J7
West Hythe Kent 13 L3
West Ilsley W Berk 19 M4
West Itchenor W Susx 10 C9
West Kennett Wilts 18 G7
West Kilbride N Ayrs 76 D2
West Kingsdown Kent 22 C10
West Kington Wilts 18 B5
West Kirby Wirral 56 E10
West Knapton N York 67 J11
West Knighton Dorset 7 Q5
West Knoyle Wilts 8 C2
Westlake Devon 5 M9
West Lambrook Somset 17 K11
West Langdon Kent 13 P1
West Lavington W Susx 10 E6
West Lavington Wilts 18 E9
West Layton N York 65 K5
West Leake Notts 41 M3
Westleigh Devon 14 H6
Westleigh Devon 16 E11
West Leigh Somset 16 F9
Westleton Suffk 35 P3
West Lexham Norfk 44 D6
Westley Suffk 34 D4
Westley Waterless Cambs 33 P5
West Lilling N York 59 P2
Westlington Bucks 31 Q11
West Linton Border 86 D10
Westlinton Cumb 71 N3
West Littleton S Glos 18 B5
West Lockinge Oxon 19 M4
West Lulworth Dorset 8 B10
West Lutton N York 60 F1
West Lydford Somset 17 N9
West Lyng Somset 17 J9
West Lynn Norfk 43 P6
West Malling Kent 22 D10
West Malvern Worcs 39 N11
West Marden W Susx 10 C7
West Markham Notts 51 Q6
Westmarsh Kent 23 P10
West Marsh NE Lin 61 L11
West Marton N York 58 B4
West Melbury Dorset 8 C4
West Meon Hants 9 Q3
West Mersea Essex 23 J2
Westmeston E Susx 11 M7
West Midland Safari Park
  Worcs 39 P7
Westmill Herts 33 K10
West Milton Dorset 7 M4
Westminster Gt Lon 21 L7
Westminster Abbey &
  Palace Gt Lon 21 L7
West Molesey Surrey 21 J9
West Monkton Somset 16 H9
West Moors Dorset 8 F6
West Morden Dorset 8 D8
West Morriston Border 80 E6
West Mudford Somset 17 N11
Westmuir Angus 93 L6
West Ness N York 66 F10
Westnewton Cumb 71 J6
West Newton E R Yk 61 L6
West Newton Norfk 44 B5
West Newton Somset 16 H9
West Norwood Gt Lon 21 L8
Westoe S Tyne 73 P7
West Ogwell Devon 5 Q6
Weston BaNES 17 Q3
Weston Ches E 49 N5
Weston Devon 6 F3
Weston Devon 6 F5
Weston Hants 10 B6
Weston Herts 33 J10
Weston Lincs 43 J5
Weston N York 58 F5
Weston Nhants 31 N5
Weston Notts 51 Q7
Weston Shrops 39 L4
Weston Shrops 48 F9
Weston Staffs 40 C3
Weston W Berk 19 L6
Weston Beggard Herefs 28 G1
Westonbirt Gloucs 18 C3
Weston by Welland Nhants 41 Q8
Weston Colville Cambs 33 P6
Weston Corbett Hants 10 B1
Weston Coyney C Stke 50 C11
Weston Favell Nhants 32 B4
Weston Green Cambs 33 P6
Weston Heath Shrops 49 P11
Westoning C Beds 32 E9
Weston-in-Gordano N Som 17 L2
Weston Jones Staffs 49 N10
Weston Longville Norfk 45 J7

Weston Lullingfields Shrops 48 H9
Weston-on-the-Green Oxon 31 M9
Weston Park Staffs 49 P12
Weston Patrick Hants 10 B1
Weston Rhyn Shrops 48 F8
Weston-sub-Edge Gloucs 30 E6
Weston-super-Mare N Som 17 J4
Weston Turville Bucks 20 D2
Weston-under-Lizard Staffs 49 P12
Weston under Penyard
  Herefs 28 H4
Weston-under-Redcastle
  Shrops 49 K9
Weston under Wetherley
  Warwks 41 J12
Weston Underwood Derbys 50 H11
Weston Underwood M Keyn 32 C6
Weston-upon-Trent Derbys 41 K2
Westonzoyland Somset 17 J8
West Orchard Dorset 8 B4
West Overton Wilts 18 G7
Westow N York 60 D2
West Park Abers 95 N3
West Parley Dorset 8 G7
West Peckham Kent 22 D11
West Pelton Dur 73 M9
West Pennard Somset 17 M8
West Pentire Cnwll 2 H4
West Perry Cambs 32 G4
West Porlock Somset 15 P3
Westport Somset 17 K11
West Putford Devon 14 G8
West Quantoxhead Somset 16 F7
Westquarter Falk 85 Q7
West Rainton Dur 73 N10
West Rasen Lincs 52 F5
Westray Ork 111 h1
Westray Airport Ork 111 h1
West Raynham Norfk 44 E5
Westrigg W Loth 85 Q9
Westrop Swindn 18 H3
West Rounton N York 65 P6
West Row Suffk 34 B2
West Rudham Norfk 44 D5
West Runton Norfk 45 K2
Westruther Border 80 E4
Westry Cambs 43 L9
West Saltoun E Loth 87 J8
West Sandford Devon 15 N10
West Sandwick Shet 111 k3
West Scrafton N York 65 J10
West Stafford Dorset 7 Q5
West Stockwith Notts 52 B5
West Stoke W Susx 10 D8
West Stour Dorset 8 B3
West Stourmouth Kent 23 N10
West Stow Suffk 34 D3
West Stowell Wilts 18 G8
West Street Suffk 34 G3
West Tanfield N York 65 M10
West Taphouse Cnwll 4 E7
West Tarbert Ag & B 83 M9
West Tarring W Susx 10 H8
West Thirston Nthumb 73 L2
West Thorney W Susx 10 C9
West Thorpe Notts 41 N3
West Thurrock Thurr 22 C7
West Tilbury Thurr 22 D7
West Tisted Hants 9 Q2
West Torrington Lincs 52 G7
West Town Hants 10 B9
West Town N Som 17 L3
West Tytherley Hants 9 J2
West Walton Norfk 43 M7
Westward Cumb 71 L6
Westward Ho! Devon 14 H6
Westwell Kent 13 J1
Westwell Oxon 30 G11
Westwell Leacon Kent 13 J1
West Wellow Hants 9 K4
West Wembury Devon 5 L9
West Wemyss Fife 86 G4
Westwick Cambs 33 L4
West Wickham Cambs 33 P6
West Wickham Gt Lon 21 M9
West Williamston Pembks 24 H7
West Winch Norfk 43 Q6
West Winterslow Wilts 9 J2
West Wittering W Susx 10 C9
West Witton N York 65 J9
Westwood Devon 6 D3
Westwood Kent 23 Q9
Westwood Wilts 18 B8
West Woodburn Nthumb 72 F4
West Woodhay W Berk 19 L8
Westwoodside N Linc 51 Q2
West Worldham Hants 10 C3
West Worthing W Susx 11 J9
West Wratting Cambs 33 P6
West Wylam Nthumb 73 K8
Wetheral Cumb 71 P5
Wetherby Leeds 59 K5
Wetherby Services N York 59 K4
Wetherden Suffk 34 G4
Wetheringsett Suffk 35 J4
Wethersfield Essex 34 B9
Wetherup Street Suffk 35 J4
Wetley Rocks Staffs 50 C10
Wettenhall Ches E 49 L4
Wetton Staffs 50 E9
Wetwang E R Yk 60 F3
Wetwood Staffs 49 P8
Wexcombe Wilts 19 J8
Weybourne Norfk 45 J2
Weybourne Surrey 10 D1
Weybread Suffk 35 L1
Weybread Street Suffk 35 L2
Weybridge Surrey 20 H9
Weycroft Devon 7 J3
Weydale Highld 110 D3
Weyhill Hants 19 K10
Weymouth Dorset 7 P7
Whaddon Bucks 32 B9
Whaddon Cambs 33 K7
Whaddon Gloucs 29 C11
Whaddon Gloucs 8 H3
Whaddon Wilts 18 C8
Whaley Derbys 51 L6
Whaley Bridge Derbys 50 D5
Whaley Thorns Derbys 51 M6
Whaligoe Highld 110 G7
Whalley Lancs 57 N2

Whalsay Shet 111 m3
Whalton Nthumb 73 K5
Whaplode Lincs 43 K5
Whaplode Drove Lincs 43 K7
Wharf Warwks 31 K4
Wharfe N York 63 P8
Wharles Lancs 57 J2
Wharley End C Beds 32 D7
Wharncliffe Side Sheff 50 H2
Wharram-le-Street N York 60 E2
Wharton Herefs 39 J10
Whashton N York 65 K6
Whasset Cumb 63 K6
Whatcote Warwks 30 H5
Whateley Warwks 40 G7
Whatfield Suffk 34 G7
Whatley Somset 7 J2
Whatley Somset 17 Q6
Whatlington E Susx 12 F6
Whatton-in-the-Vale Notts 51 Q11
Whauphill D & G 69 K8
Wheal Peevor Cnwll 2 G6
Wheatacre Norfk 45 P10
Wheathampstead Herts 21 J1
Wheatley Hants 10 C3
Wheatley Oxon 31 N11
Wheatley Hill Dur 73 P11
Wheatley Hills Donc 59 N12
Wheaton Aston Staffs 49 Q11
Wheddon Cross Somset 16 C8
Wheeler's Green Wokham 20 C8
Wheelock Ches E 49 N4
Wheelton Lancs 57 L5
Wheldrake N York 59 P5
Whelford Gloucs 18 H2
Whelpley Hill Bucks 20 F3
Whempstead Herts 33 K11
Whenby N York 66 E12
Whepstead Suffk 34 D5
Wherstead Suffk 35 J8
Wherwell Hants 19 L11
Wheston Derbys 50 F5
Whetsted Kent 12 D2
Whetstone Leics 41 M7
Whicham Cumb 62 D6
Whichford Warwks 30 H7
Whickham Gatesd 73 L8
Whiddon Down Devon 5 N2
Whigstreet Angus 93 N6
Whilton Nhants 31 N2
Whimple Devon 6 E4
Whimpwell Green Norfk 45 N4
Whinburgh Norfk 44 G8
Whinnieliggate D & G 70 B5
Whinnyfold Abers 103 M8
Whippingham IoW 9 N8
Whipsnade C Beds 32 E12
Whipsnade Zoo ZSL C Beds 32 E12
Whipton Devon 6 C4
Whisby Lincs 52 C9
Whissendine Rutlnd 42 B7
Whissonsett Norfk 44 F5
Whistlefield Ag & B 84 D4
Whistlefield Inn Ag & B 84 C5
Whistley Green Wokham 20 C8
Whiston Knows 57 J9
Whiston Nhants 32 C5
Whiston Rothm 51 K3
Whiston Staffs 40 B5
Whiston Staffs 50 D10
Whitbeck Cumb 62 D5
Whitbourne Herefs 39 N10
Whitburn S Tyne 73 P8
Whitburn W Loth 85 Q9
Whitby N York 67 J5
Whitchester Border 87 N9
Whitchurch BaNES 17 N3
Whitchurch Bucks 32 B11
Whitchurch Cardif 27 N11
Whitchurch Devon 5 K5
Whitchurch Hants 19 M10
Whitchurch Herefs 28 G5
Whitchurch Oxon 19 Q5
Whitchurch Pembks 24 E4
Whitchurch Shrops 49 K7
Whitchurch Canonicorum
  Dorset 7 J4
Whitchurch Hill Oxon 19 Q5
Whitcombe Dorset 7 Q5
Whitcot Shrops 38 H4
Whitcott Keysett Shrops 38 F5
Whiteacre Heath Warwks 40 G9
White Ball Somset 16 E11
Whitebridge Highld 98 G6
Whitebrook Mons 28 G7
Whitebushes Surrey 11 L1
Whitecairns Abers 103 J10
Whitechapel Lancs 57 K1
White Chapel Gt Lon 21 M7
White Colne Essex 34 E10
Whitecraig E Loth 86 G8
Whitecroft Gloucs 28 H7
White Cross Cnwll 2 G10
Whitecross Falk 85 R7
Whiteface Highld 107 L5
Whitefarland N Ayrs 75 N4
Whitefaulds S Ayrs 76 E8
Whitefield Bury 57 P7
Whitefield Somset 16 E9
Whiteford Abers 102 F9
Whitegate Ches W 49 L2
Whitehall Ork 111 i2
Whitehaven Cumb 70 F11
Whitehill and Bordon Hants 10 C4
Whitehills Abers 102 E3
Whitehouse Abers 102 E11
Whitehouse Ag & B 83 M10
Whitehouse Common Birm 40 E7
Whitekirk E Loth 87 L6
White Lackington Dorset 7 Q3
Whitelackington Somset 17 K11
White Ladies Aston Worcs 30 B4
Whiteleaf Bucks 20 D3
Whiteley Hants 9 N5
Whiteley Bank IoW 9 P10
Whitemire Moray 100 F5
Whitemoor C Nott 51 M11
Whitemoor Cnwll 3 L4
Whiteness Shet 111 k4
White Notley Essex 34 D11
Whiteparish Wilts 9 J3
White Pit Lincs 53 L3

Whiterashes Abers 102 H9
White Roding Essex 22 C1
Whiterow Highld 110 G6
Whiterow Moray 100 F4
Whiteshill Gloucs 29 L7
Whitesmith E Susx 11 Q7
Whitestaunton Somset 6 H1
Whitestone Cross Devon 6 B4
White Waltham W & M 20 D7
Whitewell Lancs 63 M11
Whitfield C Dund 93 M8
Whitfield Kent 13 P2
Whitfield Nhants 31 N6
Whitfield Nthumb 72 E8
Whitfield S Glos 29 J9
Whitford Devon 6 H4
Whitford Flints 56 D12
Whitgift E R Yk 60 E9
Whitgreave Staffs 40 B2
Whithorn D & G 69 L10
Whiting Bay N Ayrs 75 Q7
Whitkirk Leeds 59 J7
Whitland Carmth 25 L5
Whitlaw Border 80 C10
Whitletts S Ayrs 76 F6
Whitley N York 59 M9
Whitley Readg 20 B8
Whitley Sheff 51 J2
Whitley Wilts 18 C7
Whitley Bay N Tyne 73 N6
Whitley Chapel Nthumb 72 G8
Whitley Lower Kirk 58 G10
Whitminster Gloucs 29 K7
Whitmore Staffs 49 P7
Whitnage Devon 16 D11
Whitnash Warwks 31 J2
Whitney-on-Wye Herefs 38 F11
Whitsbury Hants 8 G4
Whitsome Border 81 J4
Whitson Newpt 28 D11
Whitstable Kent 23 L9
Whitstone Cnwll 14 E11
Whittingham Nthumb 81 M10
Whittingslow Shrops 38 H4
Whittington Derbys 51 J6
Whittington Gloucs 30 D9
Whittington Lancs 63 L7
Whittington Norfk 44 B9
Whittington Shrops 48 G8
Whittington Staffs 39 Q5
Whittington Staffs 40 F6
Whittington Warwks 40 H7
Whittington Worcs 39 Q10
Whittlebury Nhants 31 P5
Whittle-le-Woods Lancs 57 L5
Whittlesey Cambs 43 J10
Whittlesford Cambs 33 M7
Whitton N Linc 60 F7
Whitton Nthumb 73 J1
Whitton Powys 38 F8
Whitton S on T 65 P3
Whitton Shrops 39 L7
Whittonstall Nthumb 73 J9
Whitway Hants 19 M8
Whitwell Derbys 51 M5
Whitwell Herts 32 H11
Whitwell IoW 9 N10
Whitwell N York 65 M7
Whitwell Rutlnd 42 D8
Whitwell Street Norfk 44 H6
Whitwell-on-the-Hill N York 60 C2
Whitwick Leics 41 K4
Whitworth Lancs 58 B9
Whixall Shrops 49 K8
Whixley N York 59 K3
Whorlton Dur 65 K5
Whyle Herefs 39 K9
Whyteleafe Surrey 21 M10
Wibsey C Brad 58 F7
Wibtoft Warwks 41 L9
Wichenford Worcs 39 P9
Wichling Kent 22 H11
Wick BCP 8 H8
Wick Highld 110 G5
Wick S Glos 17 Q2
Wick V Glam 16 C2
Wick W Susx 10 G8
Wick Worcs 30 C5
Wicken Cambs 33 P3
Wicken Nhants 31 Q6
Wicken Bonhunt Essex 33 N9
Wickenby Lincs 52 F7
Wicken Green Village Norfk 44 D4
Wickersley Rothm 51 L3
Wicker Street Green Suffk 34 F8
Wickford Essex 22 E5
Wickham W Berk 19 L6
Wickham Hants 9 P5
Wickham Bishops Essex 22 G2
Wickhambreaux Kent 23 N10
Wickhambrook Suffk 34 C6
Wickhamford Worcs 30 E6
Wickham Green Suffk 34 H3
Wickham Market Suffk 35 M5
Wickhampton Norfk 45 N8
Wickham St Paul Essex 34 D9
Wickham Skeith Suffk 34 H3
Wickham Street Suffk 34 H3
Wick John o' Groats Airport
  Highld 110 G5
Wicklewood Norfk 44 H9
Wickmere Norfk 45 J4
Wick St Lawrence N Som 17 K3
Wicksteed Park Nhants 32 C2
Wickwar S Glos 29 J10
Widdington Essex 33 N9
Widdrington Nthumb 73 N2
Widdrington Station Nthumb 73 M3
Widecombe in the Moor
  Devon 5 P5
Widegates Cnwll 4 G8
Widemouth Bay Cnwll 14 D10
Wide Open N Tyne 73 M6
Widford Essex 22 E3
Widford Herts 33 L12
Widmer End Bucks 20 E4
Widmerpool Notts 41 N2
Widmore Gt Lon 21 N9
Widnes Halton 57 K10
Widworthy Devon 6 G3
Wigan Wigan 57 L7
Wigborough Somset 17 L12

Wiggaton Devon 6 E4
Wiggenhall St Germans Norfk 43 P7
Wiggenhall St Mary
  Magdalen Norfk 43 P7
Wiggenhall St Mary the
  Virgin Norfk 43 P7
Wigginton C York 59 N3
Wigginton Herts 20 F2
Wigginton Oxon 31 K7
Wigginton Staffs 40 G6
Wigglesworth N York 63 P10
Wiggonby Cumb 71 L5
Wighill N York 59 L5
Wighton Norfk 44 F3
Wightwick Wolves 39 Q3
Wigley Hants 9 K4
Wigmore Herefs 38 H8
Wigmore Medway 22 F9
Wigsley Notts 52 C9
Wigsthorpe Nhants 42 F12
Wigston Leics 41 N7
Wigston Fields Leics 41 N7
Wigston Parva Leics 41 L9
Wigthorpe Notts 51 N4
Wigtoft Lincs 43 J3
Wigton Cumb 71 L6
Wigtown D & G 69 L7
Wike Leeds 59 J5
Wilbarston Nhants 42 B11
Wilberfoss E R Yk 60 C4
Wilburton Cambs 33 M2
Wilby Nhants 32 C4
Wilby Norfk 44 G11
Wilby Suffk 35 L3
Wilcot Wilts 18 G8
Wilcott Shrops 48 H10
Wildboarclough Ches E 50 C7
Wilden Bed 32 F6
Wilden Worcs 39 P7
Wildmanbridge S Lans 85 N11
Wildmill Brdgnd 27 J11
Wildmoor Worcs 40 C11
Wildsworth Lincs 52 B4
Wilford C Nott 51 M12
Wilkesley Ches E 49 L7
Wilkhaven Highld 107 Q5
Wilkieston W Loth 86 D8
Willand Devon 6 D1
Willaston Ches E 49 M5
Willaston Ches W 56 G12
Willen M Keyn 32 C8
Willenhall Covtry 41 J11
Willenhall Wsall 40 C7
Willerby E R Yk 60 H7
Willerby N York 67 L10
Willersey Gloucs 30 E6
Willersley Herefs 38 G11
Willesborough Kent 13 K2
Willesborough Lees Kent 13 K2
Willesden Gt Lon 21 K6
Willesley Wilts 18 C3
Willett Somset 16 F9
Willey Shrops 39 M3
Willey Warwks 41 L9
Willey Green Surrey 20 F12
Williamscot Oxon 31 L5
Willian Herts 32 H9
Willingale Essex 22 C2
Willingdon E Susx 12 C9
Willingham Cambs 33 L3
Willingham by Stow Lincs 52 C6
Willingham St Mary Suffk 45 P12
Willington Bed 32 G6
Willington Derbys 40 H2
Willington Dur 65 L1
Willington Kent 22 F11
Willington N Tyne 73 N7
Willington Warwks 30 H6
Willitoft E R Yk 60 C7
Williton Somset 16 E7
Willoughby Lincs 53 M8
Willoughby Warwks 31 M1
Willoughby-on-the-Wolds
  Notts 41 N3
Willoughby Waterleys Leics 41 M8
Willoughton Lincs 52 D5
Willows Green Essex 34 C11
Willtown Somset 17 K10
Wilmcote Warwks 30 F3
Wilmington Devon 6 G3
Wilmington E Susx 12 B8
Wilmington Kent 21 Q8
Wilmslow Ches E 57 Q11
Wilpshire Lancs 57 M3
Wilsden C Brad 58 E6
Wilsford Lincs 42 E2
Wilsford Wilts 18 G11
Wilsford Wilts 18 G8
Wilshaw Kirk 58 E11
Wilsill N York 58 H3
Wilson Leics 41 K3
Wilsontown S Lans 85 Q13
Wilstead Bed 32 F7
Wilsthorpe Lincs 42 F7
Wilstone Herts 20 E1
Wilton Herefs 28 G4
Wilton N York 67 J10
Wilton R & Cl 66 E4
Wilton Wilts 8 G2
Wilton Wilts 19 J8
Wilton Dean Border 80 C10
Wimbish Green Essex 33 P9
Wimbledon Gt Lon 21 K8
Wimblington Cambs 43 L10
Wimboldsley Ches W 49 M3
Wimborne Minster Dorset 8 F7
Wimborne St Giles Dorset 8 F5
Wimbotsham Norfk 43 P8
Wimpole Cambs 33 K6
Wimpstone Warwks 30 G4
Wincanton Somset 17 Q9
Winchburgh W Loth 86 C7
Winchcombe Gloucs 30 D8
Winchelsea E Susx 12 H6
Winchester Hants 9 N1
Winchester Services Hants 9 N1
Winchet Hill Kent 12 E2
Winchfield Hants 20 C11
Winchmore Hill Bucks 20 E4
Winchmore Hill Gt Lon 21 L5
Wincle Ches E 50 C7
Wincobank Sheff 51 J3

Windermere Cumb....62 H3
Windermere Jetty Cumb....62 H3
Winderton Warwks....31 J6
Windhill Highld....107 L11
Windlesham Surrey....20 E9
Windmill Cnwll....3 K2
Windmill Hill E Susx....12 D7
Windmill Hill Somset....17 J11
Windrush Gloucs....30 F10
Windsole Abers....102 D4
Windsor W & M....20 F7
Windsor Castle W & M....20 F7
Windsoredge Gloucs....29 L8
Windy Arbour Warwks....31 J6
Windygates Fife....86 G3
Wineham W Susx....11 K6
Winestead E R Yk....61 M8
Winfarthing Norfk....45 J11
Winford IoW....9 P9
Winford N Som....17 M3
Winforton Herefs....38 F11
Winfrith Newburgh Dorset....8 B9
Wing Bucks....32 C11
Wing Rutlnd....42 C9
Wingate Dur....73 P12
Wingerworth Derbys....51 J7
Wingfield C Beds....32 E10
Wingfield Suffk....35 K2
Wingfield Wilts....18 B9
Wingham Kent....23 N11
Wingrave Bucks....32 C11
Winkburn Notts....51 P8
Winkfield Br For....20 E8
Winkfield Row Br For....20 E8
Winkhill Staffs....50 D9
Winkleigh Devon....15 L9
Winksley N York....65 M12
Winlaton Gatesd....73 L8
Winless Highld....110 G5
Winmarleigh Lancs....63 J11
Winnall Hants....9 N2
Winnersh Wokham....20 C8
Winnington Ches W....49 M1
Winscombe N Som....17 K5
Winsford Ches W....49 M3
Winsford Somset....16 B8
Winsham Somset....7 K2
Winshill Staffs....40 H3
Winshwen Swans....26 F9
Winskill Cumb....64 B1
Winsley Wilts....18 B8
Winslow Bucks....31 Q8
Winson Gloucs....30 E11
Winsor Hants....9 K5
Winster Cumb....62 H4
Winster Derbys....50 H8
Winston Dur....65 K4
Winston Suffk....35 K5
Winstone Gloucs....29 N6
Winswell Devon....15 J9
Winterborne Came Dorset....7 Q5
Winterborne Clenston Dorset....8 C6
Winterborne Houghton Dorset....8 B6
Winterborne Kingston Dorset....8 C8
Winterborne Monkton Dorset....7 P5
Winterborne Stickland Dorset....8 C6
Winterborne Whitechurch
  Dorset....8 C7
Winterborne Zelston Dorset....8 D7
Winterbourne S Glos....28 H11
Winterbourne W Berk....19 M6
Winterbourne Abbas Dorset....7 N5
Winterbourne Bassett Wilts....18 G6
Winterbourne Dauntsey Wilts....8 H1
Winterbourne Earls Wilts....8 H1
Winterbourne Gunner Wilts....8 H1
Winterbourne Monkton Wilts....18 G6
Winterbourne Steepleton
  Dorset....7 P5
Winterbourne Stoke Wilts....18 F11
Winterburn N York....58 C3
Winteringham N Linc....60 F9
Winterley Ches E....49 N4
Winterslow Wilts....9 J2
Winterton N Linc....60 F9
Winterton-on-Sea Norfk....45 P6
Winthorpe Notts....52 B11
Winton BCP....8 G8
Winton Cumb....64 E5
Wintringham N York....67 J11
Winwick Cambs....32 F1
Winwick Nhants....41 N11
Winwick Warrtn....57 L9
Wirksworth Derbys....50 H9
Wirral....56 F10
Wirswall Ches E....49 K6
Wisbech Cambs....43 M8
Wisbech St Mary Cambs....43 L8
Wisborough Green W Susx....10 G5
Wiseman's Bridge Pembks....25 K7
Wiseton Notts....51 Q3
Wishaw N Lans....85 N11
Wishaw Warwks....40 F8
Wisley Garden RHS Surrey....20 G10
Wispington Lincs....52 H8
Wissett Suffk....35 M2
Wissington Suffk....34 F9
Wistanstow Shrops....38 H5
Wistanswick Shrops....49 M9
Wistaston Ches E....49 M5
Wistaston Green Ches E....49 M5
Wiston Pembks....24 H5
Wiston S Lans....78 F3
Wiston W Susx....11 J7
Wistow Cambs....33 J1
Wistow N York....59 N7
Wiswell Lancs....57 N2
Witcham Cambs....33 M2
Witchampton Dorset....8 E6
Witchford Cambs....33 N2
Witcombe Somset....17 L10
Witham Essex....22 G1
Witham Friary Somset....17 Q7
Witham on the Hill Lincs....42 F8
Witham St Hughs Lincs....52 C10
Withcall Lincs....53 J6
Withdean Br & H....11 L8
Witherenden Hill E Susx....12 D5
Witheridge Devon....15 N8
Witherley Leics....41 J7
Withern Lincs....53 L7
Withernsea E R Yk....61 N8

Withernwick E R Yk....61 K6
Withersdale Street Suffk....35 L1
Withersfield Suffk....33 Q7
Witherslack Cumb....62 H5
Withiel Cnwll....3 M3
Withiel Florey Somset....16 D9
Withington Gloucs....30 D10
Withington Herefs....39 K12
Withington Manch....57 Q9
Withington Shrops....49 L11
Withington Staffs....40 D1
Withleigh Devon....6 B1
Withnell Lancs....57 L4
Withybed Green Worcs....40 D11
Withybrook Warwks....41 K10
Withycombe Somset....16 D7
Withyham E Susx....11 P3
Withypool Somset....15 P5
Withywood Bristl....17 N3
Witley Surrey....10 F3
Witnesham Suffk....35 K6
Witney Oxon....31 J11
Wittering C Pete....42 F9
Wittersham Kent....12 H5
Witton Birm....40 E8
Witton Norfk....45 M4
Witton Norfk....45 M8
Witton Gilbert Dur....73 M10
Witton le Wear Dur....65 K2
Witton Park Dur....65 L2
Wiveliscombe Somset....16 E9
Wivelrod Hants....19 R12
Wivelsfield E Susx....11 M6
Wivelsfield Green E Susx....11 M6
Wivenhoe Essex....34 G11
Wiveton Norfk....44 G2
Wix Essex....35 J10
Wixams Bed....32 F7
Wixford Warwks....30 E3
Wixoe Suffk....34 C8
Woburn C Beds....32 D9
Woburn Safari Park C Beds....32 D9
Woburn Sands M Keyn....32 D9
Woking Surrey....20 G10
Wokingham Wokham....20 D9
Woldingham Surrey....21 M11
Wold Newton E R Yk....67 M11
Wold Newton NE Lin....53 J4
Wolfclyde S Lans....78 G2
Wolferton Norfk....43 Q4
Wolfhill P & K....92 H8
Wolf's Castle Pembks....24 G4
Wolfsdale Pembks....24 G5
Wollaston Dudley....40 B9
Wollaston Nhants....32 C4
Wollaston Shrops....48 G11
Wollaton C Nott....51 M11
Wollaton Hall & Park C Nott....51 M11
Wollerton Shrops....49 L9
Wollescote Dudley....40 B10
Wolseley Bridge Staffs....40 D4
Wolsingham Dur....73 J12
Wolstanton Staffs....49 Q6
Wolston Warwks....41 K11
Wolvercote Oxon....31 L11
Wolverhampton Wolves....40 B7
Wolverhampton Halfpenny
  Green Airport Staffs....39 P4
Wolverley Worcs....39 P7
Wolverton Hants....19 P8
Wolverton M Keyn....32 B8
Wolverton Warwks....30 G2
Wolverton Wilts....8 B2
Wolvesnewton Mons....28 E8
Wolvey Warwks....41 K9
Wolvey Heath Warwks....41 K9
Wolviston S on T....66 C3
Wombleton N York....66 F10
Wombourne Staffs....39 Q4
Wombwell Barns....51 K1
Womenswold Kent....23 N12
Womersley N York....59 M9
Wonersh Surrey....10 G2
Wonford Devon....6 C4
Wonston Dorset....7 Q2
Wonston Hants....19 M11
Wooburn Bucks....20 E6
Wooburn Green Bucks....20 E6
Woodacott Devon....14 G9
Woodall Rothm....51 L5
Woodall Services Rothm....51 L5
Woodbastwick Norfk....45 M7
Wood Bevington Warwks....30 D4
Woodborough Notts....51 N10
Woodborough Wilts....18 G8
Woodbridge Suffk....35 L7
Woodbury Devon....6 D5
Woodbury Salterton Devon....6 D5
Woodchester Gloucs....29 L8
Woodchurch Kent....12 H3
Woodcombe Somset....16 C6
Woodcote Gt Lon....21 L10
Woodcote Oxon....19 Q4
Woodcote Wrekin....49 P11
Woodcroft Gloucs....28 G9
Wood Dalling Norfk....44 H5
Woodditton Cambs....33 Q5
Woodeaton Oxon....31 M10
Wood End Gt Lon....20 H7
Wood End Herts....33 K10
Woodend Highld....89 Q4
Woodend Nhants....31 N4
Woodend W Loth....85 Q8
Woodend W Susx....10 D8
Wood End Warwks....40 E11
Wood End Warwks....40 C7
Wood Enderby Lincs....53 J10
Woodfalls Wilts....8 H4
Woodford Cnwll....14 D9
Woodford Devon....16 E12
Woodford Gloucs....29 J8
Woodford Gt Lon....21 N5
Woodford Stockp....50 B4
Woodford Bridge Gt Lon....21 N5
Woodford Green Gt Lon....21 N5
Woodford Halse Nhants....31 M4
Woodford Wells Gt Lon....21 N5
Woodgate Birm....40 D10
Woodgate Devon....16 E12
Woodgate W Susx....10 F8
Woodgate Worcs....30 C2
Wood Green Gt Lon....21 L5

Woodgreen Hants....8 H4
Woodhall Invclyd....84 G9
Woodhall Spa Lincs....52 H10
Woodham Bucks....31 P9
Woodham Surrey....20 G10
Woodham Ferrers Essex....22 F4
Woodham Mortimer Essex....22 F3
Woodham Walter Essex....22 F3
Wood Hayes Wolves....40 C7
Woodhead Abers....102 G7
Woodhill Shrops....39 N5
Woodhill Somset....17 J10
Woodhorn Nthumb....73 N3
Woodhouse Leeds....58 H7
Woodhouse Leics....41 M5
Woodhouse Sheff....51 K4
Woodhouse Wakefd....59 J9
Woodhouse Eaves Leics....41 M5
Woodhouselee Mdloth....86 F8
Woodhouselees D & G....71 N1
Woodhouses Oldham....50 B1
Woodhouses Staffs....40 F4
Woodhurst Cambs....33 K2
Woodingdean Br & H....11 M8
Woodkirk Leeds....58 H8
Woodland Abers....103 J9
Woodland Devon....5 M8
Woodland Devon....5 Q6
Woodland Dur....65 J3
Woodland S Ayrs....76 C11
Woodlands Abers....95 N3
Woodlands Donc....59 M11
Woodlands Dorset....8 F5
Woodlands Hants....9 K5
Woodlands N York....59 J3
Woodlands Park W & M....20 D7
Woodleigh Devon....5 P9
Woodley Wokham....20 C8
Woodmancote Gloucs....29 K8
Woodmancote Gloucs....29 N4
Woodmancote Gloucs....30 D11
Woodmancote W Susx....10 C8
Woodmancote W Susx....11 K7
Woodmancott Hants....19 P11
Woodmansey E R Yk....60 H6
Woodmansgreen W Susx....10 D5
Woodmansterne Surrey....21 L10
Woodmanton Devon....6 D5
Woodnesborough Kent....23 P11
Woodnewton Nhants....42 E10
Wood Norton Norfk....44 G5
Woodplumpton Lancs....57 J2
Woodrising Norfk....44 G9
Wood's Corner E Susx....12 D6
Woodseaves Staffs....49 P9
Woodsetts Rothm....51 M4
Woodsford Dorset....8 A8
Wood's Green E Susx....12 D4
Woodside Br For....20 E8
Woodside Fife....86 H1
Woodside Gt Lon....21 M9
Woodside P & K....93 J7
Woodstock Oxon....31 K10
Woodston C Pete....42 H10
Wood Street Norfk....45 N6
Wood Street Village Surrey....20 F12
Woodton Norfk....45 L10
Woodtown Devon....14 G7
Woodville Derbys....40 H4
Wood Walton Cambs....32 H1
Woofferton Shrops....39 K8
Wookey Somset....17 M7
Wookey Hole Somset....17 M6
Wool Dorset....8 C9
Woolacombe Devon....14 H4
Woolage Green Kent....23 N12
Woolaston Gloucs....28 G8
Woolaston Common Gloucs....28 G8
Woolavington Somset....17 J7
Woolbeding W Susx....10 E5
Woolbrook Devon....6 F5
Wooler Nthumb....81 L8
Woolfardisworthy Devon....14 F7
Woolfardisworthy Devon....15 P9
Woolfords S Lans....86 B10
Woolhampton W Berk....19 P7
Woolhope Herefs....28 H2
Woolland Dorset....8 B6
Woolley BaNES....17 Q3
Woolley Cambs....32 G2
Woolley Wakefd....58 H10
Woolley Edge Services Wakefd....58 H10
Woolmere Green Worcs....30 C2
Woolmer Green Herts....33 J11
Woolminstone Somset....7 K2
Woolpit Suffk....34 F4
Woolstaston Shrops....39 J3
Woolsthorpe by Belvoir Lincs....42 B4
Woolsthorpe-by-
  Colsterworth Lincs....42 D5
Woolston C Sotn....9 M5
Woolston Shrops....48 G9
Woolston Somset....16 E8
Woolston Somset....17 P9
Woolston Warrtn....57 M10
Woolstone Gloucs....29 N3
Woolstone M Keyn....32 C8
Woolstone Oxon....19 K4
Woolston Green Devon....5 Q7
Woolton Lpool....56 H10
Woolton Hill Hants....19 M8
Woolverstone Suffk....35 K8
Woolverton Somset....18 B9
Woolwich Gt Lon....21 N7
Woonton Herefs....38 G10
Woore Shrops....49 N7
Wootten Green Suffk....35 K3
Wootton Bed....32 E7
Wootton Kent....13 N2
Wootton N Linc....61 J10
Wootton Nhants....31 Q3
Wootton Oxon....19 N1
Wootton Oxon....31 K9
Wootton Staffs....50 E10
Wootton Bassett Wilts....18 F4
Wootton Bridge IoW....9 P8
Wootton Courtenay Somset....16 C7
Wootton Fitzpaine Dorset....7 J4
Wootton Rivers Wilts....18 H8
Wootton St Lawrence Hants....19 P9
Wootton Wawen Warwks....30 F2
Worcester Worcs....39 Q10

Worcester Park Gt Lon....21 K9
Wordsley Dudley....39 B9
Worfield Shrops....39 N3
Workington Cumb....70 G9
Worksop Notts....51 N5
Worlaby N Linc....60 H10
Worlds End Hants....9 Q5
Worlds End W Susx....11 L6
Worle N Som....17 J4
Worleston Ches E....49 M4
Worlingham Suffk....45 P11
Worlington Devon....15 N9
Worlington Suffk....34 B3
Worlingworth Suffk....35 K3
Wormbridge Herefs....28 E3
Wormegay Norfk....43 Q7
Wormelow Tump Herefs....28 F3
Wormhill Derbys....50 E6
Worminghall Bucks....31 N11
Wormingford Essex....34 F9
Wormington Gloucs....30 D6
Wormit Fife....93 M9
Wormleighton Warwks....31 K4
Wormley Herts....21 M3
Wormley Surrey....10 F3
Wormshill Kent....22 G11
Wormsley Herefs....38 H11
Worplesdon Surrey....20 F11
Worrall Sheff....50 H3
Worsbrough Barns....51 J1
Worsbrough Bridge Barns....51 J12
Worsbrough Dale Barns....51 J12
Worsley Salfd....57 N8
Worstead Norfk....45 M5
Worsthorne Lancs....57 Q3
Worston Devon....5 M9
Worston Lancs....57 P1
Worth Kent....23 P11
Wortham Suffk....35 H2
Worthen Shrops....38 G2
Worthenbury Wrexhm....48 H6
Worthing Norfk....44 G6
Worthing W Susx....11 J8
Worthington Leics....41 K4
Worth Matravers Dorset....8 E11
Wortley Barns....50 H2
Wortley Leeds....58 H7
Worton N York....64 G9
Worton Wilts....18 E8
Wortwell Norfk....45 L12
Wotton-under-Edge Gloucs....29 K9
Wotton Underwood Bucks....31 P10
Woughton on the Green
  M Keyn....32 C8
Wouldham Kent....22 E9
Wrabness Essex....35 K9
Wrafton Devon....15 J5
Wragby Lincs....52 G7
Wragby Wakefd....59 K10
Wrangaton Devon....5 N8
Wrangle Lincs....53 L12
Wrangway Somset....16 F11
Wrantage Somset....17 J10
Wrawby N Linc....52 E2
Wraxall N Som....17 L2
Wraxall Somset....17 N8
Wray Lancs....63 L8
Wraysbury W & M....20 G8
Wrayton Lancs....63 L7
Wrea Green Lancs....56 H3
Wreay Cumb....71 N6
Wrecclesham Surrey....10 D2
Wrekenton Gatesd....73 M8
Wrelton N York....66 G9
Wrenbury Ches E....49 L6
Wreningham Norfk....45 J9
Wrentham Suffk....35 Q12
Wrentnall Shrops....38 H2
Wressle E R Yk....60 C7
Wressle N Linc....52 D2
Wrestlingworth C Beds....33 J7
Wretton Norfk....44 B9
Wrexham Wrexhm....48 G5
Wrexham Industrial Estate
  Wrexhm....48 H5
Wribbenhall Worcs....39 P7
Wrinehill Staffs....49 N6
Wrington N Som....17 L4
Writhlington BaNES....17 Q5
Writtle Essex....22 D3
Wrockwardine Wrekin....49 L11
Wroot N Linc....60 C12
Wrose C Brad....58 F6
Wrotham Kent....22 C10
Wroughton Swindn....18 G5
Wroxall IoW....9 P10
Wroxall Warwks....40 G5
Wroxeter Shrops....39 K1
Wroxham Norfk....45 L6
Wroxton Oxon....31 K6
Wyaston Derbys....50 F11
Wyberton Lincs....43 K2
Wyboston Bed....32 G5
Wybunbury Ches E....49 M5
Wychbold Worcs....30 B2
Wychnor Staffs....40 F4
Wycliffe Dur....65 K5
Wycoller Lancs....58 C6
Wycomb Leics....41 Q3
Wycombe Marsh Bucks....20 E5
Wyddial Herts....33 K9
Wye Kent....13 K1
Wyke C Brad....58 F8
Wyke Dorset....8 B3
Wyke Champflower Somset....17 P8
Wykeham N York....67 L10
Wyken Covtry....41 J10
Wyken Shrops....39 N3
Wyke Regis Dorset....7 P7
Wykey Shrops....48 H9
Wylam Nthumb....73 K7
Wylde Green Birm....40 E8
Wylye Wilts....18 E12
Wymeswold Leics....41 N3
Wymington Bed....32 D4
Wymondham Leics....42 C6
Wymondham Norfk....45 J9
Wynford Eagle Dorset....7 N4
Wyre Piddle Worcs....30 C5
Wysall Notts....41 N3
Wythall Worcs....40 E11

Wytham Oxon....31 L11
Wythenshawe Manch....57 P10
Wyton Cambs....33 J3
Wyton E R Yk....61 K7
Wyverstone Suffk....34 G4
Wyverstone Street Suffk....34 G4

Y

Yaddlethorpe N Linc....52 C3
Yafforth N York....65 N8
Yalberton Torbay....6 B10
Yalding Kent....22 E12
Yanwath Cumb....71 Q9
Yanworth Gloucs....30 E10
Yapham E R Yk....60 D4
Yapton W Susx....10 F9
Yarborough N Som....17 K5
Yarburgh Lincs....53 L6
Yarcombe Devon....6 H2
Yard Devon....15 N7
Yardley Birm....40 F9
Yardley Gobion Nhants....31 Q5
Yardley Hastings Nhants....32 C5
Yardley Wood Birm....40 E10
Yarkhill Herefs....39 L12
Yarley Somset....17 M7
Yarlington Somset....17 P9
Yarm S on T....65 P5
Yarmouth IoW....9 L9
Yarnbrook Wilts....18 C9
Yarnfield Staffs....49 Q8
Yarnscombe Devon....15 K7
Yarnton Oxon....31 L10
Yarpole Herefs....39 J8
Yarrow Border....79 M4
Yarrow Feus Border....79 M4
Yarrowford Border....79 N3
Yarwell Nhants....42 F9
Yate S Glos....29 J11
Yateley Hants....20 D10
Yatesbury Wilts....18 F6
Yattendon W Berk....19 P6
Yatton Herefs....38 H8
Yatton N Som....17 L3
Yatton Keynell Wilts....18 C5
Yaverland IoW....9 Q9
Yaxham Norfk....44 G7
Yaxley Cambs....42 H10
Yaxley Suffk....35 J2
Yazor Herefs....38 H11
Yeading Gt Lon....20 H7
Yeadon Leeds....58 G6
Yealand Conyers Lancs....63 J7
Yealand Redmayne Lancs....63 J7
Yealmpton Devon....5 M9
Yearsley N York....66 E11
Yeaton Shrops....48 H10
Yeaveley Derbys....50 F11
Yeavering Nthumb....81 K7
Yedingham N York....67 J10
Yelford Oxon....31 J11
Yell Shet....111 k3
Yelling Cambs....33 J4
Yelvertoft Nhants....41 N11
Yelverton Devon....5 L6
Yelverton Norfk....45 L9
Yenston Somset....17 Q11
Yeoford Devon....15 N11
Yeolmbridge Cnwll....4 G3
Yeovil Somset....17 M11
Yeovil Marsh Somset....17 M11
Yeovilton Somset....17 M10
Yesnaby Ork....111 g2
Yetminster Dorset....7 N1
Yettington Devon....6 E5
Yetts o'Muckhart Clacks....86 B2
Yew Tree Sandw....40 D8
Y Felinheli Gwynd....54 G7
Y Ferwig Cerdgn....36 C10
Y Ffôr Gwynd....46 G4
Yielden Bed....32 E4
Yieldshields S Lans....77 P2
Yiewsley Gt Lon....20 G7
Ynysboeth Rhondd....27 M9
Ynysddu Caerph....27 P9
Ynyshir Rhondd....27 L9
Ynystawe Swans....26 F8
Ynysybwl Rhondd....27 M9
Yockleton Shrops....48 H12
Yokefleet E R Yk....60 E8
Yoker C Glas....84 H8
York C York....59 N4
Yorkletts Kent....23 L10
Yorkley Gloucs....28 H7
Yorkshire Dales National
  Park....64 F11
York Town Surrey....20 D10
Youlgreave Derbys....50 G7
Youlthorpe E R Yk....60 D3
Youlton N York....59 L2
Yoxall Staffs....40 F4
Yoxford Suffk....35 N3
Y Rhiw Gwynd....46 D6
Ysbyty Ifan Conwy....55 M10
Ysbyty Ystwyth Cerdgn....37 M6
Ysceifiog Flints....56 D2
Ystalyfera Neath....26 G7
Ystrad Rhondd....27 L9
Ystrad Aeron Cerdgn....36 H9
Ystradfellte Powys....27 K6
Ystradgynlais Powys....26 H6
Ystrad Meurig Cerdgn....37 L7
Ystrad Mynach Caerph....27 N9
Ystradowen V Glam....27 L12
Ythanbank Abers....103 J8
Ythanwells Abers....102 E7
Ythsie Abers....103 J8

Z

Zeal Monachorum Devon....15 M10
Zeals Wilts....8 B2
Zelah Cnwll....3 J5
Zennor Cnwll....2 C7
Zouch Notts....41 L3
ZSL London Zoo Gt Lon....21 L6
ZSL Whipsnade Zoo C Beds....32 E12